# Hannah Arendt

## For Love of the World

# Hannah Arendt

## For Love of the World

*Elisabeth Young-Bruehl*

*Yale University Press*
*New Haven and London*

Published with assistance from the foundation established
in memory of Philip Hamilton McMillan of the Class of
1894, Yale College.

Designed by Sally Harris
and set in Electra type
by The Composing Room of Michigan.
Printed in the United States of America by
Vail-Ballou Press, Binghamton, N.Y.

*Library of Congress Cataloging in Publication Data*
Young-Bruehl, Elisabeth.
Hannah Arendt, for the love of the world.
English
Bibliography: p.
Includes index.
1. Arendt, Hannah.   2. Political scientists—
Biography.   I. Title.
JC251.A74Y68        320.5'3'0924   [B]        81-16114
ISBN 0–300–02660–9        AACR2
0–300–03099–1        (pbk)

10   9   8   7   6   5   4   3

# Contents

# Illustrations

vii

J. Glenn Gray

W. H. Auden

Hannah Arendt and Mary McCarthy

Heinrich Blücher shortly before his death in 1970

Hannah Arendt shortly before her death in 1975 (*Courtesy of Rhoda Nathans*)

(All pictures not otherwise credited appear courtesy of the
Hannah Arendt Estate.)

# Preface

Many of the European refugees who came to America before or during the Second World War had changed countries often and could call none home. When they told their stories of persecution and displacement, personal loss and political disaster, their American hearers glimpsed a world out of joint in novel and nearly incomprehensible ways. Each storyteller was, as Brecht said, *ein Bote des Unglücks*, a messenger of misfortune.

Those artists and intellectuals who could find the means to work soon began to make contributions, often brilliant ones. Their role in American and world culture is well known—they brought good fortune to mathematics and physics, music and painting, sociology and psychoanalysis. But while the refugees began to make new homes and mend their disrupted lives, the vast story to which their individual messages were clues remained to be told, for their generation and for future ones.

Most of the histories and analyses of Nazi Germany from the fifteen years after the war's end were written by refugee social scientists who had begun to make their marks before the war. But one book, *The Origins of Totalitarianism*, came from a woman trained in philosophy who was unknown outside a small émigré circle in New York and who had never before written a book-length work of history or political theory. The critical acclaim for Hannah Arendt's effort was enormous: "it is a masterpiece," "she is comparable to Marx." During the next twenty-four years, with her many essays and books, from *The Human Condition* to *The Life of the Mind*, Hannah Arendt won international fame and a place of preeminence among the theorists of her generation.

Always a controversial thinker, a loner who kept apart from academic schools, political parties, and ideological lines, Hannah Arendt reached an ever-widening audience. Professional and general readers came to expect rare insight from her; they felt what Hannah Arendt herself expressed in her 1968 preface to a collection of portraits: "even in the darkest times we have a right to expect some illumination. [This] may well come less from theories and concepts than from the uncertain, flickering and often weak light that some men and women, in their lives and works, will kindle under almost all circumstances and shed over the time span that was given them on earth."[1]

The light that comes from a person's works enters directly into the world and remains after the person dies. Whether it is large or small, transitory or enduring, depends upon the world and its ways. Posterity will judge. The light that comes from a person's life—spoken words, gestures, friendships—survives only in memories. If it is to enter into the world, it must find a new form, be recorded and handed down. A story must be made from many memories and stories.

I will tell Hannah Arendt's story as I have gathered it from written sources and from those still living who knew her. The history of her European generation and of our dark times is far more than a backdrop to her individual story; her life reflects it as much as her work sought to understand it. Biographies, in their nature, concentrate on one *bios*. But they presuppose that this one life, though only a part of a larger history, should be given to future generations. Posterity may judge the life too; the biographer need only judge that the story should be told.

Public recognition did not come to Hannah Arendt until she was forty-five years old, in the eighteenth year of her exile from Nazi Germany. With a mixture of astonishment and annoyance, she asked her friend and teacher Karl Jaspers: "Did I write to you that a week ago I became a 'cover girl' and had to look at myself on all the newsstands?"[2] From the day she looked at the author of *The Origins of Totalitarianism* smiling shyly from the cover of a 1951 issue of the *Saturday Review of Literature* until the day when she agreed to her first American television interview on the condition that the camera be stationed behind her back, Hannah Arendt tried to avoid living with a widely known face. Her friend W. H. Auden supplied her with one formulation of her reason: "Private faces in public places/Are wiser and nicer/Than public faces in private places."

Personal reticence and intense protectiveness for her "thinking space" might appear strange in a philosopher who praised political action and the public realm. Hannah Arendt saw no contradiction: "In matters of theory and understanding," she said, "it is not uncommon for outsiders and spectators to gain a sharper and deeper insight into the actual meaning of what happens to go on before or around them than would be possible for the actual actors or participants, entirely absorbed as they must be in the events. . . . It is quite possible to understand and reflect about politics without being a so-called political animal."[3] True as this may be, time spent as a "so-called political animal" can give the outsiders a reservoir of memories to draw upon as they watch the present players. Hannah Arendt knew that by temperament and inclination she was unsuited for political action or public life, but she had not always been a spectator: in the years before her work won her a wide audience, she had been active in Jewish politics. She had worked for the German Zionist Organization; been executive secretary of the Paris branch of Youth Aliyah, a Zionist organization which helped young refugees prepare for life in Palestine; written a political column for the New York German-Jewish newspaper *Aufbau*; and joined Judah Magnes's 1948 campaign for a binational state in Palestine. When she asked herself the theoretical question "What is politics?" her answers echoed years of wondering what Jewish politics might or should be.

But Arendt's concern for political action might never have been as deep as it was had she not met and married a very political animal—Heinrich Blücher. To this former Spartacist and Communist from Berlin, her self-educated intellectual collaborator, *The Origins of Totalitarianism* was dedicated. Kurt Blumenfeld, the German Zionist who had introduced Hannah Arendt when she was a student to his lifelong political concern, the "Jewish Question," recognized the role Heinrich Blücher had played in the thinking through of Arendt's first American book. When he received a copy of *The Origins of Totalitarianism* he wrote to tell her what joy it gave him to remember the conversations the three of them had had in New York while the book was growing, and he acknowledged his own debt to Blücher: "From 'the unpublished political philosophy of the person to whom [*Origins*] is dedicated' I still gather many things when I go strolling about in my memories."[4]

The internal dialogue of thinking has no urge to appear in public, as Hannah Arendt always claimed, but it does have an impulse to communicate with selected others. In Arendt's case the impulse that overcomes the solitariness of thinking reached out first to her husband. Those who are fortunate enough to have such a peer at hand for conversation can turn outward the inner dialogue of their thinking and reverse their original discovery that conversation can go on when companions are not present, that it can be conducted between "me and myself." Hannah Arendt's reticence, her careful protection of her privacy, kept a remarkable marriage from public view. These two strong-willed and strong-minded people ruled over the select kingdom of their conversation for thirty-five years. There were palace intrigues and policy debates, but the harmony remained. It was periodically given a brief public moment: Arendt's *Between Past and Future* was "For Heinrich after twenty-five years." They were, as their friend Randall Jarrell put it, a "Dual Monarchy."

Hannah Arendt had, as Hans Jonas remarked at her funeral, a "genius for friendship." In her own words, what moved her was the *Eros der Freundschaft*; and she considered her friendships the center of her life. Arendt dedicated her books to her friends; painted their portraits in words, contributed to their *Festschrifts*, sent them birthday poems and letters, quoted them, repeated their stories. She was fluent in the language of friendship. But the fluency had taken a long time to achieve—years in which mother tongue and friendship were often the only unchangeables in a flux of war, exile, new languages, and unfamiliar customs. In her youth she had been undiscriminating, and her gentle mother had often teased her by asking "Tell me, Hannahchen, who is now in and who is now out?" Throughout her life, she was temperamental, easily embarrassed, exacting in her judgments, and impatient; she could become, as Karl Jaspers put it, *widerborstig*, "bristly with obstinacy." With the tense urgency of those who have world history on their minds, she brushed away those who thought only of themselves. But loyalty to those with whom she had established a deep bond was fundamental to her nature, and generosity was its hallmark—its often secret hallmark, for she believed that the left hand should not know what the right is doing, just as she believed that knowing cannot know what thinking is doing. Language was her prime medium for giving—and receiving—but she also gave food packages, parties, tuition scholarships, birthday flowers, dinners, donations, and every emotion her receivers might have wished except the one she feared and despised, pity.

Friends of many sorts surrounded the Dual Monarchy, and their stories are as important for Hannah Arendt's story as their support and conversation were for her work. Some of the friends met each other, some did not; some had the esteemed title *Dichter*, "poet," some, like Karl Jaspers, the *Lieber Verehrtester*, the "dear most revered one," who slowly became *Lieber Freund*, "dear friend," changed titles over the years. In Paris, the intellectual friend they respected above all others, and mourned deeply when he died by his own hand in 1940, was the literary critic Walter Benjamin. During the war, in New York, Kurt Blumenfeld, not a thinker of the first rank but a man to whose good judgment Arendt could pay one of her highest compliments, *immer hast Du recht* ("you always get it right"), was their chief companion for arguments. Though Hannah Arendt often talked with the theologian Paul Tillich, and once went straight from a conversation to her writing table to produce a remarkable essay, "Organized Guilt," there were limits to their intellectual sympathy which they both respected: "We made an agreement that we do not have to read each other's books."[5] The novelist Hermann Broch came into their orbit in 1946, and Arendt wrote to Blumenfeld, who had departed for Palestine, that this was "the best thing that has happened since you left."[6]

Arendt first met Karl Jaspers when she was a student, and she reestablished and deepened the relationship by correspondence after the war, before she visited him on her first return trip to Europe in 1949. She went to Karl and Gertrud Jaspers's house in Basel, she told a friend, *wie man nach Hause kommt*, "as one comes home." The philosopher Martin Heidegger had been Arendt's teacher during her university years and became her friend. But he was never drawn into the circle of the Dual Monarchy, remaining what Arendt had called him in a poem written after they met in 1924, when she was eighteen, a stranger at the feast.[7]

Heidegger, Benjamin, and Broch were "poetic thinkers," men Arendt esteemed for their love of language. Each in his own way had "drifted out of the nineteenth century into the twentieth century the way one is driven onto the coast of a strange land" (as she wrote of Benjamin).[8] Blumenfeld and Jaspers were older and more fatherly men whose *humanitas* and concern for the world sustained her.

After the war, the Blüchers added American friends to the edges of the "peer group." Literary and political, rather than philosophical, affinities drew them to Randall Jarrell, Alfred Kazin, Dwight Macdonald, Philip Rahv, Robert Lowell, Harold Rosenberg, and Mary McCarthy. Most of these friendships waxed and waned in cycles over the years, but the friendship with Mary McCarthy grew steadily deeper. To her Arendt dedicated *On Violence* in 1969.

The American intellectual friends were a marvel to the Blüchers. "Their discussions are without fanaticism and their arguments are accessible to a large number of people," Arendt told Jaspers in 1946. "Each intellectual here is sure as a matter of principle that he is, as an intellectual, in opposition... he does not worship the God of Success."[9] She had developed a horror of elitist, opportunistic intellectuals during Adolf Hitler's rise to power, at a time when "the purely personal problem was not what your enemies were doing but what your friends were doing."[10] Her new American friends gave her hope for freedom in "the life of the mind." Praising a friend as *sehr amerikanisch*, "very American," to a European was one of her great pleasures.

But though the American friends were liberating, they lacked the deep personal roots in European culture that nourished Hannah Arendt's life and work. Her American citizenship was precious to her; it relieved her of her stateless condition and gave her a role in a republic, the form of government she admired above all others. But, personally, what she was most grateful for was a country in which she could have "the freedom of becoming a citizen without having to pay the price of assimilation."[11] She clung to her European background and particularly to the German language, never really exchanging her mother tongue for English. "The words we use in ordinary speech," she explained in one of her Germanic-English sentences, "receive their specific weight, which guides our usage and saves us from mindless clichés, through the manifold associations which arise automatically and uniquely out of the treasure of great poetry with which the particular language... has been blessed."[12]

In addition to her thinking "peer group"—all Europeans and all men—and the American friends, the Blüchers had a "tribe." Blücher's friends from his days in the Brandler Group, a faction of the German Communist Party, Arendt's friends from her university years, their Paris acquaintances, and a few German-speakers they had met early in America made up this group. These were the émigrés with whom German could be spoken, the friends who could respond to a quotation from Goethe with a quotation from Heine, who knew German fairy tales. The tribe celebrated birthdays together, ushered in the New Year at the Blüchers' Sylvester parties, cared about each other's children and work.

Some of the tribe summered together in the Catskills, some shared Passover seders. Well educated, but not thinking partners (with the exception of "the Hanses"—Hans Jonas and Hans Morgenthau), the tribe members were good company and deeply loyal.

The tribe's constancy was crucial: "The old friends are, after all, better than the new ones. That has become a kind of stock saying for us," Arendt said. [13] That this stock saying sprang from deep roots is apparent in the careful distinction she drew at the opening of her public farewell to W. H. Auden: "I met Auden late in his life and mine—at an age when the easy, knowledgeable intimacy of friendships formed in one's youth can no longer be attained, because not enough life is left, or expected to be left, to share with another, thus we were very good friends, but not intimate friends." [14]

The two oldest, most intimate friends, the two predecessors of the tribe, did not live in New York. Robert Gilbert, Blücher's *Jugendfreund* from Berlin, a songwriter and poet, moved to Switzerland after a brief period spent in America during the war. Anne Mendelssohn Weil, Hannah Arendt's *Jugendfreundin* from Königsberg, became a French citizen. Arendt's first book, *Rahel Varnhagen: The Life of a Jewess*, was dedicated "To Anne, since 1921." Blücher, who did not write, had no book to present to his friend, but after Blücher's death Hannah Arendt paid "Cher Robert" a written tribute when she supplied an "Afterword" to his collected poems.

The friends of every sort and also the historical figures with whom Arendt felt special affinities, like Rosa Luxemburg and Rahel Varnhagen, had one characteristic in common: each was, in his or her own way, an outsider. In Hannah Arendt's personal lexicon, *wirkliche Menschen*, real people, were "pariahs." Her friends were not outcasts, but outsiders, sometimes by choice and sometimes by destiny. In the broadest sense, they were unassimilated. "Social nonconformism," she once said bluntly, "is the *sine qua non* of intellectual achievement." [15] And, she might well have added, also of human dignity. From situations in which social conformism prevailed, she made hasty exits, often with the aid of another of her stock phrases: "This place *ist nicht für meiner Mutters Tochter* [is not for my mother's daughter];" "To public relations I have an allergy;" "Here is nothing but a *Rummel* [uproar]." Hannah Arendt maintained her independence and she expected her friends to do the same. Not many disappointed her, and a few outdid her. Jaspers had what she considered an idiosyncratic view, though it seemed quite simple to him, a former psychiatrist: "You say that only pariahs are really human, but I think: also the mentally ill."[16]

The independence of thinking and of living that she had always appreciated in her friends became even more important to Arendt as she neared the end of her life. "Our conversations are now those of people who have become older—you just a little older, I very old," Jaspers told her in 1966. "They were, as always, beautiful, but perhaps they went on a somewhat deeper level; not so exuberant as before. . . . In [them] there was both joy at the wondrousness of the world and dread in the face of evil; the search, in thinking, for the uttermost; and also such serenity."[17] Yes, she told Jaspers as she reflected on this letter and on her sixtieth birthday, which it marked, ". . . this is the beginning of old age, and I am really very content. I am a little bit like when I was a child—at last, feeling grown up. Now, that means—at last, letting go . . ."[18] Like Jaspers, in her old age Hannah Arendt needed the great philosophers, companions in the things of the mind. These companions, who had been nearby since her youth in Immanuel Kant's hometown, became friends. And the story of these friendships is the one closest to the hidden activity of her thinking self. It is the story in which Hannah Arendt's genius for friendship brought her the timeless friendships that grace the lives of people of genius.

Except for the few personal remarks she made in interviews, Hannah Arendt studiously avoided autobiography. She also had very firm notions about the suitability of biography, as a species of history, for anyone who was not an actor in the world of political affairs—a statesman, a general, or a revolutionary. Biography, she claimed, is "rather unsuitable for those in which the main interest lies in the life story, as for the lives of artists, writers and generally men and women whose genius forced them to keep the world at a certain distance and whose significance lies chiefly in their works, the artifacts they added to the world, not the role they played in it."[19] But these distinctions tell as much about Hannah Arendt's own rigid separation of the private and the public, work and action, as they do about writers, or works, or the world. Often it is an outstanding individual's distance from the world that can reveal the backstage of history and the temper of the times. "It is a curse to live in interesting times," goes an old Chinese proverb Arendt was fond of quoting, and in our all-too-interesting times, biographies of artists and writers often have the subject's efforts to achieve distance from the world—some letting go—as a central theme.

"Our eagerness to see recorded, displayed and discussed in public what were once strictly private affairs and nobody's business," Arendt once wrote as she reviewed a biography of Isak Dinesen, "is probably less legitimate than our curiosity is ready to admit."[20] She followed this warning when she wrote biographically about people she knew well. She did not write intimately. The portraits in her gallery, *Men in Dark Times*, were made by some magical inversion of a shadow-tracing technique: she traced the light cast on the darkness of our times by her friends, producing portraits purged of "mortal grossness," as though she had given the command, "thou shalt like an airy spirit go." But though she avoided gossipy "realism," she did not try to offer pedagogically designed idealizations or "lives" in the Plutarchian moralistic mode; she wrote political exemplary tales.

A biography abundant in novelistic descriptions of places, people, and periods would not be appropriate for someone like Hannah Arendt. What must be shown are the historical bases for her generalizations, the particular experiences that launched her thought, the friendships and loves that nourished her, and—if possible—her thinking manner or thinking style. The "thinking place" is as inaccessible as the "thinking ego," but something of the mode of thinking can be caught, as much or more from conversational contexts and letters as from published works.

In Hannah Arendt contrary currents met, making her thinking both rich and turbulent. In a letter which she wrote to Kurt Blumenfeld in 1947, for example, she could say "I am really quite happy, because one cannot go against one's own natural vitality. The world as God created it seems to me a good one." She felt this even though she was struggling with a book about the "brutal things" introduced into this world with totalitarianism and its "method of fabricating" death. But no sooner had she called herself *fröhlich*, "happy," than she showed her other side: "I have a kind of melancholy, which I can only grapple with by understanding, by thinking these things through."[21] Hannah Arendt struggled to hold to an attitude she called *amor mundi*, love of the world. "Philosophical biography," though it is uncomfortably close to a contradiction in terms, because of thinking's invisibility, philosophy's timelessness, is what the story of Hannah Arendt's *amor mundi* calls for.

When Hannah Arendt told stories—"anecdotes of destiny" in Isak Dinesen's phrase—they brought people to her; her stories did not take her to people. All questions of reticence, self-concealment, and extent of self-knowledge aside, Arendt did not write autobiographically because she loved and needed company. Late in her life she asked an editor who had suggested that she write her memoirs: "If I write my stories down, who will come around to hear me tell them?" She kept herself from solitude with what she called her *Scheherazaderie*—as she had done since she was a child.

But unlike her friend W. H. Auden, Hannah Arendt did not ask her correspondents to destroy her letters or make any effort to remove the traces of her private life from her papers. She put the materials for her story in the public domain, in library collections, for those in future generations who wished to come around. In her concession to posthumous publicness, as in the respect due someone whose mental life, so carefully reflected in her books, was left to posterity, there is an implicit charge to those who write about her life: see what the anecdotes of private destiny have to say about the work and the world, the public things; see what illumination they offer in our dark times. To follow this charge, the course of the life ought to be viewed from the perspective of its close: not so that the course can "explain" the ending, or vice versa, but so that both changes and continuities can appear in the light of the moment when the "privilege of judging is left to others."

The earliest document in the papers Arendt left behind begins: "Johanna Arendt was born on a Sunday evening at quarter past nine, on October 14, 1906. The birth took twenty-two hours and went normally. The child weighed 3,695 grams [8 lbs. 4 oz.] at birth."[22] With these sentences, Martha Cohn Arendt began to set down her daughter's story and this remarkable record, entitled *Unser Kind* ("Our Child"), is the main written source of information about Arendt's childhood.

The *Unser Kind* book was left in a folder with souvenirs of the years of flight and resettlement: Martha Arendt's *Deutsches Reich Reisepass*; Hannah Arendt's birth certificate, French *carte d'identité*, American passports and visas; the Blüchers' divorce papers from their first marriages and their own marriage documents; and a small book in which Martha Arendt had entered the names, birth dates and death dates of the Arendts and Cohns of her generation and that of her parents. These documents have provided a chronological framework for this biography and the guidelines for the family stories which are included in appendix 1.

Hannah Arendt carried with her through her exile years and finally put into this folder of souvenirs copies of poems she wrote between 1923 and 1926—twenty-one in all. She made typed copies and added them to the poems she wrote in New York in the 1940s and early 1950s. Next to the poems she kept a transcript of her only autobiographical piece, "Die Schatten" ("The Shadows"), which she wrote when she was nineteen, after her first year as a university student. These writings, the most personal and private that ever flowed from her own pen, have been quoted here extensively in translation. The poems have not been annotated individually in the text because the original German versions are included in appendix 2.

Other reminders of the European past had been put into folders of their own. One held several copies of a large poster announcing Hannah Arendt's completion of a doctorate in philosophy and liberal arts at the University of Heidelberg. Another folder held the printed edition of Arendt's dissertation, "Saint Augustine's Concept of Love," published by Springer Verlag in 1929. She had carried this copy with her when she fled Germany in 1933, kept it through the years she spent in France, and brought it to America, battered and stained, the one sign of her brilliant but brief German academic career.

These folders were housed in a bank of file cabinets, now in the Library of Congress, neatly labeled according to a system that kept the facets of a complicated life distinct: Manuscripts, Excerpts, Reviews, Radio and Television, Publishers, Chicago, The New School, Finances, Restitution Case, and in several drawers, Correspondence (Personal). There had been other files in this bank before Hannah Arendt deposited them in archives. To the Library of Congress, she gave two gifts, a collection of manuscripts and lecture notes and a sheaf of materials from "The Eichmann Controversy"; and to the Deutsches Literaturarchiv in Marbach, Germany, she gave a collection of letters to and from Kurt Blumenfeld, Karl Jaspers, Martin Heidegger, and others, which was completed by a donation from her own estate. Heinrich Blücher's papers and transcripts of his lectures were donated to Bard College, where he had taught for nearly twenty years. These collections of papers are the basis for the story of Arendt's years in America, her career as a political theorist, her American friendships, and her relations with the émigré tribe members. I have consulted them all except the Heidegger correspondence, which is closed to scholars.

Hannah Arendt kept her file cabinets in her bedroom, an austere, undecorated place. In the Blüchers' last apartment, on Riverside Drive, the work spaces and the conversation spaces were what was important, and everything that did not belong in these spaces was arranged to be ignored. The dining room and the library were one room; at mealtimes all the old friends looked on them from four walls of bookshelves—Plato, Aristotle, Kant, Goethe, Rilke. Most of the books now reside in a special room of the Bard College Library, just down a hill from the grove where the Blüchers' ashes are buried.

The living room and Arendt's study were also one room. Near the big windows that faced on Riverside Park and the Hudson River were a work table and a smaller table for the typewriter. Close by were the shelves that held her own works: *Rahel Varnhagen: The Life of a Jewish Woman, The Origins of Totalitarianism, The Human Condition, Between Past and Future, On Revolution, Eichmann in Jerusalem, Men in Dark Times, On Violence, Crises of the Republic*, most not only in American, but British, German, and French editions, and some in Dutch, Swedish, Spanish, Portuguese, Japanese. These books, and a cardboard box full of yellowing reprints and newspaper articles, provided the basis for the bibliography included here as appendix 3.

In the center of this spacious living room were sofas and chairs, a little bar table wheeled in from a corner, and a coffee table crowded with cigarettes, matches, ashtrays, and an array of nut dishes, mint dishes, cookie jars—the conversation center. But when visitors came, the windows drew them through the room toward Arendt's worktable. At this table Arendt's work seemed to be going on all the time, even when she was sitting with her visitors in the center of the room, talking. And the permanent audience for the work was in place on the table: photographs of Martha Cohn Arendt, of Heinrich Blücher, and of Martin Heidegger. This audience was watching, and the work was there in front of them, when Hannah Arendt died of a heart attack in her living room, while visiting with friends. The first page of "Judging," the third and final part of her last work, *The Life of the Mind*, was rolled into her typewriter—blank except for the title and two epigraphs.

Hannah Arendt's friend and literary executor Mary McCarthy edited the two existing volumes of *The Life of the Mind*, which were published in 1978. The preliminary manuscripts and the miscellany of notes for "Judging" are now in the Library of Congress; in the Deutsches Literaturarchiv there is a collection of small "thought books," full of Arendt's ruminations and quotations in Greek, Latin, English, French, and German—the notes she kept while working on her American books.

When she died in 1975, at the age of sixty-nine, Hannah Arendt was childless and a widow. Many of the American friends and most of the tribe members mingled with the crowd of mourners at her funeral, but the thinking peer group was absent—only Martin Heidegger was still alive—and the family were very few. Her cousin Ernst Fuerst and his wife came from Israel, one of their daughters from Germany, and Arendt's stepsister Eva Beerwald from England. The once large family of Arendts and Cohns—Hannah Arendt had had nine aunts and uncles and twelve cousins—had been reduced to five cousins and an aunt by marriage, living continents apart, in England, Germany, Israel, India.

Many of those who lived to mourn Hannah Arendt have contributed their recollections to this biography through interviews and letters. Only a few could tell me firsthand stories of the years before Hannah Arendt's father's death in 1913; most of the firsthand accounts of her childhood and youth date from the early 1920s and after, including those she herself provided. Stories about her adulthood are plentiful, and often exist— memories being what they are—in as many versions as there are tellers. From versions of a story not significantly different, I have woven a single story for this book and cut loose threads away. In these cases, the criteria familiar to historians—and detectives—have been employed in the weaving: inner consistency and plausibility; conformity with written sources, other stories, and documents; reliability of the storyteller in terms of vantage point and knowledge. In those few instances where irreconcilable versions of stories exist, I have noted all the versions; and the same principle of inclusiveness has governed conflicting or complementary answers given to my interview questions. (Material which appears in the text in quotation marks but without annotation is from interviews.)

It has not been my intention, as I have shaped and selected these stories, to be either definitive or definitively critical. From the rich Arendt Papers and from what my informants have told me, I have taken only what my project, a philosophical biography, required. And I have not tried to add to these ingredients a dimension of predictive criticism. At a memorial service for his friend, Hans Jonas said, quite correctly: "To call her a 'great thinker' is for none of her contemporaries to presume, nor to predict how her thought will withstand the onslaught of time."[23] I have indicated what has been written in criticism of Hannah Arendt's work, but my primary task when I have discussed her books has been contextual; I have tried to show how she came to her concerns, her subjects, how she went about making—and remaking—her books, and how she thought her way from one book to the next. Because she wrote her major works while she was living in America, and because her influence has been greatest here, my presentation of her work and of her critics is American in its focus, even though each chapter crosses the Atlantic at least once.

Stories communicated orally, letters, documents, memoirs, and also Hannah Arendt's works came into this biography in different languages and had to be translated. Much was inevitably lost in the process. In a remark she made to me when I was her doctoral student at the New School there is consolation for this conversion of the language of her philosophical and poetic homeland, German, the language of her first exile, French, the language of her second citizenship, English-with-a-German-accent, and the languages of her political forebears, Latin and Greek, all into American. I had produced a translation of a cryptic saying of Aristotle's; Hannah Arendt checked her copy of a standard Latin translation and compared it to my effort, disapprovingly. She then checked a German translation and became skeptical about the Latin. Finally, she sat back, rendered her verdict on my translation, and made a statement about her thinking style: "Ja, well, my dear, it's not exactly right, but then maybe Aristotle would think it more interesting than wrong."

# Acknowledgments

Hannah Arendt was fortunate in her friendships, and as I have written this biography, I have been fortunate in her friendships as well. Mary McCarthy, Arendt's literary executor, kindly granted me interviews, access to her letters from Hannah Arendt, and permission to quote from published work and from the unpublished materials in the Arendt estate. Lotte Kohler, who devotedly undertook the enormous task of sorting and organizing Arendt's papers and possessions, has been unfailingly generous as an informant, a reader of my manuscript, and a moral supporter.

Arendt's surviving family, Kaethe and Ernst Fuerst of Tel Aviv, Else and Manfred Braude of Cambridge, England, and Eva Beerwald of London, have supplied stories, photographs, and their warm hospitalities. Niouta Ghosh of Calcutta, a cousin, has answered my queries by letter. Arendt's first husband, Günther Anders, received me in Vienna and has since helped me often via airmail.

The members of the Arendt-Blücher tribe, most of them now living in or near New York City, have guided me, corrected me, helped me with translations from the German—in short, educated me. I have met with most of the tribe members individually and joined them for the tribal gatherings that have marked each anniversary of Hannah Arendt's death. I am in debt to them not just for their help with this book, but for that reflection of their loyalty to her that has fallen upon me: Jeanette and Salo Baron, Charlotte Beradt, Alcopley, Rose Feitelson, Minka and Peter (d. 1981) Huber, Eleonore and Hans Jonas, Charlotte and Chanan Klenbort and their children Daniel and Irene, Else and Paul Oskar Kristeller, Alice and Joseph Maier, Hans Morgenthau (d. 1980) and his daughter Susanna,

Priscilla and Robert (d. 1978) Pick, Richard Plant, Ingrid Scheib, Joan Stambaugh, and Helen Wolff. It was Anne Mendelssohn Weil who first urged me to write this biography of her friend of fifty years; she has encouraged me ever since. I regret that Robert Gilbert, Blücher's best friend, died before I was able to talk with him. His former wife, Elke Gilbert of Zurich, and his daughter Marianne Finnegan have been very kind and helpful. Many of Arendt's acquaintances, often friends of these friends, have given me interviews: George Agree, Richard Bernstein, Leon Botstein, Irma Brandeis, Roger Errera (Paris), Carl Frankenstein (Jerusalem), Nahum Goldmann (Paris), Nina Gourfinkel (Paris), Kaethe Hirsch (Paris), Yela and Henry Lowenfeld, Eva Michaelis-Stern (Jerusalem), Henry Paechter (d. 1980), Ilse Schlechter, Elizabeth Stambler, Hannah Strauss, Ernst Vollrath (Cologne). Many of Arendt's American friends have died: Rosalie Colie, J. Glenn Gray, Randall Jarrell, Robert Lowell, Philip Rahv, Harold Rosenberg. But many of those who survived Arendt have been very helpful to me; I particularly wish to thank Dwight Macdonald and William Shawn.

I read the Arendt-Jaspers and Arendt-Blumenfeld correspondences in the Deutsches Literaturarchiv in Marbach, Germany, where Ludwig Greve and his colleagues provided me with ideal conditions and, in Herr Greve's case, splendid company. Hans Saner of Basel granted me permission to quote the Jaspers materials in his care, and I thank him for that as well as for the fine editions of Jaspers's works he has prepared. As noted, I have not had access to the Arendt-Heidegger correspondence.

I consulted the Arendt Papers in the Library of Congress, Washington, D.C., but most of my notes on the papers date from the years 1976–1977 when they were being prepared for deposit in the library by Lotte Kohler, Jerome Kohn, and Lawrence May. Therefore my references to the Arendt Papers in the notes are by author, recipient or title, and date, not Library of Congress box number. I am grateful to the library's manuscript room staff for their services. And I also wish to thank the staffs of the other libraries where I worked: Olin Library, Wesleyan University; the Bard College Library; the Judaica Room of the New York Public Library; the Leo Baeck Institute (New York); the British Museum; the Centre de documentation juive (Paris); the Alliance Israélite Universelle (Paris); the Central Zionist Archive (Jerusalem); and Yad Vashem (Jerusalem). Bibliographic research to locate Arendt's early journalistic writings was done in various German libraries by Paivi and Heinz Kemner.

Among Hannah Arendt's students, there are some who have been particularly supportive: Michael Denneny, Melvyn Hill and his wife Anne, Jerome Kohn, and Lawrence May. My friend Jerome Kohn carefully and helpfully read this manuscript; the sections on Arendt's books owe much to his criticism.

My colleagues and students at Wesleyan University's College of Letters, the college secretaries, and my typist Mary Jane Arico have been patient and faithful. This book was written without financial assistance from any granting agency, but Wesleyan University provided support for manuscript preparation.

Maureen MacGrogan of the Yale University Press brought to the editing of this manuscript a rare combination of philosophical acumen and literary skill. In the page-by-page seminars she conducted, I was always the grateful student. Anne Mackinnon's careful attention to the editing in its later stages was crucial in bringing the manuscript to its final form.

I hope that those to whom I dedicate this book will take pleasure in it—as a sign of the good care they have taken of me: Hope, Robert, the two Loises, Ernie, the older Elisabeth, and the rest of my dear family.

*Chester, Connecticut*
*July 1981*

# PART 1
## 1906–1933

DURING THE YEARS SHE LIVED IN AMERICA, HANNAH Arendt seldom spoke about her childhood. Long before the last of her relatives had left the family's home in Königsberg, East Prussia, and the city had been destroyed by bombs and rebuilt as Kaliningrad, USSR, she had divided her life into "Then" and "Now" several times. With each division, the first Then, childhood, became a more secret, private matter. When she was eighteen and a student of theology at Marburg University, she made her temporal divisions in the poetic language of her teacher Martin Heidegger: "No longer" and "Not yet." As she finished her academic studies and her doctoral dissertation, she marked off a Then of Reason divorced from practical affairs and a Now of Reason in *praxis*. The year 1933 gave this division a political content: Hannah Arendt had been a German Jew and then she became a stateless person, a Jewish refugee.

When the Then of her childhood rose up behind the great divide of the Second World War, Hannah Arendt spoke of it as a matter of *Muttersprache*, "mother tongue." Language was continuity. As she told an interviewer in 1964, "After all, it wasn't the German language that went crazy."[1] That German was Hannah Arendt's *Heimat* ("home") until the end of her life was, so to speak, a political fact. But remembering the German poems she had learned by heart as a girl was also a way of not remembering, or remembering only indirectly, how her childhood had divided—with the death of her father from syphilis. There was no single moment of trauma; Paul Arendt's dying took five agonized years, from his daughter's second year to her seventh. But his death slowly brought a happy, rich childhood to an end.

Arendt told very few people about her father's death, and very few people—including even her first husband—knew that she wrote poetry. Her poems were her most private life. Hannah Arendt rejected what she called introspection, and she had many harsh words for psychological analysis; it was in and through poetry that she understood herself. In her adolescent poetry, she had wondered whether she would triumph over her early loss, her sense of being *unheimlich*, uncanny or strange:

> I regard my hand,
> Mine, and uncannily near
> But, still, another thing.
> Is it more than I am,
> Has it a higher meaning?[2]

3

But Hannah Arendt's gift was not for poetry. And poetry did not give her what she had lost with her father's death—a sense of trust. Martin Heidegger, though he gave her both the beginning of a brilliant education and a love in the tradition of German Romantic poetry, did not restore her sense of trust. Her gift for philosophy is certainly apparent in the doctoral dissertation she wrote at Heidelberg with Karl Jaspers. However, what is most striking in her work is her longing, her vision of that community-sense which Saint Augustine called "neighborly love." Such love came to Arendt only in Paris, among her émigré "tribe" and with her second husband, Heinrich Blücher. But the foundation for it was laid during her early adulthood in Germany, while she slowly turned from philosophy to politics in the company of Kurt Blumenfeld and with the support of Karl Jaspers. What she was looking for is apparent in one of the rare public statements she made about her intellectual and emotional development. She spoke to an interviewer, in 1964, about Jaspers: "You see, wherever Jaspers comes to speak, things become clear. He is open and trusting, he speaks with an intensity I haven't encountered with anyone else. . . . And, if I may say—I grew up fatherless—I allowed myself to be guided by [his reason]. God knows, I don't want to make him seem responsible for me, but if anyone has succeeded in making me reasonable, it has been him."[3]

For both Hannah Arendt and Karl Jaspers, their discussions were best, deepest, most trusting after the war, when she returned to Europe for visits. Both had, by then, come to a new, shared understanding of philosophy. "Philosophy must become concrete and practical, without for a moment losing sight of its origin," Jaspers wrote in a 1946 letter.[4] But this understanding began, for both of them, in 1933, when Hitler came to power in Germany, when they both realized that "neighborly love," too, had to become concrete and practical.

# CHAPTER 1
## *Unser Kind*
### (1906-1924)

> A large town such as Königsberg on the Pregel River,
> center of a district, containing government offices and a
> university, suitably situated for overseas trade and for
> intercourse with adjoining as well as remoter countries
> of different languages and customs—such a town is the
> right place for gaining knowledge concerning men and
> the world even without traveling.
>
> Kant, *Anthropology Treated Pragmatically*

### Königsbergers

Both sets of Hannah Arendt's grandparents, the Arendts and the Cohns,
had raised their families in Königsberg, the capital of East Prussia, a city
whose foundations dated from the thirteenth century. First built by the
Teutonic Order, a military and religious organization dating from the
time of the Crusades, Königsberg was for a time the residence of the
Order's Grand Master. In the sixteenth century, it became the residence
of the dukes of Prussia, whose castle overlooking a lake dominated the
center of the city. The lively but peaceful provincial capital was
threatened with destruction during the First World War, but when the
Russian army was repulsed it remained unharmed—until the Second
World War, when first the Jewish population and then the German
population disappeared.

Nearly five thousand Jews lived in Königsberg at the beginning of the
twentieth century, a majority of them Russian. The stretch of railroad
from Odessa to Königsberg was the shortest route from southern Russia to
the Baltic Sea, and hundreds of thousands of Russian Jews, fleeing from
anti-Jewish legislation and pogroms, used the railroad to escape. The vast
majority of the escapees went on to England and America—but many
settled in Königsberg and other eastern German cities with sizable Jewish
populations.

Jacob Cohn, Hannah Arendt's maternal grandfather, was born in 1838
in what is now Lithuania and emigrated to Königsberg in 1852, just
before the transition from the reign of Czar Nicholas to that of his son

5

Alexander II. In 1851, despite protests from Western European Jews, Nicholas had issued a classification of Jews into two groups: the wealthy or skillful "useful" and the "nonuseful." The nonuseful were subject to conscription, and during the Crimean War many fled the country. Jacob Cohn's father, who was a trader, fled and established a small tea-importing business in Königsberg, which had become the most important tea-trading center on the continent, adding Russian teas to the British-dominated world market. Jacob took over the family business and under his leadership it became J. N. Cohn and Company, the largest firm in Königsberg.

Jacob Cohn had three children by his first wife and then four more by his second wife, also a Russian emigrant, Fanny Spiero. When Jacob Cohn died in 1906, his wife, his seven children, and their children were left with the family business and a great deal of money. Until the inflation years after the First World War, the twelve cousins who were Jacob's grandchildren lived in comfort. Hannah Arendt always remembered with pleasure going, as a child, to the Cohn warehouses, sensing in the air the Russia of her mother's ancestors and being feted with a delightful item that had been added to the firm's export catalogue: marzipan.

The Königsberg to which the Cohns and so many other Russian families emigrated had been second only to Berlin as a center for the German-Jewish Enlightenment in the eighteenth century. Many Jews attended the Albertina, Königsberg's university, enrolling most frequently in the faculty of medicine but often seeking out the Albertina's most illustrious professor, Immanuel Kant. Among the educated Königsberg Jews, however, the followers of Moses Mendelssohn were the most important intellectual force. One group of followers, financed by Mendelssohn, founded a periodical in Königsberg, Ha-Me'-assef ("The Gatherer"), dedicated to presenting non-Jewish literature in Hebrew translations. This group was part of a movement called Haskalah ("Enlightenment") which had arisen in the Eastern Jewish communities and moved westward with the emigrations. Western reformers like Mendelssohn promoted the Eastern movement, but they placed less emphasis on the Hebrew language: Mendelssohn was more interested in introducing the Jews to German culture in German. For nontraditionalist German Jews, Mendelssohn became the chief exemplar of social and cultural—though not political—emancipation and he was just that for Hannah Arendt's paternal grandfather, Max Arendt, whose mother's family had come to Königsberg from Russia in Mendelssohn's time.

Mendelssohn died in 1786, before the king of Prussia met with his advisors to consider whether the Jews of Prussia should be granted citizenship. The negative decision discouraged Jews who had desired citizenship, though it left the privileged social standing of the educated, Germanized, urban Jews relatively unaffected. Many Königsbergers of the generation after Mendelssohn's, including the prominent publicist David Friedlander, converted to Christianity. In *The Origins of Totalitarianism*, Hannah Arendt remarked that men like Friedlander developed a contempt for Judaism that would never have been possible for a man of Mendelssohn's convictions and integrity. Mendelssohn, she thought, "knew that [a man's] extraordinary esteem for his person paralleled an extraordinary contempt for his people. Since [Mendelssohn], unlike Jews of following generations, did not share this contempt, he did not consider himself an exception."[1] His townsman, Friedlander, was Arendt's model for the kind of Jew she herself never wanted to be, "an exception Jew."

Napoleon's entry into Berlin marked the beginning of the end of the Friedlander generation's most illustrious social institution, the salons held in the homes of Jewesses like Rahel Varnhagen, the subject of Hannah Arendt's biography, *Rahel Varnhagen: The Life of a Jewess*. Napoleon's conquest afforded the Prussian Jews many of the civic rights recently accorded to the French Jews and the Jews of the western German states in Napoleon's Confederation of the Rhine. But when these rights were extended, the wealthy and educated Jews no longer stood out distinctly against the background of their lesser fellows. They had to strive to prove themselves "exceptions."

The Prussian Jews had hoped that the Congress of Vienna in 1815 would finally bring them full political rights. But they found themselves cast back into much the same status they had had before Napoleon's victories. Many Jews of the wealthy, educated upper class followed the example of Friedlander's generation and converted to Christianity, accepting the prevailing conservative notions of the "Christian-German" or "Teutonic-German" state. As a consequence of this wave of conversions, tensions between nontraditionalist and Orthodox Jews were greater than they had been since the days of Mendelssohn's cultural reformation. Many of the Jews who did not convert to Christianity gave their allegiance to the newly emerging Reform Judaism of men like Abraham Geiger or the Historical Judaism—known in America as Conservative Judaism—of Zechariah Frankel.

The deep divisions between Orthodox and non-Orthodox Jews continued through the period of Jewish political emancipation and through the period of Eastern emigrations, and they were still firmly in place during Hannah Arendt's childhood. Her grandparents on both sides were Reform Jews and admirers of the Reform rabbi in Königsberg, Hermann Vogelstein, one of the most influential leaders of liberal German Jewry. Along with other members of his family, Vogelstein, who had published a number of books on Jewish history, including a standard history of the Jews in Rome, provided both a cultural and a political example. He was a *German* Jew and he was a supporter of the Social Democratic Party. His son and daughter were leaders in the Jewish Youth Movement, the Camaraden, to which many of Arendt's young school friends belonged. His sister, Julie Vogelstein-Braun, edited the works of her stepson, Otto Braun, a young writer killed in the First World War who was the son of Lily Braun, a famous socialist publicist for women's issues. Both Rabbi Vogelstein and his sister emigrated to New York before the Second World War and established a philanthropic foundation which provided financial assistance to emigrants. Hannah Arendt met them again in New York, but by that time she had spent years working for the cause they had hoped would never be fostered by events—Zionism.

There were some Zionists in Königsberg during Hannah Arendt's school years, particularly in the university community. A *Verein jüdischer Studenten*, a Jewish students' club, had been founded in 1904, and many of the Jewish students joined it. The older generation, including Max Arendt, who was one of the leaders of the Königsberg Jewish community and a member of the Centralverein deutscher Staatsbürger jüdischen Glaubens ("Central Organization for German Citizens of the Jewish Faith"), did not look favorably upon the Zionists. Kurt Blumenfeld, later the president of the German Zionist Organization and Hannah Arendt's friend and mentor, met Max Arendt when he was one of the student Zionists and clashed heatedly with him about "the Jewish Question." Max Arendt would not hear any argument that cast his Germanness in doubt. Their differences remained, but the two became friends, and Blumenfeld was often a guest at the Arendts' home where he, always a jovial and exuberant man, enjoyed—as he recollected in his memoirs—getting down on the floor to play games with Max Arendt's infant granddaughter, Hannah.[2]

Hannah Arendt's father, Paul, was Max Arendt's only son by his first wife, Johanna. Neither Paul nor his sister Henriette, who moved to

Berlin, became a social worker, and married a Frenchman, was on good terms with their father's second wife, Klara—their mother's sister. Klara Arendt was a disagreeable woman, famous in her family for her willfulness and her inability to begin charity at home. When her granddaughter Hannah—named after Paul's mother, Johanna—later had many harsh complaints to make about Jewish plutocrats and philanthropists, the family's impatience with Klara Arendt sounded an echo. Martha Arendt, on the other hand, was the daughter of a simple, quiet woman, Fanny Spiero Cohn, who spoke German with a thick Russian accent and enjoyed wearing Russian peasant costumes. The Cohn women were generous and emotional. When both mother and daughter were widows, they comforted each other and went together to take the waters at Karlsbad. Their sympathy and closeness was part of the prevailing pattern in Hannah Arendt's extended Cohn family, where there were many more women than men, and where so many of the women suffered through the deaths of their husbands or children.

Paul and Martha Arendt were more educated, more widely travelled, and considerably more leftist in their politics than their parents. Both of them had become socialists when they were in their teens, while the Socialist Party was still illegal in Germany, and this commitment distinguished them from most of their contemporaries who belonged to the German Democratic Party. Paul, who took his engineering degree at the Albertina, was an amateur scholar. His library was stocked with the Greek and Latin classics, which his daughter later read with enthusiasm. Martha, like most women of her class and generation, had been educated at home and then sent abroad—she was in Paris for three years studying French and music. Neither of Hannah Arendt's parents was religious. But they sent their daughter to the synagogue with her Arendt grandparents, and they maintained good relationships with Rabbi Vogelstein and his family—for they could meet him as fellow social democrats.

Hannah's early relationship with Rabbi Vogelstein was more personal: she had a great crush on him. Martha Arendt enjoyed telling her friends that Hannah had announced her intention of marrying the rabbi when she grew up. Martha answered that if Hannah married Vogelstein she would have to do without pork, to which Hannah, never at a loss for a way to have her way, replied: "Well, then, I'll marry a Rabbi with pork." When Hannah was an elementary school student Rabbi Vogelstein appeared several times a week to give religious instruction. This instruction, which began when Hannah was seven years old, was the only formal

religious training she ever had, though she did, years later in Paris, study
Hebrew informally. Christian Sunday school had been mandatory for all
kindergarten students and she was enough influenced by this training and
by the practices at home of the Arendts' Christian maid to proclaim to
Vogelstein—to his astonishment, no doubt—that prayers were to be offered to Christ.

The rabbi was not one to be taken completely aback by a saucy child,
however, and on a later occasion when Hannah proclaimed that she no
longer believed in God he replied: "And who asked you?" Vogelstein's
appreciation that personal religious doubts and struggles were not at the
center of a sense of Jewish identity, Hannah Arendt later understood,
reflected a shift in German Jewish consciousness during the early years of
the twentieth century. Kurt Blumenfeld registered the shift in his
memoirs by quoting a remark his friend, the publisher Salman Schocken,
made in 1914: "Zur Zeit der Emancipation fragte man: was glaubst Du?
Heute fragt man nur: Wer bist du? (In the emancipation period one asked
'What do you believe?' Today one asks only 'Who are you?')"[3] And the
truthful answer to the new question was, Blumenfeld felt and Arendt
agreed: Regardless of what you believe or do not believe, you were born
a Jew.

Anti-Semitism was not very much in evidence to the assimilated Jews
of Königsberg during Hannah Arendt's childhood. The Jewish business
and professional families lived in a district called the Hufen, near the
spacious Tiergarten, in middle-class comfort. Working-class Jews, known
to even the descendants of Russian emigrants as *Ostjuden*, Eastern Jews,
lived on the south side of the Pregel River near the oldest Orthodox
synagogue, an imposing red brick building with a rather Byzantine dome.
Middle-class Jews and lower-class Jews seldom met, and very few of the
lower-class Jewish children made their way into the *Gymnasium*, where
there were only three or four Jews in each form. It was unusual for a Jew
to hold a local or provincial government appointment, but the Jews
contributed schoolteachers and artists to the larger community, in addition to the more prevalent doctors and lawyers. Jews were not appointed
to professorships at the university, though they held honorary positions
and were permitted to teach Judaic studies. Paul and Martha Arendt's
Jewish acquaintances were, unlike their parents' friends, not merchants
but professionals—doctors, lawyers, educators, and musicians. Martha
Arendt was friendly with a group of women who opened kindergartens
and elementary schools, Frau Stein and Frau Sittznik who ran the

schools Hannah Arendt attended were among them. These women were not university educated—the Albertina did not accept women students until 1906—but they had received teachers' training. Martha's generation was the first since the days of Rahel Varnhagen to produce a substantial number of female literary figures, artists, musicians; and in Königsberg there were literary circles, chamber groups, and political organizations in which women were prominent. Among Martha Arendt's friends, it was assumed that daughters should be raised and educated for careers once available only to sons.

The assimilation of secular middle-class Jews like the Arendts did not preclude the occasional confusing remark, heard in school or at play, from introducing their children to their Jewishness. Hannah Arendt came home from her elementary school one day to ask her mother if what one of her schoolmates had told her was true—that her grandfather had murdered the Lord Jesus. When Hannah Arendt reflected on such incidents as an adult, and spoke about them in a 1964 television interview, she placed them in a context that minimized their hurtfulness but stressed what she had learned from them.

I came from an old Königsberg family, [the Arendts]. But the word "Jew" was never mentioned at home. I first encountered it—though really it is hardly worth recounting it—in the anti-Semitic remarks of children as we played in the streets—then I became, so to speak, enlightened. . . . As a child—now a somewhat older child—I knew, for example, that I looked Jewish. . . . That is, that I looked a bit different from the rest. But not in a way that made me feel inferior—I was simply aware of it, that is all. And my mother, my home, was also a bit different from the way it usually is—even in comparison to other Jewish children . . . things were a little different for me—but it is very difficult for a child to determine precisely what such a difference consists of. . . . My mother was not very theoretical . . . the "Jewish Question" had no relevance for her. Of course she was a Jewess! She would never have had me christened, baptized. And she would have given me a real spanking if she had ever had reason to believe that I had denied being Jewish. The matter was never a topic of discussion. It was out of the question that it be. . . . You see, all Jewish children encountered anti-Semitism. And the souls of many children were poisoned by it. The difference with me lay in the fact that my mother always insisted that I not humble myself. One must defend oneself! When my teachers made anti-Semitic remarks— usually they were not directed at me but at my other classmates, particularly at the Eastern Jewesses—I was instructed to stand up immediately, to leave the class, go home, and leave the rest to school protocol. My mother would write one of her many letters, and, with that, my involvement in the matter ended completely. I had a day off from school, and that was, of course, very nice. But if remarks came at me from other children, I was not allowed to go home and tell. That did not count. One had to defend *oneself* against remarks from other children. And, so, these things did not become really problematic for me. There existed rules of conduct, house rules, so to speak, by which my dignity was protected, absolutely protected.[4]

Looking back over some fifty-five years, Hannah Arendt saw the anti-Semitism encountered in her Königsberg childhood as an unproblematic matter for her; she felt that she had been protected and even that she had grown up, as she later told her teacher, Karl Jaspers, without prejudices under her mother's tutelage. What stood out in her memory was the attitude she tried to maintain throughout her life, and which she tried to encourage other Jews to adopt: "One must defend oneself!"

*A Sunshine Childhood Overshadowed*

The lesson Martha Arendt taught her daughter was part of a larger project. Frau Arendt wanted to guide her daughter through what she called a *normale Entwicklung*, a normal development.[5] This ideal was not Jewish, it was German, and it stemmed from the reading matter that was obligatory for all educated Germans: the complete works of Goethe, *the* German mentor in matters of *Bildung*, the conscious forming and shaping of body, mind, and spirit. In German homes where children were expected eventually to join the *Bildungselite* ("educated elite"), small-scale preparatory versions of what Goethe had called the "Pedagogic Province" were established. Self-discipline, constructive channeling of passions, renunciation, and responsibility for others—these were the Goethean watchwords. The master's catechism was known to every child:

Was aber ist deine Pflicht? Die Forderung des Tages. [And just what is your duty? The demands of the day.]

Martha Arendt kept a careful record of her daughter's development. From the day of her birth, the Arendts' *Unser Kind* ("Our Child") book was filled with notes about physical growth, daily routines and menus, various illnesses and treatments, intellectual accomplishments, and signs of personality formation. To her parents' obvious delight, "the little daughter" grew according to the ideal schedule of the *normale Ent-wicklung*. She was healthy, alert, and cheerful, "a real sunshine child."

When Hannah Arendt was born in October 1906, Martha and Paul Arendt were living in Linden, a suburb of Hannover. Herr Arendt had a job with an electrical engineering firm and was able to buy a comfortable frame house and keep as a nursemaid a Christian woman named Ada. The Arendts vacationed during Hannah's first two summers—a stay in Lauterberg, a Harz Mountains resort, is mentioned in the *Unser Kind* book—travelled to Königsberg to visit the Cohn and Arendt grandparents, and kept up ties with friends in Berlin, where they had spent the first years of their marriage. Relatives and friends came to Hannover for visits. Until the first signs of Paul Arendt's illness appeared, the household was lively, full, and graceful: Martha Arendt played the piano, everyone, including "the little dear one," sang songs and enjoyed storytelling. Except on the harshest North German winter days, the Arendts went to a nearby park or to the central garden in Hannover for the fresh air walks considered essential to health by generations of Germans.

Martha Arendt had the ways and means to foster her daughter's physical *Entwicklung* with intense care. She recorded her successes and the occasional setbacks minutely, beginning with the first day: "After twenty-four hours, the baby was given mother's milk . . . but it did not know how to suckle, so it had to be given a little fennel tea. By the fourth day, the child was finally able to suckle. . . . During the first two weeks, it lost weight; at the end of the first week it weighed seven pounds, four ounces. It then developed as the chart indicates. . . ." Martha Arendt's notes go on in similar detail to other topics: feeding schedules, minor illnesses and difficulties with medications, physical characteristics. The Arendts watched their child with wonder: "The temperament is quiet but alert. We thought we detected sound perceptions as early as the fourth week; sight perceptions, aside from general reactions to light, in the seventh week. We saw the first smile in the sixth week, and observed a general inner awakening. The first sounds began during the seventh week. . . ."

Martha Arendt's notes are the notes of a discoverer, a mother with her first child, protective and sometimes anxious. Her protectiveness, which seems excessive by present standards, was in accord with the most progressive practices of her day. She kept her infant daughter wrapped in a heavy swaddling rug, a *Wickelteppich*, which covered her body and legs, but left her arms free. But this rug was a great improvement over the swaddling bands which mothers of German children had used until the end of the nineteenth century, tightly wrapped bands which kept both arms and legs immobile. Frau Arendt also prevented her child from sitting up until it was safe for her to do so: "I am trying to restrain her [don't sit] but so far without success. She is very uncomfortable during this." But this restraint was mild in comparison to the earlier practice of harnessing children to their beds.

Martha Arendt's observations, so careful and technical, reflect the growth, starting in the 1880s in Germany, of scientific observation of children's development. Wilhelm Preyer, whose *Soul of the Child* was published in 1881, had developed observational techniques with his own child and founded a laboratory in Leipzig where he carried out observations on others' children. Several journals devoted to child psychology were launched at the turn of the century, and soon popular accounts of the scientific articles appeared in newspapers and women's magazines. One of the most influential observational studies, written by psychologists William and Clara Stern about their three children, was published in 1914. When the oldest of the Stern children, Günther, met and married Martha Arendt's daughter Hannah in 1929, professional and amateur "results" of the same assumptions merged.

Among Martha Arendt's progressive middle-class friends, the new child-rearing techniques were much discussed. The women of her generation who were founding kindergartens and elementary schools, encouraging girls to go the educational routes long reserved for boys, and fighting for women's suffrage, were also conducting a quiet in-house rebellion against the social and religious beliefs that had explained normal childhood physical development to their parents. Events that had been ignored became important. Guidebooks and manuals for mothers at the turn of the century stressed the significance of weaning and toilet training, for example. Martha Arendt made careful notes about both.

Many of the early *Unser Kind* book entries are chiefly devoted to physical development. But Martha Arendt also included in most a few sentences about her daughter's spiritual or intellectual development. She was pleased when she saw signs of intellectual precocity, and she allowed herself to speculate, cautiously, that her child might have "some real talent." Her greatest concern, though, was for a normal sociableness, friendliness; she did not press her daughter intellectually, but tried to encourage her in her relationships with others and to control her when she was temperamental. With relief, Martha Arendt found her child "by and large easily guided" away from misbehavior. Frau Arendt's concern with sociability, which was her own great gift, recognized and appreciated by all who knew her, is already evident in her first contributions to the story of her daughter's *geistige Entwicklung* ("mental development"). At six months: "The little one does not like to be alone." At a year: "quite friendly, goes with anyone, with few exceptions, and loves to be surrounded by turbulence." At two: "She is active and cheerful most of the time, but does not like to occupy herself by herself. Has a ready temper, but is easily guided by kindness. Is a little being that needs to be loved."

By the time she was a year old, Hannah Arendt had developed a great fondness for music: "She clearly has an ear, for she loves to sit at the piano and listen, singing along in a small high voice." Part of her pleasure was certainly in the music, but listening to music was also, and continued to be, an important part of Hannah Arendt's relationship with her mother. It turned out, however, that Frau Arendt's passion for music was far greater than her daughter's abilities, and she was disappointed when she noted a year later that Hannah "still has her strong, loud voice, but is now singing off-key, unfortunately!" The situation did not improve. When Hannah was four and "a big, solid girl that people take for a school girl already," her mother admitted defeat. "Sings a great deal, with real passion, but completely off-key. She knows many texts and always recognizes a text when someone whistles it. She has rhythm but is incapable of articulating a note properly." Martha was careful not to force her daughter musically, but her disappointment is obvious.

While Frau Arendt noted her child's lack of musical ability, she began to observe with pleasure her intellectual precocity. Of the six-year-old Hannah she noted: "she learns easily, is apparently gifted, mathematics in particular is her forte. Anything theoretical in music comes to her easily enough, but her ear never corrects anything." From the first, it was Hannah Arendt's love of words and numbers that impressed her mother. The mother whom Hannah Arendt later described as "not very theoretical" raised a very theoretical child.

Hannah Arendt began to speak when she was a little more than a year old. Frau Arendt noted carefully her daughter's developing vocabulary, her joy in creating a "private language" for herself, her long struggle with the letter *r*, and, above all else, her eagerness: "Tries to imitate every sound." At a year-and-a-half: "Speaking is still quite tentative, repeats a lot but without meaning. Mostly she talks her own language which she enunciates very fluently. Understands everything."

As Hannah Arendt turned three, she made "great progress in her development"; she was able to say "just about anything... even though it may not always be intelligible to someone who is not close to her. She speaks her private language ónly rarely now, when she feels no one is observing her and when she is talking to her doll—but even then she mixes together all sorts of words. She talks to her doll the same way she is spoken to herself, usually with the same threatening expressions: Just you wait! Watch out now or you'll get it! Or: You dry? You wet? Get spanking! She never pronounces *k*, *l*, or *r*. Extremely lively, always in a rush; even with strangers, very friendly."

When Paul Arendt's illness forced him to give up his job, the Arendts moved to Königsberg. After the fall of 1910, his condition made it impossible to invite children to the house on Königsberg's quiet, shaded Tiergartenstrasse. Fortunately, Hannah Arendt started kindergarten, which kept her in contact with other children and also, as her mother noted, "offered many stimulating suggestions for playing at home." The child brought the kindergarten routines home with her, but in a very characteristic way: "She is always the teacher."

It is very clear from Frau Arendt's observations that her daughter became an increasingly eager imitator of adult roles after she started school. During the first year of kindergarten, Martha Arendt made an extended note about her four-year-old's progress, drawing up a balance sheet of abilities which very accurately forecast Hannah Arendt's later intellectual development: "There does not seem to be any artistic ability in her of any sort, nor any manual dexterity; there seems to be some intellectual precocity, however, and perhaps even some real talent. There is, for example, a sense of place, memory, an acute capacity for observation. Above all, a burning interest in books and letters. She already reads now... all the letters and numbers without any instruction, simply through asking questions in the streets and elsewhere." This entry ends with the comment: "She remains completely childlike in her behavior as well as in her questions." But by the end of the next school year, Hannah was behaving toward her sick father "like a little mother," and imitating her female kindergarten teachers. When she went to school, Hannah Arendt completely lost interest in her dolls and concentrated her attention on picture books and stories. "Her development is forced along by the sad conditions prevailing in the household, which preclude any visits by children. . . . She is extremely lively, very moved by sad stories, but loves everything cheerful."

Paul Arendt had contracted syphilis as a young man. After treatment, which consisted of inducing a malarial fever—this was prior to the German bacteriologist Paul Ehrlich's development of arsenic compounds for syphilis treatment—he was thought to be cured. Martha Cohn had known about his disease and the treatments when she married him in 1902. No symptoms of the disease had reappeared when they took the risk of producing a child, but two and a half years after Hannah's birth, Arendt had to seek treatment at the Königsberg university clinic. His condition grew steadily worse. By the spring of 1911, the disease had reached the beginning of its third stage, in which lesions develop, ataxia makes movement impossible, and paresis, a type of insanity, sets in. Arendt was institutionalized in Königsberg during the summer of 1911.

Paul Arendt had seemed to his family a severe, somewhat disagreeable man. He was scholarly and serious, aloof behind his waxed black mustache and his pince-nez. In his wife's view, he was a man of robust feelings and had what she called, in the *Unser Kind* book, "a mastery of life"—less sensitive but more controlled than Martha herself, who was a woman of passionate, overflowing warmth. Understandably, after her husband's disease reappeared, she was particularly anxious and attentive when her daughter's physical health was in question. Paul Arendt, on the other hand, was somewhat impatient with his infant daughter, as one sentence of a brief entry he made in the *Unser Kind* book illustrates: "Becomes a nuisance during the day by staying awake and demanding attention." But he also made the gentle observation, in his already uncertain, shaky script, that: "The smile looks lovable to us. Gay songs get a joyous reaction, sentimental ones incline her to tears. . . ." Typical of his style is the following: "Is very curious and shows inclination to raise upper torso; has been lifting head for a while. Shows fear reaction to sounds, loud voices, etc. very easily." His entry style is more clipped and formal, less emotional than Martha's, but not without tenderness.

Whenever Hannah Arendt later spoke of her father to friends, she portrayed him as a scholarly, gentle, kind man. But he must have been confusing and somewhat frightening to her as a child. Even walking in the Königsberg Tiergarten with him was difficult, for his equilibrium was disturbed by his disease and he often, without warning, fell down. Martha related in the *Unser Kind* book that her five-year-old daughter was patient with her father, helping him when she could and amusing him with card games. But during the years when she was clearly preoccupied with her own grief, Martha Arendt did not write about her daughter's reactions.

The written record of that story is not in the *Unser Kind* book but in Hannah Arendt's adolescent poetry. The shadow cast upon the "sunshine child" by her father's dying was deeper than Martha Arendt knew.

Hannah Arendt's beloved grandfather Max Arendt was a lively storyteller, and he made a ritual of Sunday morning storytelling walks with her in the park near his home, where she went to spend many weekends and to join her grandparents for Shabbat services at their synagogue. He recited children's poems, told fairy tales. "Sunday mornings," Martha Arendt remembered, "Grandpa takes her and Meyerchen [the dog] for a nice walk through the Glacis, which she calls the Glasis, and this remains in her memory as something beautiful long after [my] father-in-law has died." When, as an adult, Hannah Arendt talked about her father, she often presented him as her companion for walks and stories. Her grandfather was like a father to her during her own father's illness, and the storytelling was the memory-medium in which she made her own puzzling father into the father she would have liked him to be.

As books and stories became more and more important to her, Hannah Arendt's emotional need for storytelling, for playing a part, for acting, grew. For her sixth birthday she was given a marionette theatre and invited to entertain her guests, her cousins, with a play. She launched eagerly into a complicated drama, they recalled, but became so involved with her performance, so caught up in the performing, that she could not continue and stopped, dissolved in tears. It was not her story, but the performing that overwhelmed her.

In her adult years, when she lectured and debated in public, Hannah Arendt had the magnetism, the presence, of an actress, "a magnificent stage diva," as her friend, Mary McCarthy, said.[6] She had learned, slowly, to control—though never to conquer—her great stage fright by yielding to her story, to what she had to say. Throughout her life she admired, venerated, storytellers—for their stories, but even more for their reverent subservience to the perfectly crafted tale. A year after the Danish short-story writer Isak Dinesen died, Hannah Arendt recounted to a friend an occasion when Dinesen had come to New York, where she was supposed to read but did not. "She came, very very old, terribly fragile, beautifully dressed; she was led to a kind of Renaissance chair, given some wine, and then, without a shred of paper, she began to tell stories [from the *Out of Africa* book], almost word for word as they exist in print. The audience, all very young people, was over-whelmed. . . . She was like an apparition from god knows where or when. And even more convincing than in print. Also: a great lady."[7] This same great lady, through whom stories were told, provided Hannah Arendt with an epigraph for her chapter on action in *The Human Condition*, an epigraph which captures what stories—and later the writing of books—meant to Hannah Arendt when she had left her early shadows and self-consciousness behind: "All sorrows can be borne if you put them into a story or tell a story about them."

### Difficult and Sad Years

When Martha Arendt made an *Unser Kind* book entry several months before she was forced to commit Paul Arendt to the Königsberg psychiatric hospital in the summer of 1911, the stories of her daughter's physical and intellectual development were still happy ones: "Everything is functioning properly and she is always cheerful and alert." Three and a half years were to pass before Martha Arendt wrote again. Her long, retrospective entry, dated January 1914, begins abruptly:

Difficult and sad years lie behind us. The child saw and experienced the entire horrible transformation which her father suffered from his illness. She was kind and patient with him, played cards with him throughout the entire summer of 1911, did not permit me to say a harsh word to him, but wished at times her father were no longer here. She prayed for him mornings and nights without having been taught to do so.

Hannah Arendt was taken to visit her father regularly, until he deteriorated to such a degree that he could not recognize her. Frau Arendt tried to keep their life at home as normal as possible. She started to teach her daughter to play the piano, encouraged her to visit relatives, including Paul Arendt's step-sister Frieda, who was Hannah's favorite, took her to the shore in the summers, and enjoyed her progress in kindergarten, where Hannah impressed her teacher by being able, at age five, to read and write without difficulty. The child's home life was full and she was pleased with school and even more pleased with the elementary school, where she began to study in August 1913, than she had been with her kindergarten. "She is going to the Szittnick School, with great love for her teachers, especially for Miss Jander, on whom she has a little crush;

she learns very well, is ahead of her age group by a year. She also attends Sunday school, which is mandatory, where she also learns with great enthusiasm."

But even while she reported continued normal development, Martha Arendt was somewhat puzzled by her daughter; her diary entries tell as much about her own confusion as they do about her daughter's. She expressed her bewilderment in accounts of Hannah Arendt's behavior at the time of her grandfather Max Arendt's death, March 1913, and at the time of Paul Arendt's death the following October.

Illness and death of her dearly loved Grandpa. At the same time she is in bed with the mumps. His death does not touch her very much, oddly enough. She is very interested in the beautiful flowers, the many people and the funeral. She watches the cortege from the window and is proud that so many people follow her Grandpa. In the following weeks she hardly speaks of her grandfather and playmate whom she loved so much, so that I am at a loss to know whether she thinks of him at all. Until she tells me one day that we should not think of sad things too much, there is no point to being saddened by them. That is typical for her great zest for life, always happy and always satisfied, pushing everything unpleasant as far away from herself as possible. Now she also thinks of her Grandpa again, talks about him lovingly and with warmth; but whether she misses him? I don't think so.

Later in this 1914 entry, Martha noted Hannah's reaction to Paul Arendt's death:

In October [1913] Paul dies. She takes that to be something sad for me. She herself remains untouched by it. To console me she says: "Remember, Mama, that it happens to a lot of women." She attends the funeral and weeps [she told me] "because of the beautiful singing." . . . She probably derives something like satisfaction from the attentions lavished on her by so many people.—Otherwise she is a sunny, cheerful child with a good heart.

Martha Arendt was concerned that her seven-year-old daughter was not more disturbed by these two great losses, as she was concerned that Hannah did not seem to miss her when she took a ten-week trip to Paris after Max Arendt's death: "Hannah stays with both her grandmothers and hardly misses me." With more than a little relief, she noted that Hannah did miss her when she stayed with her step-grandmother Klara Arendt while Martha took a second long trip, to recuperate at Karlsbad and to tour in Vienna and London, in the spring of 1914: "When I return she is happy." Martha Arendt seems to have expected from her precocious daughter an adult comprehension of death and absence, but she also seems to have taken Hannah's attempts to give comfort and sympathy for insensitivity. She found the child's cheerful, sunny disposition hard to understand in the years of her own great grief; and then, less than a year later, when the cheerfulness disappeared, she wished it back.

Martha and Hannah Arendt were on the Baltic shore, at the Cohns' home in Neukuhren, when the First World War broke out. They returned to Königsberg "in something approaching panic." The last days of August 1914 were "terrible days full of worries knowing the Russians close to Königsberg." On 23 August, fearing that Königsberg would be captured by the advancing Russian army, they fled to Berlin, where Martha's younger sister, Margarethe Fuerst, and her three children lived. They left Königsberg by train just as the German troops who had been fighting the Russian First Army to the east were being transferred to meet the Russian Second Army to the southeast near Tannenberg. There the ferocious battle that stopped the Russian advance took place in September. The trains leaving Königsberg were chaotically packed with soldiers and fleeing East Prussians. Farmers and country gentry from the districts to the east that the Russians had overrun and ravaged carried their remaining possessions with them as they struggled for space on trains. Stories of burnt villages and plundered farms and the frightened cry "*Kosacken kommen!*" filled the air. The Arendts, with hundreds of other Königsbergers, left their house not knowing whether they would ever return.

Hannah Arendt started school that fall in a *Lyzeum*, a girl's school, in the Berlin suburb of Charlottenburg and did well despite the fact that the class was a bit more advanced than her own in Königsberg. "Here relatives and strangers give her a lot of love and spoil her. Nevertheless, an excessively great yearning remains in her for her home and Königsberg."

When Martha and Hannah Arendt were able to return to Königsberg ten weeks after their flight, the province was quiet; life returned to normal despite the war raging on the eastern and western fronts. But their personal troubles did not cease. Martha, clearly frightened and concerned, confided in her diary:

This November we . . . started her with braces to adjust her teeth since her jaw is not normal and her teeth are crooked. It is truly a time of suffering for the poor child. In March 1915 she gets sick, two days before our departure for a vacation in Berlin, with a high fever and a bad cough. She gets the measles a second time together with whooping cough (the latter, however, in mild form, without vomiting). And a middle ear infection in both ears. Dr. Fischoder treats her again and Dr. Boluminsky pierces both ear drums under anaesthesia. Terrible times, full of fears and worries. Sick for ten weeks; after that, quick recovery. During summer vacation [1915] she goes swimming and is cheerful, although she has begun to become restless in school and has all kinds of fears. Every time there is a test in school, her "knees give way." Nor does she produce written work that is up to her abilities and her oral performance is, therefore, academically much poorer this year than in previous years. I put that down to her long illness and almost torturous braces. Because she was spoiled during her sickness, she is now very difficult to handle, disobedient and boorish. I often think that I am not up to her and that gives me great pain. Whether I am too lenient or go to the opposite extreme, it is never the right thing to do and I have now decided to see less, to disregard more. I hope to get further that way. Her nervousness in school increases and I am seriously worried. She has an exceptional psychological sensitivity and suffers from almost any person she has to deal with. I see my own youth repeated in her and am saddened by that; concerning people, she will follow the same path of tears that I did. But I guess no one can be spared his fate. If only she could be like her father! The Arendts are so much more robust in their feelings and can therefore master life so much more readily than people of our kind.

Martha had been puzzled by her daughter when the Arendt robustness of cheerful feelings had prevailed over grief, when the "sunshine child" had acted more like her father, the heir of an established, assimilated, prominent family. Confronted with an image of herself as the emotional child of Russian emigrants who had struggled for their wealth and prominence, she despaired. The Goethean ideal of *Bildung* seemed hopelessly unattainable.

Hannah Arendt's illnesses continued for another year, through 1916: "Hannah is a real fever child." Fevers, severe headaches, occasional nosebleeds, and throat infections came one after another, and many trips to the doctor surrounded the twice-yearly trips to receive the newly developed Wasserman tests for congenital syphilis. Martha Arendt may well have added unnecessarily to the frightening succession of medical troubles by deciding that her daughter should attend a gymnastics class and receive massage treatments for "a slight curvature of the spine." These treatments were discontinued in the fall of 1916 "to let her recuperate somewhat."

It is testimony to Hannah Arendt's intellectual strength that she did not fall behind in school during these years of fears and illnesses. Martha noted with evident pleasure that in 1916 and 1917 Hannah was one of the best students in her school, despite her frequent absences. "During Easter vacation [1917] she comes down with diphtheria, gets a shot of horse serum which quickly reduces fever and gray film. Quarantined from school for ten weeks. The two of us, once more thrown back upon ourselves alone, have good, happy weeks. Is learning Latin from her book according to the school timetable and does so well that she writes the best test when she returns to school." But Martha's relief that her eleven-year-old's intellectual development remained satisfactory did not still her foreboding. In 1917 she recorded: "is difficult and begins to become mysterious." This note has quite a different tone than the more matter-of-fact observation entered in the *Unser Kind* book in February 1916: "She grows tremendously now, but is very, very thin and miserable despite a good appetite." But what Martha meant when she described her daughter, at the onset of her adolescence, as "mysterious" (Martha's term, *undurchsichtig*, literally means "opaque," and figuratively connotes "ununderstandable") is a matter of conjecture, for the diary ends just after this note.

Martha Arendt's last diary entry was made in the middle of the First World War. Three years had passed since the series of deaths which preceded their flight to Berlin at the beginning of the war, and the series of illnesses which immediately followed their return to Königsberg, but throughout the diary entries for these years fear of illness or death and fear of being away from home are constant motifs. The diary entries echo a story told by Arendt herself as an adult: when she was four, during the first summer after her father fell ill, she was sent to spend several weeks with her Arendt grandparents. As her mother was about to leave her at the Arendts' summer house, near Cranz on the Baltic shore, Hannah announced, with characteristic firmness and generality: "A child should not be separated from its mother." She wanted to be with her mother and at home—a wish denied again and again.

Many times, Frau Arendt had noted that her daughter fell ill just before or during trips and vacations, except for vacations they took together at their nearby seashore "which she prefers to any kind of travelling." Hannah Arendt had known many people who went away from home and never returned, who died away from home. Her father died in the hospital, her mother's brother Rafael died of dysentery on the eastern front shortly after Hannah spent a vacation week with him at the seashore—"is very impressed by the death of the uncle she had seen only a short time ago." Martha Arendt did not associate her daughter's illnesses with fear of leaving home, but she did realize that the illnesses were not attributable to what she called "external factors": "Whitsun 1915 she came home from a long walk they took in school with a fever. Whether she played robbers and princess with too much intensity or whether she was still too weak from her illness for a school outing all the way to Juditten—the fever cannot be explained by external factors. . . . After a few days it was all gone, but I had never been so beside myself with fear at any other of her sicknesses."

In Berlin, after the flight from Königsberg, Hannah Arendt had suffered from a great homesickness amidst her loving relatives; the next time a trip to Berlin was planned, four months later, she came down with a "high fever and a bad cough," followed by the series of illnesses that lasted for ten weeks. But the pattern of illnesses before trips seems to have predated the terrifying experience of fleeing Königsberg. When Hannah was six: ". . . as we were just about to leave for the Bavarian Alps she got a throat infection with a film, which the Hygienic Institute diagnosed as diphtheria. . . . Our trip was cancelled. . . . No serum injection was given and the doctor doubts that it was diphtheria in the first place." Like the next diphtheria quarantine in 1917, which allowed Hannah to stay home from school with her mother, peacefully learning her Latin, this quarantine was followed by a happy and successful return to school.

Frau Arendt, who was so puzzled and impressed by her child's cheerful disposition during the year her father and her grandfather died, did not attribute the turmoil of the years after the deaths in the family and the flight to Berlin to any darker side of her "sunshine child." But, at the same time that she wanted to explain her daughter's fearfulness in school as an effect of frequent absences and torturous braces, she recorded several stories that clearly reveal the child's bewilderment, as well as her desire to understand. "Mommy, did you know your mother's father?"—"Yes."—"Did you know your father's father?"—"No."—"Did your father know him?"—"I think so."—"You just say that. If a child were born to us now, it wouldn't know its father either." This conversation took place in January 1914, three months after Paul Arendt's death, and the following shortly afterwards: "Commenting on a miscarriage in the Deutschlander family, she says 'Why does God send a crummy child like that?'"

Martha Arendt was puzzled that her daughter did not mourn for her father when he died. What she expected was adult mourning, but what she saw was child mourning, expressed in behavior that indicates protest. It is certainly not unusual for a child's protests over the death of a parent to be manifested in her relations to the surviving parent; both an increase in closeness and dependence and an increase in negative feelings toward the surviving parent are common among children who lose a parent. Hannah's closeness to her mother is apparent in her remark that a child born "to us" would not know its father and in her need to be alone with her mother, her great enjoyment of times when, as Frau Arendt put it, "we are again thrown back upon ourselves alone." On the other hand, Martha Arendt watched her sunshine child grow difficult to handle, disobedient and boorish a year after Paul Arendt's death. His illness had made great demands for patience and self-sufficiency on the child and she had responded by behaving "like a little mother." Her resentment and her occasional wish that he go away had been controlled, and she had even chastised her mother for any harsh words. The resentful feelings were released only after Arendt's death—and then they were directed at her mother.

This interplay of treasured closeness and hostility or rejection, may very well have been aggravated by Martha's intense grief and by the long periods she spent away from home after both Max and Paul Arendts' deaths. When the "little mother" turned her attention to comforting her own mother, her comforting words were not what Frau Arendt expected. They were judged to be somewhat unfeeling. The daughter was not an adequate comforter or companion to her mother in her grief, either at the time of Arendt's funeral or in the following spring, when Martha left home, left her daughter, to recuperate at a spa. Martha was relieved when she returned from this trip to find that Hannah had missed her: her daughter's reaction was, finally, the normal, the expected one.

A number of years were to pass before Hannah Arendt was, once again, of a more robust Arendt temperament, "more like her father." As she grew older, she did become a companion to her mother and was accepted as such. But throughout her adolescence and even into her young adulthood, she was a mixture of precocious grown-upness and childlikeness. She was her mother's friend, but she also—to the great surprise of her own friends—could sometimes be found curled up in her mother's lap, like a child, listening to stories. And she was a mixture of the sort of femininity her mother fostered—warm and sentimental—and the sort of assertiveness her own intellectual gifts and intense desire for independence called for. Hannah Arendt found her mother's notions about normal development and normal femininity confining, particularly after she began her university studies. But she did not grow away from her mother until after she married Heinrich Blücher, and then only with the pain that comes when the husband and the mother are of different worlds and different temperaments entirely. While she was young, Arendt continued to be a very dutiful daughter, loyal to her mother and to her mother's great love for Paul Arendt. She joined her mother for the ceremonial celebrations of Paul Arendt's memory that were carried on throughout Martha Arendt's life, even after she remarried. When the twenty-fifth anniversary of the Arendts' marriage came in 1927, for example, Martha and her twenty-one-year-old daughter, then a doctoral candidate at Heidelberg, celebrated it together by going out for a lavish luncheon at the restaurant next door to the civil court in Königsberg where the Arendts' marriage had been registered. This was a public event; in private, Hannah Arendt's resentful sense of loss lived on. In an autobiographical sketch, "Die Schatten" ("The Shadows"), Hannah Arendt voiced her resentment—spoke of her *hilflosen, verratenen Jugend*, her helpless, be-trayed youth, her fatherless youth.[8]

At the beginning of her adolescence, as she made friends at school and began to emerge from her seclusion, Hannah Arendt's misery and mys-teriousness lessened; she had, as her mother noted, "lots of dates with friends and a predilection for reading, theatre, Punch and Judy, primitive comedies her great love." But her "excessive psychological sensitivity" never disappeared. Deep feelings of loss and betrayal find a place in memory, of course, long after time has done what healing it can do. One of Hannah Arendt's most vivid recollections of the two years her father spent at home dying, years during which she witnessed the "entire horri-ble transformation her father suffered from his illness," was of lying in bed at night listening to her mother play the piano to distract Paul Arendt from his pain. Occasionally, to close friends, the adult Hannah Arendt would tell of this. And occasionally she mentioned it unintentionally. Once, near the end of her life, one of her students asked her, in the course of a conversation about Nietzsche's views on illness, how Nietzsche had occupied himself during the last ten years of his life, as he was dying of what may have been syphilis. Her reply was that Nietzsche had been soothed by listening to his sister play the piano.

*Sturm und Drang*

Martha and Hannah Arendt lived through the years of the First World War in their house on Tiergartenstrasse. Both Hannah Arendt's widowed grandmothers kept their summer houses on the Baltic Sea for vacations, which went on as usual. Königsberg was a garrison town but no fighting took place nearby after the Russians' retreat in 1914. The fortune Jacob Cohn had left to his children protected them from the hunger and cold of wartime winters, though like most Germans they suffered from food shortages. But, by the last years of the war, Martha Arendt's income had dwindled and the Cohn business had begun to fail; she began to worry about her daughter's future.

Both to supplement their income and to provide company, Martha decided to let one of her rooms, and a Jewish student named Kaethe Fischer came to stay. Kaethe was about five years older than the twelve-year-old Hannah Arendt, bright and challenging. The girls clashed heatedly and frequently, but enjoyed tender reconciliations. Both the presence of an older and very intelligent girl in the house and demands of schoolwork that excited her—including the start of Greek classes—helped to draw Hannah Arendt out of her "mysteriousness" and self-preoccupation. And Martha Arendt's attention was also redirected, away from family troubles and toward the troubled political situation in Germany. Her home became a meeting place for social democrats during the last two years of the war and during the revolution of 1918/1919.

One of the most prominent political figures in Königsberg, Karl Schmidt, had two illustrious children: Käthe Kollwitz, the artist, and Konrad Schmidt, who edited the social democrats' official but quite conservative Berlin newspaper, *Vorwärts*. Konrad Schmidt associated with a group known by those to its political left as *Kathedersozialisten* ("academic socialists"). Among the social democratic leaders, only Eduard Bernstein, the chief theoretical opponent of the revolutionary Spartacists, led by Rosa Luxemburg, was found compatible by this group. Bernstein's reformist opinions were often expressed through a Berlin journal called *Sozialistische Monatshefte* which Martha Arendt and Paul Arendt had supported during the first four years of their marriage, when they lived in Berlin, and which they continued to read after they moved to Hannover and then back to Königsberg. The journal was for a time edited by one of their associates, Joseph Bloch, the son of a well-known Königsberg Talmud scholar, and it was the focus of a discussion group in Königsberg to which Martha Arendt belonged.[9]

Although Martha Arendt's circle was opposed to the Luxemburg group, the Spartacists, she supported the Spartacists when their rebellion led to a general strike in the first week of 1919. Hannah Arendt remembered being taken along by her mother, who was an ardent admirer of

Rosa Luxemburg, to the first excited discussions among the Königsberg circle of the news from Berlin that there had been an uprising. As they ran through the streets, Martha Arendt shouted to her daughter, "You must pay attention, this is a historical moment!"

The historical moment was tragically brief. On 15 January Rosa Luxemburg and Karl Liebnecht were captured by members of the Freikorps and killed. The Communist party, formed by a merger of the Spartacists and several splinter groups, tried to recapture the momentum of the first "Spartacus Week," but failed. The government led by President Ebert had to face not only increasing political polarization but an unstable economic situation, the beginning of a spiralling inflation.

In the year after the failed revolution, Martha Arendt decided to remarry. Kaethe Fischer moved away, and Martha prepared to move her possessions two blocks to Martin Beerwald's home on Busoldtstrasse, where she hoped to find both financial security and companionship for her fourteen-year-old daughter. Martin Beerwald's wife, Helene Lowenthal, had died of diabetes in 1916—five years before the discovery of insulin—and left him, at the age of forty-seven, with two daughters to finish raising. When the Arendts came, Clara Beerwald was twenty and Eva nineteen.

Beerwald, the son of a Russian moneylender, had been born and raised in Königsberg. He was a quiet, rather aloof businessman, a moderately wealthy partner in his brother-in-law's ironmongery firm. After his wife's death, during the later war years, Beerwald was well enough off to keep his house and even to hire a housekeeper to look after his daughters. He was fortunate in his choice, for the woman had been employed by an aristocratic country family before the war, and she was able to secure milk, butter, and eggs from that family for the Beerwalds. These rarities supplemented the usual fare—cabbages, carrots, turnips, and more turnips—which was such a shock to comfortable middle-class German citizens. An aunt of the Beerwald girls, unable to adapt to the deprivations of the war years, went mad and was institutionalized, adding to their already deeply saddened lives another sadness. Martha Arendt brought into the comfortable but emotionally bare lives of the Beerwalds her great warmth and a troop of aunts, uncles, and cousins for them to enjoy.

Martha had known the Beerwalds for a number of years, as they had lived for a time in the same two-family house as her widowed mother. She had been sympathetic to the girls when she met them, for they were

obviously in need of affection and painfully thin—not because of shortages, but because a doctor with strange nutritional theories had forbidden
them butter, eggs, and fresh bread. Hannah Arendt had met the girls for
the first time in the summer of 1915, when all three were involved with
school projects for entertaining the German troops garrisoned in
Königsberg, but they had not become friendly. Hannah had been five
years younger and completely different in temperament.

When the Beerwalds and the Arendts joined forces in February 1920,
the temperamental differences between the girls could not have been
more obvious. To Martin Beerwald, his stepdaughter Hannah was a
complete mystery; compared with his own quiet, reserved, homely
daughters, she was headstrong, frighteningly intelligent, and far too independent. He could not provide her with either intellectual guidance or
the fatherly authority she lacked in her family of widowed women. As
Beerwald was at a loss to know how to deal with Hannah Arendt, he
remained aloof and left her to her mother's care. But he could not help
becoming involved during her wilder escapades. In the first year of the
revolution at the Beerwald house, for example, Hannah gave both her
parents a day of intense worry.

Hannah had become friendly with a young Königsberger named Ernst
Grumach, who was five years older, and he told her enthusiastically
about his girl friend, Anne Mendelssohn, a descendant of Moses Mendelssohn's equally famous grandson, Felix. Hannah decided that she
would have to meet this Anne, who lived in a town to the west of
Königsberg called Stolp. But the Beerwalds refused permission for the
journey because the Mendelssohn family had an unfortunate reputation:
Anne's father, a dashingly handsome doctor, had been accused by one of
his female patients of being a seducer and the charge, which Mendelssohn both denied and attributed to anti-Semitism, had resulted in a
court case, a conviction, and two years in prison. His license to practice
was never revoked—as it certainly would have been if the case had been
adequately proven—but the prison sentence and the scandal forced him
to leave the town when he was released, to reestablish his practice elsewhere. The Beerwalds' doubts about the Mendelssohns were put to rest
when the families met, but at the time that Hannah announced her desire
to go to Stolp Dr. Mendelssohn was still in prison and the doubts stood in
the way.

Hannah Arendt, however, was not one to be thwarted in her desires.
One night, after everyone in the Beerwald house was asleep, she left the

house by her bedroom window and made the streetcar journey to Stolp on her own, arriving in time to awaken Anne by throwing a pebble against her window. The Beerwalds were frantic when they discovered her absence and had to wait a day until she turned up. The adventure was not well received; but the friendship with Anne Mendelssohn that started with it was long and close, lasting until Hannah Arendt's death fifty-five years later.

This episode was exceptionally unsettling, but even daily life at the Beerwald house was not calm after the Arendts' arrival. One day, for example, when guests were expected, a plate of sandwiches prepared for the party was left on the kitchen table. Hannah helped herself. Eva discovered the theft and was furious. Unpleasantries were exchanged and one of the girls, in anger, grabbed the pendulum of a nearby clock to continue the fight. But this tactic simply resulted in a great crash as the clock came off the wall and fell to the floor. Martha arrived, running, and the scene ended with all three in startled tears. The new sister was also temperamental about social occasions. She refused to join the others for family birthday celebrations and festivals and claimed, as a matter of principle, that she did not regard family ties as sufficient reason for sociability. But there may have been an element of jealousy in this matter of principle: the new family did require much of Martha's previously undivided attention.

Clara, the older of the Beerwald girls, required a good deal of care. She was an extremely intelligent girl who later went on from the Königin-Luiseschule, the Königsberg girls' *Gymnasium*, to study mathematics and chemistry as well as languages at various universities. People who wished her well persuaded her to turn to pharmacy rather than to try for a doctorate in chemistry, assuming that this was the more practical as well as the more ladylike route. While she prepared to be a pharmacist, Clara, who had considerable musical ability, continued the piano studies she had begun with a pupil of the renowned Berlin pianist Artur Schnabel and often entertained at private musical soirées. But Clara was physically unattractive and extremely unhappy. Martha Arendt tried to understand this unhappiness, sympathizing with her through a series of broken love affairs and unsuccessful psychiatric treatments, until Clara committed suicide by taking poison at the age of thirty. During Hannah's school years, she and Clara were distant; but later, during Hannah's university years, they became close friends. Martha and Hannah Arendt together persuaded Clara away from suicide for a number of years before she finally did take her own life.

Eva was less intellectual and less musically talented than Clara, though she played the violin well enough to join her sister and her father, who played the cello, for musical evenings. Eva did not go to a *Gymnasium*, but she trained as a dental technician and eventually operated her own dental laboratories in various provincial cities. After 1933, she opened a dental laboratory in Königsberg, and reestablished the close relationship with Martha she had enjoyed in her youth. Martha was very kind to Eva, and offered her a broad-minded understanding; she was amazed when Martha Arendt told her not to worry if she ever had a child out of wedlock, that the child would be raised in the Beerwald house. Eva had no children—her friend Karl Aron, a second cousin of Hannah's, was killed during the 1938 anti-Jewish pogroms—and did not marry; she emigrated to England and lives, now, in London.

While Martha was able to help Martin Beerwald with his daughters, he was able to provide Martha and her daughter with a secure home after the dreary and financially insecure later years of the war. His ironmongery business did well after the war and did not collapse during the years of Germany's worst inflation, 1922 and 1923. Hannah Arendt's memories of the inflation years were not memories of poverty but of help for the impoverished, of her mother's unstinting generosity. She often recalled one midnight when the household was awakened by a loud knock at the door: a man who had been reduced to begging by the rampant inflation asked the Beerwalds for coffee and was given his first full meal in days. Even when the Beerwalds had little to give, during the late 1920s when Beerwald's firm went bankrupt, their house was a refuge.

Beerwald was not able, like the Arendts and the Cohns, to keep a summer house, but he did take his family on excursions into the countryside. During the week, his firm's draft horses were used for pulling wagonloads of iron products; but on Sundays they pulled the family's landau and their driver became the coachman. Hannah made no protest about joining these family parties, and she often brought her friends along. The Beerwald house on Busoldtstrasse, which had for years been animated only by the reticent Beerwalds' music, was filled with visitors and talk. Beerwald, who was never directly involved in politics but held rather conservative views and comported himself like a Wilhelmine patriarch—complete with Bismarckian mustaches and morning coats—

found himself surrounded with Martha's social democrat friends and his stepdaughter's bright young companions, the products of a progressive generation's child-rearing techniques.

Hannah Arendt was the center of attraction for a group of talented sons and daughters—mostly sons—of Jewish professional families. Many of these young people, who were generally three or four years older than Hannah, went on to universities in western Germany and brought back stories of their teachers. Ernst Grumach, for example, attended the first lectures which Martin Heidegger gave when he became a professor at Marburg in 1922, and he told Hannah Arendt, who had already heard the rumors of Heidegger's brilliance during a stay in Berlin, of his impressions. Another of the Königsberg group, Victor Grajev, went to Marburg with Grumach, while Paul Jacobi went to Heidelberg. Gregor Segall, a frequent visitor at the Beerwalds', and later a helpful friend to Martin Beerwald during his period of financial trouble, was a good friend, and Hannah Arendt kept in touch with him after he emigrated to Palestine. Anne Mendelssohn went to Heidelberg and then to Hamburg, where she finished her doctorate in philosophy with Ernst Cassirer.

The young people were impressed by Hannah's intellectual force; she had, as Anne Mendelssohn recalled, "read everything." This "everything" covered philosophy, poetry, particularly Goethe, many, many romantic novels, German and French, and the modern novels considered inappropriate for the young by school authorities, including Thomas Mann's. The excellent memory which Martha Arendt had observed in her child became the mainstay of Hannah Arendt's school success and personal intellectual pleasure. She had begun, at age twelve, to commit a small library of poetry to memory. At that time her mother had been amazed: "she knows everything by heart." Her mother had also noted happily that Hannah Arendt had "the ambition to be better than the other students, which she had lacked up until now." She continued to have no trouble fulfilling the ambition, but the routines of school—a rigorous six-day week, with much formality and strictness—were never congenial to her.

During her years at the Luiseschule, despite her more secure family situation and her circle of friends, Hannah Arendt continued to have the troubles of the temperamental. She was, more than the usual adolescent, subject to the storms Goethe considered typical for her stage of life and *Bildung*: "Der Jüngling, von inneren Leidenschaften bestürmt, muss auf sich selbst merken, sich vorfühlen (The youth, beset by inward passions, must heed himself, find his own way)." Hannah Arendt was impressive to her schoolmates as she went about finding her own way: while they visited and chatted during school recesses and over lunch, she marched around the schoolyard, hands clasped behind her back, braids bouncing, lost in solitary thought.

At home, her displays of independence and willfulness were ceaseless. She announced to her mother that she was going to study the violin, even though her earlier forced march with the piano had convinced everyone that she lacked musical ability. Her insistence came not from love of the violin, but from love of the violin teacher, Frau Hulisch, a member of the local chamber quartet and a friend of Martha Beerwald's. Martha gave in to pressure, and the lessons began. But even love of Frau Hulisch could not triumph over Hannah Arendt's tin ear. Music remained the province of the Beerwald girls—with Eva, irritatingly enough, under the tutelage of Frau Hulisch.

Martha Beerwald seldom stood in the way of her daughter's wishes, but she always had to stand behind her when these wishes brought difficulties. She played the mediator, patching up damaged relationships, counseling patience, smoothing over quarrels. And she supported her daughter's headstrong ideas about schooling; when Hannah Arendt announced that no one should be expected to attend a Greek class and read Homer at eight o'clock in the morning, her mother helped negotiate an agreement with the school authorities. Hannah Arendt did not attend the class, but studied on her own and took a specially designed and quite exacting examination, very successfully. This arrangement allowed her to indulge a habit she had long had and kept all her life—she rose very slowly in the mornings and required solitary cups of coffee before she approached sociability. And it allowed her to follow her predilection for small study groups as opposed to large classes. In her room at the Beerwalds' the fifteen-year-old Hannah Arendt met with a group of school friends and her young cousin Ernst Fuerst to read and translate Greek texts, a *Gymnasium* version of the *Graecae* or Greek Circles commonly established in the universities of the period.

Martha Beerwald tried to make her daughter's schooling flexible, but she was not successful in this role during the episode that interrupted Hannah Arendt's career at the Luiseschule. A young teacher at the school, who was renowned for his inconsiderateness, offended the fifteen-year-old girl with a remark—the content of which was never part of Hannah Arendt's own telling of the story. What Arendt chose to emphasize was how she led her classmates in a boycott of the teacher's classes and was, as a consequence, expelled from the school. Martha Beerwald's intercession was of no help in this case; she took her daughter's side against the school principal—which was not a common parental response to breaches of Prussian discipline—but no compromise was reached.

After she was expelled, her mother arranged for Hannah Arendt to go to Berlin for several semesters of study at the University of Berlin. Old family friends and fellow social democrats, the Levins, looked after her, but she stayed in a student residence and audited courses of her own choosing. In addition to Greek and Latin classes, she attended lectures in theology—Christian theology—with Romano Guardini, one of the most vibrant and influential members of the "school" of Christian existentialists then beginning to flourish in Germany.

The Luiseschule authorities relented when their rebellious former student made an application to take the final examination, the *Abitur*, as an extraneous scholar. Martha Beerwald continued to arrange her daughter's independent path: her friend Adolf Postelmann, the headmaster of the all-male *höhere Schule*, was enlisted as Hannah Arendt's tutor for the examination. Postelmann had a devoted following at his school, which included many of Hannah Arendt's friends and Manfred Braude, the young man who later married her sole Arendt cousin, Else Aron Braude. In addition to his administrative duties, Postelmann offered courses in natural history to his students and introduced them to his great pleasures—hiking, bird-watching, petrology, astronomy. He was the only teacher Hannah Arendt had in Königsberg who was equal to the challenge of her abilities and perceptive enough to lead her to fields she could not readily grasp, like Einstein's physics!

Frieda Arendt, Paul Arendt's half-sister and the mother of Else Aron Braude, was not formally Hannah Arendt's teacher, but her influence was probably considerable. Frieda Arendt had trained to be a primary-school teacher in the years before women were admitted to the Albertina, and she was very widely read in German, French, and English literature. She supplied her niece with books. Her husband, Ernst Aron, a lawyer whose male ancestors had been the court jewelers to the dukes of Prussia at their residence in the Königsberg castle, supplied encouragement and financial assistance. After his wife's death in 1928, Uncle Ernst continued to help Hannah Arendt finance her university studies, and she remained grateful to him all her life, as she had been to Aunt Frieda, the only one of her aunts she really loved, as she once told a friend.

With Postelmann's help, the Arons' support, the two terms in Berlin, and an intense six months of all-day study, Hannah Arendt prepared for the *Abitur,* the passport to regular university enrollment, and passed it in the spring of 1924, a year ahead of her class. The examination had filled her with anxiety—she once admitted to her friend Anne Mendelssohn that it had been one of the most frightening experiences of her life—but she approached it with a display of self-assurance. Public appearances and situations involving personal or intellectual tests continued to frighten her, but she always summoned a veneer of bravado for them. In this case, the bravado continued after the trial was over: she received the little gold medals embossed with portraits of Duke Albert I of Prussia which were given to *Gymnasium* graduates, pinned them on, and made a prideful visit to her former classmates and teachers at the Luiseschule, communicating quite clearly the message that her expulsion had allowed her to race ahead of her class.

During her last year of school and while she prepared privately for her *Abitur,* Hannah Arendt advanced beyond her classmates in other ways as well. Anne Mendelssohn had moved with her family to Allenstein, and her boy friend, Ernst Grumach, became Hannah Arendt's boy friend. Hannah discovered a new use for illnesses: she feigned headaches to leave school early when Grumach came to wait for her during his last *Gymnasium* year. Her many absences from school and her special study arrangements had already made the school authorities skeptical and this intense relationship with a young man five years her senior raised disapproving eyebrows. But Martha Arendt, though she was concerned, decided not to intervene. She realized that her precocious daughter benefited from the company of older friends and the freedom to come and go as she wished. The once "thin and miserable" Hannah Arendt was in radiant good health and—when she chose to be—just as her mother hoped: sociable, friendly, and relaxed. The friendship with Grumach gave way, as Martha Arendt had anticipated, to many friendships while Grumach was away at Marburg University and while Hannah Arendt was studying in Berlin.

In the Beerwalds' Busoldtstrasse home, she now had her own room, a bedroom with a sofa and chairs, where she could entertain her guests and her Greek Circle. But though she often had company, she also spent many hours lying on the sofa reading, alone. In Guardini's lecture hall she had been introduced to the Danish philosopher and theologian Kierkegaard and was so taken with his work that she had decided to make theology her major field of study when she went on to the university as an officially enrolled student. She was, even then, critical of any form of dogmatic theology—not because she was non-Christian, but because dogmatism was non-Kierkegaardian. Arendt read Kant's *Critique of Pure Reason* and his *Religion Within the Limits of Reason Alone* when she was sixteen and soon afterward introduced herself to the emerging critical trend which Martin Heidegger and Karl Jaspers were leading. Jaspers's *Psychology of World Views* appeared in 1919, and three years later she read it avidly.

Hannah Arendt's years of independent study were years of transition. She had begun to emerge from shadows of the "sad and difficult years" in her childhood. But she was still uncertain, shy, distrustful of her new sociability and her intellectual strength. She startled her *beste Freundin* Anne Mendelssohn, with whom she had spent so many hours of intense, intimate talk, by telephoning her after a separation of several months and saying, shyly: "This is Hannah Arendt. Do you remember me?" She even addressed her friend with the formal *Sie*, though they had always used *Du* when they were together. It was the daughter Martha Arendt had called "difficult and mysterious" in the last *Unser Kind* book entry who turned, in solitary questioning, to poetry and began to develop the sense of poetry's consolation and commemoration that later was so striking in her philosophizing.

In the poetry Hannah Arendt began to write when she was seventeen, the pull of the past is a recurrent theme, a theme wrapped in Romantic imagery and Kierkegaardian angst. There is a deep but nonspecific melancholy in the poems, what she called, in the title of one poem, "Müdigkeit" ("Weariness").

> Evening falling—
> a soft lamenting
> sounds in the bird calls
> I have summoned.
>
> Greyish walls
> tumble down.

My own hands
find themselves again.

What I have loved
I cannot hold.
What lies around me
I cannot leave.

Everything declines
while darkness rises.
Nothing overcomes me—
this must be life's way.

The poems are often so abstract that ambiguity is their most salient feature. In this one, for example, *Nichts mich bezwingt* can mean "nothing at all overcomes me" or "Nothing[ness] overcomes me." These are mood poems, and whether stoical or despairing or both at once, their mood is summarized in the phrase "darkness rises." In the darkness there was very little *Trost* ("consolation").

The hour will come
when old wounds,
long forgotten,
threaten to corrode.

The day will come
when no balance
of life, or sorrow,
will reckon up.

The hours run down,
the days pass on.
One achievement stays:
mere being alive.

In one of the poems, a "hidden God" like Kierkegaard's is invoked.

No word breaks the dark—
No God lifts his hand—
And wherever I look
The land rises up.
No form dissolving,

No shadow floating.
And still I can hear it:
Too late, too late.

But even a poem which reflects a very different area of Hannah Arendt's reading, a love poem full of the flora of Romanticism, ends on a note of suffering and loss. She wrote "in the manner of a folk song":

When we meet again
White lilac will bloom.
I'll wrap you in pillows
And you will want nothing.

We'll be happy again,
The light, dry wine
And redolent linden will
Find us side by side.

When the leaves fall
Then we'll be parted.
What does wandering mean?
We must suffer it.

"In the Manner of a Folk Song" may have been addressed to Ernst Grumach, who returned to Königsberg in the summers after he began his university studies; but the temporal rhythm of happiness followed by sadness, sadness surfacing through happiness, is present in many of the poems.

One of the most personal and unconventional of Hannah Arendt's efforts captures the feeling she later attributed to a spirit she found kindred, Rahel Varnhagen, when she wrote a very autobiographical biography. In the biography of Rahel Varnhagen, Arendt presented her subject as a woman who neither avoided an irremediable, painful destiny nor let herself be seduced by worldly successes, bright dreams of the future. Rahel Varnhagen learned to live, in the present, with her past and her future, her darkest and her lightest experiences, by understanding that ambiguity points a permanent way out, that neither extreme should be taken too seriously. Rahel Varnhagen's destiny was her Jewishness, and she learned to live with it as what Arendt called a "conscious pariah." Having been born a Jew—that became Hannah Arendt's concern later in her life; but self-conscious pariahdom was her personal kingdom when she began to write poems, though she gave it another name: irony.

> My feet float in solemn glory.
> And I, I am
> Dancing too.
> Freed from the burden—
> Into the dark, into the void.
> Rooms full of past times,
> Spaces traversed
> And solitudes lost,
> Are beginning to dance, to dance.
>
> And I, I am
> Dancing too.
> Ironical rashness
> I have not forgotten.
> I know the void,
> I know the burden.
> But I dance and dance
> In ironical glory.

What *Schwere*, what burden or gravity in the spiritual sense of the word, Hannah Arendt felt she had left behind but not forgotten, what ironical rashness or impetuousness gave way to ironical glory—the poem does not tell. It may be an allegory for her impetuous relationship with Ernst Grumach, which was shrouded in such secrecy that her confidante, Anne Mendelssohn, and her cousin, Ernst Fuerst, and his wife were convinced that it had not been a love affair, while her cousin Else Aron Braude, a friend of Grumach's, was sure, from Grumach's account, that it was. A poem entitled "Farewell"—the last in the collection of poems dated Winter 1923/24—seems to recall a first love, but it is addressed throughout to "floating days" rather than to any person.

> Now let me, oh floating days, give you my hand.
> You cannot escape me, there is no escape
> Into the void or into timelessness.
>
> Yet the glowing wind is a sign more strange
> Wrapping its way around me: I do not want to
> Flee into the void of inhibited times.

Oh, you know the laugh with which I gave myself,
You know how much I silently concealed
To lie in the meadows and belong to you.

But now the blood, which was never silenced,
Calls me to ships I have never steered.
Ah, death is in life, I know, I know.
So let me, floating days, give you my hand.
You will not lose me. As a sign I leave behind,
For you, this page and the flame.

Between the past of "inhibited times" and the uncertain future with its "ships never steered," Hannah Arendt felt herself suspended, floating— *schwebende*. The poems concern not people and events, but time: past times, hours passing, floating days, futures to be marked with signs. Time speaks in the poems—"Too late, too late"—and has physical presence in them—"to lie in the meadows and belong to you [days]." The time she felt at one with, the time she gave her hand, was unworldly, floating above the world. And she even saw this time as the home of such an unlikely fellow spirit as Die Untergrundbahn, the subway in Berlin, as it went *gleichgültig schwebend* ("indifferently floating") through a station:

Coming from darkness,
coiling into the light,
quickly and rashly,
narrow and possessed
by human powers,
attentively weaving
predestined paths;
indifferently floating
above all haste.
Quick, narrow, possessed
by human powers
which it does not attend to,
flowing into the dark.
Knowing higher things,
flying, it twists:
a yellow animal.

There is a harsh struggle for general truths apparent in these poems, though they are neither good as poems nor distinctive in style. The past and the future are interrogated in the struggle for generalizations, for surety: *Ist wohl des Lebens Lauf,* this must be life's way. Like Kierkegaard, Arendt very early in her life felt existence in time—existence on life's way—as a drama. She, too, turned to irony, ambiguity, as a way out. But "out" meant into another realm, the realm of thinking. When she wrote her first poems, Arendt had spatial and temporal images for her feelings, her floating; soon she found philosophical concepts. Her "ironical glory" took another form. And she could have said of herself, as Kierkegaard once said of himself: "I have trained myself . . . always to be able to dance in the service of thought."[10]

# CHAPTER 2
# The Shadows
# (1924–1929)

How could cheerfulness stream through us if we wanted
to shun sadness?
Pain gives of its healing power where we least expect it.

Heidegger, *The Thinker as Poet*

## Passionate Thinking

Hannah Arendt's university years, from 1924 to 1929, were exactly the
years of greatest stability for the troubled Weimar Republic. By the summer of 1924 the government's program of economic stabilization had
brought to a temporary end the worst period of inflation, and a change of
government in financially troubled France had reduced the Germans'
feeling of being surrounded by vindictive extortionists. But just as this
feeling was abating, the provisions of the Dawes Plan were made known.
The plan provided an Allied loan for the continuation of the German
economic recovery and a scheme for reparations payments intended to
protect Germany from further currency devaluations; it also involved
Allied supervision of German banking and railroads and a special arrangement for German industry to contribute to the reparations payments. The Dawes Plan was dubbed a "second Versailles," particularly by
the rightist parties, and even in the midst of recovery the process of
political polarization that was eventually so disastrous for the republic
continued.

The stabilization of the currency and the acceptance of the Dawes Plan
were what was most important for the period of relative calm domesti-
cally; in international affairs it was the Treaty of Locarno, negotiated in
1926, that was crucial. The treaty included arbitration agreements between Germany, France, and Belgium for settlement of Western territo-
rial disputes and similar agreements with Poland and Czechoslovakia.
Though the Eastern agreements did not foreclose, even legally, the possibility that Germany would resort to war over the question of frontiers, the

Locarno treaty was viewed in the West as a herald of what Chamberlain optimistically called "the years of peace." In Germany, the treaty was no more popular than the Dawes Plan.

The German chancellors and ministers in the relatively stable years were confronted with a complex social and economic picture. By 1927 both production and foreign trade had reached levels which were higher than any before the war. But the country was running at a deficit. Exports lagged behind imports, reparations payments and capital investments were both largely dependent on foreign loans and while wages had risen almost 20 percent from 1924 to 1929, unemployment was high. Big industries merged, forcing many small businesses into bankruptcy; by 1925 over half of the German labor force was employed by about 2 percent of the German enterprises. The fortunes of Hannah Arendt's stepfather, Martin Beerwald, provide a good example of the result of the rise of cartels. His brother-in-law's Königsberg firm was sold to a larger firm and Beerwald was left jobless. Nearly sixty years old, he joined the larger firm as a travelling salesman, but he spent as much on railroad tickets as he made. His daughters worked, Eva as a dental technician and Clara as a pharmacist—joining the growing number of working women—and contributed what they could to their father's household. Hannah Arendt, like so many others, attended the university on a shoe-string—hers provided in part by her uncle Ernst Aron.

The university population in the mid-twenties was twice what it had been before the war, while the number of universities and *Technische Hochschulen* remained nearly the same, thirty. There had been a dramatic rise in the population after the war up to the inflation year, 1923, when there were 125,000 students; by the period of stabilization, the number had dropped back to 89,000. The inflation had cut off the careers of nearly a third.[1]

Over these years, the makeup of the university population shifted considerably: the vast majority were from financially vulnerable middle-class families rather than from upper-class families (the number of working-class students was never more than 3 or 4 percent), and many of these students, particularly in the early twenties, had to work while they studied or during the summers to make enough to subsist. By the late twenties, the students' shoestrings were a bit longer and the living conditions in and around the universities had improved somewhat, but many, like Hannah Arendt, had to depend on scholarships.

The universities themselves had barely survived the inflation of 1922 and 1923, depending on the help of emergency funds channelled through a specially created agency, the Emergency Society for German Learning (*Notgemeinschaft der deutschen Wissenschaft*), the organization which later financed Hannah Arendt's postgraduate work. The inflation emergency did little to fortify support for the Republic within the universities, where support had never been great; but even more divisive were suggestions for university reform made by the Weimar Republic's ministers of culture. Appointments of socialist professors, attempts to establish chairs in nontraditional disciplines, policies for democratizing the hierarchical structures of the professoriate and increasing the working class's access to the universities—all were treated by the majority as threats to the autonomy of the academies. The full professors, the *Ordinarien*, clung to their traditional rule.

The conservatism that dominated the universities was highlighted in the very year Hannah Arendt started her studies at Marburg. A young assistant professor at Heidelberg, E. J. Gumbel, published an account of the "Black Reichswehr," the first stage of Germany's illegal reconstruction of its army. Faculty nationalists were incensed, and they wanted Gumbel—a pacifist—removed when he went on to suggest in public lectures that the sacrifice of human lives that Germany had made in the First World War was less than honorable. Despite the efforts of men like Arendt's future teacher, Karl Jaspers, to stop them, the faculty voted to withdraw Gumbel's right to teach. "The issue was academic freedom," Jaspers later wrote. "This is uprooted once a teacher's views are subject to investigation."[2]

To Hannah Arendt, neither the example of Jaspers's commitment to practical reason in the political realm nor the general political issues of the time were of interest. She was—to her later embarrassment—extremely naive and quite unworldly. But at Marburg in the fall of 1924 she found herself in the midst of a consumingly interesting apolitical revolution, one that decisively shaped her personal and intellectual development. The young leader of this revolution, which brought to an end one of philosophy's anciens régimes, was widely known among students even though he had not as yet published a major book. Martin Heidegger, thirty-five years old, was, as Hannah Arendt put it, "the hidden king [who] reigned in the realm of thinking, which, although it is completely of this world, is so concealed in it that one can never be quite sure whether it exists at all." Her awe and sense of mystery, remembered with restraint in this 1969 description, were unrestrained in 1924.[3]

German academic philosophy in the 1920s was dominated by individuals and groups who were looking for a way to stabilize philosophy's currency, to replace a motley collection of inflated isms with a grand and certain *Ganzes*, a whole, an embracing ism. Philosophical heretics were not officially censured, but they did not—as Karl Jaspers discovered to his sorrow—find academic positions easily. "In the circle of professional philosophers," Jaspers wrote, remembering 1913 when he finally won his chair in philosophy over formidable opposition, "I was considered an alien." In the 1920s, when Jaspers stopped publishing in psychology in order to prepare himself to write his path-breaking *Philosophy*, he was "regarded as finished. The fact that I had many students seemed odd; it had to be due to qualities which earned me the title 'seducer of youth.' "[4] Jaspers came to philosophy from outside, from psychiatry; Heidegger came up through the ranks. But both had formidable forces of tradition to overcome.

There were two main species of philosophical isms in the air. On the one hand, various so-called scientisms: materialism, empiricism, psychologism, positivism; and, on the other hand, various neo-Kantianisms or formalisms, in particular the neo-Kantianism of the Baden and Marburg schools. Within these diverse cliques and schools and outside them, there developed a yearning for absolute values, for a return to systematic and certain knowledge—a renaissance of metaphysics.[5] There was a nostalgia for Hegel, for a philosophical system in which the partialness of the main camps of the day would be overcome. But while this ambitious and unoriginal synthesizing tendency grew to predominance in the 1920s, there was also an underground of those who found the academic nostalgia for a lost unity in metaphysics pretentious and stifling. Looking back over twenty years to the factions that flourished during her university years, Hannah Arendt put the matter succinctly: "Philosophy then was either derivative or it was a rebellion of the philosophers against philosophy in general, rebellion against, or doubt of its identity."[6] She rejected both the derivative metaphysicians and those who renounced philosophy in favor of a vague and misty irrationalism, and she went the way of the rebels who doubted philosophy's traditional identity.

Hannah Arendt had already been launched on this rebellious path in Berlin, where Romano Guardini was her teacher and Kierkegaard her hero. Theology had then been her choice for a main course of study. Like most German university students, she was prepared to pursue her studies at a number of different universities, sampling curricula and teachers until she found the right combination for writing her dissertation. In Marburg, she thought she had found what she wanted in one place: the "most modern and interesting" philosophical tendency, Edmund Husserl's phenomenology, and the perfect teacher, Husserl's protégé Martin Heidegger. Heidegger was developing Husserl's phenomenology in such novel directions that its boundaries threatened to give way; the man himself was equally ambitious and adventurous. Long after she had become as famous as her teacher, Hannah Arendt referred to her encounter with philosophy in Marburg as the time of her "first amour."[7] Philosophy was her first love; but it was the philosophy incarnate in the person of Martin Heidegger.

Martin Heidegger, born in 1889 to the head sexton at Messkirch in Baden, Friedrich Heidegger, and his wife, Johanna, had been precocious, as his student Hannah Arendt was. His interest in philosophy, particularly in the philosophy of Aristotle, had been kindled when he was a *Gymnasium* student in Constance and Freiburg; he had read Brentano's "On the Manifold Meaning of 'Being' according to Aristotle" when he was eighteen. After training in mathematics and logic at Freiburg University, Heidegger turned to Edmund Husserl's *Logical Investigations* (1900–1901), knowing that Husserl had been influenced by Brentano, to continue his exploration of the meaning of Being, the traditional concern of ontology. After four semesters as a theology student at Freiburg, Heidegger, like Arendt, had decided to dedicate himself entirely to philosophy.

Heidegger's interest in Husserl was stimulated in the Freiburg seminars of the neo-Kantian Heinrich Rickert. Rickert criticized Husserl's phenomenology, arguing that it was not able to relate its analyses of the contents of consciousness to the world or to historical events—a criticism which Heidegger later adopted, though not for purposes like Rickert's. Rickert's effort to establish a *Kulturwissenschaft*, a science of culture, on solid scientific principles and to write a "universal history" of cultures was quite influential. But even Rickert's followers were critical of his attempt to find a rigid system of "universal values," a whole of a Hegelian sort.

Heidegger struggled with Husserl's *Logical Investigations* while he wrote his dissertation, *Die Lehre vom Urteil im Psychologismus*, at Freiburg and passed his examinations, with Rickert as one of the examiners. In the year that Heidegger went on to obtain his *Habilitation,* or license to teach, in Freiburg, with a work entitled *Die Kategorien- und Bedeutungslehre des Duns Scotus* (1916), Edmund Husserl was appointed Rickert's successor. Heidegger became Husserl's assistant, learning directly from the master about his phenomenological method and giving seminars in which he both practiced the method and began to question it. The call that Husserl sent out through the abstract university atmosphere, through the many halls where grand systems were being contemplated, was a call to quiet revolution: "Back to the things themselves!" What this meant was that all unsettling speculative questions about the origin, historical destiny, or even reality of things in the world could be set aside or "bracketed" while the apprehension of things in consciousness was studied in a strictly scientific manner. From such study Husserl hoped to achieve a coherent and comprehensive vision without becoming caught up in the insoluble metaphysical quandaries so clearly portrayed by Kant.

Heidegger remained at Freiburg until he was appointed an associate professor at Marburg in 1922, after the Marburg faculty had considered a manuscript of his which in a preliminary way outlined his long-meditated Aristotle interpretation. He moved to Marburg with his wife, Elfriede, whom he had married in 1917, and his two young sons, Jorg and Hermann.

Paul Natorp, who had been a full professor at Marburg since 1892, was instrumental in securing Heidegger's position and, after Heidegger arrived, received him for weekly discussions. In Natorp Heidegger had an example of a fruitful, provocative return to the Greeks—particularly to Plato, whom Natorp, a Kantian, called "a Kantian before Kant." Heidegger's own return to Greek philosophy did not produce Kantian Greeks and it did not lead him immediately to the practical concerns Natorp had considered, but it did convince him that the history of ontology since the Greeks had to be critically reinterpreted so that Greek ontology could be seen clearly and adapted to the present. In the first part of the 1927 work which established his reputation among philosophers, *Being and Time,* Heidegger presented this project by outlining the phenomena, the "things themselves," that he thought would stand revealed if the philosophical underbrush of the history of ontology were cleared away. Kant's *Critique of Pure Reason* stood, for Heidegger, at the end of a long process of "forgetfulness of Being," and it provided him with the possibility for his mode of remembrance, a transcendental inquiry into the ground of Being. While he was formulating his philosophical project in the 1920s, Heidegger prepared a series of lectures on Kant which were to be the centerpiece of the second part of *Being and Time*. These were presented in his classes in 1925–26 and finally published in 1929 as *Kant and the Problem of Metaphysics*. Heidegger did not want to find the *logical* foundations of the sciences in Kant or in any Kantian before Kant as Natorp had. Instead he wanted to find the *ontological* roots of the sciences, and to do this he began with an analysis of the being that can engage in scientific theory and pose the question of Being—man, or in Heidegger's term, *Dasein*.

Paul Natorp died in 1924, the year Hannah Arendt arrived in Marburg. Heidegger by then had other friends, including the theologian Rudolf Bultmann and the philosopher Nicolai Hartmann. Bultmann and Heidegger sometimes attended each other's classes and had many students, including Hannah Arendt, in common. Hartmann attended a circle, a *Graeca*, in which Heidegger and several other Marburgers read Greek literature, a professional version of the *Graeca* Hannah Arendt had convened in Königsberg.

During the winter semester of 1923–24, Heidegger had taken a great step forward in his work on the first part of manuscript that became *Being and Time*. The work began to take shape in the lectures and seminars Hannah Arendt attended, for that year Heidegger presented a working summary of his interpretation of Aristotle's notion of *alētheia* ("truth," usually translated by Heidegger as *Un-verborgenheit*, "unconcealedness") and then led his students through a line-by-line reading of Plato's *Sophist*. A quotation from the *Sophist* stands on the first page of *Being and Time*: "You, clearly, have known for a long time what you mean when you say the word 'Being,' but we, who were once sure about it ourselves, have now become perplexed."

Heidegger had been living for nearly fifteen years in the company of those who were perplexed about the meaning of Being, and in his classes and in his writing he struggled for clarity. His students were fascinated— and quite perplexed—by this struggle. They would often convene after class to see whether anybody had understood a word of his lectures. But Heidegger's effort compelled them. Forty-five years later, looking back at Heidegger's classes on the occasion of his eightieth birthday in 1969, Hannah Arendt described the attitude of the best of the students who came to join Heidegger's quest:

The rumor that attracted them to Freiburg and to the Privatdozent who taught there, as somewhat later they were attracted to the young professor at Marburg, had it that there was someone who was actually attaining "the things" that Husserl had proclaimed, someone who knew that these things were not academic matters but the concerns of thinking men—concerns not just of yesterday and today, but from time immemorial—and who, precisely because he knew that the tradition was broken, was discovering the past anew. . . .

The rumor about Heidegger put it quite simply: Thinking has come to life again; the cultural treasures of the past, believed to be dead, are being made to speak, in the course of which it turns out that they propose things altogether different from the familiar, worn-out trivialities they had been presumed to say. There exists a teacher; one can perhaps learn to think. . . .

People followed the rumor about Heidegger in order to learn thinking. What was experienced was that thinking as pure activity—and this means impelled neither by the thirst for knowledge, nor by the drive for cognition—can become a passion which not so much rules and oppresses all other capacities and gifts, as it orders them and prevails through them. We are so accustomed to the old opposition of reason versus passion, spirit versus life, that the idea of a passionate thinking, in which thinking and aliveness become one, takes us somewhat aback.[8]

"Passionate thinking" was just what Hannah Arendt was ready to respond to. She had been restless in the presence of the Jewish tradition her grandparents lived in, uncompelled by her mother's political convictions, discontented in her *Gymnasium*. Her friends, all a few years older than she, had already begun their studies, several of them, like Ernst Grumach and Victor Grajev, with Heidegger. Her last year in Königsberg, studying for the *Abitur*, had been taxing but neither intellectually nor emotionally satisfying. She had put her discontent into a poem:

> The hours run down
> The days pass on.
> One achievement remains:
> Mere being alive.

When Hannah Arendt encountered Martin Heidegger everything changed. He was a figure out of a romance—gifted to the point of genius, poetic, aloof from both professional thinkers and adulatory students, severely handsome, simply dressed in peasant clothes, an avid skier who enjoyed giving skiing lessons. Hannah Arendt was much more "taken aback" than her retrospective account reveals by this union of aliveness and thinking.

From her one public statement about the Marburg seminars, the eightieth birthday recollection, no one would suspect that Martin Heidegger had been not just Hannah Arendt's teacher but her lover. Heidegger's reserve was even deeper. Of the years between 1923 and 1928, when he was preparing *Being and Time* and *Kant and the Problem of Metaphysics*, he said publicly only that this was his "most stimulating, composed, eventful period."[9] Twenty years after that period ended, he confessed to Hannah Arendt that she had been the inspiration for his work in those years, the impetus to his passionate thinking. But they kept this confession to themselves and agreed to keep as carefully as they had kept in 1925 the secret of their affair. The love letters they had exchanged were to be preserved but not made available to others.[10] Arendt did, however, leave among her unpublished papers the account of her year in Marburg she had written for Martin Heidegger.

In the summer of 1925, at home in Königsberg, she had written and sent to Heidegger a self-portrait, "The Shadows." The portrait, like the poems she wrote during the following year, is a last testament. Arendt tried to circumscribe her first love, to control it in words. She tried to put it in the past by telling a story. "All sorrows can be borne if you put them into a story or tell a story about them." The exorcism was not a success. Hannah Arendt had to tell someone else's story, had to write *Rahel Varnhagen: The Life of a Jewess*, before she freed herself from Martin Heidegger's spell.

*Extraordinary and Magical*

Drawn in the protective third person singular, filled with abstract locutions and Heideggerian terminology, Hannah Arendt's self-portrait is at once startlingly detached and full of anguish. Like the romantic novels she was fond of reading, the portrait is "couched in terms so general that only a mood, no real events, can be represented" (as she said years later of Schlegel's *Lucinde*).[11] The mood is captured in a poem from the same period, with the title "In sich versunken" ("Lost in Self-Contemplation").

> When I regard my hand—
> Strange thing accompanying me—
> Then I stand in no land,

By no Here and Now,
By no What, supported.

Then I feel I should scorn the world.
Let time go by if it wants to
But let there be no more signs.

Look, here is my hand,
Mine, and uncannily near,
but still—another thing.
Is it more than I am?
Has it a higher purpose?

This poem and the self-portrait both end with the same questioning: will the baffled, scornful distance to which she has retreated be surmounted? In "Die Schatten" Arendt weighed the possibilities on a heavy, melodramatic balance:

Perhaps her youth will free itself from this spell and her soul—under a different sky—experience expression and release, overcoming this sickness and aberration, learning the patience, simplicity and freedom of organic growth. But it is more likely that she will go on wasting her life in pointless experiments, and unlawful, boundless curiosity—until the end, long and fervently hoped for, surprises her and puts an arbitrary halt to this needless and futile business.[12]

The real events that precipitated this despairing mood are not told. But Hannah Arendt did offer herself two different explanations for her condition, which she called *Fremdheit*, estrangement or alienation. The first, and more immediate, was the time-dividing event which is also invoked in the poem: "Before her youth had fully blossomed, she had brushed by the extraordinary, the magical; so that she—in a matter-of-fact way that later frightened her—was accustomed to dividing her life into a Here-and-Now and a Then-and-There." Arendt's relationship with Heidegger had, abruptly and frighteningly, ended her youth, her innocence. Secondly, she attributed her *Absonderlichkeit*, her strangeness, to a trait which, over a much longer time, had become customary: "She saw something remarkable in even the most matter-of-fact and banal things. Even when the simple and commonplace things of life affected her most deeply, she never suspected, in her thoughts or feelings, that what was happening to her might be banal, a mere unnoteworthy nothing which everyone takes for granted, which is not even worth talking about."

She had not been aware of this second habit, she said, when she was growing up, for she had been too "reserved and preoccupied with her-self." When she was younger, her self-preoccupation had blocked her understanding. She "knew a great deal—through experience and watch-ful alertness, but everything that happened to her just sank to the bottom of her soul and stayed there as though encapsulated. Her tenseness and her secretiveness would not allow her to deal with events other than in dull pain or in a dreamy, enchanted isolation." Arendt did not forget what she had experienced or observed, but things "sank out of sight—some completely disappeared and some asserted themselves vaguely, without discipline or order."

Her habitual bewilderment, Hannah Arendt suggested, "was perhaps based merely on a helpless, betrayed youth." It "expressed itself in this *Auf sich-selbst-gedrücktsein* [being self-by-self oppressed] in such a way that she blocked and hid her own access and view of herself." In this tentative and complex way, Hannah Arendt acknowledged that she had been hurt: though she did not say so, it seems likely that she was thinking of her father's death and the years of unhappiness that had followed upon her loss; and that she was wondering in retrospect, as her mother had during the "sad and difficult" years, at how hidden her hurt had been. The result of her oppression and bewilderment, she claimed, was that she became, as she grew older, "more radical, exclusive and blind."

As had her mother, Hannah Arendt viewed her early childhood as a happy one, viewed herself as a "sunshine child." She spoke of the "shy and austere beginnings of her young life, when she was not yet at odds with her own groping tenderness, with social behavior,—or with express-ing her own innermost being." Then "realms of reality had opened up in her dreams, in those troubled and joyful dreams which—no matter whether sweet or bitter—were filled with a constant *Lebensseligkeit* ("joy in life")." But this period had come to an end, she said, when she had smashed the youthful dreams, exercising a "violent, destructive tyranny over herself." The sensitiveness and vulnerability which had always been hers grew "nearly grotesque." In this state, "fear of reality overcame the defenceless creature—this senseless, groundless empty fear before whose blind gaze everything becomes like nothing, which means madness, joylessness, disaster, annihilation." This fear, which she called, in Heidegger's manner, *Angst vor dem Dasein überhaupt* ("anxiety over existence in general"), was something she had known before the "violent, destructive tyranny," as she had known the many things which slipped to the bottom of her soul; but now she felt that she was "its prisoner." Her fear became "animal," so paralyzing that she could not protect herself, could only stand waiting "with an almost matter-of-fact expectancy of some brutality." Her "temptation to despair," she felt, was too strong for any involvement with art, literature, culture, any development of taste, to weigh against it or ameliorate it; it was a temptation to despair in the realm of the human as such.

What had happened was that she had let herself feel again the childlike love of life, the sense of "colorful and strange realms in which she felt at home." She had let herself feel longing and desire "but the fear had closed in around her, preyed upon her." Her radicality or estrangement, which had once helped her bear and sustain the worst, "was now so changed that everything dissolved or scattered unless she tried in docile devotion to cling to it, pale and colorless and with the hidden uncanniness [*Unheim-lichkeit*] of passing shadows."

It was at this dark point that she turned to weigh up her future possibilities, to question whether she could free herself from "this spell," or *Bann*. Longing and fear had been with her since her early youth, and fear had, before, gained the upper hand; but the immediate cause of her new imprisonment in the fear was her brush with "the extraordinary and magical." She was rather sullenly aware that her love affair, her sexual awakening, might well be misunderstood by others, who would think that she had become "uglier and more common, even to the point of being dull and licentious," so she defiantly announced her right to "indifference toward such judgment and argument." But she was sure it would be understood by Martin Heidegger, the extraordinary and magical man for whom "Die Schatten" was written and to whom it was dedicated.

Hannah Arendt was just turning eighteen when she met Heidegger and developed for him what she called in "Die Schatten" a *starre Hingege-benheit an ein Einziges*, an "unbending devotion to a single one." He was seventeen years her senior, a man of Catholic upbringing, married and the father of two sons. Even though he had commanded this brilliant young Jewess's ardent love, everything in his life and the customs he followed argued against completely accepting it. He had expressed his own devotion in letters and poems, he had let the romance flourish; but he did not let it change the course of his life. By the summer of 1925 Hannah Arendt had realized that he was to remain a stranger, no matter how deeply tied they were. In a poem, she invited him to a feast, but had to ask:

> Why do you give me your hand
> Shyly, as if it were a secret?
> Are you from such a distant land
> That you do not know our wine?

She wrote, in a melancholy but far more tranquil tone than that of "Die Schatten," a lovely "Summer Song" that shows the possibility she had thought unlikely, the possibility of "expression and release, overcoming this sickness and aberration, learning patience, simplicity and freedom of organic growth" asserting itself, despite her foreboding. She still felt caught in the dilemma of an illicit and impossible love, one that was never going to "shrink the priest's hands," but she was determined to keep alive the joy it had brought her.

> Through the ripening summer plenty
> I will go—and glide my hands,
> Stretch my painful limbs, down
> Towards the dark and heavy earth.
>
> The fields which bow and whisper,
> The paths deep in the forest,
> All command a strict silence:
> That we may love though we suffer;
>
> That our giving and our getting
> May not shrink the priest's hands;
> That in clear and noble quiet
> Joy may not die for us.
>
> The summer waters overflow,
> Weariness threatens to destroy us.
> And we lose our life
> If we love, if we live.

After her year in Marburg, Hannah Arendt went to Freiburg to spend a semester studying with Heidegger's mentor, Edmund Husserl. With more time and at a distance, she could reflect back on her "devotion to a single one" with a firmer strength, sure that even though she had been and was still deeply saddened, she was not going to be ruined or denied "organic growth." At this time she wrote one of the best of her poems:

> The evening has enwrapped me
> Soft as velvet, heavy as sorrow.

I no longer know how love feels
I no longer know the fields aglow,
And everything wants to drift away—
Simply to give me peace.

I think of him and of the love—
As though it were in a distant land;
And the "come and give" is foreign:
I hardly know what bound me.

The evening has enwrapped me
Soft as velvet, heavy as sorrow.
Nowhere is there a rebellion rising
Toward new joy and sadness.

And the distance which called for me,
All the yesterdays so clear and deep,
They no longer are beguiling.
I know a water great and strange
And a flower which no one names.
What can destroy me now?

The evening has enwrapped me,
Soft as velvet, heavy as sorrow.

In this poem, Hannah Arendt reached for that realm where German romantic poets had discovered such things as the unnameable "blue flower" and vast uncharted seas—a landscape of otherworldliness and transcendence. And she, in their manner, addressed herself with several poems to their protecting goddess, the Night.

Consoling one, lean softly to my heart.
Give me, silent one, relief from pain.
Put your shadow over everything too bright—
Give me exhaustion, shade the glare.

Leave me your silence, your cooling slackness,
Let me wrap in your dark all that is evil.
When brightness pains with new sights
Give me the strength to go on steadily.

In a less stylized and more touching poem, she addressed herself to her friends. She hoped they would not mistake the "devotion to a single one" that had consumed her emotional energies for indifference to them, and

she hoped they would know, without being told, the story behind her
story.

> Weep not for the soft sorrow
> When the look of the homeless one
> Still courts you shyly.
> Sense how the purest story
> Still hides everything.
>
> Feel the tenderest movement
> Of gratitude and faithfulness.
> And you will know: always,
> Renewed love will be given.

The friends, like Anne Mendelssohn, who knew of the love Hannah
Arendt felt for Heidegger, sympathized with her and tried to understand
Heidegger's decision to respect his obligations, particularly to his wife and
family. But the "friend" who was most deeply able to understand was a
woman to whom Anne Mendelssohn had introduced Hannah: Rahel
Varnhagen. Rahel Varnhagen was, as Hannah Arendt said years later,
while she was finishing the manuscript of her biography *Rahel Varnhagen: The Life of a Jewess*, "my closest friend, though she has been dead for
some one hundred years."[13]

Anne Mendelssohn had spoken excitedly about Rahel Varnhagen
while she was reading her way through the many volumes of the Varnhagen correspondence. These had come into Anne's hands by chance: a
book dealer in Allenstein had gone bankrupt during the inflation years
and sold his entire stock for pennies a volume. Anne had bought all the
Varnhagens. Hannah Arendt had, at the time, shown little interest in
Anne's discovery. But while she was completing her university studies
and preparing to write a monograph on German Romanticism, Arendt
encountered Rahel Varnhagen herself and found in her an "original,
unspoiled, and unconventional intelligence, combined with an absorbing
interest in people and a truly passionate nature."[14] Anne's Varnhagen
collection was transferred to Hannah Arendt.

In Rahel Varnhagen's letters and diaries Hannah Arendt saw revealed a
sensibility and a vulnerability very like her own. She sympathized with
the love Rahel had felt for the Gentile Count von Finckenstein, a love
which had been slowly and painfully refused. The count had left Rahel's
salon for the safety of his family and what he called his own conditions.

As she faced this loss, Rahel had become what Hannah Arendt felt herself becoming: a specific person. After her affair ended, Rahel was no longer a blank tablet, the outline of a destiny: "she was persuaded she had experienced life, life in general, as it was. . . . Experience had taken the place of her non-being; she now knew: *this is the way life is.*"[15] Hannah Arendt met in Rahel Varnhagen someone else for whom truths *überhaupt* rose up out of the ashes of experience, for whom even the most banal things were remarkable.

In "Die Schatten" Hannah Arendt had pronounced with characteristic generality and firmness what her own experience had taught her: "All good things come to a bad end; all bad things come to a good end. It is difficult to say which was more unbearable. For precisely this is what is most intolerable—it takes one's breath away if one thinks of it in the limitless fear which destroys reticence and prevents such a person from ever feeling at home: to suffer and to know, to know every minute and every second with full awareness and cynicism, that one has to be thankful even for the worst of pains, indeed that it is precisely such suffering which is the point of everything and its reward." This, Hannah Arendt had concluded, was the way life was: full of the suffering which Greek tragedians say brings wisdom. And her conclusion was very similar to the one Rahel Varnhagen reached: "What am I doing? Nothing. I am letting life rain upon me."[16]

Hannah Arendt came through her experience of an impossible love to her general conclusion that suffering is the point of everything and its reward; she felt that her "shy tenderness" toward the world had been ruined, that she had been deprived of her feeling of being at home. She was, as she said in the poem addressed to her friends, a "homeless one." Just this is what she found in Rahel's diaries and letters: Rahel's early efforts to be at home in the world were smashed when her love of von Finckenstein failed. But Rahel had gained from her failure: her youthful mode of dealing with the world—which Hannah Arendt called introspection—gave way to a new understanding.

Hannah Arendt's description of Rahel's early mode of introspection is very similar to her description, in "Die Schatten," of her own youthful self-absorption: "She hid and obstructed her own view and access to herself." In *Rahel Varnhagen*, the description is more elaborate and less verbally fanciful, but the same:

If thinking rebounds back upon itself and finds its solitary object within the soul—if, that is, it becomes introspection—it distinctly produces (so long as it remains rational) a semblance of unlimited power by the very act of isolation from the world, by ceasing to be interested in the world it also sets up a bastion in front of the one "interesting" object: the inner self. In the isolation achieved by introspection thinking becomes limitless because it is no longer molested by anything exterior; because there is no longer any demand for action, the consequences of which necessarily impose limits even upon the freest spirit. . . . Reality can offer nothing new; anticipation has already anticipated everything. Even the blows of fate can be escaped by flight into the self if every single misfortune has already been generalized beforehand as an inevitable concomitant of the bad outside world, so that there is no reason to feel shock at having been struck this one particular time. [17]

When Rahel lost von Finckenstein she was deprived of her shock-prevention capacity—the loss breached the bastion she had placed before her inner self. But she gave up her introspective mode slowly. Hannah Arendt wrote of her, as though commenting on the despairing conclusion of "Die Schatten" where a quick end to this "needless and futile business" of living was evoked, that she "succumbed neither to madness nor death, but inescapably to recovery which she could not allow herself to want because she did not want to forget." Rahel did not forget but reaped "the splendid harvest of despair" and went on, accepting her unhappiness, hardened but more open to the world, ready to "speak the truth." "She realized that her individual experience could be generalized without being falsified." [18]

Hannah Arendt had been, since childhood, a generalizer. But the generalizing had been of the unworldly, stoical, shock-prevention sort. She had let experiences "slip to the bottom of her soul," where they could not harm her: "We must not think too much about sad things," she had told her mother at age seven. She, like Rahel, began to learn to generalize without falsifying by confronting an experience which could not be dealt with in the two modes she had known: "dull pain" or "dreamy, enchanted isolation". But learning to tell the truth, to overcome introspective subjectivity, was not a simple matter. Rahel Varnhagen had had a guide, Goethe, who taught her "the generalizing power of poetry." Rahel needed the poet's guidance because she had been unable, after her loss, to tell the story behind her story. People had been fascinated by her personality, attracted by her original intelligence, but "apparently Rahel had not wanted them to fall prey to her magic; rather, she had hoped someone would ask how things stood with her." [19] No one asked Rahel Varnhagen, and she did not say. "Everything would be repeated, for no one had understood." Rahel Varnhagen did repeat her impossible love, did fall impossibly in love again, before she learned to tell her story with the guidance of Goethe's work and personality.

Hannah Arendt noted in *Rahel Varnhagen* how Rahel learned that poetry "converts the individual matters of which it speaks into generalities because it not only employs language as a means for communicating a specific content, but converts language back into its original substance." The function of language is preservation: "what it embodies is meant to remain, to remain longer than is possible for ephemeral human beings."[20] But this passage is pure Heidegger; it summarizes Heidegger's appreciative view of poets and poetry, which Hannah Arendt never abandoned. She did not immediately meet a Goethe to "provide her with a language she could speak"; she continued to speak Heidegger's language, and she eventually went on to write a book in that language, her dissertation on "Saint Augustine's Concept of Love," before she finally found a language of her own. And she too, like Rahel Varnhagen, had to repeat her experience, had to fall in love again, twice, before she was able to write, in her own language, *Rahel Varnhagen: The Life of a Jewess.*

*Neighborly Love*

During her year in Marburg Hannah Arendt had been isolated and estranged in her secret love for Heidegger. But she did make new acquaintances and continue her friendships with her Königsberger circle. In Heidegger's seminar, there was one other Jewish student, Hans Jonas, and in the hours they spent together puzzling over Heidegger's lectures a friendship began which lasted for the rest of Hannah Arendt's life.

After finishing his *Abitur* in Mönchen-Gladbach, near Düsseldorf, Hans Jonas had gone to Freiburg to study philosophy with Husserl. While he attended Husserl's lectures, he was assigned to a beginner's seminar with Husserl's assistant, the *Privatdozent* Martin Heidegger. In 1921, at the age of eighteen, Jonas decided that it was in Heidegger's seminars rather than in Husserl's lectures that philosophy was alive. Even though he understood very little, he too sensed that there was, in these seminars, something mysterious, a depth, an openness to new modes of thought. Heidegger intrigued him, and so did Heidegger's advanced students, like Karl Löwith, who delivered dense and difficult papers to the seminar in a slow, halting voice—he had been wounded in the lung during the war—which compounded the difficulty of grasping his meaning.

But Jonas, who had studied Hebrew during his *Gymnasium* years and was a Zionist, wanted to combine his philosophical studies with Judaic studies, as he hoped eventually to go to Palestine as a teacher. Freiburg was not the place to fulfill this ambition, so he went to Berlin, where he attended both the university and the Hochschule für die Wissenschaft des Judentums (Academy for Judaic Studies) which had been founded there in 1872. Jonas continued his philosophical studies with Eduard Spranger and Ernst Mayer and his classical training with von Willamowitz and Werner Jaeger.

After one of Spranger's seminars, Jonas was flattered to be stopped on the street for a talk by another of the students, Günther Stern, a young man whose "aura of genius" had impressed Jonas for several years. They had attended Husserl's classes together in Freiburg, but Jonas had never been able to overcome his shyness and introduce himself. Once Stern had made the gesture, a friendship was launched. The two men became very close and, after several years, Stern hoped Jonas, who had been courting Günther's sister Eva, would join his family. But, as it turned out, the friendship was matrimonially extended in another direction when Günther Stern married Jonas's friend, Hannah Arendt, six years later.

Jonas returned to Freiburg for one semester after his stay in Berlin and then followed Heidegger to Marburg in the spring of 1924. In the fall, he met Hannah Arendt in Heidegger's seminar. The two had in common not only their Jewishness but also their lack of respect for many of the young adulators who surrounded Heidegger. Arendt stayed aloof from most of the students; she was friendly only with Jonas and the young Königsbergers in Marburg and intimate only with Heidegger himself. She met Günther Stern when he came to the spring 1925 seminar after he had finished his doctorate with Husserl, for the opportunity of hearing Heidegger, but she did not then care to extend her circle of acquaintance.

Hannah Arendt's aloofness and her relationship with Heidegger did not endear her to the Heidegger cult and particularly not to its many female members. One young woman was doubly jealous of Hannah Arendt, for she had designs upon Heidegger and Ernst Grumach, who both preferred Arendt's company. Arendt was also not received with any warmth by Heidegger's wife, who resented Heidegger's relationships with his infatuated female students and disliked Jewish students of either sex. As Heidegger singled out Hannah Arendt from the others, Elfriede Heidegger became very suspicious.

Arendt stayed apart from the orthodox Heideggerians and tried to avoid generating gossip or increasing Elfriede Heidegger's hostility. She lived alone in an attic room near the university and received Heidegger, Jonas, and her Königsberg friends there. As she worked and flourished intellectually under Heidegger's tutelage, Hannah Arendt's extraordinary abilities became more and more obvious to all who knew her. Brightness of intellect was not rare in Marburg, as Hans Jonas noted, but in Hannah Arendt, the students found "an intensity, an inner direction, an instinct for quality, a groping for essence, a probing for depth, which cast a magic about her."[21] Ernst Grumach was particularly impressed, and grateful, as Arendt helped him work on the dissertation which won him his doctorate in classical philology. But her friends continued to be struck by her shyness, even childlikeness. When they came to visit, they could in one evening be treated to excellent philosophical discussions and to the charming spectacle of Hannah Arendt summoning her small roommate, a mouse, out of his hole to eat the food she provided. This mouse, she told Jonas, was as alone, *so allein*, as she was.

Outside of her classes, the student population of Marburg did not claim Arendt's attention except when it infringed on her. Anti-Semitism was not extreme, but Marburg did have a sizable reactionary movement and anti-Semitic remarks were not infrequent among the fraternity men and the National Socialist youth group members. Young rightists occasionally came into the orbit of Heidegger's followers through his wife. Günther Stern recalled meeting Elfriede Heidegger at a housewarming for their cottage in Todtnauberg in the spring of 1925. Full of good feeling after an evening of eating and singing around a bonfire, Elfriede Heidegger asked Stern, who had made an impression on her, if he would like to join the National Socialist youth group in Marburg. When Stern informed her that he was Jewish, she abruptly turned away. Hannah Arendt was careful to avoid such occasions.

Arendt was on her guard, and she appreciated the protective attentions paid her by her Jewish friends. Hans Jonas recalled how grateful she had been for his help one evening when they were dining in a student restaurant. A uniformed fraternity man came up to their table, attracted by Hannah Arendt, and asked if he could join them; Jonas caught his friend's frightened glance and refused. But she was also quite capable of setting the terms of her relationships with the Gentiles on her own. When she wanted to take Rudolf Bultmann's New Testament seminar, which required an interview with the theologian for permission, she informed Bultmann in no uncertain terms—terms, in fact, so certain that they were quoted exactly every time she and Jonas remembered the story—that "there must be no anti-Semitic remarks." Bultmann, a calm and gentle man, assured her that should any anti-Semitic remarks be made in the seminar "we two together will handle the situation."


After she left Marburg for her semester of study with Husserl—and distance from Heidegger—Arendt did not return. She could not write a doctoral dissertation with Heidegger; the personal difficulties of such an arrangement aside, both would have been compromised if their liaison had been discovered. So Heidegger directed her to Heidelberg, where his friend Karl Jaspers held a university chair in philosophy.

Hannah Arendt had started her university studies with Martin Heidegger just as he was beginning to write his masterwork, *Being and Time.* She arrived in Heidelberg just as Jaspers was beginning to draw together notes and lectures to draft his philosophical masterwork, the three-volume *Philosophy.* The goddess she often invoked, Fortune, was twice kind to her: she not only studied with the two greatest German philosophers of the generation which reached philosophical maturity between the two world wars; she was able to participate with both in the classes and discussions that shaped their finest works.

After her lesson concerning "the way life is," Hannah Arendt was challenged again in Heidelberg by the way philosophy might be, by another extraordinary example of the way reason can "order and prevail through capacities and talents." In Jaspers she met a man whose human stature was the rival of Goethe's.

Jaspers was nearly forty years old when he decided to leave behind a very successful career in psychology and neuropsychiatry to "ascend to the heights of philosophy proper."[22] His "Philosophical Memoir" tells the story of his dissatisfaction with his remarkable 1919 work, *The Psychology of World Views;* of his decision, "equivalent to starting all over"; and of the years he spent reading "the few great, original philosophical works," preparing to write his *Philosophy* (1931). But the story of Jaspers's questing, self-challenging attitude was a life story. As a young man, Jaspers had been an intern and a research assistant at the Heidelberg psychiatric hospital. A number of studies in psychopathology and an enormous *General Psychopathology,* a systematic survey and critique of the theories, methods, and topics debated among psychologists in the first decade of this century, had established Jaspers's reputation. But he was not satisfied, and he began to consider an even wider field of topics: his lectures between 1913 and 1922 ranged from empirical psychology through case studies of historical figures like Nietzsche, Strindberg, and Van Gogh, to social psychology, religious psychology, and moral psychology. *The Psychology of World Views* had emerged from one series among these lectures. It brought Jaspers close to philosophy, it became "the basis for my future thinking," he recalled. Jaspers's step into philosophy proper was prepared by a career of expanding, deepening inquiries; his life was a model of what Hannah Arendt had called "organic growth."

The lectures Jaspers gave while Hannah Arendt was his student were, as Jaspers put it, "the way to work things out." For him, lecturing was not the presentation of a finished doctrine, but a mode of communication, and "communication" itself was one of the central concepts Jaspers explored. In the seminars Hannah Arendt attended, Jaspers raised "the question of philosophy's nature, and of the dimensions in which it moves." Particular thinkers, such as Schelling, were studied, but the seminars were focused on modes of thinking, types of thinking processes. Jaspers was slowly constructing a typology of the dimensions in which philosophy moves, based not on the content of particular philosophical doctrines but on the thinking processes which grounded the doctrines.

In Jaspers's early work, the method Edmund Husserl had called "descriptive psychology" and the method Wilhelm Dilthey had called "understanding psychology" were central. But as Jaspers moved toward philosophy, the method he learned from conversations with the sociologist Max Weber became the mainstay of his thinking technique. Weber constructed "ideal types" (*Idealtypen*) or models designed to illuminate the characteristics particular to a given form of human behavior, cultural phenomenon, or social unit. Jaspers had used this technique extensively in his *Psychology of World Views* to distinguish basic types of *Weltanschauungen* ("world views") and the consequences for human behavior of each type. But he became dissatisfied with mere typologies of world views because they could not illuminate what makes people adopt a particular world view, what moves them to think, to act, to make choices. Jaspers was searching for the questions which a person must answer "in his reality, not in any contemplative view." Weber's technique continued to provide Jaspers with a framework; he used it to distinguish the dimensions of philosophizing, the types of philosophical thought processes, but his interest in the content of world views or doctrinal systems lessened. His new orientation was summarized in many different ways, but this sentence is exemplary: "Philosophizing is real as it pervades an individual life at a given moment." For Hannah Arendt, this concrete approach was a revelation; and Jaspers living his philosophizing was an example to her: "I perceived his Reason in *praxis*, so to speak," she remembered.[23]

Jaspers's concern with how individuals think and act was finally woven through a three-part schematism of "dimensions" in his *Philosophy*, which was divided, accordingly, into three volumes. One volume was dedicated to how philosophical thinking relates to the world and objects in the world, one to how it relates to the human condition, the "existential condition" of man, and one to how philosophical thinking seeks to transcend the world and man. "Philosophical World Orientation," "Existential Elucidation," and "Metaphysics" were types, but not static or fixed types; they were more like what Kierkegaard called "stages on life's way."

Jaspers formulated his "Philosophy of Existenz", his discussion of how human beings fulfill—or fail to fulfill—their human possibilities, after Max Weber died. But the presence of his friend and mentor is apparent on every page of the *Philosophy*—not just as an intellectual influence, but as a human example. "When Max Weber died in 1920," Jaspers recalled, "I felt as though the world had changed. The great man who had justified and, to my mind, animated it was no longer with us. Weber's had been the authority that never preached, never relieved you of responsibility, but encouraged what had won the approval of his strictly and lucidly humane thinking. Now it was as if it had disappeared, this ineffable, utterly trustworthy guidance for rational discussion, this authority whose depth would yield the insight into situations of the moment, and the judgment of actions and cognitions and events." Hannah Arendt felt this way when Karl Jaspers himself died in 1969, and she had to write her own *Philosophy, The Life of the Mind*, without him. But she had had, from the day when she became his student until the day when they discussed the plan for *The Life of the Mind* not long before Jaspers's death, his "trustworthy guidance for rational discussion."

Max Weber was an irreplaceable friend and guide for Karl Jaspers. But in the year Weber died, he had met in Martin Heidegger a man he hoped would challenge him intellectually as Weber had. They were introduced at the 1920 birthday celebration for Edmund Husserl, and Jaspers immediately noted how Heidegger stood out at the gathering, where there was "something petit-bourgeois, something small-minded in the air."[24] Their friendship was launched when Heidegger visited Heidelberg and then wrote a review of the *Psychology of World Views* in which he both recognized Jaspers's work as a new beginning for philosophy and criticized it for not going far enough. More than his review, Heidegger's conversations about Jaspers's work had spurred Jaspers's decision to "ascend the heights of philosophy proper." The two men exchanged letters, met to talk during the early 1920s, and after 1926 shared responsibility for the education of Hannah Arendt. But Arendt knew them together only after their friendship had begun to be problematic, after the 1927 publication of *Being and Time*. Jaspers found the book alien in tone and style: "through our work, our hidden estrangement came to light." Not until 1933 did this estrangement take on insurmountable form; when Heidegger's susceptibility to National Socialist propaganda and its anti-Semitism became apparent, the two philosophers parted ways.

For Jaspers, the early friendship with Heidegger and the presence in his classes of students like Hannah Arendt was crucial. While he was reading the Great Philosophers and thinking through his *Philosophy*—and not publishing—he came into conflict with the leading Heidelberg neo-Kantian, Heidegger's former teacher Heinrich Rickert. Rickert tried to convince his colleagues that Jaspers was not publishing because he had exhausted his ideas and talents with his 1919 work; Jaspers's university chair was, Rickert claimed, a camouflage for his incompetence. When the *Philosophy* finally appeared in 1931, Rickert was silenced, but during the years of its preparation Jaspers was grateful for the intellectual support he received from Heidegger and his students, and especially from his wife, Gertrud, and Gertrud's brother, Ernst Mayer, who were his closest intellectual collaborators.

The Mayers came from a devout, orthodox-Jewish, business family in Prenzlau which was, Hannah Arendt explained to a friend, *sehr belastet*, very troubled, by hereditary mental illness.[25] A sister had been institutionalized with a "lingering and puzzling mental illness," some years after another sister had died of diphtheria. Gertrud Mayer Jaspers herself had been deeply disturbed when her closest friend died at the age of twenty and again when her first boy friend, the poet Walter Cale, took his own life. These were, Jaspers recalled, "blows of fate which Gertrud could not reconcile with an unquestioning continuance of life." Nonetheless, she had the courage to marry Karl Jaspers when he was an unknown assistant in a psychiatric clinic suffering from an illness, bronchiectasis, for which the prognosis was grim—he was given only a few years to live. "Das ist ja auch etwas," said Arendt when she told this story ("that is really something").

Gertrud and Ernst Mayer were both intimately involved in the making of Jaspers's *Philosophy*. They talked, Ernst read each draft of the book and offered suggestions, they discussed revisions. But Jaspers also enjoyed the company of a group of Heidelberg professors who met on Sunday evenings at the home of Max Weber's widow, Marianne Weber, for *Geistertee*. After Weber's death, his widow had continued this tradition that Weber himself had instituted—a tradition of salon life reminiscent of the Enlightenment. Weber's brother, the sociologist Alfred Weber, and his colleague Emil Lederer, the archaeologist Ludwig Curtius, the psychiatrist Viktor von Weizacker, the Indologist Heinrich Zimmer, the Germanist Friedrich Gundolf, the theologian Martin Dibelius and others attended these gatherings. These were the men whose lectures Karl Jaspers recommended to Hannah Arendt. Martin Dibelius's New Testament lectures and his remarkable knowledge of Greek and Latin were particularly important to Hannah Arendt when she began to write her doctoral dissertation on Saint Augustine's concept of love.

Jaspers was sustained by his family and friends, and his circle provided Hannah Arendt with a feeling of intellectual community she had not known in provincial Marburg during the year of her "devotion to a single one." She also had companions of her own age, young people who came to Heidelberg attracted by the cosmopolitan and liberal Heidelberg spirit known throughout Germany to be tolerant of innovation and experiment. Her friend Hans Jonas came to Heidelberg to work on his first book, *Augustine and the Pauline Problem of Freedom*. And Hannah Arendt met a threesome of friends trained in philosophy and psychology: Karl Frankenstein, who later became a professor of psychology at the Hebrew University; Erich Neumann, who became a Jungian psychoanalyst and wrote many books, the best known of which is probably *The Discovery of the Unconscious*; and Erwin Loewenson, an essayist and writer of the Expressionist school. All three of the friends were attracted to Hannah Arendt, but only Loewenson, who was older than his friends by nearly twenty years, met with success in his courtship.

In 1927, Arendt and Loewenson had a brief love affair, followed by a friendship which lasted until Loewenson died in 1963. The letters they exchanged during 1927 and 1928, while Loewenson was living in Berlin and Hannah Arendt in Heidelberg, were, like the letters they exchanged after the war, while Loewenson was living in Palestine and Arendt in New York, letters of encouragement and support for intellectual projects.[26] In the early letters, Hannah Arendt discussed her dissertation topic and was sent questions, suggested readings, quotations; they spoke about the element of friendship they both held most important—loyalty. Loewenson's independent, somewhat eccentric intelligence and his remarkable literary abilities—even his letters were written in the complexly playful poetic style of his writings—were exciting to Hannah Arendt, whose predilection for masters of German prose had already flowered in the presence of Heidegger. But she was never as deeply attracted to Loewenson as he was to her. When they met, he was one of the moving forces among the Berlin-based Expressionists, but his capacities and talents were not ones through which reason prevailed. He avidly added pages to a growing collection of manuscripts, but he brought very little of his work to completion and was constantly hampered by emotional instability. As inspiring as the relationship was for Hannah Arendt, emotional instability was not what she needed after her year of emotional storm in Marburg.

The milieu Hannah Arendt entered when she met Benno Georg Leopold von Wiese und Kaiserwaldau in 1927 was, to say the least, different. Von Wiese, who was only three years older than Arendt, had just finished his first study of Friedrich Schlegel and published it with Springer, in a series edited by Karl Jaspers. His success stood before him. With his brilliant young friends, like the future Romanist Hugo Friedrich, von Wiese had been trained in literary history by Friedrich Gundolf, then the most famous and prestigious teacher of literature in Germany.

A critic and poet, Friedrich Gundolf had been a celebrated member of the enormously influential circle around the poet Stefan George. Gundolf had adulated Goethe in books and in many essays; he had written a wildly enthusiastic biography of Julius Caesar, important studies and translations of Shakespeare, and a book on the reception of Shakespeare's work in Germany. Like other members of the George circle, he had a fierce admiration for heroes, aristocrats, and ancient examples of the *Gesamtmensch* ("the whole man") whose stature shamed the cultural barbarism of the Weimar Republic. Gundolf is often criticized as a "gravedigger of the Republic" by those who look back on Weimar through the events that brought the republic to an end,[27] but during his lifetime, even though his elitism was troubling to more democratic spirits, he was a towering intellectual figure. Karl Jaspers gave an appreciative account of his friend at a seminar held shortly after Gundolf's death in 1931, in which he noted that he had often argued with Gundolf in a lively and rational way, but had remained close to him: "I cannot say 'no' to a man when I have truly said 'yes' to him."[28] Jaspers felt, and most of Gundolf's admirers would have agreed, that Gundolf's best work, particularly his last book, *Shakespeare*, was done after Stefan George had repudiated him and he had left the company of men Jaspers felt possessed "the type of spirit from which one gets no nourishment." Toward the end of his life, when Hannah Arendt attended his lectures, Gundolf was much more a man of the refined, serious, Heidelberg spirit than a man of the effete, pederastic, George circle.

In the company of Benno von Wiese and his friends, and by attending Gundolf's lectures, Hannah Arendt's ties to German Romanticism and her interest in the Jewish salons where the German Romantics had gathered at the turn of the eighteenth century grew deeper and more informed. She considered writing an extensive study of German Romanticism when she finished her doctoral dissertation, and this plan, which launched her on an enormous campaign of reading, brought her, eventually, to a specific interest in Rahel Varnhagen's Berlin salon. The interest was not academic. Arendt became, as her cousin Ernst Fuerst and his wife recalled, a modern version of the Jewish Rahel Varnhagen among her highly cultivated and aristocratic Gentile friends. With the tall, thin, fair-haired, professorial von Wiese, she was as alluringly different and unconventional—smoking her metal-stemmed modern pipe—as Rahel Levin had been with her second love, her déjà vu, Don Raphael d'Urquijo.

Unlike Marburg, Heidelberg had had a salon tradition since the turn of the century, and it had centered around the Webers. Like the Berlin salons of Rahel Varnhagen's day, the Weber circle had included many remarkable women, some of them Jews. Gertrud Jaspers was so ardently devoted to her husband and his endeavors that she was known in Heidelberg as *das Flämmchen* ("the little flame").[29] Gertrud Simmel had supported her husband, the sociologist Georg Simmel, through his difficult years of nonacceptance by traditional university faculty members hostile to sociology and then stayed on after his death in 1918. Marianne Weber and Else Jaffe, born Else von Richthofen and married to one of Weber's students, Edgar Jaffe, were both important contributors to the intellectual life and political consciousness of Heidelberg. Men and women, non-Jews and Jews (Gundolf was a Jew) came to Marianne Weber's when she reestablished the salon after Weber's death.

Benno von Wiese was accustomed to university social circles. He came from university gentry, having inherited the *noblesse de robe* of his father,

Leopold, a well-known social philosopher. He was much admired by the leading academicians, including Karl Jaspers, who hoped that the match with Hannah Arendt would be a long-lasting one. But after nearly two years, they went their separate ways, von Wiese having decided that he wanted to marry someone more dedicated to domesticity and this-worldly love than the still quite naive, nearly transcendental, and rather Heideggerian author of "Saint Augustine's Concept of Love." Von Wiese later married Ilse von Gavel. Arendt moved to Berlin, where she renewed her acquaintance with Günther Stern.[30]

Though the two men with whom Hannah Arendt had love affairs during her years at Heidelberg were of different generations, different social and religious milieus, they had in common their love of literature and German culture, their aestheticism. But Heidegger remained the representative of German culture to whom she was most deeply tied. Until she finished her doctoral dissertation in Heidelberg and moved to Berlin in 1929, whenever Heidegger wrote to her suggesting that she meet him, Arendt left her work, her friends, her obligations, to go. By the early 1930s, Heidegger's fascination with National Socialism came decisively between them. That the Nazis' nationalism was a perversion of everything admirable in German culture, Heidegger did not seem able to recognize. He was so fearful of modernization and so committed to pastoral, preindustrial values—he was, as Hannah Arendt later said, "the last German Romantic"[31]—that he could find in the Nazi evocation of primitive Germanness a compatible tendency. The German language, which he called in 1935 "at once the most powerful and most spiritual of languages," was at the center of his unworldly and politically naive cultural conservatism.[32] Because she could understand Heidegger's allegiances, and later even see the comicalness of them, Arendt remained loyal to him, even though she had to break off their relationship when he entered the Nazi party. For seventeen years, she had no communication with him. But when she did meet him again, after the war, she was able to forgive him much for his poetry. On the occasion of their postwar reunion in Freiburg, she described to a friend the nature of the bond that allowed her loyalty to survive his foolishness: "I had professional obligations [in Freiburg], and met Heidegger at my hotel. As always, I received through him the German language, uniquely beautiful. Poetry really. Man tut was man kann, one does what one can."[33]

When Hitler came to power in Germany, Hannah Arendt and Karl

Jaspers confronted the issues posed by Nazism much more directly. They had many strenuous discussions about what Jaspers's German nationalism meant to him. He had learned from Max Weber, whom he thought of as "the last genuine German nationalist," a nationalism which he felt was free of "the will to power for one's own empire" because it was dedicated to the realization of "a moral-intellectual existence that endures by power but subjects this very power to its own terms."[34] Jaspers did not share Weber's "sense of Prussian greatness" or his "soldierly spirit," however, and he came to realize after Weber's death that both political nationalism and the military mind in politics were gravely dangerous for Germany. Jaspers's Germanism had always been "a matter of language, home and background," the "great intellectual tradition" with which he had felt connected from an early age. Hannah Arendt could appreciate Jaspers's view, but she did not hesitate to tell him that he was failing to see the threat of National Socialism out of a naive trust in his fellow citizens' political maturity.

Jaspers was challenged by Hannah Arendt's refusal to accept what he called in Weberian language "the German essence."[35] She brought to her criticism her own education in the presence of a man whose knowledge and love of German culture were remarkable, but not nationalistic. This was Kurt Blumenfeld, the only other acquaintance of her Heidelberg years who shared the esteem Hannah Arendt otherwise reserved for Heidegger and Jaspers. The two German philosophers had awakened and fostered Hannah Arendt's precocious philosophical abilities and initiated her into the renewal of philosophy they had undertaken. But it was Kurt Blumenfeld who awakened and fostered her sense of her Jewish identity and introduced her to the renewal of Jewish consciousness the Zionists had undertaken.

Born in 1884, Kurt Blumenfeld was a year younger than Jaspers and five years older than Heidegger. His was, as he said in his memoir *Erlebte Judenfrage*, a Jewish family of German culture. His father had been a judge in East Prussia and his mother, like Hannah Arendt's, a talented amateur musician. Blumenfeld had set out to follow his father's profession, but while he was studying at the Königsberg Albertina his interest in Zionism came to dominate his interest in jurisprudence. He helped found a Zionist student club and began to practice his great gift for persuasion on the members of the Königsberg Jewish community council members who opposed Zionism. Hannah Arendt's grandfather, Max

Arendt, was among those of the older generation of assimilated Jews who responded to Blumenfeld's arguments with the current nationalistic maxim: "When my Germanness is attacked, I prepare for murder." Max Arendt abandoned his hostility, but he was never sympathetic to Zionism. Blumenfeld had much greater success with Hannah Arendt.

In 1909 Blumenfeld gave up his law studies to become executive secretary and chief spokesman for the Zionist Organization of Germany. He travelled throughout the country making speeches renowned for their verve and power. By the time Arendt's friend Hans Jonas invited Kurt Blumenfeld to address a meeting of the Zionist student club at Heidelberg in 1926, he was the most influential proponent of Zionism in Germany. But Hannah Arendt found herself in the audience the evening Blumenfeld spoke as a result of Hans Jonas's shyness and not from any interest in Zionism.

Jonas had issued Blumenfeld a written invitation and then telephoned Berlin to make preliminary arrangements for the occasion. Jonas was always a reticent telephoner, and his nervousness increased with long distance and esteem for the man at the other end of the line; full sentences eluded him, and Blumenfeld was forced to request that someone else do the telephoning for final arrangements. Jonas commandeered his friend Hannah Arendt for the task, and she went along to the lecture in the role of aide de camp.

The lecture did not convert Hannah Arendt to Zionism, but it did convert her to Kurt Blumenfeld. She and Jonas took Blumenfeld to dinner after his talk, and she was both flirtatious and daughterly as they ate, drank heartily, and then strolled out through the streets of Heidelberg to the beautiful Philosopher's Way that stretches across the hill opposite the town. Blumenfeld and Hannah Arendt, arm in arm, sang songs, recited poetry, and laughed uproariously—while Jonas tagged along.

Hannah Arendt admired, and continued to admire, Blumenfeld's lightly carried erudition, his vigor, and his unsentimental, ironic humor. After she left Heidelberg, he became her "mentor in politics," but he never ceased to be the man with whom she enjoyed being playful, tossing back and forth quotations from the poet who was Blumenfeld's kindred spirit, Heinrich Heine. Through the years of exile in which they were separated, Hannah Arendt treasured the memory of her happiness in Blumenfeld's company. "Do you remember," she asked him twenty years after they parted in Berlin "how in 1933 we said farewell to each other in Mampe's *Weinstube*, reciting Greek verses?"[36]

"The Jewish Question," which Blumenfeld spent the better part of his life exploring, was debated by the intelligentsia of Central Europe at the turn of the twentieth century and during its first decades. In 1912 an article entitled "German-Jewish Parnassus" appeared in a widely read journal, *Der Kunstwart*. Heated and voluminous discussions were precipitated by this piece, in which the author, Moritz Goldstein, bluntly stated the two dimensions of the German-Jewish intellectuals' situation that converged to raise the Jewish Question.[37] In a non-Jewish society, Jewish intellectuals had the uncomfortable task of preserving the intellectual property of a people which denied them the right and ability to do so. Further, Jews, in the company of other Jews, were attempting the impossible: to remain Jews without acknowledging their Jewishness. Even Jews who refused to make this attempt, Goldstein argued, faced another dilemma: in return for acknowledging his Jewishness and the anti-Semitism of the Germans, a Jew was not rewarded with a Jewish language and a Jewish culture; he still spoke German and lived in a German cultural milieu and still had to face isolation from Jews who wished their Jewishness away.

For Blumenfeld, Zionism was the only answer to the Question, but even Zionism was problematic for him. He maintained that Zionism was a matter of revelation (*Offenbarung*), not a systematic doctrine, and he publicly acknowledged his own awakening.[38] When he was young, his family's Catholic maid had informed him that each week she confessed to her priest the sin of her service to a group of "deicides." This shock, and the shame he had felt when he joined a German friend in condescending behavior toward an *Ostjude* during his school years, combined to illuminate for Blumenfeld what he called "the objective Jewish Question." No matter what their religious, cultural, or political convictions, Jews would always be perceived by non-Jews as, first and foremost, Jews. The goal of every Jew, he argued, should be to face this fact squarely, to "face the non-Jewish German unabashed, with an open visor." When Hannah Arendt later spoke and wrote about the need for Jews to refuse to humble themselves, she did so with her mother's attitude in mind and with Blumenfeld's radical Zionism echoing in her words. "Zionism," she claimed, in *The Origins of Totalitarianism*, "in the first decade after the First World War, and even in the decade preceding it, owed its... strength not so much to political insight (and did not produce political convictions) as it did to its critical analysis of psychological reactions and sociological facts. Its influence was mainly pedagogical and went far beyond the relatively small number of actual members of the Zionist movement."[39]

Blumenfeld acknowledged that his type of Zionism was problematic by calling it postassimilatory. This meant two things. First, it was a brand of Zionism for Jews who—unlike most Eastern Jews—had both emancipation and assimilation in their histories and, thus, had no base for their opposition to anti-Semitism in an existing religious or social community. And, secondly, it was for Jews who had lost contact with Jewish culture and wanted to maintain their contacts with the national culture in which they had grown up. Blumenfeld wanted Zionism to be a true national movement (a *Volksbewegung*) and he argued that emigration to Palestine should be part of every Zionist's life program, but for him this implied that a Jewish community would have to be built up, that there was no community to transplant to Zion. He questioned constantly how to build a community tolerant of the non-Jewish cultural backgrounds of its members, a community in which, as Hannah Arendt said of the place she later chose to live, America, "assimilation is not the price of citizenship."[40]

Blumenfeld's criticism of assimilation was designed to alert Jews to the pressures of life in a non-Jewish society and also to warn against reinstituting intolerance in a future Jewish society, among Jews. He wanted to eliminate inequalities from Jewish life, and one of the steps he felt was necessary to this end was a harsh critique of "philanthropic Zionism." Extending charity to Eastern Jews, persecuted Jews, victims of anti-Semitism, was not, he felt, the way to forge a national consciousness. Philanthropy simply locked into place the differences between Jews who had been successful as "parvenus" and Jews who could not or would not leave behind their "pariah" condition.

Hannah Arendt accepted the main lines of Blumenfeld's analysis of the psychological and sociological dimensions of Jewish response to anti-Semitism without difficulty, and she was particularly struck by the danger Blumenfeld sensed—that the modes and types of prejudice German Jews encountered might be repeated within Jewish ranks if assimilationist attitudes were not overcome. But emigration to Palestine was never part of her life program. Before 1933 she questioned how the Jewish Question could be, if not answered, lived with—without emigration. Her biography of Rahel Varnhagen was one way to question; but before she began

it, she posed her question in quite a different way. She considered Saint
Augustine's concept of "neighborly love," his concern for the *vita so-cialis*.

Hannah Arendt's dissertation was concerned with the concept of love
in the writings of Saint Augustine—or, rather, the concepts of love.[41]
Each of the three sections of the dissertation focused on one concept of
love: love as craving (*appetitus*), love as a relation between man and God
the Creator, and neighborly love. But the concept of neighborly love is
presented as the most fundamental, the one toward which the first two
concepts are oriented. The structure of the dissertation is dialectical:
"Thou shalt love thy neighbor as thyself" is the commandment which
both unites and transcends the other two concepts of love.

Arendt's approach was, in her own terms, "systematic," but that does
not imply that she tried to yoke Augustine to a consistency unknown to
him, to reconcile seemingly heterogeneous or even contradictory statements. Her approach seems to reflect the distinction that Jaspers made
between a system and a systematization: one can be philosophically systematic without producing a system; one can discover order without in-
sisting that there is a final, total order into which all statements or trains of
thought fit, leaving no loose ends. When Jaspers wrote his own study
of Saint Augustine in the 1950s, he emphasized the great tensions in
Augustine's thought. "Nothing is easier than to find contradictions in Augustine. We take them as a feature of his greatness. No philosophy is free
from contradiction—and no thinker can aim at contradiction."[42] Jaspers
even claimed that the contradictions in Augustine's thought were essential to its fruitfulness: "And it is because, working with the methods of
ecclesiastical thinking, he encompassed a maximum of contradictions—
even in opposition to reason—that he was able, within the authority
of the Church, to meet its needs so eminently without devising a system."
Jaspers's distinction between system and systematization is reflected in
Hannah Arendt's dissertation, and her application of the distinction is
probably reflected in Jaspers's later study. Scholarly opposition to such an
approach changed little over the thirty years between the student's dissertation and the teacher's book: both Arendt and Jaspers met the same
charge from their reviewers; they had presented the thinker Augustine and
not the Bishop Augustine.

Arendt was quite clear about what she was doing, for she insisted that
Augustine "was no theologian," and she told Jaspers that this had always

been her opinion, even when she was Rudolf Bultmann's student and heard about the current debates among Protestant theologians concerning Augustine's Christianity and its relevance for the modern world.[43] Arendt's dissertation was reviewed in some of the major journals of the time—*Philosophisches Jahrbuch, Kantstudien, Gnomon, Deutsche Literatur-Zeitung*—but not at all favorably. She had, her reviewers agreed, sinned twice: once by ignoring Augustine the theologian, and once by ignoring the contemporary theological scholars who claimed Augustine for their own. The stir in Heidelberg and in theological circles that greeted this dissertation by a twenty-three-year-old Jewess on a major figure of the Christian Church might have been, if not less, at least different had Jaspers's and Heidegger's philosophies been more widely known, for Arendt's was a work of existential philosophy, not a contribution to theology. But Arendt began her publishing career as she ended it more than forty years later—as a burr under scholarly saddles.[44]

Arendt's method of intertwining diverse and often contradictory conceptual contexts, of systematizing, is in the mode of Jaspers. Augustine's three types of love are also examined with existential concepts crucial to the three dimensions of philosophizing Jaspers had formulated. Arendt found in Augustine a world-oriented love (*appetitus*), an existential love (neighborly love), and a transcendent love (love of the Creator). She used concepts Jaspers associated with all three dimensions: desire, limitation, knowledge; communication, self-realization, thinking; origination, redemption, faith. But both the way in which Arendt wove Jaspers's orientations through her work and the language in which she expressed her ideas owe a much greater debt to Heidegger.

What Arendt owed to Heidegger is not immediately obvious and does not relate to any exposition of the concept of love in his work. Love is mentioned in *Being and Time* only once, in a footnote. Even concepts that Hannah Arendt always associated with love, like loyalty (*Treue*), are discussed by Heidegger in singular rather than plural terms: "Resoluteness," he wrote, "constitutes the loyalty of existence to its own Self."[45] But though no philosophical exploration of love by Heidegger influenced her, she may very well have been influenced by his *lack* of concern. Jaspers had noted what Arendt, in far more personal terms, knew: the Heideggerian philosophy is, as he said, "ohne Liebe: Daher auch im Stil unliebenswürdig [without love: hence also in an unloveable style]."[46] With years of critical distance, Arendt herself pointed to a grave weakness in Heidegger's early work: "The most essential characteristic of this Self is its absolute egoism, its radical separation from all its fellows."[47] This may have troubled her twenty years earlier, in 1927, in her own life.

Arendt's debt is to the deepest general level of Heidegger's thought, to the level from which he raised his fundamental questions about the relation of Being and Temporality and about man's existence as temporal. The three parts of the dissertation present love as a phenomenon of temporal existence. Love as *appetitus* is anticipatory, future-oriented; love as a relation with God the Creator is oriented to the ultimate past, the Creation. Neighborly love, love in the present tense, involves both the other modes of temporal existence and the capacities they presuppose in man—hope and memory. And these three modes of temporality, the past or "no longer," the future or "not yet," and the present, which is, in a certain sense, not at all, were as fundamental to Arendt's dissertation as they were to *Being and Time* (1927). The "Time" of *Being and Time* owes, in its turn, a great debt to Augustine's *Confessions*, as great a debt as "Being" owes to Greek ontology. With an extraordinary clarity about this lineage, Arendt did more than turn with Heideggerian impulse to the source of these very concepts; she began to develop a critical stance.[48]

While Heidegger's work is weighted toward the future experience of death, Arendt's, even though it relies upon Heidegger's time scheme, is equally concerned with birth, with what she would later call "natality." She had the beginnings of an awareness that we are shaped fundamentally by the conditions of our births, by our Neighborhood, by the group we are a part of by virtue of birth. What Hannah Arendt learned while she wrote her dissertation—learned from living, not from reading—was that, by birth, she was a Jew.

# CHAPTER 3
# The Life of a Jewess
## (1929–1933)

The truly real takes place almost unnoticed, and is, to
begin with, lonely and dispersed. . . . Those among our
young people who, thirty years hence, will do the things
that matter, are, in all probability, now quietly biding
their time; and yet, unseen by others, they are already
establishing their existences by means of an unrestricted
spiritual discipline.

Jaspers, *Man in the Modern Age* (1931)

*Defenders of Philosophy*

In January 1929 Hannah Arendt attended a masquerade ball in Berlin, a
*bal de Paris* sponsored for fund-raising by a group of Marxists who were
trying to keep a small political magazine afloat. The dance was held at the
Museum of Ethnology, and the guests came in suitably ethnological
costumes—Hannah Arendt as an Arab harem girl. She spent the evening
with the young Jewish philosopher Günther Stern, whom she had not
seen since he attended Heidegger's 1925 Marburg seminar as a postdoc-
toral student.

After a month Hannah Arendt and Günther Stern began to live together, first in Berlin and then in a small town outside the city in the
direction of Potsdam. In the summer Arendt applied for a stipend from
the Notgemeinschaft der deutschen Wissenschaft to finance her research
on German Romanticism. Her application, supported by impressive letters from Karl Jaspers, Martin Heidegger, and Martin Dibelius, was accepted just as she finished revising her doctoral dissertation for publication by Springer in 1929.

She and Stern worked together on the revision, trying to free the text of
its most complex linguistic turns, its excessively Heideggerian style. Karl
Jaspers wrote *Doktorvater* notes of encouragement and gently but firmly
instructed them to be careful at the last stage: "Proofreading is *very*
strenuous and must be done thoroughly."[1] He knew his student's impatient ways—all her life Hannah Arendt found it difficult to bring a book to

its end patiently, to attend to the details, for she was always on to something else.

The book was not, of course, a financial venture. And though her scholarship was a prestigious one, the small monthly income it assured Arendt was not enough to enable two people to find even a moderately comfortable place to live. Later, in Berlin-Halensee, Hannah Arendt and Günther Stern lived in a one-room studio which they had to vacate in the daytime when the dancing school on the first floor moved upstairs for practicing. Both they and the fledgling dancers had to make their ways around a cumbersome collection of sculptures of the "hollowed-out volumes" mode, stored in the studio by the landlady's son, Rudolf Belling, an associate of the Bauhaus. Life in this not very hollowed-out volume was cramped, uncomfortable, and occasionally embarrassing. When Professor Jaspers came to call without advance warning one morning, Arendt and Stern had no place to receive him and had to refer him to a nearby cafe while they cleared their bedroom for the dance class.

The relative economic stability of the Weimar Republic had begun to come to its dangerous end in 1928. Unemployment grew, and by the October 1929 stock market crash in New York, the economic situation was critical. The Treaty of Versailles and the hated reparations payments were once again widely blamed for Germany's "enslavement" to its enemies. The artists and intellectuals, most of them unemployed, who crowded into the cultural mecca of Germany were forced to make their meager livings free lance or to hope for stipends or help from friends. Günther Stern, who had no prospects for employment in Berlin, decided to present himself for the *Habilitation*, the first step in the direction of a university post. He worked on a lecture to present in Frankfurt, where he hoped to be asked to submit a *Habilitationschrift*, the thesis required for appointment as a *Privatdozent* or lecturer.

In September 1929, before Stern set off on his academic quest, he and Hannah Arendt were married at a civil ceremony in Nowawes attended only by their parents, Kaethe Levine, and two friends, Yela and Henry Lowenfeld, who acted as witnesses. They had agreed that they would be more comfortable appearing in Frankfurt as a married couple. The mores of the Berlin intellectuals were not—to the outrage of many who viewed the capital city as the seat of sinfulness—focused around the institution of marriage; Hannah Arendt's series of love affairs and her nine months of living with Stern out of wedlock were not at all untypical. But the provin-

cial university communities were more conservative. The Sterns's decision to marry had this conventional dimension, but there was much else
that bound them: they were both Jews of middle-class, assimilated
families; they had had similar philosophical training and shared an intellectual stance, a dedication to the revolution in philosophy Heidegger
and Jaspers promoted; both were seen as outstanding students with brilliant prospects. The intellectual accord they felt had been demonstrated
during the weeks they had spent revising Hannah Arendt's dissertation
together and it continued as they both wrote reviews of Karl Mannheim's
*Ideology and Utopia* and coauthored an article on Rilke's *Duino Elegies.*

When friends of later years, who had not known Günther Stern, asked
Hannah Arendt what had drawn her to him, she stressed two things other
than their intellectual accord. She told them that he was a kind and
gentle man, summoning the story which captured those traits: soon after
they met in Berlin, she had had a recurrence of her youthful throat
infection, a mild angina, and he had appeared with a basket of lemons
and his good humor to aid her. And, she said, her mother had been very
fond of Günther Stern, had enjoyed his company and his musical
abilities. For Martha Arendt, the marriage of her daughter to a young man
of good family and good prospects was a fulfillment of the much-desired
"normal development." Both Hannah Arendt and her mother were impressed, as well, by Günther's parents' achievements. The Sterns were
respected throughout Germany for their pioneering work in child psychology. Their *Psychology of Early Childhood,* published in 1914, was a
landmark in the history of psychological technique because it drew upon
extensive observational diaries kept by Clara Stern over six years of her
three children's young lives, and it was an important theoretical view of
the importance in children's development of both hereditary and en-
vironmental factors. Both the observational techniques and the theoretical contribution lived on in the work of a young Swiss, Jean Piaget.
Hannah Arendt never felt close to her parents-in-law and never read their
work, but she respected them both and admired Clara Stern's generous
nature. Indeed, many years later, and perhaps with some exaggeration for
pedagogical purposes, Hannah Arendt claimed that this admiration had
been one of the important factors in her decision to marry: warning a
friend's daughter against being influenced by how strong her boy friend's
mother was, she advised her to judge the young man on his own merits
and strengths.

The difficulties Günther Stern encountered in Frankfurt gave Hannah Arendt all too immediate an occasion to observe the strength of his character. He met the test well, but a blow was delivered to his hopes for an academic career. Seeking support for his work, Stern had presented a preliminary lecture to an illustrious group that included two members of the Frankfurt School, Theodor Adorno and Max Horkheimer, their friend the psychologist Max Wertheimer, and two of Frankfurt's most promising young professors, the theologian Paul Tillich and the sociologist Karl Mannheim. His audience was favorably impressed, and they not only encouraged Stern to go ahead with a *Habilitationschrift* but even suggested a subject area—the philosophy of music. The encouragement was a spur, but the suggestion proved most unfortunate.

Stern had good qualifications for the work—a knowledge of music theory and skill on both the piano and the violin—and the area was one that had received little attention from philosophers since Schopenhauer and Nietzsche. But his sponsors' suggestion left out one crucial factor: Theodor Adorno's recent Marxist work on the sociology of music. When Stern submitted a draft of his work a year later, it was only natural that the resident expert, Adorno, would be one of the readers; and it was not surprising that Adorno would find Stern's work, which approached the matter of musical theory from an angle not at all Marxist, unsatisfactory. Hannah Arendt was never sympathetic to the Frankfurt School Marxists on intellectual grounds, and this episode was only the first in a series which made personal sympathy unlikely. Hannah Arendt's opinions about people, both positive and negative, were always forceful—even if not always consistent—and she clearly meant it when she announced to Günther Stern after having made Adorno's acquaintance, "Der kommt uns nicht ins Haus! (That one's not coming into our house!)."

The Frankfurt faculty committee left Adorno out of account in 1929. They also left out of account the changing political circumstances, in which it was becoming less and less possible for a Jew to obtain a university appointment. The Frankfurt School members, most of them Jews, were well aware that the situation around them was growing ominous, but they were no more prescient than anyone else about the events which would soon send them all into exile. Paul Tillich, who discussed Stern's unsuccessful philosophy of music work with him in 1931, advised him to consider writing on another topic, perhaps on the work of Schelling, and also to wait another year before submitting anything—for, surely, by that time, the tide of National Socialism would have ebbed. This, of course, proved an underestimation of the tide, and Günther Stern was forced to find another way to make his living.

During the two years Günther Stern spent on these fruitless and discouraging negotiations, Hannah Arendt worked on her German Romanticism project and made her first excursions into journalism. The *Frankfurter Zeitung*, one of Germany's most literate newspapers, published a brief article she wrote on "Augustine and Protestantism."[2] She marked the fifteen-hundredth anniversary of Augustine's death with some rather strenuous remarks on the small role played by Augustine in contemporary Protestantism. "In Italy, in France, in Germany, the Catholic newspapers proclaim this event, meetings are held in Augustine's memory, in which both clerics and scholars give account of the meaning of his work, his role, and his effect. Among Protestants, however, he is for the most part forgotten." Protestant theologians who knew the pages dedicated to Augustine in recent years by some of the leading scholars in Germany—Harnack, Troeltsch, Holl, and Seeburg among them—would have found this assessment surprising, but the article, in a newspaper, was not addressed to them. Written for lay Protestants, it was designed to highlight the debt of Luther to Augustine: "Luther joined his conception of the believer, whose conscience stands directly before God, to Augustine." It was this heritage of concern for personal, noninstitutional conscience, that Hannah Arendt invoked.

For her, the article was a bridge between her philosophical studies and her work on the Romantics. She spoke of Augustine's *Confessions* as the ancestor, "by a detour through Pietism," of the modern autobiographical novel. "With the general movement of secularization, a religious reflection before God loses the authority which it had once been accorded and becomes simply reflection on individual life. It happened for the first time in Germany, in a representative way, with Moritz's *Anton Reiser*. Moritz, though formed by Pietism, removed the 'devotional' description of a life out of the domain of Pietistic religiosity. The concept of grace yielded fully to that of autonomous self-transformation, and the individual life story finally appeared to us in Goethe as 'imprinted form, which, living, changes itself.'" This was the development to which Rahel Varnhagen, admirer of Goethe and writer of autobiographical confessions, responded with all the passionateness of her nature. When Hannah

Arendt wrote her biography of Rahel Varnhagen, the dimension of Augustine she had left in the background of her dissertation—the confessional, personal, individual Augustine—emerged in a portrait of the modern heirs to his consciousness, the Romantics who followed Goethe. "Autonomous self-transformation" was the theme of Arendt's work, though her question was: What can this mean for a Jew?

It was in Heidelberg and Frankfurt that Arendt made her philosophical transition from the realm of Augustine to the realm of the early nineteenth-century Berlin Romantics. Stern began his *Habilitation* work in Heidelberg in 1930, and Hannah Arendt, while she worked, renewed her many acquaintances in the town. She went often to the Jaspers's home and occasionally to Marianne Weber's on Sunday afternoons. Together, the Sterns attended musical evenings at the home of Leopold Furtwängler's mother, and once had the pleasure of hearing there a piano recital by Clara Beerwald, Hannah's stepsister, which Furtwängler himself praised generously.

When Stern had made his initial drafts of his philosophy of music project, they moved to Frankfurt and participated in that university's intellectual life at the moment when the university was emerging as one of the most vital and progressive educational centers. They attended Karl Mannheim's seminars and listened to the lectures of one Protestant theologian who certainly did not neglect Augustine—Paul Tillich. Arendt actively participated in seminars and lectures, and her formidable intellectual power, manifest in complex, sometimes quite incomprehensible questions and remarks, very quickly became legendary. She had the honor of being selected by the Frankfurt students as a personage worthy of caricature in the annual student carnival—the last carnival held in Frankfurt before Hitler came to power. A young student named Richard Plant, who later became her friend in New York, where he taught German literature at City College, wrote a skit in which the persons and philosophical jargons of Theodor Adorno, Paul Tillich, and Hannah Arendt-Stern were elaborately parodied. The period in Frankfurt was, as Stern remembered it, "a very lively time"; they enjoyed their new, and far more politically conscious, professional friends, and they had a comfortable place to live, a sexton's cottage on the river Main.

When it became apparent that Stern's *Habilitation* work was not going to be successful, the Sterns moved back to Berlin. Günther decided to seek work as a journalist and began by taking to Bertolt Brecht the transcript of a radio broadcast he had made in Frankfurt on "Brecht as

Philosopher." Brecht was impressed with the piece and telephoned his friend Herbert Jhering, the influential critic for the Berlin *Börsen-Courier*, on Stern's behalf. He did this despite the fact that he viewed Stern's own credentials as a philosopher with skepticism: Stern protested his independence, but Brecht was convinced that he must be a Heideggerian, having made the quite sensible assumption that anyone who, of their own free will, undertook to even read Heidegger had to be more than passingly dedicated. Herbert Jhering was not deterred and hired him as a staff reporter for the paper's cultural section. Stern was soon producing articles on everything from mystery novels to the latest conferences on Hegel, writing so much of the cultural section that Jhering became worried. Lest the section look like a one-man show, he told Stern, they would have to do things *auf anderen Wege*. Taking the request that they find another way quite literally, Günther Stern assumed the nom de plume Günther Anders—and Günther Anders he has remained throughout a long journalistic and literary career.

One of the liveliest intellectual challenges of the time in Frankfurt was Karl Mannheim's *Ideology and Utopia*, published in 1929. For several years afterward, the book was extensively reviewed and debated, the extent of its deviation from the various shades of orthodox Marxism was variously measured, and its implications for the emergent trend called sociology of knowledge were considered. Soon after the Sterns returned to Berlin, one of the leading socialist journals, *Die Gesellschaft*, asked Hannah Arendt if she would review Mannheim's book. The editor, Rudolf Hilferding, who was friendly with Martha Arendt's social-democrat associates in Berlin, wanted a critical review, for he felt that Mannheim's work posed a threat to socialism. Hannah Arendt agreed to do the review, but she saw quite another threat in the work and wrote as a defender of the autonomy of philosophy.

Mannheim had hoped to inspire intellectuals to a critical understanding of how their thinking was anchored in their economic and social existences. An intellectual expression (*geistige Aüsserung*) in the form of an ideology could, he argued, serve the interests of a socioeconomic group trying to retain its historically gained power. The interests of a group trying to bring about change, to achieve power in the future, could be served by an intellectual expression in the form of a utopia. But both past-oriented ideologies and future-oriented utopias, Mannheim argued, would have to ignore actual, present situations, the one by failing to take account of change, the other by taking images of the future for realities. In both cases, thinking is in the service of action and thus not autonomous.

A schema more challenging to the mode of philosophizing Arendt engaged in could hardly be imagined. Mannheim used the categories of past orientation and future orientation, which had been central to Arendt's dissertation, for entirely different purposes. Augustine had looked to man's ultimate future and to his ultimate past as he sought to transcend the limitations of the human condition—desiring neither maintenance of the status quo nor change in the world. Action, for Augustine, was individual and in the service of thought or belief.

Arendt focused her criticism of Mannheim on his claim that thought is in the service of action; this was the challenge to philosophy's autonomy. She raised a logical question: how can thought, if it is anchored in a socioeconomic situation, be said to ignore that situation? If thinking can ignore the actual situation, then its root, she argued, must be elsewhere; and that would imply that thought is not simply action's servant. She then backed up her case with an illustration, presenting Augustine's notion of neighborly love as an example of a transcendent thought, neither anchored in an actual situation nor subservient to action in the world. Neighborly love, she argued, was a thought to guide action; the City of God was neither Mannheim's ideology nor his utopia.

To Arendt, Mannheim's sociology and the philosophies she thought most important, those of Jaspers and Heidegger, went in opposite directions. Heidegger's search for the Being which is the ground of all beings, the Being men have a special destiny to question, and Jaspers's search for the limit-situations in which men question the meaning of their existence—both presupposed that philosophizing is not bound by ordinary conditions. She thought that Mannheim's investigations were illuminating within the framework of ordinary conditions, but they ceased to be so when combined with the claim that the extraordinary activity of thinking is rooted in ordinary conditions. What, Arendt argued, hammering home her complaint, is the source of Mannheim's own thinking? Is it rooted in an actual situation—and thus either ideological or utopian? Has sociology itself not produced evidence of how thinking can guide and shape actions in the world, namely, in Weber's *The Protestant Ethic and the Spirit of Capitalism?*

In this dense and carefully argued review and in the article she wrote with Günther Stern on Rilke's *Duino Elegies* Hannah Arendt reached the acme of her commitment to thinking as unworldly and love as a transcendent principle. Her critique of Mannheim's work and her philosophical explication of Rilke's poem came from the same stance. Rilke was for her the Augustine of the modern, secularized world, and his *Elegies* were "the ultimate form of religious document." For Rilke, as for Augustine, men were creatures not at home in the world, struggling to transcend its transitoriness and their own mortality. Rilke had no image of God's redemptive grace, and the lovers he portrayed in his poem, seeking transcendence through love, could never rest from their efforts. Men never attained the realm of those Rilke called the "Angels." But they could, as they struggled, rise through the world's wondrous beauties, growing freer of the particularities of these beauties and themselves:

> ... is it not time that, in loving,
> we freed ourselves from the loved one, and, quivering, endured:
> as the arrow endures the string, to become in the gathering out-leap,
> something more than itself?[3]

Arendt never lost her respect for Augustine, or for Rilke, the poet of her generation, the poet of the last echo of German Romanticism. But she came to question transcendent love as a principle for living, just as she came to question the autonomy of philosophy.

*Biography as Autobiography*

By 1930, before she moved to Berlin, Hannah Arendt had decided to concentrate her attention on Rahel Varnhagen rather than pursue the topic of German Romanticism as a whole. In Berlin she was again in close contact with Kurt Blumenfeld and his Zionist associates; she had Blumenfeld as a spiritual godfather and his friends as supporters. A circle of friends was important to the work, for it was slow and arduous. Arendt used not only the published Varnhagen correspondence—selected and censored by Rahel's husband—but unpublished materials in the Prussian State Library. Rahel's impetuous handwriting and unpredictable spelling made her letters and notes difficult to read, but Arendt was rewarded for her trouble by discovering several interesting letters which shed new biographical light. One of these she published in a popular handbook called the *Deutscher Almanach für Das Jahr 1932,* along with a short piece on the Berlin salons of Rahel Varnhagen's day. The *Almanach* for 1932 was dedicated to Goethe's life and work, and Arendt's contributions were designed to show the milieu of Goethe's Berlin admirers and the attitudes of such ardent devotees as Rahel Varnhagen.

*Rahel Varnhagen* is a biography, but certainly not of any easily classifiable sort. It is not so much what its subtitle claims—"The Life of a Jewess"—as the life of a thought thought by one. Rahel's thought was, bluntly and simply: "I am a Schlemihl and a Jewess." And Hannah Arendt traced Rahel's course in thinking this thought, travelling from her initial solitary reasoning, which kept Rahel from grasping the significance of her Jewishness, to her final self-conscious understanding and acceptance of it, reached in the company of other "pariah" Jews.

Had Rahel been a woman of the twentieth century rather than the eighteenth, Arendt's biography might have been a story of conversion to Zionism. As it is, it is a twentieth-century woman's account of an eighteenth-century woman's search for a homeland of friendship. Arendt made the differences in their situations very clear in an article she published in 1933 in the Cologne *Zeitung* and then again in the *Jüdische Rundschau*: she announced that with the accession to power of Adolf Hitler a chapter in the history of German Jewry—a chapter called assimilation—had come to an end. This period had begun with Rahel Varnhagen's generation, which sought to escape Jewishness by conversion to Christianity and intermarriage with Gentiles. It ended when racism became German state policy and closed all exits.

Arendt's biography takes a complex, often obscure, route; there are only a few chronological or contextual references to orient the reader in the forest of quotations from Rahel's correspondence. Hannah Arendt's great love of quotations, which is apparent in all her books, shines on every page. The description she wrote years later of Walter Benjamin's manner of writing fits her biographical technique: "The main work consisted in tearing fragments out of their context and arranging them afresh in such a way that they illustrated one another and were able to prove their raison d'être in a free-floating state, as it were."[4] The quotations in *Rahel Varnhagen* prove not only each other's raison d'être but also that of Arendt's biographical method as a whole: to tell the story of Rahel's life as she herself might have told it. The biography is a free-floating state, unencumbered by descriptions of times and places and restricted only by commentaries on the thinking processes that gave rise to the quotations. The English novelist Sybille Bedford, reviewing it in 1958, caught its quality precisely: it is "a relentlessly abstract book—slow, cluttered, static, curiously oppressive; reading it feels like sitting in a hot-house with no watch. One is made to feel the subject, the waiting, distraught woman; one is made aware, almost physically, of her intense femininity, her frustration."[5]

The book begins at the end, by quoting a report of what Rahel Varnhagen said on her deathbed: "The thing which all my life seemed to me the greatest shame, which was the misery and misfortune of my life—having been born a Jewess—this I should on no account now wish to have missed."[6] But the story that unfolds in the book actually begins with a portrait of reason in its Enlightenment form, which "brings liberation from objects and their reality, creates a sphere of pure ideas and a world which is accessible to any rational being without benefit of knowledge or experience."[7] Before she had experienced anything, Rahel Varnhagen kept her Jewishness at a distance through such reason, which, when focused upon the self, is called introspection. Introspection can fill up a life when the world, action, or love have been rejected because they threaten to reveal the shame of one's identity; it can save from despair someone who has not yet learned to convert yearning for personal happiness into passion for truth.

Hannah Arendt's commentary on introspection as Rahel Varnhagen practiced it and Rahel's circle and its heroes applauded it is very harsh. "Introspection accomplishes two feats: it annihilates the actually existing situation by dissolving it in mood, and at the same time it lends everything subjective an aura of objectivity, publicity, extreme interest. In introspection the boundaries between what is intimate and what is public become blurred; intimacies are made public, and public matters can be experienced and expressed only in the realm of the intimate—ultimately, in gossip."[8] The introspective, confessional Rahel Varnhagen—who is known to the German literati as Rahel in the way that Rousseau is known to the French as Jean-Jacques—attracted people from different classes, with different educational backgrounds and religious beliefs. But because she lived in a shell of protective generalities she was "inwardly graceless"; she could not reveal who she really was.

As noted earlier, the critique of introspection could have been written about her own autobiographical sketch "Die Schatten"; it remained a standard part of Hannah Arendt's understanding of people. She learned later that introspection's cocoon could protect even those who, unlike Rahel, fervently embraced Jewish causes and did so in times when Jewish causes had been rendered respectable by events Rahel Varnhagen never dreamed of. For example, in a 1967 letter, she wrote harshly about a woman novelist who had supported Israel in a way Arendt found shallow: "Her partisanship is naive and childish, she talks like any unreflected [sic] Jew. But it is quite characteristic that she has reflected upon herself almost excessively and still it never occurred to her to examine herself *qua* Jewess."[9] Arendt's critique of introspection was a political critique; she was concerned to preserve the distinction between private and public matters and to show how introspection can foreclose political understanding. Introspection was, in Hannah Arendt's view, Hannah Arendt's youthful error; in Berlin, in 1931, she knew that the error urgently needed remedy.

What brought Rahel Varnhagen out of her isolation was not a political situation but the extraordinarily lucky prospect of marriage to a Gentile, Count von Finckenstein. Rahel had the chance to become someone specific, someone defined within Gentile society. The count "represented everything but was, unfortunately, nothing himself, a nullity."[10] He offered a world, but in the world of Rahel's Berlin salon he was completely out of place. After Finckenstein fled to the familiar bosom of his family, Rahel reached a new stage on her thinking way. She still generalized, but she did so on the basis of experience. To other people, the disappointed Rahel presented an austere, hard, aloof face, hoping that this would prompt her admirers to an understanding of her unhappiness rather than a fascination with her personality. It did not; they retreated before the "homeless one." And she too finally retreated—to Paris, to pleasure in simple things, and to a brief affair which began to teach her discrimination.

When she returned to Berlin, Rahel—through another crisis—reached another stage. With Finckenstein she had tried to throw off the disgrace of her infamous birth with something extraordinary—a great love, a marriage into nobility—but this time she tried to throw off her life by love of a "beautiful object," a magical act of isolation from reality.[11] She fell in love with the handsome secretary of the Spanish legation in Berlin, Don d'Urquijo, a foreigner, to whom she was not first and foremost a Jew. When d'Urquijo, overwhelmed by her intensity and confused by her salon friends, broke with her, Rahel "saw her life from the outside as a mere game . . . she could relate it in all its bareness . . . her life became a narrative to her."[12] Rahel had confessed—enormously—and gossiped about herself; now she told her story in a different way, aware of her audience, in solidarity with others; she told it having learned the power of literary generalization from her mentor, Goethe. At the same time that she learned to tell her story historically, she became interested in history and her historical milieu. "Rahel assimilated by way of Fichte's *Addresses to the German Nation.*"[13] These achievements—solidarity, storytelling, and historical consciousness—were the measure of how rich Rahel's generalizing had become. They were also the achievements which Rahel's biographer sought in quite a different form. Hannah Arendt strove for solidarity, for literary generalization—her *Rahel Varnhagen* was an effort at empathetic storytelling—and for historical consciousness. But not assimilation, not nationalism. By way of Fichte, Schelling, and the German Romantics, including Rahel Varnhagen, Arendt disassimilated, in the direction of Zionism.

At just the moment in Rahel's thought life when her inexperienced generalizing seems ready to give way to truthfulness, Arendt's story breaks off and begins again. Arendt's *Bildungsroman* has another side, a night side, for she understood that Rahel really had no *Bild*, no model to guide her development. At night, Rahel was at sea—rudderless and alone. Arendt interrupts her story with a chapter devoted to Rahel's dream life and how it made such a *Bild* impossible, to "the despair which had taken refuge in the night. . . . Moving on, assimilation, learning history, were at night a comically hopeless game. When such a gulf yawns, only ambiguity points a permanent way out, by taking neither extreme seriously and engendering, in the twilight in which both extremes are mixed, resignation and new strength."[14] In her own time, this was also Hannah Arendt's answer: neither assimilation nor Zionism, but ambiguity.

"Day and Night," the chapter in which Rahel's dreams are presented, does not have a chronological place. Even though they are filled with flashes forward and flashes backward, the other chapters in the book deal with definite periods, and their titles are combined with helpful dates. But the undated "Day and Night" describes dreams that came to Rahel over a period of fifteen years; it gives the underground of her life from the time she met Count von Finckenstein until the time, after her marriage to August Varnhagen, when she had "ceased dreaming." This odd chapter is the center of Arendt's book. Its theme—that "ambiguity points the only way out"—introduces all the variations that follow.

Hannah Arendt embraced ambiguity in political terms that were not part of Rahel Varnhagen's world. But she also chose ambiguity in emotional terms which were, in their timelessness, very close to Rahel Varnhagen's. Arendt's dreams, her youthful poetry, are full of vague foreboding and abstract despair. But Rahel Varnhagen constantly confessed what her dreams told her, that her Jewishness was ineradicable, while Hannah Arendt kept secret her own most private world. Her childhood dreams, which she had described in "Die Schatten" as "filled with a constant joy of life," no matter whether they were bitter or sweet, had been disrupted—by the loss of her father as later by the loss of a lover nearly old enough to be her father. The shadows she lived in stayed with her. She told a friend that she had once dreamt vividly, during her Heidelberg years, about the death of a well-known professor. Even the cups of coffee with which she made her daily transition into a waking state had failed to help her recognize the dream as a dream. The people she told that morning about her sorrow at the man's death were shocked at the news and telephoned the man's home. When they ascertained from the professor's startled wife that he was in his study quietly reading, Arendt had one of those moments she dreaded: a moment of intense embarrassment. Death and disappearance, homelessness—these continued to be the motifs of her dreams; and as her experiences in the world grew more and more frightening, after 1933, these motifs grew stronger. In her dream life she lived with what she called in one poem, dated 1951: "the multicolored layers in my sleep / Which fear the precipitous void of our world."

The chapter on Rahel's dream life is remarkable for its single-minded focus on Rahel's painful Jewishness. The dreams Rahel recorded are rich with much else—as her life is with elements her biographer ignored, like her family, her childhood, her less-than-beautiful physical appearance, her attraction to younger men. Arendt's opposition to introspection was politically understandable and fruitful, but it also provided justification for her distance from her own family memories, her own painful childhood and its legacy of shyness, moodiness, impatience, and incommunicativeness. Even Arendt's political conclusion, that ambiguity points the way out, was unself-conscious—for ambiguity, and its practical corollary, refusal to join a group with a program, is not without its dangers. Ambiguity can mean rootlessness, and refusal to join with others can mean inaction. In *Rahel Varnhagen* itself, Arendt's attitude produced tensions.

*Rahel Varnhagen* is a book with several fissures in it, the deepest being that between the daytime story and the story of Rahel's dreams. Another fissure opens between the story of Rahel's three marriage prospects and the story of three men who appeared in her life in all their particularity and were loved not as entryways into a world of particularity, the Gentile world, but as individuals. These three were Friedrich Gentz, the politician, Alexander von der Marwitz, an aristocrat and soldier, and Heine, the Jewish poet. Gentz showed Rahel the world of politics—into which he withdrew from her, for a Jewish mistress was not what his career called for; von der Marwitz told her the reality of their era, which he viewed with the contempt of a nobleman and conservative believer in history. These men were not nullities, though they too failed to grasp the despair felt by Rahel Varnhagen, who had no access to politics and no rank, distinction, or merit. Only Heine, the friend of her old age, understood her pariahdom: "Only galley slaves know one another."[15]

As she worked on *Rahel Varnhagen*, Arendt became more and more sensitive to the ways in which ideas from the salons of Rahel's day were being appropriated and distorted in current intellectual circles. But this past, this political story, in which Gentz, von der Marwitz, and Heine played their roles, was in the background of the biography; in the foreground were Rahel's struggle with her Jewish identity and the marriage prospects which marked the stages of her struggle. In the last two chapters of the book, however, the balance shifted, and the political implications of Rahel's hard-won and always ambiguous return to her Jewishness were brought forward. There is a fissure of quite another sort between the first eleven chapters of the book and these last two.

Before she fled from Berlin in 1933, Hannah Arendt had finished the first eleven chapters. She wrote the last two in the summer of 1938. Karl Jaspers, who read the whole book for the first time in 1952, noticed that the final chapters had quite a different tone than their predecessors and asked Hannah Arendt why.

I wrote the end of the book very irritably in the summer of 1938, because [Heinrich] Blücher and [Walter] Benjamin would not leave me in peace until I did. It is written throughout in terms of the Zionist critique of assimilation which I accepted then and which I have not until this day modified very much. . . . I had been as a young woman truly naive; I found the so-called "Jewish Question" quite boring. Kurt Blumenfeld opened my eyes to the matter.[16]

Kurt Blumenfeld opened her eyes to the matter, but the political internationalism of Blücher and Benjamin gave her the means to see the fate of the Jews more widely. In the last chapters, she brought forward clearly the ultimate irony of the assimilationist position: "In a society on the whole hostile to the Jews—and that situation obtained in all countries in which Jews lived, down to the twentieth century—it is possible to assimilate only by assimilating to anti-Semitism also."[17] This is what Rahel Varnhagen had refused to do: she had refused to be anti-Semitic. As the world in which she lived, into which she would have liked to be assimilated, grew more, not less, anti-Semitic, Rahel accepted her Jewishness more forthrightly. Hannah Arendt shows Rahel as a woman aware that anti-Semitism was not an aberration in the history of Germany or of Europe: "The fate of the Jews was not so accidental and out of the way . . . on the contrary, it precisely limned the state of society, outlined the ugly reality of the gaps in the social structure."[18] This awareness became the centerpiece of Arendt's chapter on anti-Semitism in *The Origins of Totalitarianism*: she argued that anti-Semitism is not a necessity for all times and not an accident in modern times: European nation-states and European Jewry rose, and declined, together.

## Steps in the Direction of Politics

In 1931 and 1932, Hannah Arendt's thinking became steadily more political and more historical. She spent much of her time with Kurt Blumenfeld and his Zionist friends, and she met several of the Jewish professors at the Hochschule für Politik, one of the most independent, creative centers in Germany and one of the few institutions open to students without *Gymnasium* degrees. Albert Salomon, who taught sociology at the Hochschule and also contributed regularly to *Die Gesellschaft*, became a friend and, after he joined the faculty of the New School for Social Research, a helpful supplier of letters of recommendation. Sigmund Neumann, who kept the Hochschule's newspaper archives, later wrote several studies of Nazism which Arendt admired. Neumann emigrated to America and took a position at Wesleyan University, where he offered Hannah Arendt a visiting professorship in 1961.

Arendt was invited to write a second review for *Die Gesellschaft* and one for the journal Max Weber had founded with the help of two other sociologists, Werner Sombart and Edgar Jaffe, the *Archiv für Sozialwiss-*

*enschaft und Sozialpolitik.* The *Archiv* review, for which she had been recommended by Karl Jaspers, was closely tied to her German Romanticism studies. She reviewed Hans Weil's *The Origin of the German Educational Principle*, a book which outlined the late eighteenth-century discussion of two notions of education, "development toward an ideal" (*Bild*) and "development of innate potential," which related to two traditions, the Graeco-Roman and the Pietistic.[19] Weil concentrated his attention on the way these two notions were blended together by Herder and von Humboldt, and then indicated how the principle that resulted was adopted by an "educational elite" (*Bildungselite*) in the time of Rahel Varnhagen.

In this review and in an article entitled "The Enlightenment and the Jewish Question," in which she set out the history of ideas lurking in the background of *Rahel Varnhagen*, Herder emerges as Arendt's hero. His philosophical concepts are correlative to Rahel Varnhagen's more personally expressed ideas. Against the Enlightenment elevation of "truths of reason" over "truths of history"—present in Lessing's work, adopted by Moses Mendelssohn, and then used by Jews of Rahel's generation like David Friedlander to deny the "historical" religion of Judaism—Herder emphasized the importance of history for individuals and peoples. Just as he challenged the Jews to give up the notion that their historical existence had come to an end with the destruction of the temple in Jerusalem and the notion that Judaism was a "religion of reason" awaiting amalgamation with the universal reason of mankind, so too he challenged the Germans to admit the Jews, as a people, into the German state. Herder's call for civic emancipation was of a piece with the Enlightenment claim that, without political guarantees, universalism and tolerance based on respect for mankind were inadequate assurances for individuals or peoples of diverse heritages. The respect Herder paid to individual differences and historically developed differences among peoples was not an element Hans Weil had emphasized in his discussion of Herder's education principle, but Arendt thought it crucial. Herder had affirmed that history was a process, an unfolding of variety, and that education, also, was to be a process. Education should be a striving toward harmonious images or models (often the great models of antiquity), and it should lead to the development of individuals, autonomous but aware of their place in a "chain of individuals," a tradition.

The combination in Herder's work of respect for the tradition of

Judaism and respect for individuality was very appealing to Arendt; it accorded with her developing critique of assimilationism and her growing apprehension at the success of National Socialism as a mass movement. Later she could see Herder as one of the progenitors of a tendency she deplored, the introduction of history into politics—a tendency culminating with Hegel. She had been aware, and noted it in her review, that Herder's notion of individual peoples' "organic" development might be misconstrued as a denial of autonomy, that even if man was not viewed as an "ant on the wheel of fate" he might be viewed as an ant on the wheel of his own society's development. Once history had become the book in which men looked for truth, the way was open for a thinker like Hegel to consider each people as a chapter in that book, whose author was an all-embracing fate.

The aspect of Herder's thought that Arendt never abandoned was the educational principle. She later defined a cultivated person as "one who knows how to choose his company among men, among things, among thoughts, in the present as well as in the past."[20] In Herder's notion of reason (*Verstehen* as opposed to both contemplation, *Denken*, and feeling, *Gefühl*) as a "totally new possibility of access to the world and to reality," as a capacity involving the "distance" which is necessary for judgment, she later saw a way for men to live without either absolute truths or the isms believers in absolute truths dread—historicism, relativism, subjectivism, and so forth. When she came to this view, she looked at Lessing's place in the Enlightenment quite differently. She had seen Lessing's tolerance as rooted in a conviction that diverse opinions arise from a common source which would stand revealed at the end of history; she had seen this tolerance as a rejection of "truths of history." When she realized the enormous political role nineteenth-century historical thinking played in her own time, she looked on the Enlightenment with new eyes. She thought that Lessing's insight was profound, and she explained why in the speech she gave as she accepted the Lessing Prize in 1959.

Because Lessing was a completely political person, he insisted that truth can exist only where it is humanized by discourse. . . . Every truth outside of this area [of discourse], no matter whether it brings men good or ill, is inhuman in the literal sense of the word: but not because it might arouse men against one another and separate them. Quite the contrary, it is because it might have the result that all men would suddenly unite in a single opinion, so that out of many opinions one would emerge, as though not men in their infinite plurality but man in the singular, one species and its exemplars, were to inhabit the earth. Should that happen, the world, which can form only in the interspaces between men in all their variety, would vanish altogether. For that reason the most profound thing that has been said about the relation between truth and humanity is to be found in a sentence of Lessing's which seems to draw from all his works wisdom's last word. The sentence is:

> *Jeder sage, was ihm Wahrheit dünkt,*
> *und die Wahrheit selbst sei Gott empfohlen!*
> Let each man say what he deems truth,
> and let truth itself be commended unto God![21]

That Arendt could come full circle and find in Lessing, whom she had thought of as a disparager of truths of history, this certification of human plurality and historical diversity, this political thinking, was a measure of how far she had come from the position of her review and her article, "The Enlightenment and the Jewish Question." She ceased, when she had learned a few historical truths, to be an advocate of the history of ideas. She stopped looking for either categories of thinkers or historical influences, thought genealogies, and she developed a method as informal as the title she gave it: *Perlenfischerei*, pearl fishing.[22] The pearls that were full fathom five beneath the historical surface were the sea-changed, rich, and strange jewels she sought.

Even though her review and article were written as contributions to the unworldly history of ideas she was soon to reject, Hannah Arendt was influenced by the drastic changes in the intellectual atmosphere around her. Jaspers noted her disillusionment with university trained writers late in 1931: "I think an anti-academic mood is—quite understandably— growing strong in you."[23] Arendt began to read Marx and Trotsky and to focus her attention on current affairs. In the second review she did for *Die Gesellschaft*, she tackled a contemporary political question for the first time: her assignment was to review Alice Rühle-Gerstel's *Das Frauen- problem der Gegenwart* ("The Contemporary Woman's Problem").[24]

At the beginning of her review Arendt noted a discrepancy between the achievements of the women's rights movement of her day and the condi- tions of working women. "Not only must women accept, despite their legal equality, less pay than men in comparable positions, but they are still left with tasks which are no longer compatible with their new position. These tasks are based partly on social, partly on biological facts: In addition to her profession, a woman must take care of a household and look after her children. Thus a woman's freedom to make her own living seems to imply either enslavement in the family or dissolution of the family." Rühle-Gerstel, an Adlerian psychologist, took this dilemma as her starting point and constructed a typology of the overcompensations women have employed to deal with the social and biological limitations imposed upon them. Women have become housewives, princesses, demonesses; they have used compassion, childishness, shrewdness, and anxiety. Arendt found this typology the most challenging part of the book (it is quite possible that when she described Rahel Varnhagen as a "princess" who had used her husband to enthrone herself, Arendt was recalling the typology).

But the political dimension of Rühle-Gerstel's work was what Arendt concentrated upon. Rühle-Gerstel suggested that women, who were propertyless employees of their husbands at home and almost always employees rather than employers in the marketplace, should identify themselves with the proletariat. Adlerian psychoanalysis, with its emphasis upon the means by which individuals overcome their feelings of inferiority and achieve power, was the one school of psychoanalysis which made a clear contribution to the workers' movements in Germany. Though Arendt was aware of this contribution, she had an objection to Rühle-Gerstel's program. She thought too much emphasis was placed on individuals and their employer-employee relationships when the basic unit determining women—the family, be it proletarian or bourgeois—was the immediate problem. Arendt had noted two possibilities implicit in the situation—enslavement in the family or dissolution of the family—but she did not follow up her criticism of Rühle-Gerstel's focus by presenting a program or another possibility.

Much clearer, and more significant for her future work, was her criticism of the women's movement of her day. "Women have not come forward on the political front, which is the men's front; and, furthermore, all the fronts of the women's movement are really only a single front, and that a *women's* front. Characteristically, the movement has never united to achieve concrete goals (except in the realm of charity work). The vain attempt to found a women's party shows the questionableness of the movement: it is the same questionableness as that of the youth movement, which is a movement only for youth as the women's movement is only for women. One is as abstract as the other." In this criticism, both

Mannheim's discussions of how ideologies blind groups to changes in the actual situation and Arendt's own criticism of Kurt Blumenfeld's Zionism have their echoes. A movement which does not enter into the political arena, which does not translate its ideology into concrete goals that reflect changes in the actual situation, remains abstract. "The professional woman is an economic fact, next to which the ideology of the women's movement marches along." Unless the women's movement was ready to act on the political front to achieve concrete goals it would be ineffective—all its past effectiveness, the achievement of voting rights for example, had come from such political action. Arendt was arguing against divorcing women's issues from the larger range of political concerns, just as she later argued against divorcing Jewish issues from national and international political concerns. Of the youth movement leaders who later supported the chalutz and kibbutz movements in Palestine, Arendt wrote in 1945: "The pioneers were completely content within the small circle where they could realize their ideals for themselves; they were little interested in Jewish or Palestinian politics, were in fact frequently wearied by it, unaware of the general destiny of their people."[25]

Arendt was opposed to the women's movement in the same way that Rosa Luxemburg had been. Luxemburg's friend Clara Zetkin, who was fond of quoting a line from Engel's *The Origin of the Family* that would have pleased Rühle-Gerstel—"*He* is the bourgeois in the family, the woman represents the proletariat"—was an ardent campaigner for women's rights. Rosa Luxemburg tried to convince her friend that the oppression of women, like the oppression of Jews, would only come to an end with the advent of true socialism. Arendt, without advocating socialism or any other program, thought that women's issues should be part of a larger political struggle. She never changed her mind on this point and always advocated that women pursue concrete political goals, such as legislation for equal employment opportunities, that were coordinated with the goals of other political groups. Incipient in her criticism of the women's movement is the distinction she later drew between social questions and political questions—the latter, she held, should be the focus of action.

## Days and Nights

While Hannah Arendt was formulating her reflections on the women's problem, she was experiencing a dimension of it in her own life. She and Günther Stern continued to share many intellectual interests through

1932, but the Zionist critique of assimilation was changing Hannah Arendt's attitudes toward daily life and political action as quickly as the situation of daily life was changing, and this had its effect on her marriage.

Hannah Arendt grew restless. Anne Mendelssohn Weil remembered meeting her on the street one day in 1932 and hearing her talk of emigration for the first time: the rising tide of anti-Semitism around her was making the prospect of staying in Germany less and less reasonable, she said. Anne was surprised, and answered that she had not experienced any drastic increase in hostility toward the Jews. Hannah Arendt looked at her friend in amazement, said sharply, "You're crazy!" and stomped off. But Anne Mendelssohn was certainly not alone. Few people shared Arendt's opinion that Hitler's way to power had really been opened in 1929, when he received support from the financier Alfred Hugenberg. During the general election campaign of 1930, people all over Germany had hailed Hitler as a savior. Martha Arendt reported that in Königsberg, where the townspeople feared that an invasion might follow on the Polish crisis, Hitler was dubbed the "German Margrave." The Nazis had won 107 Reichstag seats in that election, only 36 fewer than the ruling Social Democrats.[26]

Hannah Arendt's tolerance for intellectuals who failed to understand the darkening political situation grew weaker as her allegiance to the Zionists' critique grew deeper. Leo Strauss, the author of a much admired critique of a quite different sort, *Die Religionkritik Spinozas*, met with a curt rejection from Hannah Arendt for his lack of awareness. Strauss, an associate of the Hochschule für die Wissenschaft des Judentums, met Arendt at the Prussian State Library and made an effort to court her. When she criticized his conservative political views and dismissed his suit, he became bitterly angry. The bitterness lasted for decades, growing worse when the two joined the same American faculty at the University of Chicago in the 1960s. Strauss was haunted by the rather cruel way in which Hannah Arendt had judged his assessment of National Socialism: she had pointed out the irony of the fact that a political party advocating views Strauss appreciated could have no place for a Jew like him.

Günther Stern's response to the growing influence of the Nazis was far less naive than Anne Mendelssohn's and far less academic than Leo Strauss's, but still not nearly as strong as that of the Zionists. He began to work on a mammoth novel. Excerpts from Nazi party newsletters and journals provided him with the raw material for a satire of what he called the "Nazi School of Lying" (as, many years later, excerpts from the American press would provide him with material for another satire, "Visit Lovely Vietnam!"). Stern's circle of acquaintances during the months he worked on his novel consisted largely of artists, journalists, and intellectuals in and around the Communist party. Hannah Arendt's circle, meanwhile, consisted of Zionists, many of them—Blumenfeld, Robert Weltsch, editor of *Jüdische Rundschau*, Siegfried Moses, Georg Landauer, and the publisher Salman Schocken (who later employed Arendt at Schocken Books in New York)—members of the Zionistischen Vereinigung für Deutschland. Through these friends, she met others whose sympathies were with the Zionists. Waldemar Gurian, a Russian Jew who had early in his life converted to Catholicism, was trained in jurisprudence by the renowned Carl Schmidt who later became a Nazi theorist. When the Nazi influence became strong in Berlin, Gurian heeded the Zionists' critique and turned his remarkable intellectual energies to Jewish history. He continued to write brilliantly on the history of anti-Semitism both before and after his emigration to America to take up a position at the University of Notre Dame, where he founded *The Review of Politics*.

There was not, at the time, any great mutual respect between Zionists and Communists, despite the fact that Zionism and Communism were often embraced for similar reasons—rejection of hypocritical or self-deceptive ways of life, of bourgeois or assimilationist behavior. Zionists often viewed Communists as "red assimilationists" and the internationally minded Communists often viewed Zionism as a species of fascism. These ideological differences did not overtly draw Hannah Arendt and Günther Stern apart, as they were not committed without reservations to their respective camps. But their circles were separate. Several times Stern attended the Zionist discussion groups Arendt frequented, and once he delivered a lecture on Döblin's novel, *Berlin Alexanderplatz*, but he was not involved when she began to make trips to various German cities to lecture on Zionism and the history of German anti-Semitism, under Blumenfeld's auspices. Among her Zionist colleagues and with their university friends, Hannah Arendt was much admired for her intellectual abilities—enough to be known by the quite non-Zionist title "Pallas Athene." Stern did not have the same reputation, and his early promise as a philosopher had not been fulfilled.

As important in personal terms as the differences in their reputations and circles was that Stern never knew the real depth of Hannah Arendt's commitment to the issues and movements she was concerned with. She was often critical of Zionism, and even tried to discourage her friend Kathe Levin, later Ernst Fuerst's wife, from membership in the Zionist youth movement—largely on the grounds she had indicated in her *Die Gesellschaft* review, that the Blau Weiss was a youth movement, for youth, and not politically engaged. But she would not discuss with Stern the nature of her allegiance to the Zionists. During the time that she and Stern had worked on her Augustine dissertation, she had refused to say whether she was truly committed to the principle of transcendent love, and this silence continued when they wrote together about Rilke's modern version of the principle. Similarly, when Stern came home from his discussions with Bertolt Brecht and his Communist friends, where varieties of contemporary atheism and nihilism were often debated, he would report on their debates and wait for her opinion, which never came. The side of her life that was expressed in poetry was also unknown to him. Though they shared a love for poetry and she appreciated Stern's efforts—even memorized and recited his poems—he never knew that among her notebooks was one full of poetry and poetic jottings.

Günther Stern was certainly not like the "beggar by the wayside . . . *sans* name, *sans* history and *sans* face" who had married Rahel Varnhagen.[27] But, like August Varnhagen, Stern was kept away from his wife's innermost thoughts and experiences; he was her companion for the daytime, and not for the nights of her dreams. August Varnhagen was Rahel's "only reliable friend . . . the person who could accompany her understandingly in the future as well as in the present," a source of continuity and admiring acceptance. Arendt loved and needed Günther Stern in just such a way, and she may have written about the limits of this need as she described Rahel's distance from August Varnhagen:

The more Varnhagen understood [her], the more Rahel was compelled to keep back from him. A person can be understood only as a particular being with particular contours, a particular physiognomy. Everything that blurs the contour must be suppressed or the general understanding will be destroyed. And that Rahel did not want. It was not that she concealed anything definite from him, but she did not speak of the elusive misery of the nights, the confusing twilight of the days, and the painful effort it cost her to overcome her melancholia anew every single day. . . . She clung to Varnhagen as she did to the day, only to relapse over and again into the ever-recurrent, insistent and importunate dreams of the night. [28]

It was Heidegger to whom Hannah Arendt had shown her melancholy and her poetry; Jaspers to whom she had come as a fatherless child. From Günther Stern she received, gratefully, a "general understanding," a generous acceptance of her daytime self. But when her daytime self became questionable to him, they drew apart.

When the differences in their daytime circles, their interests, and their achievements, began to combine with disagreements in matters of domestic policy, the lack of spiritual openness between Arendt and Stern stood revealed. Kurt Blumenfeld, in whose company Hannah Arendt's love of life and her adventurousness—as well as her willfulness and romanticism—were always heightened, provided the occasion for one such domestic disagreement. He presented Hannah Arendt with a box of black Havana cigars, which Günther Stern considered both mannish and foul smelling. Over Stern's protests, she smoked them, at home and in public. Hannah Arendt smoking cigars was Hannah Arendt assertively unconventional, delighted by Blumenfeld's recognition of her independence and difficult for Stern to accept in the adoring Varnhagenian manner. Blumenfeld was a man of the sort Hannah Arendt called *masculini generis*. He was so self-confidently and ardently a lover of women that he had no need of stereotypical conceptions of how women should behave and he was adoringly fatherlike in his constant encouragement. In the company of such men Hannah Arendt could enjoy being *feminini generis* on her own terms.

In the midst of these tensions, family sadnesses came. In April 1932, while the two were visiting Stern's parents in Hamburg, Hannah received a telegram from Martha Arendt. Clara Beerwald, who had returned to Königsberg for psychiatric treatment in one of the worst of her depressions, had committed suicide by taking poison. Hannah Arendt left immediately for Königsberg. Clara Beerwald's death was a great shock to Martha Arendt, who had been trying for years to help her stepdaughter, to console her after one boy friend died in surgery and another left her, and after she fell in love with the psychoanalyst who had diagnosed her schizophrenia.

Martha Arendt, always deeply involved in her own daughter's life, visited Hannah often while she was living in Berlin with Günther Stern. She took an interest in Zionism, though she did not advocate it, and sympathized with Hannah Arendt's concern that emigration might be necessary. When she became aware of how apprehensive her daughter was about the deteriorating political situation and about her marriage, she sadly accepted the announcement that the marriage would remain childless. But in subtle ways, Martha Arendt's hopes for her daughter's marriage stayed in place: they visited a friend together and Martha Arendt, playing with the friend's infant girl, burst out with "Hannachen, why don't you have a little one like this?" In her own way, Martha Arendt too failed to understand the depth of Hannah Arendt's melancholy—a melancholy which was purely personal in origin but which was given a frightening political context as Hitler rose to power.

## A Zionist Rebellion

Günther Stern fled Berlin for Paris several days after the Reichstag was set afire on 27 February 1933—a work of arson attributed to the Communists and providing the pretext for a series of arrests. Stern left because he feared that the newly reorganized Gestapo would use the address book they had confiscated from Bertolt Brecht as a guidebook for a sweep through leftist Berlin. Though she had been considering emigration for months, Hannah Arendt decided to stay in Berlin; as she said years later, she felt that she could "no longer be an observer."[29] The difference between the Sterns' reactions to the crisis was not a difference in degrees of courage, but, as one friend of both put it, "a matter of personality; she was equipped for resistance with a splendid impertinence."

After Stern left, Arendt became more involved with the Zionists, whose activities became even more urgent during the anti-Jewish measures of the spring of 1933, and she offered her apartment on Opitzstrasse as a way station for fleeing enemies of Hitler's regime, most of them Communists. Aiding fleeing political figures satisfied her need to act, to resist, to declare herself in opposition to the regime and to all of the people she knew who, in various ways, collaborated with it. It was, of course, crucially important to maintain the inconspicuous normalcy of her life on Opitzstrasse. The apartment itself—which the Sterns had taken in the summer of 1932—was "endlich eine eigene Wohnung," an apartment of their own at last.[30] No comings and goings of sculptors and dancers had to be reckoned with. She received her friends and relatives: Martha Arendt came from Königsberg for several lengthy stays; Else Aron, the sixteen-year-old daughter of Paul Arendt's sister Frieda, came for her first visit to the capital. And all of this traffic gave protection to the strangers who were ushered in late at night and early in the morning. Before she was taken around to Berlin's museums and shown the city's cultural treasures, Else Aron was instructed about when and how to answer the telephone. When Martha Arendt's Social Democratic friends came to call they brought information about where to send the escapees as the various imperiled leftist groups developed a series of border stations around Germany.

The months during the spring of 1933 when Arendt participated in this underground railroad were always tense, but not without an occasional moment of comic relief at the expense of the oppressors. Anne Mendelssohn, her sister Katherine, and their mother kept a Communist "outlaw" in their apartment for several days. All went well until a neighbor spotted the man through the bathroom window, which faced on a gossipy courtyard. The police appeared and interrogated the concierge, who was, fortunately, a Communist. This man was quick-witted and impertinent enough to save all concerned by eliciting manly sympathy from the policemen for these three deprived ladies with their one male visitor: "Come now, fellows, let's be gentlemen about it!"

Comic moments were few and far between. The many successful arrests were, as Arendt recalled, "monstrous, [though] completely overshadowed by the events that followed."[31] Conscientious, thoughtful people who had had trouble grasping what was happening were shocked into the realization that legality no longer mattered. During the January when Hitler assumed the German chancellorship, Arendt and Karl Jaspers had argued heatedly about her feeling that emigration would soon be necessary. He could not understand why "you as a Jewess would want to separate yourself from the Germans."[32] She had tried to explain to him, in person and in letters, what Germany meant to her: "For me, Germany is mother tongue, philosophy and poetry. For all this I can and must be steadfast."[33] But she felt estranged from everything else, including what Jaspers called the *Deutsche Wesen*, or German essence. "Germany in its old splendor," she wrote, "is your past, but what my past is I can hardly say in a phrase. In general, every interpretation [of Germany], whether from the Zionists or the assimilationists or the anti-Semites, only covers up the real problematic of our situation."[34] Jaspers remained hopeful that he could reconcile her to her Germanness, that in a discussion he could win her "consent." He feared for her: "Man cannot live by negations, problematics and ambiguities alone."[35] He thought that her criticisms of every camp, even the Zionist camp, left her no place to stand, no foundation for positive convictions; for him, ambiguity was no way out. By April, after the Reichstag fire, when she went to visit Jaspers in Heidelberg for the last time, he did not even try to win her consent. Nazi legislation depriving Jews of civil service appointments and university posts was being put into effect while they talked.

Hannah Arendt viewed the rescue work she did in Berlin as a test of mettle as well as of wit, and she maintained throughout her life an affection for those who had seen the situation clearly and participated in the effort regardless of their attitude toward Communists as Communists. The French sociologist, Raymond Aron, for example, aided refugees headed for his country while he worked at the Maison Française in Berlin, and for this he always stood high in Arendt's esteem, even though she had deep disagreements with him in matters of political theory.

But even though Hannah Arendt's introduction into the realm of action—about which she later developed one of the most original and brilliant facets of her political theory—was her courageous participation in this escape effort, she seldom spoke of it. She was modestly aware that many people who were no more Communist than she was had been involved at greater risk; but neither modesty nor her honest regard for what others sacrificed explains her silence.

In an open letter about her controversial 1963 *Eichmann in Jerusalem*, Gershom Scholem once referred to Arendt as one of the "intellectuals who came from the German Left." And she retorted: "I am not one of the 'intellectuals who came from the German Left.' You could not have known this, since we did not know each other when we were young. It is a fact of which I am in no way particularly proud and which I am somewhat reluctant to emphasize—especially since the McCarthy era in America. I came late to an understanding of Marx's importance because I was interested neither in history nor in politics when I was young. If I can be said to 'have come from anywhere,' it is from the tradition of German philosophy."[36] Arendt had been apolitical in her youth. But she was her Social Democratic mother's daughter, and her leftist husband's wife; she had started reading Marx, Lenin, and Trotsky (according to Anne Mendelssohn Weil's recollection) in Berlin; and she did aid the Communists in the spring of 1933. What Hannah Arendt wanted to emphasize, however, at that time and later, was that she had come to her political awakening and to her resistance not as a leftist but *as a Jew*. There were both political and personal reasons for this.

Arendt's way of acting as a Jew was provided by the Zionists. In the spring of 1933, she was asked by Kurt Blumenfeld and one of his colleagues in the German Zionist Organization to do some illegal work.[37] They wanted her to collect materials at the Prussian State Library which would show the extent of anti-Semitic action in nongovernment organizations, private circles, business associations, and professional societies. She was to make a collection of the sort of anti-Semitic remarks which would be unlikely to make their way into the German or foreign press. This material, which the Zionists called "horror propaganda," would be used to substantiate the claim that the Zionists intended to make at the 18th Zionist Congress, scheduled to meet in the summer of 1933 in Prague. The message the Zionists wished to convey to German Jews and to all who would listen was summarized in their Congress's resolutions: "Never in the history of Zionism has the complete accuracy of the Zionist analysis of the general Jewish question been manifested in such a tragic and convincing manner. The events in Germany have sealed the final collapse of those illusions that presented a solution of the Jewish question through civil emancipation alone or even through deliberate assimilation—the collapse of all attempts to deny the solidarity and common destiny of the Jewish people."[38]

Blumenfeld chose Hannah Arendt because she was not officially associated with the Zionists, for he knew that if a known Zionist was arrested in the middle of this task the whole organization would be jeopardized. She was, as she told an interviewer years later, "really delighted. First of all it seemed very sensible to me, and secondly I had the feeling that here I might really be able to do something." For several weeks, she did do something—she assembled a "beautiful collection" of materials. But then on her way to a luncheon with her mother she was arrested and taken to the police presidium at Alexanderplatz. The police also brought Martha Arendt in for questioning and went to search Arendt's apartment. The police kept Martha Arendt and her daughter apart to make sure that they could not coordinate their stories, but they could not elicit from Martha Arendt any story at all. They asked her if she knew what her daughter was doing at the Prussian State Library and she firmly replied, "No, I don't know what she was doing, but whatever she was doing she was right to be doing it and I would have done the same." No more informative than Martha Arendt's terse testimony were the notebooks and manuscripts the police found in the apartment: they returned the philosophical manuscripts but it took them a number of days to break the complicated code of one notebook—a collection of quotations in Greek.

Hannah Arendt was arrested by a "charming fellow" who had recently been promoted to the political department and was not quite sure of his responsibilities. "He had some misgivings. But what was he supposed to do? He always said: 'Normally when I have someone in front of me, I just have to look the case up in our records and I know what to do. What am I supposed to do with you?'" What he did was rather unusual. On the way to headquarters, she complained that she had only a few cigarettes in her pocket and that it would be impossible for her to answer questions without cigarettes. He very politely stopped the car, bought her several packs of cigarettes, and helpfully suggested how she might smuggle them into her cell. The next day, as he was conducting the interrogation, she complained about the quality of the coffee, and a better cup was provided.

Despite this rapport, she told her captor a string of lies. "Naturally, I couldn't expose the organization. I would tell him fantastic stories and he would always say 'I got you in here and I am going to get you out. Don't hire a lawyer! The Jews don't have any money now. Save your money.' In the meantime, the organization had hired a lawyer for me. Naturally, again through associates. But I sent the lawyer away. Because this man who had arrested me had such an open, honest face, I put my trust in him and figured I would have a better chance that way than with some lawyer who would only be afraid."

Arendt's German policeman was true to his word, and she was released after eight days. But she knew very well that she was unlikely to be twice blessed with such a friend, and she prepared to leave Germany as quickly as possible. One evening's pause, Anne Mendelssohn Weil recalled, to enjoy the company of her friends and to celebrate her release with the contents of a wine *cave* left behind by a fleeing Jewish merchant was "the most drunken occasion of our lives." Kurt Blumenfeld, in high good humor, took Martha Arendt in his arms and announced to her with his usual gusto, "Now, you are someone with whom I would like to have conceived Hannah Arendt!"

Hannah Arendt and her mother left Germany, without travel documents, by way of the thick forest of the Erzgebirge Mountains, known to fleeing Jews and leftists as the "Green Front." They were headed toward Prague, which had become the capital city for exiles from Nazi Germany. The Prague-based leftist exiles had organized a network of border stations to facilitate both the exit of people from Germany and the entrance into Germany of newsletters, information, and couriers. The Arendts went to the station at Karlsbad, for a time the most important in the network and the best known within Germany. They crossed the Czech border at night, avoiding the patrol. Their escape was very simple: a sympathetic German family owned a house with a front door in Germany and a back door in Czechoslovakia; they received their "guests" in the daytime, provided them with dinner, and then ushered them out the back under the shelter of darkness.

After a brief stay in Prague, the Arendts left for Geneva where one of Martha Arendt's oldest Berlin socialist friends, a woman named Martha Mundt, lived and worked for the League of Nations. Martha Mundt offered Hannah a temporary position with her department at the League headquarters, the Bureau International du Travail. Hannah Arendt was a great success as a recording secretary: she produced minutes containing such clear and forceful speeches that the speakers laid aside the question of accuracy and were very much impressed with themselves. This new-found talent was also put to work briefly at the Jewish Agency headquarters—compounded by a new element: the speeches were in Yiddish. But Arendt did not want to stay in Geneva, in the milieu of the Social Democratic labor organizers or the Jewish Agency leadership. She wanted to go on to Paris, to join the many Zionists in exile who were gathering there.

In the months before she left Germany, Hannah Arendt's sense of what she should be doing had shifted dramatically. She stated in the 1964 Gaus interview that the burning of the Reichstag in February of 1933 and the period of illegal arrests that had followed that episode had been turning points for her. "As you know, they all ended up in the cellars of the Gestapo or in concentration camps. That was such a shock to me that ever after I felt responsible. That is to say, I no longer felt that [I] could be simply an observer." Not mentioning her work for the Communists, she said that her work for the Zionists had been a great satisfaction to her. "Well, I thought, at least I've accomplished something! At least I am not innocent, no one can accuse me of that." And this sense of satisfaction with action for the Zionist cause, with not being innocent, led her to reconsider how to accept her new-found sense of responsibility.

You see, I had been primarily occupied with academic pursuits. Given that perspective, the year 1933 made a lasting impression on me—both negatively and positively. I should give you first a negative impression and then a positive one. Many people think these days that the shock undergone by the Jews in 1933 was a function of Hitler's seizing power. As far as I and those of my generation are concerned, this is a curious misunderstanding. That was, of course, terrible. But it was political, it wasn't personal. That the Nazis were our enemies—God knows we did not need Hitler's seizing of power to demonstrate that! It was clear to everyone who was not a little crazy for at least four years prior to 1933. That a large number of Germans sympathized with the Nazis was also quite apparent to us. Therefore, we were not taken completely by surprise by the events of 1933. . . . [But] the general political realities transformed themselves into personal destiny as soon as you set foot out of the house. And, also, you know what cooperation (*Gleichschaltung*) is, of course. And cooperation meant that your friends cooperated. The problem, the personal problem, was not what our enemies might be doing, but what our friends were doing. This wave of cooperation—which was quite voluntary, or at least not compelled in the way it is during a reign of terror, made you feel surrounded by an empty space, isolated. I lived in an intellectual milieu, but I also knew many people who did not, and I came to the conclusion that cooperation was, so to speak, the rule among intellectuals, but not among others. And I have never forgotten that. I left Germany guided by the resolution—a very exaggerated one—that 'Never again!' I will never have anything to do with 'the history of ideas' again. I didn't, indeed, want to have anything to do with this sort of society again.

Arendt concluded that a *déformation professionelle* of intellectuals and their society had made them susceptible to cooperating with the Nazis.

The Germany Hannah Arendt had told Jaspers she would never leave—mother tongue, philosophy, and poetry—was entangled with her personal problem. And this made the problem all the more acute. Benno von Wiese, her literary companion from the Heidelberg years, came to the Opitzstrasse apartment and announced to her: "These are great times." Martin Heidegger, who took over the rectorship of Freiberg University in the spring of 1933, after his Social Democratic predecessor was dismissed for refusing to post the so-called Jew Notice, delivered a rectoral address celebrating "the greatness, the nobility of this national awakening." He also paid a visit to Karl Jaspers which rudely brought to an end

Jaspers's rather naive faith in the moral goodness of philosophers—for Heidegger behaved insultingly toward Jaspers's Jewish wife.[39]

In her last excursion into the history of ideas, in a 1932 article for the Cologne *Zeitung* called "An Adam Mueller Renaissance?" Hannah Arendt criticized the National Socialist intellectuals who ransacked German literature in search of precursors.[40] She argued that Rahel Varnhagen's acquaintance, Adam Mueller, did not fit the dishonest Nazi portrait drawn of him. Mueller was a Catholic, Arendt wrote, with a vision of redemptive community, and was neither an opponent of liberalism, industrialization, and enlightenment nor an advocate of the organic image of society. There was an implicit warning in her article for men like Benno von Wiese and Martin Heidegger, for she realized that the allegiance of these contemporary Adam Muellers would be used by the *Volk*-worshipping Nazis for any purposes they desired. But this article was her final attempt to send a public message into an intellectual society which had closed its ears to criticism.

Arendt's personal problem was also complicated dreadfully when Jews cooperated. She told Jaspers of one incident that rankled in her memory for many years: "[Theodor Adorno's] unsuccessful attempt at cooperation in 1933 was exposed in the Frankfurt student newspaper *Discus*. He answered with an indescribably lamentable letter, which made quite an impression, nonetheless, on the Germans. The real infamy of the matter was that he, half-Jewish [by law], had taken this step without informing his friends. He had hoped to get by with his mother's Italian family name," Adorno, instead of his father's more obviously Jewish name, Wiesengrund.[41]

Arendt later revised her assessment of intellectuals, but at the time it informed her decisions; it motivated the positive outcome of her impressions from the year 1933, the transformation of her personal problem into an unambiguous political stance. "I arrived at the conclusion which I always, at the time, expressed to myself in one sentence, a sentence which clarified it to me: 'When one is attacked as a Jew, one must defend oneself *as a Jew*.' Not as a German, not as a world-citizen, not as an upholder of the Rights of Man."[42] This is the political reason why Arendt always emphasized that her resistance in Berlin had been the resistance of a Jew.

After I realized this, I clearly intended to affiliate myself with the [Jewish] cause. For the first time. And to affiliate, of course, with the Zionists. They were the only ones who were ready. I mean affiliating with the assimilationists would have made no sense. By the way, I really never had anything to do with the assimilationists. I had concerned myself with the Jewish Question—my *Rahel Varnhagen* was finished [*sic*] by the time I left Germany, and in it, of course, the Jewish Question plays quite a part. The work signified to me that I wanted to understand. However, the Jewish problems I was discussing in that book were not my own problems. And my personal problem was political. Purely political! I wanted to do practical work—exclusively and only Jewish work. And it was according to that guideline that I oriented myself in France.

Königsberg, East Prussia, ca. 1900

Martha Cohn Arendt, 1899

Paul Arendt, ca. 1900

Hannah Arendt with her grandfather, Max Arendt

Hannah Arendt (age 8)
with her mother

Eva and Clara Beerwald
and Hannah Arendt
(age 15 or 16)

(*left to right*) Martin Beerwald,
Hannah Arendt (age 17), Martha
Arendt Beerwald, Clara
Beerwald, Klara Arendt, Eva
Beerwald, Else Aron Braude (*in
front*)

Hannah Arendt's boyfriend
Ernst Grumach, 1920

Hannah Arendt in 1924 (age 18)

Martin Heidegger, 1925/26,
drawn by Hans Jonas

(*left to right*) unknown woman,
Hugo Friedrich, Hannah Arendt,
Benno von Wiese in Heidelberg in
1928

Günther Stern (Anders) and
Hannah Arendt, ca. 1929

Kurt Blumenfeld

Hannah Arendt in 1933

Heinrich Blücher and Robert Gilbert
in Berlin

Heinrich Blücher

Hannah Arendt in Paris

Walter Benjamin                    Martha Arendt Beerwald in France, 1941

Hannah and Heinrich Blücher in New York, ca. 1950

The Blüchers with Lotte Kohler in Palenville, New York

Gertrud and Karl Jaspers in Basel, mid-1960s

J. Glenn Gray

Anne Mendelssohn Weil in 1967

W. H. Auden. Photographed by
Hannah Arendt in her Riverside
Drive apartment, 1967

Hannah Arendt and Mary McCarthy

Heinrich Blücher shortly before
his death in 1970

Hannah Arendt shortly before her death in 1975

# PART 2
## 1933–1951

FOR EIGHTEEN YEARS, HANNAH ARENDT WAS A "STATE-less person." But this period when she had no political rights—between her flight from Nazi Germany in 1933 and her receipt of American citizenship in 1951—was her most active politically. In Paris, where she worked for organizations that helped Jewish refugees emigrate to Palestine and supplied legal aid to anti-Fascists, she left behind the apolitical intellectuality of her university circles. She found a peer group that included artists and workers, Jews and non-Jews, activists and pariahs; German was their language, but they were cosmopolitan in vision. With this group, which included her second husband, Heinrich Blücher, Hannah Arendt discussed how a Jewish politics might arise in the world crisis they saw coming. When that crisis was upon them, when the Second World War began, the peer group was dispersed: some were interned briefly in French camps, some fled to unoccupied territory, all began the frantic search for visas, new homes, safety.

Hannah Arendt and Heinrich Blücher were lucky. They received American emergency visas and were able to travel across southern France to Spain, and then to Lisbon, where they set sail for New York. There she sought forums for her efforts to give a Jewish politics theoretical foundations and practical focus. In the pages of *Aufbau*, a German-language New York newspaper, she argued for a Jewish army to fight against Hitler. Neither the Jewish army nor the kind of Jewish politics she had hoped for emerged; in the terrible years of the Final Solution, she continued to write about the Jewish homeland in Palestine, but no political group took up her ideas.

At the end of the war, while working for Jewish Cultural Reconstruction, Inc., and later, when she was an editor at Schocken Books, Hannah Arendt began *The Origins of Totalitarianism*. She wrote her book and dozens of short articles and reviews, but she did not engage in political activity. Nevertheless, in the summer after the state of Israel came into existence, she joined a group headed by Judah Magnes that sought a rapprochement between the Jews and the Arabs in the new state. After this brief and frustrating effort, she retired from politics, convinced that she was, by temperament and talents, unsuited for it.

Hannah Arendt certainly was not what she called a "political animal." But what she had learned from practical activity and from being a public figure during her stateless years laid the foundations for her political theory. *The Origins of Totalitarianism* contains, *inter linea*, Hannah Arendt's political story and the story of her Paris peer group. She wrote it with her husband's help, and it contains, as Kurt Blumenfeld noted, "the unwritten political philosophy of the person to whom it is dedicated"—Blücher.

No years of Hannah Arendt's life were more difficult than the stateless ones. *The Origins of Totalitarianism* does not, of course, tell her personal story—the story of her marriage, her loyalty to absent or lost friends, her mother's death, her times of despair and hope. But it obviously was written with the passionate will to understand that presupposes a deep tempering process, the kind of process Nietzsche said either kills you or makes you stronger. Hannah Arendt, who as a young woman had divided time into "Then" and "Now" in purely personal terms, ended the 1950 preface to her first major work with a stark, strong, political charge: "All efforts to escape from the grimness of the present into nostalgia for a still intact past, or into the anticipated oblivion of a better future, are vain."

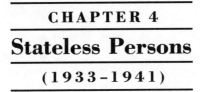

# CHAPTER 4
# Stateless Persons
# (1933-1941)

L'Affaire d'un seul est l'affaire de tous.
Clemenceau on the Dreyfus Affair

*Her People*

After arranging for her mother's safe return to Königsberg, Hannah
Arendt went to Paris in the fall of 1933 and rejoined Günther Stern. They
lived together, had common friends and activities, but their marriage was
never restored. Companionship and the difficult practical business of
securing food and lodging continued to bind them; and such bonds,
between people who hardly knew what to expect from one day to the next
at the hands of "that old trickster, World-History," were important to
them both. To friends like Hans Jonas, who visited them shortly after the
Stavisky scandals of 1934, they still presented themselves as a married
couple, and Hannah Arendt continued to use the name Hannah Stern for
her public activities. They did not finally separate until Stern left Paris for
New York in June 1936, but their *Ehelicher Verkehr*, their marital
intercourse—as Arendt's 1937 divorce papers put it—had ceased in 1933.

While Hannah Arendt involved herself in Zionist causes and issues,
Stern worked on his vast novel *Molussiche Katakomie*, which had been
on an odyssey worthy of its own pages. A copy of the partially completed
manuscript was resting with a Berlin publisher when its offices were
searched by the Gestapo early in 1933. The manuscript was confiscated,
but returned shortly afterward to Bertolt Brecht, who had submitted it to
the publisher for Stern. The Gestapo men had judged the book by its
cover, which featured a map of the magical island, a fascist utopia, where
the novel was set. That the novel was a satire, and the utopia a mock
utopia, would not have been apparent to anyone who had not read a page

115

of it. Stern recovered the novel from Brecht and gave it to Anne Mendelssohn for safekeeping. She, in turn, wrapped it in a greasy cheesecloth and hung it up in an attic among a collection of smoked bacons. Hannah Arendt took the imitation bacon with her when she left Berlin, carried it to Prague, to Geneva, and finally to Paris, where she turned it over to Stern. He took up his work again, inhaling the luxurious bacon smell its pages exuded with his spare daily breakfast. Other than this, Fascism afforded Günther Stern few comforts, and his sister Eva, who visited him in Paris after a separation of several years, was shocked at how worn down he seemed, how discouraged by life in a hostile environment, without support or recognition.

When they were not working, Hannah and Günther Stern met in the Quartier Latin cafés to talk with the friends and acquaintances who could give at least moral support. Stern introduced Arendt to Arnold Zweig and Bertolt Brecht one afternoon in a café on the rue Sufflot, under the shadow of a Pantheon for heroes not their own. They visited the literary critic Walter Benjamin, whom they had both met but not known well in Berlin. Benjamin, a distant cousin of Stern's, was more at home in Paris than most of the refugee intellectuals. As a young man, he had often travelled to the city with his father, an importer of Oriental antiques, and could speak and write French with flair. The "capital of the Nineteenth Century" suited his tastes and gave him generous spaces for his daily walking-tours, his *flâneries*. But Benjamin, too, suffered "because he did not get the 'reception' in France that was due to him," as Hannah Arendt wrote in an essay about her friend.[1] He was grateful for the few forums where French and émigré intellectuals met, like the Institut pour l'Etude du Fascisme where in 1934 he delivered his lecture "The Author as Producer" to an audience that included Hannah Arendt.

The Sterns' friends were, for the most part, German refugees, but they did have a few French acquaintances, men who looked intellectually toward the Germany they had all known before 1933. Raymond Aron, who had taught at the Institut Français in Berlin from 1931 to 1933, took a position at the Ecole Normale Supérieure as secretary for the Center of Social Information in 1934. Hannah Arendt saw him occasionally. And thanks to Aron's introductions, she and Stern were able to attend several of Alexandre Kojève's seminars at the Ecole des Hautes Etudes. These seminars were the basis for Kojève's *Introduction à la lecture de Hegel*, a volume assembled from notes taken by Kojève's students which Hannah Arendt thought fundamental to any study of Hegel. "Kojève actually believed," she told a friend years later, "philosophy had come to an end with Hegel *and* acted on [the belief]. He never wrote a book, even the Hegel book was not actually written by him. . . . He did not become a professor of philosophy. . . . In short, he did what most people don't do."[2] For Hannah Arendt, who—as Jaspers put it—had "entered increasingly, and understandably, into an anti-academic frame of mind," Kojève was a particularly impressive figure.

Jean-Paul Sartre, with whom the Sterns never became very friendly, and Alexandre Koyré, who later became a close friend of Arendt's, also attended the Kojève seminars. Koyré introduced them to Jean Wahl, his collaborator at *Recherches philosophiques*, where Stern was able to publish some book reviews and a French translation of his 1930 Frankfurt lecture, "Une interprétation de l'a posteriori." Jean Wahl was one of the first people in France to take a serious interest in Jaspers's work; others—notably Kojève and Sartre—had known Heidegger's work for some years and drawn upon it extensively.

In other times these acquaintances might have been compellingly interesting for Hannah Arendt, particularly if she had been able to dedicate herself to improving her French, which was adequate for reading but not for everyday speaking or philosophical discussions. But her attention was directed toward Jewish concerns and away from university circles, even those as refreshingly nonconformist and pariah-like as Kojève's.

Her first job, which she was able to get without a *carte d'identité*, was with an organization that had headquarters on the Champs Elysées—Agriculture et Artisanat. This organization, presided over by the French *sénateur* Justin Godart, head of France-Palestine, one of the most influential agencies contributing to the development of Palestine, offered young émigrés training in farming and crafts to prepare them for a future in Palestine. The young people were given meals at a Foyer de Jeunesse and evening courses in Jewish history, Zionism, and Hebrew. Arendt was placed as a secretary in the Agriculture et Artisanat offices.

A combination of luck and brashness had won her this job. She had presented herself at the Comité National de Secours aux Juifs Allemands and claimed a set of clerical skills she had barely heard of, much less mastered. Behavior less strident got less interesting positions. Anne Mendelssohn, who had become Anne Weil in Paris, where there was no law like the Nazi one which forbade both partners of a marriage from being employed at the same time, spent a discouraging few months selling matchbooks and tutoring in German—for the same pittance French student-tutors received from their *tapirs*. Anne looked for a better job, and Hannah Arendt tried to help her by securing a letter of reference from Kurt Blumenfeld. She wrote to Blumenfeld from her room on the rue Sainte-Jacques, the first of many little hotel rooms she briefly occupied, and described Anne's need: the letter of reference had to be suitable for "a big American insurance company. . . . I wouldn't ask you for such an absurd thing if it were not so insanely difficult to find any position here, if one did not have to absolutely leap at every opportunity."[3] Anne finally got a secretarial post at the Ecole des Hautes Etudes and a far more lucrative tutoring job—she helped an aging French duchess finish a thesis on Ernst Cassirer for the Sorbonne. Madame was very anxious to finish her degree, she told her tutor, because the Sorbonne was becoming "entirely Communist."

Hundreds of German refugees wandered through Paris, moving from hotel to hotel, looking for work of any sort. Many were caught in the vicious syndrome so well known to modern refugees: work was not available to those without the proper papers and without work the papers could not be secured. As the German refugees were joined by waves of Eastern Europeans, the situation grew more and more desperate. Slogans like "La France aux Français" and "A bas les métèques" filled the newspapers and rang out at street demonstrations—for more than half a million French were as hopelessly unemployed as the refugees.

Once she had her position at Agriculture et Artisanat, Hannah Arendt was able to make enough money to support herself and help Günther Stern. She was also able to offer work to a few wandering Jews. One was a Pole recently arrived in Paris from Palestine, Chanan Klenbort—a man who remained her friend for the rest of her life. Chanan, who had supported himself in the winter of 1934 by making boot soles in his hotel room for a Parisian factory while he wrote short stories under the pen name Ayalti, was taken on at Agriculture et Artisanat as a teacher of Yiddish and Hebrew.

Klenbort was enormously impressed by Hannah Arendt when he met her at Agriculture et Artisanat: first because she invited him for coffee at a Champs Elysées café, which was by his standards an expensive gesture, and then because she was so open-minded in conversation. She asked him if he was an anti-Zionist, as it was not common for organizations aiding emigration to Palestine to hire anti-Zionists, but when he said that he was in fact anti-Zionist (a stance he later abandoned), she offered him the job anyway. This business taken care of, they talked about their families—Arendt producing her Litvak maternal grandfather Jacob Cohen as evidence of their shared past—and about the Yiddish language, which she, unlike many well-educated, assimilated German Jews, did not look down upon. The afternoon ended with Chanan Klenbort twice hired: once by Agriculture et Artisanat and once by Arendt herself, for private tutoring in Hebrew. "I want to know my people," she told him.

Getting to know her people was a complex undertaking, because it quickly became apparent to her while she worked at Agriculture et Artisanat that each year of Jewish persecutions increased the complexities of that people's interrelations. She described the situation she had encountered in Paris: "French Jewry was absolutely convinced that all Jews coming from beyond the Rhine were what they called *Polaks*—what German Jewry called *Ostjuden*. But those Jews who really came from Eastern Europe could not agree with their French brethren and called us [German Jews] *Jaeckes*. The sons of these *Jaecke*-haters—the second generation, born in France and already duly assimilated—shared the opinion of the French upper classes. Thus, in the very same family, you could be called a *Jaecke* by the father and a *Polak* by the son."[4] Hannah Arendt transferred the Zionist critique of assimilation she had learned from Blumenfeld to this new situation as best she could, but the critique had to be adapted because so many of the people she met were veterans of two or three different assimilations. Some had been German patriots, and then perhaps Czech or Austrian patriots, before they set out to be Frenchmen. She remembered a German who, as soon as he got his bearings in Paris, founded an émigré society "in which German Jews asserted to each other that they were already Frenchmen. In his first speech he said: 'We have been good Germans in Germany and therefore we shall be good Frenchmen in France.' The public applauded enthusiastically and nobody laughed."[5] Her efforts, sometimes in what one of her *Ostjude* friends called "a doctoral tone," to point out to these assimilationists that they were not French, that they were "nothing but Jews," endeared her only to those—mostly Zionists—already familiar with the critique of assimilation. She had more effect when she joined a protest against the policy of the French Comité responsible for placing *Polaks* in whatever jobs could be found: the Comité finally gave up the practice of making German refugees obtain letters of reference from their former employers—that is, their German employers.

There were, of course, many who did not use derogatory labels for Jews of national origins other than their own. In the months between the end of her work for Agriculture et Artisanat and the beginning of her work for another Jewish organization, Youth Aliyah, Hannah Arendt was hired by a French Jewess free of *Polak*-hatred, the Baroness Germaine de Rothschild. Arendt's task was to oversee the baroness's contributions to Jewish charities, to investigate possible recipient organizations, and then to check on the use to which the baroness's money was put at the chosen organizations. Germaine de Rothschild's favorite charity was a children's home, and Arendt arranged for her visits—or visitations. She liked to appear in jewels and silks of the Rothschild red, with her limousine full of toys and candies, on the rather romantic theory that the children would feel they had been singled out for a miracle.[6] Both the baroness and her secretary, as Anne Mendelssohn Weil remembered them, "lost their heads as far as children were concerned."

Hannah Arendt liked and was liked by Germaine de Rothschild. But her attitude toward other members of the illustrious family was not friendly. The Rothschilds were the guiding force behind the Consistoire de Paris, the major religious association of native—and often upper-class—Parisian Jewry. The Consistoire had in its charge many charitable organizations for both native and immigrant Jews—a number of synagogues, over forty schools, religious law courts, kosher shops, and a seminary. Presided over by Edmond de Rothschild and then by his son Robert during the 1930s, it made major contributions to Jewish social and cultural life. It was also the association most frequently consulted by the French government when matters concerning the native Jewish communities or the refugees were discussed. But the Consistoire's leaders consistently tried to persuade the membership—and all other Jews in Paris—to refrain from joining or overtly supporting political groups.

Robert de Rothschild made this policy very clear when he addressed the Consistoire's General Assembly on 27 May 1934. He argued that the influx of immigrants presented several grave dangers to the Jewish community.[7] The first was that the immigrants, with their old-country dress, habits, and manners, would aggravate the anti-Semitism and the xenophobia of the French. The second danger was that the immigrants would continue their unfortunate political habits, involving themselves in French politics, particularly in leftist politics. Though the Consistoire, according to its own principles, should have stayed away from the French political struggles, its members did establish contacts with the right-wing groups that had attacked the Chamber of Deputies during the 6 February 1934 rioting—hoping to diminish the anti-Semitic rhetoric of the right-wingers by convincing them that the Jews were loyal to *la patrie*. For the same reason, the Consistoire also gave its support to a Jewish patriotic group—the Union Patriotique des Français Israélites.

Rothschild's speech caused a furor among many immigrants, convinced as they were of the need for political activity and protest. The Consistoire's advocacy of inconspicuous, behind-the-scenes diplomacy conducted by Jewish "notables" sounded like a call for tactics already shown to be hopelessly inadequate in their home countries. The Consistoire opposed all the actions Hannah Arendt supported—attempts to boycott German goods, efforts by the Ligue Internationale contre l'Antisémitisme to publicize anti-Semitic laws and activities in Germany, and the demonstrations (in 1936) in support of David Frankfurter, a young Jew who assassinated the head of a Swiss branch of the Nazi party. The Consistoire even refused to send delegates to the World Jewish Congress when invited to do so.

For Hannah Arendt, the Rothschilds—regardless of their personal qualities and good intentions—were of the type she called "the parvenus." In her terms, a Jew could be either a parvenu or a pariah, and she made it very clear in discussions and later in her writings that she thought only a pariah could develop a truly political consciousness, only a pariah could affirm his or her Jewish identity and seek, politically, to provide a place for Jews to live without compromising their Jewish identity. Her understanding was expressed in theoretical terms and rooted in her study of the eighteenth-century Jewish Enlightenment, but it was flavored in Paris by many personal experiences. What astounded her about so many of the Jews she worked with was their failure to think politically, to realize the necessity for Jewish solidarity in the European—the world—crisis: "I remember a director of a great charity concern in Paris who, whenever he received the card of a German-Jewish intellectual with the inevitable 'Dr.' on it, used to exclaim at the top of his voice, 'Herr Doktor, Herr Doktor, Herr Schnorrer [beggar], Herr Schnorrer!'"[8] This philanthropist could not see in a German Jew a fellow Jew; he saw only a beggar, and his vision gave him what the German-Jewish Herr Doktor would have called *Schadenfreude*, malicious pleasure in injuring another.

The distinction between politically conscious pariahs and socially ambitious parvenus came to Hannah Arendt from Kurt Blumenfeld. But it had originated with the French Jewish publicist and Dreyfusard Bernard

Lazare, whose hostility toward the Jewish leadership of his day was exemplary in its moral clarity. Lazare had risked much to stand alone in support of Dreyfus; he repudiated Jewish, even Zionist, leaders who sought, as he said, "to direct the Jewish masses as though they were children."[9] As the distinction between pariah resisters and politically malleable parvenus evolved in Hannah Arendt's thought, it lost none of its biting sharpness, but it did eventually become only a subtheme in a larger concern—a concern she took up in writings when the threat to her people had been fulfilled more horribly than anyone in the 1930s could have imagined. After the war, she distinguished the "social realm" (home of parvenus) and the "political realm" (home of pariahs) and looked only to the latter for any truly revolutionary renewal. But it was before the war, in *la nation par excellence*, the nation of the Revolution and the nation of the Dreyfus Affair, that Hannah Arendt became both more critically Zionist and more committed to revolutionary politics.

The parvenu Rothschilds and their involvement in the Consistoire became a topic in the discussions Hannah Arendt began to have in 1936 with a group of people formed in Marxist schools of theory or *praxis*. These people succeeded Blumenfeld as Hannah Arendt's political mentors. The group included Walter Benjamin, and occasionally colleagues of Benjamin's from the Institut für Sozialforschung in Frankfurt; Erich Cohn-Bendit, a lawyer; Fritz Fränkel, a psychoanalyst; Karl Heidenreich, a painter; Chanan Klenbort, the only *Ostjude* among these Berliners; and Heinrich Blücher. The discussions, which usually took place in Benjamin's apartment, 10 rue Dombasle, brought together friends of both Hannah Arendt and Heinrich Blücher; they attracted the first of the peer groups which surrounded Arendt and Blücher for the next thirty-five years.

*Heinrich Blücher*

Hannah Arendt met Heinrich Blücher in the early spring of 1936. Blücher, a Communist, had fled from Berlin by way of Prague in 1934. He had left Germany in haste, had no identity papers, and, as his friend and patroness in Paris, Lotte Sempell, put it, was "so illegal he didn't know where he lived." He stayed with friends in various hotels and apartments and comported himself when he went out as though he were his own class enemy: with suit, hat, walking stick, and the assumed name "Heinrich Larsen," he disguised himself as a bourgeois tourist. Lotte

Sempell, the daughter of a wealthy Westphalian industrialist, often provided both residence and funds and received, in Blücher's company, a political education quite different from the one that led her to write an admiring doctoral dissertation on Bismarck. The help she gave Blücher and his Marxist friends was her way of fighting Hitler. When she contemplated the further step of joining the Communist party, Blücher convinced her that the party did not accept new members in exile; and this fiction probably saved her from a fate worse than the one she met—more exile.

Lotte Sempell was convinced, from the moment Blücher told her that he had met Hannah Arendt at a public lecture, that his new interest would be more than passing. But some time went by before Blücher and Hannah Arendt met again. She was not at all reserved in conversation, but her response to Blücher was reticent—though she later liked to tell friends, with romantic exaggeration, that the courtship had been of one evening's duration. Chanan Klenbort found himself cast in the role of chaperone one evening in June 1936, shortly after Günther Stern departed for America. He was invited to Arendt's room for dinner and met there the bourgeois-in-disguise, whom Hannah Arendt jokingly called "Monsieur." Dinner was served, and dessert, and coffee, and more coffee; each time Chanan Klenbort rose to go home, he was persuaded to stay. Finally, at two in the morning, Chanan prepared to leave his hostess and her friend alone, but found himself ushered out—with "Monsieur." When Klenbort left Paris for Spain in the middle of the summer to cover the Civil War for several Parisian and Polish Yiddish newspapers, the courtship was still in progress. But when he returned at the end of the summer and was once again invited to dinner, Hannah Arendt and Blücher received him together.

Even to her closest friend, Anne Mendelssohn Weil, Hannah Arendt revealed her new relationship cautiously. Anne came to visit one afternoon and offered her reflections on recipes while her friend prepared dinner. She noticed that the amounts they were considering exceeded a single person's scale and was told, timidly, "It is easier to prepare for two," from which she was left to draw her own conclusion.

The conclusion Anne Weil drew, with pleasure, was quite accurate, and not as baffled as the one drawn soon afterward by a hotel clerk on the rue Servandoni near the Jardin du Luxembourg. Arendt went to the hotel to reserve a room for herself and her *mari*, explaining carefully that she wanted a room with two beds. The clerk's quizzical look prompted her to an elaborate and embarrassed discourse on diverse sleeping schedules, the hygienic advantages of separate beds, and so forth, to which the clerk responded with a splendid example of polite Gallic rudeness: "Ah, bien sûr, Madame. Je comprends. Mais je ne comprends pas."

From the beginning, the domestic arrangements were tailored to what most importantly and most enduringly bound them: conversation. Those who understood their bond understood the arrangements. Blücher told his Berlin friend Peter Huber, who knew his fondness for women well, that he had at last found the right companion: "We each do our work, and then we come together to discuss." Their early relationship was, as Anne Weil remembered it, "a passion," and for both of them intellectual argument was part and parcel of passion.

Hannah Arendt had been eleven years old when her mother took her to the Königsberg demonstrations in support of the Spartacists. She was thirty years old when she walked through the streets of Paris to watch the 1936 demonstrations in support of the Front Populaire government under the leadership of the Jewish Socialist, Léon Blum. Most of the political awareness she had developed in the intervening years had come in the context of her relationship with Kurt Blumenfeld and his concern with the Jewish Question. With Heinrich Blücher as her teacher, she added to her preliminary reading of Marx, Lenin, and Trotsky a feeling for "revolutionary *praxis*." Blücher—not a university man but a proletarian, not a theorist but a man of action, not a Jew but a man for whom thinking was a kind of religion—was Hannah Arendt's New World. Ten years after they met, she summarized what Blücher had meant to her intellectually, in response to words of praise Jaspers had bestowed on her own cosmopolitan and impartial political vision: "That I learned from my husband's political thinking and historical observation, and I would not have come to it otherwise, for I was historically and politically oriented toward the Jewish Question."[10]

During those ten years, from 1936 to 1946, Hannah Arendt continued to concern herself with the Jewish Question, but what she learned from Blücher became, after the Second World War, central to the political philosophizing that animated *The Origins of Totalitarianism*, *The Human Condition*, *Between Past and Future*, *On Revolution*, *On Violence*, and *Crises of the Republic*. The learning relationship was not, however, completely one-way. Blücher, an avid reader of Rosa Luxemburg, Trotsky, and Bukharin, and a convinced Communist, slowly gave up his Communism and became an incisive critic of doctrinaire Marxism.

While Hannah Arendt was being introduced to revolutionary politics in Königsberg, Heinrich Blücher was twenty years old and fighting as a Spartacist in the streets of Berlin. The stories he told her of his political past shaped her vision, both critical and constructive, her understanding of resistance and revolution, and her theory of republicanism. Blücher's stories are not easy to reconstruct: he was hesitant to tell them, particularly after he had entered America without admitting on his immigration documents that he had been a Communist, and he was given to exaggerating and embroidering what he did tell. In Heinrich Blücher, the combination of cautiousness and hyperbole was always an astonishment. Those members of the Arendt-Blücher tribe who had known him since his youth understood his storytelling for what it was—a way of finding meaning in a chaotic world. His devotees were unskeptical, and his detractors charged him with mythomania. In truth, had he had a gift for writing equal to his gift for talking, he would have made a fine novelist.

Heinrich Friedrich Ernest Blücher was born on 29 January 1899 in southwest Berlin.[11] His father, who had an equally long and historically weighty name, August Charles Heinrich Blücher, died in a factory accident several months before his only child's birth. Klara Emilie Wilke Blücher raised her son alone. He attended a _Volkeschule_ and helped his mother, who made her living as a laundress, by acting as delivery boy until he was able to continue his study at a preparatory school for teachers. In 1917, the First World War interrupted his studies, and a period in an army hospital with gas poisoning interrupted his scheduled sojourn in an officer's training program.

When the October 1918 armistice was signed, Blücher, who was nineteen, returned to Berlin and joined one of the _Soldatenräte_, the Soldiers' Councils, which, with the Workers' Councils, participated in the day of rioting on 9 November 1918 that ended with the proclamation of the German Republic. The German army had surrendered in the Forest of Compiègne and the troops returned to Germany at the beginning of December. Shortly afterward, on December 16, a National Congress of Workers' and Soldiers' Councils met in Berlin and passed a number of startling resolutions designed to create a People's army from the defeated German troops. In the hectic days that followed, these demands were largely ignored. On Christmas Eve, a battle between the Imperial army and a rebellious naval unit, helped by several thousand Berliners brought to the scene by the Spartacists, ended with the Imperial army in retreat. On Christmas Day, the Spartacists and another huge crowd took over the offices of the Socialists' paper _Vorwärts_ and used its presses to issue the call "All power to the workers and soldiers!" The Spartacist leaders, Karl Liebknecht and Rosa Luxemburg, agreed to a merger of their group with various small groups who had repudiated the new Socialist government, and a labor unit called the Revolutionary Shop Stewards. The merger gave birth to a new party in the last week of 1918: the Communist Party of Germany (KPD). Blücher, who had joined the Spartacists, joined the party.

The Communist party came into existence in the middle of a bitterly cold winter.[12] The Allies continued to blockade German ports, and food became scarcer and scarcer. Nonetheless the Communists called daily demonstrations in Berlin and tried to create the unity on the Left that Rosa Luxemburg thought should precede any mass action. Despite her strategy, on 5 January the situation took a new turn: a group of leftist leaders, calling themselves the Revolutionary Committee, proclaimed a general strike. Most of Berlin's factories and facilities were closed; some 200,000 demonstrators filled the streets and seized the railroad stations and newspapers. Red flags flew, and the rifles the Spartacists had been collecting since November appeared. "Spartacus Week" had begun. But by its end the government's miscellany of troops and volunteer units, the *Freikorps*, under the direction of the Socialist government's minister of war, had gained the upper hand in Berlin, after brutally blasting the Spartacists out of their various strongholds with heavy artillery. Karl Liebknecht and Rosa Luxemburg were captured on 15 January and murdered. As Hannah Arendt noted in an essay on Rosa Luxemburg, her death "became the watershed between two eras in Germany; and it became the point of no return for the German Left." When the election called for 19 January was over, the Social Democrats held a majority of the Reichstag seats, and the revolutionaries were forced to retreat and regroup; but they were unable, without their brilliant leaders, to prevent what Arendt called "the swift moral decline and political disintegration" of the party.[13]

Heinrich Blücher participated, with the Spartacists and then the Communist party, in the unsuccessful battles and strikes of the spring of 1919. He briefly returned to his teacher's training at a *Lehrerseminar* during the lull in the party's activities in the summer of 1919, though he never finished the program. From 1918 through the worst inflation years, 1922 and 1923, he worked occasionally as a reporter for non-Communist and Communist papers, spending what time he could on his own education.

As an adolescent, Blücher had developed a hunger for learning—not for schooling, but for learning. Whenever he had money, he bought books; whenever he could avoid work, he did—and read. His political activity had begun when he was still an adolescent, and it took a very unusual form: he, a Gentile, joined a Zionist youth group, a section of the *Blau Weiss*. At fifteen, he began to discover German poetry and read Shakespeare's plays in German translation. During the war he took up what Brecht referred to as the "Classics," Marx and Engels, and then found in the work of Trotsky the ideas which were later at the center of his own political theories. When the turbulence of the brief revolution had passed, he sporadically attended lectures at various Berlin institutions in an enormous range of subjects. At the University of Berlin he heard the lectures on military history given by Hans Delbrück, editor of the famous *Preussische Jahrbücher* and one of the Weimar Republic's most outspokenly critical supporters. This experience he shared with Kurt Blumenfeld; when they met in 1941 in New York, they both waited impatiently for Delbrück's famous axiom, "Germany cannot win a war on two fronts," to be proven a second time.

When the Hochschule für Politik was founded in 1920, Blücher attended lectures on political theory at that remarkable institution, which was alone among Germany's institutions of higher learning in accepting students without *Gymnasium* degrees. At the Berlin Academy of Fine Arts, he occasionally heard lectures on art history, one of the great passions of his later, calmer life.

Blücher's haphazard, piecemeal formal education, complemented by extensive reading, was of no help to him in the Communist party. He had remarkable skill as an orator but he was not trusted by the leadership that eventually emerged after the deaths of Liebknecht and Luxemburg. Rosa Luxemburg's consort, Leo Jogiches, became the party chairman, but was killed in the spring of 1919. Paul Levi, a lawyer and also a disciple of Luxemburg's, assumed the KPD leadership, but was forced out early in 1921. Levi's successors, Heinrich Brandler and Walter Stocker, were also committed to Rosa Luxemburg's strategies, but they were even less able than Levi to control the increasingly powerful and militant Moscow-backed Left Opposition within the party or to halt the domination of the KPD by the Russians. The party suffered a crucial defeat during the "March Action" of 1921 and then another, while Brandler was at the head of the party, in the "German October" of 1923.

Heinrich Brandler, who was Blücher's closest friend, had spent some months in prison after the March Action, and then spent a year in Moscow. After he returned to Germany and assumed the party leadership in 1923, Brandler was reluctantly prepared for what his Russian backers hoped would be a "second October" in the fall of 1923. Germany was torn by mounting inflation, by the French occupation of the Ruhr, by increasing hostility between industry and labor, by a series of strikes, and by the resignation of one government, under Cuno, and the accession of another, under Stresemann; it was hoped in Moscow and among the Berlin-based German Left Opposition members that a revolutionary situation could be made out of this chaos. Russian organizers and advisors came to Germany early in the fall of 1923, and some German party members went to Russia for military training. Some of Blücher's friends, who did not meet him until after this period, were under the impression that he had been sent to Moscow for training; others thought not. But all agreed that his role in the KPD in 1923 was to write and distribute in Germany a series of small pamphlets on armaments and guerrilla-warfare tactics.

The "German October" failed to become a "second October." A violent uprising in Hamburg was crushed, and the KPD was banned—along with a group called the National Socialists, or Nazis, which had tried to stage an opposition *Aktion* in Munich. Brandler was severely criticized in Moscow (his star set along with Trotsky's) and he and his followers were eventually excluded from KPD leadership positions as the Left Opposition, headed by Ruth Fischer, took over; the KPD was bolshevized. It was during this shift that, as Hannah Arendt noted in one of her more biting remarks, "the gutter opened, and out of it emerged what Rosa Luxemburg would have called 'another zoological species.' "[14]

The decline and fall of the German Communist party, as Blücher recounted it, provided Hannah Arendt with a clear image—one she never failed to refer to—of what any revolution cannot be without: spontaneously organized, locally based councils, or *Räte*, which are controlled neither by existing party councils—in this case, those of the Social Democratic party—nor by external, foreign organizations, in this case, the Moscow party. The *Räte* which had been crucial to the early stages of the German revolution were, as the revolution developed, left behind. By the fall of 1923, the central tenet of Rosa Luxemburg's theory of revolutionary change that "the organization of revolutionary action can and must be learnt in revolution itself, as one can only learn swimming in the water" had been completely forgotten. In 1923 the German and Russian leaders of the Communist party tried to "make" a revolution. And, as they did so, they grew more and more removed from their followers. Their power was not rooted, it did not come from below. Throughout her life as a political theorist, Hannah Arendt was harshly critical of any leadership that abandoned its local base, the true source of its power. In Paris and during her early years in America, she focused her criticism of leadership on the Jewish leadership, which she thought lacked awareness of the need for Jewish solidarity; later, she extended her criticism to the leaders of postwar Europe, of Israel, and finally of her adopted country, America.

Heinrich Brandler provided Blücher and Arendt with a paradigmatic case of a revolutionary leader gone astray. A proletarian, born in Austria-Hungary in 1881, the son of a bricklayer, Brandler was an honest, simple man, an experienced local labor-union organizer, but quite unprepared for the national leadership role into which he was thrust after Jogiches's death and Levi's expulsion. He lost his connections with his people, the workers, and became a puppet of the Comintern. Returning to Germany after nearly four years of exile in Moscow, he tried to reverse the bolshevizing trend in which he had been caught; but his Kommunistische Partei Deutschlands-(Opposition), founded in 1928, had no influence.

Heinrich Blücher joined Brandler's opposition group, the KPO, in Germany and then in Paris, where many of "the Brandler Group" went after 1933, but his friendship with Brandler deteriorated. Brandler was surprised, when he returned from Moscow in 1928, to find that his old friend was no longer the same. Blücher tried to tell Brandler about his educational pursuits and the friends he had made during the five intervening years and was greeted with an incredulous "Du spinnst! [You're crazy!]."

What Heinrich Blücher had done, from Heinrich Brandler's point of view, was to involve himself with a lot of *Luftmenschen* ("air people") of intellectual and artistic sorts, hardly sons of the proletariat. At the center of his circle was a son of Jean Winterfeld, a well-known and recently quite wealthy circus-ringmaster-turned-operetta-composer and conductor. Robert Winterfeld, who called himself Robert Gilbert, had attended a Communist rally where Blücher spoke and had been awed. Gilbert sought out Blücher after the meeting and, thinking that he was paying him a great compliment, told him that he was a natural politician. Blücher, offended, retorted: "Ich bin ein Philosoph!" Once this matter was set straight, the philosopher and the songwriter, filmmaker, and man-about-cultural-circles became fast friends and remained so until Blücher's death in 1970. With the friendship, and the munificent patronage that attended it, Blücher was free to explore all the "craziness" of Berlin.

Together, Blücher and Gilbert joined a circle around the poet Arno Holz, a founding father of the movement called Naturalism—dedicated to "raw life" rawly presented—who, by the mid-twenties, had decamped and become a prominent figure among the Expressionists and a producer of enormous, Whitmanesque, political panoramas in verse. In the diverse ranks of the Expressionist painters, Emile Nolde and Hans Hofmann were the strongest influences upon a young man both Blücher and Gilbert admired deeply, Karl Heidenreich. After his years of study with Hofmann, Heidenreich became one of the most independent producers of what the Nazis later called degenerate art. Few of Karl Heidenreich's paintings survived the Nazis' war against artists, but a few of those that did made their way into a New York retrospective for which Hannah Arendt and Heinrich Blücher wrote a catalogue foreword, a testimonial to their friend's rare strength and dedication. They praised in Heidenreich the qualities that Blücher met for the first time among his Berlin artist friends and that Hannah Arendt adapted with such fruitfulness for her own work: "He was able to preserve that quality of *Innigkeit* [intense inwardness] . . . which inspires the very best of German poetry. . . . He understood and knew how to use Juan Gris's great statement: 'if I am not in possession of the abstract, with what am I to control the concrete? if I am not in possession of the concrete, with what am I to control the abstract?'"[15]

Karl Heidenreich was best known in Berlin for his dark, brooding portraits of cultural celebrities, but he also worked with the organization which became a source of endless fascination to Blücher and Gilbert: Universum Film A. G., or UFA. This was a conglomerate of film companies established by General Ludendorff in 1917 as a propaganda factory, inherited by the governing socialists after the war, and then given its independence by them. Through the 1920s UFA was the Hollywood of Berlin. But it suffered from the competition imported into Germany in the late 1920s from the American Hollywood and was eventually bought out and turned to other propaganda purposes by Adolf Hitler's wealthy patron, Alfred Hugenberg. Heidenreich, like many of the most talented artists in Berlin, was drawn into the circle of the UFA during its unrestricted, experimental years to paint stage sets.

Blücher was and remained a dedicated moviegoer, and he wrote film reviews for various small newspapers. His love of the fruits of both the

Berlin Hollywood and the American one, his memory catalogue of film data of all sorts, and his passion for singing film scores and pop songs were tastes always a little foreign to Hannah Arendt. But the poetry and songs in which Robert Gilbert captured the days of his early friendship with Blücher were part of her vast recollection of German lyricism. "These verses," she wrote when a collection of Gilbert's poems was published in America the year after the war, "are a vivid reminder that Berlin was not the Reich, though the Reich certainly conquered and destroyed Berlin. For they recapture the dialect—a language with its own peculiar humor and full of strange, indirect, involved patterns of speech—and the mentality which formed it—extreme skepticism and keenness of mind together with simple kindness and great fear of sentimentality."[16] While Blücher rejoiced in the proximity to kitsch of many of Gilbert's poems, Hannah Arendt was more cautious: "He ... dares to touch the borderline of Kitsch and skirt the gutter—being safe against it as only a genuine poet can be. This wonderful carelessness has great precedents in German poetry. Gilbert has inherited the carelessness and, incidentally, the convincing inner goodness of Heine, the happiness and decency of Liliencron, the political passion and courage of Arno Holz."

Hannah Arendt was careful to locate Gilbert among his proper poetic peers, but she also acknowledged that it was in the company of his father, a musician in variety shows as well as a horseback-riding, circus ringmaster before he won fame and fortune for his pop songs and operettas, that Gilbert came by his "uncanny facility with rhyme and tremendous musicality." And whether it was the elder's *Puppchen, du bist mein Augenstern* ("Baby, you are the twinkle in my eye") or the younger's workingman's blues, the measure of success was popularity: their songs were sung and whistled all over Berlin. Arendt particularly admired the Gilbert song she called "the funeral song of the twenties, the street song of the unemployed," which starts off with:

> Keinen Sechser in der Tasche
> bloss'nen Stempelschein.
> Durch die Löcher der Kledasche
> kiekt die Sonne rein.
>
> [Not a penny in my pocket,
> Just my number for the dole.
> My clothes they got holes
> The sun peeks through.]

Gilbert possessed a lyricism Arendt thought "indestructible, as long as the sense of wonder we learned in childhood remains." The true poets not only have this wonder, but can celebrate it, "without pomp and circumstance." Gilbert did so with Brechtian nonchalance:

> Und wo andre längst zu Haus sind,
> wo se wohl teils Mann,
> > teils Maus sind,
> steh'ick permanent verwundert
> > mit der Klinke in der Hand.

> [While the other man is in his house
> where he is part human,
> > part mouse,
> I stand in wonder permanent
> > with the doorknob in my hand.]

What Arendt called in English "carelessness" is the *Gleichgültigkeit*, the unconcern or insouciance, about which she so often wrote in her own early poems—where it is a topic rather than a manner! In Gilbert, and in Blücher, she met this quality incarnate. And a story she was fond of telling captures the quality, which has nothing to do with apathy or passive indifference and everything to do with freedom. Blücher was very ill, and a doctor had rendered the verdict that his illness would lead, fairly shortly, to his death. Blücher announced this to his friend, and Gilbert, after pausing for only a moment said, "Well, if you are going to die soon, why don't we first take a trip to Italy?" Off they went, hitchhiking.

The stories Heinrich Blücher told Hannah Arendt about his political activities and about his excursions into Expressionist circles were, from the beginning of their relationship, part of what they came together after work to discuss. The story of Blücher's personal life came more slowly. He was always reticent about his family, though he was given to stating as a certainty what was by no means certain—that his father was descended from the Prussian general Gebhard Leberecht von Blücher, one of the outstanding military opponents of Napoleon, who had been made a prince shortly before Waterloo, his last campaign. Blücher was given to circumventing questions about his ancestors by answering in a mode that echoed his years among the Expressionist admirers of the Fauves: "I was born of a wild horse!"

From her home in the suburb of Wallitz, Blücher's mother occasionally came to visit him in Berlin, and she was sometimes invited to stay at Gilbert's. These visits were not frequent, as Blücher usually kept his mother at a distance from his friends, and some of them thought he behaved callously toward her, though they acknowledged that his situation was difficult. Klara Blücher doted on her son and wanted to be included in his life; she was demanding, unpredictable, perhaps mentally unbalanced. Blücher himself once explained to a friend that he feared having children of his own lest they be mentally ill, hereditarily *geisteskrank*. After fleeing from Germany in 1933, he never saw his mother again, and only learned after the war that she had died, in Wallitz, in 1943.[17]

Much of what Hannah Arendt slowly learned about Blücher's relations came to light as she met his Berlin friends in Paris. One of the first people he invited to their hotel room was a former Brandlerite, one of Karl Heidenreich's closest friends, Peter Huber. But it was some time before she learned how Blücher and Huber had met. Lotte Sempell, after having been Blücher's friend for months, discovered that he was married to Natasha Jefroikyn, the sister of Huber's wife. This information was later passed along to Hannah Arendt. But neither Hannah Arendt nor Lotte Sempell knew until 1937 that Natasha Jefroikyn was Blücher's second wife.

Lotte Sempell, as a non-Jewish German citizen, was free to cross the German border, so she became her exiled friends' messenger to those they had left behind in Germany. When Blücher and Hannah Arendt decided to obtain divorces, Lotte Sempell was asked to assemble the documents necessary for his divorce from Natasha Jefroikyn. At his mother's house, where she went for his birth and marriage certificates, Lotte Sempell noticed a wedding photograph in which she recognized Blücher. The young wife was Lieselotte Ostwald, Blücher's mother explained. When Lotte Sempell returned to Paris, Heinrich offered a brief explanation to her and Hannah Arendt: he had married Lieselotte Ostwald when he was too young to know better and divorced her not long after. He had married Natasha Jefroikyn under quite different circumstances. She and her sister, who had been born in Lithuania and moved to Berlin in 1920, both secured German citizenship by their marriages. After their marriage in 1932, Blücher and his wife lived together only intermittently and in the fall of 1935—as Blücher's French divorce papers put it—their *rapports conjugaux* ended.

The Jefroikyn sisters' brother, Israel, who had settled in Paris and become a French citizen, was a successful travel agent and, during the early 1930s, the respected president of the Fédération des sociétés juives de France, an organization designed to coordinate the activities of over fifty Parisian immigrant mutual-aid societies and *Landsmanschaften*. When the Jefroikyn sisters came to Paris after 1933, their brother made the acquaintance of his "Aryan" brothers-in-law and was helpful to all. Jefroikyn was impressed by Blücher, though he knew little about Blücher's Parisian life. Indeed, he knew so little that Hannah Arendt was rather embarrassed when Israel Jefroikyn, whom she had met through her work at the Zionist organization Youth Aliyah, told her one day how much he admired his sister's intelligent husband, without the slightest idea that this intelligent man was currently living with Hannah Arendt.

Another facet of Blücher's rich Berlin life turned up in the person of Fritz Fränkel, a Freudian psychoanalyst of Adlerian inclinations, who came to the discussion circle at Walter Benjamin's. Blücher had been Fränkel's assistant for a brief time in Berlin, and from his experience he extracted one tale—for Hannah Arendt's education and later for the college students he taught in America. This staple of Blücher's pedagogy concerned a woman who had taken to her bed shortly after the birth of her seventh child and refused to move or talk. Dr. Fränkel made no headway with the psychoanalytic "talking cure." So, as a last resort, he came with his assistant, Heinrich Blücher, a can of kerosene, and a bundle of rags. The rags were placed by the woman's bed, doused with kerosene, and set afire, whereupon the woman jumped out of her bed and ran across the room screaming. A neurosis, Blücher was informed, can be used to overcome feelings of inferiority or to gain power over others. According to Adler, it is so used when no compensation is successful and no overcompensation attainable.

Blücher was very impressed by the Fränkel shock technique, and he developed many less drastic variations of it himself. His fine sense for the curative powers of the unexpected was apparent to Hannah Arendt when, one morning soon after they began to live together, he offered her the opposite of the solicitous concern she had always been able to obtain from her mother. Since her adolescence, Arendt had begun her days in a melancholy mood, the residue of her nighttimes of bad dreams. Only slowly and with the aid of several cups of coffee could she reach a less dark and irritable state. On this day the limit of Blücher's patience was reached and he simply left Arendt in her mood, went back to bed, and fell immediately into an untroubled sleep. Unlike Günther Stern—or August

Varnhagen—Blücher learned slowly about his wife's "shadows." But he did so by not pressing her, not asking concernedly; what she responded to was the Berliner's "simple kindness and great fear of sentimentality."

Blücher responded to his own difficult family situation and lack of formal education not with a neurosis but with formidable compensations. His self-education was haphazard but wide and deep. "You had not been with him for five minutes before you learned something," Anne Weil remembered. And his friends—Gilbert, Heidenreich, Fränkel, and many others—who were loyal and to whom he was loyal—were a family, or as he called them, a tribe. Hannah Arendt never wrote a personal portrait of her husband, but her attitude toward him as a man and as her partner must lurk between the lines of a sketch she made of Rosa Luxemburg's companion, Leo Jogiches. Each of the details she chose from the wealth of stories she knew about Leo Jogisches and Rosa Luxemburg has a corollary in Blücher's life and in Arendt's attitude toward him:

He was definitely *masculini generis*, which was of considerable importance to her. . . . He was definitely a man of action and passion, he knew how to do and how to suffer. It is tempting to compare him with Lenin, whom he somewhat resembles, except in his passion for anonymity and for pulling strings behind the scene, and his love of conspiracy and danger, which must have given him an additional erotic charm. He was indeed a Lenin *manqué*, even in his inability to write, "total" in his case. . . . We shall never know how many of Rosa Luxemburg's political ideas derived from Jogiches; in marriage, it is not always easy to tell the partners' thoughts apart. But that he failed where Lenin succeeded was at least as much a consequence of circumstances—he was a Jew and a Pole—as of lesser stature. In any event, Rosa Luxemburg would have been the last to hold this against him. The members of the [Polish revolutionary] peer group did not judge one another in these categories. Jogiches himself might have agreed with Eugene Levine, also a Russian Jew though a younger man, "We are dead men on furlough." This mood is what set him apart from the others; for neither Lenin nor Trotsky nor Rosa Luxemburg herself is likely to have thought along such lines.[18]

Heinrich Blücher who had jokingly listed his profession on German identity forms as *Drahtzieher* ("stringpuller") and used the term as one of his code names in the Communist party, loved conspiracy and danger, and this must have given him an added erotic charm. After he left Berlin, his "total" inability to write and the frustration of his talents as a public speaker with no party or public forum made him a revolutionary *manqué.* His failure as a political figure was a product more of circumstances than lack of stature; he was a man of action who had no field for action. He may not have thought of himself as a "dead man on furlough," but he certainly was, in Paris and during his early years in New York, a man on an unwanted leave of absence, a man with the carelessness of those who realize that they do not live in times where death has much personal meaning. Hannah Arendt, who loved pariahs, who always tried not to judge in the categories of worldly success, seldom held his "failures" against him. She, too, could overlook much in gratitude—for "in marriage it is not easy to tell the partners' thoughts apart."

Blücher was volatile and opinionated; in argument, as one of his friends put it, he "went off like a little field artillery piece." But he also had a deep calm that was rooted in independence: from material possessions, in which he had almost no interest, from obligations of the soul-wearying sort, and from fixed attitudes. "Pessimists are cowards and optimists are fools," he often announced to his American students. This detachment did not imply a lack of standards or an uncritical stance; on the contrary, he was so critical that some found him impossible to abide, while a few hardy ones had the reaction that Hannah Arendt's American friend Rosalie Colie described: "He is always so critical and grim and somehow so determined about the inadequacies of things that I emerge soaked in some sort of idealism. Funny."[19]

Many of Blücher's Berlin friends came into the life he shared with Hannah Arendt. Their circles drew together; the "tribe" began to grow. And in this tribe, there was no place for the national differences, cultural barriers, ideological clashes, or class conflicts that gave the European world around it, as Arendt said, "the sordid and weird atmosphere of a Strindbergian family quarrel."[20] The tribe was a little island of cosmopolitanism and pariah-consciousness; as Rahel Varnhagen had said, quoting Goethe, "only galley slaves know one another."

Lotte Sempell, who had lost Blücher to Hannah Arendt, received them back together. Hannah Arendt became her tutor in philosophy and her companion for walks in the Jardin du Luxembourg. At a 1938 performance of a Yiddish theater troupe, Chanan Klenbort acted as interpreter for Arendt, Blücher, and Lotte Sempell. Lotte Sempell ended the evening with Klenbort, and eventually the unlikely match between a German bourgeois Protestant and a Polish shtetl Jew, which resulted in marriage and two children, was made. Lotte Sempell introduced Arendt and Blücher to the woman who later became her own closest friend, Kaethe Hirsch. The daughter of Ernst Hirsch, owner of a famous Berlin news agency, had taken a job delivering books by bicycle for the Paris lending library Biblion where Lotte Sempell went for German books. Renée and Walter Barth also came into the circle—another example of a marriage between a German Jewess of the middle class and a Protestant proletarian; Renée's mother Minna, a physician, supplied the tribe with medical advice and helpful connections among her French patients.

Through the Russian-born essayist and novelist Nina Gourfinkel, who was then a social worker and also a contributor to the Zionist periodical *La Terre Retrouvée*, Hannah Arendt made the acquaintance of a group of Russian political refugees who had left their homeland in the early 1920s. She particularly admired the work of the literary critic Rachel Bespaloff who later emigrated to America and took a position at Smith College, where she produced what Arendt thought one of the most interesting pieces ever written on Homer's *Iliad*. [21] Bespaloff's work on the *Iliad*, which is built upon a comparison of the Greek epic with Tolstoy's *War and Peace*, evokes the Christian-existentialist atmosphere of the Russian émigré circles around the philosophers Nicolas Berdyaev and Lev Shestov. Arendt shared with these Russians their intense admiration for Kierkegaard and she admired Berdyaev's *The Origin of Russian Communism*, first published in 1937, but she did not frequent their circles. She was once invited to a soiree at the home of the philosopher Gabriel Marcel, where Berdyaev was present; but when she told her friends about this evening what stood out in her memory was not the conversation but the impressive use to which the Marcels put their bathtub: they filled it with potatoes, and any of the guests who happened to be short of funds and food was invited to help himself.

Occasionally, the German émigré friends met the people with whom Hannah Arendt worked, first at Agriculture et Artisanat and then at Youth Aliyah. It was at the rue Durance office of Youth Aliyah, an organization which, like Agriculture et Artisanat, prepared young émigrés for life in Palestine, that Hannah Arendt met Juliette Stern. The wife of a very wealthy French sugar manufacturer, Juliette Stern had made a journey to Palestine early in 1935 and returned to Paris a committed Zionist. "I felt attached to this collectivity by distant fibers I thought long broken," she wrote in a 25 June 1935 article for *La Terre Retrouvée*. This experience of finding "her people" after growing up in a secular, assimilated, upper-class environment impressed Hannah Arendt; Juliette Stern was quite free of the common French suspicion of non-French Jews, and she enjoyed being introduced to Arendt's friends, the Klenborts and the Weils.

While in Palestine, Juliette Stern made the acquaintance of Henrietta Szold, an American of German Jewish ancestry who had been charged by the 18th Zionist Congress, when it met in 1933, with founding Youth Aliyah. Henrietta Szold was seventy-three years old at the time and had many, many achievements to her credit—foremost among them the medical services and training centers in Palestine her women's organization, Hadassah, had sponsored. Despite her age, she felt that she could not refuse to lead a project for saving children. The organization of Youth Aliyah was painfully slow, and Recha Freier, the Berlin rabbi's wife who had originally envisioned the program, had to keep pressing the Jewish leadership to hurry.[22] By 1935 Henrietta Szold was ready to seek financial support for Youth Aliyah from the Hadassah in America; the American women promptly responded by organizing local and national fund-raising efforts. In Paris, funds were collected for the Parisian office by the Cercle Pro-Palestinien Kadimah, under the direction of Hannah Arendt's friend Juliette Stern. The total funding was sufficient to provide Hannah Arendt, *secrétaire générale* of the Paris office, with a salary that also supported Blücher, who could not work legally in France.

Refugees from all over Europe came to the offices of Youth Aliyah hoping to be able to send their children to Palestine. Hannah Arendt, too, hoped to be able to go to Palestine, to see her people's refuge for herself. Her chance came in 1935, when she was assigned the task of accompanying a group of Youth Aliyah trainees. She and her charges set out by train from the Gare de Lyon in the late spring. They journeyed to Marseilles, where they boarded a ship bound for Haifa. The ship not only took Arendt to Palestine, it took her to her first view of a Greek temple. During a two-day stopover in Sicily, she and her young companions travelled to Syracuse, where she added to their training in the history of Judaism an introduction to Greek culture. The ruins of Syracuse always remained vivid in her memory, and she later returned several times, once with Blücher, to visit them again.

After she delivered her charges to their new homes, the Youth Aliyah work villages, Arendt made a brief visit to her cousin from Königsberg, Ernst Fuerst, and his wife Kaethe, who had arrived in Palestine only a few months before and were living in Jerusalem. Arendt toured the city and then set out on an arduous overland journey to Petra, in what was then Trans-Jordan. There she saw her first Roman temple, a beautiful building with a rose-colored facade cut into the limestone walls of a narrow wadi, and beyond it, laid out on the plain of Petra, were the ruins of a city that had once been a crossroads for Greek, Egyptian, and Arab traders.

Arendt's business was with the Zionist organizers of Youth Aliyah. She renewed her acquaintance with some of Blumenfeld's associates, such as Henrietta Szold's coworker Georg Landauer, who had been a member of the Zionist Organization of Germany, and Hans Levy. But when her business was finished, she was eager to see not Zion, but the land where many ancient peoples had settled and built cities and where many modern peoples lived. She was, and continued to be, better informed about the Romans and the Greeks than she was about the ancient Hebrews. Arendt was a Zionist for practical political reasons, because she knew that her people needed a place to live, and not for religious or cultural reasons. She was enthusiastic about the social and political opportunities Palestine offered Jewish settlers, but she opposed what she later called "Palestine-centered Zionism."

When she returned to Paris, Hannah Arendt spoke to the Parisian groups that supported Youth Aliyah and praised the new communities she had visited, the work villages and the kibbutzim. She saw in these communities "political experiments" she admired and supported. But, to her friends in Paris, she expressed reservations of a personal sort. And, many years later, in a letter recalling her visit to Palestine, she expressed the same personal uneasiness: "I still remember my first reaction to the kibbutzim very well. I thought: a new aristocracy. I knew even then... that one could not live there. 'Rule by your neighbors,' that is of course what it finally amounts to. Still, if one honestly believes in equality, Israel is very impressive."[23] The ambivalence, the political admiration and personal reservation, that she felt on her first visit to Palestine remained with her all her life; but so did a feeling she expressed in the same letter: "I knew that any real catastrophe in Israel would affect me more deeply than almost anything else."

*Lessons in Fascism*

The year 1936, when Hannah Arendt and Heinrich Blücher met and their discussion group began, was, as Blücher's Berlin friend the journalist Heinz Pol wrote, "a year of destiny for Europe."[24] The Locarno treaty was abrogated as Hitler's troops occupied the Rhineland without resistance. Soon after the Spanish Civil War began, Leon Blum's Popular Front government joined Britain, Germany, Italy, and the USSR in a nonintervention pact, which both Germany and Italy violated by aiding Franco's forces, while the Russians aided—and tried to control—the Spanish Republicans. For the French and British, who remained un-aligned, a pattern of capitulation was set, and it continued for the next three years, until the outbreak of the Second World War.

Fascist groups had organized in France after the brief period of strikes in 1936, during the formation of the Popular Front government. Even while the Left had its brief victory, France was being undermined from within. Many people of the Right who before Hitler had been anti-German and pro-war shifted toward Fascist groups—which were cer-tainly not anti-German and certainly not pro-war. The Fascist groups were of many sorts; though most were small, together they made up a powerful force. The Croix de Feu, under the leadership of Colonel de la Rocque, included not only wearers of the Croix de Guerre but many young aristocrats and members of the wealthy middle class. After the Popular Front banned the Fascist leagues in June 1936, the Croix de Feu turned into the *Parti Social Français*, led by Jacques Doriot, a former Communist turned self-styled führer, whose followers swore him an oath of personal allegiance. Both of these parties agreed in the demand that France avoid war with Germany, in hatred of the British, in fervent opposition to Russia, and in their willingness to work with German agents and business representatives in Paris. As Hannah Arendt described it in *The Origins of Totalitarianism*, their position was "peace even at the price of foreign domination."[25]

At the opposite end of the political spectrum was the Communist party, which had also undergone a shift since 1933. "The extreme Left had forgotten its traditional pacifism in favor of old nationalist slogans," Arendt thought. Between the Fascists and the Communists lay the sham-bles of what had once been the traditional French multiparty system. These parties fragmented and finally, by the 1938 Munich crisis, even the fragments were split internally. "Each party," Arendt noted, "harbored a peace faction and a war faction." The distrust for party systems that Blücher and Arendt shared, based on the dismal example of Weimar Germany, was transferred easily enough to France.

Hannah Arendt focused her political attention, defensively, on the

French Right, where anti-Semitism was prevalent and posed a threat to organizations like Youth Aliyah. Blücher looked to the Left, as he tried to find a place to stand through the series of events that made Communism, finally, impossible for him. The domination of national party groups by Russia, which had wreaked such havoc in the German KPD, was repeated in Spain and in France. The Russian government first signed the nonintervention pact that refused help to Franco's opponents, then sabotaged the Spanish Republicans. Soon after, it conducted the Moscow Trials against the Bolshevik Old Guard and the chiefs of the Red Army. Disillusioned reports brought back to Paris by friends who had gone to Spain and the newspaper accounts of the Moscow Trials marked the beginning of the end of Blücher's commitment to Communism. He slowly, reluctantly, joined the ranks of those Hannah Arendt called "former Communists." In a 1953 article, she described them:

Communism played a decisive role in their lives. Their chief responsibility was engaged there and their prominence, as long as it lasted, was the result of political activities. Among their common characteristics is that they left the Party early; they were sufficiently informed to sense, if not to know articulately, the stages by which a revolutionary party developed into a full-fledged totalitarian movement, and they had their own criteria to judge this. These criteria may not appear sufficient in the light of what we know today. They were enough then. Important among them were the abolition of inter-party democracy, the liquidation of independence for various national Communist parties and then total submission under the orders of Moscow. The Moscow Trials, which were in many respects the turning point in this whole history, concluded the process.[26]

The former Communists were, in Arendt's understanding, a totally different breed from the postwar ex-Communists for, unlike the ex-Communists, they "neither looked for a substitute for a lost faith nor . . . concentrated all their efforts and talents on the fight against Communism."

When Blücher became a former Communist, he did not turn toward Democratic Socialism; he thought this way as impossible as it had been in Germany after Rosa Luxemburg was killed by agents of the Social Democratic minister of war. The criticism he and Hannah Arendt made of the German socialists was applicable to the French socialists and communists. Arendt summarized it in *The Origins of Totalitarianism*. "The socialists kept implicitly intact the original concept of a 'nation among nations,' all of which belong to the family of mankind, but they never found a device by which to transform this idea into a working concept in the world of sovereign states. Their internationalism, consequently, remained a personal conviction shared by everybody, and their healthy disinterest in national sovereignty turned into a quite unrealistic indifference to foreign politics."[27] The French socialists' concentration on class struggle within France and their neglect of the political consequences of their own thinking left them unable to deal with international affairs and international questions—such as the Jewish Question. This state of affairs was particularly evident during the unprecedented successes of the French trade-union movement in 1936 and 1937: social reform was the order of the day, and the results were remarkable—better hours, paid vacations, increased social services, and so forth, but these successes went hand in hand with unconcern for France's rapidly deteriorating international position. The policy on the Left was as much *pas de politique* as it was, though anti-Hitler, pacifist.

While Blücher watched the French Communists change face (and then, finally, do a volte-face when the 1939 Nazi-Soviet Pact was signed), Hannah Arendt kept a wary eye on one of the most important Fascist groups, the Action Française. This Catholic group had rallied around the reactionary officers' cliques during the Dreyfus era and founded a journal (*Action Française*) to which Walter Benjamin, also an interested observer, subscribed. The Action Française members were hostile to Freemasons, Protestants, and aliens—any aliens, but particularly Jews. They provided Arendt with an example of how anti-Semitism had developed in France since the Dreyfus Affair, a development which she contrasted with the history of anti-Semitism in Germany. She began to keep a notebook with quotations, news items, statistics, and she used it to prepare lectures. She spoke several times about the history of anti-Semitism, in German, to the German branch in exile of the Women's International Zionist Organization (WIZO). By 1937, according to a brief report in *La Terre Retrouvée*, she was confident enough of her French to address meetings of WIZO in French. With the woman who headed the German branch, she "engaged the French members of the group in a lively discussion" of German and French anti-Semitism.[28] These lectures and discussions provided her with material for the first lengthy article she published in America, "From the Dreyfus Affair to France Today."

During 1936 and 1937 organizations sprang up which were dedicated to disseminating anti-Semitic propaganda throughout France, a task that until then had been largely in the hands of the Action Française. The Propagande Nationale, the Rassemblement Anti-Juif de France, the Centre de Documentation et de Propagande, and the Mouvement Anti-Juif Continental all had headquarters in Paris, though most of them were financially backed by the World Center for the Struggle against Jewry, in Erfurt, Germany. French versions of the infamous forgery called "Protocols of the Elders of Zion" were sold in the streets of Paris, while bookstores were flooded with translations of Nazi literature. Widely read Parisian weeklies like *Gringoire* and *Candide* began to weave so many anti-Semitic threads through their pro-Fascist articles that they sounded like the most blatant anti-Semitic journal, *Je Suis Partout*, which was the major French mouthpiece of the Erfurt center. The children who came to Youth Aliyah's training centers and *Foyers* were surrounded by anti-Semitism, as many had been in their home countries. As the director of the Paris branch of Youth Aliyah, Hannah Arendt had to dedicate a good deal of her energy to protecting the children from the psychological damage such an atmosphere inflicts. According to a report in the Leftist Jewish weekly *Samedi*, she lectured on "the psychology of the Jewish child" to a meeting of WIZO social workers who had responsibility for keeping the children from delinquency and despair.

Jewish children are necessarily different from non-Jewish children, because of the pressures of exterior events, which darken the milieu in which they live. The difficulties met with, in certain countries, by Jewish parents influence the children and, little by little, the characteristics that have been imposed on the parents are transmitted to the children. Among Jewish children, there is less of the gaiety typical of their little non-Jewish comrades; they often have a more penetrating intelligence, but they are also, by temperament, more credulous; often they have the well-known Jewish complex. One should, insofar as it is possible, try to provide the children with an atmosphere which is agreeable and pleasant.[29]

This was one of Youth Aliyah's most important jobs—to provide the emigrant children with an "agreeable and pleasant" atmosphere and to help them defend themselves against both the anti-Semitism of the French and the effects of this on their parents. Youth Aliyah did not have residences for its children, like those established by Ernst Papenak and described in his memoir, *Out of the Fire*. Nevertheless, the Youth Aliyah workers had to make the children comfortable in the program and try to help the children deal with the difficult transition they made daily between the program and their parents' little hotel rooms and garrets. There were never enough visas available for the children to enter Palestine. As the war drew closer, the British government, which controlled emigration to Palestine, became even more cautious: many of Youth Aliyah's charges had to wait for months, in a terrible state of suspense, to find out whether they would be able to go to the promised land.

In this atmosphere of increasing anti-Semitism and growing fear in the emigrant communities, the reaction of the Jews in Paris to the murder of a Nazi party leader in Davos, Switzerland, by a young Jewish medical student named David Frankfurter, caused a sensation. After the February 1936 murder, several large demonstrations were organized in Paris by Jewish immigrants, and a campaign was launched by the small group of Jewish Communists to protest Frankfurter's indictment. But many organizations like the Consistoire urged the Parisian Jews not to demonstrate, for fear that public protests would bring retribution.

Hannah Arendt enthusiastically joined the effort led by the Ligue Internationale contre l'Antisémitisme to provide Frankfurter with legal assistance for his December 1936 trial. The Ligue's lawyers hoped that Frankfurter's defense could be built on the principles that the French lawyer Henri Torrès had formulated when he defended Shalom Schwarzbard in October 1927. Schwarzbard, a Yiddish poet, had shot and killed Simon Petlyura, the politician who had commanded the Cossack troops that massacred fifty thousand Ukrainian Jews during the winter of 1919. Schwarzbard had then given himself up to the French police and insisted on a trial to publicize his victim's crimes to the world. In 1927 the Comité des Délégations Juives had supplied a legal staff, under Henri Torrès, which spent over a year collecting material for Schwarzbard's defense, so that both he and the lawyer could speak fully and accurately in the name of Petlyura's victims. While working on the Frankfurter case, Hannah Arendt interviewed Schwarzbard and had Chanan Klenbort translate parts of Schwarzbard's Yiddish autobiography, published in 1934.

But the years 1927 and 1936 were of different eras. Rather than being acquitted like Schwarzbard, Frankfurter was sentenced to eighteen years in prison, and the trial was not even effective as a symbol of international cooperation against the Nazis. When the Ligue Internationale contre l'Antisémitisme tried to supply a brief and a lawyer, Moro-Giafferi, the Swiss court refused, maintaining that a foreigner could not participate in the defense—even though it had no qualms about allowing the German lawyer who had defended one of Walter Rathenau's assassins to aid *la partie civile*. After the trial, two Swiss wrote a book called *L'Affaire Frankfurter* in the attempt to agitate for a retrial, but the book was not received, in the year 1937, as a "J'Accuse."[30]

Throughout 1937 and 1938, the mood of the nearly fifteen thousand refugees in Paris grew darker and darker. The end of the Popular Front government and the decline of its support group, the Jewish Popular Front, along with the collapse of all efforts to unify the Parisian Jews, brought most refugee Jews to the conclusion that political action would be not only illegal but futile. When Hitler annexed Austria on 15 March 1938, Paris was flooded by a new wave of refugees, but the Parisian Jewish communities were reluctant to protest the *Anschluss*. For fear of retribution, their policy was, also, *pas de politique*. The Jews had often learned the lesson that protests brought new outbursts of anti-Semitism from the French; this situation was all the more grave because the Austrian crisis foreshadowed the war the French so desperately did not want. The largest emigrant organization, the Fédération des sociétés juives de France, decided to appeal to the League of Nations through the World Jewish Congress for a protest against the *Anschluss* but made no public statement in Paris. Only the young contributors, most of them children of immigrant Jews, to the anti-Nazi journal *Samedi*, a Jewish successor of the Popular Front's journal *Vendredi*, denounced the French government for · its cowardice.

Even though the majority of Parisian Jews were silent in March, accusations that Jewish "warmongers" were pressing the French government into war filled the newspapers. The accusations were painful enough, but worse were the decrees against aliens promulgated by the government in April and May. The decrees restricted the number of Jews in certain trades, prohibited Jews from opening businesses, and demanded both the repatriation of unregistered Jews and the expulsion of Jews without valid work permits. Some twenty thousand Jews were affected by one or more of the regulations. Hundreds of refugees were jailed, either because they could not afford to repatriate or because repatriation was impossible; many chose suicide rather than expulsion. The Jews hoped that the international Evian conference on the refugee problem, called for June, would result in a program for resettlement, but the twenty-three nations participating offered many excuses and very few visas. Great Britain refused to change the immigration quotas for Palestine. All Jewish action seemed futile, and pleas to the democratic nations for action—or at least for assistance to the victims of Hitler's persecutions—went largely unheeded.

In November another series of decrees was promulgated against the aliens, and these particularly affected refugees who had entered France illegally, without regular visas. These new decrees came just as the Jewish communities of major German cities were attacked in retaliation for the murder of the third secretary of the German embassy in Paris. Ernst von Rath was killed by a young, German-born, Polish Jew named Hermann Grynzpan on 9 November and that night, *Kristallnacht*, Goebbels turned loose the German SA and SS, who burned synagogues, smashed windows, looted, attacked German Jewish homes, and arrested thousands of Jewish men. The Jews of Paris were shocked and terrified. The Jewish leaders quickly assured the French that Grynzpan had no connection with the Parisian immigrant community and called upon their people to be calm, not to protest the *Kristallnacht* or the French government's silence. Again, *Samedi* was one of the only public forums for protest, and the journal's criticism was very harsh—against the French for their tolerance of anti-Semitism and against the Parisian Jewish leadership for their refusal to protest, for their inability to realize that the French government's appeasement policy was not in the interest of the Jews. The paper pleaded angrily for the French Jews to realize that Nazi Germany had "declared war upon the Jews," *all* Jews.

This was precisely Hannah Arendt's position, and she was as eager to help with Grynzpan's defense as she had been with David Frankfurter's. The two lawyers who had been involved in the defences of Schwarzbard and Frankfurter, Torrès and Moro-Giafferi, accepted Grynzpan's case. But Grynzpan turned out to be a problematic defendant. The French police held him for questioning while rumors circulated that he was psychopathic and that he had been involved in homosexual liaisons with associates of his victim. Arendt retreated from the case and did not continue her work with the Ligue Internationale contre l'Antisémitisme, but what she had learned about legal procedures and practices gave her a foundation for considering the complex legal questions involved in another trial, more than twenty years later—that of Adolf Eichmann, in Jerusalem, where Grynzpan's father turned up as a witness. In her report on the Eichmann trial, Arendt speculated on what might have happened had Eichmann been assassinated by a Jew and a trial, on the model of the Schwarzbard trial, been conducted in an attempt to acquit the murderer.

In this atmosphere of frustration and fear, calls to reembrace traditional

Jewish values were made by many rabbis and, among more secular Jews, proposals were made to "return to the ghetto," to reaffirm the community values that had made life in the Eastern European shtetlach so distinctive. The proposals took many forms. No one thought of actually reestablishing shtetlach or of returning to their old—and now Nazi-threatened—countries, but most agreed that there must be some peculiarly Jewish way to meet the crises that had come, one after the other, upon the Jewish communities, and that such a Jewish way would have to be different from the way of Gentile democratic liberalism—the way of capitulation. The return-to-the-ghetto advocates wanted to isolate Jewry from its enemies and from its inconstant, unreliable allies; to seek a separate place, like Palestine, to build up a nonassimilationist tradition; or to somehow affirm Jewish identity more compellingly. The notion of the Jews as a Chosen People was recommended not as a religious tenet but as a means of psychological defense. In an apartment just a few houses from Walter Benjamin's on the rue Dombasle the historian Elias Tcherikower and his wife hosted a discussion group where the back-to-the-ghetto proposals were debated; Tcherikower and Blücher's former brother-in-law, Israel Jefroikyn, edited a volume of essays and reflections on the idea, *On the Crossroad (Oyfin Sheidweg)*.

Hannah Arendt was very critical of the return-to-the-ghetto proposals which followed the collapse of Jewish hopes in 1937 and 1938; she heard in them an echo of Germany in 1933, when "the watchwords murmured throughout Germany were: *T'schuwah*, Return, Back to Jewishness, self-knowledge." She made a set of lecture notes comparing the 1933 German situation with the 1938 situation of the Jewish refugees.[31] Acknowledging that the Jews had found their own cultural and spiritual life a bastion in the vast economic, political, and ideological upheaval of 1933, she argued nonetheless that the 1938 collapse had produced only "apathy" and "rebarbarization": "that is what 'Zurück ins Ghetto' [now] means."[32] Calls for "self-knowledge" and "return to the ghetto" might have been reasonable when the entire world was not infected with the Nazis' anti-Semitism, but present circumstances were such that even the war in Spain, where there was no Jewish Question, had been waged under anti-Semitic banners. Arendt felt that return to the ghetto—a "withdrawal from the European cultural community"—was the wrong response when the enemies of Jewry were daily becoming more powerful and influential. It was a response based on the illusion that a people's history or tradition can be reconstituted in a vacuum and not on the political insight that Jewish reconstitution could only come about in a political context, in a struggle *against* the forces that threatened destruction. Zionism as an isolated movement was no longer enough; resistance had to be mounted. Hannah Arendt's criticism of Jewish retreat and her criticism of the socialists' lack of attention to foreign affairs were at bottom the same: *pas de politique* was a slogan of defeat and the sign of a failure to realize that Europe—not just individual countries and peoples—was threatened with ruin.

Even though Hannah Arendt spoke of political action and of *Kampf* ("struggle"), neither she nor the Zionists nor the militant contributors to *Samedi* nor the Jewish Communists would—or could—mount an effective opposition or even overtly call for war. But the immigrant community of Paris was clearly expecting war. An extremely reserved January 1939 announcement appeared in *La Terre Retrouvée:* "The WIZO [Women's International Zionist Organization]... tells us that an accord between the WIZO Central Committee in London and the Central Committee of the Youth Aliyah has been reached and that now emigration work in France with young Jews from 14 to 17 years old will be assured by WIZO." No reason for this change was given. But it was clear that the organizers of Youth Aliyah, considering the deteriorating situation, had decided to move their headquarters to London because they hoped it would be a safer launch site to Palestine. They joined forces with the existing Children and Youth Aliyah Committee for Great Britain, where Günther Stern's sister Eva Michaelis was vice-chairman. Hannah Arendt was left without a job, without even her personal means of meeting the tide of anti-Semitism—aiding emigration to Palestine. The refugees in Paris waited. As the reserved, restrained Walter Benjamin wrote to Theodor Adorno in December 1938, "it is not always possible to live here without oppressive anxiety."[33]

## On the Way to Emigration

By Christmastime of 1938, Hannah Arendt had found employment with the Jewish Agency, helping Austrian, and later Czechoslovakian, refugees in Paris. She and Blücher took an apartment in the rue de la Convention, for they expected Arendt's mother to join them. Lotte Sempell Klenbort had travelled to Königsberg soon after the *Kristallnacht* to help Martha Arendt Beerwald arrange her trip to Paris. Lotte had stayed in a Christian-owned hotel, as non-Jews were forbidden to stay in Jewish homes. She told Arendt and Blücher how Martin Beerwald had walked her to her hotel in the evenings, leaving her in front of the door where the Jews Forbidden Here sign was hung. Anti-Semitic rules were observed, but Lotte Klenbort was impressed by how stunned the Königsbergers seemed after the horrible events of the *Kristallnacht*, as though the violence and destruction had, for a moment at least, filled them with foreboding. Both she and Martha Beerwald were touched when a streetcar conductor took Frau Beerwald's hand to help her up into his car.

Martha Beerwald had made the difficult decision to leave Königsberg without her husband. Her marriage had well served the purpose of providing Eva and Clara Beerwald and her own daughter with a home. But, with Clara's death, Hannah Arendt's flight to Paris, and Eva's emigration to England in 1938, that purpose was gone. Paul Arendt's brother-in-law, Ernst Aron, had been killed by the Nazis, and he had been Martha's deepest tie to her husband's family and to Königsberg. Her tie to Beerwald was not enough to hold her when she realized, after the *Kristallnacht*, that more than the glass windows of Jewish life in Germany had been shattered.

Eva Beerwald tried to arrange for her father to join her in England, but was unable to negotiate a visa. Martin Beerwald, sixty-nine years old, less politically aware than his wife and more optimistic, was then reluctant to go to Paris. He had a sister in Königsberg for whom he felt responsible; he had no deep tie to his stepdaughter; and he could neither speak French nor imagine life in Paris. Beerwald was certainly not exceptional in his reluctance to leave his home for an unknown life. Martha's sister, Margarethe Fuerst, stayed in Berlin, hoping for the best, and paid with her life for her hesitancy to join her son in Palestine: she died in a concentration camp. Martin Beerwald was more fortunate: after living undisturbed with his sister for three years, he died of a stroke in the old people's home on Synagogenstrasse, Königsberg.

Martha Beerwald had not seen her daughter for nearly five years and had not met Heinrich Blücher. When the *Kristallnacht* convinced her that Hannah Arendt would not return to Germany and that her own life was in danger, Martha wanted nothing more than to join her daughter in Paris and to take the Arendt family possessions she had carefully saved to the sparsely furnished Arendt-Blücher household. When she left for Paris in April 1939, Martha also took with her a number of gold coins, which she had had camouflaged as buttons. The buttons were sold to wealthy French acquaintances like Juliette Stern's brother and the profits sustained the rue de la Convention apartment for many months. But another of Martha Beerwald's possessions, the Iron Cross that her brother Rafael had been awarded posthumously for his World War I service, proved a liability. After some discussion about the safest way to remove this symbol of German militarism from an apartment always vulnerable to searches by the French police, Hannah Arendt wrapped it in an old coat and deposited it in a street-corner waste can. Martha Beerwald learned very quickly that her country of refuge was no more free of anti-German sentiment than of anti-Semitism.

Martha Beerwald found friends in Paris, but she concentrated her attention on her daughter, particularly as she grew more apprehensive about the war everyone expected. Arendt felt overmothered. And tensions arose in the household as Martha Beerwald and Heinreich Blücher discovered their many differences. They were as ill-matched in temperament as they were in social background and political conviction. To Martha Beerwald, Blücher seemed a rough and somewhat lazy person, and he found her bourgeois, sentimental, and incapable of letting Hannah Arendt go her independent way.

Four months after Martha Beerwald's arrival in Paris, war was declared—though it was only the phony war, the *drôle de guerre*, the Sitzkrieg, that actually began. Even though there were no battles, the German refugees felt that France immediately lost a key engagement: the French government decided to begin interning male German nationals and *réfugiés de provenance allemande* with suspicious political pasts. Blücher, along with hundreds of other refugees, was ordered to report for transport to a *prestataire* camp organized for labor in support of the French military effort. With Peter Huber and Erich Cohn-Bendit, he was sent to Villemalard, near Orléans.

When the French government began ordering refugees to report to camps, there was little to provide consolation except poetry. Walter Benjamin had been to visit his friend Bertold Brecht in Denmark the preceding spring and returned with an unpublished poem. Hannah Arendt learned it by heart, and Blücher took their copy with him to Villemalard, where he treated it like a sacred talisman with magical powers: those of his fellow inmates who, when they read it, understood it, were known to be potential friends. Brecht's "Legende von der Entstehung des Buches Taoteking auf dem Weg des Laotse in die Emigration" was "like a rumor of good tidings," Hannah Arendt remembered; "it travelled by word of mouth—a source of consolation and patience and endurance—where such wisdom was most needed."[34] As he goes into exile, the poem recounts, the sage Lao-tse meets a customs official. To this simple man, Lao-tse's young page hands on the Master's quiet wisdom:

> ... dass das weiche Wasser in Bewegung
> Mit der Zeit den mächtigen Stein besiegt.
> Du verstehst, das Harte, unterliegt.
>
> [... that the soft water's movement will
> Conquer the strongest stone, in time.
> You understand: the hard ones are undermined.]

Blücher stayed in Villemalard for nearly two months. With his fellow internees, he was billeted in the village's barns—twenty to thirty men in each—with only rotting straw for furniture, suffering from an almost incessant cold rain. One of his barnmates, and one of the men who responded comprehendingly to the Brecht poem, was Henry Paechter, a Berliner and veteran of the Communist uprising of 1918/19. Paechter remembered Blücher as a steadying influence on his comrades; in the midst of their unreasonable situation, Blücher spent his time calmly reading Kant's *Critique of Pure Reason* and talking with those who "belonged on the same applecart."

Blücher also took it upon himself to try to calm August Thalheimer, Heinrich Brandler's right-hand man and the cofounder of the KPD-Opposition, who was interned in a camp ten miles from Villemalard.[35] Blücher and Henry Paechter arranged for a pass to visit Thalheimer's camp by telling their guards the unlikely story that they, both *goiim*, wanted to join the Orthodox Jewish residents for Sabbath services. They walked the ten miles, and found Thalheimer in a deep depression; all opposition, and certainly the KPD-Opposition, Thalheimer had believed in seemed hopeless, and he found himself surrounded by campmates for whom he felt little sympathy. What strange campfellows the Orthodox Jews and the politicos were was obvious to Blücher and his friends as they watched one of the prisoners, a strapping ex-officer of the German *Wehrmacht*, stroll disdainfully through the Orthodox Sabbath service and light his cigarette on the ceremonial menorah.

Hannah Arendt was able to send letters to Blücher and to visit him and their friends, Huber and Cohn-Bendit, several times. She tried to get the camp authorities to release him when he began to suffer from bladder stones, but the situation required string-pulling of the sort only Lotte Klenbort, who had well-placed friends, was able to provide. After she left the hospital in Rambouillet where her first child, Daniel, was born in November, Lotte Klenbort arranged Blücher's release by getting the widow of a former *préfet de police* to stand as his guarantor. While she was negotiating, the only official exit from the camps was offered Blücher by a French recruiting officer: a five-year stint in the French Foreign Legion, with no guarantee of French citizenship. Blücher shouted his refusal at the startled French official and suggested, in turn, that the French draft their internees into the regular army. Such an idea, coming from a *Boche*, was of course not well received; the only Germans who fought Hitler with the French army were naturalized French citizens, like Anne Weil's husband, Eric.

On Blücher's return to Paris, he and Hannah Arendt presented the divorce papers they had applied for a year before to a Parisian civil court and were granted permission to marry. The wedding took place on 16 January 1940, two weeks before they celebrated Blücher's forty-first birthday. The timing was good, for in the chaotic period when the phony war ended and real bombs began to fall on northern France, the machinery of Parisian officialdom was not dedicated to granting marriage certificates to refugees. And those couples who did not have marriage certificates were soon faced with a dilemma: the most desirable visas, the American "emergency visas," went only to single people—singly—and to married couples.

On 5 May 1940, announcements issued by the *Gouverneur Général* of Paris appeared in all the newspapers: all men between the ages of 17 and 55 and unmarried or childless married women who had come from Germany, the Saar, or Danzig, were to report for transport to either *prestataire* of internment camps.[36] The men were to appear on 14 May at the Stadion Buffalo and the women on 15 May at the Vélodrome d'Hiver, an enormous glass-roofed sports palladium. The dreadful orders were banally specific: the "enemy aliens" were to carry food sufficient for two days, their own eating utensils, and sacks or suitcases "weighing no more than 30 kilos." Thus equipped, the refugees were ready to become what Hannah Arendt sarcastically referred to as "the new kind of human being created by contemporary history," the kind that "are put into concentration camps by their foes and into internment camps by their friends."[37]

Leaving her mother, who was over fifty-five, at the rue de la Convention apartment, Hannah Arendt went with Chanan Klenbort to the metro stop from which Parisians of easier days had travelled to the Vélodrome d'Hiver for the sports spectacles, concerts, and expos of the Popular Front's *révolution culturelle*. Along with Fritz Fränkel's mistress, Franze Neumann, and two other women Arendt was assigned to a place on the stone bleachers at the Vélodrome; the crowd of women was divided into *loges* of four each to prevent a mass action of protest.

The week the "enemy alien" women spent at the "Vel d'Hiv" was uneventful but nerve wracking. The weather was warm and they were well treated—simply but adequately fed and provided with straw-filled sacks for beds. There was nothing to do but wait. Whenever an airplane flew over the glass roof of the palladium, the women feared a German bombardment, a torrential *Kristallnacht*, and they were in a constant state of apprehension about what would be done with them. Lotte Klenbort's friend Kaethe Hirsch, whose group was lodged next to Arendt's, kept a diary: "By the end of the week, the collective nervousness had increased. No news from the outside reached us, but we would not, we believed, be turned over to the Germans. Everyone said: 'I must always remember how it would be if, instead of these French guards, SS men stood here.' Finally something happened: we were transported. We were off, out of the ready clutches of our enemies."[38] On 23 May, the women were taken by bus across Paris, along the banks of the Seine, past the Louvre, to the Gare de Lyon; it was a wrenching journey for those who had lived in Paris for years and expected never to see it again; sorrowful and fearful, many wept.

Gurs, their destination, was a camp that had been used since April 1939 for Spanish refugees and members of the International Brigade. The 2,364 women from Paris and its suburbs were added to the camp population, as were groups from elsewhere in France; by 29 June, there were 6,356 internees in all, including some children.[39]

Life in Gurs was as monotonous as the surrounding plain stretching out in every direction, broken only by the shadow of the Pyrenees in the west. Gurs was not a labor camp. But the women worked at chores as a preventive against despair. The straw-filled sleeping sacks were shaken out in the morning; the tin cans in the latrines were emptied at the end of each day; the pots for preparing the camp *spécialité, morue sèche*—a dried, salted fish—were cleaned and whatever water was left was used by the women to wash themselves, for the spring rains had made the camp a sea of mud. Hannah Arendt insisted that her barracks-mates should keep up their appearances as best they could, that their morale would decline if they took on any of the ugliness of their surroundings. The worst pitfall, Kaethe Hirsch remembered, was the temptation to "sit around and feel sorry for yourself."

Hannah Arendt did not sit about and feel sorry for herself, but she did reach one of the lowest points in her life as she contemplated the world situation. She told Kurt Blumenfeld, in August 1952, in response to a discouraged letter from him: "In general, things go well; if only world history (*Weltgeschichte*) were not so awful, it would be a joy to live. But, then, that is the case anyway. At least, that was my opinion in Gurs, where I posed the question to myself in earnest and answered myself somewhat jokingly."[40] The question was whether to take her own life.

Hannah Arendt posed her question seriously and she was not sympathetic to others in the camp who posed the question in less than full earnest—who took the question back when greeted with a grim joke. In a discussion of émigré attitudes toward suicide, she wrote:

At the camp of Gurs where I had the opportunity of spending some time, I heard only once about suicide, and that was the suggestion of a collective action, apparently a kind of protest in order to vex the French. When some of us suggested that we had been shipped there *pour crever* [to be done in] in any case, the general mood turned suddenly into a violent courage of life. The general opinion held that one had to be abnormally asocial and unconcerned about general events if one was still able to interpret the whole accident as personal and individual bad luck, and, accordingly, ended one's life personally and individually. But the same people, as soon as they returned to their own individual lives, being faced with seemingly individual problems, changed once more to this insane optimism which is next door to despair.[41]

Over the course of the summer nearly two-thirds of the internees left Gurs: some were able to secure liberation papers in June, during the German occupation of Paris, some left when their naturalized husbands or relatives presented proper identification papers, and the rest registered later in the summer with the Nazi "Kundt Kommission" for transportation back to Germany. The Nazi commission accepted only "Aryans," but even these were not always saved by this label from persecution at home.

Hannah Arendt described her own exit in a 1962 letter to *Midstream* magazine.

A few weeks after our arrival in the camp. . . France was defeated and all communications broke down. In the resulting chaos we succeeded in getting hold of liberation papers with which we were able to leave the camp. There existed no French underground at the time (the French resistance movement sprang up much later, namely when the Germans decided to draft Frenchmen for forced labor in Germany whereupon many young people went into hiding and then formed the *maquis*). None of us could "describe" what lay in store for those who remained behind. All that we could do was to tell them what we expected would happen—the camp would be handed over to the victorious Germans. (About 200 women of a total of 7,000 left.) This happened, indeed, but since the camp lay in what later became Vichy-France, it happened years later than we expected. The delay did not help the inmates. After a few days of chaos, everything became very regular again and escape was almost impossible. We rightly predicted this return to normalcy. It was a unique chance, but it meant that one had to leave with nothing but a toothbrush since there existed no means of transportation.[42]

Those who did not leave were joined in the fall by nearly six thousand Jews from Baden and Saarpfalz who had been smuggled into France by Adolf Eichmann, with the cooperation of the Vichy government. In 1942 and 1943, most of the inmates who had survived the atrocious conditions of the camp were transported to extermination centers by the Germans.

In comparison with most of the women who left the camp, Hannah Arendt was very fortunate. She had a place to go—a house near Montauban rented by Lotte Sempell Klenbort and her friend Renée Barth—which could be reached on foot and by hitchhiking. With nothing worse than painful rheumatism as a result of her days on the roads, Arendt arrived safely. Many of the women who decided to stay were afraid to leave the one place where their husbands were sure to try to find them. Gurs was, at least, an address. Those who chose to leave without a place to go simply wandered. Arthur Koestler, in the diary he used to construct his memoir of the period, *The Scum of the Earth*, described these wanderers, the majority of the escapees. On 6 July 1940, he "saw several German émigré women previously interned in concentration camp at Gurs—now released, don't know where to go, what to do. Talked to one in a café; said she is sending telegrams to all concentration camps in non-occupied France, trying to find her husband; praying that he should not be in occupied territory. Hundreds of women in her case living in Castelnau, Navarrenx, Sus, Geronce and other villages round about.

Population calls them *les Gursiennes*. Peasants lend rooms to them or let them work in the fields *au pair*. They look undernourished, exhausted, but tidy. All wear turbans *à la mode*, colored handkerchief round the head."[43]

The whole southern region was in a state of confusion. "Two simultaneous decrees: one, by the local *préfet*, pinned on the town halls of Nararreux, Sus, Susmiou, Castelnau: All ex-internee aliens of the Camp of Gurs have to leave the *Département des Basses Pyrenées* within twenty-four hours, or else be interned again. Second, from the Government: No alien allowed to travel or move from his actual domicile." Montauban became a meeting point for escapees from camps all over France because the mayor of the town was a socialist and expressed his opposition to the Vichy government by housing former prisoners. Many residences in Montauban had been vacated in the general panic and demobilization, and the mayor turned them over to the refugees. Every mattress that did not have a Frenchman on it was moved into one of these houses, where refugees slept in conditions not unlike those of the camp barracks they had just left behind.

Hannah Arendt often travelled into Montauban from the two-bedroom house where Lotte Klenbort, her infant son, the Cohn-Bendits' son Gabriel, Renée Barth, and her infant daughter had modestly set up housekeeping. She was seeking word from Heinrich Blücher. No messages arrived. But one day, by one of World-History's fortunate tricks, they did meet. On the town's main street, they embraced joyously amidst the piles of goods—mostly mattresses—and the streams of people engaged in the endless search for food, cigarettes, and newspapers. Blücher had developed a bad inner-ear infection which had to be treated in Montauban, but he was otherwise well. His camp had been evacuated when the Germans reached Paris. The French guards had started to march the internees southward, but when German planes strafed the column, the guards sensibly decided to release their charges and flee. The internees had joined the mass migration of the French, walking, driving, bicycling toward unoccupied territory.

The Blüchers lived outside of Montauban briefly and then secured a small apartment above a photographer's studio in the town. Members of the Klenbort household, which had become even more crowded, visited, as did other friends who had escaped from the camps. Peter Huber, who had been interned with Blücher, rejoined him in Montauban. Erich Cohn-Bendit came to meet his wife and the son Lotte Klenbort had taken south from Paris. (Hannah did not make the acquaintance of the second Cohn-Bendit son, Daniel, who was born in 1945, until years later, in America.) Fritz Fränkel passed through Montauban on his way to Mexico. And Anne Weil came with her sister Katherine, whom she had, as a naturalized citizen, been able to extricate from Gurs. The sisters had managed to find a relatively safe home near Souillac in an abandoned pigeon house. Eric Weil was then in Germany as a French prisoner of war.

The Blüchers were constantly on the alert, watching every change in the Vichy government's progressively more stringent anti-Semitic measures, but they also were able to read and write in relative peace and to enjoy the beautiful, dry summer weather. Blücher continued his study of Kant, and Hannah Arendt read a rather unlikely collection of authors: Proust, Clausewitz, and Simenon. This threesome, laughably diverse though it was, contributed to the projects and concerns she took with her from France to America. She was thinking forward to what the war might mean for Europe, what new Europe might come with victory and peace. Her reading of Proust was prompted by her ongoing interest in the history of anti-Semitism: a brilliant portrait of Proust's milieu appeared ten years later in the Anti-Semitism section of *The Origins of Totalitarianism*. As she considered Europe before and after the First World War, she wrote a long memo to Erich Cohn-Bendit on the post-World War I minority treaties. This memo, too, was incorporated, greatly expanded, into *The Origins of Totalitarianism*.

Toward the end of the summer of 1940, at the moment that was for the refugees "the darkest moment of the War—the fall of France, the threat to England, the still intact Hitler-Stalin pact whose most feared consequence at that moment was the close cooperation of the two most powerful secret police forces in Europe,"[44] the reading of Simenon's *romans policiers* was not just a diversion. His insight into the structures and methods of the French police proved very helpful. Some of Hannah Arendt's friends thought of her as a person overinclined to embrace conspiracy theories and too ready to see collusion behind bureaucratic incompetence; but none of the friends who heeded her warning in October 1940 against complying with the French police order requiring all Jews to register with the nearest *préfet* was ungrateful to Simenon for stimulating her distrust of police. Those who refused to register added illegality to their statelessness, but they were not, like so many of the obedient refugees, arrested after supplying their addresses on the registration forms.

Lenin had read Clausewitz's *On War* when he considered the possibility—as Arendt put it in an essay on Rosa Luxemburg—"that war, the collapse of the European system of nation states, might replace the economic collapse of the capitalist economy as predicted by Marx."[45] Arendt, reading Clausewitz, was considering the same possibility—also hopefully. She began to analyze the nation-state in theoretical terms and her criticisms became one of the mainstays of *The Origins of Totalitarianism*. The shape of this book was not clear to her in France, but she had accepted as her task the writing of a comprehensive work on anti-Semitism and imperialism, a historical investigation of what she then called "racial imperialism," the most extreme form of the suppression of minority nations by the ruling nation of a sovereign state. She began to wonder, if Hitler were defeated, whether the war might provide the opportunity for a union of nonsovereign states, a European federation, comparable to the federation she and Blücher hoped to emigrate to, the United States of America.

In October, when the order for Jews to register with local prefects was issued, the Blüchers began their quest for visas to America. Martha Arendt travelled to Montauban from Paris, and the three made several visits to Marseilles, the visa capital of France. Eventually, the Blüchers were assured of an American emergency visa, thanks in part to efforts made on their behalf in America by Günther Stern. Arendt's position with Youth Aliyah won her special consideration, and Blücher, as her husband, was given an accompanying visa; but Martha Arendt's application was not granted at the same time. The situation was dreadful: of the 1,137 names submitted to the United States Department of State, only 238 received visas between August and December of 1940.[46] The group in France that processed the refugees' visa applications, the Emergency Rescue Committee, was frantic. And even when the precious visas could be obtained, the Vichy government very seldom granted exit permits, and both the Spanish and Portuguese governments were unpredictable about issuing transit permits to refugees who had arranged to sail from Lisbon.

Hannah Arendt and Heinrich Blücher were lucky to be granted visas, but if they had not used their wits, the visas would have done them no good. By bicycle, they went into Marseilles illegally to pick up the documents. All went well until a message was sent up to them in their hotel room: Blücher was to report to the hotel desk. They knew that the police could not be far behind. Blücher went downstairs, playing the innocent, left his key, and walked out the door before anyone could stop him. Arendt followed a little later. When she was sure that Blücher was safely settled in a café, she went back to the hotel, paid the bill, and had breakfast. When the hotel clerk came over to inquire about her husband, she staged a loud scene, first shouting that her husband was already at the *préfecture* and then accusing the clerk: "You are responsible for him." She then went to pick up Blücher, and they left Marseilles immediately.

After their narrow escape, they were forced to make preparations to leave without Martha Arendt. Luckily they ran into Nina Gourfinkel, Hannah Arendt's Russian friend from Paris, who was helping distribute Swiss food packages and American Joint Distribution Committee funds among the refugees near Montauban. She agreed to look after Martha Arendt until her visa application was processed. In January 1941, the Vichy government briefly relaxed its exit-permit policy, and the Blüchers immediately took a train to Lisbon. They waited there for three months before they were able to sail for New York with tickets provided by HIAS, a Jewish immigration organization. In May, Martha Arendt's visa arrived, and she went to Lisbon in time for a ship that docked only a few weeks after the Bluchers'. Their escape was fortunate in every way—for in June 1941 the State Department once again tightened its entry policy. One of the few descriptions of the refugees' plight available to American readers, an article in the *Nation*, 17 August 1940 chastising the anti-Fascist governments for inaction, was aptly titled "Nightmare in France." But little was done to provide escape for those less fortunate than the Blüchers and Martha Arendt.

The gravity of the situation was not apparent to people an ocean removed from it, and it was not always apparent to those caught by the conditions in Europe. Hannah Arendt often told the story of Rudolf Hilferding, whom she had known in Berlin when he edited *Die Gesellschaft*, and Dr. Breitscheid. These two former leaders of the German Social Democratic party were encamped at the Hotel Normandie in Marseilles with the precious visas for America but without French exit permits. In August 1940, friends tried to convince them to obtain exit papers under false names or escape across the Pyrenees without papers before the Germans sought their extradition. Under the notorious paragraph 19 of the German-French armistice, the French were required to surrender on demand any German in France. Breitscheid and Hilferding decided to put their trust in the Vichy government; they could not believe that the French would allow them to be extradited. But six months later,

they were transported to the border between the occupied and unoccupied territories and handed over to the Germans, who executed them.
Arendt told this story and the story of those who stayed behind at Gurs
whenever she wanted to illustrate specifically the price that may be paid
for misplaced confidence and refusal to act.

Both of these stories were cautionary tales. But it was the story of
Walter Benjamin's last year in the midst of the nightmare in France that
touched the Blüchers most personally. Having been spared internment in
the spring of 1940 by the intervention of the French poet and diplomat
St.-John Perse, Benjamin travelled from Paris to Lourdes and then to
Marseilles, where he met the Blüchers and learned that his New York
colleagues at the Institute for Social Research had secured for him an
American emergency visa. He then managed to obtain a Spanish transit
permit but lacked the French exit visa. Benjamin decided to leave France
illegally with a small group by an escape route over the Pyrenees to Port
Bou which was well known to the refugees in Marseilles. But when the
group arrived at the Spanish customs station, they learned that their
transit permits were not valid; on that very day, the border had been
closed. "The refugees were supposed to return to France by the same
route the next day. . . . During the night Benjamin took his life, whereupon the border officials, upon whom his suicide had made an impression, allowed his companions to proceed to Portugal. A few weeks later
the embargo on visas was lifted again. One day earlier Benjamin would
have gotten through without any trouble, one day later the people in
Marseilles would have known that for the time being it was impossible to
pass through Spain. Only on that particular day was the catastrophe
possible."[47]

Benjamin's Spanish border guard, unlike the one in Bertolt Brecht's
poem who received the sage Lao-tse's wisdom, was not friendly; Benjamin's border guard did not ask him to write out his *Tao Te Ching* book on
his way into emigration. But in the first year of the war Benjamin had had
time to write several pieces, and one of these was a commentary on
Brecht's poem and its hopeful message:

> . . . that the soft water's movement will
> Conquer the strongest stone, in time.
> You understand: the hard ones are undermined.

This was the sage's message as he went into exile; but, as Walter Benjamin pointed out in his beautiful commentary, the sage's wisdom was

only spoken, and then written, because the sage was asked to speak and then to write, in a spirit of friendship.[48]

Brecht's poem tells how the old Lao-tse and his young page, on their way into exile, are stopped by a customs official, who asks if they have anything to declare. They have nothing. But the boy volunteers that his old master "was a teacher"—and that, the poet says, is something worth declaring. When the official asks what the old man taught, the message about the water that wears away the stone is spoken—by the boy. The official ponders the message as the travellers go on, and then he runs after them, to beg the old man to tell him more. He is only an official, he says, but he is interested to know "how to conquer." He offers the travellers supper, pencils, and paper. The sage regards this ragged fellow and decides, as Benjamin put it, that the man has a vocation for question-asking, that he is qualified to pose questions, that he is a friend. "Those who ask something deserve an answer," says the old man; and the boy adds, matter-of-factly, "it's also quite cold, and a little heat would be good." The sage has decided to do something great for the official, but he behaves as though it were nothing. He treats "the greatest things as though they were the smallest." Benjamin saw in the sage's manner the true signs of friendship: a deep look, a careful, discriminating regard; a certain carelessness or refusal to make much ado about great things; a certain distance. "Friendship does not abolish the distance between people, but it makes it vibrant; after he does a great thing *for* the customs official, the sage has nothing more to do *with* him." The sage simply writes out the eighty-one maxims of his *Tao Te Ching* and has his messenger boy deliver them to the official, whom, Brecht says, we ought to thank, because he asked for them.

Walter Benjamin's essay on the nature of friendship was written in response to Brecht's poem. His own last testament was, like the *Tao Te Ching*, a collection of maxims. The "Theses on the Philosophy of History" were written in response to another friend's work, Gershom Scholem's *Major Trends of Jewish Mysticism*.

During the winter of 1939/40, the Blüchers and Benjamin spent many hours discussing the book on Jewish mysticism which Scholem had sent to Benjamin from Palestine. They read in Scholem's work the story of the seventeenth-century Sabbatian movement. Arendt later called this movement "the last great Jewish political activity," the outgrowth of a messianic mystical tradition which, she wrote, "seems unique in its ex-

clusive concern with reality and action. . . . Jewish mysticism alone
[among mysticisms] was able to bring about a great political movement
and to translate itself into real popular action."[49] Arendt could see a
historical precedent for a future reconciliation of Jewish history with the
history of Europe, a strong argument against the back-to-the-ghetto
theorists. And she could see a transcendental principle which, unlike
Augustine's concept of unworldly love, asserted the potential of neighborly
love within this world.

Benjamin, too, learned from Scholem's book. He framed an almost
mystical notion of "time filled by the presence of the Now (*Jetztzeit*)" and
hoped that this image of time would yield a realistic, action-oriented
sense of the past and future. The "Theses on the Philosophy of History "
were written against historicism, against attempts to isolate and reconstruct, or even relive, a past time, without regard to what came after it;
and they were written against historical materialism with its "concept of
the historical progress of mankind . . . through a homogeneous empty
time." Benjamin opposed both the false images of the past that historicism had created to guide men according to the values of victorious
peoples, and the false hopes for the future that historical materialism had
constructed by engaging in the kind of soothsaying prohibited by Judaism.
He accepted the prohibition against soothsaying, but he interpreted it in
light of a Jewish messianism he had read about in Scholem's account:
"This does not imply, however, that for the Jews the future turned into
homogeneous, empty time. For every second of time was the straight gate
through which the Messiah might enter."[50]

The last time Walter Benjamin saw Hannah Arendt and Heinrich
Blücher, in Marseilles, he entrusted to their care a collection of manuscripts, including the "Theses on the Philosophy of History" which he
hoped they would be able to deliver to the Institute for Social Research in
New York. They had the honor of being their friend's messengers.

While they waited for their ship in Lisbon, the Blüchers read Benjamin's "Theses" aloud to each other and to the refugees who gathered
around them. They discussed and debated the meaning of his moment-
to-moment messianic hope. But two years passed before Hannah Arendt
responded in writing to Benjamin's last gift of friendship. In the fall of
1942, the Blüchers began to read newspaper stories from Europe that
again brought them close to the despair they had known and surmounted
in the summer and fall of 1940. They read that the Germans had built
extermination centers, that they were using gas to kill Jews, that the entire

population of Gurs had been shipped to the killing center at Auschwitz. As the hope for Europe, the hope for "real popular action" that had sustained them, receded before these reports, Hannah Arendt wrote a poem for her dead friend, a farewell and a greeting, entitled simply "W. B."

> Dusk will come again sometime.
> Night will come down from the stars.
> We will rest our outstretched arms
> In the nearnesses, in the distances.
>
> Out of the darkness sound softly
> small archaic melodies. Listening,
> let us wean ourselves away,
> let us at last break ranks.
>
> Distant voices, sadnesses nearby.
> Those are the voices and these the dead
> whom we have sent as messengers
> ahead, to lead us into slumber.

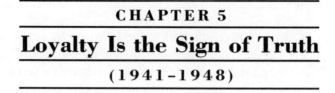

# CHAPTER 5
# Loyalty Is the Sign of Truth
## (1941–1948)

If I am not for myself, then who is for me? If I am for
myself alone, then who am I?

Hillel

### Orientations, Obligations

In May 1941, the Blüchers arrived in New York City. With the twenty-five dollars in their possession and a seventy-dollar monthly stipend from the Zionist Organization of America, they rented two small, semi-furnished rooms at 317 West 95th Street and prepared them for Martha Arendt's arrival. When the S.S. *Muzinho* docked on 21 June, they found Martha surrounded by a group of refugee children from the homes near Paris that Hannah Arendt had visited as Madame de Rothschild's secretary. Like the children, Martha Arendt was thin, haggard, exhausted from a year of hiding out in southern France, and, like the children, she was as frightened as she was relieved.

Julie Braun-Vogelstein, Martha's neighbor from Königsberg, helped the household with food packages and clothing. Paul Tillich, still as kindly as he had been in Frankfurt, directed Hannah Arendt to an organization called "Self-Help for Refugees," where she applied for a two-month placement with an American family. To survive and earn a living, some English had to be learned, and Hannah was the most likely member of the Blücher household to do the learning.

During their first week together in New York, Martha Arendt, rested enough to have recovered her sense of humor, wryly reminded her daughter of the adamant refusal she had issued during her school years in Königsberg: no, the temperamental Hannah had said, the English teacher is not for me. But the student of Greek, Latin, and French was, nonetheless, a well-equipped language learner. By the middle of July, when she had set out for the two-month stint in Massachusetts, she could manage an English postcard: "I arrived very well and am no longer frightened at all, but only highly amused. . . . Love and kisses, and letters, please."[1]

Many letters went back and forth between New York and Winchester, Massachusetts—all in German—in which the novelties of America and its language were discussed and pondered. Heinrich Blücher was not, by temperament or educational background, as well prepared to study as his wife. Until events in Europe convinced him that he would never be able to return to the Old World, he could not accept the New World as a permanent home and the new language as a necessity. Politically he was grateful for his refuge, but socially he was bewildered. He was restless, isolated, and easily irritated by his mother-in-law, who found his reluctance to learn English just one more proof that he was lazy and unsuited to the head-of-the-household role she thought he should assume. Hannah Arendt understood her husband's independent and antibourgeois spirit well; she had benefited from it while she herself was emerging from her apolitical youth and dependence on her mother. But she, too, occasionally tried to urge Blücher into English: "Und, pardon Monsieur, lernst Du noch ein bisschen Englisch?"[2]

In Winchester, as she told Blücher, Arendt found out "more about the country than about the language itself."[3] She shared her experiences in long, detailed reports on the American way. Her hostess, Mrs. Giduz, was a vegetarian, an ardent opponent of cigarette smoking, a birdwatcher, and a hiker. More Prussian, more *Wandervogel*, than the *Wandervogel* Prussians, Arendt thought, alarmed that she might have stumbled into a National Socialist home. But, as she discovered, her doting "parents" were not pro-German but simply pacifists who were completely immune to any suggestion that Americans might enter the war against Hitler on the side of the British.

After a month, the routines of the household, even when they were bent to Hannah Arendt's needs—Mr. Giduz had to take his cigarettes in the garden, while she was allowed to smoke in her room—began to be less than amusing. Arendt was irritated by Mrs. Giduz's efforts to supervise, to protect, to make her guest into the child she herself had never had. Everything about the Giduz's *Kleinbürger* ("small-town") social life was uncomfortable, including their attitude toward Negroes and their condescension, as third-generation immigrants, toward "new" Americans. But, even though their pacifism was unconscionable for a Jewish refugee struggling with newspaper reports of Hitler's successes in Europe, Arendt admired their political initiative. In the Giduz home, Hannah Arendt had her first experience of the American democratic spirit she would later praise so eloquently: she watched Mrs. Giduz sit down and write an irate letter to her Congressman protesting the internment of Japanese-born Americans. In Winchester, Hannah Arendt became aware that she could dislike American social life while admiring American political life. She formed an opinion she kept for the rest of her life: "Der Grundwiderspruch des Landes ist politische Freiheit bei gesellschaftlicher Knechtschaft [The fundamental contradiction of the country is political freedom coupled with social slavery]."[4]

Hannah Arendt bore with her American family as best she could. "I behave like a kind of steadfast tin soldier," she told Blücher. The postman brought her only respite, letters from Heinrich. Only he could share the concern that made her feel "so alone, so angry and so anxious" throughout the weeks in Massachusetts.[5]

Several days after arriving in New York, Hannah Arendt had taken the suitcase containing Walter Benjamin's manuscripts to the office on West 117th Street where Benjamin's friend Theodor Adorno and his colleagues had reestablished the Frankfurt Institute for Social Research. Alice Maier, the institute's secretary and later Hannah Arendt's friend, received her and summoned "Teddy" Adorno, who was amazed to find that Benjamin's manuscripts had survived. The writings, and particularly the "Theses on the Philosophy of History," came to play an important role in the intellectual development of the Frankfurt School; but Adorno's initial manner of dealing with them was very distressing to Hannah Arendt.

While she was in Winchester, she received a letter informing her that one of the manuscripts had been lost. Arendt was incredulous and suspected that the manuscript "had simply been suppressed."[6] This confirmed her impression that the Frankfurt institute members were not going to do what she thought they were morally obligated to do—publish Benjamin's manuscripts. She was frantic, but she did not know what to do. She wanted to send the copies she had made of the manuscripts to Salman Schocken, hoping that he would issue them "in a dignified way" through Schocken Books of Jerusalem. But this could not be done until it was clear what the institute members intended to do with their copies, "which they will never tell." Arendt finally decided to let the matter rest until overseas mail could once again be received in Palestine, and thus reach Gershom Scholem, who might be able to influence either Adorno or Schocken. "One will probably not ever be able to give [the institute members] a lecture on the subject of loyalty to dead friends," she said in a burst of anger.[7]

Hannah Arendt had never wanted to give Benjamin's manuscripts to Adorno, but she was bound by her friend's instructions. Although she was grateful to Adorno for arranging Benjamin's emergency visa to America, she clearly remembered Benjamin's fear that the institute members could not be relied upon for moral and financial support. Benjamin had become apprehensive after he submitted to Adorno an essay on Baudelaire in November 1938. The manuscript was returned to him with a call for extensive revisions. Reluctantly, Benjamin had complied, and the piece was published in a 1939 issue of the *Zeitschrift für Sozialforschung*, after being cut again and edited by Adorno. As Arendt wrote of her friend in a 1968 essay, "Benjamin was very shy in his dealings with people he had not known since his youth, but he was afraid only of people he was dependent upon." Benjamin was afraid of Adorno, and Hannah Arendt resented this deeply. She knew that, of the manuscripts she had carried to New York, Benjamin had revised one out of fear, to gain *Ruhe und Sicherheit* ("peace and quiet"), and it made her bitter to think that even this sacrifice was not enough to appease the Frankfurters, who considered Benjamin a bad Marxist, a thinker of thoughts not sufficiently dialectical.[8]

After a year, when the mail service to Palestine was restored, Arendt wrote to Scholem. Because she had not described her earlier efforts on the behalf of "Benji," Scholem, after explaining that his own efforts to stir Adorno into action had failed, simply brought the situation back to its beginning point: "Perhaps you," he suggested to Arendt, "could light a little fire under the good man?"[9] Although several Benjamin manuscripts circulated in mimeograph, not until 1945 did any of the articles appear in the institute's journal, and Benjamin's work remained uncollected until 1955. In 1968, out of continued loyalty to her dead friend, Arendt edited an English volume, *Illuminations*, and wrote an introduction for it. She was at work on a second volume, *Reflections*, at the time of her own death in 1975. Scholem and Adorno collected Benjamin's letters into two volumes in 1966. But Hannah Arendt's own carefully preserved notes from him, written in the summer before his death, were not included in the volumes, for Scholem had severed his relations with her after the publication of her *Eichmann in Jerusalem*, a book he despised.[10]

When Walter Benjamin's writings became available, many battles were fought over them. He was claimed by the Frankfurt School's heirs, though he was an unlikely Marxist, and he was claimed for Jewish literature by his Zionist friend Scholem and others, though he, like Hannah Arendt, was a pariah within the *Pariavolk*. Ideologies, he knew, and Hannah Arendt learned again and again, can prevent moments of pure recognition like the one Lao-tse and the customs official shared at the border in Bertolt Brecht's poem.

When she returned to New York from her long English lesson in Massachusetts, Hannah Arendt had more success on her own behalf than she had had on behalf of her friend. She visited the Jewish historian Salo Baron, a scholar known to many of her Berlin and Paris friends, in his Columbia University office. They discussed the situation in Vichy France, and Arendt advanced the opinion that anti-Semitism in France had been continuous from the Dreyfus Affair to Pétain. Baron suggested that she develop her thesis in an article, and, with his encouragement, she submitted her topic and her credentials in her first English letter—a stilted but impressive document—to Theodor Herzl Gaster, who was then executive secretary for the Institute of Jewish Affairs. "I enclose you a curriculum vitae out of which you perceive my general and specific qualifications."[11] She told him of her work on German Romanticism, her Varnhagen biography, and her Paris study of anti-Semitism and then cited as references Paul Tillich, Albert Salomon, Kurt Blumenfeld, Nahum Goldmann, and Martin Rosenblüth. Thereupon, with Gaster's support, she set out to write "Dreyfus und die Folgen." Gaster translated the paper and Salo Baron published it as "From the Dreyfus Affair to France Today" in the periodical he edited, *Jewish Social Studies*. Arendt was delighted. In less than a year she had in hand—to use Baron's phrase— "a *carte de visite* to the academic world."

The academic world was not, however, the world for which she wanted a *permis de sejour*. Her desire to do practical work, political work directed to the future, to a world she hoped would come into being with the end of the war, had not disappeared during the difficult three years since her job with Youth Aliyah had ended. While still at work on her Dreyfus article, Arendt began to look for a job where she would not have to rely on her still uncertain English. The German-speaking émigré community presented a complex array of possibilities, but she was careful to avoid certain sectors.[12] Chiefly, she stayed away from the group she called "Ullstein-

in-exile," the publicists who had been associated with the Ullstein publishing house in Berlin. Arendt had no patience with people who thought
of themselves as "the other Germany" and hoped to find powerful positions as *hommes de confiance* for Germany's enemies; she viewed them as
opportunists, political parvenus. Emil Ludwig, Leopold Schwarzchild,
and F. W. Foerster, Arendt thought, were typical "Vansittartites," that is,
followers of the chief "other Germany" propagandist, Lord Vansittart,
author of the *Black Record* (1941), an account of how the warlike German people had produced the Nazis and were, thus, collectively responsible for the Nazis' crimes. She was equally repelled by people like
her Berlin acquaintance, the political scientist Leo Strauss, who proclaimed adamantly that no Jew should ever, even after the war, have
anything further to do with Germany. Arendt called this "an attitude... which cares only for one's own personal dignity and honor,"
and, though it "may be satisfactory for a few scholars, it certainly cannot
satisfy a larger public." In whatever form she found it, she was opposed to
the idea of collective guilt and to any effort to read the whole German
nation out of the future of Europe. More compatible were the refugees
who advocated a future European federation, like the socialist circle
called New Beginning (*Neu Beginnen*), one of the many left-wing
splinter groups critical of the official Social Democrats in exile. Heinrich
Blücher had some contacts among the New Beginners, but Arendt felt
that, despite their reasonable future hopes for Europe, they were unconcerned about the fate of European Jewry. Despite her dissatisfaction with
the Zionist leadership in the Jewish Agency, Hannah Arendt wanted to
work with Zionist circles in America, émigré and domestic. A chance to
do this without taking on more of the wearing social work she had done in
Paris came her way in November 1941, when she was hired as a columnist for the German-language newspaper *Aufbau*.

Aufbau had begun as the news bulletin of the German Club, a New
York organization founded in 1924 to provide new immigrants with a
meeting place. As the situation of European Jews grew graver, the club
members had become concerned less with German culture and more
with the Jewish immigrant population. As they expanded their practical
efforts to aid the Jews who took refuge in America, they needed to expand
their bulletin. It was turned over to a professional editor in 1937. Two
years later, Manfred George, formerly the editor of a Berlin daily,
*Tempo*, assumed control of *Aufbau* and turned it into an impressive
weekly that reached out to German-speaking refugees all over the world

and provided the German Jewish émigré intellectuals with a forum for their political views.

Besides sponsoring *Aufbau*, the German Jewish Club, which had changed its name to the more inspiring "New World Club" at the beginning of the war, sponsored discussions and lectures on current events. Arendt's acquaintance with the newspaper began in September 1941, when she went to hear Kurt Blumenfeld speak on the question that was to command much of her attention throughout the next year: should the Jews have an army? The question had a complex history, which she set out to study and to fit into her understanding of what a Jewish politics might be.

Manfred George invited Hannah Arendt to submit an article on the issue after he recognized from an "open letter" she had submitted to the paper what a provocative journalist she might be. Her letter had been addressed to the French *littérateur* Jules Romains, who had replied heatedly to a charge made in *Aufbau*'s pages that he, like many another European intellectual, had once wished to avoid the war with Hitler through negotiated concessions. Romains's reply, in which he listed his anti-Fascist credentials and reminded *Aufbau* readers of the aid he had given to Jewish refugees in France, concluded on a self-serving note: "I hope the French Jews have not forgotten."[13]

On Romains's petulance Hannah Arendt trained a stream of unrestrained sarcasm. Surely, she chided, all "unwanted and unloved" Jews should be sorry for any harm done to the feelings of such a friend? But she was careful not to obscure her main point in mockery. The political solidarity necessary for a struggle against a common enemy is undermined when those who struggle together do not acknowledge each other as equals. Desire for gratitude, because it sets the protecting allies off from the protected allies, is a barrier to the realization that all allies are equal as anti-Fascists. Romains was behaving like the kind of philanthropist Arendt had learned to distrust in Paris or like the kind of spoiled "international celebrity" intellectual she had learned to distrust in Weimar Germany.

The need for equality and solidarity in a political struggle was also the theme of Arendt's first *Aufbau* article, "The Jewish Army—the Beginning of a Jewish Politics?" But in the article she emphasized that those equally responsible for the struggle against Hitler did not have identical needs. Because of their two-hundred-year history of assimilation and their lack of national (*völkisch*) consciousness, as well as their habit of depending upon "notables" for leadership, the Jewish people needed an army for reasons of identity as well as defense. Arendt hoped that a political strug-gle would be the beginning of a political life for the Jewish people.

Manfred George was as impressed by her article as he had been by her letter; he thought both showed "a man's strength and toughness." She soon became a regular columnist. Her biweekly columns developed ar-guments in favor of a Jewish army and summoned *Aufbau*'s readers to action. Under the recruiting-poster title "This Means You," Arendt again and again made her claim that a Jewish army would provide the Jews with a means of showing that they understood that Hitler had declared war upon the Jews; that is, with an opportunity to respond as belligerents.

Hannah Arendt, Heinrich Blücher, and Martha Arendt had to struggle to support themselves and help their friends. From her newspaper articles and the part-time teaching job she found the next year at Brooklyn Col-lege, Arendt received enough income to maintain their rooms and pro-vide food. The rooms, one for the Blüchers and one on a separate floor for Martha Arendt, did not include a kitchen, but there was a house kitchen for all the tenants to share. They ate very simply, and looked forward to the cakes Julie Braun-Vogelstein brought on Saturdays. Blücher was later fond of explaining to his students that Brecht's maxim "First grub, then ethics" meant, when stripped of Marxist irony, "First the cake and then a theory for cutting it."

Martha Arendt, who was sixty-seven years old in 1941, did most of the cooking and cleaning. She was often lonely. Occasionally, she was able to get piecework from a lace-making factory to do at home, and once she had the great satisfaction of joining the factory workers in a strike for higher pay. In the New World, where she was a worker for the first time in her life, Martha Arendt finally had a chance to practice her socialism in the marketplace. But the strike episode was atypical; she spent most of her days at home, alone. Her health was generally good during her American exile, but she had suffered a mild stroke in 1935, which had left one side of her face partially paralyzed, and the disfigurement became more and more obvious as she grew thinner and more frail. By temperament, she was lively and gregarious; during the war, she grew melancholy and anxious.

Throughout his first year in America, Blücher was disoriented. Learn-ing English was painfully difficult. He tried to find a tutor and when that failed he took to keeping notebooks where he recorded what interested him most, idioms. For page after page, he listed phrases that would not have helped even a native speaker find a job: "tickled to death," "hit the jackpot," "make a mess of it," "nifty chick."[14] When he finally found a job it was a back-breaking one: he left at dawn and arrived home in the evening covered with dust after a day of shovelling chemicals in a New Jersey factory. His paycheck was not a jackpot, and he hated the work; Hannah Arendt and her mother had to launch him in the mornings and tug his boots off in the evenings as he sat exhausted in their one armchair.

Blücher's second job was a great relief and much closer to the realm of action in which he felt at home. He was hired as a research assistant by the Committee for National Morale, an organization dedicated to urging America to enter the war. Henry Paechter, who had helped him get the position, had planned a book entitled *The Axis Grand Strategy*, designed to alarm Americans into action. While the book was under way, Pearl Harbor was bombed. To be at all timely, the book had to be rushed into print, and once Farrar and Rinehart had issued it, it was not well received. While Blücher was doing research for the book, the Committee for National Morale changed its purpose: its new assignment was to publicize the atrocity stories that were slowly making their way to America from Europe. Another form of inertia had to be combatted, as many Americans, made skeptical by their memories of unfounded tales of horror during the First World War, dismissed the stories of mass murder.

"Monsieur works, often so long that he can hardly keep his eyes open," Hannah Arendt wrote to their friends Lotte and Chanan Klenbort, who had found refuge in Uruguay until they could move to America. "But it is a very nice office, and he is working with excellent people." "Until yesterday," she told the Klenborts in one letter, "I spent half the day acting as his secretary; but this honor, unfortunately, soon came to an end, as there was less to do. . . . The last weeks have been pretty excessive. Monsieur seldom got home before ten-o'clock at night; I went for half a day to the office [of *Aufbau*] and then worked feverishly for the other half, in order that none of my contacts or possibilities be let drop. One can hardly earn a plugged nickel: everybody works hard, because the war keeps going, and the emigrants work especially hard; one can never really even feel proud of one's self."[15]

As the war intensified, communication with friends still in Europe became more and more difficult; it was almost impossible to help anyone emigrate. "It has been a long time since we had any word from Erich [Cohn-Bendit]. Here we are entirely despondent, for very very seldom is a visa granted except when the hearing has turned out well—they really only admit people who have close relatives in the country. . . . I have not heard from the Weils for ages. God knows how they are. Also, no more letters from Juliette [Stern]."[16] All over New York, when refugees met by chance on the street, way stations for their news network were instantly established. The German Jewish refugee world was a very enclosed and frightened one. Suspicion of goyim was characteristic; anti-Semitism was assumed to be, as Arendt put it, a *consensus omnium* among Americans.

*For a Jewish Army*

Fear of anti-Semitism made many of the refugees in New York reluctant to support the plan for a Jewish army. It was fear of being thought unpatriotic that inhibited American Jews. Negotiations between the Palestine-based Jewish Agency and the British for the establishment of a Jewish army had been going on secretly since the beginning of the war in 1939. But the British, fearing that an army including Palestinian Jews would eventually turn its weapons upon the Palestinian Arabs or the British army in Palestine, had stalled the negotiations and sought a compromise: two battalions, one Jewish and one Arab, on a parity basis, had been established within the Kentish regiment of the Royal Fusiliers. When the negotiating process finally collapsed in October 1941, Americans who had supported the idea of a Jewish army were reluctant to criticize the British decision or the American government's acquiescence in it.

Through the winter of 1941/42, Hannah Arendt used her *Aufbau* column to urge protest against the realpolitik of British and American opponents of a Jewish army. For both immediate and long-range reasons, she wanted the Jews to join the fight against Hitler "as a European people." Immediately, she wanted the Jews to express themselves politically—by fighting, rather than by relying on the armies of others or simply aiding the victims of the fighting with charity. In the longer range, she wanted Jews to join the Allies at any future peace conferences: "Der nicht im Krieg ist, auch nicht im Frieden ist [Those who are not in on the war are not in on the peace]."[17] And she felt that action in concert with Europeans would offer the Jews "our great chance for national emancipation," were the antagonisms that had traditionally separated European peoples to disappear in the common effort of the war against Hitler. She voiced the hope she had first formulated in Paris: that a future European federation would guarantee a homeland for the Jews. But, at the same time that she made her arguments for European solidarity, she attacked a commonly held Zionist position, another version of the back-to-the-ghetto argument she had combatted in Paris: she warned Zionists against centering their attention exclusively on Palestine, to the neglect of the Diaspora Jews who would never be Palestinians. Arendt feared that notions of the uniqueness of Jewish political conditions or the uniqueness of the Jewish people would alienate the Jews from other Europeans, especially if the notions took on nationalistic tones or invoked Germanic ideas of a people's "organic unity."

She called on the Jews to fight as a European people. But when she used the term "a people" (*Volk*) she meant it in a political, not a racial, sense: she addressed herself to *die Masse das Volk*, rather than to Jewish leaders. She summoned Jews to look to their own political traditions, to admire Moses or David without depending on other people's Washingtons and Napoleons, but she was careful to avoid any form of leader-worship.[18] Although Arendt often spoke of national consciousness, she was not a nationalist in the nineteenth-century sense; she never equated nation and state and never saw leaders as the embodiment of a nation's glory.

Two modern misconceptions, Arendt thought, inhibited action as a people that might revive the old Jewish tradition of rebellion and liberation. The first was the idea that Jewish survival depended not upon political action but upon philanthropic activities. "For two hundred years we have been led by plutocrats and philanthropists; they have regulated us, and they have represented us to the world."[19] A Jewish army, a popular army, could represent to the world a new sense of Jewish identity, one freed of the burdens of what she called philanthropic and *schnorrer* ("beggarly") habits. The second idea was that among secularized, assimilated Jews solidarity could arise only negatively, in fearful reaction to anti-Semitism. She attacked the conviction that secular Jews would lose their Jewish identity if anti-Semitism disappeared from the world, and she cited in support of her claim (August 1942) the example of the Russian Jews who had called on the Soviet government for arms and on world Jewry for help in their fight against Hitler. For twenty-five years, she argued, anti-Semitism in Russia had been decreasing, not increasing, because the Russians had made efforts to solve the problem of multinationalism politically. With this argument she was also attacking those who accepted the notion of eternal anti-Semitism, those, as diverse as

Theodor Herzl and Jean-Paul Sartre, who believed that a nation is a group of people held together by a common enemy.

Through the late fall of 1941 and into 1942, while Arendt wrote about the Jewish army for *Aufbau*, she was much impressed by the popular support in America for the idea. Only the mid-1930s boycott of German goods had filled her with similar enthusiasm and hope for the possibility of popular Jewish resistance to Hitler. She had been convinced that the Zionists were unprepared by their experience to act politically, to protest, yet she let herself hope that the call for a Jewish army would channel spontaneous popular Jewish opposition to Hitler that had not had a focus since the boycott effort had failed. "It has been one of the unfortunate facts in the history of the Jewish people that only its enemies, and almost never its friends, have understood that the Jewish Question is a political one."[20] To her, a group urging popular support for her cause—the Committee for a Jewish Army, which had a non-Jewish English soldier as its honorary chairman—looked like a group of friends who understood that Jewish indifference to political action had to end.

Neither Arendt nor the two men she worked closely with at *Aufbau*, Manfred George and Joseph Maier, who also wrote a regular column called "The Watchman," knew much about the committee, though Arendt and Joe Maier had attended several meetings with its organizational staff. They were unaware that the committee was the creation of three Palestinian Jews of the extremist Revisionist party.

The Committee for a Jewish Army was based in New York and managed by Ben Hecht. Hecht had written a column for the New York, left-liberal newspaper *P.M.*, which he often devoted to rebuking New York Jews for their misguided, would-be patriotic silence about Hitler's continuing massacres of European Jews. His outspokenness recommended Hecht to the leaders of the Revisionist party's underground group, the Irgun Zvai Leumi, who asked him, in April 1941, to head the Committee for a Jewish Army of Stateless and Palestinian Jews. Hillel Kook, alias Peter Bergson, son of a Jerusalem rabbi and nephew of the chief rabbi of Palestine, had elicited Hecht's sympathy with stories of betrayals and humiliations inflicted on the Jews of Palestine. He convinced Hecht that Chaim Weizmann and the Jewish Agency were ineffectual and that his own rebellious mentor, Vladimir Jabotinsky, was the true voice of Palestinian Jews. But Hecht, though he supported the idea of a Jewish army, would not then ally himself with what he called the "hop-headed Palestinian nationalism" of the Revisionists. In his 1954 best-seller autobiography, A *Child of the Century*, he claimed that throughout his work for various, long-titled committees his objective had always remained the same: to help make a little more impressive the simple title, Jew. And this was the feeling he aroused among a very diverse lot of supporters.

Hecht raised money in New York and Hollywood while Bergson besieged Washington. A resolution calling for a Jewish army was introduced in the House of Representatives; Secretary of State Hull announced his support; Adlai Stevenson, who was then working in the Navy Department, introduced the project to the Secretary of the Navy; the Under Secretary of War appointed military experts to consider the project. Washington support grew and then began to wane when Rabbi Stephen Wise, leader of the Zionist Organization of America (ZOA), and Congressman Sol Bloom, wanting to keep the Jewish army project in ZOA hands, launched a countercampaign. Various other attempts to raise money and enlist volunteers were quite successful but resulted in a great deal of adverse publicity. Many prominent American Jews were concerned that they would be thought unpatriotic if they supported a cause that was in opposition to British policy or if they criticized President Roosevelt and the State Department for their less than eager efforts to urge changes in the Palestine immigration quotas or denounce the massacres of European Jews by the Germans.

The position of the American Zionist leaders who opposed the committee was a complex one. After the 1940 Pittsburgh Conference of the Zionist Organization of America, which had resulted in a program of opposition to British restrictions on immigration to Palestine and in criticism of Weizmann's policy, American Zionists had become more supportive of David Ben-Gurion and more nationalistic. During the summer of 1941 they were widely criticized for drawing America toward war by their partisan publicity. After the Japanese attacked Pearl Harbor on 7 December 1941, that charge was rendered obsolete, but another arose in its place. The Emergency Committee for Zionist Affairs, created in 1939 by the World Zionist Organization, worked with the ZOA to request Jewish mobilization; as these groups became more stridently opposed to the British policy in Palestine, they met the accusation that they were harming the Allies' war effort. The Zionist leaders had to be careful as they became more vocal, and they were particularly careful to insist that that their membership avoid "individuals and groups who are not prepared to accept either the authority or the policies of the Zionist movement" (as a manifesto from the American Emergency Committee for Zionist Affairs stated in March 1942).[21] Such statements were designed to silence renegade groups like Hecht's and to keep decision-making power in the hands of the Zionist leadership.

When Arendt and Joseph Maier realized that the Committee for a Jewish Army was a Revisionist front, they formed a group of their own, Die jungjüdische Gruppe ("the Young Jewish Group").[22] The first meeting of the group was held at the New World Club's 44th Street headquarters on 11 March 1942. The announcement of this meeting that appeared in *Aufbau* was very clear about the group's stance and intentions. It was addressed "to those individuals who feel responsible for the future of the Jewish people; to those who are convinced of the bankruptcy of past ideologies and are ready to tear out their hair in order to develop a new theoretical basis for Jewish politics; to those who know that the struggle for freedom will be led neither by 'notables' nor by world-revolutionaries, but only by those who want to realize it for their own people; and to those who are truly prepared to answer for what they consider to be just."

The group's call for action was a call for a Jewish Army. Their theoretical discussions were more complex. Arendt's first step in the direction of a "new theoretical basis for Jewish politics" was a paper prepared for the group's first meeting. In her "Basic Theoretical Questions of Politics" she raised most of the questions which later formed the foundations of *The Origins of Totalitarianism, Between Past and Future,* and *The Human Condition,* questions which, in those works, applied not just to Jewish politics but to politics *überhaupt* ("in general").

Arendt and Maier led the first meeting and those that followed, but Kurt Blumenfeld was also an active participant and speaker, as was Hans Zolki, a lawyer who later handled the Blüchers' postwar restitution cases. Arendt's opening remarks were directed against past ideologies that offered pseudopolitical world views and against visions of the future that presupposed some knowledge of the course of history: "They have all made a secret pact with the *Weltgeist* [the Hegelian World-Spirit]." As though Walter Benjamin's "Theses on the Philosophy of History" were echoing in her mind, Arendt rejected historical materialism, historicism, liberalism, socialism, and even Zionism insofar as it engaged in soothsaying about the future. Freedom and justice, she asserted, are the principles of politics, and any people struggling for freedom and justice should do so without delusions about their place in history and without grandiose ideas about mankind. At a later meeting, she stressed this point in another way by arguing that the Jews' concept of themselves as a "chosen people" led to defeatism or to the dangerous notion that they would survive no matter what the catastrophe.

As the group continued its discussions in the spring of 1942, its platform became clearer. While the group members considered themselves Zionists, they were very critical of Zionism. Palestine was, for them, a "point of crystallization for Jewish politics," not the sole salvation of the Jews. On this point, Arendt and Blumenfeld quarrelled. But on the other main point of her formulation, "that all suppressed people are doubly oppressed by their enemies and their own privileged class," they agreed. Blumenfeld was optimistic about the Zionists' ability to avoid the class struggle within their ranks, and he was more convinced than Arendt was of the practical necessity for organizations like the American Joint Distribution Committee. But in their distrust of philanthropic parvenus, they always saw alike.

The Young Jewish Group continued to meet until June 1942. But its discussions of the Jewish army took place in a context ever more complex. Jewish Palestinian terrorists had attacked both the British and the Arabs and their leaders claimed for the Jews the territory east of the Jordan River promised to the Arabs by a 1922 British White Paper. When the Committee for a Jewish Army was exposed as a front for the terrorists, Arendt denounced the committee in *Aufbau*. In a 6 March 1942 article, she boldly called the Revisionists "Jewish Fascists" and asserted that their effort to raise a Jewish army was only a part of their larger effort to gain control of the Zionist organization for their own ends. This assessment was too extreme, but it was clear in the spring of 1942 that the ZOA was losing ground in the larger debate that surrounded the Jewish army issue. In May an international meeting at the Biltmore Hotel revealed the shifting consensus among Zionists.

Rabbi Stephen S. Wise called the meeting to order with a fervent plea for "the freedom of the Jews in all lands and the final establishment under the Victory Peace Conference of a free Jewish Commonwealth in Palestine."[23] Chaim Weizmann, despite his disillusionment with the British refusal to sanction a Jewish army, argued that the Jews should emphasize cooperation with Britain in the struggle against Hitler and not urge the creation of a Jewish state in opposition to British policy. But a majority of the delegates at the Biltmore Conference responded to David Ben-Gurion's passionate hope that: "A Jewish Palestine will arise. It will redeem forever our sufferings and do justice to our national genius. It will be the pride of every Jew in the Diaspora, and command the respect of every people on earth." The declaration that resulted from the Biltmore Conference endorsed this hope and also supported Ben-Gurion's demand that the British relinquish to the Jewish Agency control over immigration to Palestine. The conference was a turning point in the history of American Zionism; Ben-Gurion's vision of a Jewish state was the catalyst for American Zionism's great renewal.

Hannah Arendt attended the Biltmore Conference with Joseph Maier to prepare a report for *Aufbau*; for her it was a turning point in her relationship to Zionism. Both she and Maier were shocked by the supercharged atmosphere of the meeting and the way they were treated as they entered the hall. Security guards pushed them and demanded identification. But they were far more deeply distressed by the outcome of the debates. Arendt was no supporter of Chaim Weizmann; she rejected his attempts to preserve the status quo with the British and was particularly offended by his dismissal of what he slightingly referred to as "the so-called Jewish Army." But she was just as reluctant to accept Ben-Gurion's call for a Jewish state in Palestine.

Hannah Arendt opposed both positions represented at the Biltmore Conference. Two other positions which emerged soon after were no more satisfactory to her. A group of Reform rabbis within the American Council of Judaism completely repudiated the call for a Jewish state and all "political Zionism." Arendt thought these "protest rabbis" were simply regressive. [24] On the other hand, she could not support the position taken by Judah Magnes of the Hebrew University. Magnes argued for a binational Palestine within an Arab Federation and formalized his stance by founding a political party early in 1943.

After the Biltmore Conference, while continuing to press for the Jewish army idea in *Aufbau*, Arendt tried to formulate her own pariah position. She was aware that no existing group would take it up, but she felt that she had to contribute it to the discussions in case any American Zionists not under the sway of their leaders might respond to it. She hoped American Zionists, who had had the great advantage of living "in a land with a democratic political tradition," a tradition that might have taught them the non-Herzlian lession that anti-Semitism is "a political and not a natural phenomenon," might understand her vision of a Jewish revolutionary national movement (*Volksbewegung*). She made her appeal to the heirs of the American Revolution.

Arendt's appreciation of the American political tradition and her hope that it would inform the actions of American Zionists had grown during her first year in New York. She and many other refugees were gratefully employed in the programs opened to them at Brooklyn College, Columbia University, and the New School for Social Research; they made a little money, and they had a teaching forum. For those who had been closed out of universities since 1933, this was miraculous. In the lectures she delivered to her first American university students in a Modern European History course during Brooklyn College's 1942 summer session, Arendt recorded her gratitude and told of her astonishment at daily political life in a republic.[25] One day she lectured to her class about the Dreyfus Affair and then added a note, based on a newspaper story: "A few days ago, in one of the smaller communities of the State of New York there happened a small but remarkable event, which strongly reminded me of the Dreyfus Case. The senior students of a high school—with an overwhelming majority—elected the only Japanese—an American of Japanese origin—who was among them. This Japanese is a dull person, nobody even paid any attention to him—he is entirely incapable of holding the presidency of the school and the only reason he was elected was precisely his Japanese origin. His personality has nothing to do with the role he played [as Dreyfus's personality, she argued, had had nothing to do with the role he played]. He simply felt embarrassed. But the students wanted to show that no individual ever should suffer from his belonging to a special group. They acted according to their concept of justice." When Arendt appealed to American Zionists, she appealed to precisely that—their concept of justice.

In a 20 November 1942 article for *Aufbau*, Arendt formulated the position she hoped might attract Zionists opposed to the Biltmore Declaration; it was the third part of a long analysis entitled "The Crisis of Zionism." She called on dissident Zionists to accept the idea that Palestine should not be a British colony, part of a colonial empire, in the manner outlined in the 1917 Balfour Declaration. And then she asked them to work for the establishment of Palestine as part of a postwar British Commonwealth rather than as an autonomous state. Gandhi's work in India, she argued, should provide an instructive example. Secondly, she called for efforts to bring about a postwar European federation because she felt that only in that way would Palestine be completely guaranteed as a *jüdisches Siedlungsgebiet* ("an area for Jewish settlements"). Finally, she made a plea for legislation which would classify anti-Semitism as a punishable crime against society (*Vergehen gegen die Gesellschaft*) within such a federation.

Arendt's third "Crisis of Zionism" article was the final appearance of her "This Means You" column. In an atmosphere of growing enthusiasm for Ben-Gurion's brand of Zionism, her suggestions were without effect, and her column was replaced in the next issue of *Aufbau* by a sign of the times, a column called "Zionistische Tribune."

*The Burden of Time: Years of the Final Solution*

As each issue of *Aufbau* informed horrified readers, the times were growing darker and darker. The 18 December issue contained a report on deportation day at the internment camp of Gurs; long lists of the names of those deported followed. While the Zionists, including Arendt, were struggling for an insight into how the Jewish Question might be solved at the war's end, news was finally reaching America that an unimaginably atrocious Final Solution to the Jewish Question was being implemented in Europe.

Hayim Greenberg, the editor of *Jewish Frontier*, had published in the November 1942 issue a summary of the astonishing reports he had received from the World Jewish Congress. He editorialized desperately in January about these reports under the title "The Christian World Must Act." Ben Hecht used the same reports to try to reach a broader audience through the February 1943 issue of the *Reader's Digest*. But the "Christian World" was reluctant to believe these reports, much less to act, and the national press remained very reserved.

Ben Hecht, with Bertolt Brecht's partner, the composer Kurt Weill, the producer Billy Rose, the director Moss Hart, and a corps of actors and musicians prepared a pageant entitled "We Shall Never Die" for a March opening at Madison Square Garden. Rabbi Stephen Wise, who had been opposing Hecht's independent activities for a year, organized a separate "Stop Hitler Now" public meeting at Madison Square Garden to send out a plea for action from the American Zionist leadership. In the month before these two public events, one official and one unofficial, Arendt gave several lectures in which she urged a resolution of the Crisis of Zionism. These lectures show both her own anger at the silence surrounding the reports from Europe of mass exterminations and her reluctance to support either the Zionist leadership's approach to publicity or Hecht's emotional "We Shall Never Die" variety. "It is a well-known fact," she told a New York Hadassah meeting, "which has been stressed time and again that, since the outbreak of the war and even before, a conspiracy of silence has covered the sufferings and the losses of the Jewish people."[26] She did not explain explicitly who she thought was involved in this conspiracy, but her criticisms of the Zionist leadership were harsher than any she had made before. The Jewish Agency, she claimed, had followed a policy of appeasement "like the statesmen of all other nations—only with even less success." With many of the same arguments she later used in *Eichmann in Jerusalem*, Arendt pressed her case:

This appeasement policy had started with the transfer agreements of the Jewish Agency with the German government in 1934. It was followed by the subsequent decisions of Jews of other countries not to use their influence upon their respective governments in their relations with Germany, to help German Jewry but not to speak about the happenings which made help necessary. Long before the period of appeasement found its natural end in total warfare, the boycott movement among the Jewish masses in America and in Poland had died down. The most honest expression of solidarity had ended in disillusionment and deception, and if our politicians like the politicians of other countries have not succeeded in appeasing Hitler, they have remarkable success to report in appeasing the Jewish people in their rightful indignation and their instinctive attempts to fight back.

Arendt attacked the Zionist leadership. But unlike the flamboyantly sentimental and untheoretical Hecht, she did not make a personal attack. She was convinced that "if tomorrow we had a brand-new team of men to run our politics it is much to be doubted whether things would not go the same old way." What she opposed was the Zionists' continued reliance on outmoded political concepts and convictions.

Once again, and in the much more difficult circumstances of an atmosphere charged with mourning, fear, and anger, Arendt tried to formulate her criticisms of the Zionists' assumptions and policies. During the summer and early fall of 1943 she prepared a paper called "Can the Jewish-Arab Question Be Solved?" *Aufbau* published it in two installments that December and prefaced it with a careful little editorial note: "Without agreeing in all details with Mrs. Arendt, the tragic and difficult situation of the Jewish people demands that room be given to all opinions if they are honest and based on sound reasoning."[27]

Manfred George's note was a measure of how strongly Arendt's analysis and suggestions went against every grain. She explicitly rejected the two proposals that had been most hotly debated during the year after the Biltmore Conference. The first was the proposal of the Biltmore Declaration itself: a Jewish Commonwealth, an autonomous state, in which the Palestinian Arabs—the majority population—would be given minority status. This nationalistic solution, as she remarked rather sarcastically, "would be a novelty in the history of nation-states." The even more extreme nationalism of the Revisionist party's program, which included a proposal for relocating Arab populations, she flatly condemned because it would require "fascist organization." The second proposal she examined was a revised version of the one advanced by Judah Magnes immediately after the Biltmore Conference. This called for a binational state, in which the Jews would have minority status, to be incorporated into a federation of Arab states and affiliated with an entity vaguely called an Anglo-American union, that is, a protectorate.

Arendt rejected both proposals for the same reason: both identified the state with the national group given majority status within it. What Arendt wanted was a Palestinian entity in which there would be no majority or minority status distinctions, in which the notion of minority rights, which had been so unsuccessfully tried in the 1918 minority treaties for Central and Eastern European states, would have no new incarnation.

She had a further objection to Magnes's plan. She thought that an Arab federation would be "nothing but cover for an Empire." For British Empire protagonists such a federation could be a vehicle for British influence, for colonialism in all but name. And for the Arab ruling families it would mean an Arab empire. "In both cases the term federation suggests a phony." Appealing again to her understanding of America's revolutionary political tradition, she wrote:

A genuine federation is constituted by different and clearly distinct national and other political elements. National conflicts can be resolved in such a federation only because the insoluble majority-minority problem would cease to exist.

The United States of America was the first realization of such a federation. In that union no single state has any supremacy over another state, and all states together govern the country. In a different way, the Soviet Union has solved its nationality problem by abolishing the Russian Empire and establishing a union of equal nationalities, regardless of the size of the several constituents. The British Commonwealth of Nations, as distinct from the British Empire, may be regarded as another potential federation.[28]

Arendt recommended that Palestine become part of the British Commonwealth if and when the British actually succeeded in transforming their empire into a commonwealth. She thought that parliamentary and popular British support for the commonwealth idea and also the British offer of dominion status to India presaged this transformation.

Hannah Arendt's independent stance left her totally cut off from any possibility of action and without influence among the Zionists. Heinrich Blücher was in a somewhat more satisfying position. He had found two teaching positions through his contacts at the Committee for the National Morale. As a civilian consultant for the U.S. Army Training Program at Camp Ritchie, Maryland, he had conducted seminars on German history for German prisoners of war. Then he had been invited to another army program at Princeton University, under the supervision of Dean Christian Gauss. There he had lectured to German-speaking U.S. Army officers on the organization and structure of both the French and the German armies. These assignments, where Blücher's talent for public speaking and teaching flourished, give him credentials for a better job in New York City the next year; he was hired as a German-language news broadcaster for NBC radio. The broadcasting work was less interesting, and it involved writing—never a comfortable occupation for Blücher—but all these jobs allowed him to develop the ideas he was hoping to contribute to the project he and his wife had put at the center of their lives. While Hannah Arendt was nearing the end of her work at *Aufbau* and looking for another job, they made the first outline for their long-considered book.

*The Origins of Totalitarianism* was planned during the most despairing period of the Blüchers' lives. The news from Europe in the early months of 1943 was unbelievable. Many years later, Hannah Arendt recalled the period and her reaction to the reports of Hitler's Final Solution to the Jewish Question:

At first we did not believe it. Even though my husband had always said we should put nothing past [the Nazis]. This, however, we did not believe because it was militarily unnecessary and uncalled for. My husband was a kind of military historian at one time, and he knew something about these things. He said, "Don't listen to any of these fairy tales, they couldn't do that." A half a year later, when it was proven to us, we finally believed it. Before that, one would say to one's self—so, we all have enemies. That's quite natural. Why should a people have no enemies? But this was different. This was really as though the abyss had opened. Because one always has the hope that everything else might some day be rectified, politically—that everything might be put right again. This couldn't be. This should never have been allowed to happen. I don't mean the number of victims, but the method, the fabrication of corpses—I don't need to go further into that. This should never have been allowed to happen. And what happened was something that none of us could reconcile ourselves to. As for what happened to us, I can only say that things were occasionally difficult, we were very poor, we were persecuted, one had to flee, and one sometimes had to swindle one's way through—that's just the way things were. But we were young, and it was even a little fun at times. I couldn't put it any other way. But not that, not that. That was completely different. Personally, one could deal with everything else.[29]

Their lives went on; they went to work, struggled. But even when they went to Riverside Park to walk, to have a little fun, to enjoy the peacefulness, their vision of what was happening in Europe, what should never have happened, went with them. In the park, Arendt wrote poems. This one, untitled, was written in 1943.

> They have arisen from the standing pool of the past—
> these many memories.
> Misty figures drew the longing circles of my enchainment
> around, alluring, to their goal.
>
> Dead ones, what do you want? Have you no home or hearth in Orcus?
> Finally the peace of the deep?
> Water and earth, fire and air, are your servants as if a god,
> powerfully, possessed you. And called
>
> You up from standing waters, swamps, moors and ponds,
> Collected you, unified, together.
> Glowing in the twilight you cover the living's realm with fog,
> Mocking the darkening "no longer."
>
> We went to play, embrace and laugh and hold
> Dreams of past times.
> We, too, have grown tired of streets, cities, of the rapid
> Changes of solitude.
>
> Among the rowing boats with their loving couples, like jewels
> On woodland ponds,

We, too, could mingle quietly, hidden and wrapped in the
Misty clouds which soon

Clothe the earth, the banks, the bush and the tree,
Awaiting the coming storm.
Awaiting—out of the fog, the cloud castle, folly and dream—
The rising, twisting storm.

The Blüchers drew together and helped each other. In "Park on the Hudson," Arendt portrayed another of their many walks, their times alone for thinking and talking about what was happening. The poem is a pastoral, but its final stanza forecasts a phrase that appeared in the book they considered writing as they walked: "the burden of our time," the phrase used for the title given to *The Origins of Totalitarianism* by its British publisher.

> Fishermen are quietly fishing the rivers.
>   A branch hangs lonely.
> Drivers are blindly driving the roads,
>   Restlessly, to their rest.
> Children playing, mothers calling them.
>   Eternity is almost here.
> A loving couple passes by
>   Bearing the burden of time.

For Hannah Arendt's people, for the Jews, the European *Heimat* ("homeland") was lost forever by 1944; it was "no longer." What might be in the Europe of the future, the "not yet," was unimaginable. What might be in the Palestine of the future was beyond knowing. There was no practical action Hannah Arendt could take for her people without a base in the Zionist community. But since she lacked that, she was very grateful for an opportunity to plan for the future with a politically unaligned group. She took her first full-time salaried position in America as research director for the Conference on Jewish Relations.

The conference—later known as the Conference on Jewish Social Studies—had been proposed in April 1933 by two of the most respected Jewish scholars in America, Salo Baron and Morris Raphael Cohen. The official launching of the conference in 1936, at a meeting chaired by Albert Einstein and addressed by Baron, Cohen, Harold Laski, and Henry Morgenthau, Sr., initiated a fund drive which allowed the conference to sponsor *Jewish Social Studies* in 1939. The journal was an important part of the conference's original goal: to present data on "the position of the Jew in the Modern World" with which to counter viciously anti-Semitic Nazi propaganda.

In the early 1940s the publisher Salman Schocken asked Salo Baron whether the conference would work with the Hebrew University in an advisory capacity. The university wanted suggestions about means of recovering whatever books from European Jewish collections had survived the first years of the war. The conference members responded by establishing the Commission on European Jewish Cultural Reconstruction, and it was the research work of this commission which Hannah Arendt began to direct in 1944. She worked with Joshua Starr, the commission's first director, and a staff to prepare four installments of a "Tentative List of Jewish Cultural Treasures in Axis-Occupied Countries," published in the 1946 to 1948 issues of *Jewish Social Studies*. The commission's task was to determine how European Jewry's spiritual treasures could be recovered and given new homes.

To draw up these lists, Arendt and her coworkers interviewed Jewish refugees who had had positions in various European libraries, schools, and museums. One of their key documents, a catalogue of manuscripts in private collections that had been prepared at the Frankfurt Municipal Library, was given to them by a librarian who had taken it with him when the Nazis' 1933 law barring Jews from civil jobs had ended his career. Other refugees contributed notes and recollections, which had to be coordinated with what information was available about the Nazis' confiscation and relocation activities.

In 1940 Alfred Rosenberg and a special Nazi unit called the Einsatzgruppe Reichsführer Rosenberg ransacked Jewish cultural institutions throughout occupied Europe to supply an archive in Frankfurt dedicated to the history of the Jews and the Jewish Question. Rosenberg's activities overshadowed those of the older, Munich-based Institut zur Erforschung der Judenfrage, under the direction of the well-known historian Walter Frank, which was connected with centers inside the German universities. But when Rosenberg's collection was assembled, only part of it was deposited in Frankfurt. The most valuable holdings were sent to Berlin, where they were received by a special Gestapo department under the direction of Adolf Eichmann.

Hannah Arendt studied this complex situation while preparing the tentative lists and later used her results in *The Origins of Totalitarianism* to illustrate one of the key devices of totalitarian rule, the multiplication of offices and agencies. "None of the older institutions was ever abolished, so that in 1944 the situation was this: behind the facade of the universities' history departments stood threateningly the more real power of the Munich institute, behind which rose Rosenberg's institute in Frankfurt, and only behind these three facades, hidden and protected by them, lay the real center of authority, the *Reichssicherheitshauptamt*, a special division of the Gestapo."[30] The research done for the preparation of the tentative lists thus provided Hannah Arendt with one of her first insights into the layered, onionlike structure of totalitarian regimes. The lists provided the Commission on European Jewish Cultural Reconstruction with a basis for negotiation in its effort to recover the remains of their culture for the surviving European Jews.

Hannah Arendt became executive director of the Jewish Cultural Reconstruction organization after its establishment in 1948 and retained the position until 1952. She travelled to Europe for six months in 1949 and 1950 to direct the operation that eventually recovered 1.5 million volumes of Hebraica and Judaica, thousands of ceremonial and artistic objects, and over a thousand scrolls of law. Under the terms of the 1945 Inter-Allied Agreement, objects whose country of origin was known had to be returned to those countries, and those belonging to surviving individuals were returned to them. The third of the total that was not returnable was distributed among Jewish institutions in Israel, Europe, and other countries in the Western Hemisphere.

For Hannah Arendt, the work with Jewish Cultural Reconstruction was some consolation in the last, dreadful years of the war. But assuring a home for Jewish cultural objects did not alleviate her own sense of being *heimatlos*, without a home. She longed for the lost world, Europe. One of her simplest, saddest poems, written in 1946, turns on a famous line of Rilke's: "*Wohl dem, der eine Heimat hat,*" (lucky he who has a home).

> Sorrow is like a light that gleams in the heart,
> Darkness is a glow that searches our night.
> We need strike only the small, mournful flame
> To find our way home, like shadows, through the
>     long, broad night.
> The woods, the city, the street, the tree are
>     luminous.
> Lucky is he who has no home; he sees it still
>     in his dreams.

*Consolations*

Hannah Arendt's contributions to the preservation of Jewish culture took another form between the years of her research for the Commission on European Jewish Cultural Reconstruction (1944–46) and the trip she made to Europe on behalf of Jewish Cultural Reconstruction (1949–50). She accepted the senior editorial post at the newly established New York headquarters of Schocken Books after Max Strauss, her predecessor, suffered a disabling heart attack. Her office at Schocken was a traffic center: into it came authors and editors, German speakers and, finally, American acquaintances. Hannah Arendt came to know the world around her émigré world in the first year of a new era—after the war.

Salman Schocken and Hannah Arendt had met in Berlin through Kurt Blumenfeld and they renewed their acquaintance in New York. Before he hired her as an editor, Schocken had consulted her about various projects; she had recommended to him both Walter Benjamin's unpublished manuscripts and an edition of the writings of Bernard Lazare, the French Zionist from whom she had learned her pariah and parvenu terminology. An edition of Lazare's work appeared in 1949, under the title *Job's Dungheap*, edited and introduced by Arendt. Benjamin's work was never published at Schocken, but Arendt did have a chance to work on the second edition of Gershom Scholem's *Major Trends in Jewish Mysticism*, which Scholem had dedicated to Benjamin. The most time-consuming and difficult editorial project of her years at Schocken was a German edition of Franz Kafka's *Diaries*. Kafka's friend Max Brod had prepared the *Diaries* for publication, but his work was very sloppy and every page had to be checked against the original manuscripts. Though the Kafka work was arduous, Arendt was dedicated to it; for years she had been interested in Kafka, and her first piece in the *Partisan Review* was "Franz Kafka: a Re-evaluation" (Fall 1944).

Arendt had had reservations about working for Schocken because of their many arguments over the projects she had proposed, but she respected him more than the younger men who worked for him. "The older generation with money," she told Blumenfeld, "still has a feeling of responsibility for cultural things, which the younger generation with money really lacks."[31] Schocken was difficult: "You must realize," she warned a prospective client, "that though he is a publisher, he does not like to publish."[32] But she did develop an amused regard for the man she called "this Jewish Bismarck," and she learned how to maneuver around him.[33] Much good advice about publishers and publishing was given her by Kurt Wolff, founder of Pantheon Books, the most important émigré house. Kurt Wolff and his wife Helene became part of the Blüchers' tribe and were always receptive to Hannah Arendt's publishing suggestions.

Several exciting acquaintances developed as a result of Salman Schocken's peculiar manner of dealing with authors. Arendt met T. S. Eliot when he came for a business meeting with Schocken and his son; she was invited to attend the meeting in the role of secretary. She sat in appalled, helpless silence while Eliot was received like a travelling salesman. Rather than seizing the chance to have Eliot among their authors, the Schockens hemmed and hawed and then ended the conference abruptly with a "we'll think it over" and their apologies for having to rush off to another appointment. With great dignity Eliot rose, ushered the Schockens to their own door, and bowed formally as they made a confused exit. Then Eliot turned to a very embarrassed Hannah Arendt and said: "Well, now you and I can have a nice chat." They did, and Arendt afterwards devoted herself to reading Eliot's poems, plays, and essays in their entirety—the compliment she always paid to a new literary acquaintance.

The publisher who did not like to publish also missed an opportunity to gather in Randall Jarrell's translations of German poetry. Jarrell lived in New York during 1946 while he substituted for Margaret Marshall, the regular book-review editor of the *Nation*. The year before, Margaret Marshall had discussed Arendt's "Approaches to 'The German Problem'" (*Partisan Review*, Winter 1945) in the *Nation*, calling it "one of the best discussions of the problem of Germany and Europe I have come across." When she asked for a contribution to the *Nation*, Arendt responded by reviewing Raissa Maritain's *Adventures in Grace*.

The review was one of the sort that became characteristic of Hannah Arendt: the book was briefly mentioned in a long general discussion. Her "Christianity and Revolution" was a survey of neo-Catholic thought in France, which ranged from the antidemocratic "dilettantes of fascism" of the Action Française, to the democratic, antibourgeois publicists like Péguy and Bernanos (and Chesterton in England).[34] This survey established the context within which the neo-Thomist Jacques Maritain, neither a journalist nor a publicist, was an exception: "the case of the philosophers is slightly different and slightly embarrassing. . . . What Maritain wanted was one certainty which would lead him out of the complexities and confusions of a world that does not even know what a man is talking about if he takes the word truth in his mouth." Arendt admired Maritain, and had enjoyed a brief personal acquaintance with him under Paul Tillich's auspices—she had also sent him a review she did for *Aufbau* of his *Ransoming of Time* and a copy of her "From the Dreyfus Affair to France Today"—but she found his need for truth embarrassing because it was, in her understanding, unphilosophical. "Philosophy concerned with truth ever was and probably always will be a kind of *docta ignorantia*—highly learned and therefore highly ignorant." This last sentence was the sort of thing one can imagine Randall Jarrell clipping out and putting in his wallet as protection against the world's vast population of unlearned know-it-alls.

Jarrell's erudition was a marvel to anyone who read his poetry and criticism or heard him talk. But to Jarrell it was a small raft in a vast sea of ignorance. When he met Hannah Arendt, the living embodiment of the European education he did not have, his raft seemed even smaller to him, but she seemed like the shore. When Hannah Arendt read his poems, he trusted her completely: "Nothing anyone has said about my poems has ever pleased me more than what you've said," he told her.[35]

They met for business lunches while he was at the *Nation* and Arendt at Schocken Books. She contributed five short articles to the *Nation* during 1946, including her first enthusiastic statement about French existentialism and reviews of Hermann Broch's *The Death of Virgil* and Robert Gilbert's *Meine Reime Deine Reime*. Jarrell accepted the articles and did what Arendt called "Englishing" them. She, in turn, corrected Jarrell's translations of German poetry, sometimes giving him her own rough prose translations to work from, and guiding his reading of her favorite poets—Goethe, Rilke, Heine, and Hölderlin. She tried to arrange with "the Jewish Bismarck" for an edition of Jarrell's translations of Heine's poems but without success.

Arendt was much impressed with Jarrell's translations, and she encouraged him to improve his German—as she later encouraged W. H. Auden, with the same result. "Alas," Jarrell complained, "my German isn't a *bit* better: if I translate, how can I find time to learn German? If I don't translate, I forget about German." Arendt was a better pupil. After he left New York, Jarrell visited the Blüchers periodically and introduced Hannah Arendt to the modern English-language poets who became her favorites—Auden, Emily Dickinson, and Yeats. He read to her so that her still very uncertain ear could hear the rhythms and meters of English, and they both enjoyed noting her progress with the language from the days of their first meetings, when she had been puzzled by his possession of what sounded to her like two surnames, "Randall" and "Jarrell."

A bond developed between them which both Arendt and Jarrell treasured: a bond of shared taste and good judgment. After she had finished reading his essay "Obscurity of the Poet," she wrote to tell him that she had been "intoxicated with agreement against a world of enemies." And he replied: "I always feel this way when I see you. Someone said about somebody that 'while that man is alive I am not alone in this world'; I guess I feel that way about you." Jarrell was not alone, but he often moved from place to place, setting down only the temporary roots of the writer-in-residence. "I certainly do miss you; you'll *surely* need to come out to Illinois in the spring, won't you? To give the Ark of the Covenant to a library in Cairo, Illinois, or such."

But she did not leave New York; indeed, she hardly left her desks—the one at Schocken or the tiny one fitted into a corner of the West 95th Street apartment. She was constantly writing, during her lunch breaks, after dinner, and late into the night, producing the articles she intended to shape into *The Origins of Totalitarianism* and dozens of book reviews. In her book reviews and editorial efforts she took up another task of cultural reconstruction: introducing American literati to contemporary European literature and philosophy. At a time when a respected member of the *Partisan Review* circle could ask her at a party who "Francis" Kafka was, she worked to write clear and simple guides to this unknown world. The German language desperately needed cultural ambassadors, people who could show its treasures to America in the face of the widespread distrust of all things German. Arendt was skeptical about Germany's ability ever again to sustain great writers because the strongest impetus to literary innovation in the nineteenth and early twentieth centuries, the world of German Jewry, had been destroyed; nevertheless, she wanted America to be hospitable to Germany's remnant. In her preliminary studies for *The Origins of Totalitarianism* she presented her readers with stories of Jewish achievements—Rahel Varnhagen's, Heinrich Heine's, Bernard Lazare's— that were largely unknown. She helped make a place for these pariahs' posterity; in that, there was some consolation for what she and Karl Jaspers called the *Finis Germaniae*, the end of Germany.

Hannah Arendt's vintage year for meeting poets was 1946. As poetry had offered her consolation during the war, poets offered it afterward, during the years of slow recovery from the war's afflictions. She had met the poet and novelist Hermann Broch before she began at Schocken and had been as immediately taken with him as he with her. After they began to meet regularly she wrote in 1946 to Blumenfeld that this new friendship was "the best thing that has happened during your absence."[36]

This fortunate meeting was arranged by Broch's mistress, Anne-Marie Meier-Gräfe, whom Hannah Arendt had met in New York. The widow of a famous German art historian, Anne-Marie Meier-Gräfe was known to her friends as Buschi, and was, like Blücher, a Berliner. Her apartment was a somberly furnished evocation of the prewar Vienna where she and Broch had met. The apartment was filled with mementoes of a world Hannah Arendt had never known but had glimpsed in Stefan Zweig's autobiography, _The World of Yesterday_. The people she met there, however, were not like Zweig or the "eminent contemporaries" he had so eagerly collected in the "Golden Age of Security," while his literary fame was at its height. The events of 1933 had taken the apolitical Zweig by complete surprise and—as Hannah Arendt described it in her 1943 review of Zweig's book—destroyed a world in which "one had established oneself so comfortably."[37] The Hitler years had "razed . . . that 'reservation' for the chosen few connoisseurs who had devoted their lives to the idolatry of Art; broken . . . the trellises that barred out the _profanum vulgus_ of the uncultured more effectively than a Chinese wall." This elite world of literary cliques, which Hannah Arendt had learned to despise in Weimar Germany, had disgusted Hermann Broch long before the appearance of Hitler; he called the Vienna of this period the "metropolis of the ethical vacuum."

Hannah Arendt marked her new friendship with a review of Broch's _The Death of Virgil_. After Randall Jarrell "translated" her review from Germanic, long-sentenced English into beautiful, long-sentenced English, he encouraged her to submit a fuller piece on Broch's work to his teacher, John Crowe Ransom, at the _Kenyon Review_, which she did, after Broch's _The Sleepwalkers_ reappeared in English in 1948. The earlier review was a mark of Arendt's friendship and esteem for Broch, who wrote in that realm that she called "between past and future."

Proust is the last and the most beautiful farewell to the world of the nineteenth century, and we return to his work, written in the key of the "no longer," again and again when the mood of farewell and of sorrow overwhelms us. Kafka, on the other hand, is our contemporary only to a limited extent. It is as though he wrote already from the vantage point of a distant future, as though he were or could have been at home only in a world which is "not yet. . . ." Broch's work . . . has become something like the missing link between Proust and Kafka, between a past which we have irretrievably lost and a future which is not yet at hand.... This book... tries to span the abyss of empty space between the no longer and the not yet. And since this abyss is very real; since it has become deeper and more frightful every single year from the fateful year of 1914 onward, until the death factories erected in the heart of Europe definitely cut the already outworn thread with which we still might have been tied to a historical entity of more than two thousand years: since we are already living in the "empty space," confronted with a reality which no preconceived traditional idea of the world and man can possibly illuminate—dear as this tradition may have remained to our hearts—we must be profoundly grateful for the great work of poetry which clings so desperately to this one subject.[38]

Hannah Arendt respected Broch, but she never felt that she understood him. It impressed her that, after having been offered a contract by Alfred Knopf for the novel entitled *Der Versucher*, he would undertake a revision of the book, achieving a "purified prose of inviolable beauty and vitality."[39] But she was astonished that he would refuse to complete this same task because he regarded the novel as wholly superfluous. She could appreciate his conflicts, but it nonetheless troubled her that the fundamental trait of his nature, his ethical commitment to respond selflessly to calls for help, had led him to lay literature aside as unhelpful, an insufficient and overly subjective response to the world in which he lived. In the introduction to Broch's essays that Hannah Arendt wrote after his death, she simply recorded the story of Broch's abandonment of literature and his quest for a systematic philosophy that would offer people an "earthly absolute" to guide them to independent, unselfish living. She neither questioned nor criticized the turn, merely noting the philosophical difficulties at the base of his attempted system, specifically his artist's equation of acting with doing or making. She knew that it was impossible to question publicly Broch's ethical commitment, even though its cost to him and to literature was so great. Privately she always said that *Fortuna* had been kind to Hermann Broch only once during the years he spent responding to his friends' needs: he had taken a fall and been hospitalized so that he could not run here and there offering counsel, delivering food, succoring the emigrants.

Hannah Arendt did not rely on Broch's kindness and sensitivity herself, but she understood what such reliance might mean. For, as she admitted shyly to Kurt Blumenfeld after she had written to him about Hermann Broch: "It is always on Monsieur's perceptiveness and goodness and absolute independence from all things and all people that I rely, on his alone. (One really should not write this about one's own husband, I do it only 'once in a lifetime').''[40] She recognized in Hermann Broch those qualities of Heinrich Blücher's from which she had benefitted beyond measure.

Hannah Arendt was as impressed by Broch's love of women as by his independence. He was an inveterate ladies' man, charming, modest, beautifully mannered, gifted with *politesse du coeur*. Hannah Arendt was not surprised by the number of Broch's conquests, but she was puzzled by the pleasure he took in the embarrassing imbroglios that inevitably arose. She often discussed this pleasure of Broch's with their mutual friend, Robert Pick, an editorial assistant at Alfred Knopf. Unlike Hannah Arendt, Robert Pick had become accustomed to Broch's adventures and had even been cast, very occasionally and very reluctantly, in the role of Leporello by this Don Giovanni. When Broch attempted to include her in his female retinue Hannah Arendt's response was more startling to Pick than Broch's indiscretions had ever been. Not only had she found Broch resistible, she had declined his advances with a delicacy equal to his own: "Hermann, let me be the exception."

Hannah Arendt had been an exception for Broch long before this charming refusal was uttered. He shook his head and muttered to Robert Pick after every evening they spent with her, "No one should be *allowed* to know so much!" Hannah Arendt intimidated him, and Heinrich Blücher's passionate political arguments terrified him. "Blücher was always *shouting*," said Pick, like Broch a quiet and refined Viennese, of this wild Berliner. Nonetheless, a close friendship developed between the Blüchers—both of them—and Broch.

After Broch's death in 1951, Hannah Arendt helped deal with his considerable and chaotic literary estate; with Anne-Marie Meier-Gräfe she spent some days in Broch's New Haven studio organizing the papers later donated to Yale. The publishable works were later sent to Switzerland, where an edition of Broch's complete works was undertaken by the Rheinverlag. Arendt prepared her introduction to the two volumes of essays slowly and with difficulty. She sent her effort to Blumenfeld and warned him: "You have probably remarked to yourself that my introduction was written at a certain distance. It was an obligation of friendship. His thought, which I portrayed or tried to portray, is really quite alien to me. He knew that, and nevertheless trusted my loyalty—which is something, particularly for a poet. I did it with the best understanding and conscience I could summon. But I guarded myself against speaking out my true opinion."[41] Her true opinion—that literature's loss was not philosophy's gain—mattered less to her than her friendship. After Broch's death, Hannah Arendt was able to pay him the great respect of showing a helpfulness equal to his own.

Through Randall Jarrell and the people who managed other magazines to which she submitted her work in the mid-1940s, the *Partisan Review* and *Commentary*, the *Menorah Journal* and *Jewish Frontier*, Hannah Arendt's circle of New York acquaintances grew. Her coworkers at Schocken Books—Irving Howe, Nathan Glazer, and Martin Greenberg—introduced her to their friends. She finally met the people she had hoped to meet, such as Alfred Kazin, whose name had been disparagingly linked with hers in 1944 when both of them were branded as prime examples of "the trend of self-excoriation manifesting itself in times of sorrow and frustration."[42] Arendt had earned this criticism for statements in her review of Stephan Zweig's autobiography, in which she called into question Jewish elitism and political shortsightedness. During and just after the war, it was common for Hannah Arendt to find American Jewish intellectuals whose political convictions were close to her own and who read her work appreciatively. After 1948 the atmosphere began to change; her friendships and loyalties did not fare well in the era of Jewish nationalism.

After the war, Arendt started going to parties and discussions with the members of a loosely defined group—the New York literary and largely Jewish Left. She was excited, and a bit overwhelmed by her new milieu. "Sometimes I am defeated," she told Blumenfeld, "because I have met so many people and their names and faces float around in me in wild chaos."[43] Political accord came quickly with her new friends, and she praised them extravagantly to her European friends for their lack of fanaticism, their refusal to worship the God of Success and their commitment to a literary language accessible to readers of many persuasions and backgrounds. But, despite her regard for the new friends, misunderstandings arose easily in the emotional years at the end of the war. One such misunderstanding postponed for several years a friendship between Arendt and Mary McCarthy.

The two women had first met in 1944. Arendt followed her custom of reading whatever her new acquaintances had written, and during the next year she admired McCarthy's 1942 *The Company She Keeps*. But her admiration did not keep her from reacting violently to a remark Mary

McCarthy let slip at a party given by Philip Rahv, an editor of *Partisan Review*, in the spring of 1945, soon after Roosevelt's sudden death. Mary McCarthy was talking with a cluster of their friends about the attitudes of the French toward the Germans occupying Paris. She said that she felt sorry for Adolf Hitler, who was so absurd as to long for love from his victims. Arendt exploded: "How can you say such a thing to me, a victim of Hitler, a person who has been in a concentration camp!" Mary McCarthy's apology and her effort to explain went into the air. "I slunk away," McCarthy remembered; but Arendt went on to complain to Philip Rahv: "How can you have this kind of conversation in your home, you, a Jew?"

The reconciliation came several years later when both women were included in a small group that met with Dwight Macdonald to discuss the future of his magazine, *politics*. Arendt took the initiative by remarking, as she and McCarthy stood on the empty subway platform after a meeting, how often they formed a minority of two in the discussions: "we two think so much alike." Mary McCarthy was finally able to offer her explanation of the original remark and Arendt admitted that she had never been in a concentration camp, only in an internment camp. Soon afterwards, Arendt sealed the new understanding by sending McCarthy an appreciative note about *The Oasis*—"it is a real jewel"—at just the moment when appreciation was needed.[44] The book had stirred up much criticism, and one of the *Partisan Review* coterie who recognized facets of himself in McCarthy's characters was considering a libel suit. McCarthy and her husband, Bowden Broadwater, were then invited to squeeze themselves into the Blüchers' 95th Street rooms for a dinner.

Mary McCarthy later became one of the Blüchers' closest friends. She was one of the few Americans in whose presence Hannah Arendt overcame the shyness she felt toward those she had not known since her youth or in an atmosphere that evoked her youth, an atmosphere of German culture where the right quotation from Goethe was always at hand. Mary McCarthy had a quality which transcended cultural differences, and this Hannah Arendt described in a letter she wrote to support McCarthy's 1959 application for a Guggenheim Foundation grant. Noting the obvious, that McCarthy had "satirical talent," she went on to give a not-so-obvious explanation of the quality in which that talent was rooted: "What distinguishes her from other writers in the field is that she reports her findings from the viewpoint and with the amazement of a child who [has] discovered that the Emperor [has] no clothes. . . . She always begins by believing quite literally what everybody says and thus prepares herself for the finest, most wonderful clothes. Whereupon the Emperor enters—stark naked. This inner tension between expectation and reality... gives her novels a rare dramatic quality."[45] Their "inner tensions" were similar, and their high expectations for people and for the world, that is, the quality of their unrequited adoration, was often similarly misunderstood. Those who have never in their early lives awaited an emperor or, in their more mature lives, cultivated the ability to retain their inner tension when their expectations are no longer so high, seldom find in satire and irony anything innocent. McCarthy, like Randall Jarrell, impressed Hannah Arendt as a wide-eyed but very worldly child; the kind of person with whom she, who was more than a little of the same species, could feel (as she had said to Jarrell) "intoxicated against a world of enemies."

If there was one quality in people that attracted Hannah Arendt above all others it was innocence of a special sort: innocence in combination with wide experience, innocence preserved. In the letters she wrote and received toward the end of the 1940s and in the early 1950s—as in the portrait of Waldemar Gurian she wrote after his death in 1954 and published in the magazine he had edited, the *Review of Politics*—her attraction to the self-consciously innocent ones is everywhere apparent. She said of Gurian in her memorial essay what she might have said of all her innocents: "He was delighted when he could break down the barriers of so-called civilized society, because he saw in them barriers between human souls. At the source of this delight were innocence and courage, innocence all the more captivating as it occurred in a man who was extremely well versed in the ways of the world, and who therefore needed all the courage he could muster to keep his original innocence alive and intact."[46] Innocence courageously preserved is an unpolitical way to describe what Hannah Arendt called self-conscious pariahdom.

In Randall Jarrell the combination of innocence and experience was remarkable. He had what Arendt called an "unerring sense for quality and relevance... infallible judgment in all artistic as well as human matters," and also the innocence of one who finds that "to his everlasting surprise [the world] was as it was."[47] When Hannah Arendt met Jarrell she discovered for the first time in an American the phenomenon she had known only among refugees. Jarrell had an innocent love of his language without ever having been deprived of it, though he complicated his relationship with English by falling in love with German:

> I believe
> —I do believe, I do believe—
> The country I like best of all is German.

Jarrell loved the country of the German language—and that made him the compatriot of Hannah Arendt, who thought of herself not as a German but as a speaker of German.

It was part of Hannah Arendt's own preservation of innocence to preserve her tie to her mother tongue, and the innocents she loved were always similarly related to theirs. For Gurian, "no poetry and literature—perhaps with the exception of Rilke in his later years—could equal his love of and familiarity with Russian writers." For Walter Benjamin, as for Martin Heidegger, the mother tongue was the only one in which it was possible to think poetically. But Jarrell was certainly the first of the innocents to preserve his innocence by loving another language as unrequitedly as any troubadour ever loved his inaccessible lady. Hannah Arendt once sent him some "awfully simple" translations of Hölderlin's poems and he thanked her for them wistfully: "would that I could know what [German is] really like."

From his letters, it is clear that Jarrell was as amazed by Hannah Arendt's capacity for dramatic identification with what she observed as she was by his. All of the other innocents felt this and, in their own ways, expressed it. Mary McCarthy's correspondence with Arendt did not begin until the mid-1950s, but she did later commit to writing a description of Hannah Arendt giving a public lecture in the mid-1940s: "I was reminded of what Bernhardt must have been or Proust's Berma, a magnificent stage diva. . . . What was theatrical about Hannah was a kind of spontaneous power of being seized by an idea, an emotion, a presentiment, whose vehicle her body then became, like an actor's. And this power of being seized and worked upon, often with a start, widened eyes, 'Ach!' (before a picture, a work of architecture, some deed of infamy), set her apart from the rest of us like a high electrical charge."[48]

## The Origins of Totalitarianism

The emotional power of the book Hannah Arendt started to write in 1945 and 1946, *The Origins of Totalitarianism*, came from her ability to sustain—through four years of intense effort and over five hundred dense, difficult pages—a deep, agonized "Ach!" before the deeds of infamy she analyzed. She and Blücher viewed the book as a frontal assault on Europe's Nineteenth Century, the Bourgeois Century that had cast up the elements from which totalitarianism crystallized in Germany. She began the book while her European friends were absent, out of reach by mail, perhaps lost forever, and she finished it just before she made her first return visit to Europe in 1949. In those years, she felt, Europe's destiny hung in the balance. Arendt had dedicated her early years in America to Jewish politics. At the end of the war, she turned to more general issues: What principles should guide politics in a world shaken by such a war? Can there be a new Europe? Can there be a true comity of nations? The news that finally came from Europe—that Jaspers and his wife had survived, that the Weils were reunited and well—sustained her personally through the arduous work of writing in English. But it was her own innocence preserved, her willingness to keep her mind open and to change the main lines of her book as she learned more about what had happened in Europe during the war, that gave her book its quality of amazement and outrage. While she wrote of the past and for the future, she took as a motto a maxim of Jaspers's: Treue ist das Zeichen der Wahrheit, loyalty is the sign of truth.[49]

In the late fall of 1944 or the early winter of 1945, Hannah Arendt submitted to Mary Underwood of Houghton Mifflin the first outline of the book she intended to write. She called the book *The Elements of Shame: Anti-Semitism—Imperialism—Racism*. She also referred to it by the even more dramatic title, *The Three Pillars of Hell*. Sometimes she called it simply A *History of Totalitarianism*. Not until six years later when the book, considerably altered and enlarged from the original outline, was nearly ready for publication was its final title decided upon. But even that title, *The Origins of Totalitarianism*, seemed unsatisfactory, for the book was not a genetic study like Darwin's *Origin of Species*. Hannah Arendt wanted, and never found, a title that reflected the method of the book, which was very clearly different from those of traditional historiography. Had she been willing to settle for a title that captured not her approach but her tone, the title used over her protest when the book was released in England, *The Burden of Our Time*, would have been less confusing.

Prompted by Mary Underwood's questions about how the parts of the book were to be tied together, Arendt explained her methodological difficulty in a letter dated 24 September 1946. Historians usually presume that the events and periods they write about are parts of a sequence, an unfolding or development which is linked to the present. But, Arendt wrote, "I kept away from historical writing in the strict sense, because I feel that this continuity is justified only if the author wants to preserve, to hand down his subject matter to the care and memory of future generations. Historical writing in this sense is always a supreme justification of what has happened."[50] To justify the three subjects she was concerned with—anti-Semitism, imperialism, and racism—was impossible. Equally impossible, she thought, was simple condemnation. "A mere polemical approach has also been avoided. It is permitted only as long as the author can fall back upon a firm ground of traditional values which are accepted without questioning and on which judgments can be formed.... I no longer believe that any tradition in itself can offer us such a basis. A polemical approach, in my case, would have been simply cynical and certainly unconvincing." She could not write as the exemplary polemicist, Marx, had written *The Eighteenth Brumaire of Louis Bonaparte*, that is, as an attacker who had a better vision to offer, a new—or an old— solution to existing problems. Hannah Arendt viewed herself as a discoverer of existing problems. The three elements—anti-Semitism, imperialism, and racism—were each the expression of a problem or complex of problems for which the Nazis' answers, when they "crystallized," offered a terrifying "solution." The methodological alternative she chose was "to find out the main elements of Nazism, to trace them back and to discover the underlying real political problems.... The aim of the book is not to give answers but rather to prepare the ground."

On the ground she prepared in her first book, Hannah Arendt later built the intellectual foundations for an answer. She based this answer on the council system, a one-hundred-year-old tradition which harked back to "traditional values... on which judgments can be formed," if not to values which were "accepted without questioning." Looking back on her first book at the time of its second edition in 1958, and noting the most recent evidence of the vitality of the council-system tradition, she explained why she had added to *The Origins of Totalitarianism* a chapter on the 1956 Hungarian Revolution:

There is in this chapter a certain hopefulness—surrounded, to be sure, with many qualifications—which is hard to reconcile with the assumption of [the last section of *The Origins of Totalitarianism*] that the *only* clear expression of the present age's problems up to date has been the horror of totalitarianism. . . . [The Hungarian Revolution] has brought forth once more a form of government which, it is true, was never really tried out, but which can hardly be called new because it has appeared with singular regularity for more than a hundred years in all revolutions. I am speaking of the council-system, the Russian *soviets*, which were abolished in the initial stages of the October Revolution, and of the central European *Räte*, which first had to be liquidated in Germany and Austria before [those countries'] insecure party democracies could be established. . . . While not unaware of the role which the council-system had played in all revolutions since 1848, I had no hope for its reemergence. . . . The Hungarian Revolution had taught me a lesson.[51]

Lacking the lesson of the Hungarian Revolution and not having yet arrived at her reflections of the 1950s on the nature and possibilities of action, Hannah Arendt initially set out simply to present the elements of Nazism and the political problems underlying them.

Full-fledged imperialism in its totalitarian form is an amalgam of certain elements which are present in all political conditions and problems of our time. Such elements are anti-Semitism, decay of the national state, racism, expansion for expansion's sake, alliance between capital and mob. Behind each of these elements is hidden an unsolved real problem: behind anti-Semitism the Jewish Question; behind the decay of the national state, the unsolved problem of a new organization of peoples; behind racism, the unsolved problem of a new concept of mankind; behind expansion for expansion's sake, the unsolved problem of organizing a constantly shrinking world which we are bound to share with peoples whose histories and traditions are outside the western world. The great appeal of a full-fledged imperialism [that is, totalitarianism] was based on a wide-spread, frequently conscious, conviction that it provided the answers to these problems and [would] be able to master the tasks of our times.

In none of the drafts of *The Origins of Totalitarianism* did Arendt present these problems or pose their challenges as succinctly as in the memos to Mary Underwood. The book lacked an introductory overview, and this is one of the reasons why many of its readers felt overwhelmed by its vast historical panoramas, baffled by its many excursions into little known and seemingly unrelated issues. Similarly, the book lacked a methodological statement, an explanation of what the image of crystallization implied. A gesture in this direction was made in the Concluding Remarks of the first edition, but the clearest statement of her methodology, part of Hannah Arendt's lectures at the New School in 1954 on "The Nature of Totalitarianism," never appeared in the book. In those lectures, she said:

The elements of totalitarianism form its origins if by origins we do not understand "causes." Causality, i.e., the factor of determination of a process of events in which always one event causes and can be explained by another is probably an altogether alien and falsifying category in the realm of the historical and political sciences. Elements by themselves probably never cause anything. They become origins of events if and when they crystallize into fixed and definite forms. Then, and only then, can we trace their history backwards. The event illuminates its own past, but it can never be deduced from it.[52]

Although she was certain at the beginning of her work about the underlying questions and principles of each of the major early sections, Hannah Arendt changed her mind several times about the book's overall organization and about the content of its final sections. She started off with the three-part schema so dramatically reflected in the title *Three Pillars of Hell*, proposing eleven chapters under the headings "On Anti-Semitism," "On Imperialism," and "On Racism." The second outline suggested thirteen chapters under four headings: "The Jewish Road to the Storm-Center of Politics," "The Disintegration of the National State," "Expansion and Race," and "Full-fledged Imperialism." Only the thirteenth chapter in this scheme, called "Race-Imperialism: Nazism," touched on the vast subject matter of the third part of the final product. The book Hannah Arendt finally wrote had three parts: Anti-Semitism, Imperialism, and Totalitarianism, with the third section actually beginning where the earlier outlines stop. What Arendt knew in 1946 as race-imperialism, she later, based on a quite different understanding, called totalitarianism.

Much of the material that makes up the anti-Semitism and imperialism sections of *The Origins of Totalitarianism* had been written before 1946, and some of it had already been published in articles. The material of the third section dates from 1948 and 1949. Hannah Arendt had viewed Nazism as one logical outcome of the crystallization of the elements involved in anti-Semitism, imperialism, and racism. She had called Nazism not "totalitarianism" but "race-imperialism" (the phrase came from Franz Neumann's *Behemoth*) and she had not concerned herself with the only other regime she later thought was totalitarian— Stalinist Russia. By the fall of 1947 she had changed her plan again. The second part, on imperialism, was to be finished by the end of 1947. Then she would take up the third: "This I have to write from the beginning [that is, not based on published articles] since the really essential things— which I have to put together with Russia—are just now coming clear to me."[53]

After the war, a great deal of material on both Nazi and Russian concentration and slave-labor camps began to appear in survivors' memoirs, diaries, novels, and poems, as well as in official documents. As she read such works as Eugen Kogon's *Der SS-Staat*, David Rousset's *Les Jours de notre mort*, and an anonymous memoir of Russian camps, *The Dark Side of the Moon*, Arendt came to the conclusion that it was the concentration camps that fundamentally distinguished the totalitarian form of government from any other. The camps were essential and unique to this form of government. The imperialists' protective-custody camps and the internment camps which existed during the First World War and both before and during the Second World War in Europe and America were institutions of a fundamentally different sort. Arendt became aware of the similarities between the Nazi regime and the regime of Stalin in Russia by comparing the use both regimes made of concentration camps: "Both Nazi and Soviet history provide the evidence to demonstrate that no totalitarian government can exist without terror and no terror can be effective without concentration camps."[54] This insight is the key to the theory of totalitarianism Arendt developed in her first book.

When she became aware of the importance of concentration camps in the totalitarian regimes, Arendt prepared a memo for *Jewish Social Studies*, dated 10 December 1948, requesting support for a "Research Project on Concentration Camps." The project would include locating documents on the camps and preparing a bibliography, interviewing survivors, writing a history of the camps against the background of a survey of all types of detention and internment camps in use prior to the war, and evaluating all the assembled materials. A similar proposal formed part of a general project Hannah Arendt recommended to Elliot Cohen, the editor of *Commentary*. She asked whether *Commentary* would support a research institute to investigate not only the concentration camps but the entire spectrum of postwar Jewish issues as they related to worldwide political trends. "We [Jews] lack an intelligentsia which has been grounded in history and educated through a long political tradition," she told Cohen as she outlined her hope that a research institute could provide Jews with information to prepare them for the possibility that "world political developments may well again crystallize around hostility to the Jews."[55] Arendt's fear that the Jews might again become a precipitating element in world politics was not expressed directly in *The Origins of Totalitarianism*. She had, in fact, originally planned to include an essay called "Zionism Reconsidered" in the book, but she thought better of her plan when she realized that the essay would be extremely controversial; she also recognized that the situation of Jewry was changed dramatically by the 1948 war that brought Israel into existence as a state.

Hannah Arendt made her proposals to *Jewish Social Studies* and *Commentary* on the basis of her research on the concentration camps, summarized in a July 1948 article for *Partisan Review*. This article, "The Concentration Camps," later constituted the penultimate section of *The Origins of Totalitarianism*. But in the second edition of *Origins* the article was followed by three powerful pages in which the trajectory of Arendt's analysis reached its philosophical target: the concept of radical evil. These pages, which had originally been embedded in the first edition's Concluding Remarks, reveal Arendt's philosophical questions about the nature of evil with which she struggled until her last book, *The Life of the Mind*:

The concentration camps are the laboratories where changes in human nature are tested. . . . In their efforts to prove that everything is possible, totalitarian regimes have discovered without knowing it that here are crimes which men can neither punish nor forgive. When the impossible was made possible it became the unpunishable, unforgiveable absolute evil which could no longer be understood and explained by the evil motives of self-interest, greed, covetousness, resentment, thirst for power, and cowardice: and therefore which anger could not revenge, love could not endure, friendship could not forgive.[56]

There was no philosophical tradition within which this absolute evil could be understood. Only by an analysis of the "elements" crystallizing in totalitarianism—overpopulation, expansion and economic superfluity, and social rootlessness and the deterioration of political life—could this absolute evil be illuminated. Philosophical inquiry was postponed in the face of the threat posed by the last sentence of the book: "Totalitarian solutions may well survive the fall of totalitarian regimes in the form of strong temptations which will come up whenever it seems impossible to alleviate political, social and economic misery in a manner worthy of man."[57]

An inquiry into the "political and philosophical significance of the concept of human dignity, and the threat to its survival in our society that concentration camps constitute" was the final task of the project Hannah Arendt had suggested to *Jewish Social Studies* in 1948. The proposed research projects never came about; neither *Jewish Social Studies* nor *Commentary* was in a position to finance large-scale undertakings. But Arendt went ahead on her own, incorporating her research on the concentration camps into the third part of *The Origins of Totalitarianism* and later preparing for the second edition of the book an epilogue called "Ideology and Terror" in which she outlined her general reflections. She also used her research to try to understand the postwar political developments she had noted in the introduction to her *Jewish Social Studies* proposal. For example, she had suggested in her proposal that the violent hostility displayed by the Russians at the end of the war—a hostility found shocking by Europeans and Americans, who considered Russia an ally—was understandable only if the totalitarian nature of Stalin's regime was taken fully into account. "It is only now beginning to be realized that what makes Russian policy so hostile to the Western world is not a conflict between national interests and not even a mere antagonism in general ideology, but the fact that a totalitarian state ruled by terror cannot possibly feel secure in a nontotalitarian world."[58] This conclusion was coupled with a statement comparing democratic and totalitarian countries, a statement which flew against the Marxist analyses current at the time. Arendt claimed that the Nazis' and the Russians' reliance on terror, institutionalized in the concentration camps, was what crucially distinguished them from democratic countries:

All other differences between the institutions of democratic and totalitarian countries can be shown to be secondary and side issues. This is not a conflict between socialism and capitalism, or state-capitalism and free enterprise, or a class-ridden and a classless society. It is a conflict between a government based on civil liberties and a government based on concentration camps. The many turns of Hitler's and Stalin's political lines have been remarkable as well as confusing; the only point on which no compromises and no opportunistic changes can be expected is the use of terror, the institution of concentration camps and the permanent abolition of civil liberties, because the power of totalitarian governments is primarily based on them.

The last part of *The Origins of Totalitarianism*, which expresses the conviction that the Nazi regime and Stalin's regime were essentially the same form of government, was written in 1948 and the spring of 1949. Early in 1948, the newspapers were filled with reports on the congressional debates over what came to be known as the Marshall Plan. Winds of opinion from liberal and pro-Communist groups denouncing the plan as anti-Soviet joined with blasts from conservatives, in agreement with Senator Robert Taft, denouncing the plan as "global New Dealism." The storm gathered enormous momentum in February when a Communist coup ousted the Czechoslovakian government. For a brief period, fear of war spread across America and, for a much longer period, fear of Communism, foreign and domestic, became firmly entrenched. Across the country, nerves wore thin. Blücher, the "former Communist," was outraged by the American zealotry; Arendt tried to understand the anti-Communist rhetoric, the accusations and anger, but she also admitted that fanaticism was creating an unbearable atmosphere, "a physical nerve-torture."[59] The distinction she had drawn in her book between the Soviets' aggressive foreign policy and the Soviets' violations of the right she considered fundamental, the right of each individual and every people to be part of a polity, was lost in the rhetorical excesses of both liberals and conservatives in the United States. "Crimes against humanity have become a kind of specialty of totalitarian regimes. In the long run, it will do more harm than good if we confuse this supreme kind of crime with a long series of other crimes which these regimes also indiscriminately commit—such as injustice and exploitation, deprivation of liberty and political oppression. Such crimes are familiar in all tyrannies and will hardly ever be found sufficient to justify interference with another country's sovereign affairs."[60] Arendt felt that the Russians' aggressive foreign policy did not license intervention, but she argued, on the other hand, that Russian concentration camps "in which millions are deprived of even the doubtful benefits of the law of their own country, could and should become the subject of action that would not have to respect the rights and rules of sovereignty."[61] She did not suggest what form such action might take, though it is clear that she felt it would have to be taken by a comity of nations, not by one country alone.

By the time the Marshall Plan was accepted by Congress in April, the mood of the country had relaxed somewhat. And by the time the presidential nominating conventions appeared on the summer horizon, the Truman administration's policies for the containment of Communism seemed plausible, even if Truman himself did not seem likely to remain the director of the policy. During Truman's unexpectedly dramatic and successful campaign, Arendt worked on the final part of her manuscript and developed an analysis of the emerging "two-block" world situation for presentation in lectures. Characteristically, she avoided the extremes of American opinion, both right and left. She was staunchly antitotalitarian, as her proposal to *Jewish Social Studies* and her book indicate. But she was also very concerned about the form American opposition to totalitarianism was taking and about the emerging leftist European criticism of the American opposition, which she thought was based on a misunderstanding.

In a 1948 lecture delivered at the Rand School, a meeting place for socialists, she considered the use among disenchanted American socialists of the term "anti-Stalinism."[62] "The preference for the term anti-Stalinism, as distinguished from anti-Bolshevism or anti-totalitarianism, is significant: no anti-Nazi would have called himself an anti-Hitlerite because this would have meant he was a participant in the interior struggle of the Nazi party, a colleague of Roehm or Strasser perhaps, but no enemy of Nazism. Similarly, the term anti-Stalinism originated in the interior struggles of the Bolshevik party where, in the Twenties, one could be for or against Bukharin, for or against Zinoviev, for or against Trotsky, for or against Stalin." Hannah Arendt was worried that genuinely antitotalitarian espousers of anti-Stalinism would be perceived merely as followers of Stalin's Russian opponents and find themselves "mixed up with the wrong kind of friends against the wrong kind of enemies," despite their convictions. And, second, she feared that anti-Stalinism as a credo of a vague sort would lock its adherents into worn-out political positions. "It was bad enough, in a sense, that the whole radical movement of our time was destroyed through identification with and usurpation by the Russian Revolution; it was worse that the fixation on Russia survived the disillusionment with the Revolution. And this approach is no less outdated when the younger generation, which lacks even the political experience and sorrows behind present-day clichés, begins to adopt it for lack of anything else." Arendt noted that because American anti-Stalinists did not need to worry about domestic Bolshevism, since Bolshevism was only "a possible menace from abroad helped by domestic espionage," they had become concerned almost exclusively with foreign policy. This foreign policy orientation fundamentally distinguished American anti-Stalinists from their European counterparts.

Western Europeans who had witnessed the dedication of the

Moscow-directed Communist parties before and during the war understood that "the danger of a so-called fifth column is much more real than the danger of mere espionage." Anti-Stalinism in France, for example, often took on "a definite nationalist flavor" and led many into the De Gaulle movement, for "despite the definite totalitarian potentialities and authoritarian certainties of a De Gaulle government, they prefer... a native dictatorship to a foreign one." On the other hand, many intellectuals in France were hostile to the American brand of anti-Stalinism and even inclined to fellow-travelerism out of such hostility. They saw American anti-Stalinism as a simpleminded adherence to the status quo in America and, more ominously, to the status quo in Europe, "especially because the Marshall Plan has had the inevitable consequence of supporting otherwise tottering governments (for example, in France)." For many Europeans, Arendt felt, "the great political issue of freedom versus total domination is overshadowed by the fear of extinction." Both America and Russia, interpreted ideologically as imperialist (or fascist) and communist respectively, looked to Europeans like the enemy. In this atmosphere, even "Europeanism" or hope for European federation took on chauvinistic overtones; old nationalisms found a new and larger scope in European nationalism.

Hannah Arendt dedicated her lecture to two hopes: that American anti-Stalinists would give up their ties to past factions within the Russian revolution in order to oppose totalitarianism as more than the creation of Stalin and that critical Europeans would give up their misunderstandings of American anti-Stalinism. To the second end, she offered an interpretation of the European misunderstanding which shows clearly both what she had learned about the nation she had been living in for eight years and also how she applied a distinction fundamental for her thought to the American scene—the distinction between society and the body politic.

"The European visitor simply cannot perceive the political realities of the United States because they are so well hidden by the surface of a society whose publicity and public relations multiply all social factors as a mirror multiplies light so that the glaring facade appears to be the overwhelming reality." She recognized that European leftists would not understand how social conformists could be political independents with deep feelings of responsibility as citizens. European Marxists, accustomed to think of political forces as socially determined, were baffled by a situation in which social and political forces seldom matched and frequently contradicted each other. Arendt herself marvelled that "a Twentieth Century (and in some respects a Nineteenth Century) society lives and thrives on the solid basis of an Eighteenth Century political philosophy," almost uninfluenced by European "worshippers of history." Even Americans reared on Marxist theories, she felt, "theoretically, so to speak, cannot believe their eyes" when they look at their country. "Practically, however, they have enough sense not to oppose a form of government that they know is among the few survivors of true political freedom, and among the even fewer guarantors of that minimum of social justice without which citizenship is impossible."[63]

American intellectuals who oppose totalitarianism, Hannah Arendt argued, have failed to help Europeans understand that they are opposed to the American *social* traits which seem to Europeans potentially totalitarian: prevailing conformism, identification of individuals with jobs, concentration on achievement and success, and fantastic overestimation of publicity. They have not taught Europeans that social criticism is compatible with support for the political status quo. In the Rand School lecture she bluntly stated her own conviction, which she assumed true intellectuals shared, that "intellectually, [social] nonconformism is almost the *sine qua non* of achievement," and urged American intellectuals to hold firmly to this conviction as well as to admit their adherence to American constitutionalism, rather than persist in the rhetoric of anti-Stalinism.

When she delivered this lecture, Hannah Arendt was confirmed in a stance she never abandoned: the eighteenth-century American republican principles were to be upheld while all the domestic forces which threatened them—all of the nineteenth- and twentieth-century forces of political unfreedom as well as all the evils of mass society—were to be opposed. She was and remained both a conservative and a revolutionary, and she never lost the sense of urgency that led her to rush her views into print even though she was aware that the haste left her vulnerable to criticism from those who were either simply conservative or simply liberal.

The reflections Arendt offered in her 1948 Rand School lecture indicate that she was preparing to make a second major turn in her work. She had first turned to the concentration camps as the essential institution of Nazism and then turned to a theoretical overview: concentration camps (and terror) are essential to totalitarianism in general, *überhaupt*. This second turn, as all critics of the book have noticed, produced a grave unbalance in *The Origins of Totalitarianism*. Nazism is discussed in detail, and the bulk of the background material on anti-Semitism and imperialism is relevant to Nazism, but Stalinist Russia is discussed only in the last section. Arendt's failure to discuss Russian history or Marxist-Leninist ideology led many critics of the book's first edition in 1951 to question whether Arendt's model of developing totalitarianism was, in fact, too general to have any real explanatory power. And the detotalitarianizing developments in Russia after the death of Stalin led critics of the 1958 edition of the book to question the accuracy of Arendt's claim that the dizzying momentum of totalitarian regimes can be checked only by external resistance from nontotalitarian countries. In 1968, when she wrote a new introduction to her book, Arendt herself coined the word "detotalitarianizing" for developments in Russia.

Arendt was aware that her book lacked balance. She planned to spend 1952 and 1953 writing a separate study called "The Marxist Elements of Totalitarianism" to address the problem and provide the missing analyses. Her proposal for this book gives no indication that she intended to modify her central claim—that concentration camps are the essence of totalitarianism. What she wanted to do was to use the method she had developed in *The Origins of Totalitarianism* to draw a portrait of nineteenth-century Russia and to discuss Marxism as it was adapted in Russia, first by Lenin and then by Stalin.[64] She would have stressed the central difference between Nazism and Bolshevism, the difference between the ideology of Nature and the ideology of History, but she did not think that the differences in organization or form of government in the two regimes were essential.

The reason why Arendt let *The Origins of Totalitarianism* go to press in its unbalanced state is also clear, between the lines, in her Rand School lecture. In an atmosphere of confused opposition to Stalin, rather than to totalitarianism in general, she thought her book was urgently needed. In her 1948 article for the *Partisan Review*, she made a statement (which was incorporated into *The Origins of Totalitarianism*) that expressed the urgency: "An insight into the nature of totalitarian rule, directed by our fear of the concentration camp, might serve to devaluate all outmoded political shadings from left to right and, beside and above them, to introduce the most essential political criterion for judging the events of our time: will it lead to totalitarian rule or will it not?"[65] Arendt's concern that a *political* criterion for judgment be clearly stated overrode all considerations of adequate documentation or coherence of design. She and her teacher, Karl Jaspers, shared the feeling he expressed in 1946: "What happens today will perhaps one day found and establish a world."[66]

# CHAPTER 6

# A Private Face in Public Life

## (1948-1951)

> ... Vieles aber ist
> Zu behalten. Und Noth die Treue.
> Vorwärts aber und rükwärts wollen wir
> Nicht sehn. Uns wiegen lassen, wie
> Auf schwankem Kahne der See.
>
> [ ... But there is much
> to be borne. And one must be true.
> Neither before nor after should we
> look. But rather lie rocking.
> Like a boat cradled in the sea.]

Hölderlin

### The Europeans

The Blüchers were at Salo Baron's country house in Connecticut when the news that Paris had been liberated came over the radio. They celebrated 8 May 1945 with champagne and hoped that a new life would come to the country that Hannah Arendt admitted was the only one she felt homesick for in America. Letters from France had been few and far between in the last two years of the war, and Arendt had waited eagerly for what she always called *gute Nachrichten*, good reports, of reassembled families and safe returns to Paris. A good report had come from Anne Weil, who had been working for the French Resistance, that Eric Weil had been released from a German prisoner-of-war camp and that they were back in Paris. By the end of the summer of 1945 good news had begun to come, finally, from Germany.

Melvin Lasky, at the time a correspondent for the *Partisan Review* and stationed with the American occupation forces in Germany, took an issue of Dwight Macdonald's *politics* to Karl Jaspers. In the course of his conversation Lasky mentioned Hannah Arendt's name.[1] Jaspers was stunned. He told Lasky that the last contact he had had with her was in 1938 and asked if he and his wife could write to her through the American military post. The letter was sent in September 1945.

"Often have we thought, with sorrowful concern, about your fate over these years," Jaspers wrote in his slow, meditative style, "and for a long time have had little hope that you were still alive."[2] To Arendt's great

212

relief, Jaspers reported that her school friend Hans Jonas had appeared in Heidelberg—in the uniform of the Jewish Brigade of the British Army. Arendt was able to send a reassuring return letter, greetings for Jonas, and packages of food, coffee, and clothing through Lasky, whom Jaspers jokingly called their *Weihnachtsmann*, their Father Christmas. "Since I learned that you two have come through this whole hellish spectacle safely, it is somehow more homelike for me to live in this world," she wrote to her former teacher.[3] Both her letters and her packages were a great help to the Jasperses in the severely taxing time of shortages and confusion—moral and political—that followed on the war's end. "It is a life in fiction," Jaspers wrote, "and daily I say to myself: patience, and more patience—on no account be discouraged—if one does what one can, then a better time will always come."[4]

This serene confidence of Jaspers's had been like a beacon to those who needed some sign of hope for the future. After a visit in Heidelberg Lasky wrote: "The visitors to 66 Plock are constant and wearing. So many are looking to the Jaspers for advice and help—Mrs. Jaspers as a Jewess, the professor as a spiritual force."[5] People sensed what Hannah Arendt later described in a "Laudatio" she delivered in 1958: "There is something fascinating about a man's being inviolable, untemptable, unswayable."[6]

The political and intellectual independence Jaspers had shown during the Nazi regime, as he was barred first from university administration, then from teaching, and finally, in 1938, from publishing, had been tested to the utmost when he and his wife learned that their deportation was scheduled for 14 April 1945. The American occupation of Heidelberg on 1 April saved Karl and Gertrud Jaspers, and it left him, at the age of sixty-two, with an urgent sense of his responsibilities toward the other Germans who had to find a new life after twelve years of Nazism. He asked himself and his countrymen: "What would make their lives worth living? Would they remain Germans, and in what sense? Would they have a task?"[7] Isolated and shaken, he still had the confidence to hope, as Arendt later said, "that he [did] not represent a private opinion, but a different, still hidden public view—'a footpath,' as Kant put it, 'which someday no doubt will widen out into a great highway.'"[8]

As their correspondence continued, Arendt and Jaspers were delighted to find that their footpaths had been going the same way. She wrote to tell Kurt Blumenfeld, her second father-figure, how deeply the renewed friendship had comforted her: "Jaspers wrote an extraordinarily beautiful letter and I was somehow very relieved that the continuity of my life, or, if you will, of my feelings, on two very important points has been reaffirmed. The first such taking up of lost threads was with you in New York, and I doubt if you could have guessed what that meant for me, inwardly, how very calm it made me. The second, with Jaspers, was not unexpected. I had secretly always reckoned on it, although I had not written to him since 1933. Trust is not an empty delusion, and in the long run it is the only thing that can assure one that one's private world is not also a Hell."[9]

Hannah Arendt's understanding of her Jewishness was tied to Blumenfeld and Blumenfeld's Zionism; her philosophical consciousness was tied to Jaspers and his *philosophischer Glaube*, his philosophical faith. Jaspers's letters were invitations to return to what she called "real calm for intellectual activity," something she told him she had not known "even by hearsay for twelve years."[10] He marvelled that in those years she had been able to maintain her good judgment and open-mindedness. "In your words," he told her, "I felt not only the personal loyalty but the spirit of impartial *humanitas* which does such endless good. Tears came to my eyes as I read your letter, for I felt how rare this is—for I had just had disappointments with those who now seek together for new beginnings."[11] Arendt's refusal to countenance the "automatic mistrust" she found so many Jews displaying toward non-Jews had impressed him.

Hannah Arendt was for Jaspers what he was for her: a symbol of continuity with the years before Hitler, when Jaspers had launched upon his "ascent" to philosophy, and she had marvelled at his example. He expressed this by writing to say how much he looked forward to the day when she would return to Heidelberg and sit with him at his writing table *als Doctorandin*, as though she were once again his doctoral student. Nothing, she replied, would please her more than to find herself in that *hellen Raum*, that bright space. Four years passed before Hannah Arendt visited Jaspers in 1949, when she felt not like a doctoral student, but like a daughter: she went to the Jaspers's new house in Basel, Switzerland, she told a friend, *wie man nach Hause kommt*, as one comes home.

Though Arendt's relationship with Jaspers was familial after they met again, it always remained reverential. She wrote to *Lieber Verehrtester* ("Dear Most Revered One"), and he to *Liebe Freundin* ("Dear Friend"), though after her first visit in 1949 he used *Liebe Hannah*. They addressed each other formally, with *Sie*, until she was, to her enormous pleasure, invited to use *Du*. But fifteen years of letters and meetings passed before this invitation came during the only visit that Arendt and Blücher made together to the Jaspers's home. Their letters contained notes on their activities and works in progress, political commentaries, philosophical reflections, but very few intimate or even personal remarks. Arendt replied to the Jaspers's questions about her way of life, but she kept a certain reserve. When Gertrud Jaspers asked her, in 1946, how long she and Blücher had been married, Arendt added the three years they had lived together to the six years they had been married and replied, nine years.[12] This deference toward the Jaspers's mores—or Arendt's image of them— lessened over the years but never disappeared; it was important for her to hold the man both she and Heinrich Blücher called their *Lehrer*, their teacher, in a special position of authority. But even more important was her need to please him. "I naturally count myself especially lucky," she told Blumenfeld, "that he is in such a great measure pleased with me; because it is like a childhood dream come true."[13] Jaspers was, finally, the father she had always wanted him to be.

Soon after they began to correspond in 1945, Jaspers and Arendt became coworkers. The bond with Jaspers sustained Arendt privately, but it was also crucial to her public life, her work, and her cultural ambassadorship. During the years they had been separated, they had both come to the same task: "Philosophy must become concrete and practical, without forgetting for a moment its origin," as Japsers put it.[14] With Hannah Arendt's friend from Frankfurt, Dolf Sternberger, and in cooperation with Werner Krauss and Alfred Weber, Jaspers founded a periodical called *Die Wandlung*. He was very eager that she join the remarkable group of authors the journal published during its four years of life from 1945 to 1949—Bertolt Brecht, Thomas Mann, Martin Buber, Carl Zuckmayer, T. S. Eliot, W. H. Auden, Jean-Paul Sartre, and Albert Camus among them. Jaspers arranged for a collection of Arendt's articles to appear as a book in the *Die Wandlung* series: *Sechs Essays* published in 1948 by Springer Verlag, was Hannah Arendt's first book since *Der Liebesbegriff bei Augustin* in 1929. By the same year, Arendt had arranged for Jaspers's *Die Schuldfrage* (*The Question of German Guilt*) to be published by the Dial Press in New York. She had started to translate the short book herself with Randall Jarrell standing by to help her "English" it, but she realized that it would be better to put it in the hands of a professional translator. E. B. Ashton was hired for the first of his many fine translations of Jaspers's works.

Hannah Arendt had private doubts about Karl Jaspers's book, but her loyalty to him and her awareness that his rare inviolability was a crucial public example overrode them. She thought that some of his prewar Weberian nationalism and his Protestant piety still lingered in his desire to "redeem the German people." Heinrich Blücher's opinion was even harsher. In a strident letter to Arendt he noted the conflict which he felt Jaspers still failed to recognize in all its clarity; using Marx's *Eighteenth Brumaire* for his terminology, he spoke of "the conflict between the republican will for freedom of the few and the Cossack-slavish disposition of the many" in Germany. Germany might have been a true battleground for the "civil war between Republicans and Cossacks, which is to say, citizens and barbarians," but this was not the war that took place. Jaspers's calm effort to help his countrymen examine their consciences before God was not political enough for Blücher: "Now, before God we are all sinners. But among men there is a difference between honor and dishonor, glory and ignominy. Let us also speak of ignominy; that is a worldly thing and it is well known that it can finally only be washed away with blood."[15] The sharp antithesis between citizens and those with no concept of true political life was in Arendt's mind as she began *The Origins of Totalitarianism*. As a Jewish republican, not a former student of Augustine, she wrote of glory and ignominy, heroism and baseness. Nonetheless, she sponsored Jaspers's *The Question of German Guilt*.

These efforts at making each other's work available were part of the concern Jaspers and Arendt shared for international exchanges. *Die Wandlung* was a European, not a German, journal; it brought Europe to Germany. Jaspers had been very impressed by the European spirit he encountered at the first Rencontres Internationales in Geneva in September 1946, when he made the acquaintance of Maurice Merleau-Ponty, Lucien Goldmann, Jean Wahl, Albert Camus, and Stephen Spender. He wrote to Arendt that the conference made him hopeful for a new Europe. And she replied with the opinion that Camus, particularly, was "a new type of person, who simply and without any 'European nationalism' is a European."[16] Arendt produced two essays, one on French existentialism and another called "What is Existenz Philosophy?" which were, like Jaspers's address to the Geneva conference, "The Spirit of Modern Europe," contributions to the task of making philosophy "concrete and practical."[17] They both wrote while the chance for political cooperation between the European nations was still alive, clearly aware that the chance would pass quickly.

Both Jaspers and Arendt were eager for *Die Wandlung*'s success, but both had reservations. "My spiritual capacities are so limited and my knowledge is so scanty," Jaspers wrote with the modesty typical of him. "I say to myself: so be it, whatever one can do is better than nothing. The masses must become less troubling to me; nonetheless, everything that is essential to us originates only with individuals and small groups. The chaos grows [Das Chaos wächst]."[18] Jaspers dedicated himself to finding a style that would reach a wide public; he made every effort to live up to the noble title one of his books received in English, *Philosophy is for Everyman*. Arendt's reservation was different. She viewed publication in *Die Wandlung* as a form of return to Germany—"writing is a kind of return"—and she wanted to be sure that she, in her writing, would be welcomed as a Jew: "none of us [Jews] can come back . . . unless we are welcome as Jews."[19]

Though Karl Jaspers was relatively well known in France, thanks to the efforts of Jean Wahl and Paul Ricoeur, his prewar work was little known in English-speaking countries, and not one of his works had been translated into English. Arendt presented a brief, dense statement of his fundamental orientation and concerns in her 1946 article, written for the *Partisan Review* and included in *Sechs Essays*, "What is Existenz Philosophy?" Jaspers was pleased with the article, but it was not one of Hannah Arendt's better efforts, and she never allowed it to be collected in an English volume. Arendt had had much practice in the difficult business of writing popularly about political issues and questions, but in her thirteen years of exile from Germany she had not tried her hand at philosophy proper, certainly not at the history of ideas, and she had never attempted to adapt her philosophical prose to English. In her role as ambassador from a relatively unknown philosophical tradition, she surveyed developments within German philosophy from Kant to Hegel in the light of their importance for Husserl, Jaspers, and Heidegger. The survey was a tour de force, but so full of elliptic and overpacked statements as to be nearly impenetrable to the general reader.

The style of Arendt's essay was simply awkward up to her discussion of Heidegger, at which point it became overwrought and acerbic. She included a footnote on Heidegger's membership in the Nazi party and his subsequent activities in which she relied entirely on rumor: "In his capacity as rector of Freiburg University, he forbade Husserl, his former teacher and friend, whose lecture chair he had inherited, to enter the faculty, because Husserl was a Jew. Finally, it has been rumored that he has placed himself at the disposal of the French occupational authorities for the reeducation of the German people."[20] After she had noted these alleged activities, Arendt continued in the ironic mode that always marked her greatest disappointments: "In view of the real comedy of this development, and of the no less real low level of political thought in German universities, one is naturally inclined not to bother with the whole story. On the other hand, there is the point that this whole mode of behavior has exact parallels in German Romanticism, so that one can scarcely believe the coincidence is accidental. Heidegger is, in fact, the last (we hope) romantic—as it were, a tremendously gifted Friedrich Schlegel or Adam Mueller, whose complete irresponsibility was attributed partly to the delusion of genius, partly to desperation." This last comment, of course, reflects Arendt's criticisms of the early nineteenth-century generation that brought to an end the cosmopolitan salons of Rahel Varnhagen, and is, insofar as she identified with Rahel, a personal statement. The first comment, with its combination of innocence and grimness sounds more like an amalgam of Arendt and Blücher. Randall Jarrell had once captured in a stroke the attitude of Blücher's that allowed him to see as comic the low level of German university political thought and of Heidegger's political activity: "His automatic acceptance of everybody was a judgment of mankind crueller, perhaps, than . . . impatient rejection of everybody. [One who rejects has] great expectations for humanity, expectations which any human being disappoints; anybody satisfied [his] expectations. The thought of how he had acquired these expectations was a disagreeable one."[21]

Arendt's interpretation of Heidegger's *Being and Time* emphasized everything in the book that could be construed as egoistical and grandiose ("making Man what God was in earlier ontology"), deceptive ("Heidegger's ontology hides a rigid functionalism in which Man appears only as a conglomerate of modes of Being"), rigidly systematic and—most important—contrary to the tradition of freedom and concern for humanity which Arendt admired in Kant and in the early ideals of the French Revolution. Over against every failing of Heidegger's, Arendt set an achievement of Jaspers's. After she surveyed Jaspers's concern for communication, for modest and unsystematic Socratic exploration, for clarity and illumination and, especially, for human freedom and "a new concept of humanity," Arendt could declare that with his work "Existenz philosophy has left the period of its egoism." Nonegoistical Existenz philosophy was what Jaspers and Arendt strove for, and the concepts that are central to both their works—concepts of community, friendship, dialogue, plurality—were formulated in explicit reaction against the legacy of nineteenth-century romantic individualism, the inheritance of the tradition of solitary philosophizing far from the world and from others.

When Hannah Arendt translated her commitment to nonegoistical Existenz philosophy into *The Origins of Totalitarianism*, she produced a portrait of intellectuals like Martin Heidegger which was less ironic and more impersonal, for she saw them as part of a vast historical process. This historical segment and the others in Arendt's panoramic work were knit together by a central image: the word *superfluous* captures it.[22] Through her book's sections on anti-Semitism and imperialism, Arendt traced a pattern of social class after social class collapsing from within and shifting in relationship to the emergent bourgeoisie and the nineteenth-century nation-state governments. The aristocrats, trying to retain their social dominance, resented governments which granted legal equality to their inferiors; the petty bourgeoisie resented the loss of their meager fortunes in the disastrous, state-sponsored, foreign business involvements of the 1860s and 1870s. The classes that resented the state also resented the group they thought had secret control of state power—the Jews, the "international Jewish banking conspiracy." At the turn of the century this resentment combined with racism, ironically enough, for by then the Jews had lost most of their financial power. The racism of European colonializers rebounded upon Europe. As the traditional social classes lost their specific class interests by involving themselves in the bourgeoisie's capitalistic ventures—expansion for expansion's sake, profit for profit's sake, power for power's sake—the classes crumbled. Those who became declassé inevitably came into contact with the superfluous residue of all classes: the mob, those Karl Marx had called the *Lumpenproletariat*, who had already fallen by the wayside in the bourgeoisie's triumph. When the declassé intellectual elites of the aristocracy and of the bourgeoisie encountered the mob, the elites and the mob discovered what they had in common: ferocious resentment of bourgeois hypocrisy and pretentiousness. One of the most powerful sections of *The Origins of Totalitarianism* contains a description of the mob-and-elite bond:

What spokesmen of liberalism and humanism usually overlook, in their bitter disappointment and unfamiliarity with the most general experiences of the time, is that an atmosphere in which all traditional values and propositions had evaporated . . . in a sense made it easier to accept patently absurd propositions than the old truths which had become pious banalities, precisely because nobody could be expected to take the absurdities seriously. Vulgarity with its cynical dismissal of respected standards and accepted theories carried with it a frank admission of the worst and a disregard for all pretenses which was easily mistaken for courage and a new style of life. . . . [Those] who had traditionally hated the bourgeoisie and voluntarily left respectable society saw [in the mob's absurdities] only the lack of hypocrisy and respectability, not the content itself. [23]

This statement was Hannah Arendt's acknowledgement of the temptation offered to the politically naive, such as Heidegger, by absurd notions of preindustrial simplicity, Teutonic toughness, and tribal purity.

Behind Hannah Arendt's descriptions of class dissolution and state hatred, the eighteenth-century theme of a European order of constitutional states can be heard like a chorus of "what might have been." What was, was the opposite. The mob grew as declassés joined with it, until it became "the underworld of the bourgeois class," that is, until the bourgeois class itself began to crumble. In its earlier stage, the mob was distinguished from "the people," and in its later, larger, stage it merged with "the masses," those without class consciousness. In the eighteenth century, le peuple had also come from all social strata, but in the revolutionary period, le peuple were those citizens who concerned themselves with political action. This fundamentally distinguished them from the masses who had never been integrated into any organization based on common interests and a shared world. Arendt's story of the deterioration of the state is woven together with her story of the loss, across all classes, of common interests and a shared world. When she wrote "What is Existenz Philosophy?" Arendt had called the result of the story "egoism"; when she wrote as a historian she called it "bourgeois individualism"; later, as a political theorist, she used the term "world alienation."

Arendt's analyses move through this intricate pattern of state hostility and the disintegration of classes, or superfluity, to a discussion of the ideological roots of totalitarianism in Pan-Germanism and Pan-Slavism, the "continental imperialisms" with ideologies of "tribal nationalism," which flourished when superfluous capital and superfluous people were put in the service of national expansion. The final turn from imperialism to totalitarianism came when "the masses," following leaders cast up from the mob (like Hitler) or from their own ranks (like Himmler) become superfluous in an entirely unprecedented way. Individuals first became isolated within their classes, and then, as the classes themselves deteriorated from within, they became atomized and dehumanized. In the totalitarian machines of domination and extermination, "the masses of coordinated philistines" provided the most efficient and ignominious functionaries. "The philistine is the bourgeois isolated from his own class, the atomized individual who is produced by the breakdown of the bourgeois class itself. . . . [He is] the bourgeois who in the midst of the ruins of his world worried about nothing so much as his private security, [and] was ready to sacrifice everything—belief, honor, dignity—on the slightest provocation."[24]

It was the masses for whom an ideology like racism could become so deeply persuasive. Arendt stressed again and again that these people lacked shared social or political interests, that they were concerned only with their private security. And this made them susceptible to ideologies without immediate class interest or utilitarian content. "The revolt of the masses against 'realism,' common sense, and 'all the plausibilities of the world' [Burke] was the result of their atomization, of their loss of social status along with which they lost the whole sector of communal relationships in which common sense makes sense. . . . Before the alternatives of facing anarchic growth and total arbitrariness of decay or bowing down before the most rigid, fantastically fictitious consistency of an ideology, the masses will probably choose the latter and be ready to pay for it with individual sacrifices—and this not because they are stupid or wicked, but because in the general disaster this escape grants them a minimum of self-respect."[25] A person who chooses an ideology can consider himself part of a triumphant tribe, a member of the master race, or in the vanguard of an inevitable historical process.

The great irony of this drama of one type of superfluity following upon another was revealed in the totalitarianism section of Arendt's book, which she wrote in 1948 after reading a library of materials on the concentration camps. The totalitarians themselves became superfluous: they felt themselves to be mere instruments of Nature or History, and as functionaries in concentration camps they were just as inanimate, or soulless, as their victims: "men who can no longer be psychologically understood."[26] Those who maintained an institution which was itself superfluous, which served no utilitarian purpose and was detrimental to all their social and political goals, were caught in the same net of "lunacy and unreality" as those they slaughtered. "Totalitarianism strives not toward despotic rule over men, but toward a system in which men are superfluous."[27]

Hannah Arendt never claimed that those intellectuals who were, like Heidegger, enchanted by the mob should be absolved of responsibility for their own roles in the National Socialist revolution. But in *The Origins of Totalitarianism* she did not look on the European intellectual tradition as responsible for Nazism. Unlike many refugees who had been trained in the German universities, she did not consider totalitarianism a logical product of an aberrant philosophical development or of the decline of humanist belief. A decade after the book was published, she offered a succinct turning of the tables on the history-of-ideas analysts of totalitarianism: "European humanism, far from being the root of Nazism, was so little prepared for it or any other form of totalitarianism that in understanding and trying to come to terms with this phenomenon we can't rely on either its conceptual language or its traditional metaphors. . . . This situation, however, contains a threat to humanism in all its forms: it is in danger of becoming *irrelevant.*"[28]

This was the conclusion Hannah Arendt had come to in the years after the war, as she renewed her relationship with Karl Jaspers and tried to find a way to understand Martin Heidegger. She refused the role of philosopher for which these men had trained her. She wrote as a historian and political theorist. But a way to redirect philosophy did, slowly, present itself. Nearly a decade passed before Hannah Arendt could complete *The Human Condition*, but she turned in its direction as she finished *The Origins of Totalitarianism*, and marked the turning with a short poem.

> The thoughts come to me,
> I am no longer a stranger to them.
> I grow in them as in a place,
> As in a plowed field.[29]

## Political Theory for the Present

*The Origins of Totalitarianism* was the book on which Hannah Arendt and Heinrich Blücher were able to collaborate most fully. Blücher was without employment for most of the time between 1945 and 1949, when it was written. This distressed Martha Arendt, who thought that her daughter was assuming too much responsibility for the household finances. But Arendt herself accepted the situation, both because she understood the almost paralyzing melancholy Blücher felt—"a melancholy," as she explained to Blumenfeld, "which erupted immediately over the gas chambers"[30]—and because she knew that his contribution to their book was necessary, for him and for the book. He spent his days reading at the New York Public Library and talking with their émigré friends while she worked at Jewish Cultural Reconstruction and then at Schocken Books. At home they talked about the book. In those years Blücher was the one who could keep up their friendships with the tribe members; Arendt was with their friends vicariously through him. However, it was she who kept up their friendships with the European *Freundeskreis* ("circle of friends") when the war ended and mail could finally reach Europe.

But both Arendt's correspondences and her work on the totalitarianism section of her book were brought to a halt in the spring of 1948. World History played an ominous trick. With all the horror of the Nazis' Final Solution to describe, with the task of telling how what should never have happened had happened, Arendt considered the fate of the Palestine Jews in a state of high emotion. With the Final Solution raw in their memories, the Jews of Palestine were preparing for war. As the British withdrew from their Mandate territory, the fighting between Jews and Arabs escalated.

During the years when she was writing *The Origins of Totalitarianism*, "returning" to Germany in words and acting as an ambassador for German philosophy and literature, Arendt had seldom participated in Jewish debates about the future of Palestine. In 1946 she had written an assessment of Jewish attitudes toward statehood for the fiftieth anniversary of the publication of Theodore Herzl's *Judenstaat*. The editors of *Commentary* magazine solicited her Herzl reflection, "The Jewish State Fifty Years After," and thus made amends for their reaction to an earlier article called "Zionism Reconsidered," which they had refused to publish; but their gesture did not mean that Hannah Arendt's opinions had any more force in 1946 than they had had before. No group or party followed her lead and she was as isolated as she had been in her *Aufbau* days.

"Zionism Reconsidered," Arendt's most strenuous critique of Jewish politics—from Revisionist party extremism through *pas de politique*, kibbutzim socialism—had been submitted to *Commentary* in 1944. The editors were disturbed by it and postponed their decision for months. When Arendt protested, one of the editors, Clement Greenberg, finally admitted that he thought it "contained too many anti-Semitic implications—not in the sense that you intend them as such implications, but that the unfriendly reader might intend them as such."[31] This assessment was a clear indication of a tendency that culminated in 1948: among many American Jews, any suggestion that Zionism was proceeding under revisionist banners was anti-Semitic. The more openly Arendt pressed her claim, the more isolated she became from the American Jews she had once respected for their lack of fanaticism.

"The only difference," Arendt had said bluntly in 1944 "between the Revisionists and the General Zionists today lies in their attitude towards England, and this is not a fundamental political issue."[32] This claim was the center of her reconsideration of Zionism, but she had also, in accordance with her usual thinking procedure, swept into the past and into the future. She had outlined the sequence of events in which Jewish nationalism had grown, to the detriment of Arab Palestinians, of Diaspora Jewry, and of international understanding. "The social-revolutionary Jewish national movement, which started a half a century ago with ideals so lofty that it overlooked the particular realities of the Near East and the general wickedness of the world, has ended—as do most such movements—with the unequivocal support not only of national but of chauvinistic claims—claims not against the foes of the Jewish people but against its possible friends and neighbors." The claims Arendt had been making for a decade were assembled in this article: the Jewish leadership had betrayed the Jewish people and appeased the Nazis by failing to support the 1935 boycott and by agreeing to the transfer of German goods to Palestine; the Jewish Agency had failed to negotiate a Jewish army and had become more and more reliant on foreign powers, particularly England; the Jewish socialists had ignored political realities while they made their admirable socioeconomic experiments, the kibbutzim. "Up to now," she had concluded, "no new approaches, no new insights, no reformulation of Zionism or the demands of Jewish people have been visible. And it is therefore only in the light of this past, with consideration of this present, that we can gauge the chances of the future."

Whenever Arendt wrote about Palestine, she repeated her prophecy that political organization in the postwar world would take one of two forms, empires or federations, and that the Jewish people would only have a chance for survival if federations were formed. She had desperately urged her people to avoid establishing a Jewish state which would only be a "sphere of interest" in foreign powers' empires, "while, at the same time, alienating the goodwill of neighbors." In "Zionism Reconsidered," which had finally appeared in a 1945 issue of Menorah Journal, as in her Aufbau pieces, Arendt had claimed that American Zionists might, because of the political tradition they had grown up in, be able to divert the resurgence of European nationalism among the emigrants to Palestine. Only in America, she had argued, was there any hope for Palestine. With the same perspectives, Arendt reentered the field of Jewish politics with a May 1948 article, "To Save the Jewish Homeland: There Is Still Time." For the first time, she found an audience. The article won Arendt the admiration of Judah Magnes—a man she had criticized in 1943 but whose flexibility and honesty shone through the darkness of Palestine in 1948 like a beacon.

Judah Magnes, who spent his youth and early adulthood in America, had for decades been criticizing the 1917 Balfour Declaration, hailed by most Jews as epoch-making. He felt that the British had had no right to promise the land of Palestine to any people and that their promise to the Jews could only result in hostility from the Arabs living on the land. Magnes had also warned that dependence on British imperialism would eventually lead the Jews of Palestine astray. Magnes was not alone in his prophetic but unpopular stance. As early as 1919 (in an article for *Der Jude*), the historian Hans Kohn had criticized the Jews of Palestine for their chauvinistic attitudes toward the Arabs, and a similar criticism was made by Robert Weltsch, editor of *Jüdische Rundschau*; the two men later became Arendt's colleagues when she worked with Magnes. In 1925 a group sharing these opinions was organized in Jerusalem and was called Brit Shalom. The members, fewer than one hundred, were not political activists: many were professors and writers, often of Central and West European origin. They offered a general proposal for a binational state in Palestine in which neither Jews nor Arabs would be a minority and both would have equal rights. At the time, this proposal was considered by most Zionists to be completely unrealistic, lacking in national feeling, or—more sinisterly—a disguised pathway to an Arab state. Brit Shalom was unable to generate support for its proposal among any group and after the 1929 street battles between Arabs and Jews the binationalism proposal was ignored. Magnes and a few others continued to work for a Jewish-Arab rapprochement, but most of the Brit Shalom members despaired when another Arab revolt began in April 1936 and continued intermittently through the summer of 1939.

In August 1942 Judah Magnes founded a party called Ikhud ("Unity") in Palestine and he issued a number of policy statements in his circle's thirty-year-old monthly journal *B'ayyoth Hayom* ("Problems of Today") and in American journals. It was an article entitled "Toward Peace in

Palestine," in the January 1943 issue of *Foreign Affairs* that had introduced his party's position to concerned Americans, including Hannah Arendt. The article drew much criticism and some outrage from American Zionists.

Hannah Arendt had recognized that Magnes's proposal, which was supported by such prominent intellectuals as Martin Buber and Ernst Simon and by the revered director of Youth Aliyah, Henrietta Szold, was a justified reaction to outworn, nineteenth-century nationalist formulas. But she felt that the notion of an Arab Federation tied to a vaguely conceived Anglo-American alliance was folly and represented nothing more than a variation of Chaim Weizmann's pro-British policies. The continuity of the Ikhud party with Weizmann, she felt, had been apparent in Magnes's earlier opposition to any action which could be interpreted as unfriendly to the Arabs or to the British—including not only the formation of a Jewish army but the Jewish Agency's unofficial recruitment program for the British army.

This disagreement might have made it impossible for Arendt to work with Magnes had she not been so sympathetic to Magnes's criticisms of the Jewish leadership. Since 1943 he had wanted to break with the Jewish Agency and to offer Jews in Palestine and elsewhere more than what Arendt called "pathetic declarations about the sufferings of the Jewish people and hollow demands for 'self-government' and 'a Jewish Commonwealth,' hollow because there is no reality behind them, because they are spoken in a vacuum without regard to the hostile plans of England or the general trends of world politics."[33] Arendt respected a party like Magnes's Ikhud because it represented *political* opposition to the Jewish Agency. And she felt that political opposition was particularly important at a time when parties of other sorts were forming in Palestine. She was critical of the Aliyah Hadasha, a party largely made up of new immigrants to Palestine who had banded together, she thought, in reaction to "tribal differences" among Jews, to social discrimination against newcomers, and to poor adjustment on the part of the newcomers. "The creation of a political party based upon differences within the Jewish people in Palestine herself is no less a danger for the Yishuv than the creation of an Irish party would be for the unity of the United States." Magnes's proposal (though not his party) and the formation of Aliyah Hadasha had marked the emergence into full bloom of what Arendt had called "the crisis of Zionism" and also marked the end of the Jewish Agency's effectiveness—an end she had expected ever since the Agency failed to negotiate a Jewish army.

During a trip to America in 1946 Magnes had gathered a number of his former acquaintances into a support group. The group, which included Maurice Hexter, Hans Kohn, Erich Fromm, James Marshall, Elliot Cohen, and David Riesman, was not officially a branch of Ikhud, but it espoused the Ikhud policies. While Magnes was in America, the Revisionist party's terrorist wing, the Irgun, joined by the Haganah, attacked railroads and oil-pipeline terminals, and the Irgun blew up a wing of the King David Hotel in Jerusalem, killing nearly one hundred Britons, Jews, and Arabs. The "Jewish Rebellion" was under way.

Unable to deal with the worsening situation, the British turned to the United Nations, which dispatched a Special Commission on Palestine in the summer of 1947. Magnes was heartened when Gromyko, the Soviet Union's UN representative, spoke out in favor of a binational state, but not when the special commission failed to follow his proposals. The commission's majority favored partitioning Palestine, while its minority favored a binational state with an Arab majority. On 29 November 1947 the General Assembly voted in favor of partition, and Magnes's Ikhud group, defeated, turned its attention to the chaos in Palestine, increasing daily as the British prepared to withdraw. Magnes was unable to do anything in Palestine to stop the fighting, and his efforts to get the United Nations to impose a cease-fire were viewed as nearly treasonable. After Israel was proclaimed as a state, Magnes returned to America and lent his voice to the efforts of his New York supporters to influence the American government to bring about a truce.

Magnes accepted the State of Israel after its May fourteenth birth, but he did not abandon his dream of Jewish-Arab cooperation. When he read Hannah Arendt's article in the May 1948 issue of *Commentary*, "To Save the Jewish Homeland: There Is Still Time", he realized that he had found a colleague. When he acknowledged the article on 11 May there was no time to find an alternative to statehood. But after 14 May Magnes enlisted Hannah Arendt's support for his hope that there was still time to save the newly declared state from extinction.

In her *Commentary* article, Arendt summarized the confusing story of the events since the November 1947 UN resolution and noted the dramatic shift in American Jewish opinion as the British Mandate drew to an end. The American Jews were joining the swing toward revisionism she had noted earlier in "Zionism Reconsidered."

Jewish left-wing intellectuals who a relatively short time ago still looked down upon Zionism as an ideology for the feebleminded, and viewed the building of a

Jewish homeland as a hopeless enterprise that they, in their great wisdom, had rejected before it ever was started; Jewish businessmen whose interest in Jewish politics had always been determined by the all-important question of how to keep Jews out of the newspaper headlines; Jewish philanthropists who had resented Palestine as a terribly expensive vanity, draining off minds from other more worthy purposes; the readers of the Yiddish press, who for decades had been sincerely, if naively, convinced that America was the promised land—all these, from the Bronx to Park Avenue down to Greenwich Village and over to Brooklyn are united today in the firm conviction that a Jewish state is needed, that America has betrayed the Jewish people, that the reign of terror by the Irgun and the Stern groups is more or less justified, and that Rabbi Silver, David Ben-Gurion, and Moshe Shertok are the real, if somewhat too moderate, statesmen of the Jewish people.[34]

There was also very little left of the differences of opinion that had so deeply divided the Palestinian Jews a year earlier. Voices in Palestine opposing "the chauvinism of the Revisionists, the middle-of-the-road nationalism of the majority party, [or] the antistate sentiments of a large part of the Kibbutz movement, particularly the Hashomer Hatzair" had largely disappeared. American and Palestinian Jews alike, Arendt felt, were ready for a fight to the death and ready to label any hindrance to the pursuit of victory, she wrote in a phrase with dreadful echoes, "a stab in the back."

To Hannah Arendt this emerging unanimity, hailed by many as the end of a centuries-long "Galut mentality," was ominous: "Mass unanimity is not the result of agreement, but an expression of fanaticism and hysteria." Such unanimity can lead to all manner of miscalculations— including the one Arendt was particularly troubled by, Jewish antipathy toward America and sympathy for Russia. With sarcasm and condescension, she characterized what she considered a misunderstanding of Russian policy as a "childlike hope" on the part of a "people without political experience" for a "big brother" who would "come along to befriend the Jewish people, solve their problems, protect them from the Arabs, and present them eventually with a beautiful Jewish state with all the trimmings." Britain had turned out to be a bad big brother, as had America, and Russia was "now left as the only power upon which foolish hopes can be pinned. It is remarkable, however, that Russia is the first big brother whom even Jews do not quite trust. For the first time a note of cynicism has entered Jewish hopes." Such cynicism, Hannah Arendt thought, reflected the conviction that all Gentiles are anti-Semitic, an attitude she bluntly called "racist chauvinism." Resorting again to terms heavy with echoes of the history she was writing in *The Origins of Totalitarianism*, Arendt claimed that the Jewish "master race" is pledged "not to conquest but to suicide by its protagonists. . . . Jewish leaders can threaten mass suicide to the applause of their audiences, and the terrible and irresponsible 'or else we shall go down' creeps into all official Jewish statements, however radical or moderate their sources."

From Hannah Arendt's perspective Palestine contained potential solutions to the problems that had led to totalitarianism in Germany, the problems her book was written to expose. In the experimental societies of the kibbutzim, Arendt saw "a new form of ownership, a new type of farmer, a new way of family life and child education, and new approaches to the troublesome conflicts between city and country, between rural and industrial labor." In short, she saw answers to the problems of a mass society and the deterioration of the nation-state. In the possibility of Jewish-Arab cooperation, she glimpsed an answer to the problem underlying racism, "the problem of a new concept of man," and the problem underlying imperialism, "organizing a constantly shrinking world which we are bound to share with peoples whose histories and traditions are outside the western world." Arendt even envisioned Arab-Jewish cooperation beginning with councils, the legacy of the revolutionary tradition in Europe. "Local self-government and mixed Jewish-Arab municipal and rural Councils, on a small scale and as numerous as possible, are the only realistic political measures that can eventually lead to the political emancipation of Palestine."

In the homeland of the Jews, Hannah Arendt wished to see all of the elements which formed the foundations of her political theory: new social forms, local political councils, a federation, and international cooperation. It had been exhilarating for her to think that her own people, the victims of a totalitarian regime, could offer to the world models for institutions that might prevent totalitarianism from making another appearance. As always, the defeat of her greatest expectations and of her deepest wish for her people to be heroic was registered by Hannah Arendt in a rush of anger and irony. But she was not prepared to give up, and Magnes's group gave her a political base.

Arendt made it clear in her 1948 article that she thought President Truman's proposal for an interim UN trusteeship was the only hope to forestall statehood, to prevent partition, to stop the ascendancy of Jewish and Arab terrorists into power, and to give the possibility of a federation time to emerge from agreements among Jews and Arabs. In language that once again was heavy-handedly ironic, she argued: "This is certainly no time for final solutions; every single possible and practical step is today a tentative effort whose chief aim is pacification and nothing more." Her own next step was to help Magnes and David Riesman prepare a proposal to submit to the United Nations and its mediator in Palestine, Count Bernadotte.

Arendt also prepared a summary of the history of Ikhud for Magnes to present to his contacts at the United Nations, where he hoped to propose Ikhud as a negotiating group in the event of a UN trusteeship. Hannah Arendt participated in this effort by meeting with the UN Secretariat's appointee for Palestinian affairs, but she was not willing to be put forward as a possible chairman for a political committee representing Ikhud. "I lack quite a number of qualities a good chairman must have," she explained to Magnes.[35]

One of the qualities Arendt most saliently lacked was moderation in discourse. Like so many who write ironically, she was at her most cutting when she was most intensely involved; such involvement gives rise to ironical discourse and distinguishes it from mere sarcasm. When Arendt wrote in her undiplomatic, ironic style, her readers clearly divided into those who were offended and those who were not, those who identified with the targets of her criticism and those who did not. Perhaps more than any other mode of discourse, irony prompts those who are outraged to seek biographical explanations; the emotional distancing it seems to imply is often attributed to some character fault or personal trauma.

Typical of the kind of negative response Arendt's *Commentary* article elicited was a piece by Ben Halpern in the August 1948 *Jewish Frontier*. Halpern plucked out of the repertoire of "complexes" available to those who resort to *ad hominem* arguments the one which later critics of Arendt's *Eichmann in Jerusalem* also found: it was an "enfant-terrible complex" that had allowed her to indulge in "the outrageous sensation-mongering" of her references to Jewish "master-race" chauvinism. He added that Arendt had a "subconscious" intention to discredit "such conventionally, and hence disconcertingly successful figures as Herzl, Weizmann and Ben-Gurion." Halpern answered Arendt with his own version of the tactic he had condemned as sensation-mongering by creating three categories—the adventurer, the collaborationist, and the partisan—and then labeling Arendt a collaborationist.[36]

Ben Halpern, a self-proclaimed partisan, took as his model the "ghetto resister" and hoped that the new Jewish resisters—the Israeli soldiers—would become the ideals of Jews everywhere. Arendt tried to point out in a letter of reply that there was a difference between trying to cooperate, or "collaborate" in the "noncommital and literal" meaning of the word, with the British or the Arabs and trying to cooperate with an "anti-Semitic government" like the Nazis'. She insisted that she had recommended "collaboration" because it was essential to the future of Israel and asked her readers not to be misled by military successes into thinking that the Jews could or should be on permanent military alert against "the solid threatening opposition of many millions of people from Morocco down to the Indian Ocean."[37]

Hannah Arendt worked on her response to Halpern at the end of the summer, while she was vacationing with Julie Braun-Vogelstein at a boardinghouse in New Hampshire. Perhaps the peacefulness of the New England state which readers of *Aufbau*'s travel advertisements knew as the Switzerland of America made it possible for her to ignore Halpern's amateurish analysis of her personality and to let his misreadings pass with a mild rebuke. At any rate, she had more constructive projects to carry out.

She continued to help Magnes. Elliot Cohen, the editor in chief of *Commentary*, had asked Magnes to reply to an encouraging suggestion made by Aubrey Eban, Israel's representative to the United Nations, that Jewish-Arab collaboration would be feasible if Israel was recognized by the Arabs and that it might, then, take a form similar to that of the Benelux states in Europe. Arendt drafted a reply to Eban, which Magnes reworked to her appreciative agreement: "I admired the way you used and toned down my argument."[38] She gave him the same calming help while he was writing a sorrowful postscript to the reply, indicating that it had been written before the assassination of Count Bernadotte by Jewish terrorists—an event which damaged greatly the spirit of cooperation which Magnes had just barely begun to instill at the United Nations. She suggested that Magnes tone down an explicit analogy he wanted to draw between the attitude of the Nazis toward displaced persons and the attitude of the Jews toward the displaced Palestinian Arabs. Arendt had learned from her own use of such an analogy how little it would help their cause.

Magnes became more and more discouraged. But he and his New York circle kept planning: they debated whether to include Gentiles in their group, discussed the idea of an English edition of Ikhud's journal, and considered publishing a book of documents and speeches presenting "the non-chauvinist Zionist position from the Balfour Declaration to our day."[39] One of their key policy decisions was whether to suggest publicly that displaced Arabs should be either offered a homeland in Israel, perhaps in the Negev, or allowed to return to their own homes. Hannah Arendt was of the opinion in September 1948 that "the most urgent task of Ikhud in Palestine now is not to support Ben-Gurion as a kind of lesser evil, but rather to form and insist on a consistent opposition within the limits of a loyal opposition."[40] To inspire such a loyal opposition in America, Hannah Arendt wrote a piece for the *New Leader's* October 1948 issue, "This Mission of Bernadotte." "It might be called a momentous article," Magnes wrote to her on 7 October, "that is, it might have serious consequences if it were studied and taken to heart by anyone in whose hands decisions lay. You seem to have laid bare the inner meaning of Bernadotte's efforts and proposals. . . . Your story may be called tragic. Here was a great and good man who started full of hope and ended almost in despair. . . . It is a grave choice, this way or that. Your article has depressed me, and I am asking myself, is there really no way out?"[41] The two choices Arendt saw were stark: Bernadotte's second proposal for a UN trusteeship or a Jewish-Arab confederation along Magnes's lines. Hannah Arendt, invoking feasibility, had argued for the first.

Judah Magnes died on the morning of 27 October without having answered his own question about the way out. For his supporters, it was clear that their work could not go on without him, though they tried for a time to keep his ideas alive through the Judah Magnes Foundation. Hannah wrote to Magnes's old friend Hans Kohn, who was teaching at Smith College, on 12 November: "Magnes' death is a real tragedy at this moment. Nobody has his moral authority. I don't see anybody, moreover, who lives really in the Jewish world and who is prominent in a Jewish institution who would have the courage to speak up against what is going on now."[42] All that she herself could do was to join a group of prominent intellectuals, including Albert Einstein, who submitted a letter of protest to the *New York Times* when the Jewish terrorist, Menachem Begin, came to America in search of support for the Revisionists of his Herut party. The protest flatly compared the Revisionists "to the Nazi and Fascist parties" and repudiated the blend in their ideology of "ultranationalism, religious mysticism and racial superiority."[43]

Hannah Arendt gave her support to the Judah Magnes Foundation but would not accept its leadership. After she spoke about Magnes's efforts to a hostile audience in Massachusetts, at Hans Kohn's request, she was certain that she was not the one to lead. "I am not qualified for any direct political work," she wrote to Elliot Cohen, still shocked at having been shouted down by her audience. "I do not enjoy to be confronted with the mob, am much too easily disgusted, have not enough patience for maneuvering, and not enough intelligence to maintain a certain necessary aloofness." Furthermore, she stated firmly, "it would definitely spoil my work as a writer."[44]

Hannah Arendt could not follow Judah Magnes's example as an actor; direct political work was not her métier, and she did not have Magnes's capacity for understanding and befriending people of every sort and occupation, for moral teaching. His authority was moral, hers at that time was intellectual, and both knew well the difference. Shortly before Magnes's death, Hannah Arendt wrote to him, extending her greetings for Rosh Hashanah: "Will you permit me to tell you how grateful I am that the past year brought me the privilege of knowing you. . . . Politics in our century is almost a business of despair and I have always been tempted to run away from it. I wanted you to know that your example prevented me from despairing and will prevent me for many years to come."[45]

## Martha Arendt's Death

From Karl Jaspers and Judah Magnes, Hannah Arendt learned much about the moral authority of people who dare to enter the political realm and espouse unpopular views. Their serene self-confidence was an example to her. Both had grown up in large, community-minded, independent families, and both had the companionship of remarkable wives. Their backgrounds gave them refuge when they stood in hostile arenas. Arendt similarly, had her husband and a "tribe." But the uncertainties of mood and the temperamentalness that had been hers since childhood did not suit her for public life. Arendt knew this, and she also knew, sadly, that her mother, who had done so much to encourage her, nonetheless inhibited her.

The six months during which Hannah Arendt worked with the Magnes group were among the busiest in her life. Martha Arendt and Heinrich Blücher had been cast back on each other while she gave speeches, wrote articles, drafted Magnes's proposals, finished her editing projects at

Schocken Books, and tried to find time for the third part of *The Origins of Totalitarianism*. After she left Schocken in June 1948, her vacation in New Hampshire without her family was largely spent at the typewriter. Not only her home life but a trip to Europe for Jewish Cultural Reconstruction had been postponed while *The Origins of Totalitarianism* was finished. When she announced the postponement, Jaspers responded with a statement of the attitude he and Blücher shared: "I entirely understand, the book *must* be finished, the world-situation is dreary. . . ."[46]

In the middle of the summer vacation, Arendt returned to New York to help her mother prepare for a journey to England, where Eva Beerwald was living. They took Martha Arendt's things from the 95th Street rooms to the Queen Mary. When Arendt returned to New Hampshire, she received word from Eva Beerwald that their mother had had a serious asthma attack on board. The next day a telegram came: "Mother unchanged mostly under drugs awake suffering asthma." On 27 July a second telegram arrived: "Mother died sleeping last night arranging cremation—affectionately Eva."[47]

The death of her "Mutt" in the midst of Hannah Arendt's enormous effort to keep up with her many projects in a dreary world situation was a sadness too great to be given much attention. Martha Arendt had decided, at the age of seventy-four, to uproot herself once more and finish her life with Eva Beerwald in England. She had lived with her daughter and Heinrich Blücher in the West 95th Street roominghouse for seven years, and it had not been a happy period for her. Hannah Arendt had been preoccupied with making a living and establishing herself in a new country; she had had much to share with Blücher and little to share with her mother. "Mutt" had had even less to share with Blücher, whose reluctance to seek any sort of steady work after the war convinced her that her daughter's marriage was a *mésalliance*. Between Blücher's working-class background and Martha Arendt's bourgeois sensibility there was a gulf so great that neither Hannah Arendt's efforts to refine her husband's manners nor her efforts to lessen her mother's disapproval could bridge it. Martha Arendt thought that under Blücher's influence her daughter had become assertive and tough, and she grew melancholy in her isolation. Hannah Arendt's old friends, who had known Martha Arendt in Paris, noticed her mood but could do little for her. Lotte Klenbort could offer only sympathy when Martha sadly told her that she should enjoy her children while they were young, for they would grow estranged one day.

Hannah Arendt seldom spoke about her mother's death or the distance that had come between them in America. On 31 October she wrote to Jaspers about her work and about Magnes's death four days earlier; very much in passing she added: "I had two long vacation months during which my mother died."[48] Jaspers responded not to her surface manner but to the feelings she did not show with a gentle philosophical reflection: "It is, of course, nature's way, that the old ones die. But it is a profound change when one's mother is no longer, and the sorrow is deep, even if not devastating."[49]

Jaspers found out what little he knew about Arendt's personal life by asking questions in his letters. She never volunteered information. At his request, she had told him a little about her mother in an April 1947 letter: "It is hard for old people who do not have an independent spiritual or intellectual existence [*geistige Existenz*] to be uprooted, and I would not have done it if I had not had to."[50] In France, she said, her mother had had an easier time, for she had been able to speak French well and she had had both German and French friends. "Here, I am afraid, she lacks the proper companionship; we have so little time and we see each other really only for our evening meal. But she is lively and healthy and still physically able (though a bad fall fractured her thighbone several years ago) and she is—one of the American wonders—made very welcome here." Before and after her mother's death, Hannah Arendt always spoke well and gratefully of her. In the same letter to Jaspers she remarked: "I have her to thank for the fact that I was raised without prejudices and well-provided for." But her affection sometimes seemed to draw on the protective generalizing she had practiced as a child when she told her "Mutt" that "We should not think of sad things too much."

Only to Heinrich Blücher was Hannah Arendt completely frank about the deep ambivalence in her feelings for her mother. Their friends admired Martha Arendt's warmth and generosity, and the demands she had made upon her only child were not visible to them. But Blücher knew only too well why his wife's feelings were so mixed. She wrote to him from New Hampshire after receiving Eva Beerwald's telegram:

Naturally, I am simultaneously sad and relieved. Perhaps I have handled nothing in my life so badly as this affair. I could not simply refuse the demand, because it came to me out of love and out of a resoluteness which always made a great impression on me, and which has, surely, influenced me deeply. But naturally I could also never completely fulfill that demand, because to the radicality of it

only a radical destruction of myself and all my instincts would have been sufficient. Yet, for my whole childhood and half my youth I acted more or less that
way; as if it were the easiest and most obvious thing in the world, the most natural
thing, so to speak, to conform to all expectations. Perhaps out of weakness,
perhaps out of pity, but most certainly because I did not know how to help
myself.[51]

The demand Arendt wrote of, apparently, was that Martha Arendt continue to stay as close as possible to her daughter. For seven years this
demand had meant living a floor apart in the same roominghouse. Arendt
knew what the unavoidable arrangements—a classic triangular situation
aggravated by poverty, exile, war—had cost her husband, and she offered
him an apology:

But, when I think of you, I become dizzy. Old Frau Mendelssohn [Anne Weil's
mother] once said: Now, one truly loves a person, but cannot help him. I really
could not change everything, and never consciously deceived you, because I was
always resolute in one thing: that is, never to live with Mother. Just so: the
gas-ovens came along—or, as Robert [Gilbert] would say, World-History. That is
all for now, and it is certainly not enough.[52]

World-History had cast them all together, and Blücher, in his reply to
Arendt's plea for reassurance, acknowledged this: "Hitler and Stalin did
more than us to burden your mother."[53] Blücher, whose own mother had
made great demands on him in his youth, recognized that Arendt had
lived with obligations he had escaped.

What you have done, and what a fix you were in, I can understand only too well.
I have only to imagine how it would have been with my widowed mother, who
had quite similar tendencies—had not her craziness toward me made me suspect
that all mother-love was a type of insanity, which is naturally quite false; but the
suspicion did help me very much to avoid finding myself in your situation.

Both of the Blüchers were resolutely opposed to psychoanalytic
categories but, in their own terms, they understood that Martha Arendt's
"mother-love" and deep need for her daughter's attentions, her imposition of her own conceptions of daughterly behavior and feminine comportment, had troubled Hannah Arendt's life. In a blunt sentence
Blücher announced: "She was the one who, more than any other timid
blockhead in our circle, simply and thoughtlessly took you for a man."
Martha Arendt was accustomed to strong, intelligent women, but she was

not prepared for a daughter who, while supporting a household by working as an editor, set out to write a book like *The Origins of Totalitarianism*
and to join a group like Magnes's for political action. Blücher's bitterness
about Martha Arendt's expectations was as violent as his own expectations
for his wife were urgent. He let the bitterness burst forth after Martha
Arendt's death:

You did your best, and she would never have had enough, because when one has
the passive love of a sponge, one always feels too dry. . . . Actually, it made me
furious, her constant blood-sucking of you and her total lack of respect for your
unbelievable work. . . . Nonetheless, you are surely correct: there was once in her
a true, great and clear feeling, which was finally dissolved into a mass of muddy
sentimentalities.

In Blücher's assessment, Martha Arendt had a "private, middle-class outlook"; she lacked the Blüchers' abilities to recklessly and completely
commit themselves to politics and political theory, their abilities to sustain independent spiritual existences.

While Martha Arendt was alive, Blücher was like a man in mental
bondage. After her death, he felt free; he charged out of the domestic
prison and gave up the ideological refuge he had taken in uncritical
Americanism. In 1948, soon after his mother-in-law's death, he had what
he called—summoning an English idiom—"a brainstorm."

Blücher's "surprise attack of productivity" came in "two days and a
night." New perspectives opened to him: "I had, honestly and unsuspect-
ingly, narrowed myself completely upon the American dream," he told
his wife. Like the ex-Communists they both despised, Blücher had begun
to substitute for "the god that failed" another god—America. Philosophy
rescued him. In a long, not too coherent letter, he explained to Hannah
Arendt his realization that the assault made upon metaphysics by "the two
titans," Kant and Nietzsche, had cleared the way for philosophy to take
on a new role; Jaspers had followed these two titans, pointing to the new
role, and his work "only needs in addition the smallest dot on the i."
With a metaphor that would certainly have amused Jaspers, Blücher
pointed out his own path:

Does Jaspers remain, who with the Encompassing of Being [that is, Jaspers's
notion of *das Umgreifende*] places a huge, round, pure and crystal-clear cheese
dish over the smelly cheese of facts, a transparent glass dish, on which we, always
transcending to a certain degree, nearly hit our noses on God if we only decide

for ourselves to interrupt the loving communication of the maggots often enough—in order to persistently bump our heads against the cheese dish, singularly or in communication? Now, I will simply put this cheese dish aside, with loving respect.

Having thus announced to himself the end of metaphysics, the end of his own reliance on any "ersatz heaven," Blücher left behind the titans and the giants of modern philosophy: "Kant was a servant, Nietzsche a master, Marx a despot and Kierkegaard a slave. And I am a prospective citizen." Blücher's euphoric vision of "the new conceptual whole" that would give unity to his view is not presented in the letter, but it seems that he had in mind the task that also occupied Hannah Arendt after she finished *The Origins of Totalitarianism:* how, without metaphysical cheese dishes, to approach politics philosophically. At the time of his brainstorm Blücher had no public forum, but when he began teaching three years later, his students were the beneficiaries of it.

Blücher's emergence from his long hibernation eased Hannah Arendt's guilt, toward her mother and toward him. She could recover good memories from before the troubled years and take great joy, for example, when an old friend sent her a prewar photograph of her mother, the only one Arendt had. That photograph, made when Martha Arendt was still young and beautiful, sat on Hannah Arendt's worktables and oversaw the completion of all the books that followed *The Origins of Totalitarianism.* And that photograph was there through all the years when Hannah Arendt, in her own fashion, fulfilled many of her mother's conventional ideals. After 1948, when the Magnes group disbanded, Hannah Arendt never again took an active political role. She was suspicious of women who "gave orders," skeptical about whether women should be political leaders, and steadfastly opposed to the social dimensions of Women's Liberation.[54] Her own motherly advice to younger women was as bourgeois and conventional in its details as it was, in important matters, open-minded and unsentimental. She urged others to independence, but always, always with a qualification: for women, her maxim was *Viva la petite différence!*

The journey Hannah Arendt made to Europe in 1949 on behalf of Jewish Cultural Reconstruction confirmed in many ways the continuity of her life and feelings, including the love for her mother that had been so disturbed during their years together in New York. Her opening remark to

Eva Beerwald when they met in London for the first time in nearly fifteen years was, "Who said Kaddish for mother?"

In a discussion of Homer's *Odyssey*, Arendt once remarked that the lines that moved her most deeply were those telling how Odysseus, adrift on a wild sea, clinging to the broken frame of the boat he had made to escape Calypso's island, despaired and contemplated drowning himself by letting go. He checked himself as he remembered that if his body were lost it would receive no burial rites; he and his deeds would fade from human memory. Arendt was not a practicing Jew, but she felt for the burial and mourning sections of the Kaddish, which are usually read by the dead one's son or nearest relative, the respect she felt for rites of memory in general; for rites which are, like storytelling, a confirmation of earthly continuity.

Arendt's memorial for her mother was written years later, indirectly, in an essay about her mother's heroine, Rosa Luxemburg. She put in a phrase what she had learned from her mother—not from her mother's socialism, but from her deep loyalty. "This generation still believed firmly that love strikes only once."[55] The specificity of this lesson, the "only once," Hannah Arendt unlearned in her own life; but the general lesson, that a true love's passion must be prized above all else, no matter whether the course of events seems to confirm it or not, was her mother's great gift to her. They had heard Kaddish together at Paul Arendt's funeral in 1913, the year before World-History began to shape their lives anew.

## Confirmations

Hannah Arendt had reflected on the meaning of *Treue*, loyalty, ever since her youthful encounter with Martin Heidegger; *Rahel Varnhagen* is a story not of loyal love but of loyalty to love. In the strained, hectic, and far too public year of 1948, Arendt had tested not only her mother's loyalty, but Blücher's. When she left home for two months in New Hampshire, Blücher turned to the tribe members for company. The Klenborts, his friends from Berlin—Lotte Beradt, Karl Heidenreich, and Peter Huber—an émigré painter he met in New York named Carl Holty, a musician friend, Kurt Appelbaum, and his wife, Anne, all rallied around him. But he also turned to a vivacious and sensuous young Jewess of Russian descent. And when Hannah Arendt learned that this friendship had become an affair, her own loyalty was tested.

Blücher always made it clear to his wife that he was faithful after his fashion. Hannah Arendt did not find the fashion easy to accept, and she was very unhappy that the affair was known to some of their friends— including the one who had told her about it. Even the most limited publicity offended her. But like most of the tribe members, Hannah Arendt was a Weimar Berliner in social mores; she did not define faithfulness narrowly, maritally. She gave and expected—and got—a loyalty combined with the Berlin insouciance, *Gleichgültigkeit*. She described it herself in an essay on the Berliner, Bertolt Brecht: "To be sure, in this world there is no eternal love, or even ordinary faithfulness. There is nothing but the intensity of the moment; that is, passion, which is even a bit more perishable than man himself."[56] Blücher never wrote his own description of the Berlin credo; but it is there in Heinrich Heine's "Doktrin," a poem that had the same wry simplicity Arendt found in Robert Gilbert's poems.

> Schlage die Trommel und fürchte dich nicht,
> Und küsse die Marketenderin!
> Das ist die ganze Wissenschaft,
> das ist der Bücher tiefster Sinn.
> [Beat the drum, keep your courage,
> And kiss the canteen girls!
> That's the whole of knowledge
> And the deepest lesson of books.][57]

While she reached her understanding of Blücher's affair, Arendt had the companionship of a woman who was—as Arendt described her— "gifted with erotic genius." Hilde Fränkel, the mistress of Arendt's friend Paul Tillich, was worldly wise and innocent, like all the people with whom Hannah Arendt formed deep bonds, and she also had great warmth and graciousness. She was not, like the others with "innocence preserved," a writer and intellectual. She had Martha Arendt's loyal generosity of spirit, without Martha Arendt's sentimentality. In Anne Mendelssohn Weil's absence, Hilde Fränkel became Arendt's *beste Freundin*, and Arendt expressed her gratitude in very unreticent terms: "Not only for the kind of relaxation which comes from an intimacy like none I have ever known with a woman, but also for the unforgettable good fortune of our nearness, a good fortune which is all the greater because you are not an 'intellectual' (a hateful word) and therefore are a confirmation of my very self and of my true beliefs."[58] When she was most deeply strained by the different pulls of political life, work, and personal loyalties, Arendt most needed what a friend like Hilde Fränkel could give—a confirmation of her self.

Hannah Arendt had first met Hilde Fränkel in Frankfurt during the year she had spent there with Günther Stern. In New York, Arendt discovered her friend working as a secretary at "Self-Help for Refugees," and they renewed their acquaintance. Paul Tillich had also discovered Hilde Fränkel there and launched a love affair that lasted until Fränkel's death from cancer in 1950.

As Tillich's secretary at Union Theological Seminary after the war, Hilde Fränkel typed the manuscripts they had spent much time discussing. H. H., as Tillich called Hannah Arendt, "Hilde's Hannah"—as opposed to Tillich's own Hannah, his wife—often joined them for evenings of talk. With the help of Hilde Fränkel's adroit diplomacy, H. H. and Tillich quickly reached an agreement: their talks would be more valuable and less problematic if they were not burdened with reading each other's works. In the give-and-take of discussion, Arendt and Tillich often found themselves in accord, but each found the other's written work impossible. Tillich's Christian socialism seemed to Arendt full of contradictions and her training in Existenzphilosophie by Martin Heidegger, for whom Tillich had little respect, seemed to him something she would do well to overcome. Hannah Arendt and Paul Tillich had, nonetheless, once formed an alliance in print. In 1942, *Aufbau* had published an article by the "Ullstein-in-exile" publicist Emil Ludwig, which suggested that a corps of German-speaking American teachers ought to ready themselves to enter postwar Germany and teach the Germans to eradicate the sources of militarism in their authoritarian culture. Tillich, outraged, branded the proposal "racism in reverse" and repudiated the idea that such a thing as a "national character" or culture exists. Arendt leapt to Tillich's defense when he, in turn, was attacked in *Aufbau*'s pages. She noted Emil Ludwig's long history of affinity for imperialisms—for Pan-Germanism, for Italian imperialism in Africa between the world wars— and charged Ludwig with desiring to promote American imperialism after the war (a charge which proved prophetic). Arendt expressed her optimism about Americans' ability to see clearly what had happened in Germany by citing a recent Gallup Poll which indicated that a majority of Americans blamed Hitler and not the German people for Germany's actions. This exchange and the alliance between Arendt and Tillich that developed from it were both echoed in an article Arendt wrote at the end of the war, "Organized Guilt," in which she stated again why the notion of collective guilt was unacceptable and adapted her criticism to the postwar situation in Germany.[59]

Hilde Fränkel prided herself on her remoteness from academics and unemotional intellectuals as much as Heinrich Blücher did. She was a woman who would have been at home in an eighteenth-century salon. Without the burden of Rahel Varnhagen's two great sorrows—her shame at being a Jew and her lack of physical beauty—Hilde Fränkel was more like Rahel's great friend, Pauline Wiesel, Prince Louis Ferdinand's mistress. The letter Rahel wrote in 1816 to Pauline Wiesel, a woman who had been, as Hannah Arendt wrote of her, "much loved, because of her great beauty and amazing, dismaying naturalness," might well have been written by Hannah Arendt to Hilde Fränkel. Rahel had wondered to Pauline if there existed anyone else: "who knows nature and the world as we do... , who is surprised at nothing unusual and who is eternally preoccupied with the mysteriousness of the usual; who has loved and been loved like us; who can no longer endure loneliness and cannot do without it..., who has had the absurdly wonderful fortune to encounter one other person who sees things the same way and who is alike, though her talents are so different—which only makes it all the more amusing."[60] Hilde Fränkel's amazing and dismaying naturalness was an endless fascination to Hannah Arendt, who was flattered that her friend saw in her a kindred soul.

Throughout her life, Hannah Arendt was able, in private, to be as unconventionally sympathetic to her friends' complex lives and loves as she was to her own husband's; but whenever publicity threatened or secrets were betrayed, she retreated, often abruptly. Arendt accepted Hilde Fränkel's relationship with Paul Tillich for what it was, but she preferred not to discuss it with others who might understand it differently or not at all. When Tillich visited Hilde Fränkel at the Cape Cod boardinghouse where the Blüchers spent several summers in the late 1940s, leaving Hannah Tillich at the cottage they had rented nearby, Arendt was not disturbed; but any talk about the arrangements Tillich made with his mistress or about his other assignations in the neighborhood embarrassed her. To Blücher, in private, Arendt could be casual—"Sodom and Gomorrha is in full swing," she noted—but in public she was reticent.[61]

The Tillich who was attracted to pornographic literature, who was masochistic and had collected theories from a number of psychoanalytic experiences to explain his behavior, was not, Arendt felt, the real Tillich, and she was apprehensive that publicity would obscure all differences. "His erotic phantasy-world," she wrote to a friend years after Hilde Fränkel's death, referring to Tillich without using his name, "was absolutely contrary to his imagination. He was, in fact, not only a theologian, but an outspoken moral personality of great political and moral courage. . . . His behavior—he was married, with all the consequent complications— toward my friend [Hilde Fränkel] was excellent, so to speak, morally. When she was on her deathbed, he did not abandon her—as most of the 'Creative Individuals' she knew did; we were very close at the time, and I saw him there daily. He made a great impression on me, because I understood that, despite all the possible psychological perversities, which are very foreign to me, he was a Christian, that is, capable of Christian love. As far as my friend was concerned, she herself was not originally or ever really perverse; she was only—and it is so rare!—gifted with erotic genius and she understood, so to speak, everything. Though he was often very boring, she maintained her Scheherazade-capacity, because she really loved the man; and he had really loved her."[62] Hilde Fränkel had a storyteller's imagination, like Isak Dinesen—another woman who loved passionately a courageous but flawed man; and Paul Tillich had a moral imagination. To those gifted as the poets are, Arendt was always ready to extend the poet's understanding that, as Auden said, "the desires of the heart are as crooked as corkscrews."[63]

Hilde Fränkel's knowledge of human nature and the world, which she translated into stories full of wonderment and humor, made her a perfect confidante for Hannah Arendt, and she told Arendt she was "the only person in my life to whom I speak fully and completely."[64] Their relationship was not, like Arendt's with Tillich, an intellectual one. Hilde Fränkel appreciated Hannah Arendt simply for being, as she said, "what you essentially are—a woman."[65] They exchanged stories about what they agreed essentially concerns women, their men. "All men," wrote Fränkel, during an exchange of letters about Heinrich Blücher's poor performance as a letter writer, "whether husbands or of the sort mine [Tillich] is, are baggage. One should never get annoyed—and yet one does."[66] "Yes," Arendt replied, expressing what they both believed, "men are a pretty heavy baggage, but still one does not get on well without them."[67]

When Hannah Arendt was in Europe in 1949 representing Jewish Cultural Reconstruction she wrote many letters home, to Hilde Fränkel as well as to Blücher. "I write to no one but you and Monsieur, and I am content with that, because I really cannot. Despite my friendliness, that is how it is, and so be it. [But] I do think about Broch as well."[68] Hilde kept in close contact with Blücher while Arendt was travelling and often acted as her mediator and messenger: when she was very pressed for time, Arendt wrote to Hilde and asked her to pass the letters on to Blücher; when she was apprehensive because too much time had passed without a letter from Blücher, she asked Hilde to urge him to write. Hilde, in turn, sent reassurances which helped Arendt to trust Blücher's loyalty. After Arendt had written such strenuous complaints to Blücher that Hilde thought she "must have put the fear of Hell in him," Hilde wrote a soothing letter: "Monsieur said to me yesterday on the telephone that he is entirely confused, because he has become used to being with you, to living with you, and because he does not want to be alone any longer."[69]

Arendt's trip lasted for nearly six months, from August 1949 to March 1950, and it put a strain on all three: Arendt suffered from a great homesickness, Blücher was restless, and Hilde was distraught because her illness was growing worse and she feared she would not see Hannah Arendt again before she died. Arendt worked furiously in the Wiesbaden headquarters of Jewish Cultural Reconstruction's mission, and she travelled back and forth across Germany by train with little rest between trips, hoping not to have to extend her stay. She was as pressed, for her own reasons, as the Germans she observed were for theirs: "the Germans are working themselves dumb and stupid."[70]

As she threaded her way through her homeland, startled by the corruption and the despair, shocked by the terrible plight of the displaced persons, aware of the malaise under the surfaces of the reconstructed towns and the enormous effort everyone made to be friendly and polite, Arendt wrote her impressions to Hilde and Blücher. She intended to use these letters when she returned: "About Germany one could write a book, but I will write only an article."[71] "The Aftermath of Nazi Rule, Report from Germany," which appeared in *Commentary* in October 1950, was really a sequel to *The Origins of Totalitarianism*. Arendt described the effects of twelve years of totalitarian rule on the German people and, in what she described, found confirmation of her theory that totalitarianism is "something more than the worst kind of tyranny." Totalitarianism "kills the roots" of a people's political, social, and personal life. She had no confidence that "indigenous forces of self-help" would regenerate Germany and not even much hope that the only solution she saw to the political chaos—a federation of European states freed of nationalism and outmoded notions of sovereignty—would, if it came about, help Germany. "Neither a regenerated nor an unregenerated Germany [would be] likely to play a great role" in a European federation, she thought.[72] Arendt wrote with compassion about the Germans' inability either to face the reality of the destruction of their country or to think about the events that had brought it about, but she underestimated how much, be it ever so precarious, can be reconstructed without new roots. The economic miracle of postwar Germany lay ahead.

Arendt also wrote about her trips to France and England. Paris she found frighteningly disordered. Public services hardly functioned and the city seemed to be suffused with a "monstrous irritability and hostility." Only in the company of friends, like Alexandre Koyré, "the best and most sensible man I have met," could she relax—though Koyré and Jean Wahl eagerly invited her to lecture at the College Philosophique and planned altogether too much of a "social whirl."[73] She was delighted to see Anne Weil after nearly a decade of separation but disturbed to find her in a very difficult domestic situation; both Eric Weil and Katherine Mendelssohn were still suffering deeply from their wartime experiences: "I understood [with them] the atmosphere of Strindberg's plays."[74] Not until she went to Europe again in 1952 was Arendt's deep bond with Anne Weil reestablished.

Of all the countries Arendt visited, including Switzerland, where everything was "of course, in order," England was "the one that has survived the war morally intact. There is enormous feeling for traditions... [and for] a great history, but entirely without chauvinism." She was pleased to see her stepsister Eva Beerwald, her cousin Else Aron Braude; everything was *sehr nett*, very nice.[75]

Arendt went twice to Basel to visit Karl and Gertrud Jaspers and found them, to her great relief, secure and comfortable in the new Swiss home they had moved to in 1948. These visits offered her respite from her *Hundsarbeit*, her "dog's work," and left her "inwardly peaceful" for the first time in many years. "Philosophically and personally, especially personally," she was at home.[76] The conversations Arendt and Jaspers had about Heinrich Blücher were an important part of feeling personally peaceful. She described as best she could the husband she called her "portable home," and Jaspers was delighted. A correspondence between them began. On her second visit, Jaspers showed Arendt an admiring letter he had received from Blücher, who was one of the few people outside Europe to have read the entire Jaspers oeuvre, and Arendt was proud of her "wise and clever husband."

Jaspers also showed Hannah Arendt his correspondence with Martin Heidegger. Jaspers's generous hope that this correspondence would repair the friendship that had broken in 1933 prompted Arendt to tell him the story of her romance with Heidegger. "I told Jaspers frankly how it had been between Heidegger and me," she wrote to Blücher; and he responded with: "Ach, but that is very exciting." For Arendt, this was a confirmation of Jaspers's openmindedness and of his trust in her: "Jaspers is entirely inimitable in his unflappable reaction."[77] His sympathy for Heidegger also impressed her; she could hardly believe how carefully Jaspers tried to find the true Heidegger behind the public face. "Poor Heidegger," Jaspers said to her, "we sit here now, the two best friends he has, and see right through him [*durchschauen ihn*]."[78]

Arendt's reunion with Martin Heidegger was not peaceful, because Heidegger did not hide behind his haughty and unreliable public manner. Hilde Fränkel asked her, facetiously, which visit had pleased her more, the one in Basel or the one in Freiburg. "I was so amused by your question. . . . To be 'pleased' over Freiburg would require a kind of animal boldness—but, then, I do *not* have such."[79] She had gone to Freiburg on "absolutely necessary business. . . . Would I have gone anyway? I don't know."[80] With the romanticism that always characterized her relationship with Heidegger, Arendt used her hotel's stationery to send him a simple, handwritten summons—unsigned. He came immediately to the hotel, and there he began to recite for her "a sort of tragedy in which, presumably, I had participated in the first two acts." Heidegger did not at first seem to realize that everything they had known together "lay twenty-five years in the past," that "he had not seen me for more than seventeen years." Not for the later acts of the tragedy, which included Heidegger's year in the Nazi party, but for the first two acts, he was shame faced, like a "dog with his tail between his legs [*begossener Pudel*]."[81] When Heidegger finally entered into the present tense and spoke honestly, Arendt felt—as she told Blücher—that "we really spoke to one another, it seemed to me, for the first time in our lives."[82]

This trying but honest encounter was followed, the next day, by a "fantastic scene." Heidegger, "who is notorious for lying about everything," finally told his wife that Hannah Arendt had been "the passion of his life" and the inspiration for his work.[83] Frau Heidegger's jealousy was swift and violent. "She, alas, is simply stupid [*mordsdaemlich*]." Despite his wife's angry protests, Heidegger visited Arendt again and showered her with letters and copies of his manuscripts. He eagerly awaited her second visit to Freiburg—not, presumably, on absolutely necessary business— and then touched her deeply by understanding that she could not linger because a dying friend was waiting for her at home. He wrote a poem for Hilde Fränkel, "For the Friend of My Friend," and then a note to Arendt: "When your dearest Freundin waits so for you, your dearest Freund must not delay you, even though a farewell to him impends."[84] That was Heidegger as Arendt loved him.

Arendt's reaction to her two stays in Freiburg, to the first one and then to "the continuation of this novel," was mixed. Her loyalty to Blücher was not called into question: she told him that she had thought of him as she listened to Heidegger, and trusted that he would "judge the whole business correctly."[85] But she was oppressed by Heidegger's situation, particularly by his marriage, and she wondered how he would keep his bearings and desist from making ruinous statements in public about various people, including Jaspers. She resolved to seek Jaspers's advice, seeing in him "the only help." Arendt did not know what the reestablishment of their relationship would mean for Heidegger and herself. But she finally decided that "at bottom, I was happy at the confirmation—that I was right never to have forgotten."[86]

Hannah Arendt saw this confirmation as a sign that she had been right to be loyal to a man whose public face was as different from his private one as Paul Tillich's moral imagination was from his phantasy world. Heidegger confirmed in her what Arendt called, in a letter to Hilde Fränkel, "the level of passionateness and honesty on which one lives."[87] Arendt found her true belief in a maxim of Balzac's that she used as an epigraph for her essay on Isak Dinesen: *Les grandes passions sont rares comme les chefs-d'oeuvre*, grand passions are as rare as masterpieces. But when she wrote her Dinesen essay, in the late 1960s, she was able to add a wry reflection: Isak Dinesen was called Titania by her lover, and like Shakespeare's Titania, she was quite likely, when under a spell, to fall in love with an ass! Arendt ended her essay with a maxim of her own that marked the insight that was hers twenty years after her 1949 reunion with Martin Heidegger: "Wisdom is a virtue of old age, and it seems to come only to those who, when young, were neither wise nor prudent."[88]

The reward for the years Hannah Arendt had spent maintaining her friendships by letter or in memory while she worked on *The Origins of Totalitarianism* was the 1949 trip to Europe, the series of reunions. Since the end of the war, she had hoped for such a trip and wondered how it would be. The Europe of her friendships was the present, the home that sustained her as she worked for Europe's future by laboriously looking over its past. From the depths of her personal Europe, she had written a book bearing an epigram from Karl Jaspers's *Logik*: "Weder dem Vergangenen anheimfallen noch dem Zukünftigen. Es kommt darauf an, ganz gegenwärtig zu sein [Give in neither to the past nor the future. What matters is to be entirely present]."

For Heinrich Blücher, being entirely present was a nearly impossible task. Without a job, a political forum, or a circle comparable to that of his Brandlerite comrades, he brooded over the world situation. Before his brainstorm in 1948, he had busied himself with various frustrating projects. He drew up a declaration for a "League for the Rights of Peoples," but no group took up his idea for protecting every people's right "to life, liberty and the pursuit of creative work."[89] Blücher's emendation of his adopted country's most illustrious maxim tells the story of his own desires. Creative work was the happiness he lacked, though he did share Hannah Arendt's work on *The Origins of Totalitarianism*. By a series of lucky meetings, his chance finally came in the winter of 1949–50, in the same months that Arendt's confirmations came to her in Europe.

The painter Alcopley, who was also the medical doctor and scientific researcher Alfred L. Copley, came to New York to shift the emphasis in his double career more to the painting side. Hannah Arendt was taken to meet him by Joseph Maier's wife, Alice. He received his guests in the one-room apartment on Riverside Drive—rather like a large closet—into which he had fitted himself and his paintings. In this room his two guests constituted a crowd. But in the ample light from a large window facing on the Hudson they were able to see the paintings. Hannah Arendt was delighted, and asked Alcopley if she could bring Heinrich Blücher to see his work.

Blücher made his visit in the fall of 1945, after Alcopley had moved to a larger apartment and established his research in hematology at New York

University, Washington Square. Blücher admired the paintings so much so that he urged Dr. Alfred L. Copley to yield completely to Alcopley. The doctor did not accept Blücher's advice, but the painter did become more public when Alcopley joined eleven other artists in founding the Eighth Street Club.

In 1948, a group of artists who called themselves abstract expressionists—Baziotes, Hare, Motherwell, Rothko, and Newmann—had founded a school, "The Subjects of the Artist," at 35 West Eighth Street. The school failed financially after a year, but its popular series of Friday night lectures continued when the Eighth Street loft was taken over by another group and called Studio 35. Lectures also formed an important part of the activities of a third group, the twelve members of the Eighth Street Club, which was founded in 1949. By the winter of 1949–50 the club's lecture series, in which the speakers were more often philosophers and critics than artists, was as well known as the one going on several houses down at 35 West Eighth Street.[90]

Heinrich Blücher joined the ranks of the club's lecturers quite by chance and very reluctantly in 1950. One evening he dropped by Alcopley's third apartment, south of Greenwich Village, just as Alcopley was leaving to hear Joseph Frank and Meyer Shapiro discuss André Malraux's *La Psychologie de l'Art*. Blücher, who knew the book well, was invited to come along. In the Eighth Street loft they found about fifty people waiting restively for the speakers. When it was clear that their arrival had been delayed, Alcopley suggested to his colleagues, including the sculptor Philip Pavia, that Blücher might stand in. After much cajoling, Blücher agreed—on the condition that detailed introductory remarks be devoted to how little he wanted to speak and how completely unprepared he was. After Alcopley provided this introduction, Heinrich Blücher proceeded to give a brilliant exposition and critique of Malraux's work. Later he reported the event to Hannah Arendt in his not too sure English: "They got hold of me and I run the whole show. Es war ein überwaltigender Erfolg."[91] The delighted club members invited Blücher for several return engagements, at which he spoke to capacity crowds and had more "overwhelming successes."

For Blücher, these talks marked a turning point. The Eighth Street Club provided him with a place to speak and, as Alcopley remarked, "from this he got self-confidence." The club audiences found his ideas fascinating and, just as important, they found his heavily accented English comprehensible. Blücher even published a review of two works on aesthetics for the *Saturday Review of Literature*, the only article he ever wrote. The next year, Günther Stern, who had decided to return to Europe, arranged for Blücher to take over his course at the New School for Social Research.

One of the aims of Blücher's lectures on the philosophy of the arts was "to stimulate participation in cultural activities by responsible interpretation of works of art." Here he was on the political territory closest to his heart. Modern art, he announced, "is the common enemy for all brands of tyranny." Blücher envisioned a "cosmopolitan style" which would be adequate for experiences shared by all, for "worldwide human experiences."[92] And he happily invoked for his fascinated hearers the "discovery of a new world" by artists like Cezanne, Picasso, Kafka. Hannah Arendt told Kurt Blumenfeld, just as happily, that her husband stood at the edge of his own new world: " 'He has come into his own,' as one so beautifully says in English."[93]

Blumenfeld had written from Palestine. "When your letter came," Hannah Arendt wrote in reply, "we talked about you for hours. You and Heinrich are really the only two people I know who are entirely independent of the bourgeois conception of achievement and therefore have an understanding of people." She wrote about the success of the New School course: "It pleases him, and he has regained that old immediate contact with people, which for years (in a melancholy which erupted, immediately, over the gas chambers) has been lost to him. It is so seldom that people are able to help each other, mutually; but in our case I think it really is true that both of us would, without the other, scarcely have survived."[94]

## Foundations for Future Philosophizing

When Hannah Arendt wrote this euphoric letter to Blumenfeld, *The Origins of Totalitarianism* had just appeared to enthusiastic reviews. The long years of work were over, and as they came to an end Arendt was already preparing to move on. But she was not without what Randall Jarrell called "your 'Othello's occupation's gone' feeling."[95]

Their summer vacation the year before, in 1950, had been spent in Manomet, on Cape Cod, where Hannah Arendt had returned to her work after the exhausting months of Hilde Fränkel's dying. Alfred Kazin and an American friend of Arendt's named Rose Feitelson had helped with the final corrections on the *Origins* manuscript, and Arendt had time to read quietly, for the first time since she had been in America. "I am having a magnificent time," she wrote to Jaspers in July, "reading Plato—*Statesman, Laws, Republic.* My Greek is slowly coming back to me. I listen to a great deal of music. And I see friends. Today, unexpectedly, [Alexandre] Koyré telephoned—a great friend."[96] Other friends, including Tillich, Richard Plant, and Adolfe Lowe, an economist, came to visit, and together they read in their newspapers about another war.

Hannah Arendt had written Jaspers as she was preparing to leave for Manomet on 25 June: "Since yesterday the city has been full of war talk. We don't believe it, but with World History—with that World History that has gotten out of joint anyway—you never know."[97] The North Korean army, with full Russian support, had advanced toward the 38th parallel. Two days after she sent her letter—World-History being what it is—Truman announced that American air and naval forces would be sent to South Korea's aid. This situation strengthened Arendt's resolve to complete the work she was beginning, a study of the Marxist elements of totalitarianism that was to lead to an analysis of Stalinism. Both as a prelude to her longer work and as a summation of her book, she prepared a lecture, "Ideology and Terror," to be delivered at Notre Dame in November. By the end of the summer *The Origins of Totalitarianism* was completely "Englished" and ready to go to its editor, Robert Giroux, who had received the book at Harcourt, Brace after Houghton Mifflin, on the advice of a Harvard historian, turned it down.

At the University of Notre Dame Arendt's host was her friend, Waldemar Gurian, the editor of the *Review of Politics.* Her summer good humor and peacefulness lingered, fortunately, for she had to ease poor Gurian through the public side of her visit. "Gurian," she wrote to Jaspers, "led me around, in fear and trembling, because this was the first time a woman had clambered up to the rostrum at this Catholic place. He sweated, literally, from anxiety on a deathly cold day and it so amused me that I completely forgot to have my usual stage fright."[98]

With Waldemar Gurian Hannah Arendt continued a discussion she had been having with the sociologist David Riesman of Yale, a member of Judah Magnes's American group. Both of these men, as they read the final third of *The Origins of Totalitarianism* in its manuscript version, questioned whether Arendt's analysis implied the inevitability of totalitarianism. Even though Arendt had not claimed to have uncovered the "origins" of totalitarianism in a strictly causal sense, the title of her book and the patterns that held parts together seemed arguments for a

kind of determinism. Waldemar Gurian, like many other Europeans—
Eric Voegelin, for example—who were accustomed to considering the
spiritual dimensions of political phenomena as crucial, thought of totalitarianism as a logical product of modern secularism. Arendt's
sociopolitical theory seemed to Gurian to neglect spirituality. David
Riesman, on the other hand, taking the more empirical approach customary in American social science, questioned Arendt's statements about
totalitarianism *überhaupt* ("in general"). With many variations, these
two modes of criticism were typical of the responses that greeted Arendt's
work when it was published in 1951; a third "revisionist" mode, Marxist
in orientation, emerged when the 1958 second edition was published,
after the McCarthy era had ended.

When David Riesman read the manuscript of Arendt's "Totalitarianism" section, he was working on a book to be called *Passionless
Existence in America*. He wanted Arendt to contribute a historical chapter
dealing with the problem of changing character structure in the Western
world. This problem required greater interest in methodology than she
was ever able to summon, and his book, finally called *The Lonely Crowd*
and coauthored with Reuel Denney and Nathan Glazer, did not contain
a chapter by Arendt. The differences in their approaches are apparent in
the detailed comments Riesman made on her manuscript; his queries
pointed to evidence of flexibility and chance that escaped Arendt's broad
vision of elements crystallizing into totalitarian forms. In one of his lists of
questions, as later in a review of *The Origins of Totalitarianism* for
*Commentary*, Riesman noted: "You tend . . . to assume that Stalin and
Hitler are more calculating than I think is the case. . . . You explain as
policy what is partly the outcome of an elaborate and complex institutional arrangement." And, again: "You assume . . . that the Nazis knew
at the beginning what they wanted at the end. Were they not rather like
an upwardly mobile youth who looks only a few steps up the ladder and
for whom getting there is the most important thing? When he gets there,
he will decide what to do . . . and call in the appropriate experts."[99]
When Arendt later reconsidered the importance for individual Nazi
functionaries of the logical consistency of ideologies, in *Eichmann in
Jerusalem*, she noted what a large role local differences in European
communities, chance, and bureaucratic ambition played in the execu-
tion of the Nazis' plans. But in her later work, as in *The Origins of
Totalitarianism*, she insisted on stressing the vast "supersense" of totali-

tarian ideologies and the calculated efforts of the totalitarian leaders to "prove" this supersense by remaking reality and changing human nature.

It was the phrase "to change human nature" that disturbed critics like Waldemar Gurian and Eric Voegelin. It reflected the deepest level of Arendt's vision, the existential categories which informed her books from first to last. She saw totalitarianism as the complete denial of the spatial and temporal requirements of freedom. Totalitarian ideologies devoured both past and future, turned the past into myths of Nature or History and erased the unpredictability of the future with millennial images of these myths' fulfillments. Totalitarian terror in the concentration camps demolished all the spaces which make human movement and interaction possible. Both freedom for thought and freedom for action disappeared. Arendt made these fundamental claims explicit in her "Ideology and Terror" essay. With strokes so sure and clear that Kurt Blumenfeld marvelled—"it is really a masterpiece of political analysis!"[100]—Arendt sounded her themes:

Ideologies pretend to know the mysteries of the whole historical process—the secrets of the past, the intricacies of the present, the uncertainties of the future—because of the logic inherent in their respective ideas. . . .

By pressing men against each other total terror destroys the space between them; compared to the condition within its iron band, even the desert of tyranny, insofar as it is some kind of space, appears like a guarantee of freedom.[101]

The combination of ideology and terror demolished the world of communality and common sense, the world secured politically by laws and socially by occupational distinctions, property, individual differences, private bonds of friendship, objects fabricated by men. Arendt described this unprecedented "total dominion" without any ameliorating visions of human nature precisely because she focused her attention on the very deepest attack. This is the attack totalitarianism makes on the existential conditions for human life—a present in which to think, a space in which to act.

In a long, thoughtful review of the book written for the *Review of Politics*, the political philosopher Eric Voegelin was astonished that Arendt could think such a thing as a "change in human nature" possible. "A 'nature'," he informed her, "cannot be changed or transformed; a 'change of nature' is a contradiction in terms; tampering with the 'nature' of a thing means destroying the thing. To conceive the idea of 'changing the nature of man' (or of anything) is a symptom of the intellectual breakdown of Western civilization." Arendt replied to her fellow refugee from Germany:

The success of totalitarianism is identical with a much more radical liquidation of freedom as a political and as a human reality than anything we have ever witnessed before. Under these conditions, it will hardly be consoling to cling to an unchangeable nature of man and conclude that either man himself is being destroyed or that freedom does not belong to man's essential capabilities. Historically we know of man's nature only insofar as it has existence, and no realm of eternal essences will ever console us if man loses his essential capabilities.[102]

Voegelin had argued that Arendt's portrait of political and societal breakdown was convincing, but that she had neglected to consider the varieties of response to this breakdown, varieties which are "rooted in the potentiality of human nature rather than in the situation itself." Had she done this, he thought, she would have realized that the "spiritual disease of agnosticism is the peculiar problem of the modern masses," and she would have sought the origins of totalitarianism therein. When he accused Arendt of misunderstanding what the phrase "change of human nature" implied, he was accusing her of having been infected by this spiritual disease.

Hannah Arendt was concerned with the phenomenon—with what appears—and not with a supposed reality lying behind the phenomenon, a hidden nature or an invisible essence. When she spoke of a "change in human nature," she meant a change in human conditions radical enough to make impossible the exercise of capabilities observable under other, less radical conditions; she meant the destruction of any possibility for those capabilities to appear. Totalitarianism, she understood, would have to be worldwide—the world would have to be a concentration camp—for the goal of a change of human nature to be fully achieved. This, not any vision of human nature, was her only source of hope. Voegelin thought that Arendt's viewpoint was disturbingly secular, but, in fact, it was respectfully and nondoctrinally religious. As she later wrote in *The Human Condition*, she felt that such a thing as "human nature," or a human essence, could be known only by God; that men, who are able to know the essence of things other than themselves, cannot "jump over their shadows" to discover their own essence.[103] Desire for such a leap, she argued, distracts men from their real responsibilities to reality and the world men share. At the bottom of one of David Riesman's letters, Arendt wrote herself a brief note: "The stubbornness of reality is relative. Reality needs us to protect it. If we can blow up the world, it means that God has created us as guardians of it; just so, we are the guardians of Truth."[104]

But even though Arendt refused to view the totalitarians' goal in a theological perspective, she came close to doing so—as Voegelin noticed—when she spoke about "radical evil" or "absolute evil" and discussed the Western tradition's conceptual empty-handedness in the face of such evil. "What radical evil really is," she wrote to Jaspers in March 1951, the month her book was published, "I don't know, but it has something to do with [this] phenomenon: the superfluity of men *as men*."[105] She ventured to put forth the idea that when men aimed at the omnipotence attributed in monotheistic religions to the God who made men, they were aiming at the possibility of making men superfluous. No concept of power, she argued, not Nietzsche's, not Hobbes's, was an adequate foundation for understanding this phenomenon; and, worse, "philosophy itself is not entirely free of guilt in this business. Not of course, in the sense that Hitler somehow had something to do with Plato. . . . But in the sense that occidental philosophy never had a pure concept of politics and could not have such a concept because it always spoke of Man and never dealt with human plurality." In that reflection lay the seeds for Arendt's philosophical tasks in the 1950s, for her "Ideology and Terror" essay, for the essays collected in *Between Past and Future*, and for *The Human Condition*.

Equally important for her later work was another kind of question about "human nature" which came from liberals like David Riesman. In one of his commentaries on her manuscript, Riesman pointed out that her pages on the bourgeoisie were just as harsh as those on "the mob" and "the elite," that is, on groups that hated the bourgeoisie as much as they hated the Jews. "Perhaps," he suggested, "what leads you to this position is your contempt for the cowardice of too many of the people you describe. It seems to me, however, that you cannot ask of people that they be heroes, but only that they recognize heroism, and know a little more than they do about what they are doing."[106] This criticism, which had many an echo during the controversy over Arendt's *Eichmann in Jerusalem*, was a measure of the distress many liberals felt at Arendt's notion of "mass society." "For Miss Arendt," the sociologist Philip Reiff wrote in the *Journal of Religion*, "it is the bourgeoisie, as a style of life and as a political weapon, that has become radically evil . . . a counterimage to [Max] Weber's middle-class Puritan."[107] This controversy continued in public at a meeting arranged by the American Committee for Cultural Freedom on 28 November 1951. David Riesman offered his reservations in a paper entitled "The Limits of Totalitarian Power." "All we can do while we seek to bring down those [Communist] regimes without war is to find our way to a more robust view of man's potentialities, not only for evil, about which we have heard and learned so much, not only for heroism, about which we have also learned, but also for sheer unheroic cussed resistance to totalitarian efforts to make a new man of him."[108] Arendt criticized Riesman for thinking that such cussednesses as corruption, free enterprise, petty crime, and apathy were significant once a totalitarian regime was in place.

Beneath the surface of this controversy was a question that Arendt took up at length in her later work: how to distinguish between what she called the "social" and what she called the "political." From the realm of the social Arendt expected little, both when she wrote as a historian and when she wrote about the possibility of shouldering "the burden of our times." The political realm, not the social realm, is the realm of heroism and freedom. "One thing troubles me a little," Riesman had written in one of his 1949 letters, "namely the animus you seem at all times to show against the bourgeois and the liberal. Was Clemenceau not a liberal? Are you not a liberal?"[109] "No," Arendt noted above Clemenceau's name on Riesman's letter, "a radical." And she might well have repeated the refusal above her own name.

Arendt perceived the tradition with which she associated Clemenceau, the tradition of eighteenth-century revolutionary aspirations, as the only hope in the postwar world. It was the past she hoped to see recognized in the future. But she was not uncritical of the tradition, and she was not an advocate of the Rights of Man. "The Rights of Man," she argued, "had been defined as 'inalienable,' because they were supposed to be independent of all governments; but it turned out that the moment human beings lacked their own government and had to fall back upon their minimum rights, no authority was left to protect them and no institution was willing to guarantee them."[110] Arendt outlined the dreary story of how the Rights of Man, even when evoked in state constitutions or by liberal international groups, never became a "practical political issue," that is, were never enforceable. After the war, the situation was even more confused: "No one seems to be able to define with any assurance what these general human rights, as distinguished from the rights of citizens, really are.

Although everyone seems to agree that the plight of [stateless] people consists precisely in their loss of the Rights of Man, no one seems to know which rights they lost when they lost these human rights."

With these reflections, Arendt laid the foundations for her later political philosophy; statelessness—the condition in which she was living when she wrote her book—taught her the elements of political life. "The fundamental deprivation of human rights is manifested first and above all in the deprivation of a place in the world [a political space] which makes opinions significant, and actions effective. . . . We became aware of the right to have rights (and that means to live in a framework where one is judged by one's actions and opinions) and a right to belong to some kind of organized community, only when millions of people emerged who had lost and could not regain these rights because of the new global situation. . . . Man, as it turns out, can lose all so-called Rights of Man without losing his essential quality as man, his human dignity. Only the loss of a polity expels him from humanity." When people are left with no political space, only the "hazards of friendship and sympathy" and the "great and incalculable grace of love" offer them any confirmation of themselves and their dignity—as Arendt and the members of her émigré tribe knew well.

Following the outline of Heinrich Blücher's "League for the Rights of Peoples" proposal, Arendt argued that the right to have rights should be guaranteed "by humanity itself," as it cannot be guaranteed by Nature or by History. But his guarantee, she felt, suffered from a conceptual flaw, because it offered no bastion against the possibility that humanity itself might "quite democratically" decide to liquidate a people, and from an implausibility, because "the restoration of human rights, as the recent example of the State of Israel proves, has been achieved so far only through the restoration of national rights." Postwar efforts like the United Nations Bill of Rights were, Arendt thought, "conspicuously lacking in reality." The Nuremberg Trials had made clear the need for a "law above nations" guaranteed by a "comity of nations," and Arendt took this as her starting point as she tried to consider how such a comity might become a reality.

Arendt's reflections on the possibility of a "law above nations" were central to the Concluding Remarks of her book's 1951 edition. On her second visit to Europe in 1952, she hoped to meet people who shared her vision. She went to find French and German publishers for *The Origins of Totalitarianism*, to lecture in German universities, and to try to gauge the support among European intellectuals for the idea she had been supporting since the start of the war—European federation. Her trip, sponsored by Jewish Cultural Reconstruction, which had need of her services again for the final stages of its work, was also to include a vacation. But, like every vacation Hannah Arendt ever took, this one was a working vacation: plans for two books and half-a-dozen articles sprang up between her engagements. "Oh, pauvre ami," she said to Blücher when he tried without success to encourage her not to overwork, "I can't help it."[111]

# PART 3

## 1951–1965

"THE WORLD AND THE PEOPLE WHO INHABIT IT ARE NOT the same. The world lies in between people,"[1] wrote Hannah Arendt, fully aware that a natural, untroubled "in-between" with one's fellows had not been considered since Goethe's time as the mark of great thinkers, or even as a condition greatly desired by them. To modern people, Lessing's model man of genius—*Sein glücklicher Geschmack ist der Geschmack der Welt* ("his felicitous taste is the world's taste")—is an unknown. Even Lessing himself could not find a serene relation with the world such as the one that Goethe had attained. "His attitude toward the world was neither positive nor negative, but radically critical,"[2] said Arendt, and that was her attitude, too.

Hannah Arendt came to this attitude after a long stay in the suburb of sheer negation she had called ambiguity. She had ended *The Origins of Totalitarianism* with a forceful rejection of any reconciliation with a world in which incomprehensible, unpunishable, and unforgiveable evil—radical evil—exists. Her work in the early 1950s was a continuation in broader and more philosophical terms of the exploration that had brought her to study the radical evil of totalitarianism. Every conceptual mainstay of the European political tradition was subjected to her criticism; she rejected all the accepted verities of political philosophy and wished to salvage only the "lost treasures" of the tradition—treasures largely ignored in *praxis* and almost completely lost from theory. Less polemically, she practiced what Nietzsche had called "philosophy with a hammer."

Hannah Arendt moved toward genuinely radical criticism only when she could see the opposite of negation—only when the world, not theory, showed her positive elements. The Hungarian revolution of 1956 gave her hope that the lost treasure of the European revolutionary tradition might be recovered for the future. In *The Human Condition*, she wrote about action; for the second edition of *The Origins of Totalitarianism*, she prepared an epilogue on the council system; she planned *On Revolution*.

Theoretically, Arendt shifted her stance, using positive elements to conduct her radical critique. But the deepest chord in Arendt's attitude toward the world was not sounded anew until she found a measure of reconciliation. She underwent what she called a *cura posterior*, a cure after the fact of the war and the attempted "Final Solution" to the Jewish problem. The public sign of this cure was her questioning of radical evil in *Eichmann in Jerusalem*, but personal healing had preceded the in-

261

tellectual critique. When her marriage gained a new stability and her childhood oppression—her lack of trust—lifted, when she finally felt at home, Hannah Arendt wanted to write of her *amor mundi*, her love of the world.

## CHAPTER 7

# Being at Home in the World

## (1951–1961)

Die Mühen der Gebirge liegen hinter uns
Vor uns liegen die Mühen der Ebenen.

[The hardships of the mountains are behind us,
before us lie the hardships of the plains.]

Brecht, "Wahrnehmung" (1949)

### The Dual Monarchy

Hannah Arendt found Paris delightful in the spring of 1952, "warm, everywhere green trees." "The city is more beautiful than ever," she wrote to Blücher, inspiring in him a great homesickness for their first home together. A remarkably effective premier, Antoine Pinay, was beginning to put the Fourth Republic into economic order, and a feeling of confidence was apparent: "The French are once again happy, entirely different than two years ago."[1] The city and its people relieved Arendt of much of the dark foreboding about the *Weltlage* (world situation) she had lived with during the year following the publication of *The Origins of Totalitarianism*, the worst year of the fighting in Korea. The chance to visit her old friends lifted from her much of the sadness she had felt since the dreary summer of 1951, with its trip to New Haven to help with Hermann Broch's literary estate.

Arendt was like a creature emerging after a long hibernation; her senses awoke, she looked intently at "the wonder of the world." Her old friends were a marvel; she had many long "chatter-orgies" with Anne Weil, "once again my best friend." And she enjoyed new friends. She went to visit Chartres with "the children," Alfred Kazin and his friend Anne Birstein, who came to visit from their base in Cologne, where Kazin was teaching for a year. "Really! so beautiful. And the most heavenly Spring sent its sunshine streaming through the blue windows and made the blue even bluer. For the first time I really have eyes for architecture. I had never known what a complete wonder it is."[2]

Arendt's discovery of architecture, one of Blücher's great passions, brought them another source of intimacy. She sent him picture postcards of French buildings, and while Arendt travelled in fact he travelled in imagination. They planned a trip to Italy and Greece which they took, ten years later, when Blücher overcame his aversion to returning to Europe and visiting the new Germany. The letters they exchanged during the nearly five months Arendt spent in Europe were filled with pleasure in each other's interests and accomplishments, and they reveal the new balance that had come into their lives after Martha Arendt's death and the end of Blücher's forced retirement from public life.

All around them, they watched old personal alliances tremble and sometimes dissolve, long marriages strain and sometimes break, and they agreed that their own marriage had been kept strong by their equality and independence. Each had friends, work, a secure base from which to go out into the world. Arendt marked the security she felt about going "into the world" with a poem different in tone and mood from any she had written before. Blücher remarked that it was "like a spring song from [Ludwig] Uhland," a popular romantic poet:

> Earth poetizes, field to field
> with trees interlinear, and lets
> us weave our own paths around
> the plowed land, into the world.
>
> Blossoms rejoice in the wind,
> Grass stretches out to bed them softly.
> Heaven goes blue and greets mildly
> soft chains the sun has woven.
>
> People go about, no one is lost—
> Earth, heaven, light and forests—
> Play in the play of the Almighty. [3]

Arendt's 1952 letters home were free of anxiety about Blücher's loyalty. In the wake of the affair that preceded her trip to Europe in 1949, they had reached an agreement; there was to be no secrecy between them. The woman involved had stayed in the Blüchers' lives and in the circle of their émigré tribe, which contained others whose marriages had weathered affairs. The loyalties that bound these tribe members through years of exile and hardship ran deeper than marital conventions and customary faithfulness.

The Blüchers discussed jealousy in their letters, deploring it in others and hoping to be free of it themselves. Blücher approved and promoted Arendt's relationship with Martin Heidegger, whose wife was, in 1952, even more jealous of Hannah Arendt than she had been in 1949. Blücher reassured his wife: "Let them be jealous that there waits here at home for you your not at all jealous [husband], who, instead of being jealous, really loves you after his fashion." "Yes, love," she replied, "our hearts have really grown toward each other and our steps go in unison. And this unison cannot be disturbed, even though life goes on. These fools who think themselves loyal if they give up their active lives and bind themselves together into an exclusive One; they then have not only no common life but generally no life at all. If it weren't so risky, one should one day tell the world what a marriage really is."[4]

No statement of what the Blüchers thought "a marriage really is" was ever offered to the world, but Blücher, in an undated birthday poem, written in English, gave his wife a playful picture of their plurality and their shared religious belief:

> Now, here and now,
> As you and I are we,
> Being so mine you will be me,
> And yours so I, I must be you—
> Then look, how now and here, live and true,
> The miracle (our own!) of He and She.
>
> You more Me than me,
> I more You than you,
> So I more Me than me
> And you more You than you.
>
> Perpetual motion, We,
> Around eternity.
>
> Thus help us THEY; this grant us HE.

While Hannah Arendt was in Europe in 1952, one of the "they" was writing a portrait of the Blücher marriage. Randall Jarrell's *Pictures from an Institution*, published in 1954, presented the Blüchers as Jarrell had known them on many American Poetry Weekends. "I hope you will tell the world," he periodically wrote to his hosts, "that as far as Saturday and Sunday are concerned, you are going to be encouraging American poetry

and will have no time for anything else."[5] For Arendt, encouraging
American poetry had often consisted of retiring to the kitchen to make
dinner during verbal brawls, as Heinrich Blücher and Randall Jarrell
matched vocal power: "The voices of the two rang lustily as they tried to
outdo and especially outshout each other—who knew better. how to appreciate *Kim,* who was a greater poet, Yeats or Rilke? (Randall, of course,
voting for Rilke and my husband for Yeats), and so on, for hours. As
Randall wrote after one such shouting match 'it's always awing (for an
enthusiast) to see one more enthusiastic than yourself—like the second
fattest man in the world meeting the fattest.' "[6]

The Rosenbaums of *Pictures from an Institution* are not immediately
mistakable for the Blüchers. Jarrell explained the difference in a letter to
his friend: "Although the Rosenbaums aren't too like you and Heinrich as
individuals, I hardly could, hardly would, have made them up without
knowing you. I think I made them like you in some small specific things
and in some very big general things—in most medium-sized things
they're quite different. . . . There's almost nothing in her that corresponds
to the historian-philosopher part of you."

In *Pictures from an Institution* Jarrell revealed the Hannah Arendt who
educated him, by presenting, marvelously caricatured, her "theories" of
child-rearing. He refashioned, and made considerably more European,
his own childhood by creating a character, the young and charming
tabula rasa, Constance, who finds the education she needs in the Rosenbaums' household. Jarrell himself remained, after his childlike fashion,
an adult, the narrator, though he also created an alter ego for himself, the
novelist Gertrude Johnson, a woman whose wit was so coldly satiric that
most critics gleefully assumed she was Mary McCarthy. When Mary
McCarthy asked Jarrell about Gertrude he told her "No, it's me—like
Flaubert," but Madame Johnson does wander about in Jarrell's satire as
though she were preparing to write *The Groves of Academe.*

Mrs. Rosenbaum herself was a rather perplexing mixture. "She looked
at the world like a bird, considering; and you, too, considered; but you
could not make up your mind whether she was a Lesser Bird of Prey or
simply a songbird of some dismaying foreign kind. . . . She had almost
frighteningly deep eyesockets, so that her eyelids were like pieces of porce-
lain: when she looked at you for a moment with a bright sufficient stare,
and then looked past you, you felt you had been weighed upon her eyelids
and found wanting. She judged by standards you guessed at uneasily, and
kept her judgments to herself or gave them offhand, as if they could

hardly matter to *you;* so that you decided justice was not going to be done to you and awaited, like a child, her smile. It was an unqualified, forth-coming, outgoing smile, a smile like spring: you could not believe in it, but it was so."[7] Mrs. Rosenbaum, a Russian singer, and Dr. Rosenbaum, a Viennese composer, were, taken together, clearer. As Jarrell imagined them, he penned his perfect portrait of the Blüchers' marriage: "When I first knew them I noticed that he did little things to placate or mollify her, or to keep her from being troubled or aroused, and I decided she was the dominant member of their household, but after a while I noticed that she behaved in exactly the same way about him: they were a Dual Monarchy."

In the house of the Dual Monarchy were "the works of man," that is, books in "all the languages of the earth." "Constance felt that it was in some way the world." Both Constance and the narrator entered this world innocent and were astounded. "Visits to friends, sometimes, are like *Zwieback,* or *frijoles* or *refritos,* or twice-told tales: the friends are them-selves still, bondedly so, and you go home sounder and a little subdued, the staple of your life reestablished. Visits to the Rosenbaums weren't like this."

One thing that all who knew the Dual Monarchy could agree about was that visiting them did not reestablish the staples of life. They ques-tioned, they argued, they thought each other's thoughts aloud. In his memoir, *New York Jew,* Alfred Kazin recalled his amazement at their "open connubial excitement in some philosophical discovery unsus-pected until that moment. She confronted Heinrich even when she joined him in the most passionate seminar I would ever witness between a man and a woman living together."[8]

The passionate seminars were a private affair, carefully protected from the light of the public. Even in letters Arendt seldom wrote about her marriage, but she did include in *The Human Condition* a reflection on what marriage *überhaupt* must be to survive—a union with a space in it.

Love, by reason of its passion, destroys the in-between which relates us to and separates us from others. As long as its spell lasts, the only in-between which can insert itself between two lovers is the child, love's own product. The child, this in-between to which the lovers now are related and which they hold in common, is representative of the world in that it also separates them; it is an indication that they will insert a new world into the existing world. Through the child, it is as though the lovers return to the world from which their love expelled them. But this new worldliness, the possible result and the only possible happy ending of a love affair, is, in a sense, the end of love, which must either overcome the partners anew or be transformed into another mode of being together. Love, by its very nature, is unworldly, and it is for that reason, rather than its rarity, that it is not only apolitical but antipolitical, perhaps the most powerful of all antipolitical human forces.[9]

The Blüchers' love had been transformed into "another mode of being together" by their "child of the mind." Arendt dedicated *The Origins of Totalitarianism* to Heinrich Blücher and called it "our book." Blücher thought of his collaboration as a kind of fathering, as a remark he made about his hero, Socrates, indicates. His remark, typically, is historically dubious, but it reflects his own role: "Socrates claimed to be a midwife . . . and said he helped bring forth the child. What he really meant (and did not say) was that he engendered the child. He thought that it took two people to bring forth a thought, that without communication thought is not possible."[10]

The Blüchers had no children of their own because, as Arendt once explained to her friend Hans Jonas, "when we were young enough to have children, we had no money, and when we had money, we were too old." In Blücher's words: "We decided not to have children in times such as these. We are sad about it, but a sense of responsibility for those who might be innocent sufferers is a valuable thing."[11] By the time Arendt finished *The Origins of Totalitarianism*, she was forty-three years old, Blücher was fifty and that year, 1949, was the first year they were able to consider moving out of the small rooms on West 95th Street. Reasons of other sorts may also have been at play. Blücher feared that his mother's mental illness might be congenital, and that the inherited aneurism he had suffered from as a young man might mark a child of his for a short or sickly life. Arendt knew herself well enough to realize that her passion for work and her need for quiet would make child-rearing onerous. But it was "times such as these" that most strongly argued against children; many of their tribe-member friends either remained childless or had their children only after emigration had brought them a measure of safety.

What the Blüchers learned to value most was their equality. In his youth, Blücher had been accustomed to dominating women and seeking intellectual companions among men. Hannah Arendt, his equal intellectually, better educated, and far more disciplined, challenged his habits. Slowly a balance was struck in terms of what Blücher called the "free personality." Blücher once talked to a class about the preconditions for marriage, discussing the matter in worldly, political terms. He considered the Mosaic law according to which a man can divorce his wife by giving her a letter and then accepted Jesus' command—"What . . . God has joined together, let no man put asunder"—because he saw it as an attempt to repudiate male prerogatives and establish the equality of men and women. Jesus, he said, "established the equality of human beings in quality, in the infinite possibilities of every person, and therefore in the absolute inviolability of that person. But he knew that in order to establish this he had first to abolish the inequality between man and woman, because here every other form of inequality was anchored."[12]

The Blüchers' equality, philosophically grounded and practically instituted, was much more conveniently housed after 1951. They moved into an apartment at 130 Morningside Drive which had studies for both of them and room to accommodate guests. While Arendt was in Europe, Blücher offered her room to Mary McCarthy, to Hans Jonas, who had left Palestine for a teaching position in Canada, and to his close friend, the painter Carl Holty, whose conversation was "better than a vacation for relaxation." In his study, on Sunday evenings, he wrote his weekly letter to Arendt, reporting on their friends, on his work and his courses, his students, and, to their great joy, on the offer he received from Bard College.

James Case, Bard's president, who had heard about Blücher from Horace Kallen, the New School's distinguished professor of philosophy, sought him out with a project, the creation of a Common Course for Bard's freshman class. Case thought he had found in Blücher just what he wanted, "a Socratic man," but the Bard faculty was not sure. Blücher met with them and managed to convince them that he was not "a reactionary," as they had thought when they heard his Common Course proposal, which was hardly progressive in the then-current sense of the word.[13] At the moment when many American philosophers were retreating from political issues and starting to take up the English tendency that came to be called analytic philosophy, Heinrich Blücher, without so much as a high-school diploma, set out to restore philosophy to her ancient role as queen of the sciences. He felt that philosophy should assume responsibility for the reintegration of all the modes of human creative activity. He did not, however, propose a system for this reunification in the nineteenth-century manner; he wanted philosophy to be a critical clearinghouse for all creative ideas and their interrelations. His course was designed to introduce students to the sources of creative power, and for this purpose he selected a number of "great thinkers" who had, he felt, discovered human creative capacities not known before them, a diverse group that included Abraham, Jesus, Zarathustra, Buddha, Lao-tse, Homer, Heraclitus, and Socrates, the "arch-fathers of the free personality."

Hannah Arendt took the Common Course at home, and it is clear that her mental notes were very important to her. Many references in her works to the great thinkers had their sources in Blücher's course. When she spoke of the most fundamental of the conditions for action, she emphasized Jesus' use of the phrase in Genesis so crucial to Blücher's concept of equality, "male and female created He them," and commented: "Action would be an unnecessary luxury, a capricious interference with general laws of behavior, if men were endlessly reproducible repetitions of the same model [Adam]. . . . Plurality is the condition of human action because we are all the same, that is, human, in such a way that nobody is ever the same as anyone else who ever lived, lives, or will live."[14]

In their feeling for the most important contributions of the Greeks on the list, Homer, Heraclitus, and Socrates, the Blüchers were also in accord. But Arendt never shared Blücher's interest in the Asians, Buddha and Lao-tse, or the Persian, Zarathustra. He rushed into difficult texts, scholarly disputes, unknown languages, with the intrepidness of an autodidact; she stayed on the ground where her education had prepared her to walk with easy erudition. His insights became sharper in her books, more carefully connected to historical contexts and contrary views, more accurately based on quotations. And, in turn, he incorporated into his lectures her qualifications and suggestions. Both spoke with great sureness, with the familiarity that comes with long savoring of favorite passages, beloved stories, exemplary tales and anecdotes, drawing on the reservoir of their commonly collected treasures.

As different in style as their lectures were their modes of teaching. Heinrich Blücher was masterfully impromptu. He prepared his lectures carefully, thinking through in advance what he was going to present; but then he spoke without notes, digressing and elaborating at will, modulating his voice for dramatic effect. There was in him more than a little of the Voice of Authority, though he encouraged his students to argue and question and was far more at ease in public conversation with people of diverse sorts than his wife was. Blücher enjoyed walking back and forth on the beautiful campus of Bard as though it was an agora and he Socrates; his students collected around him, talking and disputing as their Master graced them with his aphorisms and his stories. A cult grew up around him as his students imitated his thick Berlin accent and his mannerisms or passed along his most memorable jabs at their complacencies. "Pessimists are cowards, and optimists are fools," he told them.

Often in Blücher's lectures the lesson of the Berlin analyst Fritz Fränkel's shock cures lingered; those who had settled into a pattern or had a habit of having no patterns were given warnings. To one young rebel without cause he cautioned: "You are not mad, you are not even yet neurotic. But for this you are very good material." To a young man who spent many hours talking about his grand ambition but not so many hours at his writing table, Blücher cited Norman Podhoretz's *Making It:* "What is it you really want? To write, or to have been a writer?" In his lectures there was a little shock for every shade of opinion, as one of his students recalled: "I remember the opening lecture on the theme of Christianity to what was then still partly a religious student body. I remember the rapt face of our class's most enthusiastic churchgoer as the lecture commenced. The inevitable and interminable inhaling of Heinrich's first cigarette, the words beginning to explode slowly, the gently sardonic glance at the girl with the small-town trust in her personal god. 'Jesus of Nazareth,' he began—he never said Jesus Christ . . . —'was not a God.' He paused slightly. 'He may even have been an idiot.' Another moment for the cigarette. 'In the entire history of Christianity there have been no miracles' (nothing remarkable in this for the agnostics in the class) 'except perhaps that it has lasted for almost two thousand years.' "[15]

Like any powerful personality, Blücher generated hostility and envy as well as admiration. His supporters on the Bard faculty helped him make the Common Course a success. But many of the faculty objected to the course, and to staff it Blücher often had to persuade and cajole. Many students objected to the imposition of a required course; but often the objectors returned in their senior years to take the course as auditors.

Hannah Arendt was delighted when Blücher wrote in August 1952 to tell her the news of his appointment at Bard. "I am filled with pride for my Stups the Clever and the Wise, who could persuade an American faculty. The conditions look excellent, Love, and you have done it excellently."[16] While "Stups" was reporting his own successes at the New

School and at Bard College, he also reported the ones to which he had urged her. The mail brought her notice that she had been awarded the Guggenheim Foundation grant which allowed her to continue her work for the next year without regular employment; then came an invitation to give a series of lectures at Princeton University under the auspices of the Christian Gauss Seminars in Criticism.

The Princeton invitation was the first acknowledgement from a major university of the reputation Arendt's *The Origins of Totalitarianism* had won her, and it was an unusual acknowledgement, as she was also the first woman to be invited to give the Christian Gauss seminars. When she gave her lectures in the fall of 1953, a number of the men from the university and from the Institute for Advanced Studies who attended expressed their pleasure in having a woman lecturer. Arendt responded to them very critically, annoyed at being cast in the role of the "token woman." She explained the situation to Kurt Blumenfeld, who she knew would grasp immediately the import of her criticism. "At the closing ceremony [after the lectures], and ever so slightly tipsy, I enlightened these dignified gentlemen about what an exception Jew is, and tried to make clear to them that I have necessarily found myself here an exception woman."[17] The complex history of the Jews of Germany provided Arendt with her frame of reference for rejecting the "exception woman" role; and she took this matter so seriously that when she was invited to Princeton again in 1959, to be the first woman with the rank of full professor, she threatened to refuse the invitation because the university stressed the "first woman" aspect in their report to the *New York Times*.

What the "distinguished gentlemen" of "the snobbish university *par excellence*" did not do was take it for granted that Arendt was—to use her phrase—*feminini generis*. In Germany, from the period of Rahel Varnhagen's salon until the Weimar Republic's ignominious end, "relations with Jews never came to be taken for granted." Both the "Jewish notables" who led Jewish communities and the Jewish intellectuals who were often the sons of the notables were "exception Jews," distinct from their poor and uneducated brethren but still tied to them, as much by family loyalties as religious convictions. "The 'exception Jews' of wealth felt like exceptions from the common destiny of the Jewish people and were recognized by governments as exceptionally useful; the 'exception Jews' of education felt themselves exceptions from the Jewish people and also exceptional human beings ['unique personalities'], and were recognized as such by society."[18] In *The Origins of Totalitarianism*, Arendt emphasized that for those who accepted the status of "exceptions" Jewishness became "perverted into a psychological quality," a matter of "inner experience and private emotions." The political questions raised by the existence of a group like the Jews in Germany were never answered, though Zionism was an attempt. What Arendt wanted to avoid, as a woman, was a situation in which she was distinguished from "ordinary" women by virtue of her education, thought "strange and exciting," entertainingly different, a unique personality. What she wanted for women and from women was attention paid to questions about political and legal discrimination, attention broad enough to relate women's political and legal problems to those of all groups denied equality. She became uneasy whenever she saw the "woman problem" generate either a political movement separated from others or a concentration on psychological problems. Her reaction to the Princeton appointment was not, however, political; instead of questioning why the university had never before appointed a woman to a full professorship, she emphasized the psychological dimension. "I am not disturbed at all about being a woman professor," Arendt told an interviewer, "because I am quite used to being a woman."[19]

Blücher, who had not considered the "woman problem" when he opened the invitation from Princeton, immediately saw in it a political opportunity. This, he announced with the pleasure of a strategist, would be the perfect opportunity for Arendt to make a public attack on the growing conservatism of a group of their New York acquaintances. The "Band," as Blucher called this group, already had a public forum, *Commentary* magazine.

Just before Arendt had left for Europe in April, *Commentary* had published a disturbing article by Irving Kristol, "Civil Liberties, 1952—A Study in Confusion." Kristol had described himself as a "displaced person," alienated from both the McCarthyites and McCarthy's liberal critics, who were, he argued, "lacking in sense of proportion" because they advocated "complete civil liberties for everyone" and failed to understand that this was tantamount to condoning Communist conspiracies in America. Liberals needed to learn how to make an "intelligent discrimination between one case and another," Kristol felt, and he offered as an example of discriminating judgment a Washington state guideline: "Anyone who is a member of three or more organizations officially declared subversive is considered to be a Communist." The article generated a

flurry of letters to the editor, most of them praising Kristol's clearheaded-
ness, and only a few, like one from Arthur Schlesinger, Jr., expressing
outrage. Arendt and Blücher were furious. She wrote an angry letter of
protest from Europe. When the Princeton invitation came, Blücher
thought she should use the lectures as a forum for discussion of the value
of complete civil liberties.

Princeton is really a good thing. It will restore the Band's respect for you. . . .
They will come crawling. And [William] Phillips, [Martin and Clement]
Greenberg and others will become isolated. They all write now for a maga-
zine called *Mercury* which broadcasts the neo-conservative stupidities from
Yale. They add to it their own insolent stupidities and their philistinism.[20]

Arendt eventually chose a different medium for her words of warning.
She wrote a long review of Whittaker Chambers's memoir, *Cold Friday*,
for *Commonweal*, under the title "The Ex-Communists." The review
argued forcefully against the tendency "to make of democracy a 'cause' in
the strictly ideological sense." Fighting totalitarianism with totalitarian
methods—methods ex-Communists like Chambers knew well how to
employ—would be, she said, disastrous. Addressing a peroration to the
ex-Communists in her own rough but trenchant English prose, with the
conceptual clarity brought by her study in Europe of the distinction
between acting and making, action and work, Arendt concluded:

America, this republic, the democracy in which we are, is a living thing which
cannot be contemplated or categorized, like the image of a thing which I can
make; it cannot be fabricated. It is not and never will be perfect because the
standard of perfection does not apply here. Dissent belongs to this living matter as
much as consent does. The limitations on dissent are the Constitution and the
Bill of Rights and no one else. If you try to "make America more American"
or a model of a democracy according to any preconceived idea, you can only
destroy it.[21]

Arendt published "The Ex-Communists" in March 1953, and the date
is the measure of her courage. The attorney general of the democracy in
which she was living had made a speech three days earlier in which he
announced that 10,000 citizens were being investigated for denaturaliza-
tion and 12,000 aliens for deportation as "subversives." Only a few organizations, like the American Committee for the Protection of the Foreign Born, which was at the time under investigation by the Subversive
Activities Control Board, spoke out against the ruinous effects on immi-

grants of the "make America more American" campaign. [22] The Blüchers were never investigated, but for over a year they had lived in fear. Heinrich Blücher had written to Hannah Arendt in the summer of 1952, while he was awaiting the citizenship papers that came on 7 August:

The acceptance without opposition of the dreadful new immigration bill [he referred to the revival of the McCarran-Walters Act] has demoralized the best people here, so much so that the forces of the Left, which never were really put in motion, are stunned—they actually helped serve it up. It seems that one can now deprive someone of citizenship with a simple denunciation. And in my case, absolutely nothing could stop it. [American] citizenship could, it seems to me, become the most worthless in the world at a stroke. And how soon these "Born American" people could become a Master Race. [23]

Blücher, like so many former Communists, had denied his Communist past on his immigration papers in 1941, and he knew how vulnerable this left him to informers. One of the few American intellectuals who gave him any comfort was Mary McCarthy. She was looking for financial support to enter law school—"to commit herself to the slavery of the law schools" as Blücher put it—so that she could take up the fight for civil liberties in courtrooms. "About Mary I was very pleased," Arendt agreed. [24]

In American courtrooms there has never been the kind of attention that the Blüchers thought fundamental paid to deprivation of citizenship as a means of punishment. Arendt was given an opportunity to express their views in 1957: Robert Hutchins, in his capacity as president of the Fund for the Republic, solicited her opinions on which "basic and acute issues" should be recommended as foci for scientific research sponsored by the fund. She offered a lengthy catalogue, including the basic issue she thought Attorney General Brownell's efforts to punish citizens for Communist activities had highlighted. With the authority of one who had been a stateless person, she wrote a practical epilogue to her theoretical reflections on the Rights of Man:

The basic issue involved is the following: As long as mankind is nationally and territorially organized in states, a stateless person is not simply expelled from one country, native or adopted, but from all countries—none being obliged to receive and naturalize him—which means he is actually expelled from humanity. Deprivation of citizenship consequently could be counted among the crimes against humanity, and some of the worst recognized crimes in this category have, in fact, and not incidentally, been preceded by mass expatriations. . . .

It seems absurd, but the fact is that, under the political circumstances of this century, a Constitutional Amendment may be needed to assure American citizens that they cannot be deprived of their citizenship, no matter what they do. [25]

## Varieties of Anti-Communism

While anti-Communist polemics began to build up in America, Hannah Arendt worked in European libraries on a study she called "Totalitarian Elements of Marxism." The book, which she thought would be about 90,000 words long, was conceived as a complement to *The Origins of Totalitarianism*.

The most serious gap in *The Origins of Totalitarianism* is the lack of an adequate historical and conceptual analysis of the ideological background of Bolshevism. This omission was deliberate. All other elements which eventually crystallize into the totalitarian forms of movements and governments can be traced back to subterranean currents in Western history which emerged only when and where the traditional social and political framework of Europe broke down. Racism and imperialism, the tribal nationalism of the pan-movements and anti-Semitism, have no connection with the great political and philosophical traditions of the West. The shocking originality of totalitarianism, the fact that its ideologies and methods of government were entirely unprecedented and that its causes defied proper explanation in the usual historical terms, is easily overlooked if one lays too much stress on the only element which has behind it a respectable tradition and whose critical discussion requires a criticism of some of the chief tenets of Western political philosophy—Marxism. [26]

This statement from Arendt's 1952 Guggenheim Foundation grant proposal reveals a great deal about her conclusions in *The Origins of Totalitarianism*. The stress that she laid on the unprecedentedness of totalitarianism reflected her conviction that its elements were "subterranean," not connected with the great political and philosophical traditions of the West. Had Europe's traditional social and political frameworks not broken down, the subterranean currents might have remained subterranean. Understanding their emergence required analysis in social and political terms, not in terms of the great traditions.

Hannah Arendt's book on totalitarianism had resulted in no explicit charges against the great traditions of political and philosophical thought in the West except the statement that radical evil had never been subjected to scrutiny. She had considered "philosophical implications and changes in spiritual self-interpretation" as she told Eric Voegelin, but she had maintained her distinction between historical events and intellectual events. Marxism, an outgrowth of the great tradition, presented an obvious challenge to both her method and her conclusions. Further, it presented a challenge to the adjective "great": it required that she make distinctions between the greatness of the tradition and whatever faults the greatness might conceal. Arendt abandoned neither her conviction that the unprecedented cannot be inferred from the precedented nor her warning that theories of progress and theories of doom—whether these be political, philosophical, or religious—obscure our view of the unprecedented events of our time. But she did turn her attention to Marxism, and what resulted was a strenuous critique of the whole great Western tradition. Her project for a study of the totalitarian elements of Marxism turned into a plan for laying the foundations of a new science of politics.

Less than a year after she began the study of the Marxist elements of totalitarianism, Hannah Arendt realized that the project was too narrowly conceived. Originally, she had planned her study in three sections. The first was to be a conceptual analysis dealing chiefly with Marx's understanding of man as a "working animal," the relation between his conception of work as man's "metabolism with nature" and his conception of history as man-made. Arendt intended first to explore Marx's political concepts and then their relation to his conception of history. This introductory section was to be followed by two historical analyses, one of European Marxism and socialism from 1870 through 1917 and one of the transition from Lenin to Stalin in Russia. The final section was to show how "the specifically totalitarian elements in Marxism are fully realized when both the interest of the working classes and the cause of the revolution are abandoned for the sake of the global realization of an ideology with the help of a secret police and the Red Army."

The front on which this scheme gave way was the first item, Marx's notion of man as a "working animal." Without noting that she had revised her understanding, Arendt described her research as follows: "I spent part of last year in Europe. Aside from lecturing at the universities of Heidelberg, Tubingen and Manchester, I read for six weeks in the especially rich French collections at Paris on the history of labor and the history of socialism. Here I concentrated on the theory of labor, philosophically considered, as distinguished from work. By this I mean the distinction between man as *homo faber* and man as *animal laborans*; between man as a craftsman and artist (in the Greek sense) and man as submitted to the curse of earning his daily bread in the sweat of his brow. A clear conceptual distinction as well as precise historical knowledge in this field seemed to me important in view of the fact that Marx's dignification of labor as an essentially creative activity constitutes a decisive break with the entire Western tradition for which labor had represented the animal, not the human, part of man."[27] Marx's notion of man as a "working animal" turned out to be, on closer inspection, mixed: he thought of man as a laboring animal but mingled ingredients of fabrication or work into his analysis.

The distinction Hannah Arendt drew between work and labor opened an enormous field of inquiry. "I think that unless one realizes how much the modern world, after the political revolutions of the 18th and the industrial revolution of the 19th centuries, has changed the entire balance of human activities, one can hardly understand what happened with the rise of Marxism and why Marx's teaching, nourished by the great tradition as it was, could nevertheless be used by totalitarianism." The field of inquiry became "the entire balance of human activities"—both before the eighteenth- and nineteenth-century revolutions and after. It became the *vita activa*.

*The Human Condition*, a discussion of the human activities of labor, work, and action, was the book that eventually came from this train of thought. But Hannah Arendt did not turn to it immediately; she kept working on the Marxism book. By the time she wrote her progress report to the Guggenheim Foundation, she had finished four chapters.

You will see from the chapters which I am submitting that I explain first the particular difficulties of understanding which the rise of totalitarian systems has brought with it. From there I go on to a preliminary examination of the Great Tradition in order to find the precise point on which it broke. I show this in a first analysis of Marx in the second chapter. In order to present concretely what actually distinguished the totalitarian forms of government from all others which we have known in history, I then go, in chapter 3 on Law and Power, to an examination of these two pillars of all traditional forms of government. This chapter ends with an analysis of Montesquieu, who provides me with the instruments of distinguishing totalitarianism from all—even the tyrannical—governments of the past.

The fourth chapter was "Ideology and Terror," which was eventually added to *The Origins of Totalitarianism* as an epilogue.[28]

There were to be two other chapters in the first part of the Marxism book, and then all six were to be followed by the "Marx analysis itself," which Arendt intended to prepare for the Christian Gauss Seminar in Criticism at Princeton University in the fall of 1953. The two remaining chapters were probably "History and Immortality," published several years later in the *Partisan Review* (1957), and "The Modern Concept of History," published in the *Review of Politics* (1958). Arendt's work on these two theory of history chapters, however, was delayed. Unable to prepare the "Marx analysis itself" for her Princeton lectures, she had to craft them from the first four chapters of the book, entitling them "Karl Marx and the Great Tradition." The "Marx analysis itself," which did not arrive in time to go to Princeton, went to Chicago instead. Hannah Arendt was invited to deliver the Walgreen Foundation Lectures at the University of Chicago in the spring of 1956, and there she presented the reflections on labor, work, and action that represented the first draft of *The Human Condition*.

The writing that Arendt did between 1952 and 1956 was all originally designed for the Marxism book. The book itself was never written. The "great tradition" essays were incorporated into *Between Past and Future*, and the conceptual analysis of Marx was transformed into the study of labor, work, and action in *The Human Condition*. But by the time these works were written, they no longer led naturally into a discussion of the history of Marxism from 1870 to 1917 and from Lenin to Stalin. The material she gathered for these historical analyses of Marxism was put to use when it was incorporated into another volume, *On Revolution*, which was delivered in a preliminary form at Princeton in 1959 and then published in 1962. Within the space of four years, from 1958 to 1962, Hannah Arendt released three books, *The Human Condition*, *Between Past and Future*, and *On Revolution*, all of which had grown from the original Marxism book.

These changes and expansions were intellectually exciting, but at times overwhelming. Arendt wrote to Blumenfeld about her work in November 1953, after a strenuous year of reading:

I set out to write a little study of Marx, but, but—as soon as one grasps Marx one realizes that one cannot deal with him without taking into account the whole tradition of political philosophy. The long and short of this is that I am like somebody who has attempted a little robbery, for which one might expect to get at most two years; but who, then, goes to trial before a judge with another opinion entirely and gets a prison sentence of God knows how long. For me, book writing really is like putting myself in prison, of my own free will. What we don't do of our own free will! Always, as soon as I set myself to it, the thing gets somehow shorter, at least in one sense. I will under no circumstances write a big, thick book again; it simply doesn't suit me.[29]

In fact, essays were Arendt's best medium, and she composed all of her books in essaylike sections, sometimes neglecting to make the joints between the pieces smooth when they emerged in book form. As she worked on her essays, frameworks appeared, and these held the essays together. With few exceptions, the frameworks were triptychs: work, labor, and action; the private, the social, and the political; judging, thinking, willing; all variations on the temporal categories of past, present, future. The "little Marx study" for which Arendt received her long prison sentence was conceived in a manner unusual for her: it was to start with a conceptual analysis and then turn toward a two-part historical analysis. As she worked, the plan proved confining because historical and conceptual analyses, she found out, could not be so neatly compartmentalized. The books which were written in the prison of the 1950s were much more intricately made: each concept had its historical analysis, and all the concepts she took up were set within the larger frames of their historical origination and past meaning, their present meanings, and their possible significance for the future. The historian of *The Origins of Totalitarianism* became, during the 1950s, a political philosopher. Hannah Arendt's 1953 Princeton lectures showed a searching and sweeping philosophical approach to "Karl Marx and the Great Tradition." They had words of advice for disillusioned leftists who had turned toward strident anti-Communism, but they were philosophical words.

While Hannah Arendt was in Princeton, she also prepared another series of lectures under the title "America and Europe," which were written in more accessible prose.[30] In these she summarized the lessons her trip in 1952 had taught her about European politics and European attitudes toward the political turmoil in America. Her first lesson came as she sought a publisher for *The Origins of Totalitarianism* and its urgent message about the need for a "comity of nations" and international legal guarantees for the "right to have rights." After many unsuccessful efforts, she finally found a small house in Frankfurt with a comfortingly international name, Europäischer Verlagsanstalt. Her book, in her own transla-

tion, appeared three years later, in 1955, somewhat enlarged and beautifully complemented by a prefatory statement from Karl Jaspers. She was
completely unsuccessful in France, despite the efforts of many well-
placed friends and acquaintances. The third part of *Origins*, under the
title *Le système totalitaire*, was published by Editions du Seuil in 1972,
and the first part, under the title *Sur l'antisémitisme*, by Calmann-Lévy
in 1973. The whole work never appeared in France, where *Eichmann in
Jerusalem* alone excited interest during Arendt's lifetime.

She was aware soon after her arrival in Paris that *The Origins of
Totalitarianism* would not easily find a publisher. While renewing her
acquaintances among Parisian intellectuals, she wrote Blücher a series of
reports which expressed her disappointment with what she encountered.

Tonight I'll see [Alexander] Koyré again, with whom things go a bit better,
though he has gotten much older. Sartre *et al.* I will not see; it would be
senseless. They are entirely wrapped up in their theories and live in a world
Hegelianly organized. I went to one of [Eric] Weil's Hegel seminars; pretty
boring, and full of haranguing.

Yesterday I saw Camus: he is, undoubtedly, the best man now in France. He
is head and shoulders above the other intellectuals. This goes for Raymond
Aron, too, who is so warm and friendly to me that I shall not say this aloud. Jean
Wahl as always: the intelligence of a lycée student overlaid with a thick coating of
so-called poetry.[31]

The atmosphere of the Hegelianized French Left convinced Arendt
that the hopes she had had for French existentialism at the end of the war
were premature. She began to make a series of notes which she worked
into a paper two years later and delivered to the American Political
Science Association. In "Concern with Politics in Recent European
Philosophical Thought" (1954), she surveyed various philosophical responses to the horrors of totalitarianism. Camus and Malraux received
praise for their adherence to "old virtues in the spirit of a desperate
defiance of their senselessness," but she roundly criticized both Sartre and
Merleau-Ponty for their reaction to the same senseless situation:

As philosophers, the French existentialists can lead to the point where only
revolutionary action, the conscious change of a meaningless world, can solve the
meaninglessness inherent in the absurd relationship between man and world, but
it cannot indicate any orientation in terms of its own original problems. . . . It is
because of this illusory character of all solutions which originate in their own

philosophy, that Sartre and Merleau-Ponty simply adopted, superimposed, as it were, Marxism as their frame of reference for action, although their original impulses owed hardly anything to Marxism. It is not surprising that, once they argued themselves out of the impasse of nihilism with essentially identical arguments, they parted company and adopted altogether different positions on the political scene; within the field of action, everything becomes entirely arbitrary as long as it promises revolutionary change.[32]

What Arendt continued to appreciate in the work of even those she had no sympathy for, like Sartre, was the attention paid by French intellectuals to action, to rebellion and revolution, an attention which flew in the face of the "old suspicions of philosophers."

The Frenchman other than Camus for whom Arendt expressed greatest admiration in her letters was no philosopher. Henri Frénay was a military man, one of the cabinet members in De Gaulle's resistance government and in 1952 one of the leaders of the Europe Movement. This institution, created in Paris in 1947, had brought to a 1948 Hague "Congress of Europe" nearly a thousand influential Europeans from twenty-six countries. The congress, in turn, had founded the Council of Europe, a small step in the direction of the federated Europe Arendt had hoped for. But only a small step: the council provided a meeting place in Strasbourg for national ministers, but it had no power; it sponsored important agreements, like the European Convention on Human Rights, but it was not transformed into a basis for European government. In 1952 the unification of Europe was largely an economic matter, based on the Coal and Steel Community. But in the cold-war tendency that had rigidified in America with the Korean War, a new type of unification was being debated—the European Defence Community.

Arendt wrote to Blücher her impressions of Henri Frénay (and her overestimation of his influence):

Today I saw Henri Fresnay [sic], former minister of the resistance, now the president of the Europe Movement; he will take my book to Plon [the publisher] though it probably will not succeed there. A most distinguished man: military school (St. Cyr, I think), *masculini generis*. He's the only one who could have grasped power—and out of propriety and stupidity did not do it—though he is in no way stupid, only precise and intelligent. Somehow, he understood what America is (which is nearly unbelievable); he is a modern man, and wanted a really authentic politics—and stayed with this now so forlorn Federated Europe mess.[33]

Her conversation with Frénay helped Hannah Arendt cast her "America and Europe" lectures. The unusualness of his understanding of America, his conviction that America was not imperialistically plotting the submission of Europe, was what she hoped to convey to her American audience. Most Europeans, she wanted Americans to realize, were horrified by America's military technology, its strident anti-Communism and hegemony in the Atlantic world. She feared that any European unity that came to be in such an atmosphere would arise as an act of liberation from "American imperialism" and that it would be nothing but "European nationalism."

Hannah Arendt turned from historical studies to political philosophy in the 1950s for theoretical reasons; but she did so, also, in response to what she observed in Europe. The French feared German renewal and rearmament and the Germans feared a French Europe; both seemed to her to be clinging to outmoded notions of sovereignty. In the many German universities where she lectured, she looked for people who were not party to these fears, but what she found was the old suspicions of the philosophers. "Political convictions hardly play any role there and even specific philosophic tenets about politics are conspicuously absent."[34]

Arendt's first stop on her 1952 tour was Munich, where she went to hear her old teacher, Romano Guardini. "Heard Guardini in his lecture course, with nearly 1200 people, sitting, standing, lying, packed in. He spoke, as ever, about Ethics; it was moral philosophy on the highest level but entirely inadequate."[35] She was astonished to observe the enormous number of people who attended philosophy lectures, and after she went to the cabaret in Munich where Robert Gilbert's musicals were playing— "really good, brisk performances"—she reported to Blücher that the cabaret was less popular than the universities: "The phenomenon in Germany is that every philosophy lecture brings in more people than these 'entertainments.'"[36] But most of the lectures she attended struck her as more than just inadequate. She wrote to her husband about how the generally low level of university lectures was made worse by cliquishness and mistrust within the faculties. Heidelberg, where she presented "Ideology and Terror" as a lecture, was especially distressing.

[It] was personally, for me, a success, but one finds here an immense number of things which really leave one full of evil apprehensions. I came for a discussion after my lecture with the students, who organized it themselves (the faculty, naturally, views me with mistrust). The level of the discussion was good, but only the best people came, perhaps some twenty-five out of the whole faculty. Everywhere there are sects. . . . Everybody orients himself to some kind of pseudo-political organization—where they won't learn much philosophy. In these circumstances, Karl Löwith is really good, because he knows a great deal and can make it clear. On the other side of the barricade there are people like [the sociologist Alexander] Ruestow, linked with [Dolf] Sternberger, who proclaims (this in opposition to me) "Metaphysics is superfluous." This Ruestow is impossible, as one might quickly gather from his book. Imbecility.

In Marburg I saw Bultmann and Krueger; the latter is very pessimistic about the political situation in Germany, the former resentful, but very nice and outstanding, as always. . . . Marburg is intellectually dead, and has only the pseudo-intellectuality imported from Heidelberg.[37]

Arendt wondered from whom she could expect help in the mission she had undertaken in 1952, not for Jewish Cultural Reconstruction, but for philosophical reconstruction: "From Jaspers? He would only be pulverized between the flatheaded older people [*die Plattkoepfe*] and the new-fashioned swindlers."[38] Only from the young people she met did she expect any philosophical renewal. "It looks like the younger generation, those of about twenty years, may be all right. [In Tübingen] I met a young man of nineteen who asked me questions with such precision that I was astounded by him."[39] As always, Arendt looked to "the new ones," the younger generation, for innovation, for "new beginnings." Her greatest joy was the seventeen-year-old son of her schoolmate from Königsberg, Hella Jaensch, a non-Jewish woman who had spent years in prison during the war for aiding Jewish refugees. Fritz Jaensch, a "fellow who knows his Bible from A to Z, and is a real Christian, that is, a matter-of-fact Christian," was "be it noted, the first German who, face to face, justified to me Adenauer's politics."[40]

The German people had been presented with a series of Allied accords on 26 May and, the following day, with the treaty calling for a European Defence Community (EDC). Arendt's sense of the situation was that "everybody here is against the accords with America and determined not to countenance these treaties. It is a mess." She was convinced that the Germans would refuse to raise an army "without absolute sovereignty: the people are completely nationalistic." Her pessimism did not lift, and in June she wrote that "unless Adenauer gets a two-thirds majority for the ratification of the general agreement, we can bid adieu to the Defence

Community."[41] Fritz Jaensch was later well rewarded for his independent support of Europeanism by his Tante Hannah, who helped finance his American university education, but the Germans did not do so well. To Arendt's surprise, they offered grudging support of the defense community, but, when the EDC treaty went to the French parliament for ratification, old figures from the old France that had been too trusting of Adolf Hitler emerged to obstruct the "European adventure." That phrase was from none other than Edouard Daladier, architect of the 1938 French capitulation policy. His chorus was joined by the surviving leaders of Vichy France, by many Communists, and even by Charles De Gaulle, who two years earlier had hailed the New Europe. Ironically enough, Konrad Adenauer, whose Europeanism had been so forcefully resisted within his own country, was endorsed overwhelmingly at the 1953 polls in Germany. The tables were completely turned: Germany forged ahead with both its "economic miracle" and its vision for the continent; France vetoed the EDC and witnessed an extraordinary outpouring of nationalistic scorn upon the very idea that there was such a thing as "Europe."

By the time she started to revise *The Origins of Totalitarianism* for its 1958 edition, Hannah Arendt had put her own veto upon the plans for European unity that were advanced after the defeat of the EDC in France. She saw that federation's hour was past, or, more optimistically, that its hour was in the distant future, and she turned her attention elsewhere. When she revised *The Origins of Totalitarianism* she substituted the essay "Ideology and Terror," an overview of the totalitarianism section of her book, for the first edition's Concluding Remarks, in which she had made her call for a comity of nations. She then transferred the material on the need for an international guarantee of the "right to have rights" from the old Concluding Remarks to the section dealing with the Rights of Man. Her new focus was contained in an epilogue she added to the second edition, "Reflections on the Hungarian Revolution."

Though she turned her attention to European and American revolutionary traditions, Arendt kept a watchful eye on developments in Germany. She became so distrustful of the policies of Adenauer that she began to hope that a united Europe would not emerge while he led Germany. After the EDC was defeated and Germany began to build up its own army, Adenauer, as Arendt put it, "did not have the slightest scruples about doing so under the guidance and leadership of all those officers and generals who had served Hitler so well that they had not even participated in the conspiracy against him when the war was clearly lost."[42] In Arendt's view, the end of the Occupation Statute and the restoration of the German national army was simply the beginning of the re-Nazification of Germany. She acknowledged Adenauer's contribution to the "economic miracle" and praised his insight "that Germany's best hope was the goodwill of America," but she distrusted his moral obtuseness and his realpolitik.

When Arendt looked back over Adenauer's career in 1966, while reviewing his *Memoirs 1945–1953* for the *Washington Post*, she was struck again by his simplemindedness and appalled by how crudely he reflected on the nature of totalitarianism *überhaupt*:

He tells us that "the experience we Germans have undergone with the totalitarian regime of the Nazi period . . . [and] the experience the world has accumulated with totalitarian Soviet Russia" has taught him that "totalitarian countries *especially* Soviet Russia, do not, unlike democratic countries, know law and freedom of the individual. . . . [They know] only one fact that counts and that is power." This passage seems to have been lifted from a bad high-school textbook, except that the latter, hopefully, would not have stressed that Soviet Russia is even worse than Nazi Germany.[43]

Konrad Adenauer's Dulles-like anti-Communism and his opinion that Germany should find "its appropriate place in a Christian Europe [where it would make] its contribution to the building of an effective dam against the flood of Bolshevist Marxism," was, Hannah Arendt found out when she returned to America at the end of the summer of 1952, a variation on a widely played theme.

*America and Europe: Thinking about Revolution*

Arendt attended several conferences in late 1952 and 1953 where Marxism was labeled a "secular religion." On a number of these occasions she voiced her criticisms of the position. She also wrote two articles to explain herself: a review of Waldemar Gurian's *Bolshevism* and a long article, "Religion and Politics," for *Confluence*, a magazine so heavy-handedly edited by Henry Kissinger that Arendt had to write him an irate letter of protest when he tried to rewrite her article to his own satisfaction. Without Kissinger's assistance, Arendt put her concern thus: "Communism, we are told, is a new 'secular religion' against which the free world defends its own transcendent 'religious system.' This theory has larger implications than its immediate occasion; it has brought 'religion' back into the realm of public-political affairs from which it has been banished ever since the separation of Church and State. By the same token, although its defenders are often not aware of this, it has put the almost forgotten problem of the relationship between religion and politics once more on the agenda of political science."[44] Arendt did not expect theologians to be any more helpful in this situation than philosophers had been after the war. As she read contemporary theology in 1953 Arendt raised again the issue she had left unexplored at the end of *The Origins of Totalitarianism*—"if only I knew more about the problem of evil," she lamented to Jaspers.[45]

By the summer of 1953 Arendt had been forced by three years of public discussion to amend her views on religion and politics. In a 1950 article entitled "Religion and the Intellectuals," she had suggested that the "religious revival" was a "puff of the Zeitgeist," one of the periodic puffs that arise among intellectuals after times of stifling scientism. She thought it far more significant that "an overwhelming majority" of nonintellectuals has ceased to believe "in the last Judgment at the end of time" and that the masses "are quite willing to believe—well just anything."[46] She did not change her mind about the foolishness of thinking that organized religion would be an effective "weapon against totalitarianism or 'safeguard for civilized tradition'" but she did see that the prevalent evocation of religion among antitotalitarian intellectuals was a serious concern for political science. "Confronted with a full-fledged ideology," she wrote in her *Confluence* article, "our greatest danger is to counter it with an ideology of our own. If we try to inspire public-political life once more with 'religious passion' or to use religion as a means of political distinctions, the result may very well be the transformation and perversion of religion into an ideology and corruption of our fight against totalitarianism by a fanaticism which is utterly alien to the very essence of freedom."

These careful, reasonable public statements were very different from the alarm and indignation Arendt expressed privately about the growing menace of Joseph McCarthy's fanatical anti-Communism and the vacillations of so many American intellectuals. When she returned to America from her European trip at the end of the summer of 1952, Arendt began to look for allies who shared her concern and her perceptions about "America and Europe."

Arendt had several meetings with a small group, led by Arthur Schlesinger, Jr., Dwight Macdonald, Richard Rovere, and Mary McCarthy, which convened to discuss the possibility of founding a magazine. The magazine, to be called *Critic,* was conceived as a forum for people committed neither to the Left nor the Right, but in that place where Arendt was more comfortable—which she once described in a letter to Blumenfeld as "between all stools." The only commitment required of contributors was commitment to civil liberties. For lack of financial backing, the magazine never got past the speculation stage, but Arendt took comfort in the group and the idea. She had become more and more critical of her American Jewish acquaintances like Irving Kristol, whose commitment to civil liberties was tinged with compromising views and whose arguments took on a religious ardor. She described the situation to Blumenfeld in a 1953 letter: "I met with several friends not long ago—a professor of history, two very knowledgeable journalists and a woman novelist; all non-Jews, with many Jewish friends. They set out to make a list of people who were like-minded in the fight for civil liberties. Then one said: 'Isn't it funny only Hannah of all these Jews is with us.' Our friend Elliot Cohen [the editor of *Commentary*] plays a really disagreeable role and Sidney Hook is simply unbearable. These are, of course, people with more or less well-known Communist pasts, and thus with some reason to fear. But that doesn't make it any better."[47] Many Jews, of course, and Jewish newspapers, Zionist and non-Zionist, were strenuously opposed to such things as the McCarran Act, but in Arendt's immediate intellectual circle the atmosphere was far from clear.

The political situation was considerably worse by the time Arendt wrote Jaspers a six-page, single-spaced, typewritten report in May 1953, shortly after Stalin's death. Senator Joe McCarthy had won reelection in Wisconsin by a wide margin, and many believed, because the Republican victory had been so clear while Republican opposition to McCarthy's tactics was so ambivalent, that he had great power. Democratic opposition in Congress was ominously mute, for many feared that an attack on McCarthy would produce a Republican rally around the man. In this situation of partisan stalemate, McCarthy was able to convert a minor committee, the Committee on Expenditures in the Executive Departments, into the base for his sweeping investigatory operations. The year 1953 was McCarthy's year for attacks on the Voice of America, the State Department's overseas information libraries, the Government Printing Office, and a host of individuals in various government-funded agencies.

Arendt's May letter to Jaspers was filled with evocations of Weimar. "I write everything down for you in detail," she told Jaspers, "despite my fear that you will say I am exaggerating, because it seems to me so important that you be informed." Her estimate of McCarthy's power over the Hindenburg of his day, Eisenhower, was exaggerated: "If McCarthy isn't elected President in 1956, we will have a good chance."[48] But Jaspers, who knew the source of her fears all too well, was very careful in his reply: "I thought how rightly you had prophesied in 1931, and how I did not believe you. The majority of our countrymen were, I was sure, reasonable and humane, as you also knew them to be. But the tricks of power politics and then the fear they felt when faced with a *fait accompli* left them defenceless. It could also happen in America, but, still, it is much less likely than it was with us."[49] By the summer, after McCarthy's assistants, Cohn and Schine, had completed their ridiculous whirlwind investigatory tour of American libraries in Europe, Arendt could once again appreciate the farcical aspects of the situation: "it would be better if one read it by Shakespeare, [Cohn and Schine as] Rosenkrantz and Guildenstern."[50] But she remained very frightened, particularly by the confusion among American intellectuals—so reminiscent to her of the Weimar "elites" who had allied with "the mob." "The entanglement of the intellectuals in these things is frightful," she told Jaspers in December. "The sociologists and psychologists are responsible for the conceptual morass in which everyone is sunk. Naturally, they are only a symptom of the mass society, but they also have a special significance."[51]

Arendt attended many discussions of totalitarianism and lectured at both the New School and the Rand School, offering summaries of her book's totalitarianism section. In March 1953 she went to Boston, at the invitation of another German-speaking émigré, Carl J. Friedrich, to attend a conference on totalitarianism sponsored by the American Academy of Arts and Sciences. George Kennan gave the opening address at the conference, "Totalitarianism and Freedom," and his measured statements were reassuringly close to Arendt's views: "We tend more and more," Kennan said, "to confine ourselves to military methods and to adopt our opponent's tactics. If we go too far in behaving as they do, we are lost."[52]

Arendt's own contributions to the conference were not predictive; she did not try to forecast developments within the Soviet Union, the main regime under discussion, or within America. She confined herself to clarifying points of historical and contemporary interpretation, and, most importantly, she urged the conferees to consider totalitarianism in political rather than in sociological or psychological terms. In political terms, the novelty of totalitarianism was clear, but psychologically and sociologically, totalitarian practices could be viewed as variations of tyrannical, despotic, or authoritarian methods. Arendt stressed what she had stressed in her book: that attempts to view totalitarianism within traditional frameworks would lead to misunderstanding. Similarly, she argued against using the notion of "secular religion" to characterize totalitarian ideologies. It was not, she felt, the content of ideas that mattered in totalitarian regimes but the principle of logical consistency, the process of remaking reality to "prove" a premise. In all her remarks, Arendt stressed the importance of clear distinctions and the need to keep any "model" of totalitarian regimes dynamic so that the development from a "movement" into a form of government could be traced and changes within the regime assessed.

Changes within the Soviet regime were many and very difficult to assess in 1953. The totalitarianism conference began on the very day Stalin's death on 5 March was announced by the Soviet press. A complex struggle for succession began immediately and was attended by shifts of leadership and policy in the satellite states of Eastern Europe. During the premiership of Malenkov (March 1953–February 1955) striking efforts to improve living conditions within the Soviet Union and to lessen international tensions with a "peaceful coexistence" policy led many to speculate about the extent of Soviet "liberalization." Ilya Ehrenburg's 1954 novel, *The Thaw*, lent its name to the years after Stalin's death, but Arendt remained very skeptical about what this thaw implied. She was even more cautious in her comments about how the post-Stalin developments would be received in America and elsewhere, because she feared that opposition to totalitarianism of the secular-religion variety had rigidified Western attitudes. Signs of American opposition to McCarthy during the summer of 1953 were encouraging. But just as she was beginning to see the cracks in the edifice of silence McCarthy had built in the United States Senate, Arendt was disturbed anew by events in Israel and another form of the "religion and politics" question.

In the fall of 1953, William Zukerman, the editor of the *Jewish Newsletter*, wrote to ask Arendt if she would comment on the growing Arab-Israeli tensions. Since its inauguration in 1948, the *Jewish Newsletter* had been one of the most outspoken organs of dissent within the American Jewish community. Zukerman editorialized regularly against what he called "an outburst of tribalism and conformity, which had its roots in the greatest Jewish tragedy—the Hitler extermination of European Jewry." He was concerned that "the rise of nationalism has had the same effect on Jews as on most other peoples of our age."[53] In a 19 January 1953 editorial, Zukerman, a disciple of Judah Magnes, had quoted part of Hannah Arendt's 1948 eulogy for Magnes as an indication that his criticism of Jewish nationalism was shared by others: "It has happened that the last years... coincided with a great change in the Jewish national character. A people that for 2,000 years had made justice the cornerstone of its spiritual and communal experience has become emphatically hostile to all arguments of such a nature as though they were necessarily arguments of failure."[54]

In February 1953, an explosion had injured three people in the courtyard of the Soviet legation in Tel Aviv, the culmination of the ferocious anti-Soviet sentiment, often couched in religious terms, that had grown by leaps and bounds in Israel after the late-1952 anti-Zionist trials in Prague. The Israeli government vociferously denied responsibility for the incident. The Soviets withdrew their legation and severed diplomatic relations. This was one front of tension; another was more dangerous. Throughout 1952 and 1953, hundreds of so-called Arab infiltrees, displaced people trying to return to their homeland, had been either killed or captured by the Israelis. Arab resentment of the Jewish government had escalated with the passing of a Nationality Law in March 1952 which was only too similar in its principles to the American McCarran Act; in effect, it excluded from Israeli citizenship all but about 10 percent of the Arabs living in Israel. In August, there were several attacks instigated by the Israeli Defense Ministry, "reprisal raids" on Arab settlements. One of these, at Kybia, left fifty-two Arabs dead and provoked a United Nations resolution of censure. It was on the Kybia incident in particular that Zukerman wanted Arendt to write. She felt that both the anti-Soviet feeling and the anti-Arab attacks indicated that Ben-Gurion's government had taken a step in the direction of dictatorship. But she refused to comment on the situation for the *Jewish Newsletter*, and only sent Zukerman a despairing note on 1 November: "The shortest statement to be made would be: Thou shalt not kill, not even Arab women and children. And this certainly is a little too brief. The whole business is absolutely nauseating. I decided that I do not want to have anything to do with Jewish politics any longer."[55] Kurt Blumenfeld was in melancholy agreement with her assessment of how little genuine religious feeling had to do with contemporary politics: "It seems to me we have comparable impressions of the state of the world," he wrote from Jerusalem. "The meaning of the Ten Commandments is everywhere, in Europe and in Israel, quite forgotten."[56]

Events in the Middle East and changes in Soviet policy continued to occupy Arendt's attention, though it was not until after 1956 that she left her theoretical work to speak out again as an expert on totalitarianism. She kept her resolution to have nothing more to do with Jewish politics. But while she was working on the essays that made up *Between Past and Future* and the lectures that made up *The Human Condition*, *The Origins of Totalitarianism* spoke for her in two unexpected ways.

In 1951, a man named George Agree attended Blücher's first New School *Kunstphilosophie* lectures and was included in some of the after-lecture parties with two other auditors, Rose Feitelson (Arendt's "Englisher") and Alfred Kazin. Agree was at the time moving from a period of work with the American League for a Free Palestine (ALFP), which had dissolved in 1948 with the founding of Israel, to a job with the National Committee for an Effective Congress (NCEC). Arendt knew about Agree's connection with the American League for a Free Palestine, one of the many forms the Irgun's Washington lobbying took, but she did not let memories of the old battle stand in the way of the new one.

Agree's friend from the ALFP, Maurice Rosenblatt, had founded the National Committee for an Effective Congress in 1948 to solicit campaign funds for worthy congressional candidates of either political party. After 1952 the criterion for worthiness was anti-McCarthy commitments. In 1953 the organization established a clearinghouse for information on McCarthy and McCarthyism to provide senators with research support and, when opportunities arose, to back Senate opposition to McCarthy's appointments and investigations. Around the NCEC's core an anti-McCarthy lobby slowly grew.[57]

Many strands of political analysis were woven through Agree's New York and Rosenblatt's Washington anti-McCarthy activities and research efforts. But very important to them both were Hannah Arendt's analyses in *The Origins of Totalitarianism*, for they thought of McCarthyism as a protototalitarian phenomenon. A number of prominent people from political, publishing, business, and academic circles were invited to lend their names to the NCEC letterhead. Arendt gladly lent hers. And it stayed on the letterhead until 1966, when Rosenblatt and Agree parted company, Agree taking with him those he had brought to the NCEC banner.

The second way in which *The Origins of Totalitarianism* had a political impact was not known to Arendt herself. An article by Stephan J. Pollak for the *Yale Law Review* on "The Expatriation Act of 1954" drew heavily on Arendt's discussion of statelessness. This article was cited by Earl Warren, chief justice of the Supreme Court, in his dissenting opinion in a 1957 case that upheld the expatriation act. Subsequently Warren's view prevailed in a 1958 case which found denationalization a form of punishment prohibited by the Eighth Amendment. *The Origins of Totalitarianism* was cited directly by Justice Arthur Goldberg in a 1963 majority opinion that rendered deportation for avoiding military service in wartime illegal.[58]

Arendt was always more optimistic about the ability of courts to forestall protototalitarian developments than she was about the willingness of parties to do the same. Not until the 1960s was she an active supporter of political candidates. She voted as an independent, though usually for Democratic candidates, with no enthusiasm whatsoever for parties. The McCarthy period provided Hannah Arendt with an image to add to her collection from Germany in the 1920s and France in the 1930s of how party bureaucracies, doctrinaire and protective of narrow interests, foreclose political action and turn a deaf ear to the voice of the people. Unlike many English and native American political theorists, who have lived within the relative good order of two-party systems, Arendt distrusted parties because they so quickly left the grass roots of citizen action behind. The years when America's parties were virtually paralyzed by the presence in their midst of the senator from Wisconsin confirmed Arendt's distrust. But it was not until after 1956, after the Hungarian revolution, that she began to speak publicly about how political parties might retain their roots—about the council system.

Rosa Luxemburg's notion of "spontaneous revolution" had been playing in Arendt's thoughts for several years before the Hungarian revolution gave it startling embodiment. Arendt's turn from her Marxism study to her exploration of the concepts basic to a "new science of politics" had required an enormous program of reading in philosophy and political theory. This she began when she returned from her 1952 European trip, continued during the next Guggenheim-funded year, and then supplemented as she took up her first full-time teaching appointment at Berkeley in the spring of 1955. Rosa Luxemburg's analyses of the French fin de siècle social crisis had informed Arendt's early work on the Dreyfus Affair, and *The Accumulation of Capital* had been crucial to her reflections on imperialism; but it was *The Russian Revolution* that Arendt read while she worked her critique of Marxism into *The Human Condition.*

One of Arendt's 1955 Berkeley courses, a graduate seminar called "European Political Theory," grew out of the address she had prepared for the 1954 American Political Science Association meeting, "Concern with Politics in Recent European Philosophical Thought." The other, a lecture course, was a more general history of political theory. Much of the material for both courses had already been written up for a series of (unpublished) lectures on "Philosophy and Politics" which Arendt delivered in 1954 at Notre Dame, under Waldemar Gurian's auspices. At Berkeley, and when she wrote *The Human Condition* and the *Between Past and Future* essays, Arendt was constantly thinking about what the relation between philosophy and politics should and could be in the modern world. The thinkers she returned to again and again— Machiavelli, Hobbes, Rousseau, Montesquieu, Locke, de Tocqueville, and Marx—were figures who had asked her question for their own times. She read as avidly as Rosa Luxemburg had in 1899. Writing to Leo Jogiches, Luxemburg described her state of mind at the time: "Something in me stirs and wants to come to the surface. . . . I feel in a word the need . . . to 'say something great.' . . . I badly need to write in such a way as to act on people like a thunderclap, to grip them by the head—not of course through declamation, but by the breadth of outlook, the power of conviction and the strong impression that I make on them."[59]

In her first teaching job Arendt was amazed by the strong impressions she made on the students who flocked to her lectures, turning her seminar into a class of one hundred, her lecture into a "spectacle." But most amazing to her, and most flattering, was the assessment of her lectures one young man offered: "Rosa Luxemburg has come again." She repeated this "great compliment" with obvious pleasure to Blumenfeld, and recalled it again years later when she actually undertook a project that had occurred to her while she was in Berkeley reading Luxemburg's *The Russian Revolution*—a book called *On Revolution.*[60] Her immersion in European political theory "from A to Z" had left her more convinced than ever that this tradition was not the one where she would find political insights free of the "old suspicions of philosophers." Perhaps, she thought, the American revolutionary tradition would yield what she was seeking, and what she had found only glimmers of in Luxemburg's *The Russian Revolution.* She began, in anticipation, to make bibliographic notes for a future tour of the writings of America's Founding Fathers.

In Berkeley, as earlier in Princeton, Arendt felt as much a pariah among the "cliques and factions" as Rosa Luxemburg had among the multifarious alliances in the German SPD. She began to wonder whether American universities could, given their structure and atmosphere, offer the right forum for her work or for political theory in general. She was unfavorably impressed by the pervasiveness of what she called, disparagingly, "gentility." Princeton had been "indescribably snobbish." Berkeley was better, but still estranging, as much for its hugeness as for its gentility. At the end of one hectic day, she wrote to Blücher, who was teaching full-time at tiny Bard: "You are really lucky to be teaching in a small college . . . here everything must be done in triplicate. . . . I even waited for two weeks to get keys to the office building where I work."[61] The number of *nouveaux riches* among her students startled her, and she told Jaspers that she felt herself in an excellent position to "study how easily a democracy could turn into an ochlocracy [mob rule]"[62]—again invoking the conjunction of mob and elite she thought preliminary to totalitarian movements. With some notable exceptions, the Berkeley faculty struck her as politically naive: there were, she told Blücher, liberal factions and McCarthyite factions, "but all very genteel in their positions." She hardly knew whether to be amused or frightened when a retired general, president of the university's Commonwealth Club, invited her to lecture on totalitarianism and asked her whether she was "for or against" it—not because it mattered to him particularly, but "so he could fit me into his program."[63] It was an enormous relief to her when she met a man who had no great reputation for gentility and whose robust company she enjoyed, particularly when he took her for a tour of the San Francisco docks: "Eric Hoeffner," as she called her new friend in a rush of misspelled German good-feeling, "of *The True Believer.*"[64] In addition to the young man who worked as a janitor in her apartment building and a "young village maiden" émigré from Austria who turned up in one of her classes, Eric Hoffer provided Arendt with welcome diversions from too much academic niceness.

Socially and politically Berkeley was foreign, but the philosophical climate was really distressing: "Philosophy," she told Jaspers, "has fallen into semantics—and third rate semantics at that."[65] After several months, Arendt was grasping, in Montesquieu-like terms, for a way to explain to herself all of this oddness—that is, she laid it all at the door of the nonmetaphorical climate. "In this enchanted garden . . . one's body feels quite different, that is, one really feels it, in general, not at all. It is easy to understand how the people here become so *meschugge* spiritually—it has something very much to do with this climate."[66]

Arendt's reflections on American university life have about them all of the amazement typical of Europeans unaccustomed to giantism and afflu-ence. Her distaste turned into testiness at the Hoover Institution where she went to read in the archive collections important for her revision of *The Origins of Totalitarianism.* "Thirty-eight scholars . . . come together each morning to tell each other their dreams, and for their rubbish are paid extremely well. . . . [They work in a place] which appears to be paradisiacal but which is really one of those modern hells with all the comforts. . . . The spirit of Mr. Hoover follows one everywhere, not only in the library."[67]

Despite the good relationships she formed with a few faculty members and students at Berkeley, Hannah Arendt left at the end of the semester with a firm resolution, which she never abandoned, not to become a full-time academic. "I never really wanted to be a professor," she told everyone who would listen. Through the rest of her life, Arendt did manage to secure, by many complex negotiations, a variety of special arrangements, half-time appointments, visiting lectureships; at least half of every year was left free for work and travel to Europe.[68] The demands of teaching and colleagues and community social life were not something she could comfortably meet: "You are absolutely right," she told Blücher, who had never entertained the idea of moving from New York to Bard College in Annandale-on-Hudson, "we are not cut out for this kind of life. All the time I feel as I did when I worked for Youth Aliyah [in Paris], namely, overwhelmed by the cares and anxieties of other people." Others' problems were too much by themselves, and they contributed to her main problem: "I really cannot appear in public five times a week."[69]

Arendt's resolution stayed firm, but her attitude toward teaching be-came far more favorable when she was able to arrange for less than five appearances a week and when she could go home more easily. She spoke to Blücher each Sunday by telephone from Berkeley—"across the whole continent" as she told Jaspers in wide-eyed amazement—but this did little to help their feelings of isolation. In Berkeley, Arendt was always *ein bisschen allein* ("a little lonely"). Blücher was happy with his work at Bard, but he found the company of their New York intellectual friends dreary and none of his female companions could match his wife's in-tellectual force. He wrote lonely, anxious letters. "You are absent from every nook and cranny, or really, from the very middle-point of my existence. My God, most of the people around have become so boring. One can only hope one is not also a bore."[70] He became exaggeratedly uneasy reading the newspapers. Always, when World-History threatened one of its tricks, they needed each other most. Blücher read about the ousting of Malenkov and the struggle for dominance between Khrushchev and Bulganin with alarm, and then had a moment of complete panic when he read the statement issued by Marshals Konev and Zhukov on the tenth anniversary of the end of the Second World War: the marshals outlined the devastation which a hydrogen bomb could inflict upon Europe and America. "The rumble from Russia has really frightened me, and I wanted to telegraph you to say that of course in the event of an emergency our meeting point should be Bard."

Less than a year after the "rumble," on 14 February 1956, Khrushchev presented to a closed session of the Twentieth Party Congress an indictment of Stalin for his deviation from Lenin's teachings and a dossier of his worst crimes. Many significant changes in line followed: phrases like "peaceful transition to socialism" and "differing roads to socialism" accompanied Soviet overtures to socialist neighbors and to countries of what is now called the Third World. Many Western readers of the version of Khrushchev's secret speech published by the State Department predicted the end of totalitarianism in the Soviet Union. Arendt, on the contrary, saw in the speech signals for the end of the thaw, because she expected the period of "collective leadership" to be followed—as had happened after Lenin's death—by a much more rigid and brutal regime. "That old trickster World-History" declared both predictions too simple, though Arendt was right in the short run.

As news of the Soviet developments and of the mutual cooperation pact Tito signed in Moscow reverberated through Eastern Europe, dissent turned to violent rebellion in Poland and Hungary. The Polish rebellion subsided, and the Poles remained in the Warsaw Pact. The Hungarian rebels issued calls for an end to the Russian presence in Hungary and withdrawal from the pact. Six days after fighting broke out in the streets of Budapest, the Israelis, with a dramatic military drive across the Sinai Desert, exploded the crisis Gamal Abdel Nasser's seizure of the Suez Canal had readied. French and British aircraft bombed Egyptian airbases. Both the Warsaw Pact and the Western alliance, in one week, were rocked.

Hannah Arendt was making her yearly visit to Karl Jaspers in Basel, after a trip through peaceful Holland with Mary McCarthy, when the Hungarians made their bid for freedom. She wrote to Blücher in a state of high excitement: "Finally, finally, they had to show how things really are!"[71] When they read in their newspapers that the rebels, within days of the first street demonstrations, had organized revolutionary and worker's councils, she and Blücher were amazed; for the first time since the post–World War I Berlin of Blücher's youth, councils had emerged "out of the actions and spontaneous demands of the people." A week later, when the Suez Canal dispute had turned into a war, Arendt was completely bewildered: "everything is overshadowed, except my joy about Hungary, by this crazy Israel-episode. Can you understand it?"[72] The Israeli-Sinai campaign took by surprise readers of dispatches as well as readers of newspapers, including President Eisenhower who was setting off for an election campaign tour of the South when French and British troops landed at Port Said.

Another week passed, and Arendt's amazement turned to deep fear. Although she was suspicious that the Israelis were being "imperialistic," Arendt wrote to Blücher on 5 November "with a heavy heart" and very concerned that the episode would spread beyond the Middle East:

So, World History surprises us, when we least expect it. How heavy my heart is, I prefer not to write. Also, I should not say, lest I just fly [home?]; and I might just do that all of a sudden. . . . I don't actually expect an immediate sharpening of the situation, and think that we Americans might still stay out of it. But one cannot know, and I try to keep a close eye on it. Without you, that is difficult.[73]

The cease-fire that quieted the Sinai came the next day, on 6 November, after U.S. threats of embargo, a UN resolution, and much Soviet rattling of long-range missiles. Arendt was momentarily relieved, but her sense of the future was very dark; she feared, typically, the worst possible outcome and prepared herself to face it squarely. "So, it will not then immediately come to war, and that is only because everything is in ruins, including the [Western] Alliance and the United Nations. That could very well mean, though, that now the Third World War really stands at the door; and when it comes, if it comes, it will come like this episode—without a declaration of war."[74]

When Arendt returned to America after these terrifying weeks had passed, she had a great mountain of projects to complete. On her desk sat the manuscript of *The Human Condition*, which she had delivered as lectures the preceding spring in Chicago, the manuscript of *Rahel Varn-*

*hagen*, which was being prepared with the help of a German assistant, Lotte Kohler, for publication by the Leo Baeck Institute, and a number of essays in various stages of completion. She set about these tasks, but she also resolved to write about the Hungarian revolution. She wanted to pay homage to those who had paid so dearly to show "how things really are" under a totalitarian regime's control. The Hungarian revolution had taught her a lesson about the only alternative to totalitarianism she felt the modern world had produced—the council system. "If ever there was such a thing as Rosa Luxemburg's 'spontaneous revolution,'" she later wrote in her "Reflections on the Hungarian Revolution," "this sudden uprising of an oppressed people for the sake of freedom and hardly anything else, without the demoralizing chaos of military defeat [as in Germany] preceding it, without *coup d'état* techniques, without a closely knit apparatus of organizers and conspirators, without the undermining propaganda of a revolutionary party, something, that is, which everybody, conservatives and liberals, radicals and revolutionaries, had discarded as a noble dream—then we had the privilege to witness it."[75]

## A "Laudatio" in Europe

Both the Blüchers were what one of their friends called "catastrophe-minded." The horrors they had known in their twenty years together echoed in their judgments and shadowed their vision. Though in public they spoke neither with the pessimism of cowards nor the optimism of fools, the moments when they "saw the world black," as another friend put it, gave them starting points for reflection. But these reflections were guided by *amor mundi*, by love of the world. Arendt could write elegiac descriptions of the beautiful world in one letter and catalogues of its dreariness in the next; her reactions were as diverse as those of Rahel Varnhagen's "Day and Night." The intensity of Arendt's feelings, and the quickness with which she moved between them, impressed Blücher. He called her, fondly, "the meteor" or "shooting star" (*Schnuppe*). These experiences of love and horror gave them their capacity for what the Greeks called *thaumadzein*, wonder at the spectacles of the world, and their work reveals their freedom from the old suspicion of unworldly philosophers that there is neither beauty nor meaningfulness in human affairs.

Karl Jaspers, too, was often prompted to speak out by particular events that exposed vast complexes of opinion and policy. When Hannah

Arendt visited him in the fall of 1956, he had just delivered a lecture provoked by the same rumble from Russia that had filled Blücher with foreboding the year before. His book *The Atom Bomb and the Future of Mankind,* an expanded version of the lecture, began thus:

An altogether novel situation has been created by the atom bomb. Either all mankind will physically perish or there will be a change in the moral-political condition of man. . . . Despite the apparent calm of our daily lives, the progress of the dread menace seems now irresistible. Topical aspects change quickly, but the overall aspect remains the same: either the sudden outbreak of nuclear war in a matter of years or decades, or the establishment of world peace without atom bombs. . . . Political and legal operations alone will not take us in this direction, nor will unanimous abhorrence of the bomb. We realize today that actually no start has yet been made toward achieving world peace. Do we know what is to be done?[76]

Jaspers's book, published in 1958, generated a storm of objections from German scientists and from opponents of the Western alliance, but it also won him the Peace Prize of the German book trade. Hannah Arendt was invited to give the address which accompanied the prize, and she wrote for the occasion her beautiful "Karl Jaspers: A Laudatio." The address was the second public statement she had made about her teacher and friend. The first had come a year earlier, in an article for an American volume dedicated to the philosophy of Karl Jaspers. These were the years óf their most intense collaboration. The atom bomb book is deeply indebted to Arendt's *The Origins of Totalitarianism,* and the passages in *The Human Condition,* particularly those on modern science, often draw on Jaspers's reflections. What each had learned from the other was not acknowledged in their books but when the public occasions came, they gratefully acknowledged their friendship. Jaspers had written in a "Philosophical Memoir" appended to *The Philosophy of Karl Jaspers* a tribute to Arendt's reappearance in their lives after the war and her continued visits to her second home:

She came to us, the oldsters, from the younger generation, bringing us what she had encountered and learned. An emigrant since 1933, having roamed the earth with her spirit unbroken by infinite difficulties, she knew all about the elemental terrors of an existence sundered from its native country, stripped of all rights, cast into the inhuman state of statelessness. Her inner independence made her a world citizen; her faith in the singular strength of the American Constitution—

and in the political principle which had endured, after all, as the relatively best—made her a citizen of the United States. From her I learned how to see that world of the greatest experiment in political freedom, and how, on the other hand, to see the structures of totalitarianism better than I had been able to see them before. . . . With her I could argue again, in the way I have been seeking all my life . . . argue in leaving each other radically free and ceasing to make abstract demands, because they wane in factual loyalty.[77]

Arendt hesitated about whether she should give the Frankfurt Peace Prize address, and she wrote to Blücher for advice. Plaintively, using his pet name for her, she asked "and what shall the Schnuppe do?"[78] The Meteor's worries were as complex as her temperament was meteoric. First, humbly, she thought the occasion called for a speaker of greater reputation; "I do not stand on such a level of prominence." Secondly, she wanted to keep in place the line she had always drawn so sharply between private friendship and public appearances, though she knew that Jaspers himself did not draw such a "radical distinction." Thirdly, she was "a woman, a Jew and a non-German," and she felt that all of these factors "would make a very bad impression in the publicity" and generate discussion irrelevant to the occasion. Again, she was afraid that she would be treated as an "exception woman." The issuers of the invitation did little to allay her fear when they told her "it would be so good for a woman, for the first time, to step forward in the [Frankfurt] Paulskirche." Half-jokingly and half-vainly, she told Blücher in a stage whisper that her freckles, which would be conveyed in the publicity, "were also a consideration." But, having made this girlish aside, she told him the fourth reason very simply: "*Ich habe Angst* [I am afraid]."

Only to Blücher would Arendt have written such a list and admitted her stage fright so nakedly. It was also only with him that she could discuss the fifth and most troublesome reason. She knew that her address would make public for the first time in Germany her personal accord and political solidarity with Jaspers, and she feared that her public praise of Jaspers would be interpreted as an implicit repudiation of Martin Heidegger, by her audience or by Heidegger himself. She knew she would praise Jaspers for everything Heidegger had never been: a moral example, a cosmopolitan, a model of the public philosopher. Blücher weighed Arendt's first four reasons, and then encouraged her to accept the invitation despite her misgivings. About the last reason, he was curt and clear: "One should speak there, truly, about the concept of the good European.

And that is just what Heidegger has coming to him anyhow, that *Hosen-matzdeutscher* [little-boy-in-first-pants German]."[79]

Six years of patient diplomacy preceded Blücher's burst of annoyance and Arendt's appearance at the Peace Prize ceremony—which did, in fact, bring about a measure of resentment on Heidegger's part. Amidst the many projects that had occupied Hannah Arendt during her European tours in 1949, 1952, and 1956, she had made great efforts to reestablish the friendship between Jaspers and Heidegger. Her efforts were not successful, and by 1958 she was ready to give up.

Heidegger's condition, personally and philosophically, had troubled Arendt during her first reunion with him in 1949. In that year, he had published his *Letter on Humanism*, announcing publicly for the first time that his philosophical thought had undergone a "reversal" (*Kehre*). Finding his own early work *Being and Time* too "subjective," too concerned with how man seeks to ask "the question of the meaning of Being," Heidegger had begun to think of man as a respondent to Being. Not out of a man's own spontaneity, but out of his "listening" to Being come his thinking and speaking. Arendt felt that Heidegger's change was connected to his earlier "turning against the self-assertion of man," a turning which had allowed him to speak against man's Promethean arrogance in the rector's address he gave at Freiburg in 1933. But his development of a notion of man as, in effect, a "function of Being" disturbed Arendt deeply.[80] Heidegger was, she thought, heading in the direction of a mystical view that worldly things "distract man from Being." He was, in short, becoming less and less political, even though he achieved many historical insights she valued. As Arendt and Blücher discussed Heidegger's work in their 1952 letters, they agreed that the weakest point was his concept of historicity (*Geschichtlichkeit*), which might have allowed his thought to have a political dimension. The fruit of Arendt's reflections was a passage in her address to the American Political Science Association in 1954. Since this address was never published, it is worth quoting at length the passage that deals with Heidegger's work. As clearly as anything Arendt ever wrote, this passage shows what she had learned from Heidegger and where she found the limitations of his thought:

In *Sein und Zeit* (1927) Heidegger formulated historicity in ontological, as distinguished from anthropological, terms and more recently [he] has arrived at an understanding according to which "historicity" means to be sent on one's way

(*Geschichtlichkeit* and *Geschick-lichkeit* are thought together in the sense of being sent on one's way and being willing to take this "sending" upon oneself), so that for him human history would coincide with a history of Being which is revealed in it. The point against Hegel is that no transcendent spirit and no absolute is revealed in this ontological history (*Seinsgeschichte*); in Heidegger's own words: "We left the arrogance of all Absolute behind us" (*Wir haben die Anmassung alles Unbedingten hinter uns gelassen*). In our context, this means that the philosopher left behind him the claim to being "wise" and knowing eternal standards for the perishable affairs of the City of men, because he does not really belong to it, but dwells in the proximity of the Absolute. In the context of the spiritual and political crisis of the time, it means that the philosopher, after having lost, together with all others, the traditional framework of so-called "values," does not look out for either the reestablishment of the old or the discovery of new "values."

The abandonment of the position of "wise man" by the philosopher himself through the concept of historicity is important in two respects: first, the rejection of the claim to wisdom opens the way to a reexamination of the whole realm of politics in the light of elementary human experiences within this realm itself, and discards implicitly concepts and judgments, which have their roots in altogether different kinds of human experience. This examination is, second, guided and limited by the concept of historicity which despite its obvious closeness to the political realm, never reaches its center—man as an acting being. Heidegger himself has taken the first decisive steps on this road when, in *Sein und Zeit*, he started the analyses of human existence by an extensive phenomenological description of average everyday life which does not know solitude but is constantly with and under the spell of others. These analyses exerted a certain influence on contemporary sociological inquiries and rightly so, for they retain their validity even though in the categorical opposition of the *man* (public opinion in the largest sense [*das Man*]) against the self, in which public reality has the function to hide the true realities and to prevent the appearance of truth, the old hostility of the philosopher toward the *polis* is only too apparent. Much more important, however, are other limitations, inherent in the concept of historicity itself. Insofar as it originates from a coincidence of thought and event (and the "event" plays an ever-increasing role in Heidegger's recent publications), it can throw new light on history rather than on politics, on happenings rather than on action. This seems to be the reason why this trend in philosophy is highly sensitive to general trends of the time, such as the technicalization of the world, the emergence of One World on a planetary scale, the increasing pressure of society upon the individual and the concomitant atomization of society, etc., i.e., to all those modern problems which can be best understood in historical terms; while it seems to have forgotten altogether the more permanent questions of political science, which, in a sense, are more specifically philosophic, such as what is politics? who is man as a political being? what is freedom? etc.[81]

Both Arendt and Blücher read Heidegger's postwar work with great interest, and Arendt was later very helpful to the American translators and editors who presented his work in English, particularly after her friend J. Glenn Gray began to edit Harper and Row's Heidegger series. But she always thought of Heidegger as—so she put it in a lecture on his work given at Yale University in 1951—"a philosopher's philosopher."[82] While she thought of herself as a political theorist, his later work stayed in the background of her own. When she returned to a work she considered "proper philosophy," *The Life of the Mind*, Heidegger's late work, and particularly his reflections on thinking and language, came back into the center of her concern. But never uncritically. She had reservations, always, about Heidegger's thought, and she always felt that *Being and Time*, not the later work, was his greatest contribution.

Unlike many, Arendt did not object to Heidegger's philosophical terminology, as she approved of his effort to find a new language for philosophy. She objected, however, when his language or his style seemed too involuted, too self-conscious and self-referential. When she used his reflections, as she used *Identity and Difference* in *The Life of the Mind*, she tried to translate them into simpler, more straightforward prose. Her irritation with his complexities she expressed only privately, as in a letter to Kurt Blumenfeld, the man who received over the years Arendt's many comments on the *Krankheit*, the sickness of German and German-Jewish intellectuals. Arendt diagnosed the sickness as an obsession with being a "unique personality":

When I look over the 18th Century and see Lessing and Hamann, Kant and Herder, I find not a trace in them [of this sickness]. With Goethe it takes hold a little, and God knows all those *Herren Philosophen*, Hegel, Fichte, Schelling, had to be, personally, geniuses. One can understand it with all these somewhat-geniuses and really only highly cultivated overreachers (case in point: [Gershom] Scholem), but why, why does it touch the real geniuses? I was reading yesterday the latest piece from Heidegger, on Identity and Difference, which is of great interest, but—he cites himself and interprets himself, as though he had written a Biblical text. I find it simply insufferable. And he really is a genius and not

simply highly cultivated. Also: why does he need this? This indescribably annoying manneredness.[83]

Jaspers, who had even had the temerity—it earned him a flurry of anger
from academic circles—to criticize the great Goethe for his genius-
worship, was free of this manneredness, and Arendt thought that if
Heidegger could join forces with Jaspers he would be saved from his own
weaknesses and from the followers who aggravated them with a cult.

Arendt always distrusted philosophical schools, and she found the
epigones of both Heidegger and Heidegger's teacher Husserl annoying.
The cliques and fads of the German postwar universities made her uneasy.

I am quite worried about Heidegger's fame, that is, worried for him. A "movement" or a "tendency" has come about, one which could at any moment blow
away or reorient. Basically, Heidegger is aware of this, but he sails with these
winds anyway—thought it's not unlikely that I have been able to make him a
little more distrustful. In fact, quite cautious. About [Ernst] Jünger, who was the
topic of everyone's conversation two years ago, not even a dead cat would talk
today; his books are not to be found. So it goes from one day to the next. The
same is so for Jaspers, but that also means little in the long run. Such is the
momentary German atmosphere—everyone quickly disappears. Perhaps I am
mistaken, but I think not.[84]

Arendt feared that the other side of Heidegger's fame would overtake him;
the side Alfred Kazin had reported to her during his German year: "With
Martin . . . it is sad. I couldn't be otherwise, and will not be. . . . Nevertheless, when Alfred said to me, entirely naively, that the name Heidegger seems to have become a kind of 'cuss word' in academic and other
circles, it was painful to me. I really cannot change that."[85] Arendt could
not help feeling sorry for Heidegger, but she also could not change the
fact that he had spent a year in the Nazi party or the fact that many people
were unwilling to forgive him. Even Jaspers, despite Arendt's efforts, was
reluctant to forgive him. During her 1952 visits to Basel and during a
vacation with Jaspers in St. Moritz, Arendt pressed her case: "but it is
quite clear that everything I had hoped to obtain for Martin is not going to
come off. There is nothing more to be done. Jaspers sees only the _Unheil_
("mischief") and not the other side of the coin. Or, he sees the other side
only for a moment, while I am here. What can I do? Really nothing."[86]

Arendt's sympathy for Heidegger's personal situation was constant, even though her distrust of his circle grew and she openly referred to it as "another [Stefan] George-Kreis": "What I saw and heard of the Heidegger influence in Heidelberg would be truly disastrous if it weren't so wooly-headed."[87] She felt that Heidegger was surrounded by unreliable decadents—"the only real *Mensch* he has is his brother"—and too much under his wife's control. Using the terminology she had developed to explain the fascination of the mob for the elite, Arendt gave Blücher a description of Heidegger's marriage: "It is a classic case of the mob-elite bond. . . . The whole story is really a tragedy. . . . When I imagine to myself how he relapses necessarily into such a milieu as soon as his work pauses, it makes me simply dizzy."[88] Everything about the Heideggers' domesticity saddened Arendt, but the disorder of his manuscripts and the presence of Frau Heidegger's books in his library filled her with pique: "There, on his shelves, the complete works of Gertrud Bäumer!"[89] (Frau Bäumer was a leading figure in the German Women's Movement who edited a journal the Nazis found not at all worthy of censorship). Blücher's comment upon the marriage presented in a Heideggerian phrase the biographical corollary of the Master's fundamental ontology: "How uniquely an empty wife can destroy everything: *Das Nichts nichtet* (the Nothing nothings)."[90]

Elfriede Heidegger and Heidegger's male circle worried Arendt enough that she sought whatever reassurance she could find, and, during the spring before the Frankfurt Peace Prize lecture, reassurance came from an unexpected quarter. Hannah Strauss, wife of the former Schocken Books editor Max Strauss and an expert in graphology, a science that also interested Karl Jaspers, conducted a private seminar in her home. Arendt went to the seminar one afternoon with some samples of handwriting. She was startled when Hannah Strauss, after examining one of Walter Benjamin's letters, announced that the man was self-destructive. Hannah Arendt took the sample back, not wanting to hear any more, murmuring "Yes, he took his own life not so long ago." Then she handed over a sample of Heidegger's handwriting—not a letter, but a list of books. This man, Hannah Strauss announced, was fascinated with language, with words and their origins, their etymologies: like Erasmus of Rotterdam, whose script was similar, this man vacillated in his commitments, allying himself to a cause and then retreating into his own realm, his own work. Arendt was very impressed with these accurate assessments of Heidegger's philosophical passion and political past, but she had more personal questions. "Is he married?" "Yes," Hannah Strauss answered, "but the marriage does not matter to him." "Is he homosexual?" "No, but the company of male friends is very important to him." Frau Strauss had no idea that she had, in two short sentences, helped relieve Hannah Arendt of two great fears she had about the milieu in which Heidegger lived.[91] But when her anxiety lessened, she lost her patience.

After her "Laudatio" for Jaspers in 1958, Arendt's loyalty to Heidegger began to wear thin. She had allowed herself to go intellectually unappreciated while she did what she could to sharpen Heidegger's awareness of the "momentary German atmosphere" and the quality of his associates. His interest in her work was not, apparently, great; he was startled to find out that her reputation was such that she could be invited to address the German Book Trade and he was displeased with the public recognition she received.

But his greatest surprise came when Arendt decided to let him know directly what she was capable of producing; after years of being appreciated only for her *Grossmut* ("generosity") she sent Heidegger her German translation of *The Human Condition*, *Vita Activa*. The result was a burst of hostility from Heidegger and his circle. "I know," Arendt explained to Jaspers, "that it is intolerable for him that my name appears in public, that I write books, etc. I have really fibbed to him about myself all the while, behaving as though none of this existed and as if I, so to speak, could not count to three, except when it came to giving an interpretation of his own things; in that case it was always gratifying to him when it turned out that I could count to three and sometimes even to four. But suddenly this fib became quite boring to me and I have paid for my change of mind with a knock on the nose. For a while I was really furious [at his reaction], but no longer. Now I think that I am really somehow responsible—namely, as much for the fib as for the abrupt cessation of the game."[92] Jaspers accepted this frank, generous explanation, but still could hardly believe it: "Your explanation of Heidegger's behavior is so astonishing that, had it not come from you, who know him so well, I would hardly accept it. He must have known about your books for a long time, as they have been reviewed by all the newspapers, one after another. The only new element is that he had this one directly from you—and then, such a reaction! The most unbelievable things are possible."[93]

Hannah Arendt did not explain to Jaspers why she had chosen to indulge Heidegger by behaving like a none-too-bright female, or why she suddenly grew bored with her fib. That Heidegger wished to think of her as a Muse rather than an equal, that his love for her was romantic, is clear. She complied and, further, did not publish her critical assessments of his work. Perhaps she was trying to be for him the wife his wife was not and could not be, or the lover he did not have—or both. It was more important to her to provide Heidegger with shelter from his milieu than to offer intellectual companionship; for herself she had little need of such companionship, as she had it at home with Blücher and in Basel with Jaspers. And she, too, had a Romantic, or at least a Rahel Varnhagen, in her—present since the days when her youthful love for Heidegger had brought her into *Die Schatten*.

## A Controversy in America

Hannah Arendt seldom held back her opinions for either personal or political reasons; any *Schwindel* ("fib"), no matter how well intentioned, made her uncomfortable. When she did exercise caution she usually paid dearly for it later, with some form of knock on the nose. The end of her patience was the beginning of trouble, for she came out of her silences impatiently, sharply, speaking with the "This Means You" tone of her early *Aufbau* columns. But her most pungent remarks were reserved for issues about which others had kept silent for reasons she could not accept; whenever she suspected a conspiracy of silence, she wrote furiously and sometimes disdainfully.

The same "Band" of New York intellectuals who had roused Arendt and Blücher to anger during the McCarthy years delivered her a knock on the nose in 1957, and a pitched battle began. Hannah Arendt's first experience with a public controversy came with her article on integration, "Reflections on Little Rock." It was a controversy, as the novelist Ralph Ellison noted in 1963, that gave a "dark foreshadowing of the Eichmann blow-up,"[94] the protracted controversy over Arendt's *Eichmann in Jerusalem*. In both cases, Arendt sailed upwind of strong currents, deep emotions, and unmastered pasts. She was thought unsympathetic, even callous, in the two works which burst most impatiently out of her personal sympathy for innocent victims caught up in a whirl of events they were powerless to resist. Both times she wrote without the long years of germination that had given *The Origins of Totalitarianism* its tone of tragic lament. She wrote out of sympathy for the Negro school children who had to endure the race hatred of Southern whites and for the Jewish victims of Nazi persecution; and she wrote out of moral anger at Negro parents who allowed their children to bear the burden of a racial struggle, and at Jewish leaders who "cooperated" with the Nazis. As she wrote, Arendt put to herself a personal question: what would you have done? But, in both cases, the question was asked and answered offstage; her empathetic attempt to stand in others' places and weigh up the alternatives for action preceded her writing; and the writing itself, without the questioning, seemed to many readers harsh, inappropriately judgmental, and arrogant.

When her Little Rock reflections were published, Arendt wrote a prefatory statement in which she, quite untypically and with intense embarrassment for the public display of her personal experience, warned her readers: "Since what I wrote may shock good people and be misused by bad ones, I should like to make it clear that as a Jew I take my sympathy for the cause of the Negroes as for all oppressed and underprivileged people for granted and should appreciate it if the reader did likewise."[95] The controversy grew anyway, and Arendt felt she had to bring her offstage question into view. She wrote a reply to her critics in which she retraced the path that brought her to her conclusions: "What would I do if I were a Negro mother? What would I do if I were a white mother in the South?"[96] Arendt's political theory always grew up out of just such thought exercises, attempts to capture experiences and find the experiential base of positions, decisions, and policies. But in her "Reflections on Little Rock," as later in *Eichmann in Jerusalem*, the experiences were so complex and emotion-charged that she might have saved much misunderstanding had she put her own self-questioning before her readers in the first place, had she let them see not only her theory but her struggle.

The theoretical framework of Arendt's "Reflections on Little Rock" was the one she had developed at length in *The Human Condition*, which was not widely known until after her article had appeared in a 1959 issue of *Dissent*. In the article she briefly distinguished three "spaces" for human activity—the private, the social, and the political—and indicated what meaning racial discrimination had in each. Arendt reminded her readers "that it is not the social custom of segregation that is unconstitutional, but *its legal enforcement*."[97] In society, she argued, discrimination should not be touched by law. Social equality cannot be enforced; equality "has its origin in the body politic" and can be legally enforced only there. Social groups and associations, organized in America "along lines of profession, income and ethnic origin," rather than along lines of "class origin, education and manners" as in European countries, are discriminatory by nature, by "social right," and not subject to the basic political principle of equality before the law. Arendt went even further and suggested that social discrimination, manifest in social groupings, is an important barrier against "mass society," against a society in which group distinctions and interests have disappeared. "The question," she wrote, "is not how to abolish discrimination, but how to keep it confined within the social sphere, where it is legitimate, and prevent its trespassing on the political and personal [or private] sphere, where it is destructive." Or, put in other terms: "While the government has no right to interfere with the prejudices and discriminatory practices of society, it has not only the right but the duty to make sure that these practices are not legally enforced."

Elaborated without the complex historical study provided in *The Human Condition*, Arendt's distinctions were mysterious to her critics not so much in themselves as because they led her to two shocking claims. First, she argued that legal enforcement of segregation in the private sphere—"ruled neither by equality [before the law] nor by [social] discrimination, but by exclusiveness," that is, by personal, individual choice—was the most outrageous sort of enforced segregation. Arendt, whose marriage to a Gentile could never have taken place in her home-land while the Nuremberg Laws were in force, felt that the laws against racial intermarriage which, in 1959, existed in twenty-nine out of the forty-nine states ought to be the first front for action. "Even political rights, like the right to vote and nearly all other rights enumerated in the Constitution, are secondary to the inalienable human rights to 'life, liberty and the pursuit of happiness' proclaimed in the Declaration of Independence; it is to this category that the right to home and marriage unquestionably belongs." Arendt's suggestion that blacks ought to make repeal of miscegenation laws their first political priority struck her readers as either wrong or completely impractical.

Arendt's second suggestion was just as unorthodox. She felt that the public schools were an inappropriate focus for federal interference because there the three realms intersected. Schools involve private persons' rights to raise children as they see fit, the social right of all to keep what company they wish, and the government's political right "to prepare children for their future duty as citizens." Compulsory education restricts parents' personal and social rights, but it does not imply that they cannot decide which schools their children will attend or what the social configuration of the schools will be. Arendt viewed public services like transportation as clear-cut, appropriate foci for action but warned against enforced school integration because it would set children in the middle of a confusing conflict between home and school. Such a conflict "between family prejudice and school demands abolishes at one stroke both the teachers' and the parents' authority, replacing it with the rule of public opinion among children who have neither the ability nor the right to establish a public opinion of their own." To make children the avant garde of integration was, Arendt thought, an abdication of parental responsibility: "Have we now come to the point where it is the children who are being asked to change or improve the world?"

These two stances were certainly sufficient to raise a controversy, but Arendt's third contention, confined to the political sphere alone, was what won her a reputation for being an arch conservative. Arendt charged with shortsightedness liberals who argued that the invocation of states' rights was nothing but a "Southern subterfuge" to thwart integration. "Liberals fail to understand that the nature of power is such that the power potential of the Union as a whole will suffer if the regional foundations on which this power rests are undermined. . . . And states' rights in this country are among the most authentic sources of power not only for the promotion of regional interests and diversity, but for the Republic as a whole." To many of Arendt's liberal readers, this sounded like a Republican party convention speech.

But Arendt's "Reflections on Little Rock," originally commissioned by a Jewish magazine, *Commentary*, reflected her Jewishness more than any conservatism. Her "pariah" and "parvenu" categories, though never mentioned, governed her approach. In a photograph that appeared with *Life* magazine's coverage of the Little Rock violence, Arendt had seen a black girl being escorted home from her newly integrated school by a white friend of her father's; behind the girl she saw a "mob of white children," their faces contorted, their insults, their "public opinion," almost audible. To Arendt, it was obvious that "the girl was asked to be a hero— something neither her absent father nor the equally absent representative of the NAACP felt called upon to be." The "absent father" had done what no parent ought to do: he had asked his child to go where she was not wanted, to behave like a parvenu, to treat education as a means of social advancement. This child was not given the "absolute protection of dignity" Martha Arendt had once so conscientiously given her daughter, who had been instructed to leave social situations where she was not wanted and go home.

What Arendt feared was that this black child would develop a version of the so-called Jewish complex, fear of *goyim*, a sense of inferiority and exaggerated, introspective sensibility; just the complex Arendt had tried to describe to the parents of her Youth Aliyah charges in Paris. "Psychologically, the situation of being unwanted (a typically social predicament) is more difficult to bear than outright persecution (a political predicament) because personal pride is involved. By pride, I do not mean anything like proud of being a Negro, or a Jew, or a white Anglo-Saxon Protestant, etc., but that untaught and natural feeling of identity with whatever we happen to be by accident of birth [the condition of our natality]. Pride, which does not compare and knows neither inferiority nor superiority."[98] Arendt saw in black people's struggles for integration all the dilemmas of Jewish assimilation. What she hoped was that blacks would learn that politics is not the province of whites; that the response to white domination ought to be not social but political; that action, rooted in natality, begins something new. Pride, Arendt continued, "is lost not so much by persecution as by pushing, or rather by being pushed into pushing, one's way out of one group and into another. If I were a Negro mother in the South, I would feel that the Supreme Court ruling, unwillingly, but unavoidably, had put my child into a more humiliating position than it had been in before."[99] Not something new but an interiorized psychological version of the old oppression was, she felt, the price of parvenu behavior.

Arendt advocated political action but she assumed, on the basis of her understanding of anti-Semitism and her knowledge of German-Jewish history, that even political equality would be problematic if it was achieved. The German "exception Jews," who had achieved social acceptance as exceptions, knew that political emancipation would level social differences, bringing to the fore what both the exceptions and their "backward" brethren shared—their ineradicable Jewishness. She feared that, with each step forward made by blacks, the natural, physical differences which distinguished them would become even more the focus of white resentment. And she feared that relying on the utopian idea that the world can be changed by "educating the children in the spirit of the future" would only increase the resentment and cause "needless embitterment." "Awareness of future trouble," she hastened to add, "does not commit one to advocating a reversal of the trend which happily for more than fifteen years now has been greatly in favor of the Negroes. But it does commit one to advocating that government intervention be guided by caution and moderation rather than by impatience and ill-advised measures."

Hannah Arendt did not think that the repeal of miscegenation laws would be incautious, though researchers like Gunnar Myrdal and his associates, the writers of *The American Dilemma*, had claimed that in the Southern white's "order of resentments" intermarriage ranked first, far ahead of resentment at the prospect of integrated schools. She thought the "real issue" for blacks was equality before the law and that the lack of such equality should be the focus of action. The readiness of liberals to invoke practicality or feasibility—and to argue that white resistance to intermarriage made repeal of the laws impractical—was, she thought, comparable to Thomas Jefferson's invocation of practicality when confronted with the crime of slavery. "Not discrimination and social segregation, in whatever forms, but racial legislation, constitutes the perpetuation of the original crime in this country's history." Arendt stressed the dangerous possibility that a physical difference like color could become the focus of resentment because she understood racism, a systematic, pseudoscientific ideology, to be quite a different matter from mere race prejudice or what she had called "race-thinking" in *The Origins of Totalitarianism*. Arendt feared that ill-designed integration plans would provoke white violence and that such violence might, in turn, be justified with a full-fledged racist ideology.

The controversy over Hannah Arendt's "Reflections on Little Rock" began more than a year before the article was published in the winter of 1959. It was commissioned by the editors of *Commentary* in October 1957, a month after the first civil rights legislation since Reconstruction passed Congress. While Arendt was writing, National Guardsmen and paratroopers of the 101st Airborne Division were occupying Little Rock's Central High School, the scene of violent clashes in September. By the time she had finished her article in November, the troops were being slowly withdrawn. Arkansas Governor Orval Faubus had also withdrawn to prepare another round of the battle on another front, the courts.

When the editors of *Commentary* received Arendt's article, they were as perplexed and hostile as their predecessors had been over her "Zionism Reconsidered." Apprised of the debate that had arisen in the *Commentary* offices, she offered to withdraw her article. But the editors refused her 23 November offer and decided, instead, to commission a reply from Sidney Hook, to be printed in the same issue as her article. Both the article and Hook's reply were set in galleys, and a copy of the reply sent to Arendt for her answer. But this procedure produced no calm among the editors; they first postponed the rescheduled February 1958 publication and then told Arendt that they were hesitant to publish both pieces at all. With an indignant 1 February letter, Arendt withdrew her article and announced her anger: the delays, she said, had allowed a great deal of New York literary world gossip to flourish, prevented "people from reading and having their own opinion" and deprived her of the chance to make "any adequate defense." "Controversial issues can be discussed only in an atmosphere where the good faith of all concerned is beyond doubt," she concluded, having made her distrust of the editors' good faith quite clear.[100]

After a long illness Elliot Cohen had returned to the helm at *Commentary* unsure of himself and unable to assert his authority against the editorial partners Arendt referred to collectively as "Greenberg Bros.," Martin and Clement Greenberg. Cohen's young protege Norman Podhoretz, whose collective name for the Greenbergs was "The Boss," thought the decision to reject Arendt's piece was wrong but could not prevail against his seniors. Podhoretz admitted in his 1967 memoir, *Making It*, that her piece had been judged "too controversial,"[101] but this admission came nearly ten years after Sidney Hook had made a public accusation, one *Commentary* never denied, that Arendt had withdrawn her article because she feared his criticism.

After she withdrew her piece, Arendt decided not to publish it, hoping that the situation which had provoked it was past. But June 1958 brought Governor Faubus's legal battle: the Little Rock school board sought to delay its federally mandated integration program for two-and-a-half years. The delay was finally ended by the Supreme Court, but Faubus used the opportunity of the reopened controversy to arrange a state referendum on integration, to rig the referendum, and then to turn the Arkansas public schools over to a private corporation pledged to maintain segregation. The state's black schools were closed and the white schools foundered under the corporation's mismanagement. These developments convinced Arendt that her skepticism about federally enforced integration was not misplaced and she accepted an offer from *Dissent* to publish her article.[102] In the winter 1959 issue, along with Arendt's article, her brief preparatory note about it, and two critical replies, was an outraged letter from Sidney Hook.

Hook was incensed because several phrases from his original reply to Arendt's article, which he had meanwhile revised and published separately in the 13 April 1958 *New Leader*, were quoted in Arendt's prefatory note. He chastised Arendt for quoting from the *Commentary* galleys rather than the *New Leader* text. But this was a minor moment in his effort to demonstrate that Hannah Arendt had withdrawn her article from *Commentary* "after she saw my critical reply." Hook did make nodding reference to what he chose to call "some difficulties... about the editing" at *Commentary*, but his purpose was to accuse Arendt of shrinking from his criticism and to cast doubt upon the integrity of "one who lectures Americans about their intellectual standards."[103]

Arendt's experiences with the editors of *Commentary*, with Sidney Hook's defamatory charges, and with one of the critics who offered his views in *Dissent* were startling to her. The critic, Melvin Tumin, a professor at Princeton, wrote a long harangue against "Miss A." that was very far from genteel. "Mr. Tumin," Arendt stated in her reply to her critics, "has put himself outside the scope of discussion and discourse through the tone he adopted in his rebuttal."[104] The hostile reception accorded "Reflections on Little Rock" momentarily sealed Hannah Arendt's suspicion that the open-mindedness she had so admired in American intellectuals when she arrived in New York had, during the McCarthy years, become rare.

Her adopted country was not a place where final seals were ever set, however, and Arendt had to wonder again at the room for dissent and criticism in American intellectual life when her "Reflections" received the 1959 Longview Foundation award for the year's outstanding little-magazine article. She wrote to tell Jaspers about her three hundred dollar prize and to share with him a newspaper story about another unlikely prizewinner, a black schoolgirl whose statement about the effects of racial violence on the young was as stunning to her as the Little Rock episode had been. "This prize [of mine]," she marvelled, "is really typical for this country. The New York schools gave their upper level students an essay topic—to consider how Hitler should be punished. About this a Negro girl suggested: he should be made to put on a black skin and compelled to live in the United States. For this she won first prize and a four-year scholarship to college!"[105]

Though her Little Rock article was strenuously attacked by many people, most of them liberals, Arendt gave ground to only one—Ralph Ellison. Ellison referred in passing to Arendt's essay as he replied in 1963 to a *Dissent* article by Irving Howe entitled "Black Boys and Native Sons." Arendt's "Olympian authority" was, Ellison thought, alienating; he realized that her tone was largely responsible for the intensity of her critics' responses. [106] But it was not this sort of criticism to which Arendt replied. In an interview granted to Robert Penn Warren for a 1965 volume entitled *Who Speaks for the Negro?* Ellison offered an explanation of Negro parents' attitudes toward the integration struggle that Arendt found compelling. When Warren asked him to elaborate on "the basic heroism involved in the Negro struggle," Ellison spoke about "people who must live within a society without recognition, real status, but who are involved in the ideals of that society and who are trying to make their way, trying to determine their true position and their rightful position within it."[107]

Such people learn more about the real nature of that society, more about the true character of its values than those who can afford to take their own place in society for granted. They might not be able to spell it out philosophically but they *act it out*. . . . I believe that one of the important clues to the meaning of the Negro experience lies in the idea, the *ideal* of sacrifice. Hannah Arendt's failure to grasp the importance of this ideal among Southern Negroes caused her to fly way off into left field in her "Reflections on Little Rock," in which she charged Negro parents with exploiting their children during the struggle to integrate the schools. But she has absolutely no conception of what goes on in the minds of Negro parents when they send their kids through those lines of hostile people. Yet they are aware of the overtones of a rite of initiation which such events actually constitute for the child, a confrontation of the terrors of social life with all the mysteries stripped away. And in the outlook of many of these parents (who wish that the problem didn't exist), the child is expected to face the terror and contain his fear and anger *precisely* because he is a Negro American. Thus he's required to master the inner tensions created by his racial situation, and if he gets hurt— then his is one more sacrifice. It is a harsh requirement, but if he fails this basic test, his life will be even harsher.

Arendt wrote Ellison a letter in which she acknowledged: "It is precisely this ideal of sacrifice which I didn't understand." She abandoned her judgment that parvenu social behavior was being demanded of black children by their parents when she "grasped the element of stark violence, of elementary, bodily fear in the situation."[108] The black children were not like the Jewish children of Arendt's youth who were pushed into groups where they were not wanted; black children were being initiated with an "ordeal by fire" to the realities of their violent situation.

Like all American readers of newspapers and watchers of television, Arendt had learned much in six years about the "stark violence" of black life in the South—and the North. The spring before Hannah Arendt

wrote to Ralph Ellison, Martin Luther King had led the famous
Montgomery to Selma march; all during the preceding year, 1964, there
had been riots in Northern cities; three Northern students, including the
son of the Jewish judge who signed Hannah Arendt's 1941 immigration
documents, had been murdered during a Mississippi voter-registration
drive.

Even though Ellison argued in terms she could appreciate and moved
her to amend her views, Hannah Arendt remained convinced that education should not be the sole or even the most important source of social or
political change. To argue the point in detail, she wrote "Crisis in Education" as a sequel to her "Reflections on Little Rock." Like the first book of
Aristotle's *Politics*, this essay was concerned with the relations of authority between adults and adults and adults and children. Arendt chastised
American progressive education for artificially depriving children of their
protected, prepolitical time and space, the school; for destroying the
natural authority teachers should have over children; and for enjoining
children to behave like little adults with opinions of their own. Adults
must not, she urged, forgo their responsibilities for children as children,
they must not refuse to children a sheltered period for maturation, for
being at home in the world. "Our hope always hangs on the new which
every generation [by virtue of natality] brings; but precisely because we
base our only hope on this, we destroy everything if we try to control the
new [so] that we, the old, can dictate how it will look. Exactly for the sake
of what is new and revolutionary in every child, education must be
conservative."[109] Hannah Arendt was very strict about this principle, and
she maintained it in her own political action. Some years later, when a
branch of the Student Mobilization Committee to End the War in
Vietnam contacted her for a donation, she agreed, but then she changed
her mind after reading their pamphlet: "When we talked over the phone,"
she informed the committee's fund raiser, "I was not aware that you
intend to involve high school students, and I regret to tell you that I will
not give a penny for this purpose, because I disagree with the advisability
of mobilizing children in political matters."[110] Her rule of thumb was
"from eighteen to eighty," and she was flexible only at the upper limit.

As was so often the case with Hannah Arendt, her plea for conservatism
was the vehicle for a revolutionary impulse. So-called revolutionaries,
who try to insure the longevity of their revolution through education
produce indoctrinated, unspontaneous young: "To prepare a new generation for a new world can only mean that one wishes to strike from the

newcomers' hands their own chances at the new."[111] Educators should introduce children to the world, give them the tools for understanding it accurately and impartially, so that the children can, when they mature, act in the world intelligently. When she wrote her "Reflections on Violence" in 1969, Arendt deplored the fact that black children who were not taught to do "mathematics and write a correct sentence" were encouraged to explore their identity as Afro-Americans. Though she agreed with Ralph Ellison that an ideal of sacrifice and heroism may be necessary for children who are victims of stark violence and hatred, who are homeless, she thought such an ideal quite different from the study of Swahili and the cultivation of a separatist ideology. What she hoped for others' children was what she had had herself; time for a good education before the *Judenfrage* ("Jewish Question") was personally posed in her life and before she, as a Jew, had to choose politics.

## Amor Mundi

When Hannah Arendt wrote topical essays like "Reflections on Little Rock" and "The Crisis in Education," she employed the complex schematism elaborated in *The Human Condition,* but she seldom paused to recapitulate its main elements. Her impatience paved the way for many misunderstandings and she was often taken for a cold and abstract thinker, when in fact she was dedicated to a certain kind of concreteness. She called her philosophical method "conceptual analysis"; her task was to find "where concepts come from." With the aid of philology or linguistic analysis, she traced political concepts back to the concrete historical and generally political experiences which gave rise to those concepts. She was then able to gauge how far a concept had moved from its origins and to chart the intermingling of concepts over the course of time, marking points of linguistic and conceptual confusion. To put the matter another way: she practiced a sort of phenomenology.

There are three terms in Hannah Arendt's phenomenological examination in *The Human Condition:* she speaks of the conditions of human existence, of human activities, and of the spaces in which activities take place. The conditions of human existence are: life itself, natality and mortality, plurality, worldliness, and the earth. Men are born, live, and die; they enter into the company of others, live with others, and depart from human plurality; they live upon the earth, within the world that has come to be upon the earth through human activities. All of the conditions relate to the human activities that make up the *vita activa*, labor, work, and action; but particular conditions correspond immediately to particular activities. Life itself is the condition that corresponds to the activity of labor: the biological processes of the human body, growth, metabolism, and decay, are bound to "the vital necessities produced and fed into the life process by labor." Worldliness is the condition that corresponds to the activity of work or fabrication. Men make a world upon the earth, and each durable addition to this world becomes part of the human condition of worldliness. Plurality is the condition that corresponds to action; there is no action, no political life, unless more than one person is present. And finally,

All three activities and their corresponding conditions are intimately connected with the most general conditions of human existence: birth and death, natality and mortality. Labor assures not only individual survival, but the life of the species. Work and its product, the human artifact, bestow a measure of permanence and durability upon the futility of mortal life and the fleeting character of human time. Action, insofar as it engages in founding and preserving political bodies, creates the condition for remembrance, that is, for history. Labor and work, as well as action, are also rooted in natality insofar as they have the task to provide and preserve the world for, to foresee and reckon with, the constant influx of newcomers who are born into the world as strangers. However, of the three, action has the closest connection with the human condition of natality; the new beginning inherent in birth can make itself felt in the world only because the newcomer possesses the capacity of beginning something new, that is, of acting.[112]

Men may labor or work in solitude, but if they do, they do not realize their specifically *human* qualities; they are like the laboring beasts or they are like divine demiurges. Men cannot, on the other hand, act in solitude. Plurality is the sine qua non of action. Action is dependent on the constant presence of others, it requires a public space. The public space is distinguished from the private space; or, in Greek terms, the *polis* is distinguished from the household, the place where human material needs are met by human labor and work. The household was, for the Greeks, the realm where necessity ruled; the realm of the *polis*, on the contrary, was the sphere of freedom.

The three terms of Arendt's analysis—conditions, activities, and spaces—are constants of human experience. But in different historical periods, the terms are differently connected, and the concepts men have of the terms vary with the different connections. Labor, work, and action, for example, were evaluated or hierarchically arranged by the Greeks in a different way than by the medieval Christians. Action, the highest form of activity for the Greeks, was less valued among the Christians than fabrication, while labor stayed at the bottom of the list in both cases. In the modern age, labor has been valued above both fabrication and action; *homo faber* has, in our time, given way to *animal laborans*. These shifts are correlated to shifts in the spaces for activities. The distinction between the public space and the private space, so fundamental to the Greeks and to the Romans, has become nearly obsolete. Between the two realms a hybrid which Hannah Arendt called "the social," appeared and gradually conquered. The social is a sort of household space, but one so enormously extended that it embraces whole nations: nations come to be administered as though they were vast households made up of a vast family, the nation's peoples; the social and economic matters that were once taken care of by small household groups have become the concern of national bureaucracies. The extension of the household has meant the diminution of the public space, the space of freedom. And all that is properly "private" has come to rest within individuals, as subjective experience or what Hannah Arendt called "intimacy."

The conditions of human existence—life itself, natality and mortality, plurality, worldliness and the earth—have, in these huge shifts among activities and spaces, remained relatively constant. But recently men have begun to leave the earth, to journey into outer space. They have begun to turn all human artifacts into consumables, to live in a society that destroys the worldliness of things. Plurality has, in mass or conformist societies, become less evident; human distinctiveness has become a merely "private" or subjective matter of personality. Natality and mortality are still the boundaries of human existence, but modern science has begun to act into nature, or, as Hannah Arendt put it, to initiate natural processes. At the time that Hannah Arendt wrote *The Human Condition*, this "acting into nature" was a matter of atom smashing; it is now also a matter of DNA synthesis, test-tube breeding and cloning, sperm freezing, organ transplanting, and artificial prolongation of life. What is most distinctive about the modern world is that the conditions of human existence, the most constant of the three terms of Hannah Arendt's analysis, are themselves becoming a matter of human action and potential control.

*The Origins of Totalitarianism* was not a history but rather an historical account of the elements which crystallized into totalitarianism. *The Human Condition*, similarly, is not a history of human activities, of the *vita activa*, but a historical account of the elements that have made up the *vita activa*. What is missing from the picture of the book presented so far is, very simply, the perspective from which this accounting was made. The book opens with another distinction: the *vita activa* is distinguished, along traditional lines, from the *vita contemplativa*. And the traditional hierarchy of these *vitae* is presented: the contemplative life has been considered higher, more serious, closer to divinity. For the Greeks, the *vita activa* was, first and foremost, political life, the life of action. Labor and work were the activities tied to necessity, to supplying human material needs, while action or *praxis* established and sustained the *polis*. In the Christian era, after Saint Augustine, the *vita activa* "lost its specifically political meaning and denoted all kinds of active engagement in the things of this world," and action itself was considered "among the necessities of earthly life." The only realm of freedom was the unworldly domain of contemplation; the *vita contemplativa* was the only truly free way of life. This Christian evaluation was not fundamentally different from the classical Greek; Plato and Aristotle had also valued the freedom of the philosopher from political concerns, but they had continued to maintain the traditional Greek articulation of the activities of the *vita activa*, and they granted the potential for freedom from the *vita activa* only to the philosophers, not to every child of God.

It is precisely this hierarchy of the two modes of life which Hannah Arendt had to consider before she examined the *vita activa*: "My contention is simply that the enormous weight of contemplation in the traditional hierarchy has blurred the distinctions and articulations within the *vita activa* itself and that, appearances notwithstanding, this condition has not been changed essentially by the modern break with the tradition and the eventual reversal of its hierarchical order in Marx and Nietzsche. It lies in the very nature of the famous 'turning upside down' of philosophic systems or currently accepted values, that is, in the nature of the operation itself, that the conceptual framework is left more or less intact."[113] In addition to tracing the huge shifts among activities and spaces in relation to conditions, Arendt traced the reversal of the hierarchy of the *vita contemplativa* and the *vita activa* in the modern age and arrived at the conclusion that even when the *vita activa* is elevated above the *vita contemplativa*, its articulations are still understood contemplatively, from without.

Contemplative concepts of the types of human activity are at a remove from the conditions which these activities presuppose and the spaces in which they take place; the experiential roots of such concepts are left behind. The philosopher removes himself from the world, and his concepts are thus removed from worldly experience. The phenomena of human affairs are not regarded by the contemplative with that wonder, that *thaumadzein*, which was, for Arendt, the basic condition of political philosophy.

The criticism of contemplation Arendt made in *The Human Condition* reflected a decade of questioning. She would not call herself a philosopher because she was very critical of the attitude toward politics she thought endemic to philosophy. But she questioned the contemplative attitude philosophically, as a reformer. In its simplest form, Arendt's question was: How shall we take political events, the political realm, seriously? The terms are simple, but the question is not. Arendt believed that Western philosophers, from the trial and death of Socrates through the nineteenth century, had been more concerned with how philosophy could be carried on with the least disturbance from the political realm. There is no great thinker in the tradition who did not concern himself with politics, of course, but this concern did not reflect a conviction that politics is a domain where genuine *philosophical* questions arise. The political domain was one that ought to be regulated according to precepts that arise elsewhere and are accessible to a "higher" sort of wisdom than practical wisdom. Although the nineteenth-century philosophers of history, Hegel and his followers, accorded a new seriousness to political affairs, they maintained that individual actions are parts of a universal historical process which reveals a truth that transcends the realm of the political. And this revelation was, in accordance with the tradition, made to the philosopher: the philosopher was the one who, in Hegel's view, thought the modes of the Absolute, the Transcendent itself.

In the early 1950s Hannah Arendt began to envision a new science of politics for a world in which political events—world war, totalitarianism, atomic bombings—demanded serious attention from philosophers. "A new science of politics is needed for a new world," wrote de Tocqueville in *Democracy in America*, and with each decade both the necessity and the potential scope of such a science have grown. What the nineteenth century produced was not a new science of politics but a new conception of history and this, Arendt felt, was ultimately only another way of viewing the political realm from above. To watch the agents of history play their roles in the drama of necessity was to miss the central political capacity of men: action, the capacity to begin something new whose outcome is unpredictable. "Each time the modern age has had reason to hope for a new political philosophy, it received a philosophy of history instead."[114]

What Arendt found most ominous in nineteenth-century philosophies of history was the conception of a goal of history that was not transcendent but was itself political. Rather than an Absolute making history, men were to make it themselves, fashioning history after an ideal, such as a classless society. The transformation of the means-ends categories present in Hegel's system into these political categories prepared the theoretical justifications for twentieth-century practices of the most horrendous sorts. Arendt explained that those who believe that "one cannot *make* an omelet without breaking eggs" fail to realize that—as Randall Jarrell once said—the eggs are not consulted, and the chefs make a mess. A revolution is not an omelet.

Before the Second World War European philosophy had begun to move away from its Hegelian roots, following the path of Hegel's nineteenth-century critics, such as Nietzsche. Not history in which an Absolute is revealed, but historicity (*Geschichtlichkeit*) was Heidegger's concern in *Sein und Zeit* as he set out to produce a phenomenological study of our everyday life in the company of others. But, in Hannah Arendt's view, a new science of politics demanded, first and foremost, a consideration of action, the beginning of something new which is unpredictable and thus cannot be fabricated by man or created by Being. When the originator of something new is seriously considered, the questions that follow are: What is politics? What are the conditions of political action? What are the principles of political action? What is freedom?

As she criticized the Hegelian notion of history and, less sharply, the Heideggerian notion of historicity, Arendt turned to the one thinker in the Western tradition prior to Hegel who had, she thought, taken political happenings seriously: Kant. And she collaborated in her venture with Kant's modern disciple, her own teacher, Karl Jaspers, who shared her concern for philosophy's traditional blind spots. She felt that Kant's moral philosophy was essentially political: he thought of all men, not just of statesmen or of philosopher-kings, as legislators and judges. Distinctions between rulers and ruled, the knowing few and the unknowing many, were not taken for granted by Kant—as they certainly were by Hegel and

Heidegger. Kant's concern was with the condition of human plurality, with the fact that we are not one but many and different from one another.

These Kantian notions became more and more important to Hannah Arendt as she developed her new science of politics. But initially, while she was writing *The Origins of Totalitarianism*, what had most impressed her about Kant's concern for the political was his attempt to confront the existence of evil in the world without resorting to ameliorating constructions or a vision of reconciliation with the world's evils. She had accepted Kant's notion of radical evil in *The Origins of Totalitarianism*, and she used it until she wrote *Eichmann in Jerusalem* in 1961–63, because it seemed to her the one offering from within the Western tradition of a way to take political evildoing seriously.[115]

Considering man as an acting being and looking at the conditions of human action, without neglecting the evil which the perversion of acting into a species of fabrication can bring, became the central tasks of Arendt's new science of politics. In the three works which followed *The Origins of Totalitarianism—The Human Condition, Between Past and Future,* and *On Revolution*—she took up these tasks in diverse contexts but with the same conviction: that the questioning impulse which the ancients had known as the origin of philosophy would have to be aimed directly at the realm of human affairs, at the *vita activa*. The measure of how seriously she took this conviction was the title she proposed for the manuscript that became *The Human Condition* in its English editions and *Vita Activa* in its European editions. Rejecting the philosophical tradition of *contemptus mundi*, Arendt wanted to call her book *Amor Mundi*, love of the world.

Hannah Arendt was certainly not alone in her search for a new science of politics as an alternative to the tradition of contemplation. But most American theorists at the end of the 1950s stated their effort in quite different terms. They looked for a new role for intellectuals in a moment marked by what the sociologist Daniel Bell called the "end of ideology."[116] Dozens of books on intellectuals past and present appeared in a great search for identity. Men of the Enlightenment's "party of humanity," French and Russian revolutionaries, scientists, writers on the Left, and declassé intellectuals of all periods were scrutinized by those who felt that intellectuals in America had been powerless for long enough. Out of the ferment of questioning, a migration arose: more intellectuals went to

Washington in the early years of John Kennedy's New Frontier than had ever gone during the New Deal.

In Hannah Arendt's opinion, the migration of intellectuals was no blessing, for them or for the country. "Professors today are somebodies and not nobodies," she told an interviewer in the early 1960s. But what this meant, she thought, was that they were more susceptible to the corruptions of money and society, and to parvenudom and philistinism. "I personally think that real poverty and this [recent] affluence are about equally bad for intellectuals. What they need is a reasonable amount of security; they should not be really poor and they should not be really rich, because both are distracting. . . . To the extent that the intellectuals have become a class, they have, of course, also become philistines. I don't mean all of them. Of course not. But insofar as they are nothing but intellectuals [that is, defined by their function], they are philistines. What else could they possibly be? They are just, like everybody else, members of society, and they behave accordingly."[117]

While the relation of "The Policy-Maker and The Intellectual"—as Henry Kissinger called a well-known 1961 article—was debated in American universities, Hannah Arendt took her questioning forward on more general grounds. When she had completed the manuscript of *The Human Condition* in 1958, she contemplated a book to be entitled "Introduction to Politics." This book was, as such, never written. The project was fulfilled, though not entirely, by the collection of essays called *Between Past and Future*. Arendt set out her intention in a grant application to the Rockefeller Foundation:

It will continue where [*The Human Condition*] ends. In terms of human activities, it will be concerned exclusively with action and thought. The purpose of the book is twofold: *First*, a critical reexamination of the chief traditional concepts and conceptual frameworks of political thinking—such as means and ends, authority, government, power, law, war, etc. By criticism I do not mean "debunking." I shall try to find out where these concepts came from before they become like worn-out coins and abstract generalizations. I therefore shall examine the concrete historical and generally political experiences which gave rise to political concepts. For the experiences behind even the most worn-out concepts remain valid and must be recaptured and reactualized if one wishes to escape certain generalizations that have proved pernicious.[118]

The second part of "Introduction to Politics" was designed to provide a systematic examination of the political realm and human action within it.

"Here I shall be chiefly concerned with the various modi of human plurality and the institutions which correspond to them. In other words, I shall undertake a reexamination of the old question of forms of government, their principles and their modes of being together: to be together with other men and with one's equals, from which springs action, and to be together with one's self, to which the activity of thinking corresponds. Hence, the book should end with a discussion of the relationship between acting and thinking, or between politics and philosophy."

It was this second purpose of "Introduction to Politics" which was not entirely fulfilled by *Between Past and Future*. Hannah Arendt gave a number of lectures which might have provided the basis for a discussion of the relationship between acting and thinking, or between philosophy and politics, but she did not draw these materials together for *Between Past and Future*. Later, as she was finishing *On Revolution*, the trial of Adolf Eichmann began in Jerusalem and her attention was drawn to the concrete historical experiences that finally led her to reconsider the notion of radical evil. Not until the late 1960s, when she began to give courses at the New School for Social Research on the relation of politics and philosophy and to write articles like "Thinking and Moral Considerations," did Arendt take up the relation of thinking and acting again. And it was not until the early 1970s, when she was preparing her Gifford lectures, entitled *The Life of the Mind*, that the "thinking" mode of human plurality received her full attention. Her work of the 1950s grew, as she was fond of saying, "under her hand," into three books. But the final fruit took twenty years to mature.

This history of projects and reordering of materials indicates only superficially the way in which Hannah Arendt thought and wrote—isolating key concepts, tracing them, framing them, and then widening and deepening the frames, making further distinctions, clarifying, and then reframing. Heidegger had made the claim that a great thinker thinks only one thought or asks only one question. His own, as he announced on the first page of *Sein und Zeit*, was the question of the meaning of Being. His dedication to the question occasioned the joke that he, from his cottage in Todtnauberg in the Black Forest, was keeping a watch on Being, a *Wacht am Sein*, as his military countrymen had once kept their *Wacht am Rhein*. Hannah Arendt, from a considerably more worldly vantage point, kept an action watch. She asked the question of the meaning of human action, keeping a watch on the words and deeds of men. Like Heidegger, she was aware of the unity of her mind's life. "I sometimes think," she wrote to a friend in 1972, "that we all have only one real thought in our lives, and everything we then do are [*sic*] elaborations or variations of one theme."[119] By the time Hannah wrote this to her friend, she had given up her reluctance to call herself a philosopher rather than a political theorist. In a 1964 television interview she had declared: "I am not a philosopher. My profession—if it can be called that—is political theory, I have bid philosophy my final farewell. As you know, I did study philosophy, but that does not mean that I have stuck to it."[120] But when she began to work on *The Life of the Mind* Arendt said that she was returning to her "first amour," philosophy. The final variation on her theme of action was played out in *The Life of the Mind* in sections called "Thinking," "Willing," and "Judging." In her concern with the second mode of human plurality, being together with one's self, the beginning and end of Arendt's political thinking show themselves to be one and the same. What united her thought was the love she had come to understand as the one that unites self and others—*Amor Mundi*. [121]

# CHAPTER 8

# Cura Posterior: Eichmann in Jerusalem

## (1961-1965)

> And yet, first of all, I should like to slaughter one or two
> men, just to throw off the concentration camp mental-
> ity, the effects of continual subservience, the effects of
> helplessly watching others being beaten and murdered,
> the effects of all this horror. I suspect, though, that I will
> be marked for life. I do not know whether we shall
> survive, but I like to think that one day we shall have the
> courage to tell the world the whole truth and call it by its
> proper name.
>
> Tadeusz Borowski, "Auschwitz, Our Home (A Letter)"

## The Trial Reporter

In the summer of 1960, Hannah Arendt and Heinrich Blücher vacationed at a rambling Swiss-style boardinghouse in the Catskills, several
miles from their usual haunt, the Chestnut Lawn House in Palenville,
New York. Arendt spent her days at her worktable and then joined
Blücher and several of their émigré friends for swimming or chess, the
evening meal, and expeditions to the local bar and pool parlor. Their
discussions often returned to a startling series of reports in the *New York
Times:* Adolf Eichmann had been kidnapped by Israeli agents in Argentina on 24 May; Israel and Argentina had quarreled over his extradition to
Israel; there had been debates in the United Nations over Israel's intention to put Eichmann on trial in Jerusalem. As they awaited announcement of the trial, Arendt discussed the complex legal issues in her correspondence with Karl Jaspers. Then, when it was clear that Eichmann
would be tried in Israel, she decided to propose herself as a trial reporter to
William Shawn, the editor of the *New Yorker.*

Shawn accepted Hannah Arendt's offer with alacrity, glad to have such
an illustrious and well-informed correspondent, one more qualified for
the assignment than his regulars, such as John Hersey, whose series on
Hiroshima had brought the magazine high praise in 1946. Arendt contacted Kurt Blumenfeld and asked him to keep her posted about the trial
date and any relevant discussion in the Israeli press. She then set about
rearranging her crowded 1961 schedule. "I have all the obligations possible," she told Blumenfeld, "and must in due course refuse them, but

naturally I can't just refuse them and then stand there with clean hands, declaring, as one says in East Prussia, *der Onkel kommt nicht.*"[1] Not wanting to be the uncle who doesn't show up, Arendt rescheduled a two-month stay at Northwestern University for January and February 1961, on the heels of a strenuous Plato seminar at Columbia; she cancelled a lecture at Vassar and changed the term of a one-year grant from the Rockefeller Foundation. In writing to the Rockefeller Foundation, she explained her plans: "You will understand I think why I should cover this trial; I missed the Nuremberg Trials, I never saw these people in the flesh, and this is probably my only chance."[2] Her letter to Vassar was uncharacteristically personal: "To attend this trial is somehow, I feel, an obligation I owe my past."[3] For Arendt, the opportunity to go to Jerusalem and see Eichmann "in the flesh" turned out to be more than the fulfillment of an obligation; it was, she said in retrospect, a *cura posterior.* Her first reaction to the "man in the glass booth" in Jerusalem was that he was *nicht einmal unheimlich,*[4] "not even sinister," not inhuman or beyond comprehension. She was startled. The cure, the change in her attitude toward the past, began.

While she was in Jerusalem, Arendt wrote her reactions in letters to Blücher and sent Jaspers summaries of the letters. Blücher reported to her the American press coverage of the trial, while Jaspers followed the European press. In Jerusalem, Kurt Blumenfeld translated the Hebrew press reports for her and escorted her to a series of meetings and parties where she met Israeli politicians and university people. The communications triangle Arendt had established between New York, Basel, and Jerusalem, between Blücher and Jaspers, and Jaspers and Blumenfeld, was a great source of pleasure and support. At Arendt's suggestion, Blumenfeld had gone to Basel in 1954 to meet Jaspers, and had left with a profound respect for him. "The man is, as you always told me, much greater in person than in his writings," Blumenfeld had reported to Arendt. "One can discuss with him the issue of assimilation better than with Buber, Scholem or Ernst Simon, not to mention the professors at our University."[5] Blumenfeld's admiration made him eager to hear Jaspers's opinions about the trial of Eichmann, and Arendt reported that she and Jaspers had already had a lengthy correspondence on the subject.

Jaspers had felt that the Israelis should not try Eichmann but rather turn him over to an international tribunal, perhaps under the aegis of the United Nations. He was concerned not only about the Israelis' right to "speak for all Jews" but also about the possibility that an Israeli trial might provoke a new wave of anti-Semitism if Eichmann could be successfully portrayed as a martyr by those hostile to Israel. Arendt countered that Israel could speak for the Jews, "at least for the victims," if not in a legal then "in a political sense," and then reminded him that a majority of the European Jews who had survived the Holocaust lived in Israel. She felt that it would be impossible to make Eichmann into a martyr, though she agreed that "it would be a different case if we had a law against *hostes humani generis* [enemies of mankind] and not only against murder and crimes considered analogous to murder."[6] After he had reviewed the Nuremberg judgments, Jaspers finally agreed with both her arguments, but he asked Arendt whether the word *hostes* was appropriate: "the word 'enemy' seems to me too positive, an enemy is always a 'who.'"[7] Jaspers, for whom Eichmann was less than a person, a monster, was incredulous when Arendt sent her first reactions to the trial. He was slow to give up his preconception and found some of the trial evidence indicative of Eichmann's "personal brutality." Blumenfeld, who shared the preconception, was equally reluctant.

Blücher, on the other hand, immediately understood the import of Arendt's first reports about Eichmann. Several days after the trial began, Arendt wrote about what seemed to her a startling dimension of Eichmann's character—his need for self-aggrandizement and recognition. "That the man would gladly have himself hanged *in public*, you have probably read [in the newspapers]. I am flabbergasted."[8] By the time Eichmann faced his hangman and made his farewell to the world months later, Arendt had realized how pathetically comic he was: the man who had stated that he believed in neither a personal God nor life after death, announced that *he* "would never forget" after his own death those he had known and admired. "He was *eigentlich dumm*," Arendt wrote to Jaspers, "but also somehow not."[9] She pondered this judgment—"somehow stupid, but also somehow not"—and concluded later that he was simply unable to think. What, she wanted to know, made this man stop thinking?

Blücher, whose appreciation of mordant humor came from years of reading Brecht and looking at the world with his friend Robert Gilbert's satiric vision, saw the little man's World-Historic boasting for what it was. Arendt told Jaspers that her husband had often considered the possibility that evil was "a superficial phenomenon," and it was this formula that prompted Arendt to give her book the subtitle "The Banality of Evil."[10] It was not until several years after the trial that Blücher came across the passage of Brecht's which expressed his own understanding, but when he did it gave him and Hannah Arendt the courage of their convictions. Brecht had written in his notes for *The Resistible Rise of the Man Arturo Ui:*

The great political criminals must be exposed and exposed especially to laughter. They are not great political criminals, but people who permitted great political crimes, which is something entirely different. The failure of his enterprises does not indicate that Hitler was an idiot and the extent of his enterprises does not make him a great man. If the ruling classes permit a small crook to become a great crook, he is not entitled to a privileged position in our view of history. That is, the fact that he becomes a great crook, and that what he does has great consequences does not add to his stature. . . . One may say that tragedy deals with the sufferings of mankind in a less serious way than comedy.

Arendt cited Brecht's "abrupt remarks" in an interview and then added her own remark: she said that she thought it was important in assessing Hitler and his like to remember that "no matter what he does and if he killed ten million people, he is still a clown."[11] Brecht, and Blücher, had no trouble remembering such a shocking idea, but Arendt did—she required many months of *cura posterior* to overcome her initial "I am flabbergasted."

While she was in Jerusalem attending Eichmann's trial, Arendt was too disturbed to put together her impressions of the defendant. As it dragged on, the trial depressed her: "The whole thing is *stinknormal*, indescribably inferior, worthless."[12] Completely discouraged, she told Blücher that after twenty-nine volumes by the Nazi governor general of Poland, Hans Frank, had been introduced as evidence the defense lawyer had asked whether Eichmann's name was mentioned in any of them. "No," the prosecution admitted. As the trial went on, however, she was more and more impressed by the judges, and when she heard several witnesses for the prosecution who astonished her with their simplicity and honesty, her initial interest in the trial revived: "It is again very interesting, sometimes impressive, often quite horrifying."[13] The prosecutor, Gideon Hausner, continually annoyed and embarrassed Arendt. She described him to Blücher with more than a little German Jewish disdain: "Galician Jew . . . speaks without periods or commas . . . like a diligent schoolboy who wants to show off everything he knows . . . ghetto mentality."[14] Her opinion of Hausner never altered and neither did her opinion of Eichmann's lawyer, Servatius, whom she disliked far more than

Hausner and described with a phrase she reserved for those who reminded her of Weimar—"a Georg Grosz character."[15] Not only inside but outside the courtroom, Arendt was irritated and uneasy. "There was an enormous tank parade here today, such as I have never seen; and yesterday I saw some Jewish youths around a campfire, singing sentimental songs, just as we knew it and hated it when we were young. The parallels are fatal, especially in the details."[16] It was not only Servatius who reminded Arendt of Weimar; the Israelis' militarism and nationalism revived in her the apprehensions she had had since her work with Judah Magnes in 1948.

Blumenfeld and her cousin Ernst Fuerst's family were Arendt's refuges from the strain of her reporter's life, which left her with hardly any solitude or time to write letters. The Fuersts and their two daughters took Tante Hannah touring, and Blumenfeld arranged several interesting meetings. She found the chief trial judge, Moshe Landau, a friend of Blumenfeld's, "a wonderful fellow," and was glad to meet the brother of her old friend Martin Rosenblüth, Pinhas Rosen, who was then the Israeli minister of justice. She spent a long evening talking with Israel's foreign minister, Golda Meir—an evening so long that Arendt, fatigued from a day in court, found herself in an embarrassing spot: "My problem was, simply, how to get a Foreign Minister to stop talking and go off to bed."[17] When she remembered their conversation later, Arendt had another problem, more difficult: how to understand this foreign minister's attitude toward their people. Golda Meir had added yet another dimension to the ominous feeling of déjà vu Arendt had in Israel, a feeling she did not report in the New Yorker but which certainly informed her writing.

Arendt invoked her conversation with Golda Meir in response to a letter from Gershom Scholem written the summer after Eichmann in Jerusalem appeared. Scholem accused her of having "little trace" of "love of the Jewish People." In her reply, which was published along with Scholem's letter in European newspapers and in Encounter, Arendt recalled her conversation with Golda Meir—though she agreed, at Scholem's request, to leave Meir's name and the appropriate feminine pronoun out of the published version. "Let me tell you of a conversation I had in Israel with a prominent political personality who was defending the—in my opinion disastrous—nonseparation of religion and the state in Israel. What he said—I am not sure of the exact words any more—ran something like this: 'You will understand that, as a Socialist, I, of course, do not believe in God; I believe in the Jewish people.' I found this a shocking statement, and, being too shocked I did not reply at the time. But I could have answered: the greatness of this people was once that it believed in God, and believed in Him in such a way that its trust and love towards Him was greater than its fear. And now this people believes only in itself? What good can come of that?—Well, in this sense I do not 'love' the Jews, nor do I 'believe' in them; I merely belong to them as a matter of course, beyond dispute and argument."[18]

After she left Jerusalem, Arendt met Blücher in Zurich for an event they had both looked forward to for many years—Blücher's first visit with Karl and Gertrud Jaspers. Arendt was joyful as she brought her husband to the house which had been, as she told Jaspers in a tender thank-you letter, "for me, for such a long while, just what my old European home was."[19] Arendt and Blücher were both invited by the Jaspers to use the familiar, familial, form of address, *Du*, and this prompted Arendt to ask permission for a rare display of public emotion, the dedication of *On Revolution* "To Gertrud and Karl Jaspers: in Reverence—in Friendship—in Love."

Jaspers and Blücher, despite their very different ages, temperaments, and backgrounds, struck a deep and respectful accord. Jaspers marked it to Blücher in a letter he sent to New York several months after the visit, a letter he carefully wrote and rewrote. He praised Blücher's plan for Bard's Common Course as he had always praised Arendt's books; after recognizing in the plan a conservative's desire to preserve cultural traditions, Jaspers astutely noted the radicality of Blücher's egalitarianism.[20] Blücher, too, practiced the Jasperian preaching: "Philosophy is for everyman."

On his first return to Europe since 1941, Blücher fulfilled another dream: he and Hannah Arendt went to Italy and Sicily for a tour of the museums and classical sites he had not seen since his youth—Paestum, near Naples, and Syracuse. En route to southern Italy, there was another visit which added to the sense of continuity the Jasperses had given them. Arendt told Jaspers about this reunion in Locarno: "And when I then [after Basel] saw Heinrich with Robert Gilbert, who is bound to him in the sort of friendship I have with Annchen [Anne Weil]... and with whom he spent most of the time before 1933, it was clear to me how good the bond of their youth must have been for it to have survived, even though his life could not have had the pure uncomplicated clarity of your life. An orgy of friendship!"[21]

Arendt went back to America refreshed. In Haines Falls she nearly completed the *On Revolution* manuscript, which she took to Wesleyan University's Center for Advanced Studies for the fall semester in 1961. At Wesleyan she enjoyed the company of the political scientist and student of totalitarianism Sigmund Neumann, an acquaintance from Berlin, and the new friendship of Rosalie Colie, a professor of history to whom Arendt was able to pay a remarkable compliment: "She is one of the most erudite women I have ever known."[22] Wesleyan pleased her: "good atmosphere, good students," "a paradise for scholars."[23] But, several weeks into the term, the first of a series of frightening episodes took place. Blücher, at home on Riverside Drive, suffered a ruptured aneurism in one of the blood vessels of the pia mater covering his brain. His old friend Charlotte Beradt found him in a deranged state, covered with burns from his own cigarette, pacing back and forth over a chaos of papers, books, and overturned furniture. Dr. Alfred Copley was summoned, and with his help an ambulance crew got Blücher to the Columbia Presbyterian Hospital emergency room.

By the time Hannah Arendt arrived at the hospital from Connecticut, Blücher's neurologist was ready to render his judgment. As she told Jaspers later, she immediately relayed the judgment to Blücher so that he could know "the whole truth about his illness": "50% mortality in cases like his." Blücher responded to his wife with his characteristic wry energy for life: "Reg Dich doch bloss nicht auf, Du vergisst die anderen 50%."[24] Slowly, he joined the lucky 50 percent. Arendt returned to Wesleyan to relieve Mary McCarthy who had come from her home and her new husband, James West, to take over Arendt's Machiavelli seminar. Work on the still unfinished *On Revolution* was suspended while Arendt taught three days a week and then travelled to New York for long weekends with Blücher. But by the end of December she could report to Jaspers that Blücher was nearly well and that she, with *On Revolution* just about ready, was taking up the Eichmann material, including the just released judgment of the Israeli court. Arendt and Jaspers were in agreement about the judgment, which, as he said, came from judges who were "outstanding and very intelligent, but without greatness and without philosophy."[25]

Arendt had lecture commitments at the University of Chicago during January 1962, which she had barely fulfilled when she caught a bad cold. Her work stopped while she recovered from this and from an allergic reaction to the antibiotics prescribed for it. Impatient with her own slow recovery, still worried about Blücher's health, and uneasy with the political "stillness" she observed in the wake of the Bay of Pigs invasion, Arendt was hardly able to approach the "mountain of documents" she had assembled for her Eichmann report. Then came the next blow.

A taxi in which she was riding across Central Park on 19 March was hit by a truck. The medical report filed by the doctor who attended her as she was brought to Roosevelt Hospital, covered with blood but conscious, gave a catalogue of the problems that left Arendt disabled for two months: contusion, concussion, hemorrhages of both eyes, broken teeth, right shoulder bruised, abrasions and lacerations, especially on her head, fractured ribs, and—worse for Arendt's later life—heart-muscle damage secondary to shock.[26] When Blücher arrived at the hospital, Arendt was calm. She reassured him with a story that displayed her own energy for life, the equal of his. Later, she told the story to Mary McCarthy in a letter:

When I awoke in the car [on the way to the hospital] and became conscious of what had happened, I tried out my limbs, saw that I was not paralyzed and could see with both eyes; then tried out my memory—very carefully, decade by decade, poetry, Greek and German and English; then telephone numbers. Everything all right. The point was that for a fleeting moment I had the feeling that it was up to me whether I wanted to live or die. And though I did not think that death was terrible, I also thought that life was quite beautiful and that I rather like it.[27]

The "fleeting moment" fascinated Arendt. She also told Jaspers about it: "It seemed to me that for a moment I had my life in my hands. I was quite calm: death seemed to me natural, in no way a tragedy or, somehow, out of the order of things. But, at the same time, I said to myself: if it is possible to do so decently, I would really like, still, to stay in this world."[28]

This calm acceptance and appreciation of life—so different from the feeling Arendt had had in the camp at Gurs, when she questioned whether to live or to die and answered herself "with a joke"—echoed through her work for years. It deeply informed *Eichmann in Jerusalem*, but it was most obvious in an essay she wrote about Pope John XXIII, whose funeral was held in Rome while Arendt was there in the summer of 1963, vacationing after the publication of the Eichmann book. She described this simple, proud, self-confident pope, a man whose willingness to judge and to trust his judgments was remarkable, and she found his faith inspiring. This faith, she felt, was manifest in the words he spoke on his deathbed, "his greatest words." "Every day is a good day to be born, every day is a good day to die."[29]

The philosopher J. Glenn Gray, whom Arendt had met during a

second semester at Wesleyan in the fall of 1962 and grown to respect deeply for his extraordinary book, *The Warriors*, marvelled at her portrait of "The Christian on St. Peter's Chair." Arendt's respect for the pope's last words provoked him: "I fell to wondering why you consider this his greatest insight. Then I realized that it is the same tough-minded affirmation of life in you (as in him) that I learned to admire so much at Wesleyan. . . . I guess it is only those who have such affirmation who can afford to question the worthwhileness of existence at all."[30] Gray had hit exactly upon the attitude that gave *Eichmann in Jerusalem* its power, the attitude Arendt's *cura posterior* had allowed her to display.

The interest Hannah Arendt took in the message she had given herself sustained her calm even when her surface impatience returned. She grew restless and irritable in the hospital, snapped at a nurse who had the very American audacity to call her "Honey," and concluded that "the whole place is run under the motto: we could not care less."[31] When she was well enough to receive visitors, she became apprehensive about her appearance and requested a veil to cover her blackened eyes and her stitched forehead. On hearing about her anxiety, Karl Jaspers comforted her with careful sentences: "Ultimately, one's beauty radiates through all limiting conditions. It rests finally, in one's comportment, one's look, one's expression."[32] Her vanity was not completely appeased. Even after she felt well enough to go out, she wore a patch over the blackest eye and a bandanna over her head. The poet Elizabeth Sewell, who met the distinguished philosopher for the first time at a small gathering, was astonished to find her "looking like a pirate."[33]

With her lecture obligations for the spring cancelled on doctor's orders, Arendt retired to Palenville to work. Free of any distractions, she began to assemble her source materials and her notes from the Eichmann trial. She had originally intended to write a single article for the *New Yorker*, but the mountain of documents which had been made available and her low opinion of the available press reports convinced her that a longer work was necessary. "Not a single one of the professional journalists has produced anything," she had complained to Blumenfeld when Servatius's defense plea was published, "not a single serious article on the whole story."[34]

The work proved more exciting than Arendt had expected. "I somehow enjoy the handling of facts and concrete things," she told Mary McCarthy: "I am swimming in an enormous amount of material, always trying to find the most telling quotation."[35] Nearly two years later, while the controversy over her published report was raging, Arendt told Mary McCarthy what this period of writing had meant to her—told her, tersely, what the *cura posterior* had meant. "You are the only reader to understand that I wrote this book in a curious euphoria. And that ever since I did it I feel—after twenty years—light-hearted about the whole matter. Don't tell anybody: is it not proof positive that I have no 'soul'?"[36]

## The Banality of Evil

Many people who read her five-article series in the *New Yorker*—and many more who heard about the series secondhand—concluded that Hannah Arendt was soulless, or that she lacked what Gershom Scholem called *Herzenstakt*, sympathy. They thought that Arendt felt no emotional involvement with the fate of her people. She, on the other hand, thought that she had finally been cured of the kind of emotional involvement which precludes good judgment. Deep differences of opinion about the nature of good judgment cut through the many facets of the "Eichmann Controversy." But they focused on three main topics: Arendt's portrait of a banal Adolf Eichmann; her remarks, woven through *Eichmann in Jerusalem* but concentrated in only ten of its nearly three hundred pages, on the European Jewish councils and their role in the Nazis' Final Solution; and her discussions, particularly in the first and last chapters of the book, of the conduct of the trial, the legal questions raised by it, and the political purposes it served. In the course of the controversy, each of these topics was accompanied by an emotion-laden Doppelgänger. Beside Arendt's portrait of a banal Eichmann went a portrait of someone called, in the title of an inflammatory *New York Times* review, "Man with an Unspotted Conscience." In the public controversy, comments about Jews with death wishes, Jews incapable of resistance, victims as responsible as their executioners accrued to Arendt's remarks about the Jewish councils' actions. Charges that she was anti-Israel, anti-Zionist, a Jewish self-hater, a legal purist, a Kantian moralist accompanied Arendt's reflections on the legal precedents of the trial and questions of international law.

Once the Doppelgängers had appeared in public, it was very difficult for anyone who took up the topics Arendt had posed to ignore them or to explain them. Even those critics who did not accept the distortions—and there were many of these, though their words were often lost in the fray—were hard pressed to put a distance between themselves and the allegations. Each distortion raised its own difficult questions, and each was problematic precisely because it had grown up, like all gossip or rumor, around a cause. Arendt's book did lend itself to misinterpretation more than any other she wrote: its conclusions were shocking, it contained numerous small errors of fact, it was often ironic in style and imperious in tone, and some of its most controversial passages were peculiarly insensitive. One participant in the controversy declared that "Miss Arendt was attacked not so much for what she said, [as] for how she said it."[37] There was some truth in this observation, but the substantial issues were by no means uncontroversial or uncontroverted.

The two most important and at the same time most controversial judgments Arendt made were simple, but both carried complex challenges. She reported Eichmann's story, noting his bureaucratic mentality and boastful claim that "officialese is my only language," and she judged him incapable of telling right from wrong. Thus, she implied that the Jerusalem court's "guilty" judgment, with which she certainly agreed, raised general questions about the role of motivation in deeds such as Eichmann's. Eichmann did what the laws of his state, justified by *raisons d'état*, asked of him—without knowing the laws to be wrong. The concept of *mens rea* (intent), so crucial to modern legal philosophy and procedure, has never been adequately associated with a "law of humanity" higher than state law. Even though she accepted and approved the Israeli legal proceedings, Arendt felt that only with such a "law of humanity," only with new legal and moral categories, could justice truly be rendered to individuals involved in state-instigated crimes or "administrative massacres." Secondly, Arendt reported how the moral corruption of the Nazis' totalitarian regime affected other countries and societies, including the society of the Jewish victims, and concluded that such corruption poses unprecedented challenges to judgment in general—past and present. She wrote of the past, but she addressed the crisis of judgment she saw in the present. As she put the matter to Jaspers: "Even good and, at bottom, worthy people have, in our time, the most extraordinary fear about making judgments. This confusion about judgment can go hand in hand with fine and strong intelligence, just as good judgment can be found in those not remarkable for their intelligence."[38] Inability to judge and refusal to judge were her themes in *Eichmann in Jerusalem*.

Hannah Arendt offered her report and her own judgments in full awareness that both would be controversial and that she would be accused of arrogance for making judgments in a time when anxiety about judging was so widespread. In a set of rough notes she made for a public discussion of the book, she linked her awareness to the phenomena—past and present—she had studied; she named the sources of her own lack of anxiety about judging. "For conscience to work: either very strong religious belief—extremely rare. Or: pride, even arrogance. If you say to yourself in such matters: who am I to judge?—you are already lost."[39]

The controversy precipitated by Hannah Arendt's series in the *New Yorker* raged for nearly three years, and it continues to simmer even now when the book made from the articles is in its twentieth reprinting. Almost every study of the Holocaust published since 1963 has explicitly or implicitly acknowledged the controversy and the fierce emotions that flowed through it. The term *Holocaust*, which came into common usage in the early 1960s, was the sign of a renewed effort by historians to reassess the fate of European Jewry and to provide documents for studying aspects of the Jewish resistance which the Eichmann controversy had highlighted.[40] German historians have taken up the troubling questions about the nature and extent of German resistance to Nazism which the controversy raised.[41] Psychologists and sociologists have tried to explore the phenomenon to which Arendt gave the name the "banality of evil." Legal theorists have reconsidered the questions raised by Arendt about the procedures for trying Nazi war criminals and the legal status of a "crime against humanity."[42] The compiler of a 1969 source book on the Eichmann case hardly surveyed the foothills of the mountain of relevant American, Israeli, and European publications. The controversy became so well known that a German anthology could be entitled simply *Die Kontroverse.*[43]

Controversies which have such a long and complex life are not born of a book. They may be so precipitated, as this one was by *Eichmann in Jerusalem,* but they are not understandable apart from the surrounding medium. Arendt used the image of crystallization to capture how historical elements combine, how complex factors intertwine into complexes of factors. It is an image appropriate to this controversy, in which there was a startling disproportion between the immediate cause and the ferocity of the reaction, a subtle interplay between substantial issues and matters of style, between historical questions and contemporary concerns, between political factors and social or psychological ones. In all of the criticisms made of Arendt's work, the line between fact and interpretation—not easy to locate in the most uncontroversial situations—was very vague. And her work lent itself to misunderstandings because, from its opening pages on, webs and lattices of "background information" were brought into play to make a drama out of the trial.

Arendt began her report with a description of the Jerusalem courtroom where Eichmann was tried and the contrast between those who served justice there and those who served David Ben-Gurion and the state of Israel. In the former category were the judges, in the latter Hausner and his staff; Ben-Gurion was portrayed as the stage manager of a show trial. The prosecutor, she argued, built his case "on what the Jews had suffered, not on what Eichmann had done,"[44] while the judges tried to do what justice called for: try Eichmann for his deeds. There followed a long passage full of quotations from pamphlets and newspaper articles published before the trial that Arendt used to show that Ben-Gurion had made propaganda out of the trial. In the many trial reports and studies that were published prior to Arendt's, the controversial "background" information was often mentioned, but the conflict Arendt saw between the servants of justice and the servants of Israel was not emphasized or drawn so dramatically. Much had been written in praise of the trial—though few writers had been as laudatory of the judges as Arendt was—but very little about Ben-Gurion's pretrial statements. Particularly for Jewish readers, the opening of Arendt's book was shocking: there, displayed for all, was an extremely critical account of one of Israel's most widely revered leaders. Arendt's intention was to praise the Israeli servants of justice for conducting a trial worthy of justice; but before ten pages of the book had passed, she had offered a dozen targets for charges that she was anti-Israel, anti-Zionist, and worst, unsympathetic to "what the Jews had suffered." Many of her readers were firmly convinced that she had actually found the trial a sham, a travesty.

Arendt's account of Ben-Gurion's public statements was not exaggerated. She had quoted extensively from an article he published in the *New York Times Magazine* several months before the trial, which the *Times* editor had not hesitated to call "Mr. Ben-Gurion's brief in the Eichmann case." But she had not chosen the passages which most clearly presented Ben-Gurion's method of discouraging debate about the case. His message to Jewry was quite explicit: "Now I see it argued, by Jews among others, that Israel is legally entitled to try Eichmann but ethically should not do so because Eichmann's crime, in its enormity, was against humanity and the conscience of humanity rather than against Jews as such. Only a Jew with an inferiority complex could say that: only one who does not reason

that a Jew is a human being."[45] Arendt passed over this insult to Jews—
one which was cast at her frequently during the controversy—just as she
passed over the one that followed: "Why should [Eichmann] not be tried
before an international court? Because Israel does not need the moral
protection of an international court. Only anti-Semites or Jews with an
inferiority complex could suggest that it does." Arendt had even toned
down the rhetoric of Ben-Gurion's statement, eliminating by misquotation phrases in which his emotionalism resounded. He had stated that
one of "our" motives for bringing Eichmann to trial was to educate Jewish
young people: "We want them to know the most tragic facts in our
history, the most tragic facts in world history." Arendt eliminated "the
most tragic facts in world history," and did not quote what followed: "I
don't care whether they want to know them; they ought to know them.
They should be taught the lesson that Jews are not sheep to be slaughtered
but a people who can hit back—as Jews did in the [1948] War of Independence." Arendt did not claim that Ben-Gurion viewed the trial as an
act of vengeance and a declaration to the world that Jews were not "sheep
to be slaughtered," though she pointed out repeatedly that the prosecutor
asked witness after witness at the trial what she called a "cruel and silly"
question—"Why did you not resist?"[46]

Furthermore, Arendt did not let herself voice her suspicion that Ben-
Gurion's emotional public statements were in part a cover-up for another
Israeli motive—one not made public. She thought, as she told one of her
readers, that the Israelis had known for a long time that Eichmann was in
Argentina and captured him when they did "because German [repara-
tions] payments to Israel were coming to an end—you see my mind is
considerably blacker than even you thought."[47] And in fact, after
*Eichmann in Jerusalem* appeared, there were many reports that Adenauer
and Ben-Gurion had made a deal: the trial was to focus on Eichmann,
leaving in the shadows the deeds of other ex-Nazis still at large, including
Globke, one of Adenauer's advisors, author of a commentary on the 1935
Nuremberg Laws, who was not to be summoned to the trial as a witness.
In exchange for this arrangement, West Germany was to supply Israel
with military equipment and arms. By the time Arendt's report was published, many people had forgotten that Ben-Gurion had resigned his
premiership on 16 June 1963, partly influenced by widespread public
disapproval in Israel for his policy of supplying the Israeli army with West
German equipment.[48]

But even though in these instances and throughout the book Arendt
was less critical than she might have been in her discussion of the context

of the trial, she was also less sensitive than she might have been to the emotional needs which Ben-Gurion expressed and many others shared. She wrote about the political implications of Ben-Gurion's statements, but not about the hurt from which they came or the defensive tendency to fall back on ad hominem accusations. She had long been a critic of efforts by Jews and non-Jews to substitute psychology for politics, but she did not, in this crucial instance, clarify why Ben-Gurion's effort was so dangerous. On the other two topics, the portrait of Eichmann and the portrait of the Jewish council leaders, the discrepancy between Arendt's report and the prevailing understanding, particularly among Jews, was even more pronounced and provocative. But Arendt wrote in a matter-of-course style about matters which many of her readers had been encouraged to understand quite differently.

The World Jewish Congress had widely distributed a 1961 pamphlet which was designed to show that Adolf Eichmann had been the person responsible for carrying out the Final Solution—a claim which the trial refuted. "Eichmann: Master-Mind of the Nazi Murder-Machine" was introduced by Nehemiah Robinson, later one of the contributors to the controversy, with a caveat: "Who Eichmann was, what he really amounted to, and what he did, is related in a concise but poignant way in the present study. Its aim is not to prejudice the findings and judgments of the court, but only to enlighten the public about the motivations and actions of this 'mass liquidator' of the Jews, so that it may be in a better position to follow the proceedings."[49] The portrait presented in the pamphlet—like dozens of others available before and after the trial—offered no challenge to readers who assumed Eichmann to be inhuman and monstrous; on the contrary, it was a piece of demonology. When Arendt took seriously Eichmann's own understanding of himself as a man without base motives, a man who had conscientiously done his duty, the challenge was so drastic that she herself admitted that not even the trial judges had taken it up.

The judges did not believe him, because they were too good, and perhaps also too conscious of the very foundations of their profession, to admit that an "average," "normal," person, neither feebleminded nor indoctrinated nor cynical, could be perfectly incapable of telling right from wrong. They preferred to conclude from occasional lies that he was a liar—and missed the greatest moral and even legal challenge of the whole case. Their case rested on the assumption that the defendant, like all "normal persons," must have been aware of the criminal nature of his acts, and Eichmann was indeed normal insofar as he was "no exception within the Nazi regime." However, under the conditions of the Third Reich only "exceptions" could be expected to react "normally." This simple truth of the matter created a dilemma for the judges which they could neither resolve nor escape.[50]

Arendt's declaration of the "simple truth" came before she had presented her own portrait of Eichmann. Later in the book she would give her own analysis of how the man's conscience "ceased to function"; she would try to distinguish lie from non-lie and show that she understood that the "simple truth" was not an easy one to arrive at. But, having placed her conclusion before her report, Arendt gave the impression that her vantage point had been effortlessly achieved—achieved, that is, by ignoring all contrary judgments, including the court's. And she did not consider why it would be so hard, particularly for concentration-camp survivors and those who had lost relatives and friends, to consider that a "bureaucratic murderer" might be not monstrously dedicated to evil but "unable to tell right from wrong."

The statements Arendt made about the Jewish councils were even more unfortunately placed and phrased. The widely held opinion that Hannah Arendt had accused her people of cowardice and lack of will to resist was a distortion of her criticism of the Jewish leadership, specifically the Jewish council members. Nowhere did Arendt criticize the behavior of the Jewish people as a whole; "no non-Jewish group or people behaved differently," she said in her opening pages.[51] She assumed that her assessment of the leadership would be shared by most Jews, for she knew very well that such criticism was common within Jewish circles, though as an internal issue, not for public display. After outlining Eichmann's dealings with the Jewish councils in Vienna and Budapest as evidence for his own claim that his conscience had been soothed by "the simple fact that he could see no one, no one at all, who actually was against the Final Solution," she claimed:

To a Jew this role of the Jewish leaders in the destruction of their own people is undoubtedly the darkest chapter of the whole dark story. It had been known about before, but it has now been exposed for the first time in all its pathetic and sordid detail by Raul Hilberg, whose standard work *The Destruction of the European Jews* I mentioned before. In the matter of cooperation there was no distinction between the highly assimilated Jewish communities of Central and Western Europe and the Yiddish-speaking masses of the East. In Amsterdam as in Warsaw, in Berlin as in Budapest, Jewish officials could be trusted to compile the lists of persons and of their property, to secure money from the deportees to defray the expenses of their deportation and extermination, to keep track of vacated apartments, to supply police forces to help seize Jews and get them on trains, until, as a last gesture, they handed over the assets of the Jewish community in good order for final confiscation.[52]

For many Jews, this was not the darkest chapter of the whole story, and the way in which it was told here—with the pointlessly sarcastic phrase "as a last gesture"—was not likely to persuade them that it was. Arendt wrote her "to a Jew this role of the Jewish leaders" statement because for her, as she later put it in a letter to Gershom Scholem, "wrong done by my own people naturally grieves me more than wrong done by other people."[53] It is impossible to say how widely this attitude, a prideful one certainly and a corrective to "my people right or wrong," was shared. People whose judgment Arendt respected did share the attitude; it is, for example, what led her friend J. Glenn Gray to reflect on his feelings as an American soldier in the Second World War: "The enemy was cruel, it was clear, yet this did not trouble me as deeply as did our own cruelty. Indeed, their brutality made fighting the Germans much easier, whereas ours weakened the will and confused the intellect. Though the scales were not at all equal in this contest, I felt responsibility for ours much more than for theirs."[54] But it is obvious that when such an attitude accompanies a judgment that wrong has been done by one's own people, it should not make the judgment harsher. Wrong clearly was done in many cases of cooperation with the Nazis—not just by traitors like Kastner of Budapest, but by many leaders. There were, however, a large number of debatable cases, and these were known to many of Arendt's Jewish readers. Her generalizations were, many felt, too sweeping; in the face of excruciating moral dilemmas sympathy was as important as frank acknowledgement of wrongdoing. Such sympathy seemed to be lacking in Arendt's account.

Those who charged Arendt with a lack of sympathy in *Eichmann in Jerusalem* often cited passages from *The Origins of Totalitarianism* which they thought showed a sympathetic understanding. In the first edition she had written:

Totalitarian governments have suppressed... individualistic expression of the moral person by making entirely questionable and ambiguous the very decisions of conscience. It is quite unimaginable how a man should act when he has the choice of betraying and thereby murdering his friends or surrendering his wife and children ... to the murderer, especially when his suicide would automatically mean the murder of his own family. The choice is no longer between good and evil but between murder and murder. . . . We know from many reports the extent to which the concentration camp inmates were involved in the actual crimes of the SS who left to them—the criminals, the political prisoners, the Jews in the ghettoes and the extermination camps—considerable administrative authority and thus put them into the insoluble dilemma of either sending their friends to their death or murdering people they did not happen to know.[55]

Arendt had not changed her mind, but what she wrote about in *Eichmann in Jerusalem* was not behavior in the concentration camps, the topic of this passage from *The Origins of Totalitarianism.* Distinctions were made in *Eichmann in Jerusalem* between the stages of the Nazis' murder plan: first, Jews were singled out by legislation and marks of identification, like the yellow star; then they were concentrated into ghettoes; then deported or "resettled;" and finally sent to extermination camps. Arendt's criticisms of the *Judenräte* ("Jewish councils") were criticisms of their behavior before the deportation stage, before the Nazis' reign of terror was total—when, in some cases at least, noncooperation might have made a difference in the death toll. She did not call for resistance, or noncooperation, when it was impossible. Arendt had been clear in her own mind about what might have been possible in each of these stages, though her analysis would have been much stronger had she emphasized the chronology and included a statement like the one she made privately to a reader who asked her about the council leaders: "There is one important excuse for them: the cooperation was gradual and it was difficult indeed to understand when the moment had come to cross a line which never should have been crossed."[56]

On the other hand, it should be said that Arendt's knowledge of conditions in the Eastern European ghettoes—and thus her ability to suggest how a line was crossed—was not always extensive enough to support her generalizations. Those of her critics who knew these conditions from first-hand experience or who had access to materials in Yiddish or Eastern European languages argued persuasively that her examples did not "give an accurate picture of either *Judenrat* activity or Jewish resistance."[57] The Eichmann trial itself provided Arendt with little information and that was the main reason she undertook to write about the councils, the darkest chapter. The topic of *Judenrat* cooperation was avoided at the trial—by design, Arendt felt. She thought that the prosecution had used the issue of Jewish resistance as a screen to hide the issue of Jewish cooperation.[58] In her book, she recorded the few moments when the councils came up at the trial, including one when a former Jewish council member from Hungary appeared on the witness stand and was shouted at by people in the courtroom audience. She reported that several witnesses gave testimony about the operations of the councils, but noted that the testimony suggested questions that went unasked. One of the witnesses on the camp Theresienstadt testified that Eichmann himself had made selections from among the camp inmates for "transport lists." A book, *Theresienstadt 1941–1945* by H. G. Adler, in which, as Arendt pointed out, it is stated that the transport lists were put together not by Eichmann but by the camp's Jewish council, was not part of the trial documentation; the defense did not even attempt to refute the witness's testimony.

Confronted with what she thought was a crucial gap in an extraordinarily well-documented trial, Arendt supplied an interpretation and gave her own conclusions about the importance of the Jewish councils. At the end of her account of the darkest chapter, she wrote:

The question the prosecutor regularly addressed to each witness except the resistance fighters, which sounded so very natural to those who knew nothing of the factual background of the trial, the question "why did you not rebel?" actually served as a smoke screen for the question that was not asked. And thus it came to pass that all answers to the unanswerable question Mr. Hausner put to his witnesses were considerably less than "the truth, the whole truth, and nothing but the truth." True it was that the Jewish people as a whole had not been organized, that they had possessed no territory, no government and no army, that, in the hour of their greatest need, they had no government-in-exile to represent them among the Allies . . . no caches of weapons, no youth with military training. But the whole truth was that there existed Jewish community organizations and Jewish party and welfare organizations on both the local and the international level. Wherever Jews lived there were recognized Jewish leaders, and this leadership, almost without exception, cooperated in one way or another, for one reason or another, with the Nazis. The whole truth was that if the Jewish people had really been unorganized and leaderless, there would have been chaos and plenty of misery but the total number of victims would hardly have been between four-and-a-half and six million people. . . . I have dwelt on this chapter of the story, which the Jerusalem trial failed to put before the eyes of the world in its true dimensions, because it offers the most striking insight into the totality of the moral collapse the Nazis caused in respectable European society—not only in Germany but in almost all countries, not only among the persecutors but also among the victims. [59]

Siegfried Moses, spokesman for the Council of Jews from Germany, made it plain to Arendt that this passage would be the focus of Jewish criticism—as it was. "Your formulation 'the whole truth was. . .' absolutely gives the impression of being a demonstrable assertion," Moses wrote angrily.[60] But Arendt clearly felt that her statement *was* demonstrable, that she had a responsibility to say what had not been said, and her tone just as clearly displays her anger at what she viewed as a cover-up.

Hannah Arendt's account of the trial had deep sources in her past life and thought, and the reactions of her critics drew on long-standing attitudes and issues. She disturbed a deep-rooted picture, one captured very well in Norman Podhoretz's *Commentary* summary of objections: "In the place of the monstrous Nazi, she gives us the 'banal' Nazi; in the place of the Jew as a virtuous martyr, she gives us the Jew as accomplice in evil; and in the place of the confrontation of guilt and innocence, she gives us the 'collaboration' of criminal and victim."[61] Hannah Arendt, who did not use the word *collaboration*, had neither allowed herself the comforting categories of monster and martyr nor indulged in theories of collective guilt or collective innocence. She made distinctions and respected differences within groups of people not because she was a modernistic relisher of paradox as Podhoretz charged in his review, "The Perversity of Brilliance," but because she was, as Heinrich Blücher liked to call her, a *Mädchen aus der Fremde* (Schiller's "Fair Stranger"), or, as she would have put it, a pariah. Following her own thinking, she was willing to make difficult judgments, as she had done from the first moment she saw Eichmann "in the flesh" in the Jerusalem courtroom.

## The Eichmann Controversy

Crystallization takes time. In "the controversy," too, there were clear periods, but the moments of first reaction largely determined them. Even before the last of Arendt's articles appeared in the 16 March issue of the *New Yorker*, there was a moment which marked a point of no return. On behalf of the Council of Jews from Germany, Siegfried Moses, formerly the state comptroller of Israel and a friend of Blumenfeld's, sent Hannah Arendt a letter. Moses, a scholar and an old acquaintance of Arendt's from Berlin, to whose 1962 *Festschrift* she had contributed, made what he called a "declaration of war" against Arendt and her book. Moses indicated that the council was also preparing for war on the historian Raul Hilberg's *The Destruction of the European Jews* and on the psychologist Bruno Bettelheim's "Freedom from Ghetto Thinking." Arendt warned Moses in reply that Hilberg's book would have a limited, scholarly audience and that Bettelheim's article would not lend itself to discussion on a high intellectual level; she then suggested that he attack her book alone and not confuse his war by fighting on too many fronts.[62]

The council's war began immediately with a statement of condemnation signed "The Council of Jews from Germany" and it continued shortly thereafter with a full page of articles in *Aufbau*. Meanwhile the Anti-Defamation League (ADL) of B'nai B'rith sent out a memorandum to all its regional offices, national commissions, and national committees informing them of the *New Yorker* series and alerting them to Arendt's defamatory conception of "Jewish participation in the Nazi holocaust," which, it was augured, might "plague Jews for years to come." The ADL made their chief fear quite clear: "No doubt anti-Semites will point to this Arendt document as evidence that Jews were no less guilty than others for what happened to six million of their coreligionists."[63]

While she was in Basel visiting with Jaspers, Arendt received her first war dispatch, sent on 6 March 1963 by Henry Schwarzchild, director of publications for the Anti-Defamation League and an acquaintance of Arendt's. Schwarzchild was alarmed by his organization's preparations for attack and concerned that he would have no influence on it.[64] And, indeed, the attack went on: the Anti-Defamation League issued another bulletin with an outline of *Eichmann in Jerusalem*, a superficial summary of its most controversial points, a copy (in English) of the Council of Jews from Germany statement, and an excerpt from the most mindless attack of the entire affair, a piece in the *Jewish Floridian* which attributed Arendt's peculiarities to her orbiting in the *New Yorker* set. The Anti-Defamation League had no scruples about recommending this information "for book reviews and others [sic] when the volume appears." And it seems that many reviewers accepted the ADL's advice, for the bulletin's phrases reappeared with monotonous regularity until supplanted by others made available in the July 1963 issue of another B'nai B'rith journal, *Facts*.[65] Jacob Robinson, who prepared the six-page memorandum on Arendt's "errors" for *Facts*, then set to work on a book-length manuscript which was circulated in mimeograph and later published under the title *The Crooked Shall Be Made Straight*. Robinson's work provided the information most often summoned in attempts to question Hannah Arendt's scholarship—the front on which the war was longest and most complex.

While the controversy was gathering momentum in America, Siegfried Moses flew from Israel for a meeting with Arendt in Switzerland. His purpose was to ask her if she would stop the publication of *Eichmann in Jerusalem* as a book in order to quiet the storm. She refused, and she warned Moses that her Jewish critics were going to make the book into a cause célèbre and thus do more damage to the Jewish community than anything she had said could possibly do. Several days later, she received a report from her friend Hans Morgenthau which confirmed her fear. Morgenthau had been present at a meeting where Bruno Bettelheim, one of Arendt's defenders, made the first attempt to face an angry New York audience. "The Jewish community is up in arms," Morgenthau wrote. "Reality has protruded into the protective armor of illusion and the result is psychological havoc. [Hillel House, City College of New York] has had a meeting, with Bettelheim. After ten minutes everybody was screaming, calling each other liar and threatening libel suits. It was a kind of collective psychoanalysis."[66]

All over New York, the "collective psychoanalysis" went on, in public meetings, in private discussion circles, in living rooms and offices. "People in town seem to be discussing little else," William Shawn wired Arendt.[67] But the most dramatic and widely publicized event came just before Arendt's book was issued by the Viking Press. The Israeli prosecutor for the Eichmann trial, Gideon Hausner, flew to New York to address a meeting of the Bergen-Belsen Survivors Association. As reported by the *Daily News*, his purpose was to "answer Hannah Arendt's bizarre defense of Eichmann." Hausner was joined at the meeting by Nahum Goldmann, then president of the World Zionist Organization, who told the audience of nearly one thousand that Hannah Arendt had accused European Jews of letting themselves be slaughtered by the Nazis and of displaying "cowardice and lack of will to resist."[68]

In the spring of 1963, during the early stages of the controversy, Arendt decided against answering her critics. She wanted a vacation after two years of intense work preparing the *On Revolution* manuscript and writing *Eichmann in Jerusalem*. Through March she stayed in Basel, translating *On Revolution* into German and working with Jaspers on the organization of his book *The Great Philosophers*. Then she went to Italy for visits with Mary McCarthy and James West, Nicolò Chiaramonte and the Ignazio Silones, and a reunion with Blücher in Naples. In April, the Blüchers travelled to Greece with Charlotte Beradt, spending freely the money Arendt had received from the insurance settlement of her 1962 accident and living, as she said to Jaspers, "the life of the gods"—that is, the life of leisure. Arendt played a retrospective joke on the taxi accident one evening in Patras: they had arrived in time to watch the last ferry to Delphi sail away and faced the prospect of sitting on their luggage for the night. So Arendt hired a local taxi for a godly sum to drive them all the way to

Athens under beautiful moonlight—fine compensation for the unfortunate and unfinished ride through Central Park. In Athens, they spent
their days on the Acropolis and in the National Museum. Blücher was
content to stay with the Attic Greeks while Arendt and Charlotte Beradt
went to the Minoans in Crete, but they all made tours of Salamis,
Aegina, and Delphi. Blücher's old friend from Berlin, the photographer
Ricarda Schwerin, joined them for a tour of the Peloponnese, Sparta,
Olympia, and the magnificent temple at Bassai.

From Greece, they journeyed back to Italy, where the Eichmann
controversy caught up with Arendt. She was approached by an interviewer from *Newsweek* who produced a full-page story for the 17 June
issue that further inflamed the American discussion, and she received
word from the *New Yorker* about Judge Michael Musmanno's review in
the *Times*.[69] Hermann Broch's friend Robert Pick found the Blüchers in
a Rome hotel and offered his calm reflections on the situation. With that
comfort, the Blüchers went on to Sicily and then, by boat, to the south of
France and finally to Paris—their first home.

The long trip was a very good one, the realization of a dream the
Blüchers had shared for a decade. But it was the stay in Greece—in the
homeland, as Jaspers reminded Arendt,[70] of the thinkers who had given
her concepts for communicating what she had learned about politics in
her American home—that gave Arendt the strength to face the startling
stack of mail she found waiting in their Riverside Drive apartment, a stack
so large that months were required to sort and answer it.

Arendt had a month and a half of summer vacation before she was due
in Chicago for the first semester of her appointment at the University of
Chicago's Committee on Social Thought. She made an appearance at
Columbia, where she spoke to a crowd of more than three hundred
students, Columbia faculty members, and journalists, and then retreated
to Palenville with a suitcase full of mail. She wrote gratefully to her
supporters, providing lengthy answers to questions she respected, but she
generally set aside or answered only briefly letters from the unreasonable
and overwrought, those who were convinced that she had, as one said,
"betrayed the Jews." Many of her correspondents supplied her with helpful information and stories of their own experiences, and she passed these
along to her critics: "Of course, these are *Einzelfälle* [particular cases] but
you as well as I know that in such things there is nothing but *Einzelfälle*."[71] Some of her correspondents offered sympathy for the sort of
criticism she had endured. One wry Hungarian Jewish émigré reminded
her that "washing dirty linen in public is not a Jewish failing," and told of

his own opinion—one which Arendt herself voiced in private correspondence—that "there was and is a strong link between the Establishment in Israel and the leadership which was in charge of Europe during the war."[72]

Other correspondents asked difficult questions about Arendt's attitude toward suicide, her views on "Jewish psychology," her feelings about the German people. One emotionally disturbed Russian Jew even told, chaotically, the story of her childhood of persecution and exile and then beseeched Dr. Arendt, author of a book she had heard so much about but did not dare to try reading, to "tell me, please tell me, why are they trying to kill me?" In private, all of the many dimensions of the public controversy were repeated, but in more outspoken and considerably more personal forms.

Arendt's late summer in New York and her fall in Chicago were punctuated by private exchanges, through letter and in person, with friends who did not wish to become involved in the public controversy. Several friendships were strained. Hans Jonas wrote to Hannah Arendt and then, when she did not reply, broke off communication, a sad state of affairs which lasted until Jonas's wife Lore prompted him to a reconciliation more than a year later. He and Arendt agreed to end their silence, except about *Eichmann in Jerusalem*, which they never discussed.

Silence fell over her long acquaintance with Robert Weltsch, Blumenfeld's friend, and, like Ernst Simon, Arendt's colleague in Judah Magnes's Ikhud group. In August 1963, she wrote a long, careful letter to Weltsch in which she explained her book and tried to counter his criticisms and misunderstandings. She hoped that their bond would survive the controversy, and told him so with a poem at the close of her letter:

Dear RW, all these are indeed mournful subjects—in this, at least, we agree. If I may end with a personal remark—I don't know with what you console yourself in the face of the spectre of our century. I suggest this from Gottfried Keller ["The Character Assassins"]:

> When, someday, this misery
> Like ice at length is broken,
> We will speak about it
> As we do the Black Death.
> Children will set straw men
> Upon the plain to burn;
> Joy will come from this pain
> And light from olden dread.

One thing is sure: this will be so, but only when we are all dead. Until then we must simply do what we think right.

Weltsch did not continue their correspondence after they had exchanged one more round of letters, but he did write an article for *Aufbau* in February 1964 to say that he felt enough—indeed, too much—had been said on all sides of the controversy and that the discussion should simply be closed.[73]

The art critic Harold Rosenberg, whom Arendt had known since the early 1950s, visited Arendt in Chicago and spent several hours telling her about his strenuous objections to *Eichmann in Jerusalem*, reiterating the stance he had taken in a 1961 article for *Commentary*, "Guilt to the Vanishing Point." She did not give Rosenberg a poem; she simply listened in uncomfortable silence, made not one attempt to defend herself, and then, when Rosenberg had finished, asked him to pour them both a drink so they could relax like good friends. He was startled, but understood that she had decided that she would not sacrifice their friendship to her work and the insights she had struggled for, and that she expected him to realize that their friendship should withstand their disagreements. This was Hannah Arendt practicing what she had called, in an essay entitled "The Crisis of Culture," true humanism. In that essay she considered Cicero's striking claim, "I prefer before heaven to go astray with Plato rather than to hold true views with his opponents," and wrote: "The humanist, because he is not a specialist, exerts a faculty of judgment and taste which is beyond the coercion which each specialty imposes upon us. This Roman *humanitas* applied to men who were free in every respect, for whom the question of freedom, of not being coerced, was the decisive one—even in philosophy, even in science, even in the arts." She thought that what Cicero meant was: "In what concerns my association with men and things, I refuse to be coerced even by truth, even by beauty."[74] Harold Rosenberg was impressed; he refrained from engaging publicly in the controversy and often told this story of Arendt's *humanitas*, both to praise her and to defend her from personal attacks.

It was one of the great disappointments of Hannah Arendt's life that no such accord could be reached with Kurt Blumenfeld. In early May 1963, after her stay in Greece, she had made a four-day trip to Israel to see Blumenfeld, who was hospitalized with the illness from which he died on 21 May 1963. Blumenfeld had not read Arendt's "Eichmann in Jerusalem" articles in the *New Yorker*, but, as Pinhas Rosen informed Arendt later by letter, "he had been given reports, from all sides, and he was outraged. That he was, really. He asked again and again whether he should not make his outrage known publicly, because he had written about his close association with you in his memoirs."[75] Arendt was convinced that the reports Blumenfeld had been given had completely misrepresented her work, and that Rosen, Siegfried Moses, and others had, thus, alienated her old and dear friend. During their last visit, she had tried to explain to Blumenfeld how her critics were reading her work and he had agreed that one of the *Aufbau*'s hostile writers was *ein Kotzproppen* and another *ein Idiot*.[76] She thought that had he read the articles himself he would have understood. But even though she thought that those who saw Blumenfeld during his last days had swayed him, Arendt wrote to both Moses and Rosen in restrained, respectful terms, not wanting to add to the list of broken bonds her work had cost her. Pinhas Rosen mentioned Arendt's last visit in an obituary for Blumenfeld and gave the impression that Blumenfeld had broken with her; Arendt was incensed but still tried to be patient. She wrote to Rosen, the brother of Martin Rosenblüth, Blumenfeld's friend: "It was extremely painful for me to find my last visit with Kurt, which was of a truly private and personal nature, discussed publicly. For the purpose of your obituary, this was entirely superfluous, and I would have thought you would know that it was a trespass. I don't hold it against you. But this is because I know that my feelings about the distinction between private and public are not the same as yours and others'."[77] She asked Rosen to see that her correspondence with Blumenfeld was returned to her, lest it, too, be offered up to the public without her permission, but she was careful to close her letter with a fond statement about Martin Rosenblüth, who had died shortly after Blumenfeld: "We (my husband and I) speak often of Martin, of the genuine restraint of his actions . . . of his humor and the delicacy of his sympathy and the absolute honesty of his way of thinking."[78] Rosen replied with a lengthy statement about the arrangements that were being made for Blumenfeld's literary estate; but he closed his letter with an echo of Gershom Scholem's charge: "It is a pity that you do not love the Jewish people, but only your friends."[79]

For Arendt, and for Blücher, this end to a friendship of so many years was dreadful. She was very shaken after the visit. Blücher was furious. And, back in New York in the middle of the summer, her sadness and Blücher's anger continued. Arendt told Jaspers that her husband was not always in control of his temper when she was attacked, and she even admitted that Blücher's "opinion of the Jewish people is not always what one might wish (but this only facetiously)."[80] Jaspers realized that this was said not entirely in jest. "I can understand Heinrich's anger," he said, and went on to write, with the same irritated protectiveness Blücher had displayed: "You have hit many people's most sensitive nerve endings—a lie in their very existence—and they hate you. . . . The truth will be beaten to death, as Kierkegaard said of Socrates and Jesus. Now, it has not come to this and it will not. But you have been given a *fama*, which, for you, is not the right thing, detestable. In the long run your character will, of course prevail and triumph radiantly."[81]

Jaspers was, as always, sympathetic and supportive; their friendship was deepened by the controversy. It was a great consolation to Arendt that Jaspers wanted to write about *Eichmann in Jerusalem* when the German edition appeared. All through the months she spent answering letters, making public appearances, trying to keep her feelings under control—"I can no longer trust myself to keep my head and not explode," she admitted to Mary McCarthy[82]—Jaspers wrote, calmly, carefully, about his appreciation of her work and her courage and about his plans for a book about her book. When she sent him the introduction for the German edition he sent detailed, "schoolmasterly" remarks and suggestions for rewriting. She replied: "I am *very, very* thankful for such a scrupulous reading and such attentive suggestions. I wrote it impatiently. Also with the feeling that it would really come to naught—but that happens to me frequently."[83]

Heinrich Blücher fell ill in September, just as Arendt was supposed to leave for Chicago, and this added to her apprehensiveness: "We have been together for twenty-eight years, and life without him would be unthinkable."[84] She wrote to Jaspers under great strain: "It is not now a matter of nerves or even the coincidence of this business with my concern over Heinrich's health which really paralyzes me. I am not in a position to go into the public realm because my disgust over this spectacle over-powers everything else."[85] Impatient and worried, she went to Chicago anyway, and flew back to New York every other weekend, trying all the while to keep the controversy in perspective: "I do my class, have a lot of students, and go about as though everything was normal. In the end, you believe—we believe—the truth will have its day. But this is a belief. And the question whether one will live to see the day is not separable from the belief."[86]

At the University of Chicago, Arendt was grateful for her eager, in-terested students and for the friends who would brave the hostility that surrounded her wherever she went. In the dining room of the university's faculty club, Hans Morgenthau joined her for meals, while most of the other faculty members, many of whom had invited her to their tables during a visit she had made the year before, avoided her. She was grateful to those, like the classicist Richard McKeon, who came across the room graciously and without hesitation to greet her, and to those who helped her through ordeals like Ernst Simon's address to a Chicago audience, delivered "with unbelievable lies and enormous aggressiveness."[87]

Arendt was especially grateful to Mary McCarthy, who made a visit to Chicago in November and was there on the day all the difficulties of the Eichmann controversy retreated into the background—22 November, when John Kennedy was assassinated in Dallas.

*Repercussions*

In the months after Kennedy's death, Arendt was filled with apprehension. "What stands in the balance now is nothing more and nothing less than the existence of the Republic," she wrote dramatically to Jaspers.[88] Her own experience of being hounded by her critics made Arendt very sensitive to the political and racial tensions that ran like shock waves across the country. Assassinations had helped pave the way for the destruction of the first republic she had lived in, the Weimar Republic, and like many others she feared the analogy. And more directly than Arendt expected, the analogy drew force from *Eichmann in Jerusalem*. Late in 1964, the Eichmann controversy began to assume immediate political relevance, and by 1965, after Kennedy's successor, Lyndon Johnson, had ordered American bombers to Vietnam, antiwar activists of the New Left were looking to *Eichmann in Jerusalem* for support of their claim that a new form of fascism had taken hold in America.

Within two years of the publication of *Eichmann in Jerusalem* the controversy it precipitated had extended far beyond the Jewish community. But even when the controversy widened and assumed importance in American politics, the terms set down at its beginning remained, and those terms came from Arendt's Jewish critics.

Arendt knew one of her critics' chief source books—the July 1963 issue of *Facts* prepared by Jacob Robinson, one of the three assistants who had sat at the prosecutor's table in Jerusalem with Gideon Hausner. Robinson's six-page "Report on the Evil of Banality," was later adapted for an issue of *Hadassah* and translated for *Le Monde Juif*. Arendt did not know, however, about the book-length manuscript which Robinson began in 1963 and soon made available in mimeograph to reviewers of her work. Lionel Abel, writing in the *Partisan Review*, acknowledged his debt to Robinson by citing a conversation they had had about untranslated monographs in Yiddish and Hebrew dealing with the Jewish councils. But Abel's review echoes Robinson's views more generally. His conclusion, that Eichmann "comes off much better in her book than do his victims," was right in line with the outrageous first-draft title of Robinson's book: *The Virtuous Criminal and the Victim's Crimes: Eichmann, Arendt and Jewish History.* [89]

Robinson's writings were also used by Nehemiah Robinson for a pamphlet distributed by the World Jewish Congress, by Marie Syrkin for an article in *Dissent* (though an earlier and much more persuasive piece of Syrkin's for *Jewish Frontier* was not apparently indebted to Robinson), by Norman Podhoretz for his *Commentary* review, by Gertrud Ezorsky for a *New Politics* article, by Morris Schappes for a three-part series in *Jewish Currents*, and by Louis Harap for an article in *Science and Society*—to cite only those articles where a reading of Robinson is either obvious or acknowledged. [90] But, despite this widespread indirect publication, Robinson's followers were not convinced that an audience as large—and as Gentile—as the *New Yorker's* would be reached. Irving Howe reported to *Commentary's* readers a conversation he had with Marie Syrkin: "How many *New Yorker* readers, she burst out in conversation, had ever cared to read anything of the vast literature about Jewish Resistance, martyrdom and survival during World War II? How many would ever read anything about it again? And how many—she continued—would ever know that a notable Jewish historian, Dr. Jacob Robinson, had discovered a large number of factual errors in those articles?" [91] Syrkin's questions arose from a fear that was widespread in the Jewish community of New York, particularly in Zionist circles. Konrad Kellen, writing moderately in *Midstream*, noted that the outcries of Arendt's opponents sprang from "a feeling that Hannah Arendt has wronged the victims, added insult to their injury and given food for glee and future mischief to the enemies of the Jews." [92] Fear of future anti-Semitism and worry about the future of Israel were palpable in Robinson's assessment of Hannah Arendt's book, as his first-draft summary chapter made quite clear:

The advice of Hannah Arendt to consider the past rather in sorrow than in anger is followed by reserving sorrow for Eichmann but expansively meting out anger to the Jews. . . . Our enemies have for years been engaged in a campaign of whitewashing the culprits and blaming the victims. The latter, brutally murdered not so long ago, are now being killed for a second time by the defilers. Among these enemies Hannah Arendt now places herself. [93]

Robinson's view—though not often, fortunately, the language in which he expressed it—was characteristic of the Eichmann controversy in its defensively nationalistic dimension. Walter Laqueur, who reviewed the final, published version of Robinson's book for the *New York Review of Books* in 1965, had reviewed Arendt's for the London *Jewish Chronicle* in 1963 and concluded that "the damage done by the half-truths of *Eichmann in Jerusalem* is incalculable."[94]

Robinson's followers used his material to attack Hannah Arendt, but they also seem to have realized that he had drastically overstated his case. His manuscript was clearly open to the same charges of prejudice that had been leveled, in the opposite direction, at Hannah Arendt. He revised it. His second draft carried the subtitle *Eichmann, Arendt, and the Catastrophe* and a note, "Title to be Provided." This draft was still, as Robinson admitted in his preface, "openly polemical." But readers were encouraged to rise to the polemical pitch by themselves: "The question of her use of innuendo, implied attack, smear, guilt by association, and cruel irony has been dealt with only slightingly [*sic*], since we feel that for the most part an intelligent reader armed with the facts will be able to discover for himself Miss Arendt's fiendish use of language."[95]

By the time he had produced his third draft, which was given the title *The Crooked Shall Be Made Straight: The Eichmann Trial, the Jewish Catastrophe, and Hannah Arendt's Narrative* and published by Macmillan in conjunction with the Jewish Publication Society, Robinson had left behind the most openly polemical parts of his work. He had taken out an extremely chauvinistic section on "Hannah Arendt, Zionism, and Israel," for example, and decided not to include any attempt at general conclusions. In its final incarnation, his work was an effort to prove that "Miss Arendt does not convey reliable information." Hannah Arendt's scholarly credentials and her abilities as a historian became Robinson's focuses; he called to his support nameless "scholars who have studied the Catastrophe in the myriad original sources" and "rejected her presentation." Though he intended to cast doubt on Arendt's scholarship, Robinson abandoned the facile techniques employed by critics like Lionel Abel: "There are 355 nonstylistic differences between the serialization and the book" (a fantastic exaggeration) and "no less than 600 distortions of fact." Robinson documented his every charge as extensively as possible, and he tried not to give the appearance of speaking for the prosecution or for the state of Israel.[96]

The case for the prosecution was made again by the prosecutor himself when Gideon Hausner published his *Justice in Jerusalem* in 1966. His

effort to restate his case and to keep alive a "chapter of history" he feared
was already "fading from the minds of men" was much more grandiose
than Robinson's. But it suffered from the same defect noted in Robinson's
book by the Jewish historian Léon Poliakov: "His vision of the confrontation between the Nazis and the Jews is perfectly Manichean." Poliakov
offered *Commentary*'s readers a succinct statement of Hausner's premise:

Although moderately successful as a narrative, however, *Justice in Jerusalem*
suffers perceptibly from a tendency toward oversimplification and a lack of historical perspective. Mr. Hausner's main premise is that Eichmann was the very
embodiment of anti-Semitic evil (hence perfectly suited to his role of executor of
the Final Solution) and that Germany itself, ever since the Middle Ages, has
been a hot-bed of anti-Jewish feeling. In making this second point, Mr. Hausner
compresses a millennium of German history into two pages.[97]

Poliakov then pointed out the many items in Hausner's book which
supported Arendt's portrait of Eichmann. But even Léon Poliakov, one of
the fairest and most reliable reviewers of Robinson's and Hausner's books,
could still conclude: "in the infinitely rich fabric of history, there are
situations for which such an approach and its corresponding clichés,
irritating though they may be, constitute a better approximation of the
truth than a more subtly shaded position [like Arendt's] would."

Hausner's book was not reviewed as carefully by others as it was by
Poliakov, whose 1952 *Bréviaire de la Haine* had been one of the first
studies to consider in detail the actions of the European Jewish councils.
The *New York Times Book Review*, for example, printed a laudatory piece
by the historian Barbara Tuchman, who openly accused Hannah Arendt
of "a conscious desire to support Eichmann's defense."[98] The *Times*
printed no letters of criticism. Hannah Arendt explained to Sybil
Moholy-Nagy, who had sent the *Times* a letter which was not printed,
that she had heard that Hausner had "made a great effort to influence the
editors" of the *Times* and other magazines while visiting New York to
promote his book.[99] A solitary critical letter, from Hans Morgenthau,
written on 1 June was printed on 17 July—two months after the
Tuchman review.

Throughout the controversy over *Eichmann in Jerusalem*, from its
beginning with a scathing review, 19 May 1963, in the *New York Times*
by a prosecution witness, Judge Michael Musmanno, formerly the
American prosecutor at the Nuremberg Trials, to its culmination with a
book by the prosecutor's consultant, Robinson, and a book by the prosecutor himself, the choice of reviewers was crucial. The low intellectual

level of the controversy was largely determined by the editorial policies of the major magazines and journals.

These editorial policies were not arrived at without internal dispute. There were efforts to prevent the worst excesses. When the *Times* received Judge Musmanno's review, a difference of opinion erupted among the editorial staff members about the editor Francis Brown's approval. A petition was circulated by one of the newspaper's feature editors, Gertrude Samuels, author of a biography of Ben-Gurion called *Fighter of Goliaths*, and the hesitators were overruled. Similarly, Dwight Macdonald lodged a strong protest with the *Partisan Review* editor William Phillips, but without success. Macdonald informed Phillips that Lionel Abel had already published a hostile article about Hannah Arendt in *New Politics*, entitled "Pseudo-Profundity," and that his impartiality was thus gravely in doubt. Macdonald also conveyed to Phillips Hannah Arendt's reaction to the magazine's choice in a 16 July 1963 letter (of which he sent a copy to Arendt):

[She said the review showed] "a lack of respect for me as a person and as a serious writer, and is much the worst that has happened, far worse than the *Times* review—after all, *they* don't owe me any consideration." She also asked me to tell you not to call her or write her, that she doesn't want to have anything more to do with *PR* or you or Philip [Rahv].[100]

Phillips sent Arendt a copy of Abel's review anyway, with a note dated 11 July in an envelope postmarked July 18, as Arendt noted with curiosity, circling the dates.

Perhaps William Phillips took the time to compose the *Partisan Review*'s concession to Hannah Arendt, an editorial note in which her "daringly speculative" work, which had "provoked as much controversy as any other work we can think of in the last decade," was presented as the effort of a frequent contributor and "a distinguished member of the intellectual community [the magazine] represents and is responsive to." Comments on the book and on Abel's piece, which was referred to not as a review but as a "frank polemic," were invited. These comments were published in the Winter and Spring 1964 issues. After pieces by Daniel Bell and Mary McCarthy, both in support of Arendt, had appeared, the opinion Arendt and Mary McCarthy shared moved into the center of the controversy: "It is as if *Eichmann in Jerusalem* had required a special pair of Jewish spectacles to make its 'true purport' visible," said Mary McCarthy.[101]

Mary McCarthy's statement was, in general, correct, but there were many shades of opinion within the Jewish intellectual community. Some of these were apparent at a public forum sponsored by *Dissent*, where a strident critique of *Eichmann in Jerusalem* by Marie Syrkin had been published. At the meeting, Syrkin and Lionel Abel, both Jews, were counterbalanced on the speaker's platform by Daniel Bell and Raul Hilberg, both Jews (Hannah Arendt herself had been invited, but she had declined, as had Bruno Bettelheim). After dismissing Arendt's Eichmann portrait as inconsequential, Syrkin tried to show that the *Judenräte* had not been essential to the Nazis' extermination program, that Arendt's "the whole truth" claim was quite false. Raul Hilberg, the second speaker, took the opposite view, arguing that the European Jews had refused to face the reality of their imminent destruction, that they had not responded actively as they might have. Hilberg's speech was booed loudly from the audience while Lionel Abel pounded the speaker's table in outrage. Irving Howe, the moderator, introduced Abel, who first lamented that he had ever admired Hilberg's scholarship and then made a passionate attack on Arendt's work, culminating with the bizarre opinion that Arendt had been rightly called by some unnamed friend of Abel's "the Rosa Luxemburg of nothingness." Daniel Bell's remarks, much like those he published in the *Partisan Review*, were restrained, respectful attempts to quiet the controversy. The open discussion that followed was largely devoted to denunciations of Hilberg, though Irving Howe took time to say that even the ruthless Trotsky had understood more about "the human condition" than certain philosophers who had written about it. No one from the audience rose to defend Arendt until just after Howe had closed the open discussion, when Alfred Kazin made his first public effort to defend his old friend, only to be ushered out with a roar from Lionel Abel: "Who asked you to come up here? Who asked for your opinion?"

The young Jew who sent Arendt a report on this meeting commented that *Eichmann in Jerusalem* seemed to have stirred up a generational conflict within the Jewish community.[102] This conflict was made public when Norman Fruchter published a piece called "Arendt's Eichmann and Jewish Identity" in *Studies on the Left*. Fruchter's was the voice of the young Jewish radicals who found in Arendt's work both a rebellion against "the myth of the victim which Jews tend to substitute for their history" and an analysis of what "citizen responsibility [is] necessary in every modern state to prevent the reemergence of the totalitarian movement which ravaged Germany." He wrote at the moment when comparisons between Germany of the 1930s and America of the 1960s were becoming common among the New Left—to the consternation of the Old Left. A year earlier, James Weinstein had published a piece called "Nach Goldwasser Uns?" in which the comparison was made explicit: "There are, indeed, many similarities between American society today and that of Germany in the years before and during Nazi rule." Eichmann became a symbol: "Like so many American bureaucrats and military men, Eichmann emerges from Miss Arendt's account as a man of very limited ideological commitment." Over such speeches as the one Carl Oglesby delivered at the 1965 SANE march on Washington, the New and the Old Left parted company: "Think of all the men who now engineer that war [in Vietnam]," said Oglesby, "those who study the maps, give the commands, push the buttons, and tally the dead: Bundy, McNamara, Rusk, Lodge, Goldberg, the President [Johnson] himself. They are not moral monsters. They are all honorable men. They are all liberals."[103]

The young Jewish radicals and the older generation of Jews who had been Marxist in the 1930s and anti-Marxist in the 1950s shouted over a great divide; they disagreed about Israeli policy and American Jewish support for it and they disagreed about the state of American society. But this was not the only fissure in the Jewish community that was reflected in the reactions to Arendt's book. Zionists thought Arendt anti-Zionist, and anti-Zionists tried to claim her for their own. The American Council for Judaism offered Arendt their protection and a public forum in which she could reply to her critics. She refused, writing to the council:

> You know that I was a Zionist and that my reason for breaking with the Zionist organization was very different from the anti-Zionist stand of the Council: I am not against Israel on principle, I am against certain important Israeli policies. I know, or believe I know, that should catastrophe overtake this Jewish state, for whatever reasons (even reasons of their own foolishness) this would be the perhaps final catastrophe for the whole Jewish people, no matter what opinions every one of us might hold at the moment.[104]

Arendt was not interested in anti-Zionism. But she was, as always, interested in a Zionist "loyal opposition" and she responded gratefully when Zionist readers recognized her position for what it was. She had been pleased with Marie Syrkin's first critical piece for *Jewish Frontier*—"she is the only one with whom I would like to have discussed this whole business"—because Syrkin had argued, vehemently, as a Zionist, fully aware of the two traditions of opposition to Zionism: "assimilationists of the Council-for-Judaism stripe . . . and 'radicals' of the old school, that is, opponents of 'multiple loyalty' and advocates of 'a larger international ideal.'"[105] Hannah Arendt was, as Syrkin implied, not an anti-Zionist but an internationalist.

## Unanswered Questions

The myriad currents of political opinion represented by Arendt's critics flowed over or around the larger issues Arendt had raised—and not answered. These issues loomed larger in American political life as the war in Vietnam escalated. Rosalie Colie, Arendt's Wesleyan University friend, ended a letter about the war with a plea: "Please write your morals. We need it, I do anyway."[106] For a "morals" there was—and still is—a great need, but *Eichmann in Jerusalem* could not satisfy it.

The reaction to *Eichmann in Jerusalem* of many Reform Jews, people with no overt ties to Zionism and no political commitments to the American Left, Old or New, showed *in nuce* why Arendt's book could not be a "morals," even for its admirers. One of Arendt's correspondents informed her: "I must admit that wherever I have gone in circles of Reform or Liberal Judaism, there is an automatic hostility to your volume based initially on what has been evaluated as a diatribe at the late Dr. [Leo] Baeck."[107]

In Arendt's criticism of Leo Baeck, the best and worst qualities of her book were combined: on one hand, her courageous effort to raise the most difficult questions, and, on the other hand, her often insensitive presentation and failure to put her questions clearly. The hostile reactions to her criticism of Baeck show what was most troubling about the controversy. Passages were lifted out of their contexts and turned into falsifying images of the whole book. But Arendt herself had provoked the hostility by giving an unbalanced portrait.

Rabbi Leo Baeck, the leader of the Berlin Jews and head of the Nazi-controlled Reichsvereinigung, successor to the Jewish-controlled Reichsvertretung which had been dissolved in 1939, was a man Arendt admired to some extent and a man most of her Reform critics admired without reservation. Using trial testimony and Raul Hilberg's book, Arendt briefly described the part of his behavior she found questionable, while she ignored his courageous refusal to abandon his people when he had, several times, opportunity for escape. While he was in the Theresienstadt camp with others the Nazis called *Führende Juden* ("leading

Jews") Baeck learned in August 1943 that Auschwitz was a death camp, but made what he called "the grave decision" not to tell his fellow prisoners.[108] Of this, Arendt wrote:

No one bothered to swear the Jewish officials to secrecy; they were voluntary "bearers of secrets," either in order to assure quiet and prevent panic, as in Dr. Kastner's case, or out of "humane" considerations, such as that "living in the expectation of death by gassing would only be the harder," as in the case of Dr. Leo Baeck, former Chief Rabbi [*sic*] of Berlin. During the Eichmann trial, one witness pointed out the unfortunate consequences of this kind of "humanity"— people volunteered for deportations from Theresienstadt to Auschwitz and denounced those who tried to tell them the truth as "not sane."[109]

A few sentences later, Arendt gave an example of Baeck's behavior during his last months in Berlin, describing how he had complied with a Gestapo demand for the appointment of Jewish *Ordner* ("policemen") to facilitate seizure of Jews for deportation: "Leo Baeck, scholarly, mild-mannered, highly educated, who believed Jewish policemen would be 'more gentle and helpful' and would 'make the ordeal easier' (whereas in fact they were, of course, more brutal and less corruptible, since so much more was at stake for them)."

This passage is quoted as it appeared in the revised edition of *Eichmann in Jerusalem*, from which Arendt had eliminated the phrase that infuriated so many of her readers: she had referred to Baeck as the man "who in the eyes of both Jews and Gentiles was the 'Jewish Führer.'" Raul Hilberg, probably Arendt's source, had noted that Eichmann's assistant, Dieter Wisliceny, had called Baeck the "Jewish Führer," but he did not imply that the phrase was used by others, Jewish or German.[110] Arendt's use of this phrase, with its terrible overtones, for a man repeatedly defended as a "saint" was, to say the least, ill considered; it was one of many instances where her irony provoked denunciation rather than argument.

On the other hand, Baeck's defenders gave no indication that his behavior, in Berlin or in Theresienstadt, had been criticized by anyone but Hilberg, the trial witness, and Hannah Arendt. Soon after her series began in the *New Yorker*, Hannah Arendt was surprised to receive a long letter of praise and support from Recha Freier, the Orthodox rabbi's wife who in 1932 had founded the Berlin organization which evolved into Youth Aliyah, the organization Arendt had worked for in Paris. Recha Freier, who had emigrated to Israel, told Hannah Arendt that she had recently prepared a book in English about the Youth Aliyah called *Let the Children Come*. The original Hebrew edition had contained Recha Freier's criticisms of Baeck, but the English publisher, Weidenfeld and Nicolson, had let her know that some of these passages had to be curtailed in their edition to prevent a libel suit. She informed Arendt that the materials she had used to write her book, including a collection of correspondence with the Reichsvereinigung and Baeck, were in the library at Yad Vashem; she offered to send Arendt copies and apparently did send several pages she thought particularly important. "The American-German Jews and their cohorts here have given me every conceivable slander and threat—and that is why I got the idea of sending you material for a *Nachspiel*, an afterword, that might follow your essays." The pages Recha Freier presumably sent never arrived. Arendt noted at the bottom of her letter "Israel is under mail censorship."[111]

Those who wrote about Baeck's time in Theresienstadt were, unlike Recha Freier, committed to his defense. Adolf Leschnitzer, who vehemently attacked Arendt in *Aufbau*, gave an example of the sort of moral defense offered for Baeck's decision to remain silent about Auschwitz. After noting that Baeck had thought "death was not certain for all," Leschnitzer argued that Baeck was like a doctor who decides not to inform a patient about the true nature of his illness. Jacob Robinson, commenting on Baeck's policy (which he claimed Arendt had called "a crime") and this analogy, concluded: "Although such a policy is debatable, it cannot be condemned outright."[112] Neither defender, however, debated.

Shortly after the war, Paul Tillich had made a statement which was quoted in Albert Friedlander's "Teacher of Theresienstadt": "No one can fully judge the events in the concentration camps," said Tillich. "But, in a way, I would criticize Baeck for not giving the last iota of information which he possessed. If he did know that Auschwitz meant certain death, he should have spoken out. The full existential truth should always be made available, just as the incurable patient should always be told the full truth."[113] Leschnitzer and Robinson simply stayed within the framework of the debate set down by Tillich, though they did not try to judge. Neither of them considered the witnesses' testimony cited by Arendt, which rendered the analogy inapplicable: doctors' patients are not offered a decision about whether or not to go to their deaths, whether or not to volunteer for a deportation to death. (Hilberg noted that 17,320 Jews were alive in Theresienstadt in May 1945).[114] Arendt had posed the true moral issue, though she had obscured it with needless irony and misquotation. Her critics did not take it up.

On the other hand, Hannah Arendt knew Rabbi Baeck's reputation well, and she admired him for his faith and fortitude. She said so publicly when his former student Alfred Friedlander invited her to address a group of Columbia students in July 1963. "For more than two hours," Friedlander reported, "she answered questions clearly and cogently, displaying her knowledge and awareness of Jewish and general history. She showed warm feelings toward the Jewish people and their tragic position during the Hitler days, and supplemented some portions of her book (viz., she lauded Leo Baeck highly)."[115] But the point remained: she had not balanced her written account. What had flared forth in her book was her old criticism of Baeck, a criticism which dated from her first acquaintance with him in Berlin. After the war, she had written to Blumenfeld about several concentration camp survivors she had met in New York, including Baeck: "I saw and spoke with Baeck—who is impressive because he really remains so ineffectual and so untouched. He speaks just as he did in 1932: Hitler persecuted the Jews—why? On account of their talent— the talent of the Jews, of course. And a Jew can never be a common mortal like any other. In short: the customary chauvinistic stuff of the assimilationists, then and now. We [Jews] are once again the very heart of humanity, etc. etc."[116] This old impression lay behind her criticism of the idea that Jewish policemen, because they were Jewish, would be gentle to their brethren—which she had dismissed with a sharp, and overgeneral, "of course" they were not. And this old impression lay behind her intemperate use of the word *Führer,* through which she signalled, but did not clarify, her view that Baeck's elevation of his people above others was unintentionally self-destructive.

The distance between Baeck's attitude toward his people, which Arendt thought morally and politically mistaken, and her own position—"wrong done by my people grieves me more than wrong done by other people"— is in one respect not so very great. Both valued greatness and hoped for moral action from their people. But for Baeck the moral standards were fixed, tied to a "Chosen People"; for Arendt they were not. Thus she could be accused—and she often was—of being a "Jewish self-hater" who employed a "double standard" against her people. Baeck spoke and acted within a religious tradition; Arendt, though she had a deep religious faith, could never have accepted the sort of dogmatic explanation Baeck offered to his Berlin students in 1940: "Persecution is the fate of all who come to mankind with strong, moralistic thoughts. . . . Israel is the servant of God, and incumbent on Israel is the responsibility for all people. Therefore, it is the suffering servant."[117] "The real distinction between religion and philosophy," Arendt told one of her own students, "is between the ways in which 'moral' propositions are stated. The religious statement is always an imperative which does not rely on reason but demands absolute, undisputed obedience: The [philosopher's] moral imperative is actually never imperative. Even if the philosopher wishes to impose his reasoned demands on those who do not reason—as, for instance, in Plato. In Kant you deal with a basically nonreligious morality, which is based on the absolute autonomy of human reason. Kant's morality is simply practical reason. The real imperative underlying the categorical imperative is: don't contradict yourself. And this is clearly the basic law of thinking, or a command of reason."[118] To the students who came to hear her discuss *Eichmann in Jerusalem* at the Hillel House of the City College of New York in March 1964, Hannah Arendt said (according to one listener's notes): "The justification for acting justly can't be proved. Plato recognized this, and used the myth of a future state of rewards and punishments as a kind of lie for political purposes—a carrot and stick to keep those in line who were unable to understand the real reason for acting justly. The Christian Church, in its role as a political institution, used the same myth, and for the same reasons. Now, today, with the breakdown of religious authority, the test is whether we are mature enough to go back and understand the real reason for not doing wrong . . . [namely], that it is better to suffer wrong than to do wrong; that it is impossible to live with a criminal, especially if he happens to be you . . . as Plato showed us in *Gorgias* and the *Republic*."[119] Had it been clear in Arendt's book that her concern was for what she later called "personal responsibility under dictatorship" and not obedience to any human interpretation of the Divine Will, some of her critics might have respected her stance, as the students who heard her did. Between personal responsibility for concrete judgments or actions and potentially arrogant responsibility for all people, the distance is very great.

As Hannah Arendt began to address the questions she had raised but not answered in her book, she taught courses at the University of Chicago with such titles as "Basic Moral Propositions," and later, at the New School, "On Morality." But the controversy over her book made her work very difficult. She was distracted; publicity was "for me and my way of life a first-rate nuisance."[120] But it was the low level of the controversy, the near absence of any intellectual substance, that most deeply discouraged Arendt. She wrote book reviews, she made notes, she took time off from her political reflections to reread Saint Augustine and her own *Der*

*Liebesbegriff bei Augustin* with the thought that she might publish it, revised, in English; but she could not find peace for the sustained philosophical reflection her "political morals" required. When Arthur Hertzberg, who had reviewed Arendt's book unfavorably, wrote her a letter about Jacob Robinson's *The Crooked Shall Be Made Straight* in 1966, he elicited one of Arendt's frankest statements about the controversy she had been carrying on in her own mind. Hertzberg wrote:

I want you to know that I am convinced, on further reflection, that his book is silly, and that my remarks in the *Reporter* were wrong. I think that there are issues to be discussed, and that you raised almost all of them, but so far the discussion has not been equal to the searing dignity of the subject, or the seriousness of your analysis, which has been treated quite unfairly by almost everyone, and certainly by me in a few paragraphs.[121]

Arendt, still weary from answering letters to the *New York Review of Books* about her reply to Walter Laqueur's review of Robinson's book, wrote gratefully to Hertzberg:

What you did is almost never done; it is the unexpected after which everything that had gone wrong is straightened out and is right again. . . . I had hoped for a real controversy, but you know what happened instead. If I am under attack [about the larger issues] I answer: this was not my job, this was only a report— which is partly true. But the whole truth is that I did not know the answers myself when I wrote the book.[122]

Arendt knew that the center of her questioning had to be the subtitle of her book: "The Banality of Evil." Eichmann "in the flesh" had taught her that she had overrated "the impact of ideology on the individual." She concluded that for Eichmann "extermination *per se* [was] more important than anti-Semitism or racism."[123] Noting that the content and the deadly logic of Nazism was less important to this man than the movement in which he had found a home, Arendt rejected the concept she had used in *The Origins of Totalitarianism* to point at the incomprehensible nature of the Nazis—"radical evil." As she did this, she freed herself of a long nightmare; she no longer had to live with the idea that monsters and demons had engineered the murder of millions. The banality of evil, she said in the last sentence of her book, is "fearsome, word-and-thought-defying." But its existence is not proof of an original evil element in human nature and hence not an indictment of mankind.

In her report, Arendt told how Eichmann's conscience was stilled; and this meant that she assumed that he had a conscience—like any and every man. Rewriting in political terms Rousseau's famous statement about man's "innate repugnance to see his fellowman suffer," she had spoken of Eichmann's "innate repugnance to crime."[124] Later she realized that she was going against the way of thinking that grounds evil deeds in evil natures, that claims men *do* evil because they *are* evil. "One might be tempted," Arendt wrote in a 1966 review of Bernd Naumann's *Auschwitz*, an account of the Frankfurt trials of Nazi camp functionaries, "to indulge in sweeping statements about the evil nature of the human race, about original sin, about innate human 'aggressiveness,' etc. in general—and about the German national character in particular.... [But] in any event, one thing is sure, and this one had not dared to believe any more—namely, that everyone could decide for himself to be either good or evil in Auschwitz.... And this decision depended in no way on being a Jew or a Pole or a German; nor did it even depend on being a member of the SS."[125]

The Frankfurt Nazi trials confirmed the judgment Hannah Arendt had reached in Jerusalem; nothing psychopathological or demonic, but things quite superficial, determined whether these camp functionaries would add their own personal atrocities to the mass murder they were engaged in or whether they would add small deeds of kindness—or both.

The clinical normalcy of the defendants notwithstanding, the chief human factor in Auschwitz was sadism, and sadism is basically sexual.... Only second in importance, as far as the human factor in Auschwitz is concerned, must have been sheer moodiness.... It was as though their ever-changing moods had eaten up all substance—the firm surface of personal identity, of being either good or bad, tender or brutal, an "idealistic" idiot or a cynical sex pervert. The same man who rightly received one of the most severe sentences—life plus eight years—could on occasion distribute sausages to children; Benarek, after performing his specialty of trampling prisoners to death, went into his room and prayed, for he was then in the right mood; the same medical officer who handed tens of thousands over to death could also save a woman who had studied at his old alma mater and therefore reminded him of his youth; flowers and chocolates might be sent to a mother who had given birth, although she was to be gassed the next morning. ... Death was the supreme ruler in Auschwitz, but side by side with death it was accident—the most outrageous, arbitrary haphazardness, incorporated in the changing moods of death's servants—that determined the destinies of the inmates.

Three characteristics of radical evil had recurred in Hannah Arendt's discussions in *The Origins of Totalitarianism*, *The Human Condition*, and *On Revolution*. It is unpunishable in the sense that no punishment can be adequate or commensurate; it is unforgiveable; and it is rooted in motives so base as to be beyond human comprehension. The last characteristic was the one Eichmann's trial brought into question. To groups, to classes, to the entire apparatus of totalitarian destruction, and, finally, to the totalitarian murderers whose desire to prove the statement "everything is permitted, everything is possible" rebounded even upon themselves, Hannah Arendt had once attributed the term "superfluous." In *Eichmann in Jerusalem*, she attributed superfluity to motives: when motives become superfluous, evil is banal.

Arendt did not deny that men can act from base motives. She spoke of "calculated wickedness," distinguishing it from banal or motiveless evil. When a wicked man says to himself, as Richard III does in Shakespeare's drama, "Evil be thou my good," he can still tell the difference between good and evil. The wicked man's motives, though base, are not incomprehensible—the adjective "calculated" implies this.[126] When Arendt told Gershom Scholem "evil is never radical," she did not deny wickedness; she simply implied that not even wickedness is radical, is rooted in an incomprehensible and original fault.

It is indeed my opinion that evil is never "radical," that it is only extreme, and that it possesses neither depth nor any demonic dimension. It can overgrow and lay waste the entire world precisely because it spreads like a fungus on the surface. It is "thought-defying," as I said, because thought tries to reach some depth, to go to the roots, and the moment it concerns itself with evil, it is frustrated because there is nothing. That is its "banality." Only the good has depth and can be radical.[127]

The idea of radical evil evokes the Manichean or Gnostic doctrine that both good and evil are primordial, that they are the independent and real sources of the battle between good and evil that appears in the cosmos and in each man. When Hannah Arendt rejected the idea, she moved in the direction of the doctrine that has been the chief alternative in the Western tradition: evil is merely a privation of the good; Lucifer is a fallen angel and not a being created evil. But despite her admiration for the greatest of the ex-Manichees, Arendt was no theologian, not even an Augustinian one, and she explained the privative nature of evil in secular terms. She did not agree with Plato that to know the good is to do the good. What she claimed was that thinking can condition one against evil-doing because the capacity to judge good and evil is a by-product of the thinking activity. Only in her last work, *The Life of the Mind*, did Arendt begin to present her description of how not-thinking precludes judging, blocks the ability we all have to say "this is right" or "this is wrong."

One of her most sensitive and philosophically acute readers, J. Glenn Gray, understood immediately the significance of Arendt's Eichmann portrait. He wrote on 23 March 1963: "As you know, I had to interrogate hundreds of such Nazi functionaries during and after the war, and he seemed to fit well into their mold. Hardly one's romantic image of the 'evil one.' " Then, after further reflection, he wrote again: "That [evil] has no metaphysical reality or depth is something I shall want to challenge when I see you. It strikes me as more Platonic than most of your thought. Though you established it to my satisfaction in the case of Eichmann, I wonder if you would have used such a subtitle [for your book] had Goebbels been in the dock."[128] Jaspers had similar reservations: had Arendt moved too quickly from an instance of banal evil to a concept of evil in general, *überhaupt*? He understood her position: "Now, here, you have said the definitive word against the Gnostics. You are with Kant, who [revised his notion of 'radical evil' and] said: man cannot be a devil. And I am with you." Then, in another letter, Jaspers raised his question: "I think: the notion is illuminating, and as a book title it is striking. It means: *this* man's evil is banal, not evil is banal. . . . 'What is evil' still stands behind the phrase as it characterizes Eichmann. Actually, it seems to me, your answer [to Scholem] was at once too strong and too weak. Now, we can argue with each other to both our satisfactions when you come to visit."[129]

Unfortunately, no record of their argument over this question exists. Arendt did not abandon her claim that evil is never radical, but she provided in her writings only further illustrations of banality, not a thoroughgoing argument. She never took up, for example, the philosophical problems involved in her anti-Freudian notion that sadism, which is "basically sexual," is not radical, though she did present an argument in *On Violence* for her belief that violence is "neither beastly nor irrational."[130] Apparently, she had some reservations about the generality of her claim, for she once admitted to Mary McCarthy in conversation that she thought Reinhardt Heydrich, referred to in *Eichmann in Jerusalem* as "the real engineer of the Final Solution," absolutely evil. But Arendt nonetheless continued to generalize from the position she had reached, and she made clear in many public statements what it meant: "There exists a widespread theory, to which I also contributed [in *The Origins of Totalitarianism*] that these crimes defy the possibility of human judgment and explode the frame of our legal institutions."[131] This was the theory she overcame.

Behind Arendt's conclusion lay long reflection on the other two characteristics of "radical evil" as well. She did not abandon her opinion that extreme evil, whether thought of as radical or banal, is unpunishable and unforgiveable, but she shifted the basis for her opinion with the help of one of the most enthusiastic readers of *The Human Condition*, the poet W. H. Auden.

When he read Arendt's book, Auden was amazed. He telephoned her to thank her for it and then wrote a review. "Every now and then," he declared, "I come across a book that gives me the impression of having been especially written for me . . . it seems to answer precisely those questions which I have been putting to myself."[132] Nonetheless, *The Human Condition* also raised questions for Auden and he put these to Arendt in private as he sought to make their acquaintance into a friendship. Arendt accepted both the questions and Auden's accompanying invitation to his birthday party in a letter dated 14 February 1960. She wrote a very careful letter, probably relieved to see that Auden did have questions, for his effusive, unquestioning review had made her uncomfortable, as she had admitted to Mary McCarthy after she read it: "And now I am even more embarrassed [than when Auden phoned]. Somehow I am utterly unfit for the role of author, it is a simple case of lack of suitable ideas."[133]

In *The Human Condition*, Arendt had claimed that we forgive "what was done . . . for the sake of who did it," and Auden found this formulation problematic. "I was wrong," Arendt admitted, "when I said we forgive what was done for the sake of who did it. . . . I can forgive somebody without forgiving anything."[134] Arendt might, for example, have forgiven Eichmann without forgiving any of his deeds, and she knew that she had to state clearly why she rejected this possibility. *Eichmann in Jerusalem* closed with her answer:

Let us assume, for the sake of argument, that it was nothing more than misfortune that made you a willing instrument in the organization of mass murder: there still remains the fact that you have carried out, and therefore actively supported, a policy of mass murder. For politics is not like the nursery: in politics obedience and support are the same. And just as you supported and carried out a policy of not wanting to share the earth with the Jewish people and the people of a number of other nations—as though you and your superiors had any right to determine who should and who should not inhabit the world—we find that no one, that is, no member of the human race, can be expected to want to share the earth with you. This is the reason, and the only reason, you must hang.[135]

Even if the man might have been personally forgiveable, even if it could somehow have been proven that his "inner life" was noncriminal, his decision to obey and carry out a policy of mass murder was unforgiveable: with this decision, he refused to "share the earth" with the Jews and others.

The peroration Arendt addressed to Adolf Eichmann was thought arrogant by many of her critics; she was accused of repudiating the judgment of the court and substituting her own. Arendt, who knew quite well that she had, in fact, accepted the court's judgment and also that she had as much right to offer her own judgment as any concerned individual, responded only to another sort of criticism about the peroration. A German correspondent asked her a more subtle and despairing question: did she not think that millions of people would have no qualm about sharing the earth with Adolf Eichmann or his like? She answered: "What I meant, and what cannot be easily captured in English, is that no one can be reasonably expected to [share the earth with Eichmann]. That many people do not know that this is an unreasonable expectation (*Zumutung*) does not refute the sentence."[136]

Auden questioned Arendt's notion of forgiveness and then pressed her to another distinction. Arendt had claimed that "the alternative to forgiveness, but by no means its opposite, is punishment, and both have in common that they attempt to put an end to something that without interference could go on endlessly. It is therefore quite significant, a structural element in the realm of human affairs, that men are unable to forgive what they cannot punish and that they are unable to punish what has turned out to be unforgiveable. This is the true hallmark of those offences which, since Kant, we call radical evil." This passage provoked Auden to suggest a distinction between forgiveness and judicial pardon. "You are entirely right (and I was entirely wrong)," Arendt conceded, "in that punishment is a necessary alternative only to judicial pardon. I was thinking of the absurd position of the Nuremberg [judges] who were confronted with crimes of such a magnitude that they transcend all possible punishment."[137] It may well be impossible to punish adequately a person you cannot forgive, but if you must punish a person you cannot pardon judicially—regardless of whether or not the punishment is adequate—then it follows that an argument against judicial pardon must accompany the charge "you must hang." Unpardonability, not unpunishability, is at issue, even when the framework of legal institutions is strained by a novel kind of crime, "administrative massacre." Indirectly, Arendt acknowledged this. When the Israelis hanged Eichmann—while she was in the middle of writing her book—she told Mary McCarthy, tersely: "I am glad they hanged Eichmann. Not that it mattered. But they would have made themselves utterly ridiculous, I feel, if they had not pushed the thing to its only logical conclusion."[138] Hanging was inadequate, but unpardonability had to be asserted anyway.

Philosophically and legally, the idea of the "banality of evil" was difficult to compass. But politically it was simpler. One of the commonest delusions of politics is that evil may produce some good, that the lesser evil is in some way a good or may in some future be a good. This is another version of the notion that "evil is no more than a privative *modus* of the good . . . a temporary manifestation of a still-hidden good," as Arendt wrote in *On Violence*.[139] Only rare faith or great pride—or perhaps both—can stand against the temptation to be good by evil means. As Arendt wrote of Pope John:

He had always been content to "live from day to day," even "from hour to hour" like the lilies in the field, and he now set down the "basic rule of conduct" for his new state [the Papacy]—to "have no concern for the future", to make no human provision for it", and "to take care not to speak of it confidently and casually to anyone." It was faith and not theory, theological or political, that guarded him against "in any way conniving with evil in the hope that by doing so [he] may be useful to someone."[140]

The refusal to connive with evil and the refusal to claim knowledge of the future are of a piece: it is an image of the future good, often linked to a theory of historical inevitability or an interpretation of God's will, which seduces good men into accepting an evil means. If evil is banal, no faulty nature or original sinfulness is required to become ensnarled in it; indeed, the best, not knowing what they do, are likely to become ensnarled for the sake of a future good. Arendt made her own understanding of these issues clear in a set of notes she prepared for a *Look* magazine interview:

The "banality of evil" contrasts with the notion that good can come from evil; Mephistopheles' *Geist der stets das Böse will / und stets das Gute schafft*; the devil, seen as a fallen angel, Lucifer, suggests that the best are most likely to become the worst; Hegel's whole philosophy rests on the "power of negation", for instance, of necessity to bring about a realm of freedom; and so on. European Zionists (as distinguished from views held by the American Zionists) have often thought and said that the evil of anti-Semitism was necessary for the good of the Jewish people. In the words of a well-known Zionist in a letter to me discussing the original Zionist argumentation: "the anti-Semites want to get rid of the Jews, the Jewish state wants to receive them, a perfect match." The notion that we can use our enemies for our own salvation has always been the "original sin" of Zionism.[141]

For the same *Look* magazine interview, Hannah Arendt made a list of the arguments used to justify the behavior of Jewish council members:

1) "Better, if you have to die, to be selected by your kin."—I disagree: it would have been infinitely better to let the Nazis do their own murderous business. 2) "With a 100 victims we shall save a 1,000."—This sounds to me like the last version of human sacrifices: pick seven virgins, sacrifice them to placate the wrath of the gods. Well, this is not my religious belief, and [it] most certainly is not the faith of Judaism. 3) Finally, the theory of the lesser evil. Result: good men do the worst.

These three arguments were implicit in Arendt's *Eichmann in Jerusalem*, but she did not reflect on them until after the book was published. In private, she admitted candidly that she knew her work had moral implications she had not thought out: "The writing was somehow a *cura posterior* for me. And that it was [as you say] an approach toward 'the groundwork for creating a new political morals' is true—though I would never, out of modesty, use such a formulation."[142]

With these notes toward a "political morals," Hannah Arendt began to tie the concept of the "banality of evil" to two older strands of her political theory which she had reformulated for *On Revolution*. First, she linked it to her understanding that action is perverted if it is understood as fabrication in the "you-cannot-make-an-omelet-without-breaking-eggs" manner; action is not a matter of ends and means. Secondly, she tied the concept to her historical studies of leaders who are prone to operate in a "means-are-justified-by-the-ends" manner because they have divorced themselves from their people, lost the common sense that can exist only in a common world of open discussion. The ways in which critics of her work attempted to exonerate the Jewish councils confirmed Arendt in this second of her reflections. She was, for example, astonished by Jacob Robinson's exoneration effort, and said so in a letter to the *New York Review of Books*:

Robinson's main thesis is expressed in two sentences: First, "Legally and morally, the members of the Jewish Councils can no more be judged accomplices of their Nazi rulers than can a store owner be judged an accomplice of an armed robber to whom he surrenders *his store* at gunpoint." The worst reproach one could level at the Jewish Councils would indeed be to accuse them of disposing of Jewish lives as though they *owned* them, and no one to my knowledge has ever dared to go that far before Mr. Robinson.... [Several pages later we] hear, second, that whoever "accepted appointment to a Council... did so as a rule out of feeling of responsibility," hence was by no means forced at gunpoint. Mr. Robinson's second thesis has become common property among the writers for the Jewish Establishment.[143]

Arendt herself never questioned the "feeling of responsibility" of the men, like Leo Baeck, who joined Jewish councils; she questioned whether such a feeling was accompanied by good judgment about what was best for all the Jewish people.

Hannah Arendt's "Report on the Banality of Evil" became a challenge to write her political morals. But writing a *Moralia* was not her mode. What she aimed for was a political Critique of Judgment, as she thought fixed moral codes unhelpful for reasons she outlined in a 1964 address, "Personal Responsibility Under Dictatorship." Arendt spoke of those who refused to cooperate with the Nazis, announcing the theme she later took up in *The Life of the Mind*:

The nonparticipants, called irresponsible by the majority, were the only ones who were able to judge by themselves, and they were capable of doing so not because they [had] a better system of values or because the old standards of right and wrong were still firmly planted in their mind and conscience, but, I would suggest, because their conscience did not function in [an], as it were, automatic way—as though we [had] a set of learned or innate rules which we then apply to the particular case as it arises.... Their criterion, I think, was a different one; they asked themselves to what extent they would still be able to live in peace with themselves after having committed certain deeds.... The presupposition for this kind of judging is not a highly developed intelligence or sophistication in moral matters, but merely the habit of living together explicitly with oneself, that is, of being engaged in that silent dialogue between me and myself which since Socrates and Plato we usually call thinking. . . . The total moral collapse of respectable society during the Hitler regime may teach us that those who are reliable in such circumstances are not those who cherish values and hold fast to moral norms and standards. . . . Much more reliable will be the doubters and sceptics, not because scepticism is good or doubting wholesome, but because [such people] are used to [examining things and making up their own minds]. Best of all will be those who know that, whatever else happens, as long as we live we are condemned to live together with ourselves.[144]

As she began to think about "political morals," Hannah Arendt realized that there is such a thing as a temptation not just to do good by any means but to *be* good—or a temptation to *be* moral. Those who have "highly developed intelligence" or "sophistication in moral matters"—and that might include writers of ethics—may very well be tempted by moral systems into bad judgment. In 1966 Arendt wrote about Bertolt Brecht's realization: *Schrecklich ist die Verführung zur Güte* ("terrible is the temptation to be good"). And she told how Brecht, who wanted to be good and helpful to the downtrodden, allied himself with evil and paid for his bad judgment with the loss of his poetic gift ("the poet's real sins are avenged by the gods of poetry"). Arendt argued that Brecht had understood all along what was happening to the Russian Revolution under Stalin, but that his hopes for the revolution had led him astray. For his misguided compassion, Brecht himself suggested a punishment: "In the posthumously published *Me-ti* . . . [Brecht] suggests a verdict for the 'good man' gone wrong. 'Listen,' he says after the interrogation is completed, 'we know you are our enemy. Therefore we shall put you against a wall. But in consideration of your merits and virtues, it will be a good wall, and we will shoot you with good bullets from good guns and we shall bury you with a good shovel in good soil.'"[145]

Not to go wrong requires of the good man far more than compassion, the "compassionate zeal" of the men of the French Revolution and their modern heirs. Arendt began to look for examples of people who had been good without trying to be good. Late in her life, she wrote a little summary of what she had learned to one of her finest Chicago students, William O'Grady, who had written her a letter about his own efforts to "be a very good person."

I don't quite know what you mean when you say "good," but I know that the wish to be "good" is an even greater temptation than the wish to be "wise." That is precisely what we cannot *be*. "Let not thy left hand know what thy right hand doeth" is the maxim that rules this whole realm. You probably know the Talmudic story about the 36 righteous men for the sake of whom God does not destroy the world. No one knows who they are, least of all they themselves. Every kind of self-knowledge is here absolutely ruinous. So, if you try to reflect try not to reflect on yourself, "don't trust the teller, trust the tale."[146]

As Hannah Arendt turned to the unanswered moral questions *Eichmann in Jerusalem* had posed, she began to make explicit the link between her own *cura posterior* and her concern with judgment. The attitude she had once called *amor mundi*, love of the world, took on a new richness as she explored the "life of the mind" it requires. Arendt realized that the internal harmony of thinking—"the dialogue between me and myself," as she called it—precedes judging and supplies it with its objects. Such thinking presupposes a capacity to stand back from the world of human affairs, and from what one's right hand hath done in that world, not to contemplate, but to search for meaning, to tell a meaningful story. Arendt did not become reconciled to the world in the sense that she condoned or forgave or was no longer horrified by evil deeds; but she realized that in searching for the meaning of deeds, humans win all that is possible for them as they look upon past evils—the privilege of judging. She, who had in *The Origins of Totalitarianism* rejected reconciliation as a condoning of the totalitarians, wrote in her 1968 essay on the storyteller Isak Dinesen:

"All sorrows can be borne if you put them into a story or tell a story about them." The story reveals the meaning of what otherwise would remain an unbearable sequence of sheer happenings. "The silent, all-embracing genius of consent" that is also the genius of true faith—the Hebrew Kaddish, the death prayer said by the closest relative, says nothing but "Holy is His Name"—rises out of the story because in the repetition of imagination the happenings have become what [Dinesen] would call a "destiny." . . . All her stories are actually "Anecdotes of Destiny," they tell again and again how at the end we shall be privileged to judge.[147]

In her 1951 preface to *The Origins of Totalitarianism*, Arendt had tried to find some guidance—even if only negative—in the story she told: perhaps, she reflected, this appearance of "radical evil" will shatter our illusions about what men will not do. She had tried to put past evils into the service of a future good with her rigorous charge to face reality squarely. After she wrote *Eichmann in Jerusalem*, Arendt urged reporters, historians, and particularly people of poetic imagination to a different task. "The methods used in the pursuit of historical truth are not the methods of the prosecutor, and the men who stand guard over the facts are not the officers of interest groups—no matter *how legitimate their claims*—but the reporters, the historians, and, finally, the poets."[148] The facts, no matter how horrifying, must be preserved, not "lest we forget," but so we may judge. Preservation and judgment do not justify the past, but they reveal its meaning. Arendt became (as she once said of W. H. Auden) "somehow convinced, as the bards of ancient Greece were, that the gods spin unhappiness and evil things toward mortals so that they may be able to tell the tale and sing the songs."[149] So that they may be, that is, the judges. Arendt often marked what her *cura posterior* had taught her about the value of judgment and the reconciliation of judging, by quoting part of Auden's poem on W. B. Yeats:

> Follow, poet, follow right
> To the bottom of the night,
> With your unconstraining voice
> Still persuade us to rejoice;
>
> With the farming of a verse
> Make a vineyard of the curse,
> Sing of human unsuccess
> In a rapture of distress;
>
> In the deserts of the heart
> Let the healing fountain start,
> In the prison of his days
> Teach the free man how to praise.[150]

# PART 4

## 1965–1975

HANNAH ARENDT HAD TO LEARN TO LIVE WITH THE reputation *Eichmann in Jerusalem* brought her. Praise, condemnation, and calumny came through the mail and the media. She was a public figure in the 1960s, despite her wishes, and she was preoccupied with more teaching responsibilities than ever, at the University of Chicago's Committee on Social Thought and, after 1967, at the Graduate Faculty of the New School for Social Research. From 1963 through 1971, when she was an essayist rather than a book writer, her published work was both more directly topical—because she wanted to write about the changing political life of America—and less theoretically innovative—because she was drawing on conceptual explorations already made—than at any other time in her life.

As a commentator and book reviewer, Arendt became, as one journalist put it, "the *éminence grise* of the *éminences grises*,"[1] the American intellectuals who wrote for the *New York Review of Books*, went to the Theatre for Ideas, joined various organizations in the anti–Vietnam War movement, and founded the Committee for Public Justice. Her opinions were seldom received without deep debate, but they were often sought. Arendt lectured widely, sat on panels and editorial boards, attended conference after conference—including two dedicated to her own work—and signed petitions.

During these very public years, Arendt did not tax her private life; she protected it more carefully than ever. Blücher was not always well. He had recovered from his 1961 aneurism, though not without "depression as a neurological symptom"[2] during the years of the Eichmann controversy. Arendt was anxious about his health, sometimes excessively. The Blüchers restricted their shared social life to the tribe members, and they kept their obligations in the world quite separate. Blücher, who taught until 1968 at Bard College, went his way, and Arendt went into the public realm without him. The turmoil of America in the late 1960s made them both apprehensive, as New York City, with its rising crime rate, made them seek quiet refuges in their new apartment on Riverside Drive—removed from the dangers of Morningside Heights—in Palenville, and in Switzerland.

When she could find peaceful interludes, Arendt made plans for a book to complement *The Human Condition*; she would call it *The Life of the Mind*. In this book, she wanted to consider philosophical questions about the nature of evil and the preconditions for both thinking and judging. But she had to go this way without those who made her feel at home in the world. Heinrich Blücher was with her when Karl Jaspers died; but when Heinrich Blücher died, in 1970, she was alone.

In the last ten years of her life, Arendt's always firm line between the private and the public realms became rigid. As a public person, recipient of many honors, busy to exhaustion, she spoke out often and forcefully about the Republic, America; privately, she withdrew into her "thinking space," seeking descriptions of "being together with one's self" when her self was left without those "in-betweens," those worlds, that mattered most.

# CHAPTER 9

# America in Dark Times

## (1965–1970)

Some think they're strong,
  some think they're smart,
Like butterflies they're pulled
  apart.
America can break your heart.

Auden

*The Republic*

While Hannah Arendt was trying to think her way toward a "political morals," her adopted country entered years of political and moral confusion as drastic as any in the postwar period. Many Americans in and around the New Left thought they were witnessing a reenactment of the decline of the Weimar Republic or France between the wars. Arendt resisted the analogy. In the mid-1960s, she thought that the American military presence in Vietnam would remain limited; she expected early withdrawal of troops, assuming that informed public opinion, which she viewed as solidly against the war, would prevail. In April 1965, she told Mary McCarthy that she herself was "not too interested" in the war, and soon afterwards she confidently referred McCarthy to Hans Morgenthau's article of 15 April 1965 in the *New York Times Magazine*.[1] Noting that President Johnson had expressed willingness to negotiate an end to the war, Morgenthau—who became one of two high administration officials to resign in protest over America's war policy—argued that Johnson should let Ho Chi Minh be the "Asian Tito" and that he should give up the illusory notion that North Vietnam was the aggressor in a campaign to conquer South Vietnam—as though Vietnam were not one country. Throughout 1965, Arendt adopted Morgenthau's position and wrote reassuringly to Jaspers that it would be persuasive. Jaspers was relieved that a public debate was going on without demagogy.[2] This optimism proved ill founded.

In September 1966, Arendt answered a questionnaire about the

Vietnam War sent to her by an English team who were taking an opinion poll like the one taken by W. H. Auden, Stephen Spender, Louis Aragon, and Nancy Cunard in 1937, at the time of the Spanish Civil War. On the model of *Authors Take Sides on the Spanish War*, Cecil Woolf and John Bagguley asked contributors to answer two questions for their *Authors Take Sides on Vietnam*. Arendt's opinions about what had grown during 1966 into a full-scale war, no mere matter of "military advisors," were succinct, and they showed that she rejected the American government's portrayal of the conflict in Vietnam as something other than a civil war: "1. I am against the intervention of the United States in the civil war in Vietnam. 2. The way to resolve an armed conflict is always the same: cease fire—armistice—peace negotiations—and, hopefully, peace treaty."[3]

But soon after she wrote out her simple replies, Arendt read an article which made her uneasy. Rudolf Augstein, the editor of *Der Spiegel*, condemned America's war policy but gave the impression that no Americans shared his view. Arendt was prompted to write a rare letter to the editor, in which she cautioned Augstein, one of the most important critics of the German government, to be aware that many Americans were criticizing their government's policies.

I could cite to you what appears in American publications, for example. Are people like Senator Fulbright, George Kennan, Lewis Mumford, Robert Lowell, Walter Lippmann—and I name only those I assume are known in Germany—the sort you would like to avoid [because you cannot discuss the war with them]? Don't you know how divided the country is over this question? Don't you know that the Senate Foreign Relations Committee's debates are publicized? Haven't you had in your hand an issue of the *New Republic* or the *New York Review of Books?* Don't you know how many influential television news broadcasters report on, and put before the public day after day in pictures, what is happening in Vietnam? Haven't you heard about the angry discussions in the universities, in which students and faculty alike are engaged? All these Americans, among whom I number myself, have publicly spoken out.[4]

Arendt found it hard to believe that a policy that was so openly and widely opposed could be followed to the bitter end.

Like most political analysts in the mid-1960s, Hannah Arendt underestimated the complexity of the political situation in America and the intransigence of those she later called Washington's problem-solvers and decision-makers. But by the time she had collected her late 1960s political writings for a single volume, she understood very well that she had been witnessing and writing about "Crises of the Republic" and that the Vietnam War was part of a profound change in both America's political life and the world order. When she made the last public address of her life, a fiery Bicentennial speech at the Boston Hall Forum in May 1975, only a month after the Vietnam War formally ended, Arendt was convinced that her country stood at the edge of an era she despaired to imagine. She catalogued the multitude of events that had accompanied "this disaster in Southeast Asia," and suggested to her hearers why they might perhaps agree "that among the many unprecedented events of this century the swift decline in power of the United States should be given due consideration. It, too, is almost unprecedented. We may very well stand at one of these decisive turning points of history that separate whole eras from each other. For contemporaries entangled, as we are, in the inexorable demands of daily life, the dividing lines between eras may be hardly visible when they are crossed; only after people stumble over them do the lines grow into walls which irretrievably shut off the past."[5]

This apprehensive passage, so at odds with Hannah Arendt's conviction that retrieval of the past is always possible as long as there are storytellers, marked a change of mood. In the 1960s, not just the inexorable demands of daily life but also the "unprecedented" events of the mid-century made it difficult to see clearly the conditions of the world. The events that had once been unprecedented were taken, in various ways and to various degrees, as precedents. As the cold war atmosphere of the 1950s lifted, the Nazi period and the Stalin regime were reviewed anew, combed for clues to contemporary events. America was "between past and future." In Hannah Arendt's life and work, too, proofs of Faulkner's lapidary insight—one she loved to cite—came often: "The past is never dead, it is not even past."

"What is now in the balance is nothing more and nothing less than the existence of the Republic," Arendt wrote to Jaspers on 1 December 1963, as she, like Americans everywhere, tried to understand what had happened ten days earlier in Dallas. She was "catastrophe-minded" in her shock over John Kennedy's murder. Hannah Arendt, Mary McCarthy, and Hans Morgenthau had watched the television coverage of Kennedy's funeral together in Chicago. She was impressed by her countrymen's grief, but what she stressed in her letters to Jaspers was her fear that no investigation of the assassination would dispel the speculations about

Communist conspiracies and revenge taken on a Northern "nigger-lover" (she left this expression in English for Jaspers to struggle with). For the future of the Republic, she felt that facing up to the existence of racism and fanatical anti-Communism was critical. "I imagine," she wrote to Jaspers in her annual New Year's letter, "you know more about the Kennedy murder than we do here. A week ago there appeared in the *New Republic* a detailed article about the whole business—which clarified nothing." She noted some of the conflicting evidence and concluded that "the thing forebodes ill, and probably never will be cleared up."[6] Arendt and Jaspers, who both had long experience with how cover-ups help "unmastered pasts" stay unmastered, were apprehensive about the Warren Commission. And several years after Kennedy's death, Jaspers was still warning: "The crime is unsolved. Politically, this is almost as fatal as the assassination itself. Thus far the American people as a whole have not mastered the dreadful event. . . . The most respected, most trusted and unassailable judge, Chief Justice Warren, was put in charge of the investigation. He said that the truth about the whole matter would not be fully known to the present generation—which could only mean that findings contrary to the national interest would not be made public. . . . But America is still America. The issue would not stay dead."[7]

Arendt worried privately about precedents for the decline of a Republic, but, characteristically, her public statement was more cautious. In the Christmas 1963 issue of the *New York Review of Books*, a journal which had come into being during the New York City newspaper strike of the previous winter, Arendt and others commented on the assassination and its probable consequences:

Was this "the loudest shot since Sarajevo"—as a BBC commentator, stunned by the impact of the news, said? Does this shot mean that the brief "moment of comparative calm" and "rising hope," of which the dead President spoke only two months ago in an address to the United Nations, will soon be over? Will the day come when we are forced to see in this tragedy a historical turning point? To think in terms of comparisons, to apply historical categories to contemporary events is tempting, for to anticipate the future is to escape the terrible reality and naked horror of a tragedy that is only too present. And it is misleading: for the future, which depends upon ourselves and our contemporaries, is unpredictable, and history begins only when the story it has to tell has come to its end.[8]

Arendt was sure that Kennedy's death would bring a change in the style of American politics. In private, to Jaspers, she worried about Johnson:

"Tactical abilities, provincial, unsuspecting," she said in the telegraphic mode she used when she was weary or despairing.[9] But, publicly, she emphasized, as did Hans Morgenthau in the same issue of the *New York Review of Books*, that American policy might stay constant while the style of American politics changed. "It was the style of everything [Kennedy] did which made his administration so strikingly different—different not in its formulation or pursuit of American policies, but rather in its estimate of politics as such." Kennedy had, with his respect for statesmanship, "bestowed upon the whole sphere of government a new prestige and a new dignity." This had been felt particularly by the intellectuals who were amazed to find themselves welcomed in Washington; when Robert Lowell returned to New York after Kennedy's inauguration, he told Hannah Arendt "America is green again."[10]

Finding an old-fashioned regard for honor and glory in a truly "modern man," a man of action, had allowed Hannah Arendt to overcome the many reservations she had had about Kennedy—"this Prince Hal," as she called him before he became president. She had been pleased when Kennedy won the 1960 Democratic party nomination because she felt that his only rival, Adlai Stevenson, was a *Nervenbundel*, a bundle of nerves. Watching the nominating conventions for the first time on television, Arendt decided that Kennedy "made by far the best speech of the conventions, in which he stressed the few generalities which happened to be true—that 'the old era is ending,' that 'the old slogans and the old delusions' will not do, that a policy pledged to the *status quo*—and this has been American policy since the end of the Second World War—will go bankrupt because 'today there is no *status quo*' in any part of the world."[11] Arendt, who was writing *On Revolution* at the time, had dedicated the book to just these generalities.

During the televised debate between Kennedy and Richard Nixon—who seemed to Arendt to be presenting himself as Mr. Average Citizen in the manner of the very Truman he had once castigated as a traitor—Arendt was disappointed with Prince Hal. Both candidates, she felt, "got caught in the details, did not know how to spell them out in light of principles." In a broadcast over Pacifica radio, Arendt argued that Kennedy failed to understand the basic principle that should underlie American policy and that he accepted what she took to be Khrushchev's ground rules: "Coexistence means competition between Russia and the United States in economic growth. Economic growth is to be measured by economic growth in Soviet Russia. This, I think, is totally wrong." Arendt hoped that the people of Soviet Russia would attain the "material condition [which is] the *sine qua non* of human dignity," and she thought that the people of America, "the first country in world history which held that poverty and misery are not part and parcel of the human condition," should wish this for the Soviet people and wish for themselves only enough economic growth to accommodate a growing population, rectify domestic inequalities, and provide stimuli to productivity in underdeveloped parts of the world.

Arendt was pleased to be able to vote for Kennedy in 1960, but the only program which "spelled out Mr. Kennedy's generalities" was, she thought, the one offered by another Republican, Rockefeller. The platform Rockefeller offered was "without ideological nonsense, such as capitalism versus socialism and vice versa, with full awareness of the crucial issues, and outside the hopelessly obsolete framework of both conservatism and liberalism."[12] This program was, in fact, one for which Hannah Arendt's *On Revolution*, published two years later, spelled out the principles.

Rockefeller's call for economic growth was free of the disastrous notion that "political freedom [is] a matter of free enterprise, differing from tyranny as the owner of two cars differs from the man who owns none." Just as importantly, he had formulated a "Marshall Plan for Latin America," and indicated that he favored confederations of free nations in Europe, the Western Hemisphere, and, eventually, Asia and Africa. To a trusting Hannah Arendt, this meant that he did not think in terms of "the European nation-state system" and that he might not, thus, be in principle opposed to revolutions. In Rockefeller's emphasis on a defense program that combined nuclear-deterrence capacity with increase in "conventional weapons for limited nonnuclear warfare," Arendt saw a policy that could bring about "stabilization of the atomic stalemate." This was, she thought, the "factual condition for coexistence" in military terms and the right way to achieve an eventual decrease in defense expenditures for America. She also saw in this program realization that conventional weapons would be crucial in the future; as she said in *On Revolution*, "if we don't perish altogether, it seems more than likely that revolution, in distinction to war, will stay with us into the forseeable future."[13] Long before total war was really possible, Clausewitz had written his *On War*; when it became possible, Arendt wrote her *On Revolution*.

Arendt saw one crucial lapse in Rockefeller's platform, and that was the one she had previously formulated in her controversial "Reflections on Little Rock": the lack of an endorsement of the sit-ins in the South—an endorsement of people's nonviolent action, taken according to the rules of assembly and association, as distinguished from action by the federal government against the governments of the Southern states. She was more of a republican than the Republicans were prepared to be, and that, paradoxically enough, brought her into sympathy with the Democrat, Kennedy, whose endorsement of the civil rights demonstrations in 1962 and 1963 Arendt completely approved.

As much as she admired Kennedy after he won the presidency, Arendt thought his recognition that "the end of an era" had come fell far short of a new policy. That revolutions were the phenomena most in need of understanding in the new era was her basic assumption; and that fear of revolutions would continue to be the "hidden *Leitmotif* of postwar American foreign policy" was her deepest worry.[14] When the Cuban revolution, which both she and Heinrich Blücher greeted with joy, brought fear in Washington, she was disappointed. In a 1962 *Partisan Review* symposium she expressed her judgment that:

we have not understood what it means when a poverty-stricken people in a backward country where corruption has been rampant for a very long time is suddenly released from the obscurity of their farms and homes, permitted to show their misery, and invited into the streets of the country's capital they never saw before. The mistake of the Cuban adventure did not lie so much in wrong information as in a conspicuous inability to comprehend the revolutionary spirit.[15]

That the Cuban revolution "fell so easily under the sway of Bolshevism" was, Arendt thought, the price of American incomprehension. She supported Kennedy's stand in the 1962 missile crisis, but with deep regret that such a crisis had ever been precipitated by the American antirevolutionary policy. "With Kennedy," she wrote to Jaspers in October 1962, "we have reason to be pleased, above all because he refused so obstinately to fall in line as long as another possibility existed."[16] She hoped improved relations with Latin America might follow the crisis, and when this did not prove the outcome, she branded America's late 1960s policy for Latin America "imperialistic" and found it completely at odds with Kennedy's professed rejection of a Pax Americana.

*Appearing in Public*

Like the many professors who became "somebodies" during the Kennedy years, and at times even influenced government policy, Hannah Arendt participated in national discussions frequently. She did not, however, seek positions of influence outside of university contexts. In the fall of 1963, while she was still deeply involved in the Eichmann controversy, she attended the Ninth Bi-Annual Conference of the United States National Commission for UNESCO to respond to a paper on contemporary revolutions, and she also gave a paper on revolution at a University of Chicago symposium on "The New Europe." She participated regularly in the annual meetings of the American Political Science Association. She joined the Columbia University Seminars as often as possible, went to conferences sponsored by *Jewish Social Studies*, and sat on the editorial board of the *American Scholar*.

Arendt made few trips to Washington, but she did attend several discussions at the Institute for Policy Studies, at the invitation of Maurice Rosenblatt, who had been with the National Committee for an Effective Congress. With John Nef and William McNeill of Chicago, Arendt went to the capital to discuss the Committee on Social Thought's remarkable program of seminars with the Presidential Office of Science and Technology. She joined the Board of the National Translation Center, sponsored by the Ford Foundation, and sometimes read translations from German sponsored by the center; and she acted as consultant for the National Endowment for the Humanities and for the National Book Awards Committee.

Most of Arendt's organizational commitments were to projects that were close by and in the hands of people she knew. In 1961 she succeeded Mary McCarthy as chairperson of Spanish Refugee Aid, an organization run by Nancy Macdonald which Arendt had supported since 1953. Dwight Macdonald was impressed: "How noble of you. I'm delighted, all the more because I know how you hate that kind of thing."[17] Arendt helped with Spanish Refugee Aid's fund raising, writing memos about the plight of the Spanish Civil War refugees in France and about those in Algiers who were displaced for a second time by the French-Algerian conflict. She was pleased that the organization was able to help with funds for a Spanish refugee center, the Foyer Pablo Casals, built in the French town that had once offered Hannah Arendt and Heinrich Blücher shelter, Montauban.

Dwight Macdonald also solicited Arendt's signature for a number of open letters. Along with over a dozen other New York intellectuals, they sent a protest to Soviet Premier Kosygin in 1966, when two dissident writers, Sinyavsky and Daniyel, were arrested for sending manuscripts out of the Soviet Union. Their trial and convictions constituted, Arendt said in a statement to the press, an "ugly reminder of something one had hoped had passed into history."[18] As this hope was continually thwarted, Arendt continued to provide money and support for Soviet dissenters through various committees, including Amnesty International and, in the late 1960s, PEN, whose executive board she eventually joined. The last contribution Arendt made, just two months before her death, was to the International Sakharov Hearing. She then told the director of the Radio Liberty Committee: "I believe that every development in the intellectual opposition in Soviet Russia is of great importance, and I consider Mr. Sakharov perhaps the most important member of this group, which doesn't mean that I have anything against Solzhenitsyn except that I am not sure Pan-Slavism will work."[19]

Arendt contributed generously to various causes, and often to the United Jewish Appeal and the Israel Emergency Fund—particularly during the 1967 war in the Middle East. But most of the money she gave went to individuals. The philanthropic foundation her neighbor from Königsberg, Julie Braun-Vogelstein, had established in memory of her brother was Hannah Arendt's "front organization." She arranged for the Vogelstein Foundation to offer grants, and then she supplied the foundation with funds. With this indirect support, her part-time secretary went to the New School for a master's degree, the son of her girlhood friend Hella Jaensch went to college in California, a young Austrian refugee she had met in Berkeley received college tuition, the son of her black maid Sally Davis went to a private school in Brooklyn, and the photographer Ricarda Schwerin received grants for photographic expeditions in Europe. Without secrecy, in her "Tante Hannah" role, she provided for Hans Jonas's children in her will—until Jonas received a reparations grant from the German government—and gave gifts to the Klenbort children and to the children of her cousin, Ernst Fuerst. For the other "children," her students, there were scholarships arranged, job interviews requested, and dinners given to celebrate degrees earned.

Hannah Arendt's preference was always for the small and the private. She lectured widely and went to many conferences, but all the while she was happiest with a discussion group that consisted of only four members. This was the "Greek Circle," a *Graeca* like the one she had had as a *Gymnasium* student.[20] She met once a week for many years with her editor at Viking Books, Denver Lindley, his art-historian friend, Fredrick M. Clapp, called "Tim," the founding director of the Frick Collection,

and the medievalist Helene Wieruszowski. From these sessions for translating and talking, Arendt gathered many of the details that made the
footnotes of her books almost as interesting as the texts proper, but what
she valued most was the privacy of their meetings.

Arendt was given honorary degrees at a dozen American universities,
accepted into the National Institute for Arts and Letters and the American
Academy of Arts and Sciences, awarded the Emerson-Thoreau Medal of
the American Academy in 1969, and—to her great surprise—presented
with the 1967 Sigmund Freud Preis of the Deutsche Akadamie für
Sprache und Dichtung. For sympathy toward the work of Sigmund
Freud, Hannah Arendt would certainly never have won a prize, but the
academy's citation was for excellence in German prose, and nothing
could have pleased her more. "You know," she told the academy's general secretary, "that I had to leave Germany more than thirty-four years
ago. One's mother tongue is all that one can take along from one's old
home, and I have with great effort tried to keep this unique, irreplaceable
thing intact and vital. The Academy's prize is like a recognition that this
has been well done."[21] Whenever Hannah Arendt accepted American
awards, her peers realized that German had been well kept by her, for in
the difficult business of accepting awards she waxed very Germanic. Each
acceptance speech she made began with a complex reflection on the
relation of private feelings, public recognition, the smiles of Fortuna, the
judgment of peers. All were variations on the opening of her first acceptance speech, for the 1959 Lessing Prize, made in German:

I can ignore entirely the delicate question of merit. In this very respect an honor
gives us a forcible lesson in modesty; for it implies that it is not for us to judge our
merits as we judge the merits and accomplishments of others. In awards, the
world speaks out, and if we accept the award and speak our gratitude for it, we
can do so only by ignoring ourselves and acting entirely within the framework of
our attitude toward the world, toward a world and public to which we owe the
space into which we speak and in which we are heard. But the honor not only
reminds us emphatically of the gratitude we owe the world; it also, to a very high
degree, obligates us to it.[22]

In the years when she was most often in public, Hannah Arendt formulated several rules for herself. She responded to all requests from public
relations enterprises with a standard phrase: "I am allergic to public relations." To all editors who requested reviews of books she did not like or
thought would involve her in acrimonious disputes, she sent off her

second rule: "I have a funny rule, never to review a book I do not respect."[23] There was a special rule developed for discussions of *Eichmann in Jerusalem*: she would not allow anyone who had not read the book to sit around a table she shared with readers; all spectators had to sit outside the circle and agree to be silent. She did radio interviews only with people she knew or who were known to her friends. She often refused to have transcripts from tape recordings of her lectures or discussions made available because she did not think that she was as precise on her feet as she could be in writing, and she refused to appear on television in America because she did not want to "have a face that is recognized on the street."

The television rule was broken twice. Once, shortly before her death, she agreed to make an educational television program with a group from Yale University, on the condition that she be filmed from behind—so the rule was, really, only half broken. But the other time was complete. She joined the young Swiss author of *The Deputy*, Rolf Hochhuth, for a "Camera Three" interview program on 15 March 1964. This breach of the rules was made to help a man who found himself in the same situation Arendt had been in after the Eichmann controversy swept into her life. When Karl Jaspers sent her a copy of Hochhuth's play in the fall of 1963 and informed her about the controversy it had stirred in Europe, he made the comparison explicit: "You both live now as though behind a facade, which you display to the world."[24] Jaspers had joined Hochhuth for a radio appearance in Switzerland and tried to do for his countryman what he later did publicly for Hannah Arendt—that is, to dispel misunderstandings and bring out the real issues *The Deputy* posed. Hannah Arendt took up the effort with an article for the 13 February 1964 *New York Herald Tribune* and then agreed to the television show.

The explosive subject of Hochhuth's drama was, as Arendt summarized it, "the alleged failure of Pope Pius XII to make an unequivocal public statement on the massacre of the European Jews during World War II, and . . . by implication Vatican policy toward the Third Reich."[25] The pope's silence meant that Jews—and Catholics—went to the gas chambers, as Hochhuth wrote, "abandoned by everyone, abandoned even by the Vicar of Christ." What practical difference an unequivocal statement from the pope might have made was and is a matter of speculation; what was at issue for Hochhuth was why the pope remained silent. The question rang out in theaters all over Europe after the initial Berlin production of *The Deputy* by Erwin Piscator had sent shock waves through Germany. Thousands of articles flooded European newspapers, and the American response was voluminous after the New York premiere. "It is almost certainly the largest storm ever raised by a play in the whole history of the drama," Eric Bentley remarked in his introduction to an anthology of reactions, *The Storm over "The Deputy."*

The most extreme misunderstanding of Hochhuth's play was like the most extreme misunderstanding of Hannah Arendt's *Eichmann in Jerusalem*: he was accused of holding the pope responsible for the Final Solution as she was accused of holding the Jews responsible for their own destruction. In New York, Cardinal Spellman, who admitted that he had not read Hochhuth's play, issued a statement to the press in which he claimed that the play "in effect holds Pius XII guilty of the Nazi crimes."[26] Hannah Arendt, who was keenly aware of the parallel, charged both misunderstandings to "those who have an interest in confusing the issues" through "propaganda lies." She told a correspondent: "You find the same propaganda lie spread about my book *Eichmann in Jerusalem*. Interest groups say about the Hochhuth play that Hochhuth presented the pope as being responsible for the massacre of the Jews, and they said I depicted the Jews as being responsible for their own massacre. If Hochhuth or I had said such things, we would have been insane. But, by telling such lies, people create an 'image' which is easy to refute because it is nonsense."[27] Arendt may very well have exaggerated the role of interest groups in both controversies, underestimating how easy it is for people to misunderstand without the help of institutional propaganda when their own deep needs are involved. But she had occasions to be suspicious—for example when she discovered that an inflammatory National Catholic Welfare Organization pamphlet had been written by a member of the B'nai B'rith Anti-Defamation League. Arendt suspected that the rule at work was "one hand washes the other, so that all the hands are clean."[28] But she did not have sufficient reason to conclude that there was a conspiracy to absolve either Jews or Catholics of their responsibilities—not, of course, for the Final Solution, but for what they did and did not tell their followers about the Final Solution.

Arendt saw one important difference between the Eichmann controversy and the storm over *The Deputy*: "It has been Rolf Hochhuth's good fortune that a considerable part of Catholic learned and public opinion has sided with him." This weight of opinion helped make "all protest that passivity was the best policy because it was the lesser evil, or that [Hochhuth's] disclosure of the truth comes at the 'wrong psychological moment' . . . of no avail." With some desire no doubt that such support might have come for her vision of "the whole truth" about the role of Europe's Jewish leadership, Arendt quoted the remark made by the Austrian Catholic scholar Friedrich Heer about *The Deputy*: "Only the truth will make us free. The whole truth, which is always awful."[29]

Hannah Arendt was not an uncritical admirer of Hochhuth's play; she thought it was dramatically cumbersome and put too much stress on Pope Pius XII's character. Hochhuth implied that a better man would have made a better decision, while she considered that the pope did "what most, though not all, secular rulers did under the circumstances." Jaspers, too, noted that "the Church and the papacy... [as] human institutions... did not behave any better or worse than all other political authorities."[30] Both Arendt and Jaspers spoke with one of the main—and most misunderstood—themes of *Eichmann in Jerusalem* in mind. Using the wording of her own book, she suggested that "the Vatican and its nuncios apparently thought it wise to affect rigid adherence to a normality that no longer existed, in view of the collapse of the whole moral and spiritual structure of Europe." In such a situation, Arendt thought, good men can do the worst, or certainly not the best; do the lesser evil not realizing that it cannot result in any good.

Again and again, Hannah Arendt sounded this theme. It was central to the address entitled "Personal Responsibility Under Dictatorship" which she delivered during 1964 at a number of American universities and over both BBC Radio in England and Pacifica Radio in America. She gave this address in the year after John Kennedy's death, with his realization, enunciated in 1960, that "the *status quo* no longer exists" in mind. She knew that the *status quo* of cold war between America and Russia did not exist in 1964 but she did not then see that America's "counterinsurgency" operation in Vietnam was the beginning of a new world situation. Her attention was not "between past and future"; it was on the past.

During the years 1964, 1965, and 1966, Arendt was, for the first time since 1946, not writing a book. She was travelling, lecturing, and teaching at an exhausting pace, but for her it was an *Arbeitspause*—just what she had desired since the time when she told Karl Jaspers that preparing two manuscripts, *Eichmann in Jerusalem* and *On Revolution*, for the same deadline was too much. "You once said," she reminded Jaspers, "that no one really overworks himself, and I repeat this as my epigram every day."[31]

The *Arbeitspause*, such as it was, gave Arendt a chance to take up a project that had been sitting in her desk drawer for four years. During her 1961 stay at Northwestern University, just before she went to Jerusalem, Arendt had prepared a seminar on Bertolt Brecht. Her friend, the literary critic Erich Heller, had tangled with her over the difficult question of Brecht's attitude toward Stalin—what she called his "temptation to be good"—and she had presented her view to one of Heller's seminars at Northwestern. She told William Shawn, who published her article on Brecht in the *New Yorker*: "I wrote the piece originally out of anger with a friend of mine . . . who thought he could throw Brecht out the window, and because of his 'sins' he was generous enough to let me address his students. I had to do it very quickly and mostly quoting from memory, and after had it retyped."[32]

Erich Heller was not convinced. Years later he fondly described the scene: "It may well be one of those occasions when Hannah Arendt put her very great intelligence into the service of an erroneous judgment; and when this happened, she was never simply wrong, she exploded into wrongness, with angry sparks flying about."[33] Theirs was a cordial disagreement, but the conflicts that came in the wake of Hannah Arendt's essay were not friendly. Her reflections on the case of Bertolt Brecht made Sidney Hook, who had exploded several times in the past over the case of Hannah Arendt, angry. Hook had been the object of one of Hannah Arendt's judgments because he had considered Brecht a firm Stalinist in the 1930s, citing as evidence a startling remark Brecht made to him about the defendants in the Moscow trials: "The more innocent they are, the more they deserve to die." Arendt thought that the "tricky" Bert Brecht had meant that anyone who had not opposed Stalin—that is, anyone who really *was* innocent of the crime he was charged with—bore some guilt; "there was some justice in the injustice," she said. In a letter to *Merkur*, where Arendt's article appeared in German, Hook claimed that the conversation took place in 1935, before the Moscow trials, and that Brecht was referring to the members of the political opposition to Stalin. "Only one word describes Hannah Arendt's effort to obliterate Brecht's remark and to use it as an index for his anti-Stalinist sentiments: *Unverschämtheit*, shamelessness." Arendt pointed out that Hook had not been clear about whom Brecht had had in mind—which defendants, accused of what—and that he was using the single sentence to press his own case against Brecht in a point-scoring way which had "nothing in common with thinking."[34]

On the other side of the case of Bertolt Brecht was John Willet, coeditor of the English edition of Brecht's collected works, who set out to prove that Brecht had not praised Stalin. After Arendt's essay appeared in the *New Yorker*, Willet wrote, asking her to cite her sources in the Brecht corpus. His query about Brecht's praise of Stalin and Arendt's claim that there were "odes to Stalin" went unanswered, and he raised the question again when her essay reappeared in *Men in Dark Times*.[35] Arendt then replied, citing her sources. Willet, not satisfied, wrote an open letter to the *Times Literary Supplement*. The *New York Times* reported on this letter, and interviewed Hannah Arendt for her response—which was that she was "quite satisfied" that her scholarship was not inaccurate or deceptive. She was also quite sure that mere scholarship was of no help for making judgments.[36]

Hannah Arendt had questioned Brecht's independence, his ability—or willingness—to stand back from the political realm and "say what is," "teach acceptance of things as they are." As she said in "Truth and Politics," the next essay she wrote after the Brecht piece, "out of this acceptance, which can also be called truthfulness, arises the faculty of judgment." Judgments of political matters, moral matters, and aesthetic matters all presuppose the capacity for impartiality and for what Kant called enlarged mentality, having other people's standpoints present in one's imagination. Arendt refused to think that a poet could forsake truthfulness and not himself be forsaken by the Muses, the goddesses of poetry. Neither Hook nor Willet called this position into question— which is why Arendt made her short-tempered remarks about Hook's polemicalness and Willet's membership in the club of "Brecht scholars." Only Heller raised the possibility that Brecht's loss of poetic power might have come from other sources than the loss of the Muses, "even possibilities as obvious as aging or preoccupation with other matters (as, for instance, running a theatre and training actors) or alcohol or drugs." Heller's suggestions were, from her point of view, "too psychological." As he said: "No, it had to do with ethics, and she was lovable and admirable in her moral resolution."[37]

Arendt began to work on the essay called "Truth and Politics" in 1965; it was her answer to the Eichmann controversy and her assertion of the importance for politics of the "disinterested pursuit of truth." She presented the essay at Emory University, Eastern Michigan University, St. John's College in Annapolis, and Wesleyan University. At each stop on her lecture route she gathered reactions to the Eichmann controversy, and she incorporated her reflections into an epilogue for the second edition of her book and a foreword for the German edition, and into the final version of her "Truth and Politics" essay. Arendt finished the essay during a semester at Cornell University in the fall of 1965 and then delivered the final version of it as an address to the 1966 American Political Science Association meeting. She had waited to present the essay until the last major flare-up of the controversy, the publication of Jacob Robinson's *The Crooked Shall Be Made Straight* and her reply to it through the *New York Review of Books*, had died away.

In the spring of 1966, after she had replied to several letters sent to the *New York Review of Books*, Arendt told Jaspers: "Now, hopefully, it is closed. The comical thing is that, after I openly spoke my opinion, I am flooded with letters from all the Jewish organizations with invitations to speak, to appear at congresses, and so forth—even from those I have attacked. Also, the Hebrew edition of *Eichmann* is finally out in Israel. I think that the war between me and the Jews is over."[38] This judgment was a little premature, as there was a strong reaction in France to the publication of the French edition by Gallimard in 1966. The year before, the organizers of a large exhibition at the museum of the Memorial of the Unknown Jewish Martyr in Paris had indicated that their exhibition was "not intended as a rebuttal of Dr. Arendt though it constituted one." At the opening ceremony, Nahum Goldmann claimed that Arendt and other writers had misrepresented what the exhibition—"Jews in the Struggle against Hitlerism"—represented correctly.[39] When the French edition of *Eichmann in Jerusalem* was issued, the attempts to refute were less extensive but more shocking. *Le Nouvel Observateur*, for example, ran two pages of letters under the title "Hannah Arendt, est-elle une Nazi?" But, in America, the Eichmann controversy died down in 1966 and then disappeared with the 1967 war in the Middle East. The issues, of course, remained, and they were presented in contexts as diverse as novels—Saul Bellow's *Mr. Sammler's Planet*—plays—Robert Shaw's *Man in a Glass Booth*—conferences on the Holocaust, and college courses. Arendt herself retired from the field. When she was offered two volumes on the Nazi period to review in 1969 she said, simply, that she had "the feeling that I've done my share in trying to understand and come to terms with the whole period. Let others try now."[40]

## On Revolution

During the summer of 1966 Arendt went to Palenville for two months of swimming, walking, and visiting with the tribe members. She was relaxed except for the few times she became panicky about Blücher's health—once, for example, refusing to go on a Sunday drive because he looked pale. She preferred to stay at the Chestnut Lawn House, free of any travel anxiety, content with light fiction—she read Agatha Christie and Simenon, while Blücher went through half-a-dozen of his favorites, Westerns. Arendt also read the two volumes of Peter Nettl's brilliant biography of Rosa Luxemburg which Robert Silvers of the *New York Review of Books* had suggested she review.

As she read, Arendt underlined and made marginal notes, marking surprising passages from Rosa Luxemburg's correspondence, quarreling with Nettl, and clearly enjoying coming to know better a spirit she found so kindred. Where Nettl remarked "Curiously, her work was largely free of slogans," Arendt put a huffy "indeed" in the margin to defend Rosa Luxemburg's seriousness. Where he simply recorded that "with regard to trade unions, Rosa Luxemburg once again followed the classical Marxist notion of limiting their role," Arendt added her judgment: "and was *wrong.*" She pointed out to Nettl how many of Luxemburg's theses were "anti-Marxist"—particularly her thesis that capitalist reproduction is impossible in a closed economy and must reach out imperialistically to underdeveloped, precapitalist economies—and chastised him for "still complaining" when he argued that Rosa Luxemburg was only a critic and not a political theorist with an alternative vision of socialism. In the margins, Arendt recorded her agreement with observations about beliefs and methods she and Luxemburg shared: "[She] was more afraid of a deformed revolution than an unsuccessful one"; "She was at all times concerned with the ethics of revolution"; "She always began with an historical analysis." The details Nettle provided about Rosa Luxemburg's "Polish peer group," the Polish Social Democrats who were "a group of intellectual peers long before [they] became a political party," fascinated Arendt, as did the portrait of Luxemburg's companion Leo Jogiches, who was the "one and only one person with complete access [to her], from whom nothing must be hidden."[41]

Arendt decided to review the biography and spent the last part of the summer writing "not quite a small book, thank God."[42] The contributions Blücher made to the article were enormous; the article in part his statement about the German revolution of 1918/19, the revolution of his youth, as it was in part Arendt's statement about the Blücher-like mainstay of Rosa Luxemburg's life, Leo Jogiches. But the most provocative parts of the review were given over to a discussion of Rosa Luxemburg's political ideas and their abiding value.

Arendt considered many of Rosa Luxemburg's most controversial ideas—called "errors" by many Marxists—including her positions on the "national question," the controversy between the revolutionists and the reformists, and the "mass strike" tactic. These discussions led up to the "republican question," which separated Luxemburg most decisively from all others: "Here she was completely alone, though less obviously so, in her stress on the absolute necessity of not only individual but public freedom under all circumstances."[43] What Rosa Luxemburg learned from the 1905 Russian revolution and the workers' councils that sprang up in it was the value of "spontaneity" and the principle that "good organization does not precede action but is the product of it." What she did not conclude, while Lenin did, was that revolutions in nonindustrialized countries can be effectively led by small, tightly organized groups, and that a war can create revolutionary conditions and is thus to be welcomed as a precipitant. Rosa Luxemburg could never accept the utility of war, and she argued the point with Lenin during the First World War: she "did not believe in a victory in which the people at large had no part and no voice."

And haven't events proved her right? Isn't the history of the Soviet Union one long demonstration of the frightful dangers of "deformed revolutions?" Hasn't the "moral collapse" which she foresaw—without, of course, foreseeing the sheer criminality of Lenin's successor—done more harm to the cause of revolution as she understood it than "any and every political defeat . . . in honest struggle against superior forces and in the teeth of the historical situation" could possibly have done? Wasn't it true that Lenin was "completely mistaken" in the means he employed, that the only way to salvation was the "school of public life itself, the most unlimited, the broadest democracy and public opinion," and that terror "demoralized" everybody and destroyed everything?

These were the questions Hannah Arendt had put to herself as she wrote *On Revolution*, which ended with an ardent advocacy of republicanism and of spontaneous and voluntary associations within republics.

Republicanism was the core of Arendt's survey of Rosa Luxemburg's political ideas, but she was also careful to set out in some detail the consequences of Luxemburg's non-Marxist theory of the inevitability of imperialism: "Hence, capitalism was not a closed system that generated its own contradictions and was 'pregnant with revolution'; it fed on outside factors [precapitalist economies], and its *automatic* collapse could occur, if at all, only when the whole surface of the earth was conquered and could be devoured." As Arendt noted in the margin by Nettl's discussion of *The Accumulation of Capital*, "the 3rd factor destroys the dialectical process." Arendt had used this theory of Rosa Luxemburg's in the imperialism section of *The Origins of Totalitarianism*, and she continued to hold it in 1966, when she judged that the American involvement in Vietnam, escalating while she wrote, and the American policies in Latin America, so contrary to the country's "old anticolonial sentiments," were imperialistic. [44]

Peter Nettl was very perplexed by the fact that Rosa Luxemburg did not relate her economic analysis of capitalism and its consequent imperialism to her political programs. He noted that in this instance, as in Luxemburg's earlier contributions to the revisionist debate, there was a "methodological and analytical break between politics and economics." One way to overcome the break was to transpose her economic formulae into the political field; and this was done by hostile critics who manufactured a doctrine, Luxemburgism, in which "spontaneity" was taken to mean that a revolutionary party had no real role in an *automatic* process—an "every-man-his-own-party" anarchism. Nettl pointed out that Luxemburgism was a Bolshevist travesty invented to dismiss Rosa Luxemburg as a theorist. But he did not find another way to reconcile her political program and her economic analysis. Hannah Arendt did not consider the problem, though she claimed that Lenin's assessment of the imperialism theory was a "fundamental error" and not sufficient to refute "an eminently faithful description of things as they really were."

The problem Nettl saw did not exist for Hannah Arendt because of the assumptions she made about Rosa Luxemburg's thinking. She thought that Luxemburg had given up the Marxist "theory of crises," that her break with Marxism was both economic and political, and that "her commitment to revolution was a primarily moral matter." This meant, Arendt said, "that she remained passionately engaged in public life and civil affairs, in the destinies of the world. Her involvement with European politics outside the immediate interests of the working class, and hence completely beyond the horizon of all Marxists, appears most convincingly in her repeated insistence on a 'republican programme' for the German and Russian Parties." Arendt saw Luxemburg's political program— republicanism—as a corollary of her rejection of the Marxist economic dialectic, the antithetical relation of capitalists and proletarians. In Hannah Arendt's own terms, republicanism was a political ideal that transcended all the Marxist visions of either capitalism or socialism.

Building on Rosa Luxemburg's insight that capitalism is not a process which begins from a unique expropriation by the nascent bourgeoisie and then continues ineluctably to the point of collapse, Arendt emphasized that expropriation is repeated again and again. There is only one way to stop it:

All our experiences—as distinguished from theories and ideologies—tell us that the process of expropriation which started with the rise of capitalism does not stop with the expropriation of the means of production; only legal and political institutions that are independent of economic forces and their automatism can control and check the inherently monstrous possibilities of this process. . . . What protects freedom is the division between governmental and economic power, or, to put it in Marxian language, the fact that the state and its constitution are not superstructures.[45]

What protects freedom, Arendt concluded, is a republic with a constitution. She had argued in *On Revolution*, and implied in this passage from a 1969 interview, that a "rational, nonideological economic development" is possible, and that a republic must achieve it and keep it.[46]

Arendt's review of Nettl's biography was an epilogue to *On Revolution*. And the year it was published, 1966, was one in which the topic of revolutionary theory and practice was central to both academic political science and American policy debates. In the late 1960s, *On Revolution* itself found new audiences.

Published in the spring of 1963, shortly after *Eichmann in Jerusalem* had appeared in the *New Yorker*, *On Revolution* was an overshadowed sibling. But its main point was not lost on reviewers. The historian Hans Kohn, one of Judah Magnes's supporters and a man whose criticisms of nationalism were much like Arendt's, summarized the book's argument for readers of the *New York Times Book Review*: "The contest today in the world is not about economic systems but about freedom and authoritarianism. This Dr. Arendt makes abundantly clear."[47] There were few reviewers, however, who were willing to let such a claim go unchallenged, and even fewer who thought that the claim was based on cogent political or historical analyses. "Needless to say, [*On Revolution*] has been almost completely ignored by the professionals," Arendt told Norman Jacobson, the Berkeley political scientist whose interest in John Adams had been suggestive to Arendt in 1955, when she began to consider writing her book.[48]

Many professionals agreed with E. J. Hobsbawm's opinion that historians or sociologists would be "irritated, as the author plainly is not, by a certain lack of interest in mere fact... a preference for metaphysical construct or poetic feeling over reality."[49] Many aspects of the book drew criticism: Arendt's claim that the American Revolution was, in fact, a revolution—something which, at least since de Tocqueville, has been much disputed—and also an ideal one; her assessment of the heritage of the French Revolution; her interpretation of Rousseau and the French revolutionary theorists; her neglect of Marxian categories; her failure to discuss the role of religious establishments in America, or even to mention the existence of classes. Those who pressed past the factual questions focused on the point Hans Kohn had summarized, arguing that Arendt's distinction between matters economic and matters political was either theoretically misguided, or, for all practical purposes, conservative. "Arendt seems to be working, with her formidable arsenal of knowledge and insight, toward a kind of Burkean Toryism, with overtones of nostalgia for an agrarian, hierarchic society of freeholders and eloquent town councils," wrote the ubiquitous critic George Steiner.[50]

Few of Arendt's readers considered why she had come up with what seemed to them such an odd combination of progressive and conservative ideas based on such a questionable historical foundation. Only Bernard Crick of the University of London, who thought of Arendt as "the most original mind in modern political literature," not only admitted that he was embarrassed by Arendt's admiration of the Founding Fathers, but offered an explanation: "Every German American does it once in gratitude."[51] *On Revolution* was, certainly, an act of gratitude. Arendt's portrait of the Founding Fathers was fabulous in the literal sense of the word, but her fable was of a very specific sort: a political fable. Merle Fainsod, a political scientist, was one of the few who recognized that Arendt's lack of concern with "the history of revolutions as such, with their past, their origins and course of development" was intentional and that she was concerned with what he called "meaningful revolution"— meaningful for the present and future. In Arendt's words: "We want to learn what a revolution is—its general implications for man as a *political* being, its *political* significance for the world we live in, its role in modern history."[52]

Jaspers, who had once admitted to Arendt that if he could be anything other than a German he would be an American and who was often mentally in exile in America, read her fable for the political one it was. After struggling with her text—"die englische Sprache!" he sighed—he wrote his reaction to the book he called, because of its dedication, "also Gertrud's and my book": "I grasp the main feature of your intention. It seems to me a book that in the profundity of its political conviction, mastery and accomplishment, stands near, perhaps above, your totalitarianism book. . . . On the whole, your vision is, finally, a tragedy— which does not leave you without hope."[53] Blücher's judgment, written as he sent his wife the proof-pages produced from her much reworked manuscript, was similar: "It is, so to speak, looking better, and really is, as [Alfred] Kazin said, your best book. Clear, well-presented, good political judgment. If it has an effect, it will be one of long duration."[54] Jaspers and Blücher saw that *On Revolution* was a book of warning, a cautionary tale, an effort to preserve the political realm and the council-system, the "lost treasure" of revolutions.

*On Revolution* did have a delayed effect, but it was a mixed and muted one. The book was widely read in the mid- and late-1960s by students interested in political theory. At Berkeley, in the early days of the free speech movement, Arendt's book and Albert Camus's *The Rebel* were virtually required reading. The students responded to Arendt's advocacy of what the American Students for a Democratic Society called "participatory democracy" and what Rudi Dutschke of the German SDS (Socialist Students League) called "Democracy at the bottom"—councils of people everywhere, discussing and deciding. The book was discussed in student publications and in peace movement journals like *Peace News*. But, like the socialist Michael Harrington, who had reviewed *On Revolution* for the *Village Voice* in 1964, many who accepted the last part of the book, "The Revolutionary Tradition and its Lost Treasure," rejected the first part, with its critique of the social revolutionaries' overriding concern with "the Social Question." "Arendt *si*; Arendt, *no*," concluded Harrington, and many concurred.[55]

Some of Arendt's readers who became involved with community organizing in the late 1960s adapted her work to their projects. A New York group, working in Brooklyn, established a journal called the *Public Life* and acknowledged their debt to two American political theorists: Thomas Jefferson and Hannah Arendt. One member of this group, Walter Karp, went on to write political analyses of the American party-system, *Indispensable Enemies*, for example, which were grounded in Arendt's discussions of the council-system. She, in turn, recommended to her own admirers the work of those who came to their theoretical conclusions after much practical experience, like Milton Kotler, whose 1969 book *Neighborhood Government* was far ahead of its time.

Among academic political theorists, *On Revolution* was widely read but much criticized. In theoretical terms, as opposed to the terms of political organizers, *On Revolution* was problematic because of its method. Hannah Arendt practiced a kind of phenomenology, though she seldom used the term and usually felt that the less said about method the better. "I am a sort of phenomenologist," she once said to a student, "but, ach, not in Hegel's way—or Husserl's." When she studied political phenomena—revolutions, in this case—she assumed that each had essential characteristics and that a perception of these characteristics was possible. For such a perception, words were a good place to begin, not because conceptual language reveals the phenomenon in any straightforward way, but because, as Heidegger maintained, words carry the record of past perceptions, true or untrue, revelatory or distorting. Thus Arendt pointed out that "revolution" originally meant restoration, but during the course of the eighteenth century "revolution" gained its definitive spirit: *new* beginnings. She assumed that if different words exist for phenomena, the phenomena are distinct. But she also assumed that if words for distinct phenomena have come to be used synonymously there is a reason for the confusion, that is, that some overriding concept has subsumed the different words. She noted, for example, that "power," "strength," "force," "authority" and "violence" have lost their clarity because of a conviction that "the most crucial political issue is, and always has been, the question of Who rules Whom?" The various words indicate "the means by which man rules over man; they are held to be synonyms because they have the same function."[56]

In the 1960s academic critics often referred to Arendt's method as "essentialism" and they questioned it in much the same way that more empirically minded critics and opponents of "Germanic" metaphysicality had questioned Max Weber's method of constructing ideal types. Her concept of revolution was seen as an unjustified generalization which neglected key differences among phenomena. Her claim that a revolution is characterized, essentially, by a rebellion and then an act of political foundation for the preservation of freedom was called idealistic, metaphysical, antisocialist, antiprogressive, anti-Marxist.

To take just one representative example: Chalmers Johnson criticized "the extreme imprecision and narrowness of Arendt's idea of freedom used to *define* revolutions." He thought that "the constructing of definitions at the outset is a sterile and often tautological balancing of different impressions." In his 1966 book, *Revolutionary Change*, and elsewhere, Johnson constructed a typology of revolutions which included conspiratorial coups d'état, mass peasant risings, millenarian rebellions (utopist rebellions led by messianic figures), reactionary rebellions or restorations, the rare "Jacobin Communist Revolution," as well as the new type of revolution in the twentieth century, "militarized mass insurrection" led by a guerrilla elite. The goal of revolutions in Arendt's terms—constitution-making—is, of course, not essential to these types; but "who rules whom?" is common to them all, regardless of their historical periods. Johnson thought that all revolutions involve the overthrow of an "intransigent elite"—that is, they involve a change of rulership. Like most theorists, Johnson accepted a premise that Arendt rejected, a definition of politics as "a struggle for power," in which "the ultimate kind of power is violence," as C. Wright Mills wrote in *The Power Elite*. [57]

Hannah Arendt discussed revolutions not in order to outline their histories or distinguish their types but in order to present an ideal for practice. She was as opposed to the view of politics as a power struggle as she was to the idea embraced by many young people who rejected power politics and sought a more personal mode. She argued with her professional social-science critics, on the one hand, and with "the new ones" on the other. Commenting on one of her Chicago students' papers, she took her stance clearly: "At the end of your paper you finally define your notion of politics, and you say that it is a 'mode of self-expression.' I don't doubt that many people agree with this definition, especially among the young; I certainly don't." [58]

## Reviewing Totalitarianism

While *On Revolution* was finding a cool reception among many historians and social scientists, *The Origins of Totalitarianism*, where Arendt had first practiced her method, was being reconsidered by political scientists who found Arendt's concepts problematic for similar reasons. Both books were criticized by those loosely described, by adherents and critics alike, as revisionists. With the later book the concept in question was "revolution," with the earlier it was "totalitarianism."

Throughout the 1950s the most widely discussed postwar studies were Arendt's book and *Totalitarian Dictatorship and Autocracy* by Carl J. Friedrich and Zbigniew K. Brzezinski. Especially during the McCarthy years, the most hotly debated issue was the extent to which Nazism and Bolshevism were similar as forms of government. By the beginning of the 1960s the general term totalitarianism was rejected by many as vague and polemically anti-Communist. The reasons for this rejection had been articulated in the 1950s, but, as the cold war climate lifted, the rejectors became more vocal and influential. By 1968, the second edition of the *Encyclopedia of the Social Sciences* carried an entry on "Totalitarianism" by Herbert J. Spiro, who ventured the prophecy that "a third encyclopedia of the social sciences, like the first one [in 1935], will not list 'totalitarianism.'"[59]

When it was published, Arendt's *The Origins of Totalitarianism* had been criticized by leftists and liberals for its claim that "up to now we know only two authentic forms of totalitarian domination: the dictatorship of National Socialism after 1938, and the dictatorship of Bolshevism since 1930." That National Socialism was totalitarian was not at issue; the nature of Stalinism was. The historian H. Stuart Hughes, who praised the book highly, questioned Arendt's knowledge of Soviet economic history: "If she had consulted some of the professional economic analyses, she might have been less ready to dismiss the first Five Year Plan [1928–1933] as 'insanity.'"[60] Arendt had, in fact, consulted the most thoroughly documented study then available, Dallin and Nicolaevsky's *Forced Labor in Soviet Russia*. Reviewing the book for the *Review of Politics*, Arendt argued as she had in her book that "no other aspect of totalitarian regimes is more difficult to grasp than its emancipation from the profit motive and its nonutilitarian character in economic matters."[61] To the annoyance of her later revisionist critics, including H. Stuart Hughes, who had in the meantime decided that Arendt's book was amateurish, "over-wrought, highly colored and constantly projecting interpretations too bold for the data to bear,"[62] Arendt restated her opinion with new evidence in the last edition, 1968. "Finally," she wrote in the 1968 preface, "all doubts one might still have nourished about the amount of truth in the current theory, according to which the terror of the late twenties and thirties was 'the high price of suffering' exacted by industrialization and economic progress, are laid to rest by this glimpse into the actual state of affairs and the course of events in one particular region [provided by Fainsod's *Smolensk under Soviet Rule*]."[63] After she had reviewed the documents and studies which had appeared between 1949 and 1968, Arendt was convinced that "the Nazi and Bolshevik systems look even more than before like variations of the same model."

While Arendt stood her ground on the matter of Soviet economic policy, her critics, rather than analyzing the policy in any detail, tried to attribute her assessment to what Hughes called cold war hysteria. Hughes's attack, recorded in *The Sea Change*, is a summary and collection of paraphrases of articles written during the 1960s. From a piece by Adler and Paterson provocatively entitled "Red Fascism: The Merger of Nazi Germany and Soviet Russia in the American Image of Totalitarianism, 1930s–1950s," Hughes took the following explanation: "In the late 1940s and early 1950s, the term ['totalitarianism'] served to ease the shock of emotional readjustment for Americans or Englishmen—or émigrés—who had just defeated one enemy and were now called upon by their governments to confront another. If it could be proved that Nazism and Communism were very much the same thing, then the cold war against the late ally would be justified by the rhetoric that had proved so effective against the late enemy."[64] Arendt's review of the literature in 1968 and her reasons for arguing (long after the supposed "shock of emotional readjustment") that the Nazi and Bolshevik systems were variations of the same model were not noted in Hughes's argument.

Through all of the articles attacking the "unitotalitarianism" theory, as Robert Burrowes called it, runs a theme of annoyed, defensive ideological critique.[65] Adler and Paterson, in their "Red Fascism" piece, summarized it: "Miss Arendt... avoided the important distinction between one system proclaiming a humanistic ideology and failing to live up to its ideal and the other living up to its antihumanistic and destructive ideology all too well."[66] This seems to be the crux of the revisionist complaint against Arendt, that she failed to see in Bolshevist Russia Marxism gone haywire, a good ideology perverted. To brand "totalitarianism" as a shibboleth enforcing cold war attitudes in America, was to release Marxism, as an ideology, from anathema. But Arendt's insight rested on another level: when a nation's means overwhelm its end, as when good men do the worst after adopting a "less evil" means, the result, not the motive, is what matters. This level was not touched by her revisionist critics.

A less politically charged version of what the political scientist Michael Curtius labeled the "Retreat from Totalitarianism" emerged during the 1960s. What Curtius and others found troubling about the concept "totalitarianism" was not that it stood in the way of appreciation for Marxism as an ideology, but that it was, when first used, less than adequate to describe reality and, after Stalin's death, not adequate at all. The shortcomings of the concept signalled to these critics that the social sciences were in methodological crisis.

Curtius's essay and another by Benjamin Barber were collected in a volume called *Totalitarianism in Perspective: Three Views.*[67] The third view was offered by Carl J. Friedrich, the editor of the volume, who noted in his introduction that the papers had been generated by a panel held during the 1967 American Political Science Association convention. Barber's essay set the problem: "Where one theorist perceives in totalitarianism only an inappropriate pejorative antonym for laissez-faire, another [Arendt] speaks darkly of the 'absolute evil' that accompanies the 'final stages of its evolution.' Still a third, trying to utilize the concept in a theory of development, complains that it 'has been applied so loosely as to become virtually meaningless in communicating any specific meaning.'" Employing the terminology that had gained currency in political theory in the early 1960s, Barber differentiated between "phenomenological" and "essentialist" definitions of totalitarianism, that is, between those concerned with something called "limited performance characteristics" or measurable behavioral and institutional characteristics, and those concerned with "relatively abstract and nonmeasurable attributes of a regime," like ideology. Barber noted a number of other factors differentiating types of definitions: whether they emphasized the novelty of totalitarianism or saw it as an old pattern in modern dress, whether they emphasized social and economic conditions or political conditions, whether they focused on one or many causal factors, whether they were oriented toward "the convergence theory" (the notion that advanced societies of all sorts are headed toward centralization and bureaucratic control) or not, and so forth. Barber's recommendation—the "extirpation" of "totalitarianism" from the vocabulary of political theory—was designed to encourage objective exploration of the "theoretical implications" of concepts. Such was the way to bring political theory out of its "analytic wilderness." Curtius came to a similar conclusion in his article, but Friedrich argued that if a term like "totalitarianism" was carefully used, understood as "a relative rather than an absolute category," it should be maintained.

This debate about whether the term "totalitarianism" should be abandoned because of its vagueness and susceptibility to propagandistic use had in common with the pro-Marxist criticism a desire to overcome cold war simplicities, but its main focus was on the role political science plays in policy decisions. In search of a purer and more objective political theory, free of unquantifiables, many theorists retreated from the concept of totalitarianism in quite another sense than Curtius intended: they stopped asking any questions mathematical "models" could not answer or "game theory" scenarios register. Others, in search of a Marxism relieved of the burden of historical perversions, turned to Marxist theorists of totalitarianism like Franz Neumann for their historical insights and to various stripes of neo-Marxism for predictions about the future. Arendt's work was of little use to either the new quantitative empiricists or the new Marxists. [68]

During the late 1960s, Hannah Arendt had many occasions for discussion of the views she had advanced in *On Revolution* and *The Origins of Totalitarianism*. One of the most interesting for her was a conference held at Harvard on the fiftieth anniversary of the 1917 Russian revolution. She was flattered to be invited as she was the only layman among a group mainly composed of Sovietologists and historians. (Characteristically, she noted to Jaspers that she was the only one *nicht vom Fach*, not from the profession, and did not say she was the only one not male.)[69] Arendt's assignment was to comment on a paper by Adam Ulam, a professor of government at Harvard, called "The Uses of Revolution." Her reply contained several statements about the view that for twenty years had separated her from most students of the Russian revolution and the Bolshevist regime. She mentioned a debate that had taken place among her fellow participants over the continuity of the revolution:

While I was listening to this debate I was struck by the fact that its protagonists had one thing in common, namely, that both believed in an unbroken continuity of Soviet Russian history from October 1917 until Stalin's death. In other words, those who were more or less on the side of Lenin's revolution also justified Stalin, whereas those who were denouncing Stalin's rule were sure that Lenin was not only responsible for Stalin's totalitarianism but actually belonged in the same category, that Stalin was a necessary consequence of Lenin. This implicit consensus seems to me highly characteristic of what has been called "the mainstream of Western thought" on the matter, and it is noteworthy that it stands in contrast to recent voices in the Soviet Union [who denounce all attempts to justify Stalin and view him as the betrayer of Communism].[70]

Stalin's economic policies—his "liquidation of the peasant class"—as well as his attacks on both Russian and foreign Communist party bureaucracies and on the Red Army officers, were, Arendt argued, discontinuous with Lenin's theory and practice; only Stalin's regime was, properly speaking, totalitarian. Theoretically, what Arendt was arguing against was the assumption of continuity—on the part of Lenin's heirs as well as the historians she addressed: "The lesson learned from the French Revolution has become an integral part of the self-imposed compulsion of ideological thinking today . . . [the revolutionaries] knew that a revolution must devour its own children, just as they knew that a revolution would take its course in a sequence of revolutions, or that the open enemy was followed by the hidden enemy under the mask of the 'suspects,' or that a revolution would split into two extreme factions . . . [and be] 'saved' by the man in the middle. . . ."[71] The continuity theory put into practice minimized or eliminated contingency, new beginnings—what might have been.

By the last time she discussed Stalin at a scholarly meeting, a Columbia University seminar in 1972, Arendt was more than ever convinced of this discontinuity, not because new source material had come to light, but because for the first time since the war books by Russians living in Russia, not émigrés, had become available in the West. She noted that Medvedev's *Let History Judge*, Nadezhda Mandelstam's *Hope Against Hope*, and Solzhenitsyn's novel, *The First Circle*, although they added nothing theoretically, "changed the whole taste" of the period for Western historians:

[They] do away with a number of theories about Stalin, including the following: 1) That Stalin was necessary to unite the country; 2) That Stalin was necessary to unite the Communist party which was chronically susceptible to splits; 3) That Stalin was necessary for industrialization; 4) That Stalin (and Stalinism) was a [necessary outcome] of a revolution; and 5) That Stalinism was the outcome of Leninism. All these myths, including the myth of the personality cult, somehow have the effect, Professor Arendt stressed, of denying the *sheer criminality* of the whole regime. . . . Sheer criminality was used as a principle of organization . . . and criminality as a principle is very different from reasons of state. . . . Thus, we are left with not the question "what is evil?" but rather with the question "what are the organizational principles of evil?" . . . While we know some elements of this process [in which people support evil and march into self-destruction], such as the need to atomize and sow distrust, there are many other aspects which we don't understand. In conclusion, Professor Arendt suggested that in a mass society it would be worthwhile for political theorists to think about—and ask *why*—people act against their own self-interest, for this is exactly what they did in the Stalinist case.[72]

At this 1972 conference, Arendt was clearly speaking from the framework of *Eichmann in Jerusalem* as a study of how evil is organized and how people become caught up in its organization. She was also clearly apprehensive about the extent to which criminality had invaded the government and society of America in the present. She spoke on 26 April, two months before the burglary at the Democratic Party Headquarters which eventually precipitated the Watergate affair, but after she had reviewed the *Pentagon Papers*. Arendt insisted on making distinctions between periods in the history of Russia for the same reason that she stressed the periods in the history of America: notions of necessary development and continuous evolution are the modern intellectual devices which, above all others, obscure the unpredictability of action and alleviate the responsibility of making judgments. Medvedev, a Marxist, was willing to let history judge. Arendt called for men to judge—and hoped that that would prevent them from supporting evil. During the years between the 1967 discussion and the one in 1972, Arendt had made this call for judgment repeatedly and praised those she thought had issued the call to themselves.

## On Violence in 1968

I want to say only two things: First, that I am quite sure that your parents, and especially your father, would be very pleased with you if they were alive now; Second, that should you run into trouble and perhaps need money, then we and Chanan Klenbort will always be ready to help as far as it lies in our power to do so.[73]

On 27 June 1968, Hannah Arendt sent this message to Daniel Cohn-Bendit, the younger son of her old friends. After both the reactionary and the Communist press in France had castigated "Dani the Red" as a "Jew," a "German," and an "undesirable," the French government refused to allow him to stay in the country where his parents had taken refuge and where he had been born in 1945, in Montauban. Cohn-Bendit returned to Germany, since 1958 the country of his citizenship, and wrote *Le Gauchisme: remède à la maladie sénile du communisme* with his brother Gabriel.

Cohn-Bendit left France after *les événements* of the spring, 1968, which had begun when he and other students at Nanterre protested the university's educational and social regulations. After the police dislodged them from an occupied building, they took refuge in the Sorbonne; a police action at the Sorbonne then precipitated riots in the Latin Quarter. Throughout the month of May, the streets of the Latin Quarter teemed with demonstrators. Barricades went up, paving stones and tear gas filled the air. First in Paris and then all over France universities closed, while thousands of factory workers and civil servants went on strike. Many heads were bloodied—though no shots were fired and there were no deaths—before Charles de Gaulle announced that he intended to remain in power and won a landslide election victory.

On the walls of Paris slogans from the *manifestations* Hannah Arendt had seen in the Front populaire days reappeared: Tenez bon camarades; La lutte continue. One poster, with a picture of Cohn-Bendit, carried a proud reply to the government in the spirit of Clemenceau's statement about Dreyfus, "the affair of one is the affair of all": Nous sommes tous "indésirables." And the French Revolution was, of course, also echoed: the young rebels were called *enragés*, and their faction was as far from "senile" Communism as the original *enragés* had been from the *indulgents*.

Hannah Arendt and Heinrich Blücher watched their television and read their newspapers avidly. "We have recently witnessed," she wrote in retrospect, "how it did not take more than the relatively harmless, essentially nonviolent students' rebellion to reveal the vulnerability of the whole [French] political system, which rapidly distintegrated before the astonished eyes of the young rebels. Unknowingly, they had tested it; they intended only to challenge the ossified university system, and down came the system of governmental power, together with that of the huge party bureaucracies. . . . It was a textbook case of a revolutionary situation that did not develop into a revolution because there was nobody, least of all the students, prepared to seize power and the responsibility that goes with it. Nobody except, of course, de Gaulle."[74] De Gaulle was no Robespierre, but rather the man of the middle, the savior.

Hannah Arendt was impressed that what the French called *les événements* were "essentially nonviolent." She had been arguing publicly in America for the effectiveness of nonviolent action, trying, without much success, to point out the dangerous confusion of "power" and "violence" in the manifestos of the American New Left. On 17 December 1967, she had participated in a discussion on "The Legitimacy of Violence," joining Noam Chomsky, Conor Cruise O'Brien, and Robert Lowell on a panel chaired by Robert Silvers of the *New York Review of Books*. The discussion took place in the 21st Street loft where the Theatre for Ideas, a gathering place for New York intellectuals since 1961, had its home.

Arendt set out the distinction between power and violence that had been central to *On Revolution* and then drew the lesson:

Generally speaking, violence always rises out of impotence. It is the hope of those who have no power [no consent or support from the people] to find a substitute for it—and this hope, I think, is in vain. By the same token, it is a dangerous illusion to measure the power of a country by its arsenal of violence. That an abundance of violence is one of the great dangers for the power of commonwealths, especially for republics, is one of the oldest insights of political science. To maintain that this country, for instance, is the most powerful on earth because it possesses the largest arsenal of destructive instruments is to fall prey to the common and erroneous equation of power and violence.[75]

She pointed to three justifications for violence: Marx's claim that violence is a necessary part of a society's revolutionary birth pains; Sorel's claim that violence is essentially creative and therefore the proper mode for society's producers, the working class, as opposed to society's consumers; and Sartre's claim that violence is essential to man's creation, is "man recreating himself." Elaborating on distinctions she had made in *The Human Condition*, Arendt rejected Marx's confusion of action and natural processes like giving birth or laboring, Sorel's confusion of action and fabrication, and Sartre's extension of Marx's position—his argument that not labor but violence creates man.

Arendt's remarks were abstract and theoretical, as were those of the other panelists, and she was not surprised when Susan Sontag, speaking from the audience, questioned them: "It's personally hard for me to understand how in December 1967 in New York the discussion has at no point turned actively to the question of whether we, in this room, and people we know are going to be engaged in violence." "I'm very glad you brought up this question," Arendt said, "[as it is] of course in the back of all our minds."[76] She went on to agree with Noam Chomsky that nonviolence was essential to the peace movement for tactical reasons—because of the government's arsenal, its capacity to make protest "suicidal," and because "violence antagonizes the uncommitted"—and to add a reason of her own: "the enormous power of nonviolence." She felt that American officials would exercise the kind of restraint shown by the English when they were confronted with Gandhi's nonviolent movement, "which could, however, have been broken, as one of the imperialist officers did propose, by administrative massacres." She thought that Americans would realize that administrative violence directed against citizen nonviolence would be "the end of the republic." On the other hand, Arendt roundly condemned those who wanted to use violent protest as a pretext to try to bring about the end of the republic: "that is precisely where the line should be drawn, between legitimate and illegitimate tactics."

The panelists were in agreement about the tactical importance—if not the power—of nonviolence. But Tom Hayden, who had been in Newark, New Jersey, as a community organizer for SDS during the 1967 summer riots, was impatient. "It seems to me that until you can begin to show— not in language, not in theory, but in action—that you can put an end to the war in Vietnam, and an end to American racism, you can't condemn the violence of those who can't wait for you."[77] Hayden argued that there was, or shortly would be, a place for violence in the peace movement— "the resistance movement I think is a better term for it"—and also that the Newark riots were a justified response to a demonstrable failure of nonviolent efforts to effect change. Arendt was not convinced: "As for riots helping effect social change, riots have, of course, occurred throughout history, and they have never led to anything; nothing blows away so quickly, and leaves so little trace." She cautioned Hayden to be careful about judging domestic challenges facing the peace movement: "In this respect Europeans could teach Americans quite a few lessons. Up until now there has been no torture here, nor do concentration camps exist, nor terror."

Hannah Arendt held fast to her side of the argument with Tom Hayden, but she shifted her stance somewhat after reflection on a point made by Conor Cruise O'Brien, who came to the meeting still stiff from a bit of police violence that had come his way at a demonstration. O'Brien quoted a remark made by one of his Irish countrymen: Sometimes "violence is the only way of ensuring a hearing for moderation." When Hannah Arendt wrote her "Reflections on Violence" in 1969, she cited this remark approvingly: "Violence does not promote causes, neither history nor revolution, neither progress nor reaction; but it can serve to dramatize grievances and bring them to public attention."[78] She acknowledged that ghetto violence might do this. But she was careful to suggest that "violence, contrary to what its prophets try to tell us, is more the weapon of reform than revolution." The student riots in France had brought only reform of the university system, she noted, and the riots at Columbia University had brought only a study of that university's policies.

The April 1968 demonstrations at Columbia University received an excited endorsement from Hannah Arendt when they began. She was impressed with the students' desire to rid the university of its Institute for Defense Analysis affiliation, its tie to war-related research, though she was not sure about what they meant with their calls for the university to be more responsible in its relations with the surrounding community of Harlem, which was alive with mourning for Martin Luther King, Jr., who had been shot on 4 April. Chanan Klenbort met her in a Broadway restaurant between her Riverside Drive apartment and Columbia's main gate on the first day of the students' occupation of buildings. "The students are demonstrating," she announced happily, "and we are all with them." Klenbort, far more cautious than Arendt—in moments of irritation, she would say that both he and Heinrich Blücher were "just old ex-Communists!"—reminded her that she was, in fact, eating dinner in a restaurant and not out demonstrating. Hannah Arendt was not a demonstrator. Crowds and mass meetings made her uneasy, and she kept carefully to her chosen role of spectator. When some of the tribe members, also in their sixties, went to Washington to march in antiwar demonstrations, she declined.

Within several days, Arendt was disappointed with the course of events at Columbia. Two years before, at Chicago, she had supported the efforts of her students to stop the university administration from reporting students' class ranks to the Selective Service Administration—for those ranking high received exemption from the draft. The students felt that the Vietnam fighting was being left to the poor and not to those who were, so to speak, "exception students." Long a critic of any who accepted exception status socially or politically, Hannah Arendt went with one of her students, Michael Denneny, to an occupied building on the Chicago campus, climbed the stairs to the students' headquarters two at a time— "as excited as a girl," Denneny recalled—to talk to them about their thoughts and plans. She told the students a story she had related in *Eichmann in Jerusalem*: when the French Jewish war veterans of World War I were offered exemption from deportation by the Nazis, they issued a statement. "We solemnly declare that we renounce any exceptional benefits we may derive from our status as ex-servicemen."[79] Very impressed with her students, and with the student movement in general, Arendt praised them three years later, in "Reflections on Violence": "A student rebellion almost exclusively inspired by moral considerations certainly belongs among the totally unexpected events of this century."[80] Her Chicago students were also impressed with her; her course, Basic Moral Propositions, was the only one they voted to exempt from their boycott of classes.

But the Columbia takeover went in a direction Arendt could not accept. She felt that the Columbia students had lost sight of their goals and combined their legitimate protest against university support for defense research with an illegitimate attack upon the university itself. Many times Arendt had argued that universities—like the courts—must be institutions apart, "outside the power struggle." "Very unwelcome truths have emerged from the universities," she wrote in "Truth and Politics," "and very unwelcome judgments have been handed down from the bench time and again; and these institutions, like other refuges of truth, have remained exposed to all of the dangers arising from social and political power. Yet the chances for truth to prevail in public are, of course, greatly improved by the mere existence of such places and by the organization of independent, supposedly disinterested scholars associated with them."[81] Arendt made it quite clear that she thought university administrations, not students, were responsible for corrupting the universities, for linking universities to business and government enterprises. But she thought that the students who wanted to give the universities over to the "people" were simply calling for another ownership, not independence; and that those who wanted to close the universities because of their corruption were threatening not only the possibility of an independent locus for the pursuit of truth but their own "only possible basis" for action. Arendt did not object to the occupation of buildings—"sit-ins and occupations of buildings are not the same as arson or armed revolt, and the difference is not just one of degree"[82]—because she felt that universities were the "property" of students, as well as faculty and administrators; but she did object to the threat of armed revolt that came when Columbia's Hamilton Hall was taken over by black students allegedly supplied with arms from the Harlem community.

On the subject of universities and their responsibilities to minority communities, Hannah Arendt was and remained a "conservative." She was opposed to the open admissions policy when it was instituted at City College and whenever it was called for elsewhere. She felt that "serious violence" entered onto American campuses "with the appearance of the Black Power movement. . . . Negro students, the majority of them admitted without academic qualification, regarded and organized themselves as an interest group, the representatives of the black community. Their interest was to lower academic standards. They were more cautious than the white rebels, but it was clear from the beginning (even before the incidents at Cornell University and City College in New York) that violence for them was not a matter of theory and rhetoric. . . . [T]here stands a large minority of the Negro community behind the verbal or actual violence of the black students."[83] Arendt felt that accession to demands for open admissions and for Black Studies courses were a threat to academic standards and a disservice to blacks who needed not "African literature and other nonexistent subjects" but training in basic skills— reading, writing, and arithmetic. She was afraid that blacks would, "in about five or ten years," come to see Black Studies as "another trap of the white man to prevent Negroes from acquiring an adequate education."[84]

Hannah Arendt had never considered what she called the "Negro Question"—thinking of it as comparable to the Jewish Question—from a position acceptable to either liberals or conservatives. She thought that what happened in the late 1960s was the result of the situation she had addressed in "Reflections on Little Rock" a decade before. She explained in a letter to Mary McCarthy:

I am pretty convinced that the new trend of Black Power and anti-integration, which comes as such a rude shock to our liberals, is a direct consequence of the integration that preceded it. Everything went about all right so long as integration was what was called tokenism and actually was integration of the relatively small percentage of Negroes who could be integrated without seriously threatening the normal standards of admission. The general civil-rights enthusiasm led to inte- grating larger numbers of Negroes who were not qualified and who understood much quicker, of course, than others, full of good will, that they were in an intolerable competitive situation. Today the situation is quite clear: Negroes demand their own curriculum without the exacting standards of white society and, at the same time, they demand admission in accordance with their percent- age in the population at large, regardless of standards. In other words, they actually want to take over and adjust the standards to their own level. This is a much greater threat to our institutions of higher learning than the student riots. . . . The trouble with the New Left and the old liberals is the old one— complete unwillingness to face facts, abstract talk, often snobbish and nearly always blind to anybody else's interest. . . . The hypocrisy is indeed monumental. Integrated housing is of course quite possible and absolutely painless on a certain level of income and education, and it is a fait accompli in New York precisely in the expensive apartment buildings. No trouble whatsoever. The trouble begins with the lower-income groups, and this trouble is very real. In other words, those who preach integration, etc., are those who are neither likely nor willing to pay the price. And then look down their educated noses upon their poor benighted fellow citizens, full of "prejudices."[85]

This was not snobbish talk but it, too, was abstract. Arendt's generaliza- tions were built upon the case of City College, without much experience with the by no means monolithic "interest" of the black community. She cited the black civil-rights leader Bayard Rustin's call for "remedial training" rather than "soul courses," but she assumed that his was a solitary voice. No more than others was she able to propose an approach to integrated education that offered the combination of basic courses and programs designed to recognize the particular needs of minority students. But ten years after she wrote, as she anticipated, black leaders like the Reverend Jesse Jackson did begin to work for the kind of local programs she would have approved; through organizations like PUSH for Excellence a call went out for public schools, parents, and students to review their commitments to academic achievement.

Arendt had little experience with community schools or public universities and their conflicts, but she did have at least one chance to observe how the complexities of the late 1960s played upon the nerves of moderate blacks. One evening in October 1968 she and the other editorial board members of the *American Scholar* listened, stunned, to two hours of Ralph Ellison's anger. Hiram Haydn, the editor, recalled in his memoir, *Words and Faces*, how Ellison had taken exception to an editorial decision, claiming that an article should have been shown to him before it was accepted: "Then he plunged into an attack as vague as it was angry, at the general tendency not to recognize accurately people's qualifications. He made so many sweeping generalizations, spoke with so much forcefulness, went so far afield from his starting point that it was difficult to follow him. It was impossible to quiet him." Several board members tried to calm Ellison, without success; "Hannah Arendt said good night and left, telling me she was too upset to stay." None of the fifteen men and women knew what had moved Ralph Ellison, but Haydn ventured that "this was one manifestation of the lonely burden that certain black men of a transitional generation have carried. Disclaimed by the new militants, yet too genuinely liberal for black conservatives, widely accepted by the white community, yet always aware of that *one* difference, these aristocrats of the mind and spirit have often achieved greatly in our society, yet have belonged really to no community except the small one of their peers. The strain of this isolation must eventually tell on anyone, and I believe that October evening was one time when the load was too great."[86]

The Theatre for Ideas discussion of violence and the chaotic events of 1968 prompted Hannah Arendt to elaborate on her distinction between power and violence, between the human ability to act in concert and the use of instruments, which can be the prerogative of a group or an individual. "I would never have written my essay on violence, without the discussion that made me aware of the confusion of all of us in this matter."[87] She began to write the essay in the summer of 1968, after she had finished her first year of teaching at the New School for Social Research. Her appointment allowed her to do what she had wanted to do for several years—stop commuting to Chicago, leaving her husband for weeks at a time. In Blücher's honor, her first New School seminar had been "Political Experience in the 20th Century," a course designed to track the experience of a hypothetical individual—actually Blücher—born at the turn of the century and living through its "dark times."

While Arendt wrote *On Violence*, she reflected often on the changed atmosphere she lived in. "For the first time," she told Mary McCarthy, "I meet middle-aged, native-born Americans (colleagues, quite respectable) who think of emigration."[88] The atmosphere was well reflected in the title of the first fall 1968 Theatre for Ideas discussion: "Democracy: Does It Have a Future?" Arendt felt that democracy did have a future, and a present—unlike Herbert Marcuse, who claimed at the the discussion that "it certainly does not have a present. . . . American society has become progressively insane"[89]—but she was finding daily life very difficult. She and Blücher did not want to emigrate, but they did consider various plans for buying a house in Palenville or spending part of the year in Switzerland: "It has to do with old age and the wish to live less exposed than is possible here. Also, to have more comfort than is possible in big cities."[90] Blücher was not well. He had several mild heart attacks during the spring of 1968 and was hospitalized briefly in June, just in time to miss being awarded his one and only academic degree, an honorary doctorate from Bard College. A delegation from Bard came to the Riverside Drive apartment when he was well enough to receive them and presented the degree; then the Blüchers went to Palenville for two months, postponing until the next summer a trial-run stay near Locarno in southern Switzerland.

*On Violence* was drafted that summer, but Arendt also began to write sketches for what she called, in a letter to Mary McCarthy, "a kind of second volume of *The Human Condition*," that is, *The Life of the Mind*.[91] She had been making notes during the New School course and during a brief stay at Chicago, where she had agreed to give some lectures and continue supervision of her doctoral students. But the teaching demands, despite her appreciation of her students—"the only joys one now has are students"[92]—left her tired. The dreary *Weltlage* ("world situation") interrupted her concentration: "I have a feeling of futility in everything I do. Compared to what is at stake, everything looks frivolous. I know this feeling disappears when I let myself fall into the gap between past and future, which is the proper temporal locus of thought. Which I can't do while I am teaching, and have to be all *there*."[93]

Like most Americans who opposed the Vietnam War and feared the domestic law-and-order forces, Arendt thought that the election campaigns of 1968 were disastrous. She had had high hopes for Eugene McCarthy's presidential-primary campaign, and had made contributions to it, as she had to the senatorial campaigns for George McGovern and Frank Church. She would have voted for McCarthy, whom she considered "a true patriot," or for Robert Kennedy, had Kennedy lived to seek his party's nomination. And had Nelson Rockefeller run against the Democratic nominee, Hubert Humphrey, she would, not being a party voter, have favored him. Given the choice between Humphrey and Richard Nixon, she voted, without enthusiasm, for Humphrey, but her traditional distrust of the party system was more than ever confirmed by the choice. "After the people had made their views so clear," she said at another Theatre for Ideas discussion, "both parties did not draft the guy with the most appeal but the guy with the most power inside the party. I have come to the conclusion that it is the party machines that really make us impotent."[94]

With that conclusion in mind, Arendt watched the antiwar movement in 1969 with great hope, thinking that in its successes might lie the party machines' defeats. After the October 1969 moratorium demonstrations in Washington, she had a moment of optimism:

One feels once more the hopes one had during the McCarthy campaign. But this is better because it bypassed the whole party system altogether and rested solely on the Constitutional right of the people to assemble and petition. Hence, one is tempted to conclude, the Constitution is still alive and the party system, though of course not dead, has become a nuisance . . . *Potestas in populo* . . . The whole business organized by the new generation, who now perhaps really will come into their own, lose the "extremists" with their hollow rhetoric, and perhaps rediscover the republic, the public thing.[95]

Arendt's moment of optimism came after she had already concluded that the powerlessness of the Democratic party was revealed in the violence used against demonstrators during its Chicago convention. But her optimism was not long sustained. The "nuisance" of the party bureaucracies was overshadowed by the dangers of the government bureaucracies that Arendt wrote about in her next political essay, "Lying in Politics: Reflections on the *Pentagon Papers*."

## Farewell to Jaspers

The year President Nixon announced the first troop withdrawals from Vietnam, 1969, was a year of comparative domestic peace. Although there were some summer riots and shoot-outs between Black Panthers and police, arousing anxious memories of 1968—the year of assassinations, police violence, and student rebellions—1969 seemed a calm after a storm or, some thought, before another storm. For Hannah Arendt, it was a sad year.

While she started her New School courses entitled "Philosophy and Politics," she completed an eighty-sixth birthday letter to Karl Jaspers, saying how sorry she was to be unable to join him for a celebration. Three days after his birthday, Jaspers, who had been seriously ill for several weeks, died. Gertrud Jaspers, whose ninetieth birthday was the same day, 26 February, sent a brief message to their friends: "Heute starb mein Lebensgefährte Karl Jaspers [Today my life's companion Karl Jaspers died]."[96]

Hannah Arendt, as was her custom and the custom of her European peers, wore a black dress to Basel, where a funeral service for Jaspers took place on 4 March. She wore black for several months, but she also wore bright-colored scarves, because of a story Gertrud Jaspers told her at the funeral. Several days before he died, Jaspers and his wife discussed what she should wear to his funeral; they agreed on her best black dress, for custom's sake, but they also agreed that she should wear a white collar—because his was a good death! Jaspers was careful to send another, and more impersonal, message to the memorial service that was held the day after the funeral. He dictated and left a brief *Nekrolog* in which he gave thanks, for their generosity and support, to his parents and those who had educated him, his wife, his friends, and those in the places he had lived before, during, and after the Nazi period. He spoke of himself in the past tense and in the third person, with the same slow, measured dignity that had always marked his public addresses.

The loss of the political fatherland left him in a baseless condition where he, with his wife, reached out for the sources of human being in general; through friendship with individual beloved people in Germany and dispersed over the whole globe; and through the dream of a common world-citizenship.

In Basel, in its European tradition, in the freedom he had as a guest to find a calm asylum, was the last blessing given him. He gave all his strength in these years to the continuation of his unconcluded philosophical work, in which he—more sensing than really knowing how, searching, not resting—sought a part in the problem of the era: sought a way out of the end of European philosophy into a future world-philosophy.[97]

Two other of Jaspers's students, one from the years after the war, Jeanne Hersch, and one from his last years, his research assistant Hans Saner, joined Arendt as speakers at the Basel University memorial service. Arendt spoke of Jaspers's life and writing, of Jaspers as a philosopher and a citizen—a man who was drawn late in his life into political action-through-speech. Then she spoke of natality and mortality, standing in the place where she, as a thinker, always stood, "between past and future."

We do not know, when a man dies, what has come to pass. We know only: he has left us. We depend upon his works, but we know that the works do not need us. They are what the one who dies leaves in the world—the world that was there before he came and which remains when he has gone. What will become of them depends on the way of the world. But the simple fact that these books were once a lived life, this fact does not go directly into the world or remain safe from forgetfulness. That about a man which is most impermanent and also perhaps most great, his spoken word and his unique comportment, that dies with him and thus needs us; needs us who think of him. Such thinking brings us to a relationship with the dead one, out of which, then, conversation about him springs and sounds again in the world. A relationship with the dead one—this must be learned, and, in order to begin this, we come together now, in our shared sorrow.[98]

"A relationship with the dead one" was hard indeed for Hannah Arendt to learn. She had dreaded Jaspers's death for years. When he was seriously ill in 1965, she visited him and wrote to Mary McCarthy afterwards: "Always thinking it could be the last time, and, though I doubt it, it was the first time I thought along these lines constantly. And was at the same time more at home there than ever. As though the approach of death makes everything easier: what considerations could conceivably count?"[99] Paul Tillich died that year, and considering his death made her very anxious about Jaspers and about Heidegger. Jaspers realized how apprehensive she was, and he comforted her, even in the letters which contained frank, detailed descriptions of his failing health, for he thought—as she did—that the precariousness of his situation should not go unmentioned. In 1966 he wrote to reassure her after he noticed she was "in an anxious farewell mood, different than before." He told her how much he looked forward to seeing her, and perhaps Blücher, the next year, but added: "We always say farewell, and never farewell." To keep her from worrying, Jaspers sent along his wife's wry reflection on their situation: "We wished to grow old together, now we must endure it." And, always supportive, he commented on Arendt's many activities and encouraged her, writing in 1968 with a trembling hand his fatherly message: "Send us, when you have time, new reports."[100]

Until 1967 Jaspers had been able to keep writing—usually by dictating while he lay on his *Arbeitsofa*—and answering the critics of his last book, published in English as *The Future of Germany* with a preface by Hannah Arendt.[101] The book was his farewell to politics, and he hoped, then, to be able to return to his other homeland, philosophy. But this required that Hannah Arendt release him from a promise, the partly drafted book about *Eichmann in Jerusalem*, which he felt was beyond his strength. She did this, of course, and he thanked her: "I am not only freed of a book (that is only an external, though a very important result) but also from a kind of captivity, from, above all, politics and [its] customs. Now I am in the free air, and can turn back to Philosophy as my *Arbeitsthema*—and therefore I am well."[102]

After Jaspers died, Hannah Arendt tried to regain the "free air" of philosophy, the life of the mind, but politics kept her earthbound. She finished *On Violence* and then did the German translation, *Macht und Gewalt*. After her essay appeared in the *New York Review of Books* several letters came to Robert Silvers, and these had to be answered. The philosopher Raziel Abelson of New York University had challenged her: "It is never clear what, if anything, Miss Arendt is for or against. At one point, she seems merely to be championing the cause of intellectual clarity." Professor Abelson supposed, finally, that she must have been "blessing the Establishment" by identifying power with authority—which, in fact, were two of the terms she had tried, at length, to distinguish.[103] Arendt made an effort to untangle Professor Abelson's misreadings, and wearily concluded that he did not believe in making distinctions. Hans Morgenthau sent a sympathetic note after he read this exchange: "I read your polemic against your critics. It is really not worth it! What an idiocy to assume that when you write you must of necessity champion a cause. We are all intellectual streetfighters: we are either for or against something or other. So if we don't make it clear on which side of the barricades we stand we have failed."[104]

Arendt knew the value of "mere" clarification in "dark times." Jaspers had been the great clarifier of his generation—and of her life. She dearly missed the man she had described to Edward Levi of the University of Chicago in 1966, when she wanted Levi to support the University of Basel's suggestion that Jaspers be awarded the Nobel Prize for Peace.

Jaspers is in many respects a unique figure; he is today the only great European who speaks about political issues without any commitment to a specific party or cause. His political convictions are the natural consequences of his philosophy, and they are centered around freedom and reason. This is, about the two concepts that are central to his philosophy. To award him the Peace Prize would have a twofold political significance: it would mean the recognition of the importance of philosophy for politics and it would mean to give the Prize to a German against the Germany of the Twentieth and late Nineteenth centuries. As Jaspers is rightly worried about the development of the Federal Republic . . . this gesture would almost certainly force attention on what he has to say upon the political milieus in Germany, as distinguished from the general public where his success has always been great.[105]

## Moral and Political Action

For Karl Jaspers, Hannah Arendt had been, as he once said, the confirmation of his life as a professor, his *Professorsein*. Her own rewards as a teacher were very different, because she was not, like Jaspers, primarily a teacher. In addition, her students were Americans and thus at a cultural remove from her, as well as being more than twice the distance in age she had been from Jaspers. But in the late 1960s, while she and her students watched the political scene in America with great apprehension, she let herself become more personally involved with the "new ones." Some of the European aloofness, traditionally overcome only when students have become colleagues, disappeared. She made her home more homelike for those she had singled out of her overpacked New School classes for special attention and those who had won her regard at Chicago. Her grief at the time of Jaspers's death was not hidden from her young ones; she told stories about her teacher, encouraged a doctoral dissertation on his work, began to quote him in her dense, difficult lectures.

To those who came for advice, she offered her own version of Jaspers's independence of mind. But she was also unpredictable and volatile. One of her students told her about a network of people organized to smuggle draft-dodgers and U.S. Army deserters out of the country, to Canada or Sweden, and explained that participating in the network was going to mean absences from class. Arendt's first reaction was stereotypically Jewish grandmotherish: "But you will be arrested! And, Gott in Himmel, I do not wish to read your prison memoirs." Then she calmed down, asked many questions about the organization in a conspiratorial whisper, and finally said, with obvious pridefulness: "Perhaps you have learned a little something in my classes to help you write *good* prison memoirs."

Her encouragement was generous, and her criticism was delivered with the respectful, if harsh, assumption that anyone who could not accept it well should not continue under her tutelage. To one doctoral student whose nearly finished manuscript she had read promptly and carefully, she gave one of her awesome judgments: "Well, my dear, if this was right, it would be revolutionary, but I am afraid it is just wrong." Her comments on students' political activities were just as sharp: "Action is not like reading a book; you can do that alone, but when you act you act with others, and that means you leave aside all this theorizing and keep your eyes open." For those who never measured up intellectually or politically she offered the distinction Kant made between ignorance and stupidity: "for stupidity, there is no cure." The mixture of parental concern and imperiousness in Arendt was continually disconcerting to her students, as was the combination of great intellectual sureness and nervousness— stage fright—in public, even in classrooms. Her vulnerability and shyness were difficult to discern, in part because she had so little patience with weakness in others; she retreated abruptly when faced with insecurities or neuroses she could not or would not understand.

Arendt was never without her apprehensions about public appearances, but during the Vietnam War years she responded promptly when called upon to join discussions. Alarmed by the many verbal attacks made by the forces of Law and Order—particularly by Vice-President Spiro Agnew— upon Vietnam War protestors and the constitutional right to assemble, the Theatre for Ideas planned a session on "The First Amendment and the Politics of Confrontation." Arendt joined Attorney General Ramsey Clark and Ron Young, an organizer for the 15 November 1969 "March Against Death" in Washington, on the panel for the evening. She came after a brief spell in the free air of philosophy, a break after two weeks of lecturing in Chicago, during which she had "great laziness—reading Plotinus and Schelling and this and that," as she told Mary McCarthy.[106] Her respite left her more rested than usual, despite the fact that Blücher's health worried her again, this time because of an attack of phlebitis.

She was vigorous and forceful during the Theatre for Ideas discussion, giving the audience a taste of the wit she usually reserved for her students. She told Ron Young, who felt that it was the people who insisted on their right to assemble, not the Constitution, that had made the November peace march possible:

You are entirely right. Without the people to enforce it, the whole edifice crumbles. But without the First Amendment in the Constitution, the government would have found it very easy simply to prohibit the whole business. For those few lines on the books do still stand between us and tyranny. . . . All in all, it seems to me that you *under*estimate the seriousness of the situation in a fantastic way. What concerns me are your illusions. What concerns me is that you really don't know how fast you must hold on to this First Amendment. And show it to the government, and the people, time and again. Can it be that you have cried wolf so many times that you do not see when he really comes around the corner?[107]

The audience laughed, but Young protested that the best way to defend the First Amendment was "a vigorous and dangerous struggle against the Vietnam War." Arendt held on: "But your right to carry out this struggle is guaranteed precisely through the First Amendment. Without that you would have to rely on the good will of the government. I wouldn't do that if I were you. I would much rather have a legal leg to stand on." Ron Young was not alone in his position. Joan Simon, a young writer for *Ramparts* and other magazines, asked: "If you can murder, as they did in My Lai, what does free speech mean?"

Hannah Arendt was concerned about what she thought were the illusions of the agonized young advocates of "confrontational politics." She suggested that Martin Luther King's actions had "confronted the American people with the gap or the contradiction between the Constitution, the law of the land, and the actual ordinances and laws and practices of the south. . . . That was a real confrontation. And it was effective." She thought this kind of confrontation a very different matter than civil disobedience, which stemmed from a decision "made by *individuals* according to their conscience." Arendt spoke about this distinction at the Theatre for Ideas, and then, thinking further, decided she was wrong.

She was prompted to further reflection by the Theatre for Ideas discussion itself and by an invitation to participate in a 1 May 1970 conference at New York University. "Is the Law Dead?" was the conference's bleak title, but the topic Arendt chose from those suggested did not commit her to the bleakness; it was "The Citizen's Moral Relation to the Law in a Society of Consent."

During the summer of 1970, Arendt reworked her address into an article, "Civil Disobedience."[108] In it she argued that there is a difference between civil disobedience and conscientious objection. Both involve individual decisions, but only the civil disobedient, not the conscientious objector, also relies on the decisions made by others; the civil disobedient is a member of a group that shares a conviction.

For practice, this theoretical distinction between a "good man" and a "good citizen," a moral stance and a political affiliation, was important to Arendt because she knew that protest action had to come from groups of people acting together and also because she thought that the ability of the Republic to admit civil disobedience was an index of its accord with the "spirit of the American laws." Unlike the case she had cited at the Theatre for Ideas, the civil-rights movement, the anti-Vietnam War demonstrations were aimed at federal not state practices and laws—the constitutionality of the war, for example, was at issue. Arendt acknowledged that it is impossible to expect any legal system to justify violations of the law, but she thought that a "political approach" to the problem of civil disobedience could show "a recognized niche for civil disobedience in our institutions of government." She compared civil disobedience with membership in a voluntary association, noting that pressure groups and special-interest lobbies are given the kind of recognition that could well be given to "civil-disobedient minorities." Arendt was aware that the First Amendment "neither in language nor in spirit covers the right of association as it is actually practiced in this country," so she suggested: "if there is anything that urgently requires a new constitutional amendment and is worth all the trouble that goes with it, it is certainly this."

Hannah Arendt, who had last suggested a constitutional amendment in 1949 when she proposed one to guarantee that no citizen could have his or her citizenship revoked, did not specify the form an amendment guaranteeing the "right of association" should take. She was not unaware that groups bound to corporate interests rather than united by political convictions were potentially dangerous, but her purpose was to insure for all associations the recognition enjoyed by the lobby groups. "The fact is that pressure groups are also voluntary associations, and that they are recognized in Washington, where their influence is sufficiently great for them to be called an 'assistant government.'. . . This public recognition is no small matter, for such 'assistance' was no more foreseen in the Constitution and its First Amendment than freedom of association as a form of political action." Blanket Constitutional sanction for associations might well have made the "assistance" given to the government by interest groups even more troubling, but, in principle, Arendt's attempt to carve out a niche for groups wanting "to bring a law believed to be unjust or invalid . . . into court or before the bar of public opinion" was certainly respectful of the "spirit of the American laws." Noting that the Supreme Court can invoke the so-called political-question doctrine in order to refuse to review actions of the legislature and the executive, she argued that "the establishment of civil disobedience among our political institutions might be the best possible remedy for this ultimate failure of judicial review."

When Arendt made her proposal to the "Is Law Dead?" conference, it was not well received. Eugene V. Rostow, the convener of the conference, said flatly "the use of illegal means to achieve political ends cannot be justified." Robert Paul Wolff of Columbia was not concerned with an institution for civil disobedience; defending anarchism, he simply said that "no one, not even a citizen of a true democracy, has an obligation to obey the law." Ronald Dworkin felt that the policy of the government had nothing to do with the "spirit of the laws"—a point which did not take into account any situation except the one of the moment. The moment was not ripe for a long view like Arendt's. "The Vice-President [Agnew] is wrong in lumping together civil and uncivil disobedience," said Harris Wofford of Bryn Mawr. "He is dangerously polarizing our politics." And the polarization was quite apparent at the conference. The *New York Times* recorded Eugene Rostow's view: "Mr. Rostow, noting that a 'demonstration of mass hysteria' was perhaps under way at Yale this weekend, said: 'Perhaps we are too fevered, too involved, to take an analytical look at individual liberty.'"[109]

There was no mass hysteria at Yale University that weekend; the "convocation" over the upcoming trial of Black Panther leader Bobby Seale was peaceful. Arendt was encouraged by that but discouraged by the atmosphere of the conference. The discussion had been calm, but the mood was defeatist. "The law may not be dead," one member of the audience had suggested, "but it's pretty dormant."

In small matters, the law was not dormant, as Arendt discovered when she threatened the Bar Association of New York, the sponsor for the conference, with a legal action to prevent publication of her address. She won her point without resort to the awkward task of getting "a lawyer [to go] against the Bar Association," and went off to the peace and quiet of Switzerland to give "Civil Disobedience" the revision and lengthening she thought it needed.[110]

The distinction between moral decision and political action she had elaborated in the article received another review in Tegna, above Locarno, where Arendt, looking out from the Casa Barbete over an alpine meadow, felt much closer to the "free air of philosophy." She wrote an essay called "Thinking and Moral Considerations" that summer, a long reflection on individual moral decisions and how they are made. She had considered civil disobedience, political action against or in opposition to a law, and distinguished it from "the counsels of conscience [which] are not only unpolitical; they are always expressed in purely subjective statements. When Socrates stated that 'it is better to suffer wrong than to do wrong,' he clearly meant that it was better *for him*. . . . Politically, on the contrary, what counts is that a wrong has been done; to the law it is irrelevant who is better off as a result—the doer or the sufferer."[111] That summer of 1970, Arendt gave Socrates and the subjective statements of conscience their due. And she made the first step toward *The Life of the Mind*, where her essay came to rest in the "Thinking" volume.

*Blücher*

Hannah Arendt was delighted with the summer. Blücher was well, though he tired easily, was a bit deaf in one ear, and was not without apprehension about his health. Mary McCarthy came for a visit, as did Anne Weil. All enjoyed the tranquility of the small boardinghouse and the picturesque town with its small inn for their luncheons and its quiet streets. The Blüchers sometimes went to Locarno to visit Robert Gilbert, taking a little train Arendt fondly called "Bimmel-Bammel" down the mountainside. Arendt would like to have stayed "with my books for many more months—no teaching, no demands, no household. And, please, a little boredom—boredom is so healthy in small doses."[112]

But teaching, demands, and household started up again in September. Arendt offered a lecture and a seminar on Kant's *Critique of Judgment* designed to help her further the reflections she had written into "Thinking and Moral Considerations." To the Platonic description of thinking as a "dialogue between me and myself," Arendt added Kant's concepts of disinterestedness or impartiality and "enlarged mentality" as she tried to discover that link between thinking and judging which she had gestured toward at the end of her essay. She was in search of a way to reunite the moral and the political, the "good man" and the "good citizen," the subjects of "Thinking and Moral Considerations" and "Civil Disobedience."

On Friday, 30 October, Arendt presented "Thinking and Moral Considerations" to a meeting of the Society for Phenomenology and Existential Philosophy at the New School. That evening, with this "demand" behind, she and Blücher entertained J. Glenn Gray at home. Blücher ate and drank his schnapps, talked with his usual gusto, despite having had some pain in his chest earlier in the day. But during their luncheon on the next day he suddenly felt ill and was barely able to make his way to the couch before a heart attack came. Terrified, Arendt called for an ambulance. Blücher was very calm, he held his wife's hand and told her, quietly, "This is it."

Blücher died that evening in Mount Sinai Hospital. He was seventy-one. Arendt called his old friend Peter Huber, who took a series of photographs of Blücher, with Arendt by his bedside. Lotte Kohler took her home, and there she sent telegrams to close friends: "Heinrich died Saturday of a heart attack. Hannah."

One characteristic of Blücher's dominated all others in the memories of those who knew him as companions or students, in his youth or his old age: his argumentativeness, his passion for debate, his willingness to follow an idea to the edge of its reasonableness and even beyond. The letters of condolence that came to Hannah Arendt Blücher after word of his death spread among their acquaintances—letters, as she put it, "from all strata of the past"—reveal a man who was not different things to different people but the same man in varying intensities to all. The portrait by the Blüchers' American friend Dwight Macdonald is remarkable for its dash and vigor, but quite of a piece with the others in its perception:

He was to begin with a true, hopeless anarchist both in mind and in temperament—always ready to respond to a stimulus (or an argument, bad or good) in a reckless, wholehearted way that was never so reckless or emotional—except in *form*, at times, but O ye Pharisees & Scribes & precisionists—as to miss the main target, The Point—and his aim was all the more admired by me bec. he didn't seem to draw a bead at all, like those Zen archers, but just let fly "at random"—rationally—but not at all randomly in terms of his experience up to that moment, [which] was brought to bear, without his conscious thought perhaps (or perhaps not unimportant) wholly on the subject—his arrow hit the center most times, as I saw it. . . . His low-keyed grumblings and flashing-eyed shoutings (how desperately precise his enunciation was when he felt himself driven into an argumentative corner from which he saw an existential exit denied him by the Rules of the Game!) were a humanistic *obligato* to many arguments I've been present at, and taken part in, conducted on a plane that was intellectually higher, or rather more rule-respecting, than Heinrich's, but—when you came to think about it later—lower in terms of imagination, and common sense, than his. Also I liked one quality, among others, he shared with you: the ability to commit himself to a position, passionately, and damn the horses—or the expense![113]

Blücher was a talker, not a writer. His self-education had not prepared him for writing professionally, and the path events and his talents sent him on did not require it. Some of his friends thought he had a writing block, others thought he did not write as a matter of Socratic principle; but it seems quite likely that the "cannot" and the "will not" each had their weight in him. Near the end of his life, he tried his hand at writing aphorisms; had he had time to practice, this might have been an apt medium for him, as whittling is for retired lumberjacks.

Blücher liked to argue and debate in small groups, and he liked to plant ideas for action in others, to conspire and work in secret. His gregariousness was balanced with a rare ability to enjoy solitude. Hannah Arendt's admiration for pariahs, great as it was, was less than Blücher's; but like his wife, he deplored excessive concern with one's isolated personality. He told his students "We cannot run after ourselves. We must see ourselves reflected in others. . . . The surest way of losing ourselves is to run after ourselves. In seeking the self we get lost in the labyrinth and are consumed by the Minotaur."[114] But while Hannah Arendt stressed the political dimension of "ourselves reflected in others," Blücher stressed the individual path by which true consciousness of self is obtained. She admired the Greek *polis*, he admired the men who were that *polis*, the men portrayed in Greek statuary, "the free-standing man." "To make up one's mind is the fundamental creative capability of man. By this, every individual begins to make himself into a free personality." With much less hesitation than Hannah Arendt, for whom trying to fabricate one's personality as though it was a work of art reflected a Romantic misunderstanding, Blücher spoke often of artistic creativity as the basic capacity of men. It is not surprising to find a self-made man putting self-making at the center of his thought, but it is remarkable that not egoism but, so to speak, alterism flowed from this center. Blücher did not view being a free-standing man as a possibility for the egoist, only for those who practiced what he called "erotics." There are, he said, two concerns without which philosophical activity is not possible: "erotics (friendship) and politics." "If they are not related, as in our time—and we have parted with them entirely," he said in 1967, "then we must integrate them again into some kind of human ethical responsibility. . . . We have neglected our primary duty: namely, to care for the human (i.e., political) relations that can only come into existence when men are free."

The kind of friendship which Blücher thought of as a part of erotics, was, for him, the basis of political action; in this he followed Aristotle, for whom *philia* bound those who acted together. He formulated a scale of relationships every person should be capable of, organized like a series of concentric circles flowing from the center. "Accepting the whole human being from within—love; accepting the whole personality from without—friendship; accepting an independent person—political relationship; accepting an individual as a member of society; accepting strangers as coworkers." These circles evolve in a person's life from the central experience of love. In his last lecture, in 1968, a lecture in which his relationship with Hannah Arendt is often anonymously invoked, Blücher said that "friendship means love without *eros*. The *eros* is overcome. It was there in the beginning, but it has been overcome and it doesn't count any more. What counts now is the mutual insight of two personalities who recognize each other as such; who in effect can say to each other 'I guarantee you the development of your personality and you guarantee me the development of mine.' That is the basis of all real community thinking, and such a community can only start with friends, in the relation of the elder with the younger."

What Blücher wanted his students to experience was this friendly relation of the elder with the younger, this preparation for political relationships, this education for politics. He wanted to teach his students what his life had taught him and what he thought he had taught his wife. "I was born in 1899," he often told them in his thick Berlin accent, "and am exactly as old as the 20th century. When I talk to you about Hellas, I am really talking about the 20th century." Blücher carried the great grudge he held against the late nineteenth century and much that he had seen in the twentieth century and gave his students what he thought they needed—examples. He told them about the free-standing Greeks and their heirs in later times.

Blücher never really overcame his hatred of Europe's bourgeois civilization and certainly not of Germany's particular path. But he did, in his later years, grow mellower about bourgeois comforts. He overcame his feeling that it was corrupting to own furniture, to enjoy clothing, to develop a taste for food and wine—he even marched around the Bard campus in a Burberry mackintosh, very pleased with this touch of elegance. But he remained unfailingly rigorous in his likes and dislikes and uncomplicated in his opinions: "he did see things *plain*," said Arendt's friend, Rosalie Colie, "both in their ideas and in their earthiness."[115] When Blücher disapproved of the way his students chose to indulge themselves in a "luxury society," he did not hesitate to say so. He thought that bourgeois society offered many "antiphilosophical" temptations and that drug-taking was one of the worst: "To ruin and destroy your perceptions [i.e., your senses] and then say you want to pursue the truth: are you crazy? The experiences you have you will not be able to communicate. They are not in the region of human speech; they are hallucinations. . . ." This judgment was respected by some, not by others. "I decided to study law," one of his last students recalled, "and came to him to ask advice. 'I think our society is headed for cataclysmic events,' I said, 'I can't see the law remaining stable for many years. Of what use would it be to be trained in it?' 'The use,' he said, 'is that you will be one of the ones to remember what it was.' "[116]

Friends and students from all strata of the past came to Heinrich Blücher's funeral at the Riverside Chapel on 4 November 1970. It was a simple ceremony, a time for sharing memories. Horace Kallen, who had helped Blücher and Bard College find each other; Blücher's colleagues, Ted Weiss, the poet, and Irma Brandeis; two of his students; and Mary McCarthy, who came from Paris, spoke of him.

Hannah Arendt was grateful for this ceremony, though it was not what her first impulse had demanded. To her friends' astonishment, she had wanted a Jewish funeral service for her non-Jewish husband, with Kad-dish spoken. Her childhood came forth in that wish. Memories of her father's death wove through her bereavement; she remembered how her mother and her grandmother had lived with the illnesses and deaths of their husbands. Even when nearly a year had passed and the anniversary of Blücher's death approached, she thought in the frame of the past. "I dream sometimes of a spa and I think, in my old age I should, as my mother and my grandmothers did at my age, treat myself to a cure. That tempts me very much, though I don't know exactly what I should under-take a cure *for.*"[117]

The only cure there was for being alone was friendship. The tribe members came frequently to the Riverside Drive apartment. Anne Weil came from France for a long stay the winter after Blücher's death. And she helped Hannah Arendt keep up with her traditional social events— there was a small New Year's party, and a party for the students in the New School seminar on Kant's *Critique of Judgment*. With help from Arendt's part-time maid, Sally Davis, Anne Weil did the shopping and cooking, and, most importantly, spoke German, with East Prussian idioms she and her friend had known since their youth. Life went on; as Anne Weil said, "Hannah just put one foot in front of the other." But there were moments when she stumbled.

Anne Weil came back one evening from a shopping expedition and opened the door with Blücher's key. Hannah Arendt, talking in the living room with one of her students, heard the familiar sounds and called out the familiar instructions—"Heinrich, leave your galoshes by the door." When Anne Weil came into the living room, Arendt gasped and sank back in her chair. But she said nothing.

She rarely spoke about how she felt. But she did tell Mary McCarthy, after coming home from a Bard College memorial service for Blücher in November, how it was to live without fearing for her husband.

The truth is that I am completely exhausted, if you understand by that no superlative of tiredness. I am not tired, or much tired, just exhausted. I function alright now but know that the slightest mishap could throw me off balance. I don't think I told you that for ten years I had been constantly afraid that just such a sudden death would happen. This fear frequently bordered on real panic. Where the fear was, and the panic, is now sheer emptiness. Sometimes I think without this heaviness inside me I can no longer walk. And it is true I feel like floating. If I think even a couple of months ahead I get dizzy. I am now sitting in Heinrich's room and using his typewriter. Gives me something to hold on to. The weird thing is that at no moment am I actually out of control.[118]

She kept her control and finished the semester of teaching. Looking weary and strained, she ended the semester with her reflections on Kant's attitude toward the French Revolution, and Marx's. Marx, she said wryly in the last lecture, "never made allowance for the unexpected."

Hannah Arendt was offered a two-week stay at Saint John's Abbey in Minnesota by a former student from Chicago, Father Chrysostom Kim. She went there in February 1971. The peaceful setting, the deep, still winter, calmed her; and the prospect of several weeks in Sicily the next spring, with Mary McCarthy and James West, gave her something to look forward to. Arendt finished the final version of "Thinking and Moral Considerations" for publication in *Social Research*. This gave her something to give to W. H. Auden—she dedicated the essay to him. And she asked Father Kim to issue an invitation to him for the next year. These were two of many gestures Arendt made to comfort Auden for her refusal to marry him.

Less than a month after Blücher's death, Auden went to Arendt's apartment to make his proposal, to suggest that the two of them—both alone—take care of each other. He had spent many late afternoons with Arendt and Blücher, talking and staying so long that a dinner invitation was usually extended, but he was not an intimate, and his life outside of her apartment was largely unknown to Arendt. She had been to his East Village apartment only once, for a dinner party to which T. S. Eliot and an odd assortment of Auden's young friends had come. The evening was chaotic, right down to the moment when Auden, possessing only one spoon for his demitasse, circulated it around the table for everyone to use. Arendt had mothered him—once taking him off to Saks and forcing him to buy a second suit—but she certainly did not wish to do so regularly.

She was shocked by Auden's proposal and by his condition. He came "looking so much like a *clochard*" that the doorman accompanied him to her apartment. He "said he had come back to New York only because of me," she told Mary McCarthy, "that I was of great importance to him, that he loved me very much. . . . I had to turn him down. . . . I am almost beside myself when I think of the whole matter. . . . I hate, am afraid of, pity, always have been, and I think I never knew anybody who aroused my pity to this extent."[119]

Three years later, a month before the third anniversary of Blücher's death, Arendt went to a memorial service for W. H. Auden at the Cathedral Church of Saint John the Divine. Auden had died at his summer home in Austria on 28 September 1973. During the service, Arendt took out a pencil and wrote on her copy of the program two of Auden's lines she had called up from her memory, for herself and for Auden:

> Sing of human unsuccess
> In a rapture of distress.

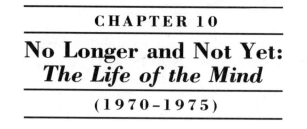

# CHAPTER 10

# No Longer and Not Yet: The Life of the Mind

## (1970-1975)

> All of us reason about and understand what people necessarily must be; we dream about, are bewitched by, what they accidentally and incomprehensibly are.
>
> Randall Jarrell, *Pictures from an Institution*

### The Consolation of Philosophy

In the five years she lived after Heinrich Blücher's death, Hannah Arendt never lost her ardent interest in the political realm. The summer after his death, she wrote a long analysis of the *Pentagon Papers*, "Lying in Politics"; during the summer before her own death, she followed the revolution in Portugal with the same intensity she had given twenty years earlier to the revolution in Hungary. But her mood was different. She longed for peace and quiet. Often she invoked the words that had been so appropriately spoken at Heinrich Blücher's memorial service: "We must go now, I to die, you to live, but which is better is known to the god alone," the somber words of Socrates' farewell in the *Apology*. Arendt's loneliness was, to those who knew her well, palpable. She had asked her friends from the tribe, when they gathered at her apartment the evening after Blücher's death, "How am I to live now?"

That evening she had no answer. But, slowly, she came to the answer that had been part of the Western tradition for many hundreds of years before Boethius wrote *On the Consolation of Philosophy*. Arendt did not wish to think the world away, in the Stoic manner, or to think herself away from the world; she did not ask philosophy to "compensate for the frustrations of politics, and, more generally, of life," as she wrote in *The Life of the Mind*, describing Boethius's need. But, like Karl Jaspers, she longed for the "free air" of philosophy. "During the last months I have often thought of myself—free like a leaf in the wind—*frei wie ein Blatt im Winde*. And all the time I also thought: Don't do anything against this, that is the way it [is], let no 'autocratic will' interfere."[1]

Hannah Arendt wrote this description of her lonely freedom to Mary McCarthy six months after Heinrich Blücher's death. But then she reflected further on her metaphor and wrote a retraction, sitting in the Riverside Drive apartment she had refused to give up because Blücher's absence was "there and alive in every corner and at every moment":

It is of course only half true. For there is, on the other hand, the whole *weight* of the past (*gravitas*). And what Hölderlin once said in a beautiful line:

> Und vieles
> Wie auf den Schultern eine
> Last von Scheiten ist
> Zu behalten.

"And much/as on your shoulders/a burden of logs/is to bear and keep."—In short: remembrance.

As she wrote these reflections, Arendt was in her usual place—between past and future, between memory and the unknown that lies ahead. But she was more deeply weighed down by personal loss than she had ever been and less inclined than ever to try to look into the future. Out of her own feelings, she sought a notion of "Thinking" that could range over the past and find in it a meaningful story and a notion of "Willing" that was free of autocracy.

When she came to write the "Willing" volume of *The Life of the Mind*, Hannah Arendt searched through a vast literature for an example of Willing conceived as a nonautocratic and noncommanding faculty. She found what she was seeking in the work of Duns Scotus: "I have a seminar this afternoon about Duns Scotus and since I have high respect for the gentleman, I am properly frightened. So, instead of preparing for class or just being afraid (by far the best preparation) I sat down to the typewriter."[2] She began to write Mary McCarthy a report about the spring 1972 bombing of Cambodia, and got only half way through the letter when news reached her that George Wallace had been shot. "Who will get his votes?" she wondered, while her reflections on Duns Scotus went undeveloped.

Throughout the early 1970s, Hannah Arendt struggled for a little freedom from political news. But she withdrew into her "thinking space" only to be called back by the frightening press of events. Philosophically, Arendt struggled for an image of how the mind can withdraw from the world without ignoring or demeaning it. In *The Life of the Mind*, she contrasted the Boethian, Stoic mode of seeking consolation for the world's evils with Hegel's mode. Rather than retreating from the world, Hegel absorbed it into his notion of the mind, *Geist*. This reconciliation through dissolution of the world into thought was even less appealing to Arendt than the Stoic mode. But she did speak of reconciliation as one of thinking's gifts. In the 1950s, as she explored the philosophical foundations of the historical work she had done in *The Origins of Totalitarianism*, she had strenuously rejected reconciliation, seeing it as a failure to be serious about the world and human action. But after the *cura posterior* of the Eichmann book reconciliation emerged in Hannah Arendt's thought as a possibility: "reconciliation of man as a thinking and reasonable being," she said in 1972, "this is what actually happens in the world."[3] Thinking, which prepares us to make judgments about the world, even about the most horrible things that happen in the world, was what Arendt's theme became in the 1970s.

For both Jaspers and Arendt philosophizing was an activity of solitude, though not of solitude far from friends. In the last years of her life, she relied on her friends more than ever for continuity, comfort, and reconciliation. In the fall of 1973, several months after Auden had died and on the occasion of Philip Rahv's death, she wrote to Mary McCarthy:

I must admit that I mind this defoliation (or deforestation) process. As though to grow old does not mean, as Goethe said, "gradual withdrawal from appearance"—which I do not mind—but the gradual (rather, sudden) transformation of a world with familiar faces (no matter, friend or foe) into a kind of desert, populated by strange faces. In other words, it is not me who withdraws but the world that dissolves—an altogether different proposition.[4]

As her forest thinned, Arendt spent more time with the tribe members in New York and, whenever possible, with two American friends who lived farther away—Mary McCarthy and J. Glenn Gray. These two were Arendt's chief companions for the work that came from her time in the "free air," *The Life of the Mind*. Mary McCarthy read parts of the book, heard parts of it in lectures, and finally edited it after Arendt's death. J. Glenn Gray took up the role from which first Jaspers and then Blücher had departed: he encouraged Arendt, discussed her work with her, supported her in person, by letter, and over the telephone.

J. Glenn Gray was deeply flattered when Hannah Arendt compared him to Karl Jaspers. He was not, as he understood, an intimate friend, for he had not known Hannah Arendt since youth; but her feeling that he and Jaspers thought in the same way brought Gray very close to her personally as well as philosophically. She had sensed when she met Gray at Wesleyan University in 1961 that he was someone with whom she could, as she told him, "let my hair down."[5] Gray was comfortable, unpretentious and discreet, careful about imposing himself. His respect for Arendt's privacy had always impressed her; when she went to his home in Colorado he arranged her visit with great care, adhering strictly to her request that there be "no singing"—no lectures, no public performances—only good talk with him and his Colorado College colleagues. She was not surprised to find that Gray's wife, Ursula, a German woman he had met while he worked for the American occupation forces, was a companion for him as Gertrud Jaspers had been for Karl Jaspers.

Gray's thought, like Jaspers's, was clearly and simply rooted in his experience. His reflections on men in battle, *The Warriors*, had germinated in him for nearly fifteen years after he returned to America from Europe, where he had gone as a soldier in the same year, 1941, that he finished his Ph.D. in philosophy at Columbia. "This much time was needed," Hannah Arendt noted in her preface to the second edition of *The Warriors*, "to learn 'simplicity,' to unlearn 'the simplication of abstract thinking,' to become fluent in the art and language of 'concrete' thoughts and feelings." Arendt felt that Gray was, after his learning and unlearning, able "to comprehend that both abstract notions and abstract emotions are not merely false to what actually happens but are viciously interconnected; abstract thinking is strictly comparable to the inhumanity of abstract emotions, the love and hate of collectives—my people, *the* enemy, especially in wartime, or, finally, in a mood of disillusionment, either hatred of or blind allegiance to 'mankind collectively [which] is doubtless as predisposed to injustice as nations are.'"[6] Arendt herself had struggled with hatred of *the* Germans and with claims that one should love *the* Jews or act for the sake of the abstraction, "Mankind," just as Karl Jaspers had struggled with his prewar notion that there was a "German essence." All, in their lives at home, were helped past abstractness: Arendt by her non-Jewish German husband, Jaspers by his Jewish German wife, and Gray by his German wife, to whom he dedicated his book—"To Ursula, formerly one of 'the enemy.'"

Gray valued his family, his friends, and his students at Colorado College as Arendt, after Blücher's death, valued her tribe and her students. During the early 1970s their moods often ran parallel. "Like you," he wrote to Arendt, "I get on best with my students, after my own family, and find that I have to fight against misanthropy as I get older. If I didn't have these, and a few friends, like you above all (so far you have never disappointed me), I would reiterate Kant's complaint about his old age—to the effect that a man of good will finds himself avoiding people from increasing disillusionment with the species. There are really few who hold up to one's expectations."[7] His gratitude to Hannah Arendt ran very deep, and it did much to sustain him. He wrote to her after she had sent him the introduction to his *The Warriors,* an introduction which helped the book find a much wider audience than it had had in its first small printing: "You seem to understand me, Hannah, better than I understand myself. . . . You have done me the greatest service a friend can do for another."[8] Gray did not, of course, mean just the service of the introduction itself, but the service of understanding and communication the introduction represented. When he wrote Hannah Arendt long letters of meticulous, thoughtful criticism of *The Life of the Mind* in the 1970s, Gray repaid this service in kind. And he gave it for the parts of the book which were most difficult for Hannah Arendt to write—her assessment and critique of Martin Heidegger in the "Willing" volume.

Gray had spent the year of 1967 in Freiburg, working with Heidegger on a project Hannah Arendt had urged upon him—the editorship of Harper and Row's series of Heidegger's works in English. Gray had accepted the editorship in 1965, on the condition that Hannah Arendt would check and approve the translations. Together, they paid Heidegger the service of understanding which they both took as the mark of philosophical loyalty. But the work also brought Heidegger the renewal of Arendt's personal loyalty, and for this J. Glenn Gray was the mediator.

After Heidegger's sharp reaction to the copy she sent him of her German translation of *The Human Condition* in 1961, Hannah Arendt had stayed away from Freiburg. Gray gave her the opportunity to return by arranging a lecture in the early summer of 1967, having convinced her that Heidegger had mellowed and moved away from the university infighting and cliquishness she found so distasteful. As a result of her visit, a new accord was struck between Arendt and Heidegger. She marked it a year later by agreeing to contribute to Heidegger's eightieth birthday *Festschrift* and by taking Heinrich Blücher to meet him for the first time; he marked it the next year by sending her a poem when Blücher died.

Arendt certainly had questions about Heidegger's character and opinions that her contribution to the 1969 *Festschrift* did not raise. She noted that many who retire from the world into a "thinking space" and celebrate the serenity (*Gelassenheit*) of their sojourns are blind to political realities and given to foolish opinions. Good judgment, she felt, presupposes a withdrawal from the world for thinking, but it does not necessarily follow from such a withdrawal. Lenient with Heidegger in her *Festschrift* article,[9] Arendt was much franker to J. Glenn Gray in private. Gray asked many Germans who had known Heidegger before the war about his Nazism and even considered writing a book about his political past. Arendt cautioned him about asking too many questions of Heidegger himself, knowing that his mistrust was easily aroused. She then went on to offer an explanation of why Heidegger had left an offensive sentence praising National Socialism in the postwar editions of his *Introduction to Metaphysics* (she did so without knowing that Heidegger and his German publisher had suggested that the sentence be extirpated from the American translation): "He probably left the sentence in to explain in an underhand way what he thought National Socialism was, namely, an encounter between global technology and modern man. The idea, as I said, is grotesque, but he is not the only one. I found a very similar notation in [Walter] Benjamin. The trouble with these gentlemen was, and no doubt always has been, that they couldn't read books like *Mein Kampf*— too boring—and preferred to read slightly crazy but highly interesting books by Italian futurists who later turned fascists."[10] Arendt told Gray that she felt that Heidegger's Nazism was a confused business; his 1933 speech accepting Freiburg's rectorship was, she thought "not Nazi . . . [but] a very unpleasant product of nationalism."[11] They agreed that Heidegger lacked both political judgment and discernment about people, and Gray, who then knew nothing of Hannah Arendt's youthful relationship with him, admitted that his personal regard for Heidegger was sometimes mixed with bewilderment.[12]

During his year in Freiburg, Gray tried to understand the paradoxes of Heidegger's personality and philosophy. He found the late works of Heidegger very perplexing, thinking that they represented a "flight from philosophical concepts" and an idolization of language as a nearly autonomous force.[13] But he sympathized with Heidegger's great and independent effort to rethink the philosophical foundations of the Western tradition, a tradition that Heidegger himself, Gray, and Arendt thought had ended. It amazed Gray that a man of Heidegger's genius could associate with mediocre minds so blindly, but he did not know whom to hold responsible for Heidegger's behavior. "If the Germans didn't kow-tow to him so much, they might get better results. For thus far he has been about as human and simple a man to talk with as I have found. I realize from the seminar that he can be different, but the students treat him so deferentially he consents to play the role."[14] Gray found the Freiburg philosophers a very discouraging lot, far removed from the pedagogical ideal he had written about in a book called *The Promise of Wisdom* and striven to attain in his classrooms at Colorado College. He was almost naively disconcerted by the academic politicking and intellectual pretentiousness of Heidegger's colleagues at Freiberg.[15] In such a tragicomical milieu, Gray thought Heidegger's brother was the only person with his feet on the ground, and he was delighted to report to Hannah Arendt Fritz Heidegger's bemused assessment of his brother: Martin was, when young, *normal wie jeder andere*, ("normal as everybody else") that is, he liked sports, girls, drinking, but then he discovered the phenomenological method of Husserl and ever after went circling around "Being" *wie eine Katze um den heissen Brei* ("like a cat around hot mush").[16] Arendt herself came to a more intellectual assessment of what had happened to Heidegger in his later years; she told Mary McCarthy she was convinced that "the so-called late Heidegger" was entirely influenced by the work of the German mystic, Meister Eckhart, and she knew well enough that universities are not designed for helping mystics return to earth from their philosophical flights.[17]

When Hannah Arendt set out to write about Martin Heidegger's philosophy in *The Life of the Mind*, she emphasized the differences between his early and late work, tracing his main concepts across the "turn" (*Kehre*) he had made during the Nazi years. She saw Heidegger during the years she worked on her book, but the meetings were very unsatisfactory; Heidegger's wife would not leave them alone to talk. J. Glenn Gray sympathized with her irritation, for his own talks with Heidegger had often been inhibited by Mrs. Heidegger's presence.[18] Gray also gave his support to Arendt's decision to write frankly her criticisms of Heidegger's work and to "let the chips fall where they may." He urged her on by citing Heidegger himself: "Heidegger has somewhere a wonderful phrase about Hegel, 'whose rationalism cannot be sufficiently praised or blamed.'"[19]

Arendt focused her criticism on Heidegger's notion of the Will, which he interpreted in terms of autocracy or the will-to-power and associated with technology's inevitably destructive domination. Rejecting the technological mode and rejecting the Will, Heidegger had turned to thinking. Heidegger's view that willing and thinking are necessarily in conflict was one that Arendt wanted to criticize, as she wanted to reject both his repudiation of willing in favor of thinking and his contention that thinking itself is a kind of acting. She thought that Heidegger had once nearly avoided the repudiation of willing she so disliked; his praiseworthy but ultimately unsuccessful effort had come just after the war, before the "reality of Adenauer's Germany" had crushed Heidegger's—and Jaspers's—brief hopes for a new Germany and a new Europe. For a moment, she felt, Heidegger had turned away from his preoccupation with Being to a concern for beings and for history—even for politics—and to the possibility that, in privileged eras, eras of transition, men can become "mindful of what is destined." The moment passed, and Heidegger went on to repudiate willing, which, in Arendt's terms, meant rejecting the possibilities of politics, of action that begins something new.[20]

The possibility Heidegger had turned away from was the one Hannah Arendt wanted to take up in *The Life of the Mind*. She worked in a period that completely lacked the hopefulness that Heidegger had felt immediately after the war. America, and the world, in the early 1970s seemed bleak to Arendt; and it was Mary McCarthy to whom she turned for comfort in the bleakness.

The spring after Heinrich Blücher's death, Arendt went to Sicily with Mary McCarthy and her husband, James West. Before she left America, she completed negotiations with the New School's graduate faculty for a teaching schedule, a salary, and a pension plan that permitted her to turn down a lucrative offer from the City University of New York. Except for one professor who felt that she was "a journalist, not a philosopher," her new colleagues were delighted. The only drawback was that she, like most of them, was near retirement. The situation at the former "University in Exile" was precarious as the generation of exiles that had given the institution its fame began to be thinned by death and retirement. And the New School was not the only institution suffering from the old age of its pillars. When Arendt went to Washington in the spring to celebrate the twentieth anniversary of the National Committee for an Effective Congress, she met the congressmen who had opposed Senator Joseph McCarthy in the 1950s and won praise in Robert Griffith's book, *The Politics of Fear*. These men, Fulbright, Symington, Ervin, and others, were Arendt's age, nearing retirement, and she wondered who would replace them. Within two years, as the Watergate scandal broke, she was to find out that they did not need replacing so quickly. When she had considered Senator Sam Ervin's role in the Watergate Hearings she told her publisher, William

Jovanovich: "I am developing a crush on Senator Ervin . . . long live old age. Old people, if they are halfway sensible, are almost impossible to intimidate—their careers are behind them, and they will die soon anyway—a very nice and comforting thought under certain circumstances."[21]

This nice and comforting thought was one that came to Arendt herself a number of times during the early 1970s, but not during the vacation in Sicily. It was such a pleasant and restorative visit that Arendt decided to do something she had done before only with the Jasperses—be the long-term houseguest of friends. She agreed to join the Wests at their summer house in Castine, Maine, for a month, after she made a trip to New Haven to receive an honorary degree from Yale University. Mary McCarthy offered a little apartment over her garage, removed from the household traffic, ideal for working, and there Arendt wrote "Lying in Politics: Reflections on the Pentagon Papers." The alternative was perfect, for Arendt had felt that she could not return to Tegna, in Switzerland, where she and Blücher had spent their last summer together.

In her "Lying in Politics" essay, as in an interview she had granted to Adalbert Reif in Germany just after the Sicilian venture, Arendt spoke in a mood of defiance, unintimidated, with no thought for whom she would please or displease. She sent her criticisms to the Right and to the Left, noting the forms of thoughtlessness that cross all political lines. She focused on the mental manner of the "problem-solvers," those Washington policymakers who were "remarkably free from the sins of ideology" but treated hypotheses as reality and theories as established facts. She noted the pervasive "inability or unwillingness to consult experience and to learn from reality" of people who never imagined the consequences of their actions and commands. In the Reif interview, as earlier in "Reflections on Violence," Arendt focused on the sins of ideology prevalent among the New Left students in America and in Germany. The young people who would like to be revolutionaries "are so fond of loose, theoretical talk," Arendt held, that they "go peddling obsolete conceptions and categories mainly derived from the nineteenth century" without stopping to analyze actually existing conditions.[22]

After she had delivered her "Lying in Politics" as a lecture at the Council for Religion and International Affairs in Washington and published it as an essay in the New York Review of Books, Arendt received requests for speaking engagements from all over the country. Even young people who were disturbed by her earlier criticisms of the New Left welcomed "Lying in Politics" as an oasis of sanity in America's dark times. She went to a number of universities in the winter of 1971/72 to deliver the lecture or to discuss it. Crisscrossing the country, she spoke at Haverford and Carleton, Notre Dame and Harvard. Her reflections were debated at forums like the one held by the *Partisan Review*, where Hans Morgenthau and Noam Chomsky conducted a session devoted to the Pentagon papers. At just the moment that she wanted to find peace and quiet for *The Life of the Mind*, Arendt was besieged. She accepted the price of her reputation dutifully, but impatiently.

Arendt gave courses that fall at the New School on "The History of the Will" and began to write out the manuscript of "Willing." But her speaking engagements distracted her from the work. She went to a conference at the New School on "The Intellectual and Political Phenomenon of Weimar," a dinner party at the home of Dorothy Norman for Prime Minister Indira Gandhi of India, an informal discussion at a Danforth Foundation conference on the politicizing of the universities, the December meeting of the American Historical Association where she chaired a panel on women in Weimar, a January conference at the Museum of Modern Art on "Institutions for a Post-Technological Society." This schedule, heavy in comparison to many of Arendt's academic semesters, left her tired. She made her tiredness considerably worse by ignoring the advice of her doctor, who told her in December 1971 that she had angina. Matter-of-factly, she reported the news to Mary McCarthy:

And also my angina business is confirmed; or so my doctor believes. By no means bad enough to get excited about. But of course the usual talk—slow down, stop smoking, etc. Since I am certainly not going to live for my health, I'll do what I think is right—avoid everything which could bring me in an unpleasant situation, by which I mean a situation in which I am forced to make a fuss. Cut down on smoking or even cut it out if it does not bother me or prevent me from writing. If that is not possible, *tant pis*. (This incidentally just among ourselves; here nobody knows about this.)[23]

Hannah Arendt did exactly what she thought was right, which meant that she did not stop smoking and did not cancel any of her engagements. But when word reached her that her application for restitution from the German government had been granted with a German Supreme Court ruling—the *lex Arendt*, which established the precedent for all applications from professors whose careers had been interrupted by the Nazi takeover in 1933—she did make a sensible resolution. She used part of the money to ease her day-to-day life: she hired secretaries to type both her English and her German correspondence and moved much of her entertaining out of her apartment and into restaurants. When she did entertain at home, she hired a waiter in addition to her maid and gave parties that would have been much too elegant for Blücher's tastes. Finally, she made a reservation for a long, restful stay in the summer of 1972 at the Casa Barbete in Tegna.

Arendt's decision to return to Tegna was a mark of her exhaustion; she could no longer mourn for Blücher as she had in the year after his death. She told Mary McCarthy, in January 1972, that she was not surprised at how Miriam Chiaramonte mourned the death of her brilliant husband Nicolò, one of McCarthy's closest friends: "Miriam is quite in tune with Jewish mourning . . . [the Jews] are expressive, demonstrative, and know how to lament. And lamentations (of which I am perhaps no longer capable) are what we owe the dead ones precisely because we go on living."[24] Arendt went to Bard College yearly on the anniversary of Blücher's death and sat on the stone bench she had ordered placed near his tombstone. But she did not lament. She just sat, quietly, thinking, and did what she said the thinker does, "make the absent present."

## This Thinking Business

Before she left for the summer, Arendt received more unexpected and pleasing letters. Invitations to accept honorary degrees came from Dartmouth, Fordham, and Princeton. And then Edward Wright of Aberdeen University in Scotland wrote to ask her if she would deliver the spring 1973 Gifford Lectures. Wright's invitation was such a model of British understatement that Hannah Arendt had to send her New School research assistant off to a library to find out what the Gifford Lectures were. She was amazed and flattered when she surveyed the list of luminaries who had lectured in Aberdeen, beginning in 1888 with the German Orientalist, Max Müller, and including such philosophers as Royce, James, Bergson, Whitehead, Dewey, Gilson, and Marcel. But she responded with an understatement of her own, the invitation was accepted with the comment that it was, indeed, an "exciting proposition."[25]

Knowing that she would have to have her "Thinking" manuscript finished in less than a year, Arendt set off for Europe in July. She made her family visits—to Gertrud Jaspers in Basel, and then for a week to the

Fuersts in Israel—and her visit to Heidegger. And then she retired to the Casa Barbete in Tegna to work under the supervision of the innkeeper, Mrs. Jenny. She interrupted her stay in Tegna for three weeks in August to go to the equally beautiful and restful Villa Serbelloni near Lake Como, the residence of the Rockefeller Foundation's international seminars. Arendt later thanked the Rockefeller Foundation for their hospitality by agreeing to join Paul Freund, Irving Kristol, and Hans Morgenthau for a discussion designed to launch the foundation's new humanities fellowships. Her remarks at that discussion, reported in the *New York Times*, reveal clearly the attitude she had brought to her work on *The Life of the Mind*. She addressed the "crisis of values" in America by speaking of the proper way to read and to teach the great works of Western literature and philosophy. "To look to the past in order to find analogies by which to solve our present problems is, in my opinion, a mythological error. If you cannot read these great books with love and pure motives, just because you are fond of the life of the spirit—of the life of man—it won't do you any good and it won't do the students any good."[26]

Many of those who read Arendt's "Thinking" section of *The Life of the Mind* when it appeared, first in the *New Yorker* and then as a book, found it surprisingly unpolitical in comparison to her works from the 1950s and 1960s. And it certainly was, in the sense that it reflected Arendt's conviction that thinking involves a purposeless withdrawal from the world, with "pure motives," with love. Arendt felt that thinking was a very different matter than knowing. Knowing—scientific cognition—has an object and a purpose, while thinking is objectless and self-referential. Similarly, she thought that knowing's result, truth, is a very different thing than thinking's "result," meaning, or a meaningful story.

One of the key questions Arendt had about this self-referential thinking process was how it related to its own mode of manifestation in the world, language. Indeed, throughout *The Life of the Mind* she had to deal with the oddness of describing in language what cannot be seen: the mental activities of thinking, willing, and judging. In her work Arendt had always had a problem establishing her point of view: in *The Human Condition* she had tried to write about the *vita activa* without assuming the traditional stance, without writing from the point of view of the *vita contemplativa*; in *The Life of the Mind*, she had to write about the *vita contemplativa* from somewhere. But where? Indirectly, the topic came up at Princeton in April 1972 when Hannah Arendt went with Elizabeth Hardwick to hear the French novelist Natalie Sarraute give the Christian

Gauss lectures. Sarraute, a close friend of Mary McCarthy's, was a writer Arendt admired for the same kind of rigorous honesty she found in Mary McCarthy's work. In a review of Sarraute's *The Golden Fruits* in 1964, Arendt had cited the advice given to Alyosha by Father Zossima in *The Brothers Karamazov:* "Master, what must I do to gain eternal life?" "Above all, do not lie to yourself."[27] In the year she reviewed *The Golden Fruits*, Arendt herself took this advice as a buffer against the inauthentic intellectual milieu Sarraute satirized and Arendt detested, having just suffered from it by way of the "Eichmann Controversy." In her novels, Sarraute performed the magic trick of making the invisible psychological realm visible, a part of the "surface world" of linguistically describable appearances. At Princeton, in the question period after Sarraute's lecture, Arendt wanted to know about this magic. "But when you take the invisible and put it into words, then it is in the realm of 'appearances,' no?" "Not precisely," Madame Sarraute answered, as Elizabeth Hardwick recalled, with a "sly little smile."[28]

When Hannah Arendt tried to describe the "thinking space" in a metaphor, she too finally had to do so with a sly little smile. She offered the spatial metaphor of the "timeless now," suspended between past and future, which she called a "perfect metaphor." Then she had to admit that this is, really, a contradiction in terms; phenomena are precisely *not* mental, and metaphors are supposed to bridge the gap between the mental and the phenomenal or worldly. Metaphors are *not* to stay within the mental realm. Hannah Arendt never did solve the problem of perspective, never did say where she was standing as she portrayed the mental realm. Her critics, however, found her unidentified point of view problematic for other reasons.

To write about thinking as she did in the fall of 1972 was not an easy task. Withdrawal from the world for thinking was difficult, and her commitment to it was often called into question. The challenges came in quick succession at an October conference in Toronto organized by the Toronto Society for the Study of Social and Political Thought. The "Conference on the Work of Hannah Arendt" at York University, where one of Arendt's University of Chicago students, Melvyn Hill, was a professor, consisted of four papers, two of them by political theorists Arendt knew and respected highly—Richard Bernstein of Haverford College and Ernst Vollrath of Cologne University and the New School—and much discussion. Arendt was on the defensive in the discussion, for her interlocutors wanted to know why she, as a political theorist, rejected both the desire to influence others as a teacher and the desire to act. She spoke from a position that the activists in the group found very disturbing:

I don't believe we [political theorists] have, or can have, such influence in your sense. I think that commitment can easily carry you to a point where you do no longer think. There are certain extreme situations where you have to act. But these situations are extreme.... And I think... the theoretician who tells his students what to think and how to act is... my God! These are adults! We are not in the nursery.[29]

The young activists were puzzled, but so were old friends like Hans Morgenthau, who asked Arendt a question many of her readers had asked themselves over the years:

*Morgenthau:* What are you? Are you a conservative? Are you a liberal? Where is your position within the contemporary possibilities?
*Arendt:* I don't know. I really don't know and I've never known. And I suppose I never had any such position. You know the left think I am conservative, and the conservatives sometimes think I am left or a maverick or God knows what. And I must say I couldn't care less. I don't think the real questions of this century will get any kind of illumination by this kind of thing.

Those of Arendt's friends who attended the conference were not surprised by her stance, or rather her lack of stance. Morgenthau himself, Mary McCarthy, William Jovanovich, and Jonathan Schell, William Shawn's "Talk of the Town" political columnist at the *New Yorker,* had known for years that their friend defied labeling. But all could understand the sense of urgency Arendt's young interlocutors felt.

The fall of 1972 was a time that called out for commitments. Just before she went to Toronto, Arendt had attended a convocation sponsored by the Committee for Public Justice, an organization to which she also made financial contributions. At the convocation, plans for a May 1973 program at the New York University School of Law on "Secrecy in Government" were discussed. The committee members knew that the trial of the Watergate burglars, scheduled for January 1973, would bring into the public view a potentially explosive instance of government secrecy. But they did not know that by the time their May conference started the Ellsberg-Russo trial would be ending and the Senate Watergate hearings beginning; they did not know that the October 1972 agreement to end American military operations in Vietnam would have been violated by bombings both of North Vietnamese cities and of neutral

Cambodia. As Anthony Lewis of the *New York Times* pointed out in his opening remarks for the May conference's public record: "Vietnam and Watergate . . . those two great series of events—we might better call them earthquakes—changed the feelings of millions of Americans toward their institutions."[30]

Hannah Arendt could not attend the May 1973 conference; she was due in Aberdeen for the Gifford Lectures on 21 April. But before she left, she made donations to various antiwar groups, including the Fellowship for Reconciliation, which placed advertisements in the *New York Times* entitled "Congress End the War." This donation was just as necessary but less personal than the one she had made a year before to the Fellowship for Reconciliation's "Auction for Peace." Then she had given up for auction one of the few volumes from her father's library that had survived: her 1795 first edition of Kant's *Zum Ewigen Frieden* ("*Perpetual Peace*").

Hannah Arendt had been very reticent about discussing her "Thinking" work before she went to Aberdeen for the Gifford Lectures. At the Toronto conference and again, in January 1973, at another conference dedicated to her work, she simply stated that she was trying to get clear about "this thinking business." At the second conference, sponsored by the American Society for Christian Ethics, she had formulated her main thesis in response to two papers about her work and its relevance to the "radicality of the crisis" in the churches. "Thinking," she told her audience, "prepares us ever anew to meet whatever we must meet in our daily lives."

So I think that this "thinking," about which I wrote and am writing now— thinking in the Socratic sense—is a maieutic function, a midwifery. That is, you bring out all your opinions, prejudices, what have you; and you know that never, in any of the [Platonic] dialogues did Socrates ever discover any child [of the mind] who was not a wind-egg. That you remain in a way empty after thinking. . . . And once you are empty, then, in a way which is difficult to say, you are prepared to judge. That is, without having any book of rules under which you can subsume a particular case, you have got to say "this is good," "this is bad," "this is right," "this is wrong," "this is beautiful," and "this is ugly." And the reason why I believe so much in Kant's *Critique of Judgment* is not because I am interested in aesthetics but because I believe that the way in which we say "that is right, that is wrong" is not very different from the way in which we say "this is beautiful, this is ugly." That is, we are now prepared to meet the phenomena, so to speak, head-on, without any preconceived system. And, please, including my own![31]

At Aberdeen, Arendt delivered a series of dense, difficult lectures, but the main theme was as straightforward as this synopsis: she advocated what she called *Denken ohne Geländer* ("thinking without a bannister").[32] Hannah Arendt never found it easy to say how thinking prepares us for judging, but she worked toward such a statement with the clear sense that "Judging," the projected third part of *The Life of the Mind*, would link her philosophical reflections to the political realm. Judging, she held, is the truly political activity of the mind.

When Arendt left Scotland after the first series of Gifford Lectures, she returned to Tegna. Her judgment, like that of all Americans, was severely tested by the Watergate Hearings. She was distracted and anxious. "I had the impression that Nixon would actually emerge as victor in the guise of saviour of the nation from Watergate, to be blamed not on him or on the White House, but on Congress," she told Mary McCarthy in one of the meandering English sentences typical of her when she was living in a German-speaking place.[33] But as the summer of 1973 passed, she was relieved: "I just read excerpts of [Nixon's] speech and a few comments on the reaction, and I am reassured. He seems to have been again on the defensive, without answering in detail—which, of course, he cannot do anyhow—and to me the whole thing sounded like he was afraid." She was sympathetic to the widespread apprehension in America that impeachment proceedings against the president would bring chaos: "Since Nixon actually behaved like a tyrant, his downfall would be a kind of revolution. I, too, feel that the consequences would be quite unpredictable and possibly of great magnitude."[34] Arendt was angry at the Democrats for not taking more initiative in the electoral realm: "They believe that the Republicans will hang themselves and they can afford to do nothing. Which is a great mistake." And she suspected that the Watergate Hearings would confuse the political situation in America even as they clarified it: "The overwhelming number of scandals which come to light is in a way self-defeating. Everybody, so it must *seem*, did more or less what Nixon did, and where all are guilty, no one is."[35] Arendt anticipated the despair which would soon be translated into the view that "all politicians are corrupt."

Even though she had a restful summer, and a good two-week vacation on the island of Rhodes with Hans Morgenthau, Arendt was not able to find the proper peace for her work on "Willing." Morgenthau himself disconcerted her. For years they had enjoyed each other's company, and after Blücher's death he often took Arendt out for dinners in their favorite New York restaurants. For his companionship and political talk, Arendt was always grateful, but when he suggested that they convert their friendship into a marriage, she refused. Her refusal was not given with any guilt or pity, but when Morgenthau suffered from a series of illnesses in the next few years, Arendt was intensely solicitous, calling him frequently and consulting often with his daughter, Susanna. They did not vacation together again after the time in Rhodes, but Morgenthau continued in his role as escort. Arendt always praised him with the phrase she reserved for men of action—*masculini generis*—but she felt that he was without the kind of "real understanding of people"[36] she had loved in Blücher.

When Arendt returned to Tegna, from Rhodes, her work on the "Willing" manuscript went very slowly. She was not on the familiar territory of thinking, where she could "simply trust my instinct and my own experience." She had a large collection of notes and pieces from a Chicago seminar in 1972 and from her fall 1971 courses at the New School, "Selected Readings on the History of the Will" and "History of the Will," a lecture and a seminar. But her pieces lacked a clear order and a definite direction. Lost in a forest of interpretations of Augustine, Aquinas, and Duns Scotus, she could not see the trees, particularly the neighboring nineteenth-century trees about which she and J. Glenn Gray had many a quarrel. In her path stood Hegel.

Arendt expected that she would be distracted in the fall of 1973 as she took up Hegel's political writings. She had two courses to do on Greek political theory, a mass of complicated negotiations at the New School over replacing the faculty in philosophy, diminished by one more with the death of the phenomenologist Aron Gurwitch, and a number of meetings with lawyers to arrange to buy her Riverside Drive apartment. She anticipated that the Watergate scandals would occupy much of her attention, and she knew she had another meeting of the Committee on Public Justice, on "Watergate as Symbol," to attend. For October, she had scheduled a week of filming sessions with French Television—her ban against television interviews not extending to European countries, where she would not have to worry about being recognized on the street. But she did not expect and could not anticipate the personal and political episodes of that fall which struck her most deeply—the death of W. H. Auden, and the October War in the Middle East.

Arendt met her classes as usual the week after Auden's death on 28 September, but she was haggard and unsure of herself. The students who had known her at the time of Blücher's death were surprised to find that she was without the public composure she had summoned then; she wept when one of them came forward to offer to accompany her to Auden's memorial service at the Cathedral of Saint John the Divine. At the memorial service, dressed in black, listening to the poets who assembled to read from Auden's poetry and to the choir which sang the Anglican Chant of Psalm 130 and Benjamin Britten's "Offertory Anthem," with Auden's wonderful text, she was lost in melancholy. To Mary McCarthy, she revealed her anguish: "I am still thinking of Wystan, naturally, and of the misery of his life, and that I refused to take care of him when he came and asked for shelter."[37]

When she sat down to write her own memorial for Auden, in preparation for a testimonial meeting of the American Academy of Arts and Sciences on 14 November, Arendt tried to explain to herself why Auden had tried so desperately in his last years to pretend to have been "lucky." She focused upon Auden's ability to let himself feel in full vulnerability the curse of "human unsuccess" and to:

> Sing of human unsuccess
> In a rapture of distress.

Without, of course, revealing how she had come by her knowledge, she said: "Now, with the sad wisdom of remembrance, I see him as having been an expert in the infinite varieties of unrequited love."[38]

## De Senectute

During the 1967 war in the Middle East, Hannah Arendt had been intensely proud of the Israeli victories. Usually critical of Israeli policy, she behaved, as one of her friends remarked, "like a war bride." Arendt distinguished sharply between aggressive and defensive military involvement, and she thought the 1967 war as reasonable as the 1956 one had been foolish. Reflecting on the Six Day War in October 1967, she wrote to Mary McCarthy, "Any real catastrophe in Israel would affect me more deeply than almost anything else."[39] In 1973, when Egypt and Syria invaded Israeli territory on Yom Kippur, the catastrophe seemed imminent, and Arendt feared that Israel might this time be destroyed. The war began on 6 October, the day that Arendt started the week-long interview with Roger Ererra for French Television, and the script of the interview reflects her preoccupation. "The Jewish people are united in Israel," she said, and even went on to explain, without criticism, that Judaism was a *national* religion.[40] She and Roger Ererra, a Sephardic Jew and editor of the "Diaspora" series for Calmann-Lévy Publishers in Paris, went together to a meeting at the Columbia University School of Law where various suggestions for aiding the Israeli cause were considered. Arendt made a contribution to the United Jewish Appeal, as she had in 1967, and made arrangements to be able quickly to offer financial assistance to her relatives in Tel Aviv if the war threatened their safety. When the tide of the fighting turned in the second week of October, she tried to take up her "Willing" manuscript again: "I have some trouble to get back to work chiefly of course because of this unexpected outbreak of 'history,'" she wrote to Mary McCarthy.[41]

Hannah Arendt wrote to Mary McCarthy ironically, echoing her long-neglected Hegel critique, the heart of which was her claim that Hegel's view of history precluded the unexpected. Events like the Yom Kippur invasion stood for Arendt as the marks of how far Hegel's philosophy of history had strayed from common sense and the needs of a "new science of politics." Hegel's insistence on the primacy of the future and his commitment to History as Progress entailed a mental "no" to present events; the present could be nothing but an unactualized form of a Whole to be revealed in the future. Hannah Arendt interpreted Hegel's *Geist* as a Will, inherently hostile to that thinking which, through remembrance, draws upon the past for its images. Her project in the "Willing" volume of *The Life of the Mind* was to analyze the history of the antagonistic relations between Thinking and Willing, between the "thinking space" and the political realm where contingency and unexpectedness are always disconcertingly present. With her analysis, she hoped to be able to suggest a peace treaty between Thinking and Willing, a mode of mutual appreciation. To do this, she had to show the insufficiency of Hegel's critics, Nietzsche and Heidegger, who simply avoided conflict by believing that Thinking is itself a kind of acting. Arendt wanted to maintain the distinctions of the Thinking and Willing faculties, but not their competition for ascendancy in the life of the mind. Her method of criticizing Nietzsche and Heidegger for "willing-not-to-will" was to prepare the way for seeing "men of action" as exemplars of the proper attitude toward the future— that is, an attitude welcoming novelty.

One way to think out the relationship of Thinking and Willing occurred to Hannah Arendt as she watched the Watergate hearings and contemplated their probable aftermath in America. Again and again, she was impressed by the role the "old ones" played in the crisis. During the hearings, she admired Senator Sam Ervin's crusty, Bible-quoting style. When Nixon fired the Watergate special prosecutor, Archibald Cox, and tried to invoke executive privilege as a means to keep his tape recordings of White House conversations from the public, Arendt felt that the "old ones" of the Supreme Court saved the day. She signed a petition organized by Political Scientists for Impeachment in November 1973, and hoped that the "old ones" in Congress would push impeachment proceedings forward.

At a February 1974 Columbia University "Conference on the Humanities and Public Policy Issues," Hannah Arendt noted that the decay of the Republic had brought about a situation in which "the only place where a citizen still functions as a citizen is as a member of a jury."[42] During a week spent doing jury duty in New York shortly before, she had been deeply impressed by the fairness and impartiality of her fellow jurors. Like the jurors she had served with, the Supreme Court justices set aside their prejudices, political allegiances, and debts to give what the judicial traditions of the Republic called for—impartial reflection. Arendt was convinced that she could see in the courts the "Judging" she intended to consider in the last volume of *The Life of the Mind*. As she questioned how such Judging relates to Willing and Thinking, the other two mental faculties, she turned to Cicero's *De Senectute*, wondering whether his treatise might give her a portrait of the harmony of mental faculties in old age.

In Cicero's treatise, Old Cato tells his friends that "great deeds are not done by strength or speed or physique; they are the products of thought and character and judgment. And far from diminishing, such qualities actually increase with old age." Arendt agreed and, as she read, she thought that she might write a sequel to *The Life of the Mind*, a modern *De Senectute*, not only to oppose the tendency of contemporary youth to denigrate old age and the tendency of books like Simone de Beauvoir's *The Coming of Age* to lament it, but to argue that equanimity like Old Cato's should inspire good judgment in people of any age.

In *The Life of the Mind*, Arendt noted that old age, from the perspective of the Will, means the loss of a future. Futurelessness need not, however, be a cause for anguish; it can yield up the past, the course of one's life, for inspection and reflection. The backward glance of the "thinking ego" elicits the past's meaning and shapes it into a life story.

From the point of view of Thinking, old age is a time for meditation, for detachment from the clamor of self-interest and the distortions of partisanship. But Arendt felt that anyone who ceases to worship the future and ends a blind adherence to doctrines of Progress can gain for him or herself the joy thinking finds in remembrance and the "result" of thinking's meaningfulness, a coherent story. Old age can bring the feeling of being "free as a leaf in the wind," but one can also decide—as Pope John XXIII, for example, did—to live "from day to day." Judgment, which presupposes that one has withdrawn from the world for thinking, need not be at war with Willing, but it suffers if the Will is dominant in the mind's trinity.

Hannah Arendt's *The Life of the Mind* is, to put the matter very simply, a treatise on mental good governance. Through a complexly woven series of reflections and analyses, Arendt tried to present an image of the three mental faculties checking and balancing each other like three branches of government. No one faculty should dominate the other two; each should live and have its being in freedom. The precondition for such mental harmony is the internal freedom of each of the three faculties. Each has a self-relation, an inner duality which must not become a relation of dominance. Neither partner in the thinking dialogue should silence or refuse to hear the other; neither the I-will nor the I-nil should autocratically command unconditional obedience of its other half. And, in the judging faculty, neither the individual spectator's "I" nor the opinions of others brought imaginatively into mental view should prevail; judging is a mental interplay of self and imagined others who share the self's world. In the manuscript of *The Life of the Mind*, the internal freedoms of the faculties are very clearly and thoroughly presented. But the image of interfaculty relations is incomplete; Hannah Arendt did not live to write the "Judging" section and so the relation of this faculty to Thinking and Willing is not presented. The ideal—good governance, equality between the faculties—is clear, but a constitution for the mental republic was not drawn up.

The "Willing" manuscript had to be ready for the second series of Gifford Lectures by the first week of May 1974. From January to mid-April, Arendt kept her obligations to a minimum. Just before she left for Scotland, she flew to Milwaukee for a speaking engagement and then received a visit from Mary McCarthy in New York. But by then she had her lectures in hand. The outline, which she had submitted to the Gif-

ford Lectures committee earlier, indicates that the lectures were organized just as the published manuscript is, with the exception of the
fourth and last section, which included Arendt's discussion of Nietzsche,
Heidegger, and the exemplary "men of action," the American Founding
Fathers. Arendt later decided to restructure and expand this section. Two
realizations brought her to the conclusion that she should work into the
chapter a much more complete discussion of Heidegger's work. First, she
understood, in Scotland, that if she was ever going to write an extensive
critique of Heidegger, she would have to do it for *The Life of the Mind*;
and, second, in 1975 she concluded that the eighty-five-year-old Heidegger, growing deaf and unwell, would be unlikely to live to read and be
offended by her critique.

Arendt's first consideration was the product of her stay in Scotland. In
the middle of her "Willing" lecture, still weary from her flight to London,
family visits, and her trip to Aberdeen, she suffered a nearly fatal heart
attack. William Jovanovich, who was present at the lecture, rushed to her
aid and supplied her with some of the medication he carried for his own
heart condition. She was rushed to the nearest hospital and placed in an
intensive-care unit.

Lotte Kohler flew to Scotland from New York and took over the role of
companion from Mary McCarthy who had come from Paris. All were
impressed by Hannah Arendt's recalcitrance as a patient. She made a good
recovery, but she took up her cigarettes as soon as the oxygen tent was
removed from her room, refused to eat sensibly or cut down on her daily
coffee intake, and mustered an irritated bravado which thwarted all efforts
to keep her calm. Disdainful remarks about people who live for their
health and allow fusses to be made about them were as numerous in her
sickroom as letters and telegrams from well-wishers. After she was released from the hospital and lodged in a hotel, she was impatient and
wanted to leave for Tegna before her doctor thought it safe for her to
travel. When she was finally given permission to depart on 27 May, Mary
McCarthy accompanied her to London and Elke Gilbert joined her there
for the trip to Tegna.

Once she was safely in the Casa Barbete, Hannah Arendt grew calmer.
She rested and gratefully received a train of concerned visitors—Robert
Gilbert, her two Königsberg friends Hella Jaensch and Anne Weil, Hans
Jonas and his wife Eleonore, and Hans Morgenthau. But, after a month
of quiet, she insisted on making a strenuous trip to Freiburg to see
Heidegger. The visit was not a success, as Elfriede Heidegger again would

not leave Arendt alone with her husband, and Arendt returned to Tegna depressed and angry. But the month of August was relaxing enough to allow her to put this disappointment behind. She did, however, begin to give serious thought to a critique of Heidegger's work.

After the summer of her recovery from the heart attack, Arendt curtailed her work schedule and urged her friends to visit her. She took great care both to revive old friendships that had lapsed during her busy, preoccupied years of work on *The Life of the Mind* and to repair those that had suffered in the controversy over *Eichmann in Jerusalem*. Her new venue was launched with several good days of visiting in New York with J. Glenn Gray. Almost every evening, after she had finished her day's work, Arendt arranged for a visit from one or two of the tribe members or an expedition, with company, to the cinema, the theatre, concerts. Lotte Kohler visited frequently, and called often on the telephone to exchange news. The Klenborts, Lotte Beradt, Rose Feitelson, Alcopley, Hans Morgenthau, the Jonases, the Barons, the Hubers, and others came frequently; most were on hand for the tribe's traditional New Year's party, hosted for 1975 by Rose Feitelson. Arendt went for dinners with Robert Pick, who was not well enough to come to her, and they reminisced about their old friend, Hermann Broch. Younger and newer friends—the novelist Renata Adler and the philosophy professor Joan Stambaugh, as well as a number of students—"the children" as Arendt called them— were taken out to dinner at various New York restaurants. One of the most pleasant of the many social events Arendt attended through the fall of 1974 and into the beginning of 1975 was a Passover seder at the home of Louis Finkelstein, director of the Jewish Theological Seminary. Many of the people at the seder, including Finkelstein himself and several of his colleagues, had not seen Hannah Arendt socially since the publication of *Eichmann in Jerusalem*. Radiantly happy to be welcomed, Arendt listened with her friends to the Haggadah and joined in the singing of the traditional Passover songs.

*The Last Year*

In the spring of 1975, Fortuna smiled upon Hannah Arendt's old age, offering recognition for her work as a historian of totalitarianism and as a political theorist. She was invited to Copenhagen to receive the Danish government's Sonning Prize for Contributions to European Civilization. The prize brought her $35,000 and the distinction of being both the first

American citizen and the first woman to receive an honor that had been bestowed upon Winston Churchill, Albert Schweitzer, Bertrand Russell, Karl Barth, Arthur Koestler, Niels Bohr, and Laurence Olivier. At a dinner in Washington given by the Danish Embassy on 11 March, she discussed plans for the Copenhagen ceremony with the Danish ambassador, and then, in haste, she prepared her acceptance speech.

Every time she accepted one of Fortuna's prizes, Arendt spoke about what it means to go into the public realm, when public recognition demands such an appearance. She found it necessary to tell her Danish hosts how uncomfortable she was with the persona fame causes one to assume. "The masks or roles which the world assigns to us, and which we must accept and even acquire if we wish to take part in the world's play at all, are exchangeable; they are not inalienable . . . they are not a permanent fixture annexed to our inner self in the sense in which the voice of conscience, as most people believe, is something the human soul constantly bears within itself."[43] Arendt had long viewed public recognition as a temptation, though she seldom said publicly why this was so. But as she received a Prize for Contributions to European Civilization, she wanted to state her reason: she reminded her audience that the European "society of celebrities" which had existed between the wars, basking in what Stefan Zweig called the "radiant power of fame," was a good deal less able to understand the political catastrophes of the 1930s than the "nonfamous multitude." Deprived of their fame, many of these luminaries lost their footing entirely. "Nothing is more transient in our world, less stable and solid, than that form of success which brings fame; nothing comes swifter and more easily than oblivion."

In the 1930s Hannah Arendt had formed an intense dislike for the elites of Europe, whose distance from the nonfamous multitudes brought them blindness and sometimes susceptibility to collaboration with oppressors. Since that time she had resolved to avoid being or desiring to be an "exception." She was by temperament ill-equipped for public life, as she well knew, and she also required privacy for thinking: "Thinking has no *urge* to appear and even a very restricted impulse to communicate with others." These realizations had been Arendt's for all the years of her life outside Germany. What she added to them in the last years of her life, and noted in her Sonning Prize speech, was that our ability to make judgments depends upon our ability to step back from the temptations and noisy displays of the public realm without becoming "antipublic" or desirous only of "secrecy and anonymity." One must be able to maintain both a public persona and an inner self; for through the public persona the inner self manifests itself as something "entirely idiosyncratic and undefinable and still unmistakably identifiable, so that we are not confused by a sudden change of roles."

After she had distinguished the persona and the inner self, Arendt wrote for her Danish audience a farewell:

When the events for which the [persona] was designed are over, and I have finished using and abusing my individual rights to sound through the mask, things will snap back again; and I—greatly honored and deeply thankful for this moment—shall be free not only to exchange roles and masks as they may be offered by the great play of the world, but even to go through it in my naked "thisness," identifiable, I hope, but not definable and not seduced by the great temptation of recognition *as* such and such, that is, as something which we fundamentally are *not*.

In the theoretical terms of *The Life of the Mind,* what Hannah Arendt spoke of here was the "reflexivity" of the faculty of judgment. She was invoking her concept of Judging as a relation between the capacity to feel pleased (or not pleased) and the capacity to reflect approvingly or disapprovingly on such feelings. As a matter of "purely personal, individual inclination," Hannah Arendt was displeased with recognition, but, upon reflection, she did not approve of her displeasure; she judged it something to be overcome. In order to show her Danish hosts why she had felt uneasy with their honor, she cited W. H. Auden:

> Private faces in public places
> Are wiser and nicer
> Than public faces in private places.

But Arendt also made it clear that her judgment had nothing to do with the "delicate question" of merit. Her merit was for her Danish hosts to judge. "We are not fit to judge ourselves and our accomplishments," she said, for no one can judge how he or she appears to others. Being judged and judging are, of course, not the same. But what no one should neglect to judge *about* themselves is whether they will let the public persona and the inner self stay distinct, so that the inner self can do what it is able to do only in freedom—judge.

Although she overcame her aversion to publicity, Arendt needed prodding to prepare for her trip to Copenhagen. Mary McCarthy, who, escorted by William Jovanovich, was Arendt's guest for the prize ceremony, insisted that Hannah Arendt buy a new dress. "I bought the dress," she reported irritably. Then she said that an announcement of the Sonning Prize printed in the *New York Times* had prompted dozens of people to telephone or write their congratulations and made it difficult for her to find enough peaceful hours to type out her speech. "Mary, believe me the whole thing is a nuisance."[44] She became so nervous about the occasion that she asked her doctor for a small number of tranquilizers to take on the trip.

Yela Lowenfeld, who had been a witness at Hannah Arendt's marriage to Günther Stern, was one of the people who wrote to extend her congratulations. In her note she reminded Arendt that once, in Berlin, Arendt had shyly revealed that she hoped one day to fulfill her father's dream for her by becoming a famous scholar. Yela Lowenfeld was surprised when Arendt, thanking her for the note, said that she had forgotten this confidence.[45] Hannah Arendt herself was just as surprised when her father's sister-in-law, Charlotte Arendt, seventy-six years old, appeared at the Copenhagen ceremony, having travelled from her home in Berlin in order to tell Hannah Arendt that her father would have been immensely proud of his only child. And, if this flood of memories was not enough, a letter from the mayor of Hanover, Germany, claiming pride in the honor given to "a native," was sufficient to make Hannah Arendt tremble as she gave her address.

The Danish newspaper reports of the Sonning Prize ceremony noted neither Hannah Arendt's complicated attitude toward public recognition nor her nervousness. They dwelt upon the high praise she had given in her speech to the Danish people's courageousness during the war. The Danes had refused to acquiesce to Nazi demands for deportation of Jewish refugees and had, instead, smuggled large number of Jews out of the country to the safety of Sweden. The Nazi officials in Denmark were, as Arendt put it, "overpowered by what they most disdained, mere words, spoken freely and publicly. This happened nowhere else."

The power of mere words, spoken freely and publicly, was much on Hannah Arendt's mind in the spring of 1975. As soon as she returned from the 18 April Sonning Prize ceremony, she had to prepare for another public appearance, at the Boston Hall Forum. For this occasion Hannah Arendt wrote, "in great haste and in great anger," a fusillade of words about the state of the American Republic.[46]

Arendt went to Boston on 20 May 1975 at the invitation of the city's mayor, Kevin White, to speak at a Bicentennial ceremony, a birthday party for America. It was an inauspicious moment for a party. Americans everywhere were still astonished by the series of events "like a Niagara Falls of history." President Nixon's resignation in August 1974, following upon the spectacle of America's honorless withdrawal from the lost war in Vietnam, was succeeded by President Ford's effort to give the nation a healing period by pardoning Nixon. On the first of January 1975, criminal proceedings against John N. Mitchell, John D. Ehrlichman, and H. R. Haldeman had resulted in convictions; the former president got only a book contract for his memoirs. By the time Hannah Arendt spoke in Boston, few in her audience disputed her judgment that the American Republic's power had declined through the recent "years of aberration" to a point unknown since the Second World War.

After she delivered her "Home to Roost" address, Arendt responded to questions from the audience and then from the participants in a seminar at Parkman House. Her address was broadcast five days later over National Public Radio, praised in a *New York Times* editorial by Tom Wicker, and then published in the *New York Review of Books*. By the end of the year, when the *Times* quoted the address in its "Abstract for the Year," Arendt's reflections had reached an enormous number of people and she had received fan letters from all over the nation.[47]

Shortly after she returned from her trip to Boston, Hannah Arendt set out for Europe. She went, first, to the Deutsches Literaturarchiv in Marbach, Germany, where she had arranged to deposit a collection of her letters to and from Jaspers, Kurt Blumenfeld, and Erwin Loewenson, her old friend from Berlin, who had died in 1963. She stayed in Marbach for four weeks in order to fulfill her obligation as one of the executors of Karl Jaspers's estate, sorting through and organizing much of his correspondence for eventual publication.

The month in Marbach was exhausting. Arendt worked full weekdays in the archive, stopping only for lunches with the director, the poet and essayist Ludwig Greve. Greve's hospitality and good conversation were essential. The little town of Marbach might otherwise have proved imprisoning, as Arendt's activities were pretty much confined to the half-acre park that held the archive, her small furnished apartment, the Schiller Museum, and a tourist restaurant. She was not accustomed to working in libraries—she had not done so since her uncomfortable weeks at the Hoover Institution in 1955—or to being situated far from friends, without company in the evenings. She took her evening meals alone in the town's one hotel. Ludwig Greve drove her once to Stuttgart, where they visited an elderly couple she had known during her youth in Berlin, but she was otherwise too much alone with the many memories that reading Jaspers's letters stirred in her. When Mary McCarthy came for a few days at the end of the month, she found Arendt nervous, uncharacteristically insensitive, and in a mood to be always right—even about the species names of the trees in the Schillerhof park!

Despite the debacle of her 1974 visit, Arendt decided to visit Martin Heidegger in Freiburg on her way to Tegna. She found him unwell. Concerned about her husband, Elfriede Heidegger was cordial to Hannah Arendt, and at long last a truce was reached between the two women, a reconciliation. But Arendt left Freiburg disheartened. "I came home very depressed," she wrote to Mary McCarthy from Tegna. "Heidegger is now suddenly very old, very changed from last year, very deaf and remote, unapproachable as I never saw him before. I have been surrounded here for weeks by old people who suddenly got very old."[48]

Anne Weil journeyed to Tegna from her summer retreat near Montreux, aged from a heart attack she had suffered the year before. The friendship she and Arendt had enjoyed for over fifty years was still strong—they shared again the story of how Arendt had telephoned Nice from New York the day after Anne Weil's heart attack, somehow knowing long-distance that something was wrong—but their visit was overcast with anxiety about health. With the frankness they had always known, they made an agreement that neither had to attend the other's funeral, an agreement Anne Weil honored less than six months later. Robert Gilbert was also much older and unwell in the summer of 1975. But Elke Gilbert, who came for a visit from her home in Zurich, was miraculously youthful though older in years than Hannah Arendt. With Elke Gilbert, Arendt went down the mountainside to Locarno on the little train she called "Bimmel-Bammel" with childlike pleasure, for movies and, on a lark, to the circus. After more youthfulness, in the forms of Albrecht Wellmer, a Frankfurt School scholar, his wife and two of Arendt's New School students, enlivened the Casa Barbete, Arendt felt restored and went back to work—reading the posthumously published fragments of Kant's work.

In the simple but comfortable room she took each year at the Casa Barbete, with its desk facing out upon a deep valley and snow-covered alpine peaks beyond, Arendt worked on the critique of Heidegger she

wanted to include in the "Willing" volume and on a set of notes on Kant
for the "Judging" volume. She was not pushed, for she had arranged to
postpone the interrupted Gifford Lectures until the spring of 1976, and
she was convinced that she would not ever have to face Martin Heidegger's disapproval of her pages about him. "It is warm here," she wrote to
Ludwig Greve, missing his company, "but not hot, now and then a rain
shower, many cats going back and forth, and each morning there are two
robins who come to my terrace for the breakfast crumbs. In short, it is
paradisaically beautiful. . . . I read with extraordinary pleasure good old
Kant, and trouble myself with no one else. That makes me happy."[49]
Feeling "extremely lazy," she worked only in the late mornings, after a
slow breakfast, and in the early afternoons. In the evenings, after a nap,
she had dinner with the other Casa Barbete guests or with friends who had
come to see her, and then retired with a variety of newspapers in German
and French to read about the revolution in Portugal. Arendt had toward
the Portuguese revolution just the sense of wonder and enthusiasm she
was reading about in "good old Kant," who had written many notes to
himself about the fountainhead of modern revolutions—the French.

Hannah Arendt stayed quietly in Tegna until she was due at an international symposium sponsored by the Fondation internationale des sciences humaines in Jouy-en Josas, near Paris, on 27 September. Her
departure from her paradise was abrupt: the symposium was ominously
entitled "Terrors of the Year 2000," and the paper for which she was to be
*contre-rapporteur*, "Les Terreurs politiques," by Ulrich Matz of Cologne,
was an unsettling speculation about the future of terrorism. But it was the
present tense of New York that most personally jarred Hannah Arendt.
When she returned to her Riverside Drive apartment, she was reluctant to
go out alone; the neighborhood had become dangerous, particularly for
the elderly, who lived in fear after a rash of muggings. She had endured a
mugging attempt in the elevator at Lotte Kohler's apartment in 1971, and
she had no wish, in her frailer health, to brave one again.

Hannah Arendt spent most of her days at home, working on her manuscript. Her routine of inviting guests for the evenings was kept, almost
desperately. When an empty evening threatened, she called one of the
tribe members; if no one was available, she visited over the telephone—
something she had never been comfortable doing before. Every other
Sunday, she called Mary McCarthy in Paris; when she reached an impasse in her work, she called J. Glenn Gray in Colorado to ask his advice
or to discuss the lengthy criticisms of her manuscripts he sent in letters.

In the calm but rather bleak fall, Hannah Arendt's sixty-ninth birthday celebration was a highlight. The tribe gathered in full force, and some old friends, like Joe and Alice Maier, who had been at a distance for years joined them. Thanksgiving, too, was pleasantly spent with Lotte Kohler at the Jonas's home. But Arendt was uneasy enough about continuing on in her apartment that she surprised everyone by announcing that she was going to accept an invitation for the following year to spend a semester at Smith College. Her friends argued that the winter in Northhampton, Massachusetts, would be too harsh, but Arendt was determined to spend most of her time away from New York after she officially retired from the New School, with a $1,000-per-month pension, in the fall of 1976.

It was not the expected burglary or mugging that sealed Hannah Arendt's resolve to find a haven away from the city; it was a fall. The day after Thanksgiving, as she was walking into her apartment building from a taxi, Arendt tripped on the edge of pothole and fell onto the street. A crowd assembled and the doorman went off to summon the police while Arendt waited, collecting her strength and checking to see that she had broken no bones. Before the police arrived, she got up, made her way through the crowd and entered her building.

With her characteristic desire not to have a fuss made—her motto in these matters was *Kein Mitleid* ("no pity")—Arendt did not summon any of the tribe. When Lotte Kohler telephoned two days later, Arendt mentioned the fall, but claimed that she was in little pain and in no need of seeing her doctor. She had, in fact, made an appointment for the next day, Monday, but when the day brought a rainstorm, she cancelled it. Lotte Kohler came for dinner on Tuesday, and found Arendt busily assembling her notes for the "Judging" manuscript, which she intended to start typing out the next day.

Convinced that her fall had not harmed her, Arendt received Salo and Jeanette Baron for dinner on Thursday, 4 December. She left her typewriter, with the first page of her "Judging" manuscript rolled into it, to greet them.[50] After dinner, they retired to the living room to discuss the Barons' arrangements for liquidating Jewish Cultural Reconstruction, which had not been in operation since 1957. Arendt had rejoined the board of *Jewish Social Studies* when Jeanette Baron took over the presidency, and there were also editorial matters to consider. The Barons, to Arendt's enthusiastic agreement, reported that the journal would sponsor a volume of essays by Phillip Friedman, a Jewish historian who had died in 1960 leaving many uncollected articles. She called Friedman the best

Jewish historian of his generation and talked eagerly about his work, much of which had been helpful to her as she wrote *The Origins of Totalitarianism*.

The Barons were startled when, after a brief spell of coughing, Arendt sank back into the living room chair where she had settled to serve their after-dinner coffee and lost consciousness. On a medicine container the Barons found the name of Arendt's doctor, who came at once and summoned Lotte Kohler. But before Lotte Kohler arrived, Hannah Arendt had died from a heart attack without regaining consciousness.

## The Work of Comprehending

Hannah Arendt's funeral was held in the Riverside Memorial Chapel, at Amsterdam Avenue and 76th Street, on 8 December 1975. As she had requested, the funeral was like Heinrich Blücher's. In the same place, with a similar plain pine coffin covered by white roses, her funeral, too, was a ceremony of remembrances by friends.

Hans Jonas and Mary McCarthy spoke, representing the émigré tribe members and the American friends. Jonas evoked the young woman he had met in Martin Heidegger's Marburg seminar: "How I remember this singular newcomer! Shy and withdrawn, with strikingly beautiful features and lonely eyes, she stood out immediately as exceptional, as unique in an as yet indefinable way. Brightness of intellect was no rare article there. But here was an intensity, an inner direction, an instinct for quality, a groping for essence, a probing for depth, which cast a magic about her. One sensed an absolute determination to be herself, with the toughness to carry it through in the face of great vulnerability."[51] Mary McCarthy, too, wanted to evoke her friend's physical presence: "When she talked it was like seeing the motions of the mind exteriorized in action and gestures as she would flex her lips, frown, pensively cup her chin."[52]

Jerome Kohn, Arendt's last research assistant at the New School for Social Research, spoke for her students, saying what they had felt: "She was one of the great teachers of our times. Her knowledge was vast and she gave it gracefully." William Jovanovich, Arendt's publisher, portrayed her as a public figure: "She was passionate in the way believers in justice can become and that believers in mercy must remain. . . . She followed wherever serious inquiry would take her, and if she made enemies it was never out of fear." Jovanovich halted, his voice shaking, and tearfully told the mourners, "As for me, I loved her fiercely."[53]

In the crowded room, among the three hundred mourners, there were many who had felt fiercely about Hannah Arendt; though they were seldom without memories of anger or hurt or bewilderment, they felt, as Jonas said, that "the world has become colder without your warmth." She was, for those who loved her, part of the "world," not just of the circles of family and friends and colleagues in which they had known her. They were aware that there were many strangers at the funeral, Arendt readers, even a contingent of them in denim overalls wearing Farm Workers buttons. These were from the "world." It was not—and still is not—easy for those who loved her to locate their Hannah Arendt in the multifaceted light of Hannah Arendt's public *fama* or in the many layers of privacy which she had kept around what some of her friends would have called her *Innigkeit*, some her *vivida vis animi*, and some her soulfulness. The night before the funeral, friends and family had debated fiercely whether Jewish prayers should be said for her—as she had debated whether they should be said for her non-Jewish husband! The conclusion of the debate was a compromise: Arendt's Israeli niece read a psalm in Hebrew and then it was read in English by the Klenborts' son, Daniel.

That such a debate arose is not surprising; in the "world" there are many worlds, and Hannah Arendt lived in not a few of them. Different mourners wished her remembered and wished to remember her in the terms of their own relationship with her. As time passed, the friends and family—from coming to know each other and from reading and hearing about her—formed new contexts for their memories. At a memorial service at the New School in April 1976, as in the many obituaries that appeared during the winter of 1975/76, some vision of Hannah Arendt's life and work, some summary or signpost indicating her significance, was sought. When her ashes were buried in May 1976 at Bard College, the friends gathered again and heard Hans Jonas, J. Glenn Gray, and Leonard Krieger of Chicago continue the work of comprehending. Since then, in articles, in three American essay collections and one French collection, in two book-length critical studies, at conferences, in seminars, over dinner tables, the comprehending has gone on, for those who knew Hannah Arendt and for those who did not.[54]

Mary McCarthy undertook the intricate editorial conversion of Arendt's Gifford Lectures manuscripts into *The Life of the Mind*. McCarthy rightly did not try to remedy the uneven quality of the manuscripts, or their lack of transitions, summaries, and clear highlights, but she did produce a readable and almost always accurate book. Only in unimportant details, which faithfully reflect Mary McCarthy's image of Hannah Arendt, was she unfaithful to the manuscripts. The poker player's phrase "When the chips are down" did not fit Mary McCarthy's image—though Arendt had used it in print and loved to use it in seminars—so she made a change: "I can see her (cigarette perched in holder) contemplating the roulette table or chemin-de-fer, so it is now 'when the stakes are on the table'—more fitting, more in character."[55] This is fine, though Arendt's students laughed; they remembered her saying, often and with great emphasis, "wen de cheeps are down, you must make some choices." The more excited she got about these "cheeps," the more she relied on American idioms and street talk to categorize them. As Randall Jarrell said of the German learner in his *Pictures from an Institution*, "there is no such happiness as not to know an idiom from a masterstroke."

When Mary McCarthy's work was finished, she and William Shawn prepared an edition of the "Thinking" volume for the *New Yorker*. William Jovanovich issued both volumes in a handsome boxed set in 1978. The publication of *The Life of the Mind* did not make the task of comprehending Hannah Arendt's oeuvre easier. Like Martin Heidegger's *Being and Time*, a book which can be seen in retrospect to mark the end of an epoch in European philosophy, Arendt's one work of "proper philosophy" (as she jokingly referred to it) is missing its final, third part. But Heidegger lived for nearly fifty years after his work appeared and he wrote many works exploring the pathways he had laid down in his magnum opus. Arendt's work must remain rough-hewn, without benefit even of the changes she might have made in the first volumes had her impatience not gotten the better of her. (Arendt once told Chanan Klenbort that she could have said in two pages what it had taken her two volumes to say—so it is fortunate that there are two volumes at all.) Mary McCarthy did decide to include in the second volume excerpts from a lecture course Arendt gave at the New School on Kant's political philosophy, and this is a gesture toward the missing "Judging."

Judging is what Hannah Arendt, as a political theorist and a political commentator, spent the greater part of her writing life doing. The clearest clues to what she might have said about her activity are in the essays she wrote about others who judged—Rosa Luxemburg, Bertolt Brecht, Karl Jaspers, and the entire gallery of *Men in Dark Times*. Like these people, Arendt was judged for her judging in the most various ways. Long before her death, the camps of contemporary assessors had formed; after her death, messages came from them all.

From those to her political right came charges that she was too critical of American institutions and too unconcerned with the basic shaping factor in American foreign policy—the need to fight Communism. From those to her political left came, predictably, the opposite charges: she was too conservative, elitist, cold-warriorish, wedded to class differentiations. Nathan Glazer's "Hannah Arendt's America" in *Commentary* is representative of the former, H. Stuart Hughes's *The Sea Change* of the latter.[56] In between and much closer to Arendt in spirit are political theorists like Richard Bernstein, Norman Jacobson, George Kateb, Hannah Pitkin, Judith Shklar, and Sheldon Wolin who, though they have quarreled with Arendt over matters of theory and *praxis*, have done so respectfully and without polemic. In Germany, Arendt's most influential admirer and critic is Jurgen Habermas of the Frankfurt School, who met Arendt in 1968 at the New School and has since many times—most recently at the 1980 New School commencement—acknowledged his debt to her. Though she is not often cited, Arendt's work is read among the young French *nouveaux philosophes*; an issue of the journal *Esprit* was dedicated to making her work more widely known.

Among philosophers, the English Channel is often wider than the Atlantic Ocean. Those sympathetic to Continental traditions are more likely to respect Arendt's work, particularly *The Life of the Mind*, than those trained in English or Anglo-American philosophy. Stuart Hampshire of Oxford has declared himself unable to understand why Americans take Arendt seriously as a "political theorist and public philosopher." "She seems to me to be inaccurate in argument and to make a parade of learned allusion without any detailed inquiry into texts," he has said. *The Life of the Mind* was, for Hampshire, a locus of "metaphysical mists."[57] In the camps of the historians, too, there are divisions of response to Arendt's work that run along both political lines and the less ascertainable lines separating speculators from empiricists, those who write of the past for the present and the future and those who write for the record.

The most vehement divisions of opinion about Hannah Arendt are the ones that came into being with the publication of *Eichmann in Jerusalem*. Arendt received few of the customary marks of recognition bestowed by the Jewish community upon its illustrious dead. In 1978, when a young Jewish student of Arendt's work edited a collection of her writings on Jewish issues, including two fragments from the Eichmann controversy, the old differences of opinion flared forth again. Ron Feldman presented his collection, *The Jew as Pariah*, with the conviction that the Eichmann controversy has "obscured for too long the real depth of [Arendt's] contribution to understanding the Jewish experience in the modern age." He hoped to help retrieve her from "a modern form of excommunication from the Jewish community."[58] In a 1979 review of *The Jew as Pariah* for *Encounter*, the historian Walter Laqueur repeated a claim he had made in 1965: "Hannah Arendt was mainly attacked not for *what* she said but for *how* she said it." But his claim had always had a deeper anchor:

The Holocaust is a subject that has to be confronted in a spirit of humility; whatever Mrs. Arendt's many virtues, humility was not one of them. "Judge not, that ye be not judged"—but Hannah Arendt loved to judge, and was at her most effective in the role of *magister humanitatis*, invoking moral pathos. And thus she rushed in where wiser men and women feared to tread, writing about extreme situations which she in her life had never experienced, an intellectual by temperament always inclined to overstatement, most at ease when dealing with abstractions, at her weakest when dealing with real people in concrete situations.[59]

With formulas like these a sacred preserve has been made of Holocaust history, one where those who did not experience its extreme situations— and certainly those who are not Jewish—are criticized for judgments out of accord with the ethos of the preserve and the prerogatives of the survivors. Hannah Arendt wrote, said Laqueur, "as an outsider, lacking identification." Sadly, many within the Jewish community still accept such judgments. But others share Feldman's hope that there will be more room one day for the opinions of pariahs among this brilliant people.

Classics—so one rule of thumb goes—are those books that are reborn for each new generation. *The Origins of Totalitarianism*, now thirty years old, has had time to show itself two generational steps along that way. A generation of revisionist historians set out to mark its limitations in the 1960s, and they have current heirs; a generation of post-Vietnam War readers has read it in a new world situation. No one who wishes to study totalitarianism can ignore it. In 1975, *The Human Condition* was given the Lippincott Award of the American Political Science Association for its "exceptional quality" and its significance "after a time span of at least fifteen years from publication." For political theorists, this is Arendt's most provocative book. Though Justice William O. Douglas was ready to predict in 1962 that *On Revolution* would eventually be considered a "classic treatise,"[60] it still awaits a generation of current readers to step in that direction. *Eichmann in Jerusalem* has stirred controversy and compelled interpretation since its publication, and there is no sign that it has lost its power to excite. It has not, however, been reborn for philosophical consideration—except by Hannah Arendt herself in *The Life of the Mind*.

Essay collections like *Between Past and Future, Men in Dark Times,* and *Crises of the Republic* do not have the weight or the longevity of book-length studies. Arendt's essays, individually, have special readerships and continue to be printed as parts of essay collections. She herself once remarked that *Between Past and Future* was the best of her books. She believed in its form: as its subtitle indicates, it contains "exercises in political thought," and it was thus not systematic.

It is Arendt's urge to systematize that makes *The Life of the Mind* such a difficult and disturbing book. Arendt used to say of Martin Heidegger that he indeed had taken apart, "destroyed," the tradition of Western philosophy—and then been unable to make a new assembly. She did not say this disparagingly, for she did not hope for a new philosophy, and she was keenly aware of the fortitude required to live so freely, with no more than fragments shored against your ruin, setting out with only *Wegmarken*, pathmarks, for guidance. Had her "Judging" section been written— it is tempting to say had Arendt been *able* to write "Judging"—she would have had to say systematically how the mental faculties interrelate, even how they *should* interrelate. But this was not a question congenial to Arendt's spirit. She was a critic in the original sense of the Greek word κριτής, a judge or interpreter who can make distinctions, separate things out, give meanings. She was not a philosophical or political visionary. There is no utopian impulse in her work, though she took political hope from the existence of councils, the spontaneous outgrowths of revolutions. "Die Welt kann nur durch die gefördert werden, die sich ihr entgegensetzen," said the old Goethe. "The world only goes forward because of those who oppose it."

In the last days of her life, Hannah Arendt's thoughts were far from the earthly immortality that some of the critics of the world win for themselves or are given as their stories are told and retold. She was, on the contrary, writing an addendum to the penultimate chapter in the "Willing" volume of *The Life of the Mind*. In that chapter she had discussed, quite critically, Martin Heidegger's "will-not-to-will." She was clearly opposed to his notion that Being, forever changing, has a history of manifestation in the thinking of actors, "so that thinking and acting coincide." Arendt felt that Heidegger had come to this notion after turning away from quite a different one that he wrote about in his 1946 commentary, "The Anaximander Fragment."

She recalled the years immediately after the Second World War when her teachers, Heidegger and Jaspers, hoped a new era would dawn. "We live as though knocking at gates that are still closed," Jaspers said at the famous 1946 *Rencontres philosophiques* in Geneva. "What happens today will perhaps one day found and establish a world." The moment of hope passed quickly; the era that began was not one of peace and world order. In that moment, while Jaspers dedicated himself to his philosophy for everyman, Heidegger envisioned men as living together in a common destiny, in a time between the two absences before birth and after death, in a space in which history unfolds. In this vision, Being is not forever changing; it is the hidden Eternal which has no history. Only when men retire from the realm of history, "the realm of errancy," into thinking do they have access to the hidden Being. Then they forego that will to self-preservation which is the source of all disorder in history.

What Heidegger had for this brief moment was the idea of history— human history, not Being's history—that Arendt had always found lacking in his philosophy. She would not have called history "errancy," and she thought the term marked Heidegger's concept as a "mere variation," no true variant of his basic convictions. But she was clearly compelled by the image of sojourning between absences, between what she herself had called "natality" and "mortality." Those who think of themselves as "lingering awhile" and sharing a destiny with others do not will otherwise and do not treat life as the highest good, to be preserved at all costs. In political terms, such people have courage and the impartiality for good judgment.

In his essay on the Anaximander fragment Heidegger had sounded the basic theme of the work Hannah Arendt once said she would turn to when her "proper philosophy" was finished. Cicero's *On Old Age* was to be her model. In that text, too, she found the theme she was exploring in the last days of her life. "As I approach death," says Cato, "I feel like a man nearing harbor after a long voyage; I seem to be catching sight of land."

# The Cohns and the Arendts
# of Königsberg

# MARTHA COHN'S FAMILY

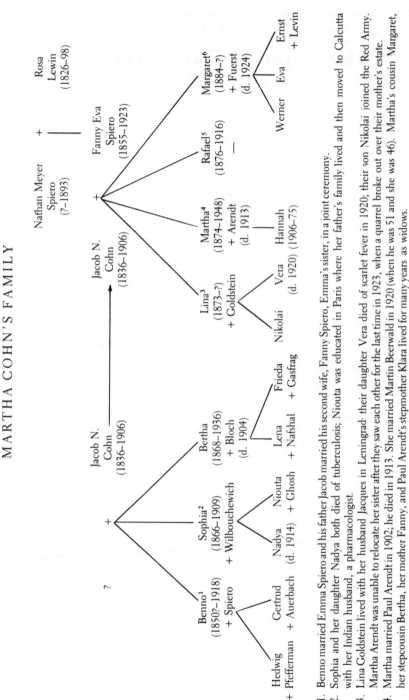

1. Benno married Emma Spiero and his father Jacob married his second wife, Fanny Spiero, Emma's sister, in a joint ceremony.

2. Sophia and her daughter Nadya both died of tuberculosis; Niouta was educated in Paris where her father's family lived and then moved to Calcutta with her Indian husband, a pharmacologist.

3. Lina Goldstein lived with her husband Jacques in Leningrad: their daughter Vera died of scarlet fever in 1920; their son Nikolai joined the Red Army. Martha Arendt was unable to relocate her sister after they saw each other for the last time in 1923, when a quarrel broke out over their mother's estate.

4. Martha married Paul Arendt in 1902; he died in 1913. She married Martin Beerwald in 1920 (when he was 51 and she was 46). Martha's cousin Margaret, her stepcousin Bertha, her mother Fanny, and Paul Arendt's stepmother Klara lived for many years as widows.

5. Rafael died of dysentery on the eastern front in 1916 and was posthumously awarded an Iron Cross.

6. Margaret was widowed in 1924 and raised her three children in Berlin. She died in a Nazi concentration camp.

# PAUL ARENDT'S FAMILY

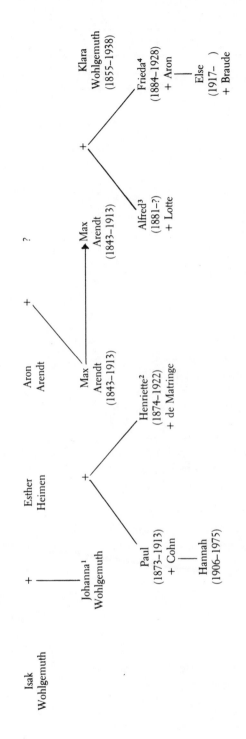

Isak
Wohlgemuth

Johanna[1]
Wohlgemuth +

Esther
Heimen

Aron
Arendt +

?

Klara
Wohlgemuth
(1855–1938)

Paul
(1873–1913)
+ Cohn

Henriette[2]
(1874–1922)
+ de Matringe

Hannah
(1906–1975)

Max
Arendt
(1843–1913)

Max
Arendt
(1843–1913)

Alfred[3]
(1881–?)
+ Lotte

Frieda[4]
(1884–1928)
+ Aron

Else
(1917–  )
+ Braude

1. Paul Arendt's mother (died circa 1880) was the sister of Max Arendt's second wife, Klara. The Wohlgemuth sisters were the daughters of Isak Wohlgemuth (a Russian by birth) and Esther Heimen. Hannah Arendt was named after her father's mother.

2. Henriette Arendt worked as a nurse in Berlin (1895–1903) and then (1903–1909) as a police assistant social worker specializing in care for home-less children. She married a Frenchman named René de Matringe in 1915. A bibliography of Henriette Arendt's writings about her social work experience has been compiled by Dr. Renate Heuer of the Bibliographia Judaica in Frankfurt.

3. Alfred Arendt, a businessman, married a Christian widow named Lotte, who was able to care for Martin Beerwald in Königsberg after Martha Arendt Beerwald left for Paris in 1939.

4. Frieda, Hannah Arendt's favorite aunt, married Ernst Aron, a lawyer and descendant of a family that had been court jewelers to the dukes of Prussia. Ernst Aron was killed by the Nazis. (His younger brother, Karl, a close friend of Hannah Arendt's stepsister Eva Beerwald, was also killed.)

# German Texts of Arendt's Poems

This section includes only poems that are quoted or referred to in the text.

*Winter 1923/24*

Im Volksliedton

Sehn wir uns wieder
Blüht weisser Flieder,
Ich hüll Dich in Kissen
Du sollst nichts mehr missen,

Wir wollen uns freune,
Dass herber Wein,
Dass duftende Linden
Uns noch beisammen finden.

Wenn Blätter fallen,
Dann lass uns scheiden
Was nützt unser Wallen?
Wir müssen es leiden.

*Winter 1923/24*

[Untitled]

Kein Wort bricht ins Dunkel—
Kein Gott hebt die Hand—
Wohin ich auch blicke
Sich türmendes Land.

Keine Form, die sich löset,
Kein Schatten, der schwebt.
Und immer noch hör ich's:
Zu spät, zu spät.

*Winter 1923/24*

Trost

Es kommen die Stunden
Da alte Wunden
Die längst vergessen
Drohn zu zerfressen.

Es kommen die Tage,
Da keine Wage
Des Lebens, der Leiden
Sich kann entscheiden.

Die Stunden verrinnen,
Die Tage vergehen,
Es bleibt ein Gewinnen
Das blosse Bestehen.

*Winter 1923/24*

Traum

Schwebende Füsse in pathetischem Glanze
Ich selbst,
Auch ich tanze,
Befreit von der Schwere
Ins Dunkle, ins Leere.
Gedrängte Räume vergangener Zeiten
Durchschrittene Weiten
Verlorene Einsamkeiten
Beginnen zu tanzen, zu tanzen.

Ich selbst
Auch ich tanze.
Ironisch vermessen
Ich hab nichts vergessen,
Ich kenne die Leere,
Ich kenne die Schwere,

Ich tanze, ich tanze
In ironischem Glanze

*Winter 1923/24*

Müdigkeit

Dämmernder Abend—
Leise verklagend
Tönt noch der Vögel Ruf
Die ich erschuf.

Graue Wände
Fallen hernieder,
Meine Hände
Finden sich wieder.

Was ich geliebt
Kann ich nicht fassen,
Was mich umgibt
Kann ich nicht lassen.

Alles versinkt
Dämmern steigt auf.
Nichts mich bezwingt—
Ist wohl des Lebens Lauf.

*Winter 1923/24*

Die Untergrundbahn

Aus Dunkel kommend,
Ins Helle sich schlängelnd,
Schnell und vermessen,
Schmal und bessessen
Von menschlichen Kräften.
Aufmerksam webend
Gezeichnete Wege,
Gleichgültig schwebend
Ueber dem Hasten.

Schnell, schmal und bessessen
Von menschlichen Kräften
Die es nicht achtet,
Ins Dunkle fliessend,
Um Oberes wissend
Fliegt es sich windend
Ein gelbes Tier.

*Winter 1923/24*

Abschied

Nun lasst mich, o schwebende Tage, die Hände Euch reichen.
Ihr entfliehet mir nicht, es gibt kein Entweichen
Ins Leere und Zeitenlose.

Doch legt eines glühenden Windes fremderes Zeichen
Sein Wehen um mich, ich will nicht entweichen
In die Leere gehemmter Zeiten.

Ach Ihr kanntet das Lächeln mit dem ich mich schenkte.
Ihr wusstet wie vieles ich schweigend verhängte,
Um auf Wiesen zu liegen und Euch zu gehören.

Doch jetzt ruft das Blut, das nimmer verdrängte
Hinaus mich auf Schiffe, die niemals ich lenkte.
Der Tod ist im Leben, ich weiss, ich weiss.

So lasst mich, o schwebende Tage, die Hände Euch reichen.
Ihr verlieret mich nicht. Ich lass Euch zum Zeichen
Dies Blatt und die Flamme zurück.

*Winter 1924/25*

In sich versunken

Wenn ich meine Hand betrachte
—Fremdes Ding mit mir verwandt—
Stehe ich in keinem Land,
Bin an kein Hier und Jetzt
Bin an kein Was gesetzt.

Dann ist mir als sollte ich die Welt verachten,
Mag doch ruhig die Zeit vergehen,
Nur sollen keine Zeichen mehr geschehen.

Betracht ich meine Hand,
Unheimlich nahe mir verwandt,
Und doch ein ander Ding.
Ist sie mehr als ich bin,
Hat sie höheren Sinn?

*Summer 1925*

Sommerlied

Durch des Sommers reife Fülle
Lass ich meine Hände gleiten
Meine Glieder schmerzhaft weiten
Zu der dunklen, schweren Erde.

Felder die sich tönend neigen
Pfade die der Wald verschüttet
Alles zwingt zum strengen Schweigen:
Dass wir lieben wenn wir leiden.

Dass das Opfer, dass die Fülle
Nicht des Priesters Hand verdorre,
Dass in edler, klarer Stille
Uns die F r e u d e nicht erstarre.

Denn die Wasser fliessen über,
Müdigkeit will uns zerstören
Und wir lassen unser Leben
Wenn wir lieben, wenn wir leben.

*Summer 1925*

[Untitled]

Warum gibst Du mir die Hand
Scheu und wie geheim?
Kommst Du aus so fernem Land,
Kennst nicht unseren Wein?

Kennst nicht unsere schönste Glut
(Lebst Du so allein?)
Mit dem Herzen, mit dem Blut
Eins im andern sein?

Weisst Du nicht des Tages Freuden
Mit dem Liebsten gehen,
Weisst Du nicht des Abends Scheiden
Ganz in Schwermut gehen?

Komm mit mir und hab mich lieb
Denk nicht an dein Grauen,
Kannst Du Dich denn nicht vertrauen
Komm und nimm und gib.

Gehen dann durchs reife Feld
(Mohn und wilder Klee)
Später in der weiten Welt
Tut es uns wohl weh,

Wenn wir spüren, wie im Wind
Stark Erinnerung weht
Wenn im Schauder traumhaft lind
Unsere Seele weht.

*Summer 1925*

Spätsommer

Der Abend hat mich zugedeckt
So weich wie Samt so schwer wie Leid.

Ich weiss nicht mehr wie Liebe tut,
Ich weiss nicht mehr der Felder Glut,
Und alles will entschweben
Um nur mir Ruh zu geben.

Ich denk an ihn und hab ihn lieb
Doch wie aus fernen Landen
Und fremd ist mir das Komm und Gieb
Kaum weiss ich was mich bangt.

Der Abend hat mich zugedeckt
So weich wie Samt so schwer wie Leid.

Und nirgends sich Empörung reckt
Zu neuer Freud und Traurigkeit.

Und alle Weite die mich rief
Und alle Gestern klar und tief,
Kann mich nicht mehr betören.

Ich weiss ein Wasser gross und fremd,
Und eine Blum die keiner nennt
Was soll mich noch zerstören?

Der Abend hat mich zugedeckt
So weich wie Samt, so schwer wie Leid.

*Winter 1925/26*

## An die Freunde

Trauet nicht der leisen Klage,
Wenn der Blick des Heimatlosen
Scheu Euch noch umwirbt.
Fühlt, wie stolz die reinste Sage
Alles noch verbirgt.

Spürt der Dankbarkeit und Treue
Zartestes Erbeben.
Und Ihr wisst  in steter Neue
Wird die Liebe geben.

*Winter 1925/26*

## An die Nacht

Neig Dich Du Tröstende leis meinem Herzen
Schenke mir Schweigende Lindrung der Schmerzen.
Deck Deine Schatten vor Alles zu Helle—
Gib mir Ermatten und Flucht vor der Grelle.

Lass mir Dein Schweigen die kühlende Löse,
Lass mich im Dunkel verhüllen das Böse
Wenn Helle mich peinigt mit neuen Gesichten,
Gib Du mir die Kraft zum steten Verrichten.

1942

W.B. [Walter Benjamin]

Einmal dämmert Abend wieder,
Nacht fällt nieder von den Sternen,
Liegen wir gestreckte Glieder
In den Nähen, in den Fernen.

Aus den Dunkelheiten tönen
Sanfte kleine Melodeien.
Lauschen wir uns zu entwöhnen,
Lockern endlich wir die Reihen.

Ferne Stimmen, naher Kummer—:
Jene Stimmen jener Toten,
Die wir vorgeschickt als Boten
Uns zu leiten in den Schlummer.

1943

[Untitled]

Aufgestiegen aus dem stehenden Teich der Vergangenheit
Sind der Erinn'rungen viele.
Nebelgestalten ziehen die sehnsüchtigen Kreise meiner Gefangenheit
Vergangen, verlockend, am Ziele.

Tote, was wollt Ihr? Habt Ihr im Orkus nicht Heimat und Stätte?
Endlich den Frieden der Tiefe?
Wasser und Erde, Feuer und Luft sind Euch ergeben, als hätte
Mächtig ein Gott Euch. Und riefe

Euch aus stehenden Wässern, aus Sümpfen, Mooren und Teichen
Sammelnd geeinigt herbei.
Schimmernd im Zwielicht bedeckt Ihr mit Nebel der Lebenden Reiche,
Spottend des dunklen Vorbei.

Spielen wollen auch wir; ergreifen und lachen und haschen
Träume vergangener Zeit.
Müde wurden auch wir der Strassen, der Städte, des raschen
Wechsels der Einsamkeit.

Unter die rudernden Boote mit liebenden Paaren geschmückt auf
Stehenden Teichen im Wald
Könnten auch wir uns mischen—leise, versteckt und entrückt auf
Nebelwolken, die bald

Sachte die Erde bekleiden, das Ufer, den Busch und den Baum,
Wartend des kommenden Sturms.
Wartend des aus dem Nebel, aus Luftschloss, Narrheit und Traum
Steigenden wirbelnden Sturms.

*1943*

Park am Hudson

> Fischer fischen still an Flüssen
> In der ganzen Welt.
> Fahrer fahren blind auf Wegen
> Um die ganze Welt.
> Kinder laufen, Mütter rufen,
> Golden liegt die Welt.
> Geht ein liebend Paar vorüber
> Manchmal durch die Welt.
>
> Fischer fischen still an Flüssen
> Bis zum Abendrot.
> Fahrer fahren blind auf Wegen
> Eilig in den Tod.
> Kinder selig in der Sonne
> Spielen Ewigkeit.
> Manchmal geht ein Paar vorüber,
> Mit ihm geht die Zeit.
>
> Fischer fischen still an Flüssen—
> Einsam hängt der Ast.
> Fahrer fahren blind auf Wegen
> Rastlos in die Rast.
> Kinder spielen, Mütter rufen,
> Ewigkeit ist fast.
> Geht ein liebend Paar vorüber,
> Trägt der Zeiten Last.

*1946*

[Untitled]

Die Traurigkeit ist wie ein Licht im Herzen angezündet,
Die Dunkelheit ist wie ein Schein, der unsere Nacht ergründet.
Wir brauchen nur das kleine Licht der Trauer zu entzünden,
Um durch die lange weite Nacht wie Schatten heimzufinden.
Beleuchtet ist der Wald, die Stadt, die Strasse und der Baum.
Wohl dem, der keine Heimat hat; er sieht sie noch im Traum.

*1951*

[Untitled]

I

Unermessbar, Weite, nur,
wenn wir zu messen trachten,
was zu fassen unser Herz hier ward bestellt.

Unergründlich, Tiefe, nur,
wenn wir ergründend loten,
was uns Fallende als Grund empfängt.

Unerreichbar, Höhe, nur,
wenn unsere Augen mühsam absehn,
was als Flamme übersteigt das Firmament.

Unentrinnbar, Tod, nur,
wenn wir zukunftgierig
eines Augenblickes reines Bleiben nicht ertragen.

II

Komm und wohne
in der schrägen, dunklen Kammer meines Herzens,
dass der Wände Weite noch, zum Raum sich schliesst

Komm und falle
in die bunten Gründe meines Schlafes,
der sich ängstigt vor des Abgrunds Steile unserer Welt.

Komm und fliege
in die ferne Kurve meiner Sehnsucht,
dass der Brand aufleuchte in die Höhe *einer* Flamme

Steh und bleibe.
Warte, dass die Ankunft unentrinnbar
zukommt aus dem Zuwurf eines Augenblicks.

1951

[Untitled]

Die Gedanken kommen zu mir,
ich bin ihnen nicht mehr fremd.
Ich wachse ihnen als Stätte zu
wie ein gepflügtes Feld.

1951

H.B. [Hermann Broch]

Wie aber lebt man mit den Toten? Sag,
wo ist der Laut, der Ihren Umgang schwichtet,
wie die Gebärde, wenn durch sie gerichtet,
wir wünschen, dass die Nähe selbst sich uns versagt.

Wer weiss die Klage, die sie uns entfernt
und zieht den Schleier vor das leere Blicken?
Was hilft, dass wir uns in ihr Fort-sein schicken,
und dreht das Fühlen um, das Ueberleben lernt.

1952

Fahrt durch Frankreich

Erde dichtet Feld an Feld,
flicht die Bäume ein daneben,
lässt uns unsere Wege weben
um die Acker in die Welt.

Blauten jubeln in dem Winde,
Grass schiesst auf, sie weich zu betten,
Himmel blaut und grüsst mit Linde,
Sonne spinnt die sanften Ketten.

Menschen gehen unverloren—
Erde, Himmel, Licht und Wald— —
jeden Frühling neugeboren
spielend in das Spiel der Allgewalt.

# Arendt's Doctoral Dissertation: A Synopsis

Hannah Arendt's doctoral dissertation, *Der Liebesbegriffe bei Augustin*, printed in Gothic script, filled with untranslated Latin and Greek quotations, and written in Heideggerian prose, is not an easily accessible work. E. B. Ashton drafted a translation of it in the early 1960s, but Arendt did not want the translation revised for publication. She hoped to add new material to the work and thus make the old material clearer. In 1965 she gave up the project, discouraged by the amount of work required and preoccupied with other tasks.

I will offer below a synopsis of the dissertation designed to do three things: show its basic structure and intent; indicate how the thinking methods Arendt had learned from her teachers Heidegger and Jaspers are revealed in it; and suggest how the work relates to Arendt's later philosophical and political concerns. I will not try to criticize or evaluate Arendt's contribution to Augustine scholarship.

Neither Jaspers nor his student ever began the exploration of a phenomenon or concept without spatial tracing. They asked about the place of a phenomenon or concept in the scientifically explorable world; they asked about the existential conditions which define or are defined by a phenomenon or concept; and they asked how the unknowable, transcendent, ultimately mysterious realms bordering on a phenomenon or concept could be approached.

Neither Heidegger nor his student ever began the exploration of a phenomenon or concept without temporal tracing. They asked not just about the historical developments, the histories of phenomena and concepts, but, more fundamentally, about experiences of time, in time, which lay at the sources of phenomena or concepts. Past, present, and future, not as "tenses" but as experiences, frame all of Arendt's books, until the last, *The Life of the Mind*, which is framed by concern for future-oriented willing, past-oriented judging, and thinking as an experience of "now."

The interlacing of Jasperian spatial systematizations and Heideggerian temporal framings is intricate in Arendt's study of Augustine's concept of love, but the propositions with which the work begins are quite simple. One form of love, *Appetitus* or craving, is related to a definite object, something known, which is sought for its own sake. Because we seek the object for its own sake, not in relation to or as a means toward other things, it is a good, a *bonum*. Once the craving is satisfied, it ends— unless it is threatened with loss, mingled with fear or dread of some evil or *malum*. The good is that which will make men happy, and it is the will to be happy that guides desire toward the good, away from evil. Different men may have different opinions about what is good and what is evil, but they all agree in wanting to live happily. Life itself, then, is a good for all; and all necessarily fear losing it. If it were impossible for men to lose their lives, they could be happy; if death did not threaten men, they could live without fear. Life without fear, *metu carere*, is the ultimate goal of love as *appetitus*.

The first tension in Augustine's thought which is revealed in the dissertation is already present in this dense sequence of propositions: life without death, or a present in which the future is anticipated without fear, is impossible. A living man who craves anything on this earth, who hopes for secure possession of anything, is doomed to frustration, for both he and the things of this world are perishable. A present without a menacing future, which would be in itself the *summum bonum*, the Highest Good, is—eternity. Love as craving must shun the earth and all things mutable, all merely relative goods. Augustine's conception of love as craving led him, Hannah Arendt argued, into a contradiction: eternity is desired as a future object. But Augustine conceived eternity, nonetheless, as a Now, the neo-Platonic *nunc stans*, in which past and future meet and disappear, a timeless present.

Desire for everlasting life, the right object of desire, is called by Augustine *caritas*, while wrong desire for perishable objects is called *cupiditas*. But caritas is problematic because it renders the earth and earthly things a desert for men; they must sacrifice "being at home in the world" for their right desire, for their freedom. Augustine, like the Stoics, thought of freedom as self-sufficiency, independence from perishable things. Again, it is a Greek current that flows through Augustine's thought—this time Stoic rather than neo-Platonic. Indeed, Hannah Arendt argued that Augustine explicitly rejected Plotinus's notion of freedom as cessation of desires, which implies that only the mind (*nous*), relating to itself and not to anything exterior, is free.

Augustine's distinction between *cupiditas* and *caritas*, and his elevation of *caritas* and its freedom, led him into another difficulty. Freedom or self-sufficiency cannot be attained in this world; but, even more, when a man withdraws from the world into himself, he falls short of self-sufficiency in a crucial way. He becomes a question to himself. And the answer to the question he asks, "What am I?" can only be God-given.

Self-questioning and self-love bring man near to God, allowing him to know what he is not, what he as a mortal being lacks: an eternal essence. The right love of self—that is, *self*-love as a form of *caritas*—aims not at the present, mutable self but at that self which will live forever. The temporal self must be negated if a man is to project his true self toward an absolute future.

By filling his present life with desire for the future, man anticipates a timeless present, everlastingness. Adopting the Roman understanding of time, Augustine conceived of the future as coming into the present, running "backwards" into the past; the image of time's movement is the opposite of the linear image that accompanies the word *progress*. When the future is, so to speak, rushing in, the present self is negated, and the world forgotten. For Augustine, Hannah Arendt claimed, Temporality and Being are opposites: Temporality must be overcome for man to Be. This tension was fundamental to Augustine's thought—and to Heidegger's.

Augustine had tried to think of man as free, self-sufficient; but, in order to do this and to continue to think of love as craving, he had to suffer the tension of the thought that the self must be transformed, the temporal self forgotten. Put in other terms: when man uses the world to try to reach, through *caritas*, the enjoyment of extratemporality, he breaks his bonds with things and men, with God's creation. And this severance makes another form of love, neighborly love, a very complex one.

Two categories, usage (*uti*) and enjoyment (*frui*)—or, simply, means and ends—follow from the definition of love as craving. The world is used to attain enjoyment, which is, ultimately, enjoyment of God, *Deo frui*. Two further categories are related to this enjoyment: we love the highest good, the *supra nos*, as opposed to both what is *iuxta nos*, beside us (our selves and our neighbors) and also to what is *infra nos*, beneath us (our bodies). Our selves, our neighbors, and our bodies are to be loved for the sake of the highest good; but this means that love of our neighbors for their own sakes is impossible and that our neighbors are *used* (not enjoyed) when we desire rightly. Love as desire, love whose object is in the future, makes the commandment "Love thy neighbor as thyself" meaningless.

The first part of Arendt's dissertation ends at this impasse. The notion of love as desire founders when the desired "happy life" is projected into the absolute future and the present self is viewed as a mere means for its attainment, the obstacle to be overcome. So, Hannah Arendt began her investigation again, circling back to the beginning. The proposition that every *appetitus* is tied to a definite object was reexamined. The happy life, if it is to be the object of desire, must be known; but, if this is so, knowledge must precede desire, knowledge must present the object of desire. Put in another way: past knowledge is the basis for a projection into the future. Desire transcends the present toward the future, but it can do so only because memory transcends the present, guarding the past. And, further, knowledge of the "happy life," unlike knowledge of something perceivable, of which we have a "corporeal image," a worldly experience, implies memory of a different sort than memory of perceivables. Augustine constructed the possibility of a transmundane memory on the basis of an analysis of the working of memory in general.

For example: when we are sad, we remember joyful times hopefully, as we remember sadness fearfully when we are joyful. The past is remembered as part of the present—so to speak, inspirationally. As the past is made present, it is transformed into a future possibility; what has been can be again. Desire for a happy life involves an answer to the question "whence is the holy soul happy?" This question is, ultimately, the question "who made me?" In the "camps and vast places of memory," as Augustine said, the creature finds his Creator; he finds the Creator in himself as the determinant of his being, the reason for his existence.

At this turn in her interpretation, a contrast which became fundamental to Hannah Arendt's later work was revealed, a contrast which provided one of the most forceful conceptual frameworks for *The Human Condition*. With the clarity that comes with years of familiarity, years of thinking and rethinking, Arendt stated the contrast in her 1963 notes for revision of the dissertation thus: "The decisive fact determining man as a conscious remembering being is birth or natality, that we have entered the world through birth, while the decisive fact determining man as a desiring being is death or mortality, the fact that we shall leave the world in death. Fear of death, and the inadequacy of life are the springs of desire, whereas, on the contrary, gratitude for life having been given at all—a life cherished even in misery—... is the spring of remembrance. What ultimately stills the fear of death is not hope or desire but remembrance and gratitude: 'Give thanks for wanting to be as you are that you may be delivered of what you do not want to be. For you are willing to be and unwilling to be miserable.'"[1]

Natality and mortality became, in Hannah Arendt's later political thought, the springs of action as initiation of something new and of action as striving for immortal words and deeds. Actions renew the lives of men and also lend men what immortality they, as mortals, can have: they live on in human memory. She shifted the emphasis from the theological side of these existential determinants, which is predominant in the context of the Augustine dissertation, to the political side. Or, to put the matter differently, she considered the political life as that for which we should be grateful.

The shift in Arendt's dissertation from love as *appetitus* to love as memory of our nature as God's creatures has another important echo in Arendt's later work. To the confusion of many of her readers, Arendt argued in *The Human Condition* that action is not a matter of means and ends, as fabrication is. This claim seemed to imply that action does not involve planning or policy-making. But what Arendt meant, I think, is that action conceived as planning alone is as insufficient as love conceived as *appetitus* alone. Ends-means categories, like *uti-frui* categories, result in neglect—for the sake of the future—of present being-with-others or neighborly love. Recalling the past or the source of action or love— natality or creatureliness—gives men a principle rather than an end for their orientation. We act so that action is possible, which means that freedom is the principle of action. Planning is not precluded, but action that fails to achieve its end may nevertheless be meaningful or great ("greatness" is Arendt's criterion in *The Human Condition*). Action engaged in only for the sake of an end may, on the other hand, adopt any means or pervert human relations by making them into a means (as men become *uti* for the sake of *Deo frui*).

In *The Human Condition*, Arendt left the Augustinian or theological dimension of the question of man's nature aside—acknowledging that theological constructions come up inevitably when man's nature or essence is questioned, because only from a point of view "outside" man can man's nature be considered—and turned her attention to the conditions of human existence, life itself, natality and mortality, worldliness, plurality and the earth. She paid the theological approach its due, however, by also acknowledging that these conditions of human existence can never " . . . 'explain' what we are or answer the question of who we are for the simple reason that they never condition us absolutely."[2] Hannah Arendt did not suppose that man has a humanly *knowable* nature, nor did she suppose that man or nature can be scientifically explained by or reduced to the conditions which largely determine man's nature. Philosophy steers a middle course, *thinking* about man rather than seeking to *know* him from an extrahuman perspective or from an investigation of his human context. This distinction between thinking and knowing, philosophy and science, was one that both Heidegger and Jaspers made.

Hannah Arendt's concern for natality, which is equal to, and often greater than, her concern for mortality, emerged in her study of Saint Augustine but it was later brought urgently to the center of her thought by her political experiences. Initiation of something new, action, is the human possibility that offers a glimmer of hope in political situations that could so easily lead to complete despair. "The miracle that saves the world, the realm of human affairs, from its normal, 'natural' ruin is ultimately the fact of natality, in which the faculty of action is ontologically rooted. It is, in other words, the birth of new men and the new beginning, the action they are capable of by virtue of being born. Only the full experience of this capacity can bestow upon human affairs faith and hope, those two essential characteristics of human existence which Greek antiquity ignored altogether, discounting the keeping of faith as a very common and not too important virtue and counting hope among the evils of illusion in Pandora's box. It is this faith in and hope for the world that found perhaps its most glorious and most succinct expression in the few words with which the Gospels announced their 'glad tidings': 'A child has been born unto us.'"[3] For Arendt, temporality, far from having to be overcome for man to be, is the source of his possibility for action in which his being is intensified. It is as though she quoted to Augustine (and Heidegger) one of her favorite lines from Pindar: "become what you are"— gratefully acknowledge what the fact of having been born grants you.

Hannah Arendt brought "natality" into the conceptual light in her later work, retrieving it from philosophical neglect. In this she departed from

Heidegger: for him, mortality, rather than natality, was the crucial existential condition. Heidegger did not concern himself with action or, in general, with the political realm. Hannah Arendt was very much influenced by the descriptions of everyday life in *Being and Time*, but she thought they did not go far enough. Heidegger presented the "thrownness" of man toward death, his headlong rush into the future that comes toward him, but he did not present the force of the past, the presence of beginnings.

The contrast between natality and mortality emerged in Arendt's dissertation as she turned from considering love as craving to considering it as a relation to God. In the "camps and vast palaces of memory," the creature finds his Creator, his answer to the question "who made me?" The Creator, the ultimate origin of man, is also, for Augustine, his ultimate end. God is "outside" of man in this twofold sense; but man can concentrate this "outside" into himself by remembering the past and anticipating the future; he can annihilate both time and his subjection to it. *Caritas* is this form of extraworldly right desire. But, where *caritas* is actualized— which requires God's grace—man casts off his individuality, his own individual past. Helping a humbled man, who has the will but not the power to overcome his ties to self and world, God shows his love of man. He re-creates him, makes him a *nova creatura*. Accepting God's love, the creature loves as God loves—and this means that he loves men not as individuals but as God's creatures. He loves his neighbor (*das Nächste*) neither for the neighbor's sake nor for his own sake; he loves in isolation, denying both his own self and other selves. Man loves the eternal in himself and in others, and thus all men are loved equally as they are, so to speak, equally occasions for love.

In this context, a question obviously arises: why does neighborly love play such a large role in Augustine's thought if it is merely a mode of extraworldly relation? What makes men *neighbors*, what specifically binds them to one who loves them all equally? Hannah Arendt took up this tension in Augustine's work by introducing another train of thought. All men are kin, Augustine held, by virtue of their common descent from Adam; and, to all men, certain social relations are prescribed by virtue of the "law of Christ," the new Adam. Man's historical origin is the First Man, and he relates to this past through the generations. When he relates to this past, rather than to the Creator Himself, man realizes that love is due to all men because they are his worldly kin, because all have both a common nature and a common sinfulness. Further, the appearance in the world of the new Adam, Christ, offers salvation to all men, who participate equally in sin, and not to individuals solely on their merits. Both shared descent and shared salvation bind men to each other. The Christian's life in the world embodies his constant tie to the past and thus to the original kinship, his equal share of the original sin which explains death. (That is, death is not simply an inevitability; it is necessary as the wages of sin.) But estrangement in the world through *caritas* can give rise to a new togetherness, a society beside and over against the society of the historically kindred: the City of God. Men share a common peril, death, and love each other in common knowledge of this peril. But even in this unity of love there remains a distance or indirectness: each believer faces his death alone, no other man can save him. In neighborly love, men love one another because in doing so they love Christ, their Saviour; neighborly love is an unworldly, transcendent love, in the world but not of it.

Arendt's dissertation ends with a summary statement of the twofold relation between worldly existence with others and the extraworldly stance of self- and world-denial. Considering the first relation, Arendt claims that we meet others as fellow members of the human race, but that we only become neighbors to others when we are isolated in our singular relation to God. When an individual is lifted out of the matter-of-course dependence in which all men live among others, his association with others is subject to the explicit obligations of original kinship with them. Considering the second relation, Arendt claims that the possibility of isolation also enters as a fact into the history of mankind. Isolation thus becomes historic itself—even though it is isolation that enables us to detach ourselves from human history and from the continuity of generations. Only in this twofold relationship can we understand the neighbor's relevance. In individual isolation, we realize that the other is our neighbor as a member of the human race. But this mere coexistence of believers in the same God turns into the common faith, the communion of all the faithful, when we realize that our origin in the human race is complemented by our origin in God's love, our natality by our redemptive rebirth.

Hannah Arendt revised her dissertation only as far as the beginning of the second part which deals with the past-oriented relation of creature and Creator. The third section, which deals with neighborly love, the most condensed and difficult, would probably have required the most explication—as the dense sequence of thought just summarized illustrates. The concerns of the third part are restated in much less compact prose and much more clearly—at a distance—in *The Human Condition*. And a glance at this later statement will show in another way the critical stance that Hannah Arendt eventually reached: "To find a bond between people strong enough to replace the world was the main political task of early Christian philosophy, and it was Augustine who proposed to found not only the Christian 'brotherhood' but all human relationships on charity. . . . [The] bond of charity between people, while it is incapable of founding a public realm of its own, is quite adequate to the main Christian principle of worldlessness and is admirably fit to carry a group of essentially worldless people through the world . . . provided only that it is understood that the world itself is doomed and that every activity is undertaken with the proviso *quandiu mundus durat* ("as long as the world lasts")."[4] What she was concerned with in the dissertation was simply how the Christian principle of worldlessness could be adequate to carry a group of essentially worldless people through the world, with how the worldless experience of charity could unite men. Her later concern with the founding of public realms was rooted not in any Christian philosophy, but in Greek and Roman thought. "For unlike the common good as Christianity understood it—the salvation of one's soul as a concern common to all—the common world is what we enter when we are born and what we leave behind when we die. . . . But such a common world can survive the coming and going of generations only to the extent that it appears in public. It is the publicity of the public realm which can absorb and make shine through the centuries whatever men may want to save from the natural ruin of time."[5] The common world—the world existing between men—lasts as long as men care for it and are able to save it. Deeds, for example, last as long as there are men who tell of the deeds in stories. Deeds reflect human natality by initiating, beginning something new, and they overcome human mortality by living on past the doer's death in human memories. Hannah Arendt's completely non-Christian understanding of the common world gave her a measure by which to judge the loss of the public realm in the modern age: "There is perhaps no clearer testimony to the loss of the public realm in the modern age than the almost complete loss of concern with authentic immortality."[6] Striving for authentic, that is, earthly immortality or fame is thought to be a species of vanity, a private vice. She came to understand modern "dark times" as times in which the public realm has atrophied, and publicity, far from enhancing human endeavors, trivializes them:

"Das licht der Öffentlichkeit verdunkelt alles [The light of the public obscures everything]," as Heidegger put it.

Neither Hannah Arendt's critical position nor the conclusions she drew from it are apparent in her dissertation. She kept the promise she made in her introduction that the inquiry would be "analytical throughout." Arendt described her approach as "purely philosophical," by which she meant that she was not going to consider Augustine's "dogmatic subservience" to Scriptural and ecclesiastical authority. She dealt with his conversion to Christianity only in terms of the movement in his thought from the "pretheological" notion of love as craving to the theological notion of love as a relation of creature and Creator. Not only the dogmatic elements of Augustine's thought but the events in Augustine's life, as such, play no role in the dissertation, which is as resolutely abstract as it is apolitical and atheological.

When she revised her dissertation, Hannah Arendt must have felt this abstractness as a weakness, for she added several references to Augustine's life, transferring them from the footnotes into the body of the text. She included passages from Augustine's *Confessions* about his loss of a close friend; his fear of death, which "recalled him from carnal pleasure" and prepared him for his conversion; and his dependence on the writings of Saint Paul ("the more Christian Augustine grew in the course of a long life, the more Pauline he became"). Arendt also incorporated many of the quotations from Augustine's works that had appeared in her footnotes and material that had been set aside in an appendix into her first chapter, making the text richer and less elliptical, as well as less abstract. All of these revisions reflect the same fundamental insight: the kind of "purely philosophical" approach she had followed could avoid dogmatic concerns and reach the existential experiences, the temporal experiences, from which philosophical thought arises; but it could do this only in general terms, ahistorical and impersonal. Arendt had been looking for a universal, a universal bond among men, an ontological foundation, a transcendent principle guiding men who are in the world but not of it. She continued to look for such a universal or transcendent principle, and to defend the autonomy of philosophy, until her experience taught her that philosophy, pure philosophy, can be dangerously blind to history, to the political realm; until her association with Zionism taught her to question the foundation of "neighborly love" in political terms.

With Martin Heidegger Hannah Arendt had had an experience of the "extraordinary and wonderful" which seemed to divide time into a "then" and a "now"—an experience of the fears and frustrations of *appetitus*. And she was able to find in Augustine, as later in the poet Rilke, an image of that division transcended, that mode of love translated into a transcendental love. But the historical events which cast Hannah Arendt into political action raised questions that would not yield to such a "purely philosophical" solution.

# Notes

The libraries where documents are located are abbreviated as follows:

Library of Congress     Arendt Papers, Library of Congress, Washington, D.C.
Marbach     Arendt Papers, Deutsches Literaturarchiv, Marbach, Federal Republic of Germany
Bard College     Bard College Library, Annandale-on-Hudson, New York

Materials appearing in quotation marks in the text but not cited in the notes are from the author's interviews. If there is a documentary source that complements or augments the interview material, it has been cited. Because the material gathered from interviews is presented in the text in composite form, in which differences in the interviewees' languages and minor differences of recollection do not appear, the material has not been attributed to particular individuals. The method of dealing with interview material is described in the preface, and the names of those interviewed are given in the acknowledgments.

Further information about the books and articles by Hannah Arendt that are cited in the notes can be found in the bibliography.

## Notes to Preface

1. Hannah Arendt, Preface, in *Men in Dark Times* (New York: Harcourt, Brace & World, 1968), p. ix (hereafter cited as *Men in Dark Times*).
2. Arendt to Jaspers, 14 May 1951, Marbach.
3. Arendt's unpublished address on receiving the Sonning Prize, 1975, Library of Congress.
4. Blumenfeld to Arendt, 18 March 1951, Marbach.
5. Arendt to Alex Morin, University of Chicago Press, 18 April 1958, Library of Congress.
6. Arendt to Blumenfeld, 17 July 1946, Marbach.
7. Arendt's untitled poem, dated 1924, Marbach: "Kommst Du aus so fernem Land / Kennst nicht unseren Wein?"

8. Arendt, "Walter Benjamin: 1892–1940," in *Men in Dark Times*, p. 172.

9. Arendt to Jaspers, 29 January 1946, Marbach.

10. From Arendt's 1964 interview with Günther Gaus, "Was bleibt? Es bleibt die Muttersprache," collected in Gaus, *Zur Person* (Munich: Feder, 1964) (hereafter cited as Gaus interview.)

11. Arendt's unpublished address on receiving the Sonning Prize, 1975, Library of Congress.

12. Ibid.

13. Arendt to Blumenfeld, 1 February 1959, Marbach.

14. Hannah Arendt "Remembering Wystan H. Auden," *New Yorker*, 20 January 1975, p. 39.

15. From Arendt's unpublished and untitled address at the Rand School, 1948, Library of Congress.

16. Jaspers to Arendt, 5 March 1960, Marbach.

17. Jaspers to Arendt, 11 October 1966, Marbach.

18. Arendt to Jaspers, 3 November 1966, Marbach.

19. Arendt, "Rosa Luxemburg: 1871–1919," *Men in Dark Times*, p. 33.

20. Arendt, "Isak Dinesen: 1885–1963," *Men in Dark Times*, p. 98.

21. Arendt to Blumenfeld, 19 July 1947, Marbach.

22. Martha Cohn Arendt's diary, *Unser Kind*, Library of Congress.

23. Hans Jonas, "Acting, Knowing, Thinking," *Social Research*, Spring 1977, p. 26.

## Notes to Introduction to Part 1

1. Gaus interview.

2. Arendt's poems are in the Deutsches Literaturarchiv, Marbach. All translations are the author's. Dr. Herbert Arnold's assistance is gratefully acknowledged. Succeeding quotations from the poems will not be noted individually; German texts of the poems quoted can be found in appendix 2.

3. Gaus interview.

4. Jaspers to Arendt, 18 September 1946, Marbach.

## Notes to Chapter 1

1. Hannah Arendt, *The Origins of Totalitarianism* (New York: Harcourt Brace Jovanovich, 1973), p. 58, n. 12. (All references are to the 1973 reprint of the 1966 new edition unless otherwise indicated; hereafter cited as *Origins*.)

2. Kurt Blumenfeld, *Erlebte Judenfrage* (Stuttgart: Deutsche Verlags-Anstalt, 1962), p. 45 (hereafter cited as *Erlebte Judenfrage*).

3. Blumenfeld, *Erlebte Judenfrage*, p. 93.

4. Gaus interview.

5. Martha Arendt's *Unser Kind* diary is in the Arendt Papers, Library of Congress. All translations are the author's. I wish to thank my colleague, Dr. Herbert Arnold, for his assistance. Succeeding quotations from the diary will not be individually noted.

6. Mary McCarthy, "Saying Good-bye to Hannah," *New York Review of Books*, 22 January 1976, p. 8.

7. Arendt to Richard Wandschneider, 16 July 1964, Library of Congress.

8. Arendt's "Die Schatten" is in the Arendt Papers, Library of Congress. See also chapter 2, n. 12.

9. Martha Arendt's group may also have had contacts among the Independent Socialists (one of the groups that later joined the Spartacists in the German Communist
party), who moved their headquarters to Königsberg after expulsion from Berlin in 1917.
The Königsberg workers had protested the war and the terrible burdens it brought them
during 1917 and had been fired upon by the German army. See David Morgan, *The
Socialist Left and the German Revolution* (Ithaca: Cornell University Press, 1975), pp.
332–33.

10. Kierkegaard quoted in Karl Jaspers, *Reason and Existenz*, trans. William Earle
(New York: Noonday Press, 1955), p. 43.

## Notes to Chapter 2

1. Fritz K. Ringer, *The German Inflation of 1923* (Oxford: Oxford University Press,
1962), pp. 104ff.

2. Karl Jaspers, "Philosophical Memoir," in P. A. Schlipp, ed., *The Philosophy of
Karl Jaspers* (La Salle, Ill.: Open Court, 1957), p. 50 (hereafter cited as "Philosophical
Memoir").

3. Hannah Arendt, "Martin Heidegger at Eighty," *New York Review of Books*, 21
October 1971, p. 51 (hereafter cited as "Martin Heidegger at Eighty").

4. Jaspers, "Philosophical Memoir," p. 33.

5. For a portrait of the main intellectual trends in the German universities of the
Weimar Republic, see Fritz K. Ringer, *The Decline of the German Mandarins* (Cambridge: Harvard University Press, 1969).

6. Hannah Arendt, "What is Existenz Philosophy?" *Partisan Review* 13 (Winter
1946):34 (hereafter cited as "What is Existenz Philosophy?").

7. Arendt to Fr. Pierre Riches, 21 August 1974, Library of Congress.

8. Arendt, "Martin Heidegger at Eighty," p. 51.

9. Cited by Walter Biemel, *Martin Heidegger, An Illustrated Study*, trans. J. L.
Mehta (New York: Harcourt Brace Jovanovich, 1976), p. 15. Heidegger's autobiographical piece, "My Way To Phenomenology" was translated for inclusion in Joan Stambaugh,
ed., *On Time and Being* (New York: Harper & Row, 1972).

10. The Arendt-Heidegger correspondence is in the Deutsches Literaturarchiv in Marbach; Arendt arranged for her letters to be sent to the archive after her death. Heidegger's
confession of his debt to Arendt was related by Arendt to Blücher in an 8 February 1950
letter: "This now seemed to him to have been the passion of his life [Dies nun einmal die
Passion seines Lebens gewesen sei]." Library of Congress. For a description of the 1949
reunion Arendt had with Heidegger in Freiburg, see chapter 6 below.

11. Hannah Arendt, *Rahel Varnhagen: The Life of a Jewish Woman*, rev. ed. (New
York: Harcourt Brace Jovanovich, 1974), p. 21 (hereafter cited as *Varnhagen*).

12. "Die Schatten" is in the Arendt Papers, Library of Congress. Quotations from it
will not be noted individually. Translations are the author's, but assistance from Anne-
marie Arnold is gratefully acknowledged.

13. Arendt to Blücher, 7 July 1936, Library of Congress. Arendt repeated this statement to friends, including Dr. Lotte Kohler, who helped prepare *Rahel Varnhagen* for
publication.

14. Arendt, *Origins*, p. 59.

15. Arendt, *Varnhagen*, p. 53.

16. Ibid., p. 21.

17. Ibid., p. 10.

18. Ibid., p. 114.

19. Ibid., p. 80.

20. Ibid., p. 114.

21. Hans Jonas, "Hannah Arendt: 1906–1975," *Social Research*, Winter 1976, pp. 3–5.

22. This and the following autobiographical remarks, which are not individually annotated, are from Jaspers's "Philosophical Memoir."

23. Gaus interview.

24. This and the following remarks about Heidegger are from a chapter Jaspers prepared for his "Philosophical Memoir" but chose not to include in it. The chapter was included in a reissue of the "Philosophical Memoir": *Philosophische Autobiographie* (Munich: Piper Verlag, 1977), pp. 92–111. (English translation in *Graduate Faculty Philosophy Journal*, Spring 1978, pp. 107–28.)

25. Arendt to Blumenfeld, 10 October 1954, Marbach. Jaspers's reflections on his wife's family in "Philosophical Memoir," and also Hans Saner, ed., *Karl Jaspers in Selbstzeugnissen und Bilddokumenten* (Hamburg: Rowohlt, 1970).

26. The Arendt-Loewenson correspondence is in the Deutsche Literaturarchiv, Marbach. Several additional letters given to the author by Professor Karl Frankenstein of Hebrew University will be deposited in the archive.

27. Peter Gay, *Weimar Culture: The Outsider as Insider* (New York: Harper & Row, 1968), p. 48.

28. Hans Saner, ed., *Karl Jaspers in Selbstzeugnissen und Bilddokumenten* (Hamburg: Rowohlt, 1970), p. 118.

29. Martin Greene, *The Von Richthofen Sisters* (New York: Basic Books, 1974), pp. 29ff.

30. Benno von Wiese is currently writing his memoirs, which will have pages on his relationship with Hannah Arendt.

31. Arendt, "What is Existenz Philosophy?" p. 46.

32. Martin Heidegger, *Introduction to Metaphysics*, trans. R. Mannheim (New Haven: Yale University Press, 1959), p. 199. Arendt discussed this passage of Heidegger's with J. Glenn Gray in a letter dated 25 March 1967, Library of Congress: "He probably left the sentence in to explain in an underhand way what *he* thought National Socialism was, namely, the encounter between global technology and modern man. The idea, as I said, is grotesque, but he is not the only one. I just found a very similar notation in Benjamin. The trouble with these gentlemen was, and always has been, that they couldn't read books like *Mein Kampf*—too boring—and preferred to read slightly crazy but highly interesting books by Italian futurists who later all turned fascists."

33. Arendt to Blumenfeld, 1 April 1951, Marbach.

34. These and the following remarks about Max Weber are from Jaspers, "Philosophical Memoir."

35. Jaspers to Arendt, 3 January 1933, Marbach.

36. Arendt to Blumenfeld, 29 March 1953, Marbach.

37. Arendt discussed Goldstein's article in "Walter Benjamin: 1892–1940," in *Men in Dark Times*, pp. 183ff. For a brief review of Kurt Blumenfeld's career and writings, see Shaul Esh, "Kurt Blumenfeld on the Modern Jew and Zionism," *Jewish Journal of Sociology*, December 1964, pp. 232–42.

38. The following stories are based on Blumenfeld's *Erlebte Judenfrage*.

39. Arendt, *Origins*, p. 79, n. 61.

40. Hannah Arendt, address delivered upon receiving the 1975 Sonning Prize, Library of Congress.

41. For a synopsis of Arendt's dissertation, see appendix 3.

42. This and the following quotation from Karl Jaspers, *Plato and Augustine* (New York: Harcourt, Brace & World, 1962), p. 111.

43. Arendt to Jaspers, 13 July 1955, Marbach. In a discussion of Bultmann, the nature of theology, and the inability of most theologians to think politically, Arendt remarked, "Augustin war noch kein Theologe."

44. For a survey of the critical reviews that greeted Arendt's dissertation, see Robert Meyerson, "Hannah Arendt, Romantic in a Totalitarian Age, 1928–1963" (Ph.D. diss., University of Minnesota, 1972).

45. Martin Heidegger, *Being and Time*, trans. Robinson and MacQuarrie (New York: Harper & Row, 1962), p. 443. Heidegger does, of course, have a general and inter-personal concept of *Sorge* ("care"), as the fundamental concept of his exposition of being-in-the-world.

46. Karl Jaspers, *Notizen zu Heidegger*, ed. Hans Saner (Munich: Piper Verlag, 1978), p. 34, n. 9.

47. Arendt, "What is Existenz Philosophy?" p. 50.

48. A copy of the preliminary translation of Arendt's doctoral dissertation which was prepared by E. B. Ashton is in the Arendt Papers, Library of Congress. Arrangements for publication of the dissertation in English were never consummated; Arendt wanted to revise the work and began to do so in 1964, but she never completed the project. The revisions she did make, in marginal notes on the manuscript, carried her critical stance so far that the intention of the dissertation was blocked. To produce a coherent text, she probably would have had to begin again.

## Notes to Chapter 3

1. Jaspers to Arendt, 4 August 1929, Marbach.

2. The following quotations, which are not individually annotated, are from Hannah Arendt, "Augustin und Protestantismus," *Frankfurter Zeitung*, no. 902, 12 April 1930.

3. Rainer Maria Rilke, *Duino Elegies*, trans. J. B. Leishman and Stephen Spender (New York: Norton & Co., 1963), p. 23.

4. Hannah Arendt, "Walter Benjamin: 1892–1940" in *Men in Dark Times*, p. 202.

5. Sybille Bedford, "Emancipation and Destiny," *The Reconstructionist*, 12 December 1958, pp. 22–26. (One of the finest portraits of Varnhagen's era is Bedford's novel *A Legacy*.)

6. Arendt, *Varnhagen*, p. 3.

7. Ibid., p. 9.

8. Ibid., p. 21.

9. Arendt to McCarthy, 7 October 1967 (in McCarthy's possession).

10. Arendt, *Varnhagen*, p. 58.

11. Ibid., p. 88.

12. Ibid., p. 104.

13. Ibid., p. 127.

14. Ibid., p. 143.

15. Ibid., p. 227. (The quotation is from Goethe.)

16. Arendt to Jaspers, 7 September 1952, Marbach.

17. Arendt, *Varnhagen*, p. 224.

18. Ibid., p. 183.

19. The following quotations, which are not individually annotated, are from Hannah Arendt's review in *Archiv für Sozialwissenschaft und Sozialpolitik* 66 (1931): 200–05. For

Arendt's later reflections on Herder and the "education principle," see *Origins*, pp. 57–58.

20. Hannah Arendt, "The Crisis in Culture," in *Between Past and Future*, 2d ed. (New York: Harcourt Brace Jovanovich, 1968), p. 226 (hereafter cited as *Between Past and Future*).

21. Arendt gave this address as she accepted the 1959 Lessing Prize of the City of Hamburg; it is collected in Arendt, *Men in Dark Times*.

22. Arendt to Blumenfeld, 21 July 1960, Marbach.

23. Jaspers to Arendt, 16 January 1931, Marbach.

24. The following quotations in the text are from Hannah Arendt's review in *Die Gesellschaft* 10 (1932): 177–79.

25. Hannah Arendt, "Zionism Reconsidered," *Menorah Journal* 33 (August 1945), p. 169.

26. "Margrave" here has the original meaning, "guard of the frontier districts," that it had when Charlemagne established the function. In 1930 the Nazis won a majority in the Königsberg local government.

27. Arendt, *Varnhagen*, p. 147.

28. Ibid., pp. 156–57.

29. Gaus interview.

30. Arendt to Jaspers, 1 January 1933, Marbach.

31. Gaus interview.

32. Jaspers to Arendt, 3 January 1933, Marbach.

33. Arendt to Jaspers, 1 January 1933, Marbach.

34. Arendt to Jaspers, 6 January 1933, Marbach.

35. Jaspers to Arendt, 10 January 1933, Marbach.

36. The exchange of letters between Arendt and Scholem was published in English in *Encounter* 22 (January 1964): 51–56, after it had appeared in several German journals; it is reprinted in R. Feldman, ed., *The Jew as Pariah* (New York: Grove Press, 1978).

37. Arendt described this episode in the Gaus interview, but her version is supplemented here with details related to the author in interviews.

38. Central Office of the Zionist Organization, *Resolutions of the 18th Zionist Congress* (London: 1934), p. 11, British Museum, London. The *Resolutions* presented an understanding of the situation couched in terms Arendt thought anachronistic: "The suppression of the rights of the Jews by all the powers of the state, unique in its scope and inconceivable in the twentieth century, represents a new and terrible manifestation of the century-old Jewish question depicted by the great creator of Zionism Theodor Herzl, the solution of which is the aim and content of the Zionist movement," p. 9.

39. In Jaspers to Arendt, 9 March 1966, Marbach, there is a description of Heidegger's behavior in 1933. Jaspers claimed that Heidegger, *selber nie Antisemit* ("himself never an anti-Semite"), was disturbed on his last visit not so much by Gertrud Jaspers's Jewishness as by the fact that she spoke her opinions about the Nazis so frankly and openly. Jaspers concluded: "I can never forget his completely unchivalrous behavior toward Gertrud in that situation." (Heidegger's 1966 interview with *Der Spiegel*, published after his death in 1976, does not cast much light on his personal attitudes in 1933; see "An Interview with Martin Heidegger," *Graduate Faculty Philosophy Journal* (Winter 1977), p. 5–27.)

40. Hannah Arendt, "An Adam Mueller Renaissance?" *Kolnische Zeitung*, no. 501, 13 September 1932, and no. 510, 17 September 1932.

41. Arendt to Jaspers, 4 July 1966, Marbach.

42. This and the following quotations are from the Gaus interview.

## Notes to Chapter 4

1. Arendt, "Walter Benjamin: 1892–1940," in *Men in Dark Times*, p. 173.
2. Arendt to William O'Grady, 1 May 1969, Library of Congress.
3. Arendt to Blumenfeld, 28 November 1933, Marbach.
4. Arendt, "We Refugees," *Menorah Journal* 31 (January 1943): 74 (hereafter cited as "We Refugees").
5. Arendt, "We Refugees," p. 75.
6. For descriptions of Germaine de Rothschild's charity projects, see Ernst Papanek, *Out of the Fire* (New York: William Morrow and Co., 1975).
7. Reported in David Weinberg, *Les Juifs à Paris de 1933 à 1939* (Paris: Calmann-Lévy, 1974).
8. Arendt, "We Refugees," p. 73.
9. Arendt, Introduction to *Job's Dungheap*, by Bernard Lazare (New York: Schocken Books, 1948).
10. Arendt to Jaspers, 18 November 1945, Marbach.
11. In addition to interviews, several documents provided the dates and factual information in the following account of Blücher's youth: documents prepared for the Blüchers' restitution cases and marriage and divorce papers, both in the Arendt Papers, Library of Congress; an autobiographical sketch called "Beschreibung Eines Durchschnittlichen Lebens" and a collection of obituaries, both at Bard College; and a letter from Arendt to P. Witonski, 12 January 1971, Library of Congress.
12. The following account of the German Communist Party comes chiefly from Peter Nettl, *Rosa Luxemburg* (Oxford: Oxford University Press, 1966) and Ossip K. Flechtheim, *Die KPD in Der Weimaren Republik* (Frankfurt: Europaische Verlagsanstalt, 1971).
13. Hannah Arendt, "Rosa Luxemburg: 1871–1919," in *Men in Dark Times*, p. 36.
14. Ibid., p. 55.
15. The 1971 catalogue foreword, a joint production, is signed "Hannah Arendt." (Selected Artists Galleries, 655 Madison Avenue, New York.)
16. Hannah Arendt, "The Streets of Berlin," *Nation*, 23 March 1946, p. 350. The poems and comments cited below are taken from Arendt's "Nachwort" for Robert Gilbert, *Mich hat kein Esel im Galopp verloren* (Munich: Piper, 1972).
17. Blücher did try to contact his mother after the war, but a long letter dated April 1946 was returned to him with the information that his mother had died in 1943. He visited Wallitz in 1963 on his first return to Germany and wrote a brief description of the town. (Both of these documents are now in the Library of Congress.) Arendt, worried that his guilt at the time of his mother's death would depress Blücher, wrote him a strenuous letter (Arendt to Blücher, July 1946, Library of Congress): "Had you done otherwise, you would have had to have decided at age 15 . . . to be a good son. And that would have been both wrong and inhuman—because this whole parent-child business becomes automatically so as the child grows up. . . . Believe me, being a good son is a lifetime profession. . . . I know I am being 'like an axe,' but I am worried that you will sink again into a kind of melancholy, with this as the precipitating cause."
18. Arendt, "Rosa Luxemburg," *Men in Dark Times*, pp. 45–46.
19. Colie to Arendt, 21 May 1965, Library of Congress.
20. Arendt, *Origins*, p. 268.
21. Bespaloff's *On the Iliad* was translated into English by Mary McCarthy and published by the Bollingen Foundation in 1947; Arendt's friend Hermann Broch wrote the introduction.

22. Recha Freier told Youth Aliyah's story in *Let the Children Come* (London: Weidenfeld and Nicolson, 1961). For her correspondence with Hannah Arendt, see chapter 8 below.

23. Arendt to Mary McCarthy 7 October 1967 (in McCarthy's possession).

24. Heinz Pol, *Suicide of Democracy* (New York: Reynal & Hitchcock, 1940). (Pol, the photographer Ricarda Schwerin, now living in Jerusalem, and several other Berlin leftists had joined Blücher in Prague in 1933. Pol settled in New York, as did his first wife, Blücher's friend Charlotte Beradt.)

25. This and the following descriptions of the French political configurations are from Arendt, *Origins*, pp. 263ff. For further background information, see Louis Bodin and Jean Touchard, *Front Populaire: 1936* (Paris: Armand Colin, 1972).

26. Arendt, "The Ex-Communists," *Commonweal* 57 (20 March 1953): 596.

27. Arendt, *Origins*, p. 264.

28. Brief reports in *La Terre Retrouvée*, 15 January 1937, 1 February 1937. In 1 March 1937, p. 19: "Mme Stern a terminé en français son cours sur les causes historiques de l'antisémitisme allemand."

29. *Samedi*, March 1937. Translated by the author.

30. David Weinberg described the Frankfurter incident in *Les Juifs à Paris de 1933 à 1939*. See also reports in *La Terre Retrouvée* (15 December 1936) by Emil Ludwig, who also wrote a book called *The Davos Murder* (New York: Viking Press, 1936). *L'Affaire Frankfurter* by Pierre Bloch and Didier Meran (Paris: Denoël, 1937) was reviewed in *Samedi*, 19 June 1937. Frankfurter himself published an autobiography.

31. Arendt's unpublished remarks on the back-to-the-ghetto theorists are in the Arendt Papers, Library of Congress.

32. Arendt's notes (in German) are in the Arendt Papers, Library of Congress. What she meant by "rebarbarization" is clear in her 1959 Lessing Prize speech, where she described first the fraternity of pariah peoples and then their great liability: "so radical a loss of the world, so fearful an atrophy of all the organs with which we respond to it—starting with the common sense with which we orient ourselves in a common world to ourselves and others and going on to the sense of beauty, or taste, with which we love the world—that in extreme cases, in which pariahdom has persisted for centuries, we can speak of real worldlessness. And worldlessness is always, alas, a form of barbarism." *Men In Dark Times*, p. 13.

33. Cited from English translations of some of the Adorno-Benjamin correspondence which appeared in the *New Left Review* 81 (1973): 46–80.

34. Arendt, "Bertolt Brecht: 1898–1956," *Men in Dark Times*, p. 245.

35. It is possible that Blücher's contribution to the "mass society" theory in Arendt's *The Origins of Totalitarianism* was indebted to his former Brandlerite colleague August Thalheimer's 1930 essay "Über den Fascismus und Kapitalismus" [reprinted in W. Abendroth, ed., *Faschismus und Kapitalismus* (Frankfurt: Europaeische Verlagsanstalt, 1967)]. Thalheimer had recognized the insufficiencies of the standard Marxist explanation of Italian fascism as a capitalist conspiracy and argued that it was an autonomous, mass-mobilizing movement.

36. Copies of the official announcements relating to internment can be found in Barbara Vormeier's appendices to Hannah Schramm, *Menschen in Gurs* (Worms: Verlag Georg Heintz, 1977), pp. 159–385.

37. Arendt, "We Refugees," p. 70.

38. Kaethe Hirsch's description is available in Schramm, *Menschen in Gurs*, pp. 332–34.

39. For descriptions and photographs of Gurs, see Joseph Weill, *Contribution à l'histoire des camps d'internement dans l'Anti-France* (Paris: Éditions du Centre, 1946).

40. Arendt to Blumenfeld, 6 August 1952, Marbach.

41. Arendt, "We Refugees," p. 72.

42. Arendt, letter to the editor of *Midstream*, Summer 1962, p. 87, in response to an article by Bruno Bettelheim.

43. This quotation and the following one are from Arthur Koestler, *Scum of the Earth* (New York: Macmillan Co., 1941), p. 275.

44. Arendt, "Walter Benjamin," in *Men in Dark Times*, p. 153.

45. Arendt, "Rosa Luxemburg," in *Men in Dark Times*, p. 171.

46. For further information see Henry Feingold, *The Politics of Rescue: The Roosevelt Administration and the Holocaust, 1938–1945* (New Brunswick, N.J.: Rutgers University Press, 1970).

47. Arendt, "Walter Benjamin," in *Men in Dark Times*, p. 53, n. 9.

48. Benjamin's commentary is available in English: Walter Benjamin, *Understanding Brecht* (London: New Left Books, 1973). The quotations following are from this translation.

49. Hannah Arendt, "Jewish History, Revised," *Jewish Frontier*, March 1948, p. 38.

50. Walter Benjamin, "Theses on the Philosophy of History," in Hannah Arendt, ed., *Illuminations* (New York: Harcourt, Brace & World, 1968), pp. 255–66.

## Notes to Chapter 5

1. Arendt to Blücher, 18 July 1941, Library of Congress.

2. Arendt to Blücher, undated, ca. July 1941, Library of Congress.

3. Arendt to Blücher, undated, ca. July 1941, Library of Congress.

4. Arendt to Jaspers, 29 January 1946, Marbach.

5. Arendt to Blücher, undated, ca. July 1941, Library of Congress.

6. Arendt to Blücher, undated, ca. July 1941, Library of Congress.

7. Arendt to Blücher, undated, ca. July 1941, Library of Congress.

8. Arendt, "Walter Benjamin: 1892–1940," in *Men in Dark Times*, p. 167, n. 5.

9. Gershom Scholem to Arendt, 6 February 1942, Library of Congress.

10. Benjamin's notes to Arendt are with the Arendt Papers, Library of Congress, as is the original manuscript of the "Theses on the Philosophy of History," which Benjamin wrote in his delicate, small script on several newspaper wrappers of different colors.

11. Arendt to Gaster, 5 October 1941, Marbach.

12. The following survey of German émigré political groupings is based on an unpublished, undated manuscript of Arendt's, "German Émigrés," Library of Congress.

13. Romain's letter appeared in *Aufbau* 7/2 (1941), pp. 5–6. Arendt's reply: "Der Dank vom Hause Juda? Offener Brief an Jules Romain," *Aufbau*, 25 October 1941.

14. One of Blücher's notebooks is in the Bard College Library.

15. Arendt to Klenbort, 18 August 1942 (in Klenbort's possession).

16. Ibid.

17. Hannah Arendt, "Papier und Wirklichkeit," *Aufbau*, 10 April 1942.

18. Hannah Arendt, "Moses oder Washington," *Aufbau*, 27 March 1942.

19. Hannah Arendt, "Mit dem Rucken an der Wand," *Aufbau*, 2 July 1942.

20. Arendt, *Origins*, p. 56. The Zionist Organization of America published appeals for a Jewish army in the *New York Times*, 16 February 1942, p. 13; 11 March 1942, p. 7;

13 March 1942, p. 9. An appeal signed by 1,521 prominent individuals appeared on 17 November 1942, p. 23.

21. Cited in the *Jewish Frontier* editorial for March 1942, discussing the American Emergency Committee for Zionist Affairs manifesto.

22. Copies of the announcements and position papers for the Young Jewish Group cited below are in the Arendt Papers, Library of Congress.

23. This and the following quotations, from reports of the Biltmore Conference, are from Melvin Urofsky, *American Zionism: From Herzl to the Holocaust* (New York: Doubleday Anchor, 1976), p. 399.

24. These and the following remarks about American Zionism are from Hannah Arendt, "Can The Jewish-Arab Question Be Solved?" *Aufbau*, 17 December 1943; the article is written in English.

25. The Brooklyn College lecture notes (in English) are in the Arendt Papers, Library of Congress.

26. The Hadassah lecture (in English, dated in Arendt's hand) is in the Arendt Papers, Library of Congress.

27. Hannah Arendt, "Can the Jewish-Arab Question Be Solved?" *Aufbau*, 17 December 1943.

28. Ibid.

29. Gaus interview.

30. Arendt, *Origins*, p. 402.

31. Arendt to Blumenfeld, 2 August 1945, Marbach.

32. Arendt to Michael di Capua, 25 October 1967, Library of Congress. This letter concerned Jarrell's Heine translations, which Schocken Books did not publish.

33. Jaspers to Arendt, 19 September 1948, Marbach.

34. Arendt, "Christianity and Revolution," *Nation*, 22 September 1945, p. 288.

35. This and the following quotations are from Jarrell's letters to Arendt, Library of Congress. None of the letters is dated, though Arendt wrote approximate dates on them when she prepared her essay "Randall Jarrell: 1914–1965," now in *Men in Dark Times*, in 1965. They will be quoted without individual annotations.

36. Arendt to Blumenfeld, 17 July 1946, Marbach.

37. This and the following quotations are from Hannah Arendt, "Portrait of a Period," *Menorah Journal* 31 (Fall 1943): 308.

38. Hannah Arendt, "No Longer and Not Yet," *Nation*, 14 September 1946, p. 300.

39. Hannah Arendt, "Hermann Broch: 1886–1951," in *Men in Dark Times*, p. 114.

40. Arendt to Blumenfeld, 19 July 1947, Marbach.

41. Arendt to Blumenfeld, 31 July 1956, Marbach.

42. "Magazine Digest," *Contemporary Jewish Record*, April 1947, p. 205.

43. Arendt to Blumenfeld, 19 July 1947, Marbach.

44. See Doris Grumbach, *The Company She Kept* (New York: Coward-McCann, 1967), p. 130.

45. Arendt to Henry Allen Moe, Guggenheim Foundation, 22 February 1959 (copy in McCarthy's possession).

46. Hannah Arendt, "Waldemar Gurian: 1903–1954," in *Men in Dark Times*, pp. 258–59.

47. This quotation and the lines of Jarrell's poetry from Hannah Arendt, "Randall Jarrell: 1914–1965," in *Men in Dark Times*, p. 266.

48. Mary McCarthy, "Saying Good-bye to Hannah," *New York Review of Books*, 22 January 1976, pp. 8, 10.

49. The motto is cited by Arendt in "Karl Jaspers zum fünfundachtzigsten

Geburtstag," in K. Piper and H. Saner, eds., *Erinnerugen an Karl Jaspers* (Munich: Piper Verlag, 1974), p. 314.

50. Arendt to Underwood, Houghton Mifflin, 24 September 1946. Unless indicated otherwise, the following discussion of *Origins* is based upon this letter and a number of undated outlines which are in the Arendt Papers, Library of Congress.

51. Hannah Arendt, "Totalitarianism," *Meridian* 2/2 (Fall 1958): 1 (the *Meridian* was the newsletter of Meridian Books.)

52. Hannah Arendt, "The Nature of Totalitarianism," unpublished lecture, 1954, Library of Congress.

53. Arendt to Jaspers, 4 September 1947, Marbach.

54. Cited from Arendt's 10 December 1948 draft of "Memo: Research Project on Concentration Camps," with addenda in her hand, Library of Congress. Arendt to Jaspers, 31 October 1948, Marbach; mentions a project envisioned by Salman Schocken on concentration camps.

55. Arendt to Cohen, undated, ca. 1948, Library of Congress. This letter accompanied a copy of the "Memo: Research Project on Concentration Camps" noted above.

56. Arendt, *Origins*, pp. 458–59.

57. Ibid., p. 459.

58. This passage and the following one are quoted from Arendt's introduction to "Memo: Research Project on Concentration Camps." See note 54 above.

59. Arendt to Jaspers, 11 March 1949, Marbach.

60. Arendt, *Origins*, 1st ed. (1951), p. 440.

61. Ibid.

62. This and the following quotations are from Arendt's unpublished lecture inscribed "Rand School, 1948" in her hand, Library of Congress.

63. Mary McCarthy elaborated on this position in two essays: "America the Beautiful: The Humanist in the Bathtub" and "Mlle. Gulliver en Amérique," in *Humanist in the Bathtub* (New York: Farrar, Straus & Co., 1951).

64. For a discussion of the proposed "Marxist Elements of Totalitarianism" book, see chapter 6 below.

65. Hannah Arendt, "The Concentration Camps," *Partisan Review*, July 1948, p. 63.

66. Karl Jaspers, *The European Spirit*, trans. Ronald G. Smith (London: SCM Press, 1948), p. 30.

## Notes to Chapter 6

1. Lasky to Macdonald (and forwarded to Arendt), 31 July 1945, Library of Congress.

2. Jaspers to Arendt, 10 October 1945, Marbach.

3. Arendt to Jaspers, 18 November 1945, Marbach.

4. Jaspers to Arendt, 12 March 1946, Marbach.

5. Lasky to Macdonald (and forwarded to Arendt), 31 July 1945, Library of Congress.

6. Arendt, "Karl Jaspers: A Laudatio," in *Men in Dark Times*, pp. 76–77 (hereafter cited as "Laudatio").

7. Karl Jaspers, *The Question of German Guilt* (New York: Dial Press, 1947), p. 16.

8. Arendt, "Laudatio," p. 77.

9. Arendt to Blumenfeld, 14 January 1946, Marbach.

10. Arendt to Jaspers, 18 November 1945, Marbach.

11. Jaspers to Arendt, 2 December 1945, Marbach.

12. Arendt to Gertrud Jaspers, 30 January 1946, Marbach.

13. Arendt to Blumenfeld, 6 August 1952, Marbach.

14. Jaspers to Arendt, 18 September 1946, Marbach.

15. Blücher to Arendt, undated, ca. July 1946, Library of Congress.

16. Arendt to Jaspers, 11 November 1946, Marbach.

17. As noted in chapter 2, Arendt's "What is Existenz Philosophy?" appeared in the *Partisan Review* 13 (Winter 1946); "French Existentialism," was published in the *Nation*, 23 February 1946.

18. Jaspers to Arendt, 18 and 22 November 1946, Marbach.

19. Arendt to Jaspers, 29 January 1946, Marbach.

20. In private, Arendt was even more strenuous about Heidegger. Arendt to Jaspers, 9 July 1946, Marbach, relates a story about Heidegger told to Arendt in Paris by Jean-Paul Sartre and then notes Heidegger's *ausgesprochen pathologischer Einschlag* ("well-known pathological strain").

21. Randall Jarrell, *Pictures from an Institution* (New York: Alfred A. Knopf, 1954), p. 169. For a discussion of this novel as a portrait of the Blüchers, see chapter 7 below.

22. For more detailed expositions of Arendt's *Origins*, see Margaret Canovan, *The Political Thought of Hannah Arendt* (New York: Harcourt Brace Jovanovich, 1974) and Stephen J. Whitfield, *Into the Dark: Hannah Arendt and Totalitarianism* (Philadelphia: Temple University Press, 1980).

23. Arendt, *Origins*, p. 334.

24. Ibid., p. 338.

25. Ibid., p. 352.

26. Ibid., p. 441. That the Nazis might be psychologically understandable is the assumption of Arendt's *Eichmann in Jerusalem*. See chapter 8 below.

27. Ibid., p. 457.

28. Arendt, xerox of unpublished notes for a lecture on *Eichmann in Jerusalem*, Library of Congress.

29. This short poem, dated 1952, and written while Arendt was in France (see chapter 7 below), seems to refer to the train of thought which eventually led to *The Human Condition*.

30. Arendt to Blumenfeld, 1 April 1951, Marbach; for the context of this letter see chapter 7 below.

31. Greenberg to Arendt, 28 February 1944, Library of Congress.

32. This statement and the following quotations are taken from "Zionism Reconsidered," *Menorah Journal* 33 (August 1945): 137–53.

33. This and the following quotations come from Arendt's unpublished 1943 address to a Hadassah meeting, "The Crisis of Zionism," pp. 7, 10, Library of Congress.

34. This and the following quotations are from Hannah Arendt, "To Save the Jewish Homeland: There Is Still Time," *Commentary*, May 1948, pp. 398–406.

35. Arendt to Magnes, 3 August 1948, Library of Congress.

36. Ben Halpern, "The Partisan in Israel," *Jewish Frontier*, August 1948, pp. 6–9.

37. Arendt's reply to Halpern was published in *Jewish Frontier*, October 1948, pp. 55–56. It has been collected in Ronald Feldman, ed., *The Jew as Pariah* (New York: Grove Press, 1978), pp. 237–39.

38. Arendt to Magnes, 1 September 1948, Library of Congress. Eban's article appeared in the September 1948 issue of *Commentary* and Magnes's reply (partly drafted by Arendt) was published in the October 1948 issue.

39. Arendt to Magnes, 22 October 1948, Library of Congress.

40. Arendt to Magnes, 17 September 1948, Library of Congress.

41. Magnes to Arendt, 7 October 1948, Library of Congress.

42. Arendt to Kohn, 12 November 1948, Library of Congress.

43. Albert Einstein et al., letter to the editor, New York Times, 4 December 1948, p. 12. (Arendt may have drafted this letter, as one of the signers, Zellig Harris, thanked her for it in an undated letter to her; Library of Congress.)

44. Arendt to Cohen, 24 November 1948, Library of Congress. Arendt felt that only an appeal through the synagogues would be effective in combatting the Revisionists' terror campaign: "You know that I am not religious in my accepted institutional sense of the word; but I am quite sure that there is simply no other force to be mobilized against the welter of superstition and mean savagery, against this mixture of plain stupidity and plain wickedness." But she also suggested a cadre of trained "tough guy" lecturers "who know how to talk the language of the mob," be sent around the country.

45. Arendt to Magnes, 3 October 1948, Library of Congress.

46. Jaspers to Arendt, 22 May 1948, Marbach.

47. Both telegrams and other correspondence from Eva Beerwald are in the Arendt Papers, Library of Congress.

48. Arendt to Jaspers, 31 October 1948, Marbach.

49. Jaspers to Arendt, 6 November 1948, Marbach.

50. This and the following quotations are from Arendt to Jaspers, 23 March 1947, Marbach.

51. Arendt to Blücher, 27 July 1948, Library of Congress.

52. Ibid. The last sentence alludes to a line of Brecht, "Dies ist nun alles und ist nicht genug."

53. This and the following quotations are from Blücher to Arendt, 29 July 1948, Library of Congress.

54. At a discussion of Women's Liberation that took place among the American Scholar's editorial board members in 1972, Arendt passed Hiram Haydn a note: "The real question to ask is, what will we lose if we win?" This, she told him in a 5 May 1972 letter (Library of Congress), was a "well-considered wisecrack."

55. Arendt, "Rosa Luxemburg," in Men in Dark Times, p. 45.

56. Arendt, "Bertolt Brecht," in Men in Dark Times, p. 231.

57. Heine's poem is cited in Arendt, "Nachwort," for Robert Gilbert, Mich hat kein Esel im Galopp verloren (Munich: Piper, 1972).

58. Arendt to Fränkel, 8 January 1950, Library of Congress. These letters, so uncharacteristically intimate, were written while Hilde Fränkel was dying and desperately in need of Arendt's affection and attention.

59. Arendt's letter appeared in Aufbau 8/31 (1942): 6. Arendt, "Organized Guilt," Jewish Frontier, January 1945, pp. 19–23.

60. Arendt, Varnhagen, p. 206.

61. Arendt to Blücher, 26 July 1950, Library of Congress, referring to the summer after Hilde Fränkel's death. Paul Tillich's wife, Hannah Tillich, was not so reticent; see her memoir, From Time to Time (New York: Stein and Day, 1973). On the other hand, Tillich's biographer, Wilhelm Pauck, presents his love affairs quite obliquely; see Paul Tillich (New York: Harper & Row, 1976).

62. Arendt to Hella Jaensch, 12 June 1965, Library of Congress.

63. Arendt put the matter another way in her 12 June 1965 letter to Hella Jaensch: "Eros is a powerful god, and appears in many forms; in every struggle he comes out the victor, as Sophocles said and I agree. He is not one of the great Olympians; Aphrodite is greater."

64. Fränkel to Arendt, undated, ca. New Year's Day 1950, Library of Congress.

65. Fränkel to Arendt, 14 February 1950, Library of Congress.

66. Fränkel to Arendt, 23 January 1950, Library of Congress.

67. Arendt to Fränkel, 4 February 1950, Library of Congress.

68. Arendt to Fränkel, 27 December 1949, Library of Congress.

69. Fränkel to Arendt, 7 December 1949, Library of Congress.

70. Arendt to Fränkel, 20 December 1949, Library of Congress.

71. Arendt to Fränkel, 4 February 1950, Library of Congress.

72. Arendt, "The Aftermath of Nazi Rule, Report from Germany," *Commentary* 10 (October 1950): 353.

73. Arendt to Fränkel, 3 December 1949, Library of Congress.

74. Arendt to Fränkel, 18 January 1950, Library of Congress. Arendt never established a good relationship with Eric Weil, and she found Anne Weil's patience with her very troubled husband so disturbing that she was quite relieved when Anne Weil secured a position with the Common Market in Brussels and was much of the time separated from Eric Weil.

75. Arendt to Fränkel, 8 January 1950, Library of Congress.

76. Arendt to Fränkel, 20 December 1949, Library of Congress.

77. Arendt to Blücher, 18 December 1949, Library of Congress.

78. Arendt to Blücher, 26 December 1949, Library of Congress.

79. Arendt to Fränkel, 2 March 1950, Library of Congress.

80. Arendt to Fränkel, 10 February 1950, Library of Congress.

81. Ibid.

82. Arendt to Blücher, 8 February 1950, Library of Congress.

83. Ibid.; Arendt to Fränkel, 10 February 1950, Library of Congress.

84. Arendt to Fränkel, 2 March 1950, Library of Congress.

85. Arendt to Blücher, 8 February 1950, Library of Congress.

86. Arendt to Fränkel, 10 February 1950, Library of Congress.

87. Arendt to Fränkel, 2 March 1950, Library of Congress.

88. Arendt, "Isak Dinesen," in *Men in Dark Times*, p. 109.

89. A typescript of the "League for the Rights of Peoples" proposal is with the Blücher Papers, Bard College Library. The manuscript is undated, but it seems to be referred to in a 9 June 1947 letter written to Arendt by Hermann Broch [H. Broch, *Briefe*, ed. Robert Pick (Zurich: Rhein-Verlag, 1957), p. 352].

90. For background on the Eighth Street Club, see Irving Sandler, *The Triumph of American Painting* (New York: Harper & Row, 1970), pp. 212ff.

91. Blücher to Arendt, 22 February 1950, Library of Congress. This success renewed Blücher's energy for work, which had also been given a great boost by the correspondence with Jaspers about the "Great Philosophers" series Arendt had initiated.

92. These course descriptions are taken from the New School for Social Research catalogue for 1951–52. The *Saturday Review* article appeared in the 17 April 1951 issue.

93. Arendt to Blumenfeld, 1 April 1951, Marbach.

94. Ibid.

95. Jarrell to Arendt, undated, ca. 1951, Library of Congress.

96. Arendt to Jaspers, 11 July 1950, Marbach.

97. Arendt to Jaspers, 25 June 1950, Marbach.

98. Arendt to Jaspers, 25 December 1950, Marbach.

99. Riesman to Arendt, 7 June 1949 and 8 June 1949, Library of Congress; Riesman's review of *Origins* appeared in *Commentary*, April 1951, pp. 392–97.

100. Blumenfeld to Arendt, 12 May 1953, Marbach.

101. Arendt, "Ideology and Terror," *Review of Politics*, July 1953, pp. 303–27; the essay was used as an epilogue to the 1958 edition of *Origins*.

102. Eric Voegelin's review and Arendt's reply to it were published in *Review of Politics*, January 1953, pp. 68–85.

103. Hannah Arendt, *The Human Condition* (Chicago: University of Chicago Press, 1970), p. 10 (hereafter cited as *The Human Condition*).

104. Arendt's handwritten note on Riesman to Arendt, 8 June 1949, Library of Congress.

105. This quotation and the following one are from Arendt to Jaspers, 4 March 1951, Marbach.

106. Riesman to Arendt, 26 August 1949, Library of Congress.

107. Philip Reiff, "The Theology of Politics," *Journal of Religion* 32 (1952): 119. For a summary of the critique directed against Arendt's concept of mass society, see Daniel Bell, *The End of Ideology* (New York: Free Press, 1960), chap. 1.

108. See David Riesman, *Individualism Reconsidered* (Glencoe, Ill.: Free Press, 1954), pp. 409ff. for a description of this meeting and a reprinting of Riesman's address.

109. Riesman to Arendt, 26 August 1949 with Arendt's handwritten additions, Library of Congress.

110. This and the following quotations are from Arendt, "The Rights of Man: What are They?" *Modern Review* 3/1 (Summer 1949): 24–37. (The essay was incorporated into the Concluding Remarks section of the first edition of *Origins*.)

111. Arendt to Fränkel (for Blücher), 3 December 1948, Library of Congress.

## Notes to Introduction to Part 3

1. Arendt, "On Humanity in Dark Times: Thoughts about Lessing," in *Men in Dark Times*, p. 12.

2. Ibid., p. 15.

## Notes to Chapter 7

1. Arendt to Blücher, 11 April 1952, Library of Congress.

2. Arendt to Blücher, 17 April 1952, Library of Congress.

3. Blücher to Arendt, 10 May 1952; the poem is in Arendt to Blücher, 1 May 1952, both in Library of Congress.

4. Blücher to Arendt, 7 June 1952 and Arendt to Blücher, 13 June 1952, both in the Library of Congress. Blücher's poem is also in the Library of Congress.

5. Jarrell's letters, Library of Congress, are undated. They are not individually annotated in this account.

6. Arendt, "Randall Jarrell: 1914–1965," in *Men in Dark Times*, p. 265.

7. This and the following quotations are from Randall Jarrell, *Pictures from an Institution* (New York: Alfred A. Knopf, 1954).

8. Alfred Kazin, *New York Jew* (New York: Alfred A. Knopf, 1978), p. 198.

9. Arendt, *The Human Condition*, p. 242.

10. From Blücher's notes for a course called "Why and How Do We Study Philosophy?" given at the New School, 1952. Notebook in the Bard College Library.

11. Blücher to his mother, Klara Blücher, April 1946, Library of Congress.

12. From the transcript of Blücher's Bard lectures on Jesus and Abraham, Bard College Library.

13. On his Bard College invitation and interview, Blücher to Arendt, 26 July 1952 and 2 August 1952, Library of Congress. Blücher's notes for the Common Course introduction and transcripts of his lectures are in Bard College Library.

14. Arendt, *The Human Condition*, p. 8.

15. Martin Self to the Reverend Kline, Bard College president, 14 December 1970, copy in Arendt Papers, Library of Congress.

16. Arendt to Blücher, 7 August 1953, Library of Congress.

17. Arendt to Blumenfeld, 16 November 1953, Marbach.

18. Arendt, *Origins*, p. 64.

19. Cited in Arendt obituary, *New York Times*, 5 December 1975.

20. Blücher to Arendt, 10 May 1952, Library of Congress. Blücher reports in this letter what he has heard about the in-house battles among the little-magazine staffs in New York, applauding Philip Rahv (who urged a response to the Kristol article be made in *Partisan Review*). There is no copy of Arendt's letter of protest in the Arendt papers, and no letter from her was printed in *Commentary*.

21. Hannah Arendt, "The Ex-Communists," *Commonweal*, 20 March 1953, p. 599.

22. For a report, see *I. F. Stone's Weekly Reader* (New York: Vintage Press, 1974), pp. 34ff.

23. Blücher to Arendt, 5 July 1952, Library of Congress.

24. Blücher to Arendt, 17 May 1952 and Arendt to Blücher, 24 May 1952, both in Library of Congress.

25. Arendt to Hutchins, Fund for the Republic, 27 January 1957, Library of Congress.

26. Arendt, "Project: Totalitarian Elements of Marxism," undated, ca. winter 1952, to Guggenheim Foundation, Library of Congress. The following account is based upon this document.

27. This and the following quotations are from Arendt to Henry Allen Moe, Guggenheim Foundation, 19 January 1953, Library of Congress.

28. Of these four chapters, only "Ideology and Terror" remained, as Arendt kept working, in anything like its original form. "Ideology and Terror" was published in the *Review of Politics* in July 1953, while a different version came out in German in a Festschrift for Karl Jaspers entitled *Offener Horizont*. The final version appeared as the penultimate chapter of *The Origins of Totalitarianism* at the time of the book's second edition, 1958. The other three chapters underwent revisions to make them fit for separate publication, outside of the framework of the Marxism book. The first became "Understanding and Politics," published in the *Partisan Review* in 1953. The second became "Tradition and the Modern Age" and was also published in the *Partisan Review*, 1954. The third chapter, on law and power, was refocused considerably, and retitled accordingly ("What was Authority?") for a volume edited by Carl J. Friedrich for the American Society of Political and Legal Philosophy, *Nomos I: Authority* (New York: Bobbs-Merrill, 1958).

29. Arendt to Blumenfeld, 16 November 1953, Marbach.

30. The three-part "America and Europe" series appeared in *Commonweal* 60/23, 24, 25 (September 1954).

31. Arendt to Blücher, 24 April 1952 and 1 May 1952, Library of Congress.

32. The unpublished manuscript of "Concern with Politics in Recent European Philosophical Thought," 1954, is in the Arendt Papers, Library of Congress.

33. Arendt to Blücher, 1 May 1952, Library of Congress.

34. Arendt to Blücher, 18 May 1952, Library of Congress.

35. Ibid.

36. Arendt to Blücher, 20 June 1952, Library of Congress.

37. Arendt to Blücher, 18 July 1952, Library of Congress.

38. Arendt to Blücher, 1 August 1952, Library of Congress.

39. Arendt to Blücher, 13 June 1952, Library of Congress.

40. Arendt to Blücher, 6 June 1952, Library of Congress.

41. Arendt to Blücher, 30 May 1952 and 13 June 1952, Library of Congress.

42. Hannah Arendt, "The Negatives of Positive Thinking: A Measured Look at the Personality, Politics and Influence of Konrad Adenauer," *Book Week, Washington Post,* 5 June 1966, p. 1.

43. Ibid., p. 2 (emphasis added by Arendt).

44. Hannah Arendt, "Religion and Politics," *Confluence,* September 1953, p. 105. Arendt to Henry Kissinger, 14 August 1953, Library of Congress.

45. Arendt to Jaspers, 13 July 1953, Marbach.

46. Hannah Arendt's contribution to "Religion and the Intellectuals, A Symposium," *Partisan Review,* February 1950, p. 113.

47. Arendt to Blumenfeld, 2 February 1953, Marbach.

48. Arendt to Jaspers, 13 May 1953, Marbach.

49. Jaspers to Arendt, 22 May 1953, Marbach.

50. Arendt to Jaspers, 13 July 1953, Marbach.

51. Arendt to Jaspers, 21 December 1953, Marbach.

52. George Kennan, in a discussion of his "Totalitarianism in the Modern World," *Totalitarianism,* ed. C. J. Friedrich (New York: Universal Library, 1954), p. 34.

53. William Zukerman, *Voice of Dissent: Jewish Problems, 1948–1961* (New York: Bookman Associates, 1964) in an anthology of pieces from the *Jewish Newsletter.*

54. Hannah Arendt, "The Conscience of the Jewish People," *Jewish Newsletter* 14/8 (21 April 1958): 2. (This piece, written in 1958 for the tenth anniversary of Magnes's death, seems to be based on a 1948 eulogy given by Arendt, of which no copy exists.)

55. Arendt to Zukerman, 1 November 1953, Library of Congress.

56. Blumenfeld to Arendt, 26 October 1953, Marbach.

57. The National Committee for an Effective Congress is described in Robert Griffith, *The Politics of Fear* (Rochelle Park, N.J.: Hayden Books, 1970). On Arendt, see ibid., p. 226.

58. Stephen J. Whitfield, *Into the Dark: Hannah Arendt and Totalitarianism* (Philadelphia: Temple University Press, 1980), pp. 110ff.

59. Peter Nettl, *Rosa Luxemburg* (London: Oxford University Press, 1966), p. 167.

60. Arendt to Blumenfeld, 31 July 1956, Marbach.

61. Arendt to Blücher, 21 February 1955, Library of Congress.

62. Arendt to Jaspers, 6 February 1955, Marbach.

63. Arendt to Blücher, 12 February 1955, Library of Congress.

64. Arendt to Blücher, 19 February 1955, Library of Congress.

65. Arendt to Jaspers, 5 February 1965, Marbach.

66. Arendt to Blücher, 12 February and 19 February 1955, Library of Congress.

67. Arendt to Blücher, 21 February and 4 April 1955, Library of Congress.

68. Arendt's two full-time appointments were at the University of Chicago (1963–67) and the New School (1967–75), but she usually taught only one semester of each year.

69. Arendt to Blücher, 8 March and 14 April 1955, Library of Congress.

70. This quotation and the following one are from Blücher to Arendt, undated, ca. May 1955, Library of Congress.

71. Arendt to Blücher, 24 October 1956, Library of Congress.

72. Arendt to Blücher, 31 October 1956, Library of Congress.

73. Arendt to Blücher, 5 November 1956, Library of Congress.

74. Ibid., with addendum dated 6 November.

75. Hannah Arendt, "Reflections on the Hungarian Revolution," *The Origins of Totalitarianism* (New York: Meridian Books, 1958), p. 482.

76. Karl Jaspers, *The Future of Mankind* (Chicago: University of Chicago Press, 1961), p. vii.

77. Karl Jaspers, "Philosophical Memoir," p. 66.

78. This and the following quotations are from Arendt to Blücher, 25 May 1958, Library of Congress.

79. Blücher to Arendt, 1 June 1958, Library of Congress.

80. Arendt used the "function of Being" phrase in her 1946 "What is Existenz Philosophy?" essay and then again in her discussion of Heidegger's postwar work in *The Life of the Mind* (New York: Harcourt Brace Jovanovich, 1978), 2: 172–94.

81. The manuscript for "Concern with Politics in Recent European Philosophical Thought" is in the Arendt Papers, Library of Congress.

82. Lecture notes for a 1951 Yale University "Heidegger and Jaspers Seminar," Library of Congress.

83. Arendt to Blumenfeld, 16 December 1957, Marbach.

84. Arendt to Blücher, 25 July 1952, Library of Congress. Arendt also wrote to Dolf Sternberger (28 November 1953, Library of Congress) and to Hugo Friedrich (7 July 1953, Library of Congress) with explanations of Heidegger's thought and appeals for understanding.

85. Arendt to Blücher, 20 June 1952, Library of Congress.

86. Arendt to Blücher, 1 August 1952, Library of Congress.

87. Ibid.

88. Arendt to Blücher, 6 June and 13 June 1952, Library of Congress.

89. Arendt to Blücher, 13 June 1952, Library of Congress.

90. Blücher to Arendt, 30 June 1952, Library of Congress.

91. The meeting, which Ms. Strauss reported to Blumenfeld, is discussed by him in Blumenfeld to Arendt, 21 May 1958, Marbach.

92. Arendt to Jaspers, 1 November 1961, Marbach.

93. Jaspers to Arendt, 11 November 1961, Marbach.

94. Ralph Ellison, *Shadow and Act* (New York: Random House, 1964), p. 108.

95. Hannah Arendt, "Preliminary Remarks" to "Reflections on Little Rock," *Dissent*, Winter 1959, p. 46.

96. Hannah Arendt, "A Reply to Critics," *Dissent*, Spring 1957, p. 179.

97. This and the following quotations, unless otherwise noted, are from Arendt, "Reflections on Little Rock."

98. Arendt, "A Reply to Critics," p. 179.

99. Arendt made her comparison between Jews and blacks explicit in an unpublished letter to Matthew Lipman, 30 March 1959, Library of Congress: "One could even state it as a law: Political equality always spelt social discrimination, whereas social recognition was always paid for by political inequality. The Prussian Jews knew that this would be the case even before the whole business started in earnest; precisely the more assimilated among them who felt they could no longer live outside Gentile society tried desperately to prevent legal and political emanicipation. . . . Social discrimination does not force me to agree; if I wish I can live as a pariah and many people at all times have preferred such a life. But legislation does force me and is therefore a political matter."

100. Arendt to Editors of *Commentary*, 1 February 1958, Library of Congress.

101. Norman Podhoretz, *Making It* (New York: Random House, 1967), p. 233.

102. The editors of *Dissent* decided to publish Arendt's article because "we believe in freedom of expression even for views that seem to us entirely mistaken" (as they said in an editorial note).

103. Sidney Hook, letter to the editors, *Dissent* 6/2 (Spring 1959): 203.

104. Arendt, "A Reply to Critics," p. 179.

105. Arendt to Jaspers, 3 January 1960, Marbach.

106. Ralph Ellison, *Shadow and Act* (New York: Random House, 1964), p. 108.

107. This quotation and the following extract are from Robert Penn Warren, ed., *Who Speaks for the Negro?* (New York: Random House, 1965), pp. 342–44.

108. Arendt to Ellison, 29 July 1965, Library of Congress.

109. Hannah Arendt, "The Crisis in Education," in *Between Past and Future*, rev. ed. (New York: Viking Press, 1968), pp. 192–93.

110. Arendt to Sara Johnston, Student Mobilization Committee to End the War in Vietnam, 2 February 1970, Library of Congress.

111. Arendt, "Crisis in Education," p. 177.

112. Arendt, *The Human Condition*, pp. 8–9.

113. Ibid., p. 17.

114. Ibid., p. 298, n. 62.

115. Arendt wrote in her unpublished 1954 address, "Concern with Politics in Recent European Philosophical Thought" (Library of Congress): "It is as though in this refusal to own up to the experience of horror and take it seriously, the philosophers have inherited the traditional refusal to grant to the realm of human affairs that *thaumadzein*, that wonder at that which is as it is, which, according to Plato and Aristotle, is at the beginning of all philosophy and which even they refused to accept as the preliminary condition for political philosophy. For the speechless horror at what men may do and what the world may become is in many ways related to the speechless wonder or gratitude from which the questions of philosophy spring."

116. See Daniel Bell, *The End of Ideology* (New York: Free Press, 1962).

117. From an interview with Alfred Alvarez, collected in his *Writers Under Pressure* (London: Penguin Books, 1965), p. 115.

118. This quotation and the following one are from Arendt to Thompson, Rockefeller Foundation, 7 April 1956, Library of Congress. Arendt sometimes referred to the book in German letters as *Einleitung in die Politik* and sometimes *Einführung in die Politik*; the latter title may well indicate that she thought of it as a counter to Heidegger's *Einführung in die Metaphysik*.

119. Arendt to Richard Bernstein, 31 October 1972, Library of Congress.

120. Gaus interview.

121. Jaspers to Arendt, 13 August 1955, Marbach, mentions *Amor Mundi* as a possible book title: *Ein schöner Titel*.

## Notes to Chapter 8

1. Arendt to Blumenfeld, 23 October 1960, Marbach.

2. Arendt to Thompson, Rockefeller Foundation, 20 December 1960, Library of Congress.

3. Arendt to Vassar College, 2 January 1961, Library of Congress.

4. Arendt to Blücher, 15 April 1961, Library of Congress.

5. Blumenfeld to Arendt, 6 September 1954, Marbach.

6. Excerpts from Arendt to Jaspers, 23 December 1960 and Jaspers to Arendt, 12 December, 16 December, 31 December 1960, Marbach. Jaspers used his correspondence with Arendt for thinking through the position on the Eichmann trial he took in an interview with François Bondy, "Karl Jaspers Zum Eichmann-Prozess," *Der Monat* 12 (May 1961): 15–19.

7. When Jaspers read newspaper accounts of Eichmann's activities in Hungary, he wondered whether Arendt's impression of the man was correct (Jaspers to Arendt, 8 June

1961, Marbach): "You are by this time back in Israel [after a visit to Basel]. In the meantime, Eichmann has shown another aspect, also personally brutal. Ultimately, can such a functionary for bureaucratic murder be, personally, without inhuman characteristics . . . ? You will not have an easy time coming to a truly adequate portrait of the man."

8. Arendt to Blücher, 20 April 1961, Library of Congress.

9. Arendt to Jaspers, 29 December 1963, Marbach.

10. Arendt to Jaspers, 29 December 1963, Marbach.

11. Bertolt Brecht's *The Irresistible Rise of the Man Arturo Ui* was cited by Arendt in a 1973 interview with Roger Ererra, excerpted for the *New York Review of Books*, 26 October 1978, p. 18. She also cited Brecht's remarks in "Bertolt Brecht," in *Men in Dark Times*, p. 247.

12. Arendt to Blücher, 20 April 1961, Library of Congress.

13. Arendt to Blücher, 25 April 1961, Library of Congress.

14. Arendt to Blücher, 15 April 1961, Library of Congress.

15. Arendt to Blücher, 25 April 1961, Library of Congress.

16. Arendt to Blücher, 20 April 1961, Library of Congress.

17. Arendt to Blücher, 26 April 1961, Library of Congress.

18. The exchange of letters between Gershom Scholem and Arendt appeared in *MB*, Tel Aviv, 16 August 1963: 3–4, *Neue Züricher Zeitung*, 19 October 1963, *Aufbau*, 20 December 1963, and *Encounter*, January 1964: 51–56. The German exchange was shown to *Encounter*'s editor by Isaiah Berlin (John Mander to Arendt, 5 September 1963, Library of Congress). On Golda Meier as the "socialist," see Gershom Scholem to Arendt, 6 August 1963, Library of Congress.

19. Arendt to Jaspers, 6 August 1961, Marbach.

20. Jaspers to Blücher, 31 July 1961, Library of Congress.

21. Arendt to Jaspers, 6 August 1961, Marbach.

22. Arendt to Oxford University, Lady Margaret Hall, 19 February 1967, Library of Congress.

23. Arendt to Jack Paton of Wesleyan, 30 November 1961, Library of Congress. Arendt arranged this stay at Wesleyan for the fall of 1961 and the fall of 1962 in order to be there when Sigmund Neumann was in residence; but Neumann died, after a long illness, early in the fall of 1962.

24. Arendt to Jaspers, 1 November 1961, Marbach.

25. Jaspers to Arendt, 5 January 1962, Marbach.

26. Report by Jack Allen Kapland, M.D., dated 17 July 1963 and filed for insurance claims, Library of Congress.

27. Arendt to McCarthy, 4 April 1962 (in McCarthy's possession).

28. Arendt to Jaspers, 31 March 1962, Marbach.

29. Hannah Arendt, "The Christian Pope," *New York Review of Books* 4/10 (17 June 1965): 5–7 (included in *Men in Dark Times*).

30. Gray to Arendt, 12 June 1965, Library of Congress.

31. Arendt to McCarthy, 4 April 1962 (in McCarthy's possession) and Nicola Chiaramonte to Arendt, 10 April 1962, Library of Congress.

32. Jaspers to Arendt, 5 April 1962, Marbach.

33. Sewell to Arendt, 20 October 1965, Library of Congress, enclosing a copy of her "Envoi" to "Cosmos and Kingdom," which was dedicated to Arendt. Arendt to Sewell, 14 November 1965: "One never deserves such things, and they always come unexpected,": Library of Congress.

34. Arendt to Blumenfeld, 16 August 1961, Marbach. Jaspers's opinion of the

Jerusalem court's judgment was also a spur (Jaspers to Arendt, 1 May 1962, Marbach): "So, the trial has become just a sensation, not a true event [*Ereignis*]."

35. Arendt to McCarthy, 20 May 1962 (in McCarthy's possession). Arendt to Jaspers, undated, ca. June 1962, Marbach: "I have a great desire for a fundamental pause in my work; nevertheless, I cannot deny that the Eichmann story pleases me."

36. Arendt to McCarthy, 23 June 1964 (in McCarthy's possession).

37. Walter Laqueur in a letter to the editor of *New York Review of Books*, 3 February 1966, p. 24 and in "Re-reading Hannah Arendt," *Encounter* 3, no. 3 (March 1979): 73–79.

38. Arendt to Jaspers, 29 December 1963, Marbach.

39. Notes for a lecture given at Wesleyan University, 11 January 1962, that is, before *Eichmann in Jerusalem* was written, Library of Congress.

40. Examples of books on Jewish resistance spurred by the controversy: Reuben Ainsztein, *Jewish Resistance in Nazi-Occupied Eastern Europe* (New York: Harper & Row, 1975) which says of Arendt and Bruno Bettelheim "their writings on the subject of Jewish behavior under the Nazis are much more within the competence of psychologists and psychoanalysts than historians. . . ."; Yuri Suhl, ed., *They Fought Back* (New York: Schocken Books, 1975). See also Verena Wahlen, "Select Bibliography on Judenräte under Nazi Rule," *Yad Vashem Studies* 10 (1974): 277–88.

41. The German reaction to *Eichmann in Jerusalem* is not discussed in this chapter. On this subject: Golo Mann's review of *Eichmann in Jerusalem* in *Die Neue Rundschau* 4 (Frankfurt am Main, 1963); Arendt's correspondence about this review with Emil Henk, March–April 1964, Library of Congress; and Jaspers to Arendt, 25 July and 12 August 1963, Marbach, in which Jaspers suggests: "Deine Formulierung 'der Widerstand gegen das Regime selbst nie zum Prinzip geworden,' ist, meine ich, eine nicht richtige Verallgemeinerung." Though Jaspers thought Arendt had generalized mistakenly about the German resistance, he was angry about his friend Golo Mann's review (Jaspers to Arendt, 13 December 1963, Marbach), which he found "ironisch, kalt, herzlos, Besserwissen. . . ." (On Jaspers's suggestion, Arendt added new material on the German resistance to her 1965 revision of *Eichmann in Jerusalem*.) A discussion of Arendt's book was sponsored by the Friends of Hebrew University in Berlin (see *Tagsspiegel*, 14 November 1964, "Schatten der Vergangenheit" for a report) after the German edition appeared and there was much public discussion—as Jaspers said in a letter to Arendt 27 July 1964, Marbach, *eine grosse Unruhe*. Arendt went to Germany for a television interview with Günther Gaus on 28 October 1964. Cf. Günther Gaus, *Zur Person: Porträts in Frage und Antwort* (Munich: Feder Verlag, 1964). Earlier, Arendt had been interviewed briefly in New York, 24 January 1964, by Thilo Koch.

42. References to *Eichmann in Jerusalem* are legion in studies of behavior in extreme situations, but see especially Stanley Milgram, *Obedience to Authority* (New York: Harper & Row, 1974). This psychologist suggested: "After witnessing hundreds of ordinary people submit to authority in our own experiments, I must conclude that Arendt's conception of the *banality of evil* comes closer to the truth than one might dare imagine. . . . This is, perhaps, the most fundamental lesson of our study: ordinary people, simply doing their jobs, and without any particular hostility on their part, can become agents in a terrible destructive process." A case for Eichmann as a psychopath was popularly presented by Michael Selzer, "The Murderous Mind," *New York Times Magazine*, 27 November 1977, pp. 35ff.

43. Randolph L. Braham, *The Eichmann Case: A Source Book* (New York: World Federation of Hungarian Jews, 1969) contains a list of articles about and reviews of

*Eichmann in Jerusalem* (pp. 144–74), but this is not complete even for English items prior to 1969. *Die Kontroverse* was published by Nymphenburger, Munich, in 1964.

44. Hannah Arendt, *Eichmann in Jerusalem* (New York: Viking Press, 1965), p. 6. (All references are to this revised edition, hereafter cited as *Eichmann*, unless otherwise indicated.)

45. See "The Eichmann Case as Seen by Ben-Gurion," *New York Times Magazine*, 8 December 1960. See also an article by the prosecutor, Gideon Hausner, "Eichmann and his Trial," *Saturday Evening Post*, 2, 10, and 17 November 1962.

46. Arendt, *Eichmann*, p. 12.

47. Arendt to Samuel Merlin, 8 May 1965, Library of Congress. See also Arendt to Jaspers, 14 March 1965, Marbach.

48. For background information on the Israeli-German exchanges: *Der Spiegel*, 24 February 1965; on German arms shipments to Israel, *New York Times*, 21 January 1965 and 3 May 1966. The rumor of protection for Globke was repeatedly denied: I. Deutschkron, *Bonn and Jerusalem* (Philadelphia: Chilton Books, 1970), pp. 139–40.

49. A copy of "Eichmann: Master-Mind of The Nazi Murder-Machine" (1961) is in Yad Vashem Library, Jerusalem.

50. Arendt, *Eichmann*, p. 26.

51. Ibid., p. 11.

52. Ibid., pp. 117–18.

53. Arendt's open letter to Gershom Scholem in *Encounter* (see note 18).

54. J. Glenn Gray, *The Warriors* (New York: Harcourt Brace Jovanovich, 1967), p. 6.

55. Arendt, *Origins*, p. 452.

56. Hannah Arendt to Judah Goldin, Judaic Studies, Yale University, 18 July 1963, Library of Congress. Before *Eichmann in Jerusalem*, Arendt had discussed the Jewish councils in print only once, in a review of Léon Poliakov's *Bréviaire de la Haine* for *Commentary*, March 1952. She wrote: "Nowhere does Mr. Poliakov's integrity and objectivity show to better advantage than in his account of the ghettos and the role of their *Judenräte*, or Jewish councils. He neither accuses nor excuses, but reports fully and faithfully what the sources tell him—the growing apathy of the victims as well as their occasional heroism, the terrible dilemma of the *Judenräte*, their despair as well as their confusion, their complicity and their sometimes pathetically ludicrous ambitions. In the famous and very influential *Reichsvertretung* [*sic*: actually, *Reichsvereinigung*] of German Jews, which functioned smoothly until the last Jew had been deported, he sees the forerunner of the *Judenräte* of the Polish ghettos; he makes it clear that the German Jews, in this respect too, served the Nazis as guinea pigs in their investigations of the problem of how to get people to help carry out their own death sentences, the last turn of the screw of the totalitarian scheme of total domination."

57. Arthur Donat, "An Empiric Examination," *Judaism* 12, no. 4 (Fall 1963) is polemical, but informative.

58. This was Arendt's impression while she was attending the trial, not just in retrospect. She wrote to Jaspers from Jerusalem her first impressions, 13 April 1961, Marbach: "The trial could drag out for months, because of the way the prosecutor goes on, and, for all that, the really essential aspects of the whole devilish business could be hindered from coming to light; for example, the fact of the collaboration of Jews, the overall organization [of the Final Solution] and comparable matters."

59. Arendt, *Eichmann*, pp. 125–26.

60. Moses to Arendt, 24 March 1963 (from Jerusalem).

61. Norman Podhoretz, "Hannah Arendt on Eichmann," *Commentary*, September 1963, pp. 201–08.

62. Moses to Arendt, 7 March 1963 (from Jerusalem); Arendt's reply to the letter, 12 March 1963 (both in the Library of Congress).

63. For the Council of Jews from Germany statement see *Aufbau*, 12 March 1963; further *Aufbau* articles appeared on 29 March 1963 and in *Nach dem Eichmann Prozess*, Tel Aviv, 1963. Copies of the *ADL Bulletin* for 11 March and 27 March are in the Arendt Papers, Library of Congress, and many of the *Aufbau* pieces are collected in *Die Kontroverse* (Munich: Nymphenburger, 1964).

64. Schwarzchild to Arendt, 6 March 1963, Library of Congress.

65. "A Report on the Evil of Banality: The Arendt Book," *Facts* 15, no. 1 (July–August 1963) reprinted in part in *Die Kontroverse*, pp. 223–32. As noted, copies of *ADL Bulletin* in Arendt Papers, Library of Congress.

66. Morgenthau to Arendt, 31 March 1963, Library of Congress. (Permission to quote from the Morgenthau letters courtesy of Susanna and Matthew Morgenthau.)

67. Shawn to Arendt (telegram), 8 March 1963, Library of Congress.

68. Reports on Hausner's visit in *New York Daily News*, 20 May 1963 and *New York Times*, 20 May 1963.

69. Michael Musmanno, "Man With An Unspotted Conscience," *New York Times Book Review*, 19 May 1963, pp. 40–41 and letters to the editor 23 June 1963, pp. 4–5, 22; 14 July 1963, pp. 28–30.

70. Jaspers to Arendt, 16 May 1963, Marbach.

71. Arendt to Felix Bing, 18 July 1963, Library of Congress.

72. Gerschon Weiler to Arendt, 1 July 1963, Library of Congress.

73. Arendt to Robert Weltsch, 29 August 1963, Library of Congress; Weltsch's "Wenn Grauen zur Statistik wird . . ." in *Aufbau*, 7 February 1964.

74. Hannah Arendt, "The Crisis in Culture," in *Between Past and Future*, pp. 224–25.

75. Rosen to Arendt, undated, ca. July 1964, Library of Congress.

76. Arendt to Rosen, 27 June 1964, Library of Congress, reports this conversation. Arendt's cousin Ernst Fuerst was under the impression that she did not see Blumenfeld at the hospital in May 1963, but was, rather, refused the visit by Blumenfeld himself.

77. Arendt to Rosen, 30 August 1964, Library of Congress.

78. Ibid.

79. Rosen to Arendt, undated, ca. July 1964, Library of Congress.

80. Arendt to Jaspers, 20 July 1963, Marbach.

81. Jaspers to Arendt, 25 July 1963, Marbach.

82. Arendt to McCarthy, 16 September 1963 (in McCarthy's possession).

83. Arendt to Jaspers, 14 May 1964, Marbach.

84. Arendt to McCarthy, 16 September 1963 (in McCarthy's possession).

85. Arendt to Jaspers, 20 October 1963, Marbach.

86. Ibid.

87. Arendt to Jaspers, 20 October 1963, Marbach. See Ernst Simon, "Hannah Arendt—An Analysis," *Judaism* 12 (1963): 387–415. See also Arendt to Shereshewsky, 8 July 1965, about *NER*; and Arendt to Steven Schwarzchild, editor of *Judaism*, about Simon's article, 6 September 1963, Library of Congress. Jaspers had a conversation with Ernst Simon (Jaspers to Arendt, 16 November 1963, Marbach), who listened *aber hörte immerlich nicht zu*.

88. Arendt to Jaspers, 1 December 1963, Marbach.

89. Lionel Abel, "The Aesthetics of Evil," *Partisan Review*, Summer 1963, p. 219. Robinson's two draft manuscripts are available at Yad Vashem Library, Jerusalem; Abel mentions Robinson's manuscript in a letter, *Partisan Review*, Spring 1964, p. 275.

90. On Nehemiah Robinson's report for the World Jewish Congress see Fruchter's piece cited in note 103 below. For the other articles see: Marie Syrkin, "Hannah Arendt: The Clothes of the Empress," *Dissent*, Autumn 1963, pp. 344–52; Norman Podhoretz, "Hannah Arendt on Eichmann," *Commentary*, September 1963, pp. 201–08; Gertrud Ezorsky, "Hannah Arendt Against the Facts," *New Politics*, Fall 1963, pp. 53–73 (and the reply by Robert Olson in the next issue); Morris Schappes, "The Strange World of Hannah Arendt," *Jewish Currents* 17, nos. 7, 8, 9 (Fall 1963); Louis Harap, (untitled), *Science and Society*, Spring 1964, pp. 223–27.

91. Irving Howe, "The New Yorker and Hannah Arendt," *Commentary*, October 1963, pp. 318–19.

92. Konrad Kellen, "Reflections on *Eichmann in Jerusalem*," *Midstream*, September 1963, pp. 25–35.

93. As noted, a copy of Robinson's 1963 draft is in the Yad Vashem Library, Jerusalem. (These quotations from pp. 245 and 247.)

94. Walter Laqueur, "The Shortcomings of Hannah Arendt," *Jewish Chronicle* (London), 11 October 1963, p. 7.

95. Robinson's untitled second draft, p. ix.

96. Jacob Robinson, *The Crooked Shall Be Made Straight* (New York: Macmillan Co., 1965), p. viii. Robinson's book had many titles, but certainly the most unusual was its title in French: *La Tragédie juive sous la croix gammée à la lumière du procès de Jérusalem (Le récit de Hannah Arendt et la réalité des faits)*.

97. Léon Poliakov, "The Eichmann Trial," *Commentary* (January 1967).

98. Barbara Tuchman, "The Final Solution," *New York Times Book Review*, 29 May 1966, pp. 3, 12.

99. Arendt to Moholy-Nagy, 5 July 1966, Library of Congress.

100. Macdonald to Phillips, 16 July 1963, Arendt's copy in Library of Congress. Abel's "Pseudo-Profundity," a review of Arendt's *Between Past and Future*, appeared in *New Politics* 1/1 (Fall 1961): 124–31.

101. Mary McCarthy, "The Hue and Cry," *Partisan Review*, Winter 1964, p. 82. In the circles McCarthy and Arendt knew, McCarthy's judgment may have been correct. Arendt noted to Jaspers in a 24 November 1963 letter, Marbach: "It is a serious matter that now almost all the non-Jews have taken my side and that not a single Jew will do so publicly, even if he is for me completely." But Arendt also noted, in the same letter, that her Jewish students were understanding.

102. Harris Dienstfrey sent a copy of his unpublished article to Arendt, 25 March 1964, Library of Congress. Irving Howe described the *Dissent* forum as a more decorous affair in *Partisan Review*, Spring 1964.

103. Norman Fruchter, "Arendt's Eichmann and Jewish Identity," *Studies on the Left* 5 (1965) and replies in the Fall 1965 issue. James Weinstein, "Nach Goldwasser Uns?" *Studies on the Left* 4 (1964): 59–64; Carl Oglesby in Paul Jacobs and Saul Landau, eds., *The New Radicals* (New York: Random House, 1966), pp. 257ff. See also Sol Stern, "My Jewish Problem—and Ours," *Ramparts* 10/12 (August 1971): 30–40.

104. Elmer Berger of ACJ to Arendt, 4 June and 13 June 1963 and her reply to the first letter on 11 June 1963, Library of Congress. Arendt drafted a reply to the second ACJ letter on 19 July 1963, Library of Congress, but did not send it: "I will do nothing, so long as an organized campaign is going on.... I have decided it would be neither wise nor proper for me to step into this whole business."

105. Marie Syrkin, "Miss Arendt Surveys the Holocaust," *Jewish Frontier*, May 1963, pp. 7–14. Arendt's opinion of this article is in her letter to Herman Pomrenze, 27 January 1964, Library of Congress.

106. Colie to Arendt, undated, letter from Iowa, Library of Congress.

107. Gunther Lawrence to Arendt, 24 July 1963, Library of Congress. Lawrence also offered his services as a lecture tour organizer. Hannah Arendt replied on 8 September 1963, Library of Congress: "I don't go on lecture tours, I am not the kind of person to do that, and I also don't want to make that kind of money out of a publicity which I personally regard as an unhappy incident."

108. For Hilberg's criticism of Baeck, see *The Destruction of the European Jews* (New York: New Viewpoints, 1973), pp. 122–25, 297. For Baeck's "grave decision," see Leonard Baker, *Days of Sorrow and Pain: Leo Baeck and Berlin Jews* (New York: Macmillan Co., 1978), p. 311.

109. This quotation and the following one are from Arendt, *Eichmann*, p. 119.

110. Hilberg, *Destruction of the European Jews*, p. 292.

111. Freier to Arendt, 20 March 1963, Library of Congress. Arendt may have had an exaggerated notion of Israeli censorship, but she continued to have reason for suspicion. In a 23 October 1963 letter to Jaspers, Marbach, she said: "Letters from and to me do not get through the Israeli censorship. . . . Only letters to people who are thought reliable— Hebrew University, etc.—and to my family get through." Israel Shahak of Hebrew University wrote on 3 March 1967 to tell her that he could find no copies of *Eichmann in Jerusalem* in paperback in Jerusalem, not even at Hebrew University Library, Library of Congress.

112. Dr. Adolf Leschnitzer, *Aufbau*, 29 March 1963; Jacob Robinson, *The Crooked Shall Be Made Straight*, p. 206.

113. Tillich's statement in Friedlander's "Teacher of Theresienstadt" is cited by Baker, *Days of Sorrow and Pain*, p. 311.

114. Hilberg, *Destruction of the European Jews*, p. 283.

115. Albert Friedlander, "The Arendt Report on Eichmann and the Jewish Community," *Central Conference of American Rabbis Journal* 11/2 (October 1963): 55.

116. Arendt to Blumenfeld, 14 January 1946, Marbach. Blumenfeld's opinion of Baeck (as reported by Arendt to Pinhas Rosen, 27 June 1964, Library of Congress) was: "Baeck war ein durch und durch verlogener Bursche, aber er hatte Mut [Baeck was a thoroughly mendacious fellow, but he had courage]."

117. Baker, *Days of Sorrow and Pain*, p. 263.

118. Arendt to Auraam-Makis Koen, a University of Chicago student, 3 July 1972, Library of Congress.

119. Notes prepared by George McKenna and annotated by Hannah Arendt, Library of Congress.

120. Arendt's notes for an interview with *Look* magazine, Library of Congress. Samuel Grafton wrote requesting the interview on 19 September 1963, Library of Congress; Arendt consented but then refused when the magazine wanted to send a Jewish rather than a Gentile interviewer: Arendt to Jaspers, 20 October 1963, Marbach.

121. Hertzberg to Arendt, 31 March 1966, Library of Congress.

122. Arendt to Hertzberg, 8 April 1966, Library of Congress.

123. Arendt to Mary McCarthy, 20 September 1963 (in McCarthy's possession).

124. Arendt, *Eichmann*, p. 93.

125. This passage and the following extract are from Hannah Arendt, introduction to *Auschwitz*, by Bernd Naumann (New York: Frederick A. Praeger, 1966).

126. For "calculated wickedness" see Arendt's notes for a lecture at Wellesley College, 16 March 1964, Library of Congress and *The Life of the Mind* (New York: Harcourt Brace Jovanovich, 1978), 1: 3–5.

127. See the Arendt-Scholem exchange, note 18 above.

128. Gray to Arendt, 23 March 1963 and 18 April 1964, Library of Congress.

129. Jaspers to Arendt, 10 October and 13 December 1963, Marbach.

130. Hannah Arendt, *On Violence* (New York: Harcourt Brace & World, 1970), p. 63. In *Civilization and its Discontents*, of course, Freud argued that there is a radical instinct, the death instinct, which underlies the aggression manifest in sadism and masochism.

131. Two very clear statements of the legal dilemmas are Ernst von den Haag, "Crimes Against Humanity," *National Review*, 27 August 1963, pp. 154–57 and Ronald Berman, "Hostis Humani Generis," *Kenyon Review*, Summer 1963. Arendt wrote to Berman on 20 September 1963 to praise him for "the most perceptive and, if you will permit my saying so, the most intelligent review that appeared," Library of Congress.

132. W. H. Auden, "Thinking What We Are Doing," *Encounter*, June 1959, pp. 72–76.

133. Arendt to McCarthy, 11 November 1959 (in McCarthy's possession).

134. Arendt to Auden, 14 February 1960, Library of Congress. (Arendt's files do not contain the letter from Auden to which she was replying.)

135. Arendt, *Eichmann*, p. 279.

136. Arendt to Herr von Kuhnelt-Leddihn, 18 July 1963, Library of Congress: "... was ich meinte und was im Englischen nicht so gut ausdrückbar ist, ist dass es niemandem *zugemutet* werden kann. Dass viele nicht wissen, dass dies eine Zumutung ist, spricht nicht gegen den Satz."

137. Arendt, *The Human Condition*, p. 241 and Arendt to Auden, 14 February 1960, Library of Congress.

138. Arendt to McCarthy, 7 June 1962 (in McCarthy's possession).

139. Arendt, *On Violence*, p. 56.

140. Hannah Arendt, "A Christian on St. Peter's Chair," in *Men In Dark Times*, pp. 64–65.

141. Notes for an interview with *Look* magazine (see note 120 above). For the reference to "a well-known Zionist," see Robert Weltsch to Arendt, 16 August and her reply, 29 August 1963, Library of Congress. Arendt discussed Weltsch's letter with Samuel Merlin in a 12 December 1963 letter, Library of Congress.

142. Arendt to Herr Meier-Cronemeyer, 18 July 1963, Library of Congress: "Das Schreiben war mir damals eine cura posterior. Aber, dass es mir wirklich darauf ankommt, 'die Grundlagen einer neuen politischen Moral zu schaffen,' ist natürlich wahr, wenn ich es auch so aus Bescheidenheit nie formuliert habe."

143. "The Formidable Dr. Robinson," in Feldman, ed., *The Jew as Pariah* (New York: Random House, 1979), p. 159 (emphasis added). Arendt suspected that many leaders performed their administrative tasks with a prejudice for those they thought most worthy. At her 26 March 1964 discussion at Hillel House, CCNY, Arendt said: "... as to those who went through with the grim business of putting names on death-lists, the case has been made for them—at least they stuck it out. Kastner argued that it took more courage to shoulder this terrible responsibility than to face death. He likened himself, Baeck and others to captains on a sinking ship. But the analogy is a false one, for 'women and children first' is an arbitrary rule, one followed without need to choose. But Kastner and others made choices themselves, and decided that Jewish notables, including their friends, were more entitled to life than un-notables. Such choices are best left to God." (From notes prepared by George McKenna, Library of Congress. See also undated [1963?] letter to Gideon Czapski, Library of Congress.)

144. "Personal Responsibility under Dictatorship" was delivered in Boston on 15 March 1964 and broadcast over Pacifica Radio; The BBC broadcast was published in the

*Listener* 6 August 1964, pp. 185–87, 205. Reaction to *Eichmann in Jerusalem* was also very strong in England. The British sector of the World Jewish Congress held a conference called "Answering Hannah Arendt" in October 1963 at which four emigrés offered testimony on the Jewish councils to refute Arendt, and the Association of Jewish Refugees in Great Britain published many reports and reviews in *AJR Information*.

145. Arendt, "Bertolt Brecht," in *Men in Dark Times*, p. 248.

146. Arendt to O'Grady, 16 July 1975, Library of Congress.

147. Arendt, "Isak Dinesen," in *Men in Dark Times*, p. 104.

148. Hannah Arendt, "Truth and Politics," in *Between Past and Future*, p. 263.

149. Arendt's memorial address for W. H. Auden appeared in the *New Yorker*, 20 January 1975, and was collected in Stephen Spender, *W. H. Auden: A Tribute* (New York: Macmillan Co., 1975).

150. W. H. Auden, "In Memory of W. B. Yeats," *Collected Shorter Poems, 1927–1957* (New York: Random House, 1966).

## Notes to Introduction to Part 4

1. Philip Nobile, "A Review of the *New York Review of Books*," *Esquire*, April 1972, p. 121.

2. Arendt to Jaspers, 1 December 1963, Marbach.

## Notes to Chapter 9

1. Arendt to McCarthy, 2 April and 28 April 1965 (in McCarthy's possession). Blücher was not at all opposed to the early American involvement in Vietnam, and he refused to sign petitions protesting the war until after 1965.

2. Arendt to Jaspers, undated, ca. April 1965, and Jaspers to Arendt, 28 May 1965, Marbach.

3. Arendt to Woolf and Bagguley, 14 September 1966, Library of Congress.

4. Augstein's editorial, "Die Moral des Schreckens," appeared in *Der Spiegel*, 12 September 1966, p. 18; Arendt's letter appeared 17 October 1966, pp. 12–13.

5. Hannah Arendt, "Home to Roost," *New York Review of Books*, 26 June 1975, p. 5.

6. Arendt (in a postscript) to Jaspers, 29 December 1963, Marbach.

7. Karl Jaspers, *The Future of Germany*, trans. E. B. Ashton (Chicago: University of Chicago Press, 1967), p. 144.

8. Hannah Arendt, untitled, *New York Review of Books*, 26 December 1963, p. 10.

9. Arendt to Jaspers, 24 November 1963, Marbach.

10. As reported in Arendt to Jaspers, 5 February 1961, Marbach.

11. This and the following remarks on the presidential nominating conventions are from Arendt's "Reflections on the National Conventions, 1960," with addenda, broadcast over Station KPFA, Berkeley, California, on 28 September 1960, transcript in Library of Congress, and from Arendt to Loewald, an elaboration on the radio broadcast, 28 September 1960, Library of Congress.

12. Arendt to Jaspers, 22 August 1960, Marbach, notes that she thought Rockefeller made the best impression, but that she would vote for Kennedy.

13. Hannah Arendt, *On Revolution*, rev. 2d ed. (New York: Viking Press, 1965), p. 8. All subsequent references are to this edition, hereafter cited as *On Revolution*.

14. Arendt, *On Revolution*, p. 219.

15. Hannah Arendt, "The Cold War and the West," *Partisan Review*, Winter 1962, p. 19.

16. Arendt to Jaspers, 29 October 1962, Marbach.

17. Macdonald to Arendt, 22 October 1960, Library of Congress.

18. Noted in *Facts on File* for 10–16 February 1966, p. 55. Report on the letter of protest, *Facts on File*, 30 December 1965–5 January 1966, "Soviet Union."

19. Arendt to Valerio, Radio Liberty Committee, 14 October 1975, Library of Congress.

20. The Greek Circle is described in "Talk of the Town," *New Yorker*, 22 December 1975, p. 27.

21. Arendt to Johann, General Secretary, German Academy, 6 July 1967, Library of Congress.

22. Hannah Arendt, "On Humanity in Dark Times: Thoughts about Lessing," in *Men In Dark Times*, p. 3.

23. Arendt to Berman, *Kenyon Review*, 15 October 1964, Library of Congress. Arendt had a working rule, which she did break a number of times, to her regret: she refused interviews. After one concession, which produced an article in which she was misquoted (Phillip Nobile, "A Review of the *New York Review of Books*," *Esquire*, April 1972), she wrote to Denis Wrong, 5 April 1972, Library of Congress: "The fact is that if you happen to be a 'public figure,' you are an outlaw . . . you can be slandered or misrepresented in any way. . . . I would never have let the guy into my apartment if he had told me that he was writing for *Esquire*."

24. Jaspers to Arendt, 25 October 1963, Marbach.

25. Arendt's *Herald Tribune* article was collected in Eric Bentley, ed., *The Storm Over "The Deputy"* (New York: Grove Press, 1964), pp. 85–94.

26. Cardinal Spellman's statement in Bentley, *Storm Over "The Deputy*," p. 37.

27. Arendt to J. Maguire, University of Colorado student, 30 October 1964, Library of Congress.

28. Arendt to Renate Rubinstein (her Dutch translator for *Eichmann in Jerusalem*), 24 January 1966, Library of Congress.

29. Arendt's article in Bentley, *Storm Over "The Deputy*," p. 94.

30. Karl Jaspers, "On *The Deputy*" in Bentley, *Storm Over "The Deputy*," p. 100.

31. Arendt to Jaspers, 7 January 1963, Marbach.

32. Arendt to Shawn, 14 April 1965, Library of Congress. Arendt exaggerated a little: much of her article came from a piece on Brecht she had written for the *Kenyon Review*, Spring 1948, pp. 304–12. The quotations below are from Arendt, "Bertolt Brecht," in *Men in Dark Times*.

33. Erich Heller, "Hannah Arendt as a Critic of Literature," *Social Research*, Spring 1977, pp. 147–59.

34. The exchange between Arendt and Hook appeared in *Merkur*, 23/259 (1969): 1082–84. Hook restated his case in *Encounter*, March 1978, p. 93.

35. John Willett, "The Story of Brecht's Odes to Stalin," *Times Literary Supplement*, 26 March 1970.

36. Two reports in the *New York Times*, 28 March 1970, p. 25. Arendt wrote to one of the reporters, Henry Raymont, 30 March 1970, Library of Congress, with further corrections and arguments.

37. Heller, "Arendt as a Critic," p. 154.

38. Arendt to Jaspers, 26 March 1966, Marbach.

39. *New York Times*, 7 February 1965, p. 20. *Le Nouvel Observateur* printed extracts

of Arendt's *Eichmann* (5 and 12 October 1966) and then letters to the editor (26 October 1966).

40. Arendt to Silvers of the *New York Review of Books*, 14 December 1969, Library of Congress.

41. All the above from Arendt's marginalia in her copy of Peter Nettl, *Rosa Luxemburg* (Oxford: Oxford University Press, 1966), now in the Bard College Library.

42. Arendt to Silvers, undated, ca. August 1966, Library of Congress.

43. This and the following quotations are from Arendt, "Rosa Luxemburg," in *Men in Dark Times*, pp. 33–56.

44. Hannah Arendt, "Lying in Politics: Reflections on the Pentagon Papers," *Crises of the Republic* (New York: Harcourt Brace Jovanovich, 1972), p. 41 (hereafter cited as *Crises of the Republic*).

45. Hannah Arendt, "Thoughts on Politics and Revolution," *Crises of the Republic*, p. 173.

46. Arendt, *On Revolution*, p. 60.

47. Hans Kohn, "The Search for Freedom Is Not Enough," *New York Times Book Review*, 14 April 1963.

48. Arendt to Jacobson, 13 November 1964, Library of Congress.

49. E. J. Hobsbawm, untitled review, *History and Theory* 4/2 (1965): 252–58.

50. George Steiner, "Lafayette, Where Are We?" *Reporter*, 9 May 1963, pp. 42–43.

51. Bernard Crick, "Revolution vs. Freedom," *London Observer*, 23 February 1964.

52. Merle Fainsod, "For Spaces of Freedom," *American Scholar*, Spring 1963, pp. 316–17; Arendt, *On Revolution*, p. 37 (emphasis added).

53. Jaspers to Arendt, 5 May 1963, Marbach.

54. Blücher to Arendt, 3 April 1963, Library of Congress.

55. Harrington, untitled review, *Voice Books*, 9 May 1963, p. 11.

56. Arendt, *On Violence*, p. 43.

57. See Chalmers Johnson, *Revolutionary Change* (Boston: Little, Brown, 1966) and C. Wright Mills, *The Power Elite* (New York: Oxford University Press, 1956).

58. Arendt to Marc Cogan, 13 March 1970, Library of Congress. To the same student she wrote on 19 February 1968, Library of Congress: "[You accept] the old, well-worn opposition of passion to reason. But it would be unfair to charge you with this, since it is so deep in the Anglo-Saxon tradition and everything you were taught."

59. Herbert Spiro, "Totalitarianism," *International Encyclopedia of the Social Sciences*, vol. 16 (New York: Macmillan Co., 1968).

60. H. Stuart Hughes, "Historical Sources of Totalitarianism," *Nation*, 24 March 1951, p. 281.

61. Hannah Arendt, "Totalitarian Terror," *Review of Politics*, January 1949, p. 112.

62. H. Stuart Hughes, *The Sea Change: The Migration of Social Thought, 1930–1965* (New York: McGraw-Hill Paperbacks, 1977), p. 123.

63. Arendt, *Origins*, p. xxxi.

64. Hughes, *Sea Change*, p. 120.

65. Robert Burrowes, "Totalitarianism: The Revised Standard Version," *World Politics*, January 1969, p. 276.

66. Les K. Adler and Thomas G. Paterson, "Red Fascism: The Merger of Nazi Germany and Soviet Russia in the American Image of Totalitarianism, 1930s–1950s," *American Historical Review*, April 1970, p. 1049.

67. The following quotations are from Carl J. Friedrich, Michael Curtius, and Benjamin Barber, *Totalitarianism in Perspective: Three Views* (New York: Praeger Publishers, 1969).

68. For a survey of the critiques of postwar studies of totalitarianism, see Elisabeth Young-Bruehl, "The Use and Abuse of 'Totalitarianism'," forthcoming.

69. Arendt to Jaspers, 13 April 1967, Marbach.

70. Hannah Arendt, "Comments," in Richard Pipes, ed., *Revolutionary Russia* (Cambridge: Harvard University Press, 1968), p. 345.

71. Arendt, *On Revolution*, p. 51.

72. From the minutes for the Columbia University Seminar on Stalinism, typescript (Columbia University, New York City, April 1972) in Library of Congress.

73. Arendt to Cohn-Bendit, 27 June 1968, Library of Congress.

74. Arendt, *On Violence*, pp. 49–50.

75. Transcripts from some of the Theatre for Ideas discussions are available in Alexander Klein, ed., *Dissent, Power, and Confrontation* (New York: McGraw-Hill, 1971); this quotation, p. 99.

76. Ibid., p. 123, and report in *New York Times*, 17 December 1967, p. 16.

77. Ibid., p. 131, for this and the following quotations. (Hayden is referred to as "man in the audience," though he is identified in the *Times* report.)

78. Hannah Arendt, *On Violence* (New York: Harcourt Brace & World, 1970), p. 79. This is an expanded version of "Reflections on Violence," 1969.

79. Arendt, *Eichmann*, p. 132.

80. Arendt, *On Violence*, p. 23.

81. Arendt, "Truth and Politics," in *Between Past and Future*, p. 261.

82. See Arendt, "Thoughts on Politics and Revolution," in *Crises of the Republic*, p. 170. When the New School's Graduate Faculty was occupied by students in 1970, Arendt was adamantly opposed to allowing police on the premises. To one of her émigré colleagues, who favored a police "bust," she said: "You forget, these are not criminals, these are our children."

83. Arendt, *On Violence*, pp. 18–19.

84. Ibid., p. 96.

85. Arendt to McCarthy, 21 December 1968 (in McCarthy's possession).

86. Hiram Haydn, *Words and Faces* (New York: Harcourt Brace Jovanovich, 1974), p. 19.

87. Arendt to Shirley Broughton, organizer of the Theatre for Ideas, 10 July 1969, Library of Congress.

88. Arendt to McCarthy, 9 February 1968 (in McCarthy's possession).

89. Klein, *Dissent, Power, and Confrontation*, pp. 33ff. and *New York Times*, 9 October 1968.

90. Arendt to McCarthy, 21 December 1968 (in McCarthy's possession).

91. Arendt to McCarthy, 9 February 1968 (in McCarthy's possession).

92. Cited in J. Glenn Gray to Arendt, 7 October 1975, Library of Congress.

93. Arendt to McCarthy, 9 February 1968 (in McCarthy's possession).

94. *New York Times*, 25 May 1969.

95. Arendt to McCarthy, 17 October 1969 (in McCarthy's possession).

96. Hans Saner, *Karl Jaspers in Selbstzeugnissen und Bilddokumenten* (Hamburg: Rowolt, 1970), p. 67.

97. *Gedenkfeier für Karl Jaspers*, Basler Universitätsreden, vol. 60 (Basel: Helbing & Lichtenhahn, 1969), p. 4.

98. Ibid., p. 20.

99. Arendt to McCarthy, 20 October 1965 (in McCarthy's possession).

100. Jaspers to Arendt, 11 October 1966 and 17 June 1968, Marbach.

101. Karl Jaspers, *Wohin treibt die Bundesrepublik?* (Munich: Piper, 1966) and *Antwort. Zur Kritik meiner Schrift "Wohin treibt die Bundesrepublik?"* (Munich: Piper,

1967). (The English translation, *The Future of Germany*, contains material from both
· texts.)

102. Jaspers to Arendt, 11 October 1968, Marbach.

103. Letters about "Reflections on Violence," *New York Review of Books*, 19 June 1969, p. 38.

104. Morgenthau to Arendt, 5 June 1969, Library of Congress.

105. Arendt to Levi, 2 May 1966, Library of Congress.

106. Arendt to McCarthy, 4 February 1970 (in McCarthy's possession).

107. This and the following quotations are from Klein, *Dissent, Power, and Confrontation*, pp. 17–20.

108. Arendt's "Civil Disobedience" was published in the *New Yorker*, 12 September 1970, and then collected in *Crises of the Republic*. The following quotations are taken from the latter title, pp. 43–82.

109. This report based upon the *New York Times*, 1 May 1970, p. 37.

110. Arendt to McCarthy, 30 June 1970 (in McCarthy's possession).

111. Hannah Arendt, "Thinking and Moral Considerations," *Social Research*, Fall 1971, p. 440. And see "Civil Disobedience," in *Crises of the Republic*, p. 51.

112. Arendt to McCarthy, 2 November 1970 (in McCarthy's possession).

113. Macdonald to Arendt, 18 November 1970 (xerox copy in Mary McCarthy's possession).

114. This and the quotations of Blücher throughout this section are from his lecture notes, in Bard College Library.

115. Colie to Arendt, undated, ca. November 1970, Library of Congress.

116. Martin Self to the Reverend Kline of Bard College, 14 December 1970, copy in the Library of Congress.

117. Arendt to Johannes Zilkens, 23 October 1971, Library of Congress.

118. Arendt to McCarthy, 22 November 1970 (in McCarthy's possession).

119. Ibid.


## Notes to Chapter 10

1. This and the following quotations are from Arendt to McCarthy, 28 May 1971 (in McCarthy's possession). The Hölderlin poem quoted is "Reif sind in Feuer getaucht..." (see epigraph to chapter 6).

2. Arendt to McCarthy, 15 May 1972 (in McCarthy's possession).

3. From Arendt's responses to questions at a conference on her work, published in Melvyn Hill, ed., *Hannah Arendt: The Recovery of the Public World* (New York: St. Martin's Press, 1979), p. 303.

4. Arendt to McCarthy, 23 December 1973 (in McCarthy's possession).

5. Arendt's 1961 stay at Wesleyan was quite relaxed. John Cage, also in residence at what he called "Sig's Motel" (the Center run by Sigmund Neumann), supervised the recreation of the Center Fellows, which consisted of playing hide-and-seek. Hannah Arendt was a great success on the day she chose to hide in the broom closet.

6. Hannah Arendt, introduction to *The Warriors: Reflections on Men in Battle* by J. Glenn Gray (New York: Harper & Row, 1966), p. xiii.

7. Gray to Arendt, 7 October 1975, Library of Congress.

8. Gray to Arendt, 8 February 1966, Library of Congress.

9. Arendt was reluctant to publish the Heidegger *Festschrift* article in America, and nearly two years passed before she did (*New York Review of Books*, 21 October 1971). She

knew that her willingness to forgive Heidegger for his year in the Nazi party would not be well received. Much has been written about Heidegger's political views; the issues are well put and well balanced in Georg Romoser, "Heidegger and Political Philosophy," *Review of Politics*, April 1967, pp. 261–68; and close in spirit to Arendt's view is William Barrett, "Homeless in the World," *Commentary*, March 1976, pp. 34–43. Arendt's opinion of Jean-Michel Palmier's *Les Ecrits politiques de Heidegger* (Paris: Editions de l'Herne, 1968) was not high (Arendt to Joel Beck, a student, 28 June 1971: "A pretty bad book. Also, it is by no means accurate").

10. Arendt to Gray, 25 March 1967, Library of Congress. Arendt was not aware that Heidegger, prompted by his German publisher, had suggested that the sentence be removed from the English translation. Yale University Press decided to leave the sentence in.

11. Ibid.

12. Gray to Arendt, 1 March 1967, Library of Congress.

13. Gray to Arendt, 19 February 1975, Library of Congress.

14. Gray to Arendt, 25 January 1967, Library of Congress.

15. Gray to Arendt, 2 April 1967, Library of Congress.

16. Gray to Arendt, 25 January 1967, Library of Congress.

17. Arendt to McCarthy, 25 February 1974 (in McCarthy's possession). Arendt's judgment was probably influenced by Reiner Schürmann, *Meister Eckhart: Mystic and Philosopher* (Bloomington: Indiana University Press, 1978; original French edition, 1972).

18. Gray to Arendt, 28 July 1974, Library of Congress.

19. Gray to Arendt, 21 January 1975, Library of Congress.

20. Arendt's discussion of Heidegger is in volume two of *The Life of the Mind* (New York: Harcourt Brace Jovanovich, 1978), pp. 172–93. Arendt's opinion of her assessment of Heidegger, "I am afraid I am right," is cited in Gray to Arendt, 9 March 1975, Library of Congress.

21. Arendt to Jovanovich, 18 July 1973, Library of Congress.

22. Hannah Arendt, "Lying in Politics," collected in *Crises of the Republic*, pp. 9–42, and "Thoughts on Politics and Revolution" in the same volume, pp. 164–92.

23. Arendt to McCarthy, 8 December 1971 (in McCarthy's possession).

24. Arendt to McCarthy, 22 January 1972 (in McCarthy's possession).

25. Wright to Arendt, ca. June 1972, and Arendt to Wright, 20 June 1972; both in the Library of Congress.

26. *New York Times*, 1 April 1975, p. 31.

27. Hannah Arendt, "Nathalie Sarraute," *New York Review of Books*, 5 March 1964, p. 5.

28. Hardwick to McCarthy, 9 April 1972 (in McCarthy's possession).

29. This and the following quotation are from Hill, *Hannah Arendt*, pp. 333–34.

30. Anthony Lewis, introduction to *None of Your Business: Government Secrecy in America*, Norman Dorsen and Stephen Gillers, eds. (New York: Viking Press, 1974), p. 4.

31. Transcript of Arendt's remarks to the American Society for Christian Ethics, Richmond, Va., 21 January 1973, Library of Congress.

32. Hill, *Hannah Arendt*, p. 314.

33. Arendt to McCarthy, 17 August 1973 (in McCarthy's possession).

34. Ibid.

35. Ibid.

36. Arendt, writing about Blücher, to Blumenfeld, 1 April 1951, Marbach. Arendt's attitude toward Morgenthau is well captured in Hans Jonas's reflection on her "womanly

sensitivity": "When on occasion I demurred to her often quick and cutting judgments on a person, an act, or a situation, saying that I needed proof, she used to exchange with my wife a glance of mutual understanding, compounded with exasperation and compassion, perhaps even tenderness, and then say, "Ach, Hans!" Only very recently I felt moved to ask her on one such occasion, "Hannah, please tell me, do you find me stupid?" "But no!" she answered with almost horrified eyes—and then added, "I only think you are a man." (Hans Jonas, "Acting, Knowing, Thinking," *Social Research*, Spring 1977, p. 26.)

37. Arendt to McCarthy, 30 September 1973 (in McCarthy's possession).

38. Arendt's memorial for Auden was published in the *New Yorker*, 20 January 1975, pp. 39–40.

39. Arendt to McCarthy, 21 December 1968 (in McCarthy's possession).

40. Excerpts from Arendt's interview with Errera appeared in *New York Review of Books*, 26 October 1978, p. 18. The full transcript is in the possession of French Television.

41. Arendt to McCarthy, 16 October 1973 (in McCarthy's possession).

42. Hannah Arendt, "Public Rights and Private Interests," in Mooney and Stuber, eds., *Small Comforts for Hard Times: Humanists on Public Policy* (New York: Columbia University Press, 1977).

43. This and the following quotations are taken from the typescript of Arendt's Sonning Prize address, Library of Congress.

44. Arendt to McCarthy, 10 March 1975 (in McCarthy's possession); notice of the Sonning Prize in *New York Times*, 6 March 1975, p. 42.

45. Arendt to Lowenfeld (in Lowenfeld's possession).

46. Arendt to John Silber, president of Boston University, 2 October 1975, Library of Congress.

47. Hannah Arendt, "Home to Roost," *New York Review of Books*, 26 June 1975, pp. 3–6; Tom Wicker's column, *New York Times*, 25 May 1975; "Abstract for the Year," *New York Times*, 26 December 1975, p. 3.

48. Arendt to McCarthy, 22 August 1975 (in McCarthy's possession).

49. Arendt to Greve, 20 July 1975 (in Greve's possession).

50. Only two epigrams for the "Judging" manuscript were actually typed. The first was *Victrix causa diis placuit, sed victa Catoni*, the dictum of Cicero's that Arendt had always associated with the German politician Friedrich Gentz (she mentions it in *Rahel Varnhagen*, p. 84). The second was a passage from Goethe's *Faust*, 2 (act 5), cited here from the George Madison Priest translation (New York: Alfred A. Knopf, 1941):

> Könnt ich Magie von meinen Pfad entfernen,
> Die Zaubersprüche ganz und gar verlernen,
> Stünd'ich Natur vor Dir, ein Mann allein,
> Da wär's der Mühe. wert ein Mensch zu sein.

> [Could I all magic from my pathway banish,
> Could quite unlearn its spells and bid it vanish,
> Nature, could I face thee, in thy great plan,
> Then were it worth the pain to be a man.]

51. Hans Jonas, "Hannah Arendt: 1906–1975," *Social Research*, Winter 1976, pp. 3–5.

52. Mary McCarthy, "Saying Good-bye to Hannah," *New York Review of Books*, 22 January 1976, p. 8.

53. Kohn's and Jovanovich's remarks cited in *New York Times*, 9 December 1975, p. 32.

54. The essay collections: *Social Research*, Spring 1977; Melvyn Hill, ed., *Hannah Arendt: The Recovery of the Public World* (New York: St. Martin's Press, 1979); *Response*, Summer 1980; and *Esprit*, June 1980. The books: Margaret Canovan, *The Political Thought of Hannah Arendt* (New York: Harcourt Brace Jovanovich, 1974) and Stephen J. Whitfield, *Into the Dark: Hannah Arendt and Totalitarianism* (Philadelphia: Temple University Press, 1980). Whitfield's notes and bibliography refer to most of the work on Arendt in English.

55. Mary McCarthy, postface to *The Life of the Mind* by Hannah Arendt (printed in both volumes).

56. Nathan Glazer, "Hannah Arendt's America," *Commentary*, September 1975, pp. 61–67; H. Stuart Hughes, *The Sea Change: The Migration of Social Thought, 1930–1965* (New York: McGraw-Hill Paperbacks, 1977).

57. Stuart Hampshire, "Metaphysical Mists," *London Observer*, 30 July 1978, p. 26.

58. Ronald Feldman, introduction to *The Jew as Pariah*, by Hannah Arendt (New York: Grove Press, 1978), p. 48.

59. Walter Laqueur, "Re-reading Hannah Arendt," *Encounter*, March 1979, p. 77.

60. William O. Douglas, *San Francisco Chronicle*, 21 January 1962.

## Notes to Appendix 3

1. This and subsequent quotations from Arendt's notes are taken from her marginalia on E. B. Ashton's draft translation, Library of Congress.

2. Arendt, *The Human Condition*, p. 11.

3. Ibid., p. 247.

4. Ibid., p. 53.

5. Ibid., p. 55.

6. Ibid., p. 55.

"Dilthey as Philosopher and Historian." *Partisan Review* 12/3 (Summer 1945): 404–06. (A review of H. A. Hodges, *Wilhelm Dilthey: An Introduction*.)

"Imperialism, Nationalism, Chauvinism." *Review of Politics* 7/4 (October 1945): 441–63. (Used in *The Origins of Totalitarianism*, Part 2.)

"Nightmare and Flight." *Partisan Review* 12/2 (Spring 1945): 259–60. (A review of Denis de Rougemont, *The Devil's Share*.)

"Organized Guilt and Universal Responsibility." *Jewish Frontier*, January 1945, pp. 19–23. (Reprinted in Roger Smith, ed. *Guilt: Man and Society*. New York: Doubleday Anchor, 1971.)

"Parties, Movements and Classes." *Partisan Review* 12/4 (Fall 1945): 504–12. (Used in *The Origins of Totalitarianism*, Part 2.)

"Power Politics Triumphs." *Commentary* 1 (December 1945): 92–93. (A review of Feliks Gross, *Crossroads of Two Continents*.)

"The Seeds of a Fascist International." *Jewish Frontier*, June 1945, pp. 12–16.

"The Stateless People." *Contemporary Jewish Record* 8/2 (April 1945): 137–53. (Used in *The Origins of Totalitarianism*, Part 2.)

"Zionism Reconsidered." *Menorah Journal* 33 (August 1945): 162–96. (Translated into German for *Die Verborgene Tradition* and reprinted in M. Selzer, ed. *Zionism Reconsidered*. New York: Macmillan Co., 1970, pp. 213–49.)

1946

"Expansion and the Philosophy of Power." *Sewanee Review* 54 (October 1946): 601–16. (Used in *The Origins of Totalitarianism*, Part 2.)

"French Existentialism." *Nation*, 23 February 1946, pp. 226–28. (Anthologized in *One Hundred Years of the Nation*.)

"The Image of Hell." *Commentary* 2/3 (September 1946): 291–95. (A review of *The Black Book: The Nazi Crime Against the Jewish People* compiled by the World Jewish Congress et al. and Max Weinreich. *Hitler's Professors*.)

"Imperialism: Road to Suicide." *Commentary* 1 (February 1946): 27–35.

"The Ivory Tower of Common Sense." *Nation*, 19 October 1946, pp. 447–49. (A review of John Dewey, *Problems of Men*.)

"The Jewish State: 50 Years After, Where Have Herzl's Politics Led?" *Commentary* 1 (May 1946): 1–8.

"The Nation," *Review of Politics* 8/1 (January 1946): 138–41. (A review of J. T. Delos, *La Nation*. Montreal: Editions de l'Arbre.)

"No Longer and Not Yet." *Nation*, 14 September 1946, pp. 300–302. (A review of Hermann Broch, *The Death of Virgil*. Translated by J. S. Untermeyer.)

"Privileged Jews." *Jewish Social Studies* 8/1 (January 1946): 3–30. (Reprinted in Duker and Ben-Horin, *Emancipation and Counteremancipation*. New York: Ktav Publishing House, 1947).

"Proof Positive." *Nation*, 5 January 1946, p. 22. (A brief review of Victor Lange, *Modern German Literature*.)

"The Streets of Berlin." *Nation*, 23 March 1946, pp. 350–51. (A review of Robert Gilbert, *Meine Reime Deine Reime*.)

"Tentative List of Jewish Cultural Treasures in Axis-Occupied Countries." *Supplement to Jewish Social Studies* 8/1 (1946). (This was prepared by the Research Staff of the Commission on European Jewish Cultural Reconstruction headed by Arendt.)

"Tentative List of Jewish Educational Institutions in Axis-Occupied Countries." *Supplement to Jewish Social Studies* 8/3 (1946). (This was also prepared by the Research Staff of the Commission on European Jewish Cultural Reconstruction headed by Arendt.)

"The Too Ambitious Reporter." *Commentary* 2 (January 1946): 94–95. (A review of Arthur Koestler, *Twilight Bar* and *The Yogi and the Commissar*.)

"What is Existenz Philosophy?" *Partisan Review* 8/1 (Winter 1946): 34–56.

1947

"Creating a Cultural Atmosphere." *Commentary* 4 (November 1947): 424–26.

"The Hole of Oblivion." *Jewish Frontier*, July 1947, pp. 23–26. (A review of *The Dark Side of the Moon*.)

1948

"About Collaboration" (a letter). *Jewish Frontier* 15 (October 1948): 55–56.

"Beyond Personal Frustration: The Poetry of Bertolt Brecht." *Kenyon Review* 10/2 (Spring 1948): 304–12. (A review of Bertolt Brecht, *Selected Poems*. Translated by H. R. Hays; an article based on this review, printed in *Die Neue Rundschau* 61 (1950): 53–67 was translated for P. Demetz, ed. *Brecht*. Englewood Cliffs, N.J.: Prentice-Hall, 1962, pp. 43–50.)

"The Concentration Camps." *Partisan Review* 15/7 (July 1948): 743–63. (Anthologized in *Partisan Reader*, 1945–1953 and used in *The Origins of Totalitarianism*, Part 2.)

"Jewish History, Revised." *Jewish Frontier*, March 1948, pp. 34–38. (A review of Gershom Scholem, *Major Trends in Jewish Mysticism*.)

"The Mission of Bernadotte." *New Leader* 31 (23 October 1948): 808, 819.

"To Save the Jewish Homeland: There Is Still Time." *Commentary* 5 (May 1948): 398–406.

1949

"The Achievement of Hermann Broch." *Kenyon Review* 11/3 (Summer 1949): 476–83.

"'The Rights of Man': What Are They?" *Modern Review* 3/1 (Summer 1949): 24–37. (Used in *The Origins of Totalitarianism*, Part 2.)

"Single Track to Zion." *Saturday Review of Literature* 32 (5 February 1949): 22–23. (A review of Chaim Weizmann, *Trial and Error: The Autobiography of Chaim Weizmann*.)

"Totalitarian Terror." *Review of Politics* 11/1 (January 1949): 112–15. (A review of David J. Dallin and Boris I. Nicolaevsky, *Forced Labor in Soviet Russia*.)

1950

"The Aftermath of Nazi Rule, Report from Germany." *Commentary* 10 (October 1950): 342–53. (Anthologized in *The Commentary Reader*.)

"Mob and the Elite." *Partisan Review* 17 (November 1950): 808–19. (Used in *The Origins of Totalitarianism*, Part 3.)

"Peace or Armistice in the Near East?" *Review of Politics* 12/1 (January 1950): 56–82.

"Religion and the Intellectuals, A Symposium." *Partisan Review* 17 (February 1950): 113–16. (Reprinted as a part of *Partisan Review*, Series 3, 1950, pp. 15–18.)

"Social Science Techniques and the Study of Concentration Camps." *Jewish Social Studies* 12/1 (1950): 49–64.

1951

"Bei Hitler Zu Tisch." *Der Monat* 4 (October 1951): 85–90.

"The Imperialist Character." *Review of Politics* 12/3 (July 1950): 303–20. (Used in *The Origins of Totalitarianism*, Part 2.)

"The Road to the Dreyfus Affair." *Commentary* 11 (February 1951): 201–03. (A review of Robert F. Byrnes, *Anti-Semitism in Modern France*.)

"Totalitarian Movement." *Twentieth Century* 149 (May 1951): 368–89. (Used in *The Origins of Totalitarianism*, Part 3.)

1952

"The History of the Great Crime." *Commentary* 13 (March 1952): 300–04. (A review of Léon Poliakov, *Bréviaire de la Haine: Le IIIê Reich et les Juifs*.)

"Magnes, The Conscience of the Jewish People." *Jewish Newsletter* 8/25 (24 November 1952): 2.

1953

"The Ex-Communists." *Commonweal* 57/24 (20 March 1953): 595–99. (Reprinted in *Washington Post*, 31 July 1953.)

"Ideology and Terror: A Novel Form of Government." *Review of Politics* 15/3 (July 1953): 303–27. (Included in the 1958 edition of *The Origins of Totalitarianism*. A German version appeared in *Offener Horizont: Festschrift für Karl Jaspers*. Munich: Piper, 1953.)

"Rejoinder to Eric Voegelin's Review of *The Origins of Totalitarianism*." *Review of Politics* 15 (January 1953): 76–85.

"Religion and Politics." *Confluence* 2/3 (September 1953): 105–26. (Cf. Arendt's reply to criticism of this article in *Confluence*, pp. 118–20.)

"Understanding and Politics." *Partisan Review* 20/4 (July-August 1953): 377–92.

"Understanding Communism." *Partisan Review* 20/5 (September-October 1953): 580–83. (A review of Waldemar Gurian, *Bolshevism*.)

1954

"Europe and America: Dream and Nightmare." *Commonweal* 60/23 (24 September 1954): 551–54.

"Europe and America: The Threat of Conformism." *Commonweal* 60/25 (24 September 1954): 607–10.

"Europe and The Atom Bomb." *Commonweal* 60/24 (17 September 1954): 578–80.

"Tradition and the Modern Age." *Partisan Review* 22 (January 1954): 53–75. (Drawn from a series of lectures delivered at Princeton as the Christian Gauss Seminars in Criticism, 1953, and used in *Between Past and Future*.)

1955

"The Personality of Waldemar Gurian," *Review of Politics* 17/1 (January 1955): 33–42. (Reprinted in *Men in Dark Times.*)

1956

"Authority in the Twentieth Century." *Review of Politics* 18/4 (October 1956): 403–17.

1957

"History and Immortality." *Partisan Review* 24/1 (Winter 1957): 11–53.

"Jaspers as Citizen of the World." In *The Philosophy of Karl Jaspers*, edited by P. A. Schilpp. La Salle, Ill.: Open Court Publishing Co., 1957, pp. 539–50. (Reprinted in *Men in Dark Times.*)

1958

"The Crisis in Education." *Partisan Review* 25/4 (Fall 1958): 493–513. (Reprinted in *Between Past and Future.*)

"The Modern Concept of History." *Review of Politics* 20/4 (October 1958): 570–90. (Reprinted in *Between Past and Future.*)

"Totalitarian Imperialism: Reflections on the Hungarian Revolution." *Journal of Politics* 20/1 (February 1958): 5–43. (Reprinted in *Cross Currents* 8/2 [Spring 1958]: 102–28, and added to the 1958 edition of *The Origins of Totalitarianism.*)

"Totalitarianism." *Meridian* 2/2 (Fall 1958): 1. (Arendt's reflections on *The Origins of Totalitarianism* at the time of its second edition.)

"What Was Authority?" In *Authority*, edited by C. Friedrich. Cambridge: Harvard University Press, 1959. (Reprinted in *Between Past and Future.*)

1959

"Reflections on Little Rock." *Dissent* 6/1 (Winter 1959): 45–56. (Included in the same issue are criticisms by David Spitz and Melvin Tumin. In *Dissent* 6/2 [Spring 1959]: 179–81, Arendt replied to her critics. The article was reprinted in *Public Life: A Journal of Politics* 4/3–4 [May–June 1973]: 92–97.)

1960

"Freedom and Politics: A Lecture." *Chicago Review* 14/1 (Spring 1960): 28–46. (Revised for *Between Past and Future.*)

"Revolution and Public Happiness." *Commentary* 30 (November 1960): 413–22. (Used in *On Revolution.*)

"Society and Culture." *Daedalus* 82/2 (Spring 1960): 278–87. (Reprinted in *Between Past and Future.*)

1962

"Action and 'The Pursuit of Happiness'." In *Politische Ordnung und Menschliche Existenz: Festgabe Für Eric Voeglin*. Munich: Beck, 1962. (Used in *On Revolution.*)

"The Cold War and The West." *Partisan Review* 29/1 (Winter 1962): 10–20.

"Revolution and Freedom: A Lecture." In *In Zwei Welten: Siegfried Moses Zum Fünfundsiebzigsten Geburtstag*. Tel Aviv: Bitaon, 1962. (Used in *On Revolution.*)

1963

"A Reporter at Large: Eichmann in Jerusalem." *New Yorker*, 16 February 1963, pp. 40–113; 23 February 1963, pp. 40–111; 2 March 1963, pp. 40–91; 9 March 1963, pp. 48–131; 16 March 1963, pp. 58–134. (This five-part article, revised, was published as *Eichmann in Jerusalem: A Report on the Banality of Evil.*)

"Kennedy and After." *New York Review of Books* 1/9 (26 December 1963): 10.

"Man's Conquest of Space." *American Scholar* 32 (Autumn 1963): 527–40.

"Reply to Judge Musmanno." *New York Times Book Review* 8/4 (23 June 1963). (Arendt's exchange with Musmanno was reprinted in Freedman and Davis, eds. *Contemporary Controversy*. New York: Macmillan Co., 1966, pp. 312–17.)

1964

"*The Deputy*: Guilt by Silence." *New York Herald Tribune Magazine*, 23 February 1964, pp. 6–9. (Reprinted in *Storm over "The Deputy*," edited by Eric Bentley.)

"Eichmann in Jerusalem." *Encounter*, January 1964, pp. 51–56. (An exchange of letters between Arendt and Gershom Scholem.)

"Nathalie Sarraute." *New York Review of Books* 2/2 (5 March 1964): 5–6. (A review of Nathalie Sarraute, *The Golden Fruits*. Translated by Maria Jolas.)

"Personal Responsibility under Dictatorship." *Listener*, 6 August 1964, pp. 185–87, 205.

1965

"The Christian Pope," *New York Review of Books* 4/10 (17 June 1965): 5–7. (A review of Pope John XXIII, *Journal of a Soul*. Translated by D. White; included in *Men in Dark Times*.)

"Hannah Arendt—Hans Magnus Ernzenberger: Politik und Verbrechen: Ein Briefwechsel." *Merkur*, April 1965, pp. 380–85.

1966

"The Formidable Dr. Robinson: A Reply to the Jewish Establishment." *New York Review of Books* 5/12 (20 January 1966): 26–30. (Arendt's response to letters about this article appeared in the 17 March 1966 issue.)

"A Heroine of the Revolution." *New York Review of Books* 7/5 (6 October 1966): 21–27. (A review of J. P. Nettl, *Rosa Luxemburg*; included in *Men in Dark Times*.)

Introduction to *Auschwitz*, by Bernd Naumann. New York: Frederick A. Praeger, 1966. (Reprinted in Falk, Kolko, and Lifton, eds., *Crimes of War*. New York: Random House, 1971.)

Introduction to *The Warriors* by J. Glenn Gray. New York: Harper & Row, 1966.

"The Negatives of Positive Thinking: A Measured Look at the Personality, Politics and Influence of Konrad Adenauer." *Book Week, Washington Post*, 5 June 1966, pp. 1–2. (A review of Konrad Adenauer, *Memoirs 1945–1953*. Translated by Beate Ruhm von Oppen.)

"On the Human Condition." In *The Evolving Society*, edited by Mary Alice Hinton. New York: Institute of Cybernetical Research, 1966, pp. 213–19.

"Remarks on 'The Crisis Character of Modern Society'." *Christianity and Crisis* 26/9 (30 May 1966): 112–14.

"What Is Permitted to Jove." *New Yorker*, 5 November 1966, pp. 68–122. (A study of Bertolt Brecht, reprinted in *Men in Dark Times*.)

1967

Preface to *The Future of Germany* by Karl Jaspers. Chicago: University of Chicago Press, 1967.

"Randall Jarrell: 1914–1965." In *Randall Jarrell, 1914–1965*. New York: Farrar, Straus & Giroux, 1967. (Reprinted in *Men in Dark Times*.)

"Truth and Politics." *New Yorker*, 25 February 1967, pp. 49–88. (Reprinted in *Between Past and Future*, 2d edition, and in David Spitz, ed., *Political Theory and Social Change*. New York: Atherton Press, 1967, pp. 3–37.)

1968

"Comment by Hannah Arendt on 'The Uses of Revolution' by Adam Ulam." In *Revolutionary Russia*, edited by Richard Pipes. Cambridge: Harvard University Press, 1968.

"He's All Dwight: Dwight Macdonald's *Politics*." *New York Review of Books* 11/2 (1 August 1968): 31–33.

"Is America by Nature a Violent Society? Lawlessness Is Inherent in the Uprooted." *New York Times Magazine*, 28 April 1968, p. 24.

"Isak Dinesen: 1885–1962." *New Yorker*, 9 November 1968, pp. 223–36. (Reprinted in *Men in Dark Times*.)

"Walter Benjamin." *New Yorker*, 19 October 1968, pp. 65–156. Translated by Harry Zohn. (Reprinted in *Men in Dark Times*.)

1969

"The Archimedean Point." *Ingenor*, College of Engineering, University of Michigan, Spring 1969, pp. 4–9, 24–26.

"Reflections on Violence." *Journal of International Affairs*, Winter 1969, pp. 1–35. (Reprinted in *New York Review of Books* 12/4 [27 February 1969]: 19–31. Expanded as *On Violence* and reprinted in *Crises of the Republic*.)

1970

"Civil Disobedience." *New Yorker*, 12 September 1970, pp. 70–105. (Reprinted in *Crises of the Republic* and in E. V. Rostow, ed., *Is Law Dead?* New York: Simon and Schuster, 1971, pp. 213–43.)

Letter in reply to a review by J. M. Cameron, *New York Review of Books* 13 (1 January 1970): 36.

1971

"Lying and Politics: Reflections on the Pentagon Papers." *New York Review of Books* 17/8 (18 November 1971): 30–39. (Reprinted in *Crises of the Republic*.)

"Martin Heidegger at 80." *New York Review of Books* 17/6 (21 October 1971): 50–54. (Originally in German, *Merkur* 10 [1969]: 893–902. Translated by

Albert Hofstadter. Reprinted in English in Michael Murray, ed., *Heidegger and Modern Philosophy*. New Haven: Yale University Press, 1978.)

"Thinking and Moral Considerations: A Lecture." *Social Research* 38/3 (Fall 1971): 417–46.

"Thoughts on Politics and Revolution." *New York Review of Books* 16/7 (22 April 1971): 8–20. (An interview conducted by Adelbert Reif in the summer of 1970, translated by Denver Lindley; reprinted in *Crises of the Republic*.)

1972

Nachwort for *Mich Hat Kein Esel im Galopp Verloren* by Robert Gilbert. Munich: Piper, 1972.

"Washington's 'Problem-Solvers'—Where They Went Wrong." *New York Times*, 5 April 1972, Op-Ed page.

1974

"Karl Jaspers zum fünfundachtzigsten Geburtstage." In *Erinnerungen an Karl Jaspers*, edited by H. Saner. Munich: Piper, 1974, pp. 311–15.

1975

"Home to Roost." *New York Review of Books*, 26 June 1975, pp. 3–6. (Reprinted in S. B. Warner, *The American Experiment*. Boston: Houghton Mifflin Co., 1976, pp. 61–77, with Arendt's comments.)

"Remembering Wystan H. Auden." *New Yorker*, 20 January 1975, pp. 39–40. (Reprinted in *Harvard Advocate* 108/2–3, pp. 42–45; and in *W. H. Auden: A Tribute*. London: Weidenfeld & Nicolson, 1974/5, pp. 181–87.)

1977

"Public Rights and Private Interests." In *Small Comforts for Hard Times: Humanists on Public Policy*, edited by Mooney and Stuber. New York: Columbia University Press, 1977. (Response to a paper by Charles Frankel in the same volume.)

"Thinking." *New Yorker*, 21 November 1977, pp. 65–140; 28 November 1977, pp. 135–216; 5 December 1977, pp. 135–216. This three-part article comprises the first volume of *The Life of the Mind*, 1978.

1978

"From an Interview," with Roger Errera, *New York Review of Books* 25/16 (26 October 1978): 18.

## COLUMNS AND ARTICLES IN AUFBAU

| | |
|---|---|
| 25 Oct. 1941 | "Der Dank vom Hause Juda" (an open letter to Jules Romain), p. 7. |
| 14 Nov. 1941 | "Die jüdische Armee—der Beginn einer jüdische Politik?" pp. 1, 2. |
| 28 Nov. 1941 | "Aktive Geduld, " p. 2. |
| 24 Dec. 1941 | "Ceterum Censeo . . . ," p. 2. |

10 Jan. 1942    "Ein erster Schritt," pp. 15, 16.
6 Mar. 1942    "Wer ist das 'Committee for a Jewish Army,'" p. 6.
27 Mar. 1942    "Moses oder Washington," p. 16.
3 Apr. 1942    "The Case Against the Saturday Evening Post: Cui Bono?" p. 3.
10 Apr. 1942    "Papier und Wirklichkeit," pp. 15, 16.
24 Apr. 1942    "Ganz Israel bürgt füreinander," p. 18.
8 May 1942    "Des Tuefels Redekunst," p. 20.
22 May 1942    "Die 'sogenannte jüdische Armee,'" p. 20.
5 June 1942    "Ein christliches Wort zur Judenfrage," p. 19.
19 June 1942    "Keinen Kaddisch wird man sagen," p. 19.
2 July 1942    "Mit dem Rücken an der Wand," p. 19.
12 July 1942    "Wenn man dem kleineren Übel nicht widersteht," p. 20.
31 July 1942    Eintreten *für* Paul Tillich (in a debate with Emil Ludwig), p. 6.
14 Aug. 1942    "Konfusion," p. 17.
28 Aug. 1942    "Die Rückkehr des russischen Judentums, 1," p. 18.
11 Sept. 1942    "Die Rückkehr das russischen Judentums, 2," p. 18.
25 Sept. 1942    "Was geht in Frankreich vor?" p. 18.
23 Oct. 1942    "Die Krise des Zionismus, 1," p. 18.
6 Nov. 1942    "Die Krise des Zionismus, 2," p. 17.
20 Nov. 1942    "Die Krise des Zionismus, 3," p. 17.
26 Feb. 1943    "Französische politische Literatur im Exil, 1," pp. 7, 8.
26 Mar. 1943    "Französische politische Literatur im Exil, 2," p. 8.
3 Sept. 1943    "Die wahren Grunde für Theresienstadt," p. 21.
17 Dec. 1943    "Can the Jewish-Arab Question Be Solved?, 1," p. 1.
31 Dec. 1943    "Can the Jewish-Arab Question Be Solved?, 2," p. 1.
21 Apr. 1944    "Für Ehre und Ruhm des jüdischen Volkes," pp. 1, 2.
19 May 1944    "Balfour Deklaration und Palistina Mandat," p. 16.
2 June 1944    "Das Ende Eines Gerüchts," pp. 1, 16.
16 June 1944    "Sprengstoff-Spiesser," p. 19.
30 June 1944    "Gäste aus dem Niemandsland," pp. 15, 16.
14 July 1944    "Das neue Gesicht eines alten Volkes," pp. 1, 2.
28 July 1944    "Die Tage der Wandlung," p. 16.
11 Aug. 1944    "Eine Lehre in seche Schüssen," p. 15.
25 Aug. 1944    "Neue Vorschläge für jüdische-arabischen Verständigung," pp. 13, 14.
8 Sept. 1944    "Die jüdischen Partisanen im europäischen Aufstand," p. 15.
22 Sept. 1944    "Vom 'Salz der Erde': Waldo Frank's jüdische Deutung," pp. 13, 14.
6 Oct. 1944    "Von der Armee zur Brigade," pp. 15, 16.
3 Nov. 1944    "Frei und Demokratisch," pp. 15, 16.
15 Dec. 1944    "Die Entrechten und Entwürdigten," pp. 13, 16.
16 Mar. 1945    "Völkerverständigung im Nahen Osten: Eine Basis jüdischer Politik," pp. 1, 2.

20 Apr. 1945    "Die jüdischen Chancen," pp. 7, 8.
31 July 1953    "Gestern waren Sie noch Kommunisten . . . ," p. 19.
 7 Aug. 1953    "Gestern waren Sie noch Kommunisten . . . ," pp. 13, 16.
20 Dec. 1963    "Sie haben mich misverstanden" (answer to critics of *Eich-mann in Jerusalem*), pp. 17, 18.

# Index